LAW, AUTONOMY, AND VULNERABILITY

SUPPORTING AND PROTECTING OLDER ADULTS IN JAPAN

LAW, AUTONOMY, AND VULNERABILITY

SUPPORTING AND PROTECTING OLDER ADULTS IN JAPAN

YUKIO SAKURAI

COMMON GROUND

First published in 2025
as part of the Aging & Society Book Imprint

Common Ground Research Networks
University of Illinois Research Park
2001 South First Dr, Suite 201 L
Champaign, IL 61820 USA

Library of Congress Cataloging-in-Publication Data

Names: Sakurai, Yukio author
Title: Law, autonomy, and vulnerability : supporting and protecting older
   adults in Japan / Yukio Sakurai.
Description: Champaign, IL : Common Ground Research Networks, 2025. | "June
   2025." | Includes bibliographical references and index.
Identifiers: LCCN 2025041359 (print) | LCCN 2025041360 (ebook) | ISBN
   9781969318009 hardcover | ISBN 9781969318016 paperback | ISBN
   9781969318023 adobe pdf
Subjects: LCSH: Older people--Legal status, laws, etc.--Japan | Older
   people--Protection--Japan | Older people--Services for--Japan | Autonomy
   (Psychology) in old age--Japan | Capacity and disability--Japan |
   Vulnerability (Personality trait)--Japan | Guardian and ward--Japan |
   Older people--Legal status, laws, etc.
Classification: LCC KNX1529 .S25 2025 (print) | LCC KNX1529 (ebook) | DDC
   342.5208/774--dc23/eng/20250905
LC record available at https://lccn.loc.gov/2025041359
LC ebook record available at https://lccn.loc.gov/2025041360

ISBN: 978-1-969318-00-9 (HBK)
ISBN: 978-1-969318-01-6 (PBK)
ISBN: 978-1-969318-02-3 (PDF)
DOI: 10.18848/978-1-969318-02-3/CGP

Cover Design: Phillip Kalantis-Cope

ACKNOWLEDGMENTS

The author wishes to express sincere gratitude to the broader research community for their invaluable guidance and support. Special thanks are extended to Adrian D. Ward (Scotland); Anita Smith, John Chesterman, Piers Michael Gooding, and Terry Carney AO (Australia); Fusako Seki and Teruaki Tayama (Japan); and Michael Ludwig Ganner (Austria) for their insightful comments and generous engagement during the preparation of this study. Deep appreciation is also extended to the author's family, whose unwavering support has been a constant source of strength throughout this journey.

   This book originated as the author's doctoral dissertation submitted to Yokohama National University, Japan, in March 2022, and has since been revised and updated in 2025. Its objective is to clarify the legal concept of adult support and protection legislation by examining its theoretical foundations, legislative development, and community-based implementation frameworks. The legal framework discussed herein is grounded in the principles of adult guardianship, supported decision-making, and the prevention of elder abuse. Rather than restricting human rights, it aims to support and protect older adults within their regional and cultural contexts. This work aspires to contribute to the development of forward-looking legislation suited to super-aged societies, drawing upon both domestic and international discourse. Although the primary focus is on Japan, the analysis may offer insights applicable to other nations confronting similar demographic challenges.

TABLE OF CONTENTS

DESCRIPTION

This book examines the potential of adult support and protection legislation to serve as a comprehensive legal framework that integrates adult guardianship, supported decision-making, and elder abuse prevention—particularly in response to the limitations of Japan's current guardianship system. It clarifies the legal concept of advocacy for vulnerable adults at the intersection of civil law and social security law, drawing on two analytical perspectives: (1) the vulnerability–autonomy approach developed in common law jurisdictions, and (2) a comparative legal analysis of Japan and Australia's legislative responses to diminished capacity. The central research question asks: What legal and policy frameworks can respect the will and preferences of vulnerable adults while enabling effective, community-based implementation? To address this, five sub-questions—introduced in the opening chapter—are examined throughout the study.

The analysis involves three main areas. First, it conceptualizes adult support and protection legislation as a rights-based, integrated structure that promotes individualized support through the least restrictive means. Second, it emphasizes the importance of institutional safeguards and social norms that prioritize supported decision-making, reserving guardianship as a measure of last resort. This includes an examination of soft-law instruments and their normative evolution into binding legislation, with particular reference to Australia's experience. Third, it proposes a model for community-based support, centered on quasi-public core agencies that coordinate with courts, municipalities, and local support centers.

This book makes three key contributions. First, it offers a conceptual and normative foundation for adult support and protection legislation, addressing under-theorized areas in the Japanese context. Second, it analyzes Victoria's Guardianship and Administration Act 2019, demonstrating how empirical research and stakeholder engagement can reinforce supported decision-making within a guardianship framework. Third, it proposes an operational model for community-level adult protection, highlighting the mediating role of core agencies between informal and formal interventions. A distinctive feature of this study is its legislative roadmap for Japan, illustrating how supported decision-making principles can be progressively codified into binding law, with guardianship limited to a subsidiary role. The study concludes by identifying limitations—including the need for further research on safeguards and comparative advocacy models—which are left for future inquiry.

Keywords: vulnerability, autonomy, guardianship, supported decision-making, elder abuse

The Outlines of the Study

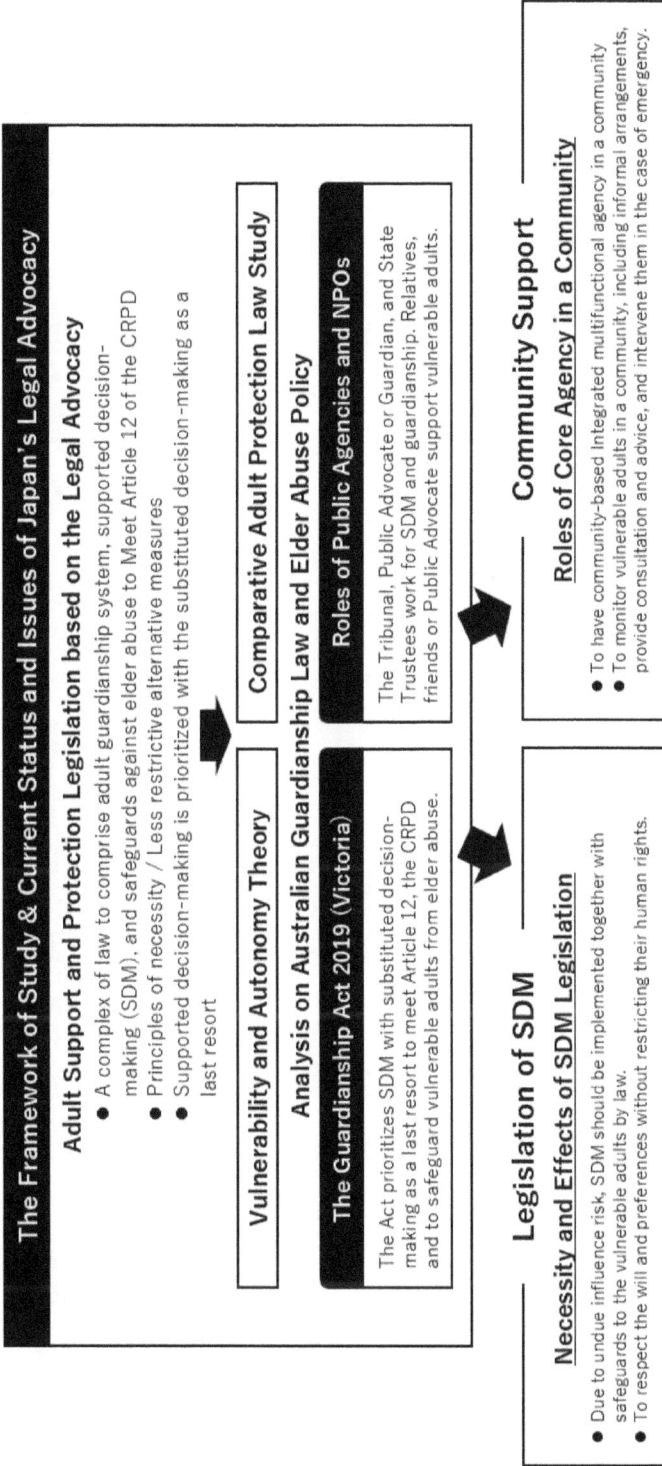

The Framework of Study & Current Status and Issues of Japan's Legal Advocacy

Adult Support and Protection Legislation based on the Legal Advocacy

- A complex of law to comprise adult guardianship system, supported decision-making (SDM), and safeguards against elder abuse to Meet Article 12 of the CRPD
- Principles of necessity / Less restrictive alternative measures
- Supported decision-making is prioritized with the substituted decision-making as a last resort

Comparative Adult Protection Law Study

Vulnerability and Autonomy Theory

Analysis on Australian Guardianship Law and Elder Abuse Policy

The Guardianship Act 2019 (Victoria)

The Act prioritizes SDM with substituted decision-making as a last resort to meet Article 12, the CRPD and to safeguard vulnerable adults from elder abuse.

Roles of Public Agencies and NPOs

The Tribunal, Public Advocate or Guardian, and State Trustees work for SDM and guardianship. Relatives, friends or Public Advocate support vulnerable adults.

Community Support

Roles of Core Agency in a Community

- To have community-based Integrated multifunctional agency in a community
- To monitor vulnerable adults in a community, including informal arrangements, provide consultation and advice, and intervene them in the case of emergency.

Legislation of SDM

Necessity and Effects of SDM Legislation

- Due to undue influence risk, SDM should be implemented together with safeguards to the vulnerable adults by law.
- To respect the will and preferences without restricting their human rights.

Future Tasks: Legal Issues of SDM and Contemporary Issues of the Legal Advocacy

Source: Made by the Author

ACRONYMS

ABA	American Bar Association
AD	advance decision
ADR	alternative dispute resolution
AGAC	Australian Guardianship and Administration Council
ALRC	Australian Law Reform Commission
APS	Adult Protective Services
ASPA	Adult Support and Protection (Scotland) Act 2007
ASU	Adult Safeguarding Unit
AWIA	Adults with Incapacity (Scotland) Act 2000
CAPA	Child and Adult Protection Authority
CHS	Community Health Service
CRPD	Convention on the Rights of Persons with Disabilities
DPA	durable power of attorney
DSCV	Dispute Settlement Centre of Victoria
ECHR	European Court of Human Rights
ELDA	Act on Decisions on Life-Sustaining Treatment for Patients in Hospice and Palliative Care at the End of Life of 2016 (South Korea)
EPA	enduring power of attorney
EU	European Union
FINRA	Financial Industry Regulatory Authority
FTMH	Fast Track Mediation and Hearing service
ILO	International Labour Organization
IMCA	independent mental capacity advocate
JAGA	Japan Adult Guardianship Law Corporate Association
LDP	Liberal Democratic Party
LPA	lasting power of attorney
MCA	Mental Capacity Act
MCI	mild cognitive impairment
NGA	National Guardianship Association
NGN	National Guardianship Network
NGO	non-governmental organization
NPO	not-for-profit organization
NSW	New South Wales

OPA   Office of the Public Advocate
OPG   Office of the Public Guardian
PaCS   Pacte Civil de Solidarité
PEAS   Protecting Elders' Assets Study
PoA   power of attorney
PRAA   Patient Right to Autonomy Act (Taiwan)
SAAR   safeguarding adults at risk referral
SAB   Safeguarding Adults Board
SDM   supported decision-making
SDM-WG   Supported Decision-Making Working Group
SIRS   Serious Incident Response Scheme
STL   State Trustees Limited
UAGPPJA   Uniform Adult Guardianship and Protective Proceedings
                Jurisdiction Act
UGCOPAA   Uniform Guardianship, Conservatorship, and Other Protective
                Arrangements Act
UGPPA   Uniform Guardianship and Protective Proceedings Act
ULC   Uniform Law Commission
UN   United Nations
UNOHCHR   The United Nations Office of the High Commissioner for
                Human Rights
VCAT   Victorian Civil and Administrative Tribunal
VLRC   Victorian Law Reform Commission
WCAC   World Congress on Adult Capacity
WCAG   World Congress on Adult Guardianship
WHO   World Health Organization

TABLES AND FIGURES

NOTES

English Translation of Japanese Law and Terms:

   In accordance with the *Japanese Law Translation* (the Ministry of Justice of Japan) <http://www.japaneselawtranslation.go.jp/?re=02>

Exchange Rate:

   For simplicity, exchange rates are set as US$1.0 = Japanese yen 144.00 and A$1.0 = 92.00 Japanese yen, based on market rates as of May 1, 2025.

Fiscal Term:

   Based on *April to March* in Japan and *July to June* in Australia.

KEY TERMS

Dementia: A syndrome in which there is deterioration in memory, thinking, behavior, and the ability to perform everyday activities (WHO).

Elder Abuse: A single or repeated act, or lack of appropriate action, occurring within any relationship where there is an expectation of trust, which causes harm or distress to an older person. It can be of various forms: physical, psychological/ emotional, sexual, financial, or simply reflect intentional or unintentional neglect (WHO).

Informal Arrangements: Usually involving family members, friends, or other supporters (Australian Law Reform Commission, *Equality, Capacity and Disability in Commonwealth Laws Final Report,* 'ALRC Report 124').

Legal Capacity: The ability to hold rights and duties (legal standing) and to exercise these rights and duties (legal agency) (GC1).

Mental Capacity: The decision-making skills of a person, which naturally vary from one person to another and may be different for a given person depending on many factors, including environmental and social factors (GC1).

Persons with Disabilities: Persons with disabilities include those who have long-term physical, mental, intellectual, or sensory impairments, which in interaction with various barriers may hinder their full and effective participation in society on an equal basis with others (Article 1 of CRPD).

Support: A broad term that encompasses both informal and formal support arrangements, of varying types and intensity (GC1).

Supported Decision-Making: Supported decision-making emphasizes the ability of a person to make decisions, provided they are supported to the extent necessary to make and communicate their decisions. It focuses on what the person wants. (The terms 'supporter' and 'representative' are recommended by the ALRC and are contained in the Commonwealth decision-making model set out in this Report [ALRC Report 124]).

Undue Influence: Undue influence is characterized as occurring, where the quality of the interaction between the support person and the person being supported includes signs of fear, aggression, threat, deception, or manipulation (GC1). It is defined as an 'excessive persuasion that causes another person to act or refrain from acting by overcoming that person's free will and results in inequity' (California Welfare and Institutions Code section 15610.70).

Will and Preferences: The 'best interests' principle is not a safeguard which complies with Article 12 (CRPD) in relation to adults. The 'will and preferences' paradigm must replace the 'best interests' paradigm to ensure that persons with disabilities enjoy the right to legal capacity on an equal basis with others (General Comment No. 1 by UN Committee on CRPD, 'GC1').

INTRODUCTION

This introductory chapter explores the current state of aging societies and identifies the emerging challenges associated with demographic shifts, such as increased vulnerability among older adults. It highlights the growing necessity of examining legislation aimed at the support and protection of vulnerable adults, with particular attention to the aging population. Furthermore, it outlines the analytical framework employed in this study, detailing its objectives, scope, and methodology. A review of prior research relevant to this field is also provided, situating the study within the broader academic discourse. Finally, this introductory chapter offers an overview of the overall structure and content of the study, guiding readers through the key themes and arguments to be discussed.

1. Background of the Study

(1) Issues in Japan

The Civil Code of Japan (hereinafter referred to as the 'Civil Code') governs adults[1] who are presumed to possess mental capacity[2] and autonomy.[3] This is based on the underlying assumption of the Civil Code that human beings should have capacity and autonomy and are expected to behave as rationally as possible. In this framework, individuals who lack full capacity and autonomy—such as those with impaired intellectual or mental capacity, dementia,[4] or higher brain

---

[1] The term 'adults' refers to people having reached the age of 16, 18, or 20, according to how relevant local law defines an adult, and living without any cognitive disability.

[2] The term 'mental capacity' is used in the study, which refers to 'the decision-making skills of a person, which naturally vary from one person to another and may be different for a given person depending on many factors, including environmental and social factors' (General Comment No. 1 by the United Nations Committee on Convention on the Rights of Persons with Disabilities). The term 'legal capacity' refers to 'the ability to hold rights and duties (legal standing) and the ability to exercise these rights and duties (legal agency)' (Ibid); See Lanny Vincent, 'Differentiating Competence, Capability and Capacity' (2008) 16(3) *Innovating Perspectives* 1–2.

[3] Refers to Section '2.3.1 Capability Approach and Autonomy.' Autonomy is close to the right to self-determination. Some psychologists state that the notion of autonomy is 'regulation by the self.'

[4] The term 'dementia' is used in this study, which is a syndrome characterized by deterioration in memory, thinking, behavior, and the ability to perform everyday activities (WHO); 'dementia' is the umbrella term for a number of neurological conditions, with the major symptom being a decline in brain function, and is categorized as a 'Neurocognitive Disorder' (NCD) in the *Diagnostic and Statistical Manual of Mental Disorders, Fifth Edition* (*DSM-5*) published by the American Psychiatric Association (APA) in 2013. Dementia Australia, *Diagnostic Criteria*

dysfunction—are regarded as exceptions. Those who fall short of the required mental capacity must be placed under the supervision of others, such as guardians, according to the relevant degree of incapacity.

Japan's adult guardianship system was implemented on April 1, 2000, with the aim of upholding values such as respect for self-determination, the utilization of the principal's[5] remaining capacity, and normalization,[6] while ensuring that support[7] and protection[8] are provided only to the extent necessary.[9] The duties of adult guardians are limited to legal acts such as property management and the conclusion of contracts on behalf of the principal. Adult guardians are supervised by family courts, to which they must submit annual reports regarding their activities.[10] The adult guardianship system may uniformly restrict the principal's ability to act in exchange for the guardian's substitute decision-making,[11] the right to revoke contracts, or the right to consent to particular transactions. These are protective measures rooted in the Civil Code's 'capacity doctrine,' which corresponds to the principal's assessed mental capacity.[12] This doctrine—the principle of restricted legal agency[13]—originates in Roman law and has long been employed to protect the interests of individuals lacking full capacity.[14] However,

---

for Dementia (Web Page, n/a) <https://www.dementia.org.au/information/for-health-professionals/clinical-resources/diagnostic-criteria-for-dementia>.

[5.] The term 'the principal' in this study refers to 'the represented person' or 'the person who is supported by others.'

[6.] The term 'normalization' is not used any longer because it may hint a discrimination toward people with disabilities. This term is used in this study to show the historical background of the adult guardianship system in Japan. Wolf Wolfensberger, 'A Contribution to the History of Normalization, with Primary Emphasis on the Establishment of Normalization in North America between 1967–1975' in Robert John Flynn and Raymond A. Lemay (eds), *A Quarter-Century of Normalization and Social Role Valorization: Evolution and Impact* (University of Ottawa Press, 1999) 3–69.

[7.] 'Support' is a broad term that encompasses both informal and formal support arrangements, of varying types and intensity (General Comment No. 1 by UN Committee on CRPD).

[8.] 'Protections' are laws and other official measures intended to protect people's rights and freedoms. Collins, *Protection* (Web Page, n/a) <https://www.collinsdictionary.com/dictionary/english/legal-protection>.

[9.] Refers to the Ministry of Justice of Japan, Civil Affairs Bureau Counselor's Office, *Commentary on Proposal Overview for Revision of Adult Guardianship System* (Kinzai Institute for Financial Affairs, Inc., 1998) Appendix 1 (in Japanese).

[10.] Refers to the Ministry of Justice of Japan website: Ministry of Justice of Japan, *Adult Guardianship System and Adult Guardianship Registration System* (Web Page, October 15, 2020) (in Japanese) <http://www.moj.go.jp/MINJI/minji95.html> and (in English) <http://www.moj.go.jp/EN/MINJI/minji17.html#a1>.

[11.] 'Substituted decision-making' enables a proxy to make decisions on behalf of a person with insufficient mental capacity.

[12.] In Japan, the guardianship system adopts the capacity doctrine in the Civil Code while the supported decision-making guidelines for adult guardians (October 2020) include the term 'decision-making capacity' and suggest that the adult guardians should adopt supported decision-making in decision-making process of principals and apply substituted decision-making as a last resort (refers to Section 1.3.2 (2) b 'Seven Principles').

[13.] Those who are protected by law include persons with guardianship, conservatorship, and assistance, in addition to minors. These persons are determined by the family courts in Japan (Articles 8, 12, and 16 of the Civil Code).

[14.] Charles P. Sherman, 'The Debt of the Modern Law of Guardianship to Roman Law' (1913) 12(2) *Michigan Law Review* 124, 131.

the paternalistic[15] aspects of the adult guardianship system have increasingly come under criticism from human rights institutions, including the United Nations Committee on the Rights of Persons with Disabilities (hereinafter referred to as the 'UN Committee') and international non-governmental organizations (hereinafter referred to as 'NGOs').

In addition to such institutional critiques, public trust in the adult guardianship system has eroded due to instances of misconduct by guardians, including fraudulent acts against principals and the misappropriation of their property.[16] As of December 2024, there were approximately 253,941 users of the adult guardianship system in Japan,[17] corresponding to an estimated 2 to 3 per cent of the potential user population.[18] In most cases, support for individuals with insufficient mental capacity is provided through 'informal arrangements,'[19] typically by relatives or nursing home managers. Japanese adults with diminished capacity tend to prefer such informal, family-centered support arrangements over formal legal and policy-based approaches. However, individuals relying on informal arrangements do not benefit from the legal protections afforded by the statutory guardianship system, leaving them vulnerable to potential abuse.

Due to the limited growth in the use of the adult guardianship system over the years, the Act on Promotion of the Adult Guardianship System (Act No. 29 of 2016, hereinafter referred to as the 'Promotion Act') was enacted on April 15, 2016. Based on the Promotion Act, the Basic Plan for Promoting the Adult Guardianship System (hereinafter referred to as the 'Basic Plan') was approved by the Cabinet of Japan on March 24, 2017,[20] and subsequently renewed as the

---

[15.] The term 'paternalistic' expresses the character of paternalism, which is 'the interference of a state or an individual with another person, against their will, and defended or motivated by a claim that the person interfered with will be better off or protected from harm.' Gerald Dworkin, 'Paternalism' (Online, September 9, 2020) in Edward N. Zalta (ed), *The Stanford Encyclopedia of Philosophy Archive Fall 2020 Edition* <https://plato.stanford.edu/archives/fall2020/entries/paternalism/>; the English law principle of parens patriae is important. Erica Wood, 'History of Guardianship' in Mary Joy Quinn (ed), *Guardianship of Adults: Achieving Justice, Autonomy and Safety* (Springer Publishing Co., 2005) 17, 48.

[16.] Refers to Section 1.2.1 (1) 'Adult Guardianship System in Japan-*Issues of Adult Guardianship System.*'

[17.] Refers to the Courts of Japan, *The Annual Overview of Adult Guardianship Cases in FY2024* (Web Page, March 2025) (in Japanese) <https://www.courts.go.jp/toukei_siryou/siryo/kouken/index.html>.

[18.] One research project estimated approximately 2 per cent based on the 0.25 million adult guardianship users vs. 12.00 million potential users of the adult guardianship in 2023. The Regional Guardianship Promotion Project (joint research between the Division of Lifelong Learning Infrastructure Management, Graduate School of Education, the University of Tokyo and the Regional Guardianship Promotion Center), *The Gist of the Adult Guardianship System* (Web Page, n/a) (in Japanese) <https://kouken-pj.org/about/agingsociety/#1>.

[19.] Refers to Section 1.1.1 (1) e 'The CRPD and the Adult Guardianship System.' In Japan, it is sometimes called 'de facto adult guardianship.' The term 'informal arrangement' is used in Australia, involving family members, friends, and other supporters (ALRC Report 124).

[20.] Refers to the Ministry of Health, Labour, and Welfare of Japan, *Basic Plan for Promoting the Adult Guardianship System* (Web Page, March 24, 2017) (in Japanese) <https://www.mhlw.go.jp/file/06-Seisakujouhou-12000000-Shakaiengokyoku-Shakai/keikaku1.pdf>.

Second Term Basic Plan on March 25, 2022, covering the period until March 2027.[21] The Basic Plan is intended to enhance access to legal protections for adults with insufficient mental capacity by establishing regional collaboration networks[22] across the country.[23] As part of this initiative, core agencies[24] are being established within communities to serve as focal points, assisting individuals in accessing family courts and lodging guardianship petitions. These core agencies play a central role in advocacy[25] activities aligned with the objectives of the Basic Plan. Operational improvement programs for the system are also being implemented. Although the reform of the Civil Code and related laws governing the adult guardianship system was not addressed in the original Basic Plan, the Second Term Basic Plan has acknowledged the possibility of such reforms in the near future.

People are generally less familiar with the family courts responsible for operating the adult guardianship system. Although the Basic Plan may provide certain benefits to users, it is unlikely that the system will be significantly promoted through the Basic Plan alone. It is anticipated that the number of adult guardianship users will increase at a greater pace than in recent years, with statutory curatorship and assistance-type cases growing more than statutory guardianship-type cases. However, no such results had been realized as of December 2024.[26] One reason for this limited progress is the wide range of individual circumstances among vulnerable adults, which the adult guardianship system does not adequately

---

[21] Refers to the Ministry of Health, Labour, and Welfare of Japan, *The Second Term Basic Plan for Promoting the Adult Guardianship System* (Web Page, 2022) (in Japanese) <https://www.mhlw.go.jp/stf/seisakunitsuite/bunya/0000202622_00017.html>.

[22] This study uses the term 'adults with insufficient mental capacity,' which is used on the Ministry of Justice of Japan website. Ministry of Justice of Japan, *Adult Guardianship System and Adult Guardianship Registration System* (Web Page, October 15, 2020) (in Japanese) <http://www.moj.go.jp/MINJI/minji95.html> and (in English) <http://www.moj.go.jp/EN/MINJI/minji17.html#a1>.

[23] The term 'regional collaboration network' refers to a community system, involving relevant agencies and practitioners, which finds people who need support and properly advocate them to the necessary support measures, including the adult guardianship system, in addition to establishing a consultation desk in a community. Ministry of Health, Labour, and Welfare of Japan, 'Guidance for Formulating a Basic Plan for Promoting the Adult Guardianship System in Municipalities' (Web Page, March 2019) 3 (in Japanese) <https://www.mhlw.go.jp/content/000503082.pdf>.

[24] Refers to Section 5.2.1 'Roles and Legal Status of a Core Agency for Community Support.' In this study, a 'core agency' is positioned as a multi-functional agency to work for legal advocacy in community support, in addition to the role that is stipulated in the Basic Plan to promote the adult guardianship system.

[25] The term 'advocacy' refers to 'public support for an idea, plan, or way of doing something.' Cambridge Dictionary, *Advocacy* (Web Page, n/a) <https://dictionary.cambridge.org/ja/dictionary/english/advocacy>.

[26] There is no change in the structure in which the statutory guardianship type accounts for approximately 71 per cent of the total adult guardianship system in Japan. In December 2024, the number of adult guardian cases increased slightly to 253,941 (1.8 per cent increase from 2023), and the breakdown by type was guardianship 179,373 (70.6 per cent, 0.8 per cent increase from 2023) and 54,916 curatorship (21.6 per cent, 5.4 per cent increase from 2020), assistance 16,857 (6.6 per cent, 6.3 per cent increase from 2023), and voluntary guardianship 2,795 (1.2 per cent, 0.3 per cent increase from 2019). The Courts of Japan, *The Annual Overview of Adult Guardianship Cases in FY2024* (Web Page, March 2025) (in Japanese) <https://www.courts.go.jp/toukei_siryou/siryo/kouken/index.html>.

accommodate. Therefore, a one-size-fits-all policy for adult guardianship cannot be assumed to be effective under the current conditions.

Instead, multiple options for consumer choice[27] should be provided to allow individuals to choose the support that best meets their needs within community-based services.[28] Such options may include community monitoring programs, support programs for self-reliance in daily life, supported decision-making schemes, the adult guardianship system, elder abuse[29] prevention measures, and others. Public agencies play an essential role in raising awareness of these available options. Providing a reasonable number of choices, rather than overwhelming individuals with too many, would be most effective.[30] Individuals can then independently assess and select appropriate law or policy instruments based on their particular needs. This relationship between individuals and public agencies reflects the values of autonomy and citizen participation in public policy, which aligns with contemporary developments in social security law based on contractual principles.[31]

The Second Term Basic Plan, covering the period from April 2022 to March 2027, was approved by the Cabinet on March 25, 2022. This Second Term Basic Plan emphasizes the concept of 'advocacy support,'[32] aiming to promote a range of optional measures for community support, including but not limited to the adult guardianship system. It can be observed that the focus of adult guardianship promotion efforts has shifted from merely promoting the adult guardianship

---

[27.] The term 'consumer choice' refers to 'the range of competing products and services from which a consumer can choose.' Collins, *Consumer Choice* (Web Page, n/a) <https://www.collinsdictionary.com/jp/dictionary/english/consumer-choice>.

[28.] Refers to Section 5.2.1 (4) 'Contributions of Civil Society for Community Support.'

[29.] The term 'elder abuse' refers to 'a single, or repeated act, or lack of appropriate action, occurring within any relationship where there is an expectation of trust which causes harm or distress to an older person. It can be of various forms: physical, psychological/emotional, sexual, financial, or simply reflect intentional or unintentional neglect' (WHO).

[30.] The theory on consumer behavior, an increase in choices does not always lead to his or her own interests, is known as 'Jam study' in the US. This implies that people tend to be more satisfied with reasonably less choice with greater satisfaction. Sheena Iyengar and Mark R. Lepper, 'When Choice Is Demotivating: Can One Desire Too Much of a Good Thing?' (2000) 79(6) *Journal of Personality and Social Psychology* 995, 1006.

[31.] Refers to Section 1.1.1 (2) 'Previous Research in Social Security Law.' 'The social security law' is a general term for legislation in Japan that regulates legal relationships, such as social insurance (pension, health care, and aged care), public assistance, health care and public health, and social welfare, which includes the social welfare law and legal advocacy.

[32.] The term 'advocacy support' is defined as 'support activities which have a common foundation for support and activities centered on the person, which are support for exercising their rights through supported decision-making and support for recovering from infringement of their rights in dealing with abuse and unfair property transactions, for adults with insufficient mental capacity to participate in the community and live independent lives.' Ministry of Health, Labour, and Welfare of Japan, *The Second Term Basic Plan for Promoting the Adult Guardianship System* (Web Page, 2022) (in Japanese) <https://www.mhlw.go.jp/stf/seisakunitsuite/bunya/0000202622_00017.html>.

system to promoting multiple support options, following seven years of expert deliberations.

Another important issue concerns how to establish adult protection laws and policies that respond to the needs of adults with insufficient mental capacity who lack relatives or close friends to support them, possess no financial assets, or may suffer abuse at the hands of family members or acquaintances. Such difficult cases[33] have become increasingly common nationwide, presenting significant challenges to local governments and communities. In some instances, public agencies must intervene to provide emergency protection for these vulnerable adults. Preventive measures, including the enhancement of the adult guardianship system and the development of comprehensive elder abuse prevention policies, must also be considered. It is understood that complex cases require a combination of tailored measures, mobilizing local human resources within local governments and communities to ensure an effective response.

It is therefore evident that addressing the diverse needs and circumstances of vulnerable populations requires the implementation of multiple law and policy measures. A single approach, such as reliance solely on the adult guardianship system or informal arrangements, is insufficient to respond effectively to the wide-ranging demands and complexities faced by vulnerable individuals. A more flexible and multifaceted framework is necessary to ensure that support and protection measures are tailored to the specific needs of each individual.

(2) Adult Support and Protection Legislation

There is growing international recognition of human rights as a universal value, accompanied by increased activity from international NGOs and not-for-profit organizations (hereinafter referred to as 'NPOs'). In particular, General Comment No. 1, adopted on April 11, 2014, regarding Article 12 (Equal Recognition Before the Law) of the Convention on the Rights of Persons with Disabilities (hereinafter referred to as 'CRPD'), emphasizes respect for the autonomy and self-determination of adults with impaired mental capacity.[34] It recommends abolishing substituted decision-making and promoting supported decision-making, which upholds the will and preferences of the individual. Supported decision-making

---

[33.] Difficult cases include five categories: financial problems, the need for living supports, family problems, service usage problems, and community and workplace problems, which are clarified by empirical studies. Individual support, parallel support, collaborative support, intermediation and formation support are implemented. Noriharu Unuma and Kaoru Sekine, 'A Study of Difficult Cases in Adult Guardianship: Analyses the Contents and Support Methods through Corporate Guardianship by the Council of Social Welfare' (2022) 12 *Kogakkan University of Japanese Studies* 1, 28 (in Japanese).

[34.] Refers to 1.2.1 (2) 'The CRPD and the General Comment No. 1.'

enables a person to make decisions with appropriate support and assistance, thereby emphasizing what the individual wants rather than what others consider to be in their best interest.[35]

In several developed countries facing similar demographic challenges as Japan—such as an aging population and a growing number of older adults with dementia—legislative reforms to civil codes or guardianship laws have aimed to provide structured support and protection to vulnerable adults.[36] In this study, such legal frameworks are collectively referred to as *adult support and protection legislation*. This form of legislation recognizes individual vulnerability[37] and seeks to offer support and safeguards tailored to the needs of each person, while minimizing restrictions on their rights. It promotes the use of the least restrictive alternatives to achieve these objectives.[38]

In countries undertaking legal reform in this area, a comprehensive understanding of autonomy and self-determination is typically integrated into the legislative process. Considerations include the potential financial burden on national and local governments, the views of professionals such as legal practitioners, social workers, and healthcare providers, and collaboration with civil society. In common law jurisdictions, unless there is clear evidence of incapacity, decision-making capacity is presumed. In this context, adult guardianship is treated as a measure of last resort, and supported decision-making is promoted as a more appropriate legal mechanism to respect the will and preferences of the individual.

This study reviews the laws and policy developments in selected developed countries that incorporate the values of the CRPD. These examples may offer insights and implications for future legislative developments in Japan.

---

[35] The 'will and preferences' paradigm must replace the 'best interests' paradigm to ensure that persons with disabilities enjoy the right to legal capacity on an equal basis with others (General Comment No. 1 by UN Committee on CRPD).

[36] This study uses the term 'older adults' as the APA recommends using.

[37] Refers to Section 2.3.1 'Vulnerability.'

[38] The 'least restrictive alternative' comes from the *Shelton v. Tucker* case in which the U.S. Supreme Court on December 12, 1960, ruled (by a 5-to-4 decision) that the Arkansas statute requiring all public-school educators to disclose every institution to which they were affiliated over a five-year period was unconstitutional. J. M. Johnston and Robert A. Sherman, 'Applying the Least Restrictive Alternative Principle to Treatment Decisions: A Legal and Behavioral Analysis' (1993) 16(1) *The Behavior Analyst* 103, 115.

2. Framework of the Study

(1) Purpose of the Study

This study aims to examine the potential integration of adult support and protection legislation into the broader legal framework encompassing adult guardianship, supported decision-making, and the prevention of elder abuse involving vulnerable adults. The research is grounded in the challenges facing Japan's current adult guardianship system.

It focuses on the following three key areas:

(a) Conceptual Foundations: This section defines adult support and protection legislation by drawing on previous research and comparative legal analysis, thereby establishing the theoretical foundation for the study.

(b) Legislative Development: This section investigates the legislative evolution of supported decision-making in Japan, with particular attention to comparative legal perspectives.

(c) Operational Implementation: This section explores the role of community-based social resources in the practical implementation of adult support and protection legislation.

(2) Methodology

This study first clarifies the concept of legal advocacy[39] for vulnerable adults, encompassing the adult guardianship system, supported decision-making, elder abuse prevention, and relevant public policies. The legal domain under consideration spans both civil law and social security law, areas that intersect in addressing the needs of adults with diminished mental capacity.[40] The analysis proceeds along two axes: (1) the theoretical frameworks of vulnerability and autonomy as developed in common law jurisdictions, and (2) a comparative legal analysis between Japan and Australia regarding legislation supporting and protecting vulnerable adults.

[39.] The term 'advocacy' holds multifunctional meanings, such as self-advocacy, legal advocacy, social advocacy, and systemic advocacy. Karen Williams and Sue Field, 'Advocacy and the Rights of the Vulnerable Older Person' (2021) 12 *Journal of Aging Law & Policy* 1, 37.

[40.] 'The concept of diminished competence varies depending on the professional disciplinary domain.' This study focuses on the concept of diminished competence from a legal perspective (i.e., law and policy) and from a social perspective (i.e., function-based review). Terry Carney, 'Guardianship, "Social" Citizenship and Theorising Substitute Decision-Making Law' (2012) in Israel Doron and Ann M. Soden (eds), *Beyond Elder Law: New Directions in Law and Aging* (Springer Science & Business Media, 2012) 1–17, 3.

In Chapter 1, the study conducts a systematic review of Japan's adult guardianship system and related legal and policy frameworks. This includes civil law theory concerning guardianship, social security law theory on advocacy, and the core functions required to support and protect vulnerable adults. The author's theoretical position regarding both civil law and social security law is articulated. Through this review, the legal-policy scope and the principal functions of the system for supporting and protecting adults with insufficient mental capacity are delineated. Based on this groundwork, the research framework of the study is outlined below.

First, the primary focus of this study is on legal acts performed by or involving the adult principal. The research applies an interdisciplinary legal approach grounded in both civil and social security law. Legal issues arising after the death of the principal are excluded from the scope. Drawing on international developments—particularly Australia's legal reforms—this study develops a legislative theory tailored to Japan, informed by comparative legal analysis.[41]

Second, the study examines the legal and policy frameworks related to the adult guardianship system, supported decision-making, elder abuse prevention legislation, and relevant programs such as the 'Support Program for Self-Reliance in Daily Life' and the 'Community-Based Integrated Care System.'[42] These are collectively referred to as 'legal advocacy,' a subcategory of advocacy focused specifically on legal actions that protect the interests of the adult principal. Elder abuse prevention law, functionally linked to the adult guardianship system, is included in this category and is listed in Table 1 (List of the Main Functions to Support and Protect Vulnerable Adults). In contrast, areas such as consumer contract law and trust law, which indirectly support vulnerable adults and require separate comprehensive analysis, are excluded.

Third, the discussion proceeds on the assumption that the current civil and related laws concerning the adult guardianship system remain unchanged. The study focuses on supported decision-making, which centers on respecting the will and preferences of the principal. It posits that supported decision-making should evolve into an independent legal framework coexisting with the guardianship system. This discussion is based on current guidelines from the Ministry

---

[41.] Refers to Section '5.1 Introduction.'

[42.] Refers to Section 1.2.3 (2) 'Relevant Policy in Community Support.' The 'support program for self-reliance in daily life' is a social welfare system that supports people with insufficient mental capacity to use simple welfare services and manage their financial arrangement for daily use. A structure called 'the community-based integrated care system' is to comprehensively ensure the provision of health care, nursing care, prevention, housing, and livelihood support in a community. Ministry of Health, Labour, and Welfare of Japan, *Establishing the Community-Based Integrated Care System* (Web Page, n/a) <https://www.mhlw.go.jp/english/policy/care-welfare/care-welfare-elderly/dl/establish_e.pdf>.

of Health, Labour and Welfare of Japan, which already incorporate supported decision-making into healthcare and end-of-life care contexts.[43]

Fourth, although the COVID-19 pandemic has had widespread effects on society, its specific impact on the systems studied remains insufficiently understood and lacks comprehensive academic analysis. Therefore, the effects of the pandemic fall outside the scope of this study.

Adult support and protection legislation has become a pressing social issue both domestically and internationally in the context of an aging society. Following the adoption of the CRPD by the UN, matters concerning adult guardianship systems and supported decision-making have emerged as common challenges among the 192 State Parties to the CRPD. In this respect, the research theme of this study addresses a global concern.

Recognizing this, the author considered international academic engagement essential from the outset of the research. Accordingly, this study has been prepared in English to facilitate scholarly exchange. In particular, feedback from Australian scholars has been incorporated into the development of the study.[44] It is hoped that this work will contribute to the international academic discourse by introducing Japanese legal and policy approaches to guardianship and related issues, thereby inviting further insights and suggestions from researchers abroad. Through such two-way exchange, the broader significance of this study may be realized.

(3) Why Australian Law Is Examined

This study includes a comparative legal analysis of legislation enacted in Japan and Australia to support and protect vulnerable adults. Australian law is examined because two leading states—Victoria and New South Wales ((hereinafter referred to as 'NSW')—have revised, or are in the process of revising, their guardianship and supported decision-making laws for the first time in over thirty years. In particular, the State of Victoria enacted the Guardianship and Administration Act 2019 in May 2019. This legislation, which incorporates supported decision-making into the guardianship framework, was developed in response to a reference made by the Attorney-General of Victoria to the Victorian Law Reform Commission (hereinafter referred to as 'VLRC') in May 2009. The process took approximately a decade, during which pilot projects for supported decision-making were implemented in local communities.[45]

---

[43]. Supported decision-making in health care and terminal care is discussed in the medical law or bioethics in Japan.

[44]. The corresponding experts in Australia are Anita Smith, John Chesterman, Terry Carney AO, and Piers Gooding.

[45]. Refers to Section '4.3 Victoria and NSW State Acts Incorporating Supported Decision-Making.'

Australia is also pursuing state-level elder abuse prevention legislation in line with national policy. Within this context, guardianship and supported decision-making are positioned as legal mechanisms for the prevention of elder abuse. These three components—adult guardianship, supported decision-making, and safeguards against elder abuse—are therefore closely interconnected. Analyzing Australia's ongoing legislative developments can offer valuable insights into the purpose and potential structure of adult support and protection legislation, even though the reforms remain in progress.[46]

Furthermore, public agencies in Australian states and special territories—such as Civil and Administrative Tribunals (which operate independently of the state court system), Offices of the Public Advocate or Public Guardian,[47] and Public Trustees or State Trustees Limited—play central roles in administering guardianship systems. These public agencies are responsible for managing guardianship, facilitating accessible dispute resolution, and overseeing property administration. They are also actively involved in implementing supported decision-making and elder abuse measures, in accordance with legislative reforms. Working in partnership with local governments and communities, these public institutions provide day-to-day support and protection for vulnerable adults.

Academic institutions and professional societies in Australia contribute through both theoretical and empirical analysis of these developments. Lessons drawn from the Australian legislative experience—such as the roles of public agencies, respect for the principles of the CRPD, the institutionalization of supported decision-making, mechanisms for dispute resolution, and the involvement of community-based NPOs—may inform Japan's efforts to develop a coherent legislative framework for adult support and protection.[48]

(4) Comparative Law and Its Limits

Comparative law is a legal discipline that analyzes the similarities and differences between the laws of two or more countries from both theoretical and practical perspectives.[49] It is valuable not only for understanding the current

---

[46.] Refers to Section '4.5.1 Discussion on Australian Adult Support and Protection.'

[47.] The status and role of 'public guardian' varies according to country. In the US, a public guardian might be an entity, such as volunteer, agency, or attorney, which receives most, if not all, of its funding from a governmental entity. A public guardian directly advocates principals. In the UK, a public guardian is an executive public agency under the Ministry of Justice, which indirectly advocates principals through registered guardians and directly advocates guardianship policymaking and relevant programs. Australia, Canada, and Singapore adopt the U.K. system. Pamela Booth Teaster and Stephanie Chamberlain, 'Public Guardianship: Policy and Practice' (2020) 1(1) *Journal of Elder Policy* 155, 174.

[48.] Refers to Section '4.5.2 Implications from Australian Legislative Project.'

[49.] Surveys of a discipline of comparative law studies: Rodolfo Sacco, 'Legal Formants: A Dynamic Approach to Comparative Law (I)' (1991) 39(1) *The American Journal of Comparative Law* 1, 34; Rodolfo Sacco, 'Legal

state of legal systems but also for informing legal development by drawing on insights from other jurisdictions. Comparative legal studies can offer useful suggestions from jurisdictions facing similar challenges. As Israel Doron[50] observes, 'Comparative law is interesting, but even the term "guardianship" has different legal meanings in each jurisdiction, and the society, culture, and history behind the law are also different. Analyzing laws comparatively is really difficult, considering the background of the law.'[51] Indeed, conducting comparative legal research requires a conscious awareness of these challenges and strategies to address them.

In this regard, it is essential for researchers to engage directly with the target jurisdictions in collaboration with local research partners, in order to understand the context and experiences of the individuals concerned. Equally important are relationships with legal practitioners, which help researchers grasp not only legal theory but also how the law operates in practice. Comparative legal studies, therefore, can be understood as a multidimensional dialogue between researchers and practitioners across jurisdictions.

(5) Research Surveys

This research is based on a review of legal literature in both English and Japanese, as well as interviews with experts. Numerous prior studies have examined the adult guardianship system and supported decision-making, including works by Arai (2010, 2021), Tayama (2010, 2021),[52] Suga (2013), Kamiyama (2015, 2020), Doron (2002), Van Puymbrouck (2017), Ho and Lee (2019), Scholten and Gather (2018, 2021), Scholten (2025), and Kohn (2021). In the field of social security law, relevant contributions include Kawano (1999), Hirata (2012), Akimoto (2012), and Kikuchi (2020). Studies employing the vulnerability approach include seminal works by Fineman (2008, 2012), Kohn (2014), Herring (2016), and Clough (2017). Foundational normative

---

Formants: A Dynamic Approach to Comparative Law (Installment II of II)' (1991) 39(2) *The American Journal of Comparative Law* 343, 401; Sue Farran and Esin Örücü, 'The Continuing Relevance of Comparative Law and Comparative Legal Studies' (2019) 6(2) *Journal of International and Comparative Law* 171, 182.

[50.] Israel Doron is a faculty member who studies medical errors, social work research, and safety and health in the workplace at the faculty of law, Gerontology Department, University of Haifa. Israel Doron, 'Elder Guardianship Kaleidoscope–A Comparative Perspective' (2002) 16(3) *International Journal of Law, Policy, and the Family* 368, 398.

[51.] Israel Doron remarked as in the text in his online lecture at the Elder Law Society Japan meeting held on February 26, 2022, and the WCAC2022 in Edinburg on June 7 to 9, 2022.

[52.] Refers to Section '1.1.1 (1) g. Future Developments.' Teruaki Tayama remarks that 'the adult guardianship system should be transformed into an adult protection law that may be cooperative with social welfare law, which does not restrict human rights and is easy to understand.'

and theoretical perspectives are also drawn from Sen (2005, 2009), Dworkin (2015), and Herring (2017).[53]

Australian guardianship studies—such as those by Carney and Tait (1997), Chesterman (2013, 2019), Field et al. (2018), and Gooding and Carney (2021)—are closely aligned with and often reflected in the reports of national and state law reform commissions. Although comparative legal analyses of adult protection legislation exist primarily in common law jurisdictions—for example, Martin et al. (2016), Montgomery et al. (2016), S. Donnelly et al. (2017), and M. Donnelly (2022)—studies specifically addressing the legal concept of adult support and protection legislation, including supported decision-making, remain limited (Chesterman 2013 a, 2013b. 2019 a, 2019b).[54]

Although substantial prior research exists on individual topics such as the adult guardianship system, studies that take a comprehensive approach to legal policy for adult support and protection—including supported decision-making—remain limited. Accordingly, this study focuses on legal policy concerning adult support and protection in Japan, including supported decision-making, with particular attention to the concept of 'adult protection law' (Tayama 2021), which intersects both civil law and social security law.

To supplement the legal analysis, expert interviews were conducted as part of international fieldwork. These included four research visits to Australia—Adelaide (2016), Melbourne (2017 and 2019), and Melbourne, Brisbane, and Sydney (2023)—as well as participation in the Australian Guardianship and Administration Council (AGAC) conference held in Canberra in March 2019, where the author presented preliminary research findings and conducted expert interviews.[55]

The interviewed experts were affiliated with universities, research institutes, and public agencies such as the Office of the Public Advocate, civil and administrative tribunals, and State Trustees Limited. Selection criteria for interviewees included affiliation with the AGAC, the World Congress on Adult Guardianship (WCAG), or a relevant academic society. In addition to interviews conducted during international conferences and meetings outside Australia, expert input was also gathered through email correspondence

---

[53.] No citations are shown here regarding previous studies to avoid duplication of those cited in the text.

[54.] From the interview of John Chesterman by the author in the Victorian OPA on March 5, 2019. John Chesterman recognizes that adult guardianship, supported decision-making, and legal measures against elder abuse are closely interrelated in the law system, although he does not use the term 'adult support and protection.'

[55.] Interviews: Guardianship law experts in Melbourne (Victoria) on March 1 to 3, 2017, and March 4 to 12, 2019, in Trieste/Singapore in May/July 2017, and Vienna/Innsbruck in September 2019. The author joined a supported decision-making facilitation training (two weeks), conducted by Cher Nicholson in Adelaide (South Australia) in February 23 to March 4, 2016.

between January 2020 and January 2023, due to travel restrictions caused by the COVID-19 pandemic.

(6) Research Questions

The central question addressed by this study is: 'What is the framework and value of adult support and protection legislation that respects the will and preferences of vulnerable adults with insufficient mental capacity, and how can such legislation be effectively implemented at the community level?' To explore this question, five research sub-questions are presented and will be examined in the subsequent chapters:

(a) What is the appropriate framework for researching legal systems that support and protect older individuals with insufficient mental capacity from the perspective of interdisciplinary legal studies—namely, civil law and social security law—and what are the existing systems and issues in Japan? (Chapter 1)

(b) What insights can the vulnerability approach and related normative theories, including those found in safeguarding legislation, offer for understanding the legal and policy systems affecting older individuals with insufficient mental capacity in a super-aged society? (Chapter 2)

(c) How have developed countries and regions responded to the challenges of adult guardianship systems, supported decision-making, and prevention of elder abuse, and what are the implications of these responses for conceptualizing adult support and protection legislation in an international context? (Chapter 3)

(d) How have Australian states responded to issues surrounding adult guardianship, supported decision-making, elder abuse prevention, and legal advocacy policies, and what are the implications of the legal concepts and values underlying adult support and protection legislation in the Australian context? (Chapter 4)

(e) What legislative concepts and normative values are feasible for Japan's adult support and protection legislation, and how might these be implemented in the context of community support—particularly with a focus on supported decision-making—drawing on lessons from Australian legal reforms and international comparisons? (Chapter 5)

The primary limitation of this study lies in the potential constraints posed by Japan's civil law tradition in adopting concepts developed in common law jurisdictions. However, this limitation does not diminish the academic significance of undertaking such a comparative legal analysis.

3. Composition of the Study

Chapter 1: Legal Advocacy and Challenges in Japan establishes the research framework and examines legal advocacy, including the adult guardianship system and related issues in Japan. After the *Introduction*, Section 1.1 systematically reviews the adult guardianship system, related laws and policies, theories of civil law, social security law perspectives on advocacy, and the key functions necessary to support and protect vulnerable adults. The research framework is then constructed. Section 1.2 outlines the legal framework and challenges of the adult guardianship system and the Promotion Act, the concept and guidelines of supported decision-making, and the elder abuse prevention law, along with related advocacy measures. Section 1.3 synthesizes the chapter's findings.

Chapter 2: Vulnerability Approach and Autonomy provides the theoretical foundation for the study. Following the *Introduction*, Section 2.1 gives an overview of vulnerability, focusing on population aging and the older as a global issue, with particular attention to Japan's super-aged society. Section 2.2 reviews how legislation and policy should respond to aging, drawing on the vulnerability approach and previous studies. This section also analyzes safeguarding laws in common law jurisdictions to identify effective protective measures. Section 2.3 discusses relevant normative theories such as the capability approach and individual/relational autonomy, exploring how to harmonize respect for self-determination with public welfare. Section 2.4 concludes the chapter.

Chapter 3: Adult Support and Protection in the International Context examines adult support and protection legislation from a comparative law perspective. After the *Introduction*, Section 3.2 reviews the 2000 Protection of Adults Convention and reforms in countries such as Switzerland, Austria, Scotland, the US, and Australia. Section 3.3 *Analysis of Adult Support and Protection Legislation*, analyzes similarities and differences in these reforms to identify the core concept of adult support and protection. A working definition of adult support and protection is then presented. Section 3.4 concludes the chapter.

Chapter 4: Adult Support and Protection in the Australian Context focuses on Australian law. After the *Introduction*, Section 4.2 outlines the legal framework of Australia and reviews current and past guardianship laws in Victoria and New South Wales (NSW). Section 4.3 discusses achieved and proposed reforms in these states. Section 4.4 examines national and state policies addressing elder abuse. Section 4.5 analyzes the values and principles behind Australia's adult support and protection legislation, referencing the multidimensional model of elder law, and summarizes implications for Japan. Section 4.6 concludes the chapter.

Chapter 5: The Idea of Adult Support and Protection in Japan proposes a legislative framework for adult support and protection in Japan and examines the values underpinning it. After the *Introduction*, Section 5.2 analyzes the legal status and roles of a core agency and supported decision-making (SDM) as essential elements of the legislative structure. It compares combined models of guardianship and SDM in Australia, Europe, and Japan to clarify Japan's current stance. It then outlines a preliminary legislative proposal and a step-by-step path toward implementation. Section 5.3 presents the proposed legislative architecture, illustrating how community-based mechanisms, including dispute resolution, might function. Section 5.3.3 explores the value framework behind the legislation, referencing a modified version of the multi-dimensional model of elder law. Section 5.4 concludes the chapter.

The study ends with a Conclusion, summarizing the key findings and contributions.

CHAPTER 1

Legal Advocacy and Challenges in Japan

This chapter systematically reviews the adult guardianship system and related legal and policy frameworks in Japan. It clarifies the theoretical foundations of civil law and social security law as they pertain to legal advocacy for vulnerable adults. Section 1.1 presents a review of these legal theories and identifies the core functions necessary for adult support and protection. Based on this framework, Section 1.2 examines current legal advocacy measures and relevant policies in Japan. Particular attention is given to supported decision-making (SDM) as a legal concept distinct from guardianship, with consideration of its future legislative potential in light of international developments.

1.1 Research Framework of the Study

1.1.1 Theoretical Review

(1) Previous Research in Civil Law

This section provides an overview of previous research on the adult guardianship system and related topics published between 2000 and 2022 by Japanese scholars grounded in civil law theory. It aims to clarify key legal issues through the lens of their theoretical discussions. The author's position is then presented in relation to these scholarly perspectives.

a. Legal Interpretation of the Adult Guardianship System

In April 2000, the adult guardianship system came into force, and the legal interpretation of the text accompanying the operation of the system was discussed. Jun Sunaga (2004)[1] provides a comprehensive review of the legal issues of the adult guardianship system in his 'Interpretation and Operation of the Adult

---

[1] Jun Sunaga was a Japanese civil law scholar (1930–2016). Jun Sunaga, 'Interpretation and Operation of the Adult Guardianship System and Legislative Issues' (2005) 2 *Adult Guardianship Law Research* 3, 26 (in Japanese).

Guardianship System and Legislative Issues,' representing the concerns of re-searchers and practitioners in Japan at that time. This is the keynote lecture at the first annual conference of Japan Adult Guardianship Law Corporate Association[2] (hereinafter referred to as 'JAGA') held in Tokyo on May 29, 2004.

Sunaga discusses various issues of legal interpretations and operations regard-ing the statutory guardianship and voluntary guardianship systems.[3] Namely, Sunaga discusses issues of the statutory guardianship system: 'Necessity of further flexibility of the system,' 'Discretion of the family courts for starting the protection system,' 'Theoretical issues of legal acts in daily life,' 'Costs and remunerations of adult guardians,' and 'Issues on the limits of obligations and power of adult guardians for personal protection.' Then, Sunaga discusses issues of the voluntary guardianship system: 'Capacity required to conclude voluntary guardianship,' 'Will the voluntary guardianship contract be familiar to a proxy?' 'Is an appointment of a sub-agent of the person allowed?' 'Designation of adult protection required by a voluntary guardianship contract,' 'Granting the right of consent to a voluntary guardian,' 'Does the scope of duties of the voluntary guardian includes long-term care (aged care),' 'Limitations to what can be executed by the voluntary guardian,' and 'Effect of voluntary guardianship contracts that do not comply with the provisions of the Voluntary Guardianship Contract Law.'

Among these issues, Sunaga discusses 'the obligation and the limited scope of personal protection by adult guardians' in the greatest detail. Personal protection by adult guardians was the greatest attention from researchers and practitioners. In addition, Sunaga is of the opinion that amendments to relevant laws or leg-islation should be considered to improve matters that cannot be resolved by legal interpretations. Namely, Sunaga discusses possible legislative issues for the statutory guardianship and voluntary guardianship systems: 'Consent and substituted decision-making for medical practice,' 'Improve national negative attitude to the adult guardianship system,' 'How multiple adult guardians should exercise their duties,' 'The ideal way of guardianship and voluntary guardian-ship,' 'Requests for the appointment of a supervisor for a voluntary guardian,' 'Immediate and flexible protection measures,' and 'Order of the family court in the event of serious or emergency medical practice.'

It is understood that the Civil Law scholars, including Sunaga, and practitioners have discussed various issues regarding the adult guardianship system, since its enforcement in April 2000, not only for legal interpretations and operation but

---

[2] The Japan Adult Guardianship Law Corporate Association (JAGA) is a national association of scholars and practitioners interested in issues concerning Adult Guardianship Law and policy (President: Prof. Dr. Makoto Arai). The JAGA has approximately 1,000 members, including academics, legal practitioners, social workers, notaries, accountants, court clerks, and medical doctors. JAGA <https://jaga.gr.jp/en/>.

[3] Refers to Section 1.2.1, 'Adult Guardianship System and the Promotion Act.'

also ideas of amendments to relevant laws or legislation. Some issues discussed by Sunaga remain unchanged as the current issues.

b. Duty of Adult Guardians: Property Management and Personal Protection

Makoto Arai (2010)[4] shows two contrasting views on the roles of the adult guardianship system. For the traditional and the majority view, Eiichi Hoshino[5] and Takashi Uchida consider that the roles of the adult guardianship system are mainly property management for people with property. This view is influenced by Sakae Wagatsuma[6] who contributed to the Civil Code studies, including the older incapacity/quasi-incapacity system, to protect property of the principal's family and limit the scope of personal protection by adult guardians. It can be said that Hoshino and Uchida's view respects the stability of the Civil Code rather than structural change of the Civil Code in changing social environments.[7] Uchida states that, 'we should not have an excessive illusion in the Civil Code regarding the welfare function of the elderly and people with disabilities. The government's responsibility for welfare must be taken outside the Civil Code.'[8]

The other influential view is advocated by Shoichi Ogano[9] and Yasushi Kamiyama.[10] They focuses on the life support function of the adult guardianship system in a changing social environment, such as an aging society and a national with an increasing number of people with dementia.[11] Ogano classifies the contents

---

[4.] Makoto Arai, 'Construction of the Adult Guardianship Law System: What We Learn from the Comparison of the German Adult Guardianship Law and Japan's Adult Guardianship System' in Makoto Arai (ed), *Generation and Development of the Adult Guardianship System* (Yukikaku, 2021) 3–20 (Reprint from the previously published article: Makoto Arai, 'Construction of the Adult Guardianship Law System: What We Learn from the Comparison of the German Adult Guardianship Law and Japan's Adult Guardianship System' (2010) 33 *Adult Guardianship Practices* 5–6 (in Japanese).

[5.] Eiichi Hoshino was a Japanese civil law scholar (1926–2012).

[6.] Sakae Wagatsuma was a Japanese civil law scholar (1887–1973).

[7.] Eiichi Hoshino remarks in his interview that 'In the first place, the capacity doctrine is a system for managing people's assets. Therefore, it is written in Wagatsuma's civil law textbook that these systems are for those who have property and not to protect those who do not have any property. It is natural that property management is central [in the adult guardianship system].' Eiichi Hoshino, 'Adult Guardianship System and Legislative Process: Interview of Professor Eiichi Hoshino' (2000) 1172 *Jurist* 2–16, 6 (in Japanese).

[8.] Takashi Uchida, *Civil Law I: General Rules and General Remarks on Property Rights* (University of Tokyo Press, 4th ed, 2008) 119 (in Japanese).

[9.] Shoichi Ogano, *Adult Personal Custody System Theory: Guarantee of Rights in Japanese Legal System and Prospects for Adult Guardianship* (Shinzansha Publisher, 2000) (in Japanese).

[10.] Yasushi Kamiyama, *Professional Guardian and Protection of Personal Affairs* (Civil Law Study Group, 2008) 66 (in Japanese).

[11.] There are views to positively capture the personal protection of adult guardians in the Civil Code. Noriko Mizuno, *Obligation of the Adult Guardian to Personal Protection* (Online, 2001) (in Japanese) <http://www.law.tohoku.ac.jp/~parenoir/shinjou-kango.html>, Akiko Watanabe, *Adult Guardianship of Personal Custody* (Shinzansha Publisher, 2015) (in Japanese).

of personal protection affairs into three categories—social welfare-related affairs, medical-related affairs, and living-related affairs—which describe the ideal form of personal protection affairs. Kamiyama assumes that it is necessary for adult guardians to manage property for life support of their principals, and property management and life support are inextricably linked. These views appear in response to emerging needs of vulnerable adults as the national population ages. In this sense, these views are considered reasonable, but the point is in what law these requirements are positioned within the law system of Japan.

The former view (Hoshino/Uchida) has been regarded as a majority view in the civil law, staying status quo that property management is central in the adult guardianship system and considering personal protection by means other than civil law (i.e., the welfare law), and the latter view (Ogano/Kamiyama) suggests considering personal protection within the Civil Code as much as possible and some complementary measures other than civil law, in addition to property management. The above contrasting views on personal protection can be regarded as an extension of the debate over personal protection in the Civil Code Subcommittee of the Legislative Council when the draft law was deliberated on before December 1999.[12]

In the deliberations regarding draft amendments to the Civil Code by experts from 1995 to 1997 at the research group organized by the Ministry of Justice of Japan, gaps between the opinions of the experts were found in three issues, namely the statutory guardianship types (a single type of assistance or multiple types), the voluntary guardianship system, and the scope of duty of adult guardians for personal protection of principals.[13] Eiichi Hoshino, chair of the research group and of the Civil Code Subcommittee of Legislative Council, coordinated the experts' deliberations and concluded on the framework of the adult guardianship system.[14]

Consequently, the multiple statutory guardianship types, including assistance, have been adopted and voluntary guardianship has been newly introduced. The scope of duty of adult guardians for personal protection remains minimal, although Article 858 (Respect for the intention and personal consideration of the

---

[12] The deliberations of the Civil Code Subcommittee of the Legislative Council are analyzed by these articles: Toshiki Nishimori, 'Purpose of the Corporate Guardianship System from the Perspective of the Legislative Process-Focusing on the Deliberation of the Adult Guardianship Subcommittee-' (2013) 22(2) *Yokohama Law Review* 231, 55 (in Japanese); Atsushi Omura, 'Study Group on the Adult Guardianship System and Eiichi Hoshino: Eiichi Hoshino Research Survey (Part 2)' (2017) 134(11) *Journal of the Law Association* 2254, 2280 (in Japanese).

[13] Hoshino (n 7).

[14] Ibid 4. Eiichi Hoshino remarks that the guiding principles of the adult guardianship system are 'harmony between protection and autonomy/self-determination' and 'strike a balance between the protection of the principal and the protection of a third party, that is, the other party of the contract.'

adult ward) exists in the Civil Code.[15] The adult guardianship is primarily subject to property management of principles.[16] There are many voices of practitioners seeking specific guidelines for the performance of adult guardians' duties.[17] Recently, the debate regarding the scope of duty of adult guardians for personal protection was deliberated on by experts in the adult guardianship promotion project, which is discussed later.[18]

c. Legal Position of the Adult Guardianship System in Japan Law System

The debate over personal protection is closely tied to the legal nature and position of adult guardianship within Japan's legal system. Teruaki Tayama (2010)[19] states that 'the adult guardianship system is a civil law system whereby an adult guardian appointed by the family court exercises authority that interferes with the autonomous sphere of the principal. Such interference is not unlawful as long as it is grounded in statutory authority; however, if the guardian violates the duty of due care as a prudent manager, the specific act becomes unlawful,'[20] thereby highlighting the public aspect of the adult guardianship system. Tayama further argues that 'the adult guardianship system should not be confined to the civil law domain but should also be developed in cooperation with social welfare law and the values of the social security system enshrined in the Constitution,'[21] precisely because of its public character. The statutory guardianship system is separately prescribed in the General Provisions and the Family Law sections of the Civil Code, while the voluntary guardianship system is governed by the Act

---

[15.] The duty of adult guardians includes legal acts and excludes non-legal acts, such as meals and aged care. The principal's daily life and choices, including purchase of daily necessities (Article 9 of the Civil Code), identification (i.e., marriage, divorce, adoption, etc.), personality (i.e., religion, voting, etc.), where the principal lives, and the principal's consent to medical treatment are not included in the duty of adult guardians. Consequently, adult guardians have only a few duties in regard to their principal's personal protection. Ministry of Justice of Japan, Civil Affairs Bureau Counselor's Office, *Commentary on Proposal Overview for Revision of Adult Guardianship System* (Kinzai Institute for Financial Affairs, Inc., 1998) 39–43 (in Japanese).

[16.] There is an opinion that Article 858 is regarded as the 'guideline' for the responsibility of adult guardianship. One secretariat officer of the Ministry of Justice of Japan remarked that 'adult guardianship is subject to property management.... It is based on the understanding that the duty of personal consideration that adult guardians bear, stipulated in Article 858, provides guidelines for carrying out such an adult guardianship duty.' Osamu Kaneko, 'Scope of Adult Guardianship and Obligation to Custody' (2010) 63(8) *Law Plaza* 9, 17 (in Japanese).

[17.] Yasuhiro Akanuma, 'Adult Guardian's Duties and Limitations' (2015) 1406 *Hanrei Times* 5, 15 (in Japanese).

[18.] Refers to Section 1.2.1 (3), 'The Basic Plan and the Interim Verification Report.'

[19.] Teruaki Tayama, 'Legal Position of the Adult Guardianship System: Its Private Law and Public Law Aspects' in Kazutoshi Kobayashi, Hidefumi Kobayashi and Akira Murata (eds), *Legal Issues in an Ageing Society: A Collection of 80-Year-Old Commemorative Papers for Dr. Jun Sunaga* (Sakai Shoten, 2010) 1–29 (in Japanese).

[20.] Ibid 14.

[21.] Teruaki Tayama refers to laws of the social welfare law in his text, such as the *Social Welfare Act* (Article 2-3-12 support program for self-reliance in daily life) and Act on Mental Health and Welfare for the Mentally Disabled (Article 22-1 protection system). Tayama (n 19) 26.

on Voluntary Guardianship Contracts, and the adult guardianship registration system is regulated by yet another statute. Consequently, the adult guardianship system forms a complex legal framework. The statutory guardianship system, involving the family courts, embodies a public aspect and is partly intertwined with administrative law and social welfare legislation adjacent to the Civil Code, which contributes to its difficulty for the general public to comprehend. In light of this complexity, Tayama suggests that 'there is no objection to establishing adult guardianship legislation that is more easily understood, consolidated as a coherent package, and positioned within a unified domain of law.'[22]

d. Research on the Mental Capacity Act 2005 and the Consumer Contract Law

Research on the adult guardianship system from a new perspective has emerged. This is a study by Fumie Suga on the Mental Capacity Act 2005 (hereinafter referred to as 'MCA 2005') in England and Wales. Suga introduced the MCA 2005 to Japan. The law was enacted in 2005 based on the accumulation of common law cases; deliberated on by experts and came into force in 2008. It is a legal system that formulates SDM, which is not based on the capacity doctrine.[23] The underlying premise of this law is that 'a person must be assumed to have capacity unless it is established that he lacks capacity' (section 1(2)a, MCA 2005), when a third party can then support the principal in decision-making. It allows agency decisions by a third party only if it is determined by proof that the principal is incapable of making decisions.

Suga, along with Yasushi Kamiyama, proposes a combination of 'small adult guardianship' and 'large support' based on comparative law research in the UK, Germany and other European countries, encouraging the adoption of new trends in Japan, such as SDM without restrictions on the rights of the principals.[24] In anticipation of the Convention on the Rights of Persons with Disabilities (hereinafter referred to as 'CRPD'), Suga advocated for a legal device that combines the adult guardianship system and SDM. Suga's discussion has become known by researchers and practitioners in Japan.[25] Suga has since shifted her research

---

[22] Teruaki Tayama's opinion may be based on the German care law, which forms a unique territory within their civil code.

[23] Fumie Suga, *The Doctrine of Autonomous Support in the English Adult Guardianship System: Towards a Society Pursuing the Best Interests* (Minerva Shobo, 2010) (in Japanese).

[24] Fumie Suga and Ohara Institute for Social Research (Hosei University), *New Grand Design of Adult Guardianship System* (Hosei University Press, 2013) (in Japanese); Fumie Suga, 'Comparative Legal Consideration on Adult Guardianship System in the International Trends: Suggestions for Reconsidering the Agency Decision System from the Idea of Self-Determination Support' (2014) 76 *Private Law* 198, 204 (in Japanese).

[25] This research led to the 'Guidelines for Adult Guardians Based on Supported Decision-Making,' which was introduced in October 2020.

focus from the adult guardianship system to consumer protection legislation that supports vulnerable adults without restricting human rights.[26]

Japan's consumer contract law, which was reformed in 2018, protects the rights of vulnerable adults in a more unique way than the guardianship system does when concluding a contract. The theoretical background of the consumer contract law is similar to that of the guardianship system.[27] This law is different from the Civil Code as a general contract law that presupposes equal relationships between the parties in private law. If there is any disparity between the contracting parties, the law may protect the interests of vulnerable contracting parties based on three theoretical regulations: capacity of a person, contract contents, and contract indication.[28] These legal methods are exceptions to private autonomy, which presupposes equal and horizontal transactions between the parties, and revokes or invalidates the contract as necessary for unequal relationship between the parties. It can be said that this is a vertical relationship that intervenes in private autonomy. Public intervention is also seen in the guardianship system and the abuse prevention law. Public intervention in consumer contract law is carried out, taking after prescribed procedures only when it is deemed necessary due to disparity between the contracting parties, and accountability is imposed on the public agencies.

e. The CRPD and the Adult Guardianship System

Keisuke Shimizu (2017)[29] states that 'the revision of the Civil Code in 1999… was nothing more than a restructuring of the older incapacity/quasi-incapacity systems within the framework of the existing legal concept prepared by the theory of civil law so far. In contrast, the changes that the CRPD requires of member state parties, including Japan, are on a larger scale.'[30] The impact of

---

[26.] Fumie Suga, *New Consumer Law Research: Legal System and Enforcement System for Inclusion of Vulnerable Consumers* (Seibundo, 2018) (in Japanese).

[27.] This paragraph is based on these two articles: Kazuma Yamashiro, 'Mental Capacity of Contracting Parties and Consumer Law: Issues on Capacity-Type Contract Regulations' (2021) 9 *Review of Consumer Law* 83–110, 110 (in Japanese); Kazuma Yamashiro, 'The Mental Capacity of Contracting Parties and Consumer Law: Following the Logic of CRPD in Private Law' (Japan Association of Private Law Symposium Material: Civil Code and Consumer Law in Transition) (2021) 1199 *NBL* 24–31, 28–31 (in Japanese).

[28.] Kazuma Yamashiro argues that capacity is a valid requirement for legal action of adults and limits the possibility of forming legal relationships with others based on private autonomy. The indication doctrine can be used to support adults with insufficient mental capacity without excluding them from the legal action domain. This trend may manifest itself either by reducing the function of *the principle of restricted legal agency* and expanding the response to defects in the manifestation of intention, or by recognizing *the principle of incapacity of intention* as a discipline regarding the manifestation of intention.

[29.] Keisuke Shimizu, 'The Convention on the Rights of Persons with Disabilities and Civil Law Theory' (2017) 14 *Adult Guardianship Law Review* 40, 50 (in Japanese).

[30.] Ibid 40–1.

the CRPD on civil law theory based on the keywords 'capacity, representation, and support' is extracted in sequence. This is Shimizu's report at the thirteenth annual conference of JAGA held in Tokyo on May 28, 2016, which includes the following points of discussion.

First, in the theory of capacity, Shimizu points out that the doctrine of restricted capacity to act could violate Article 12 of the CRPD due to the CRPD's concept of legal capacity and examines in which part of the Civil Code the statutory guardianship system should be placed.[31] Regarding mental capacity, 'The creation of a provision for invalidation of incapacity in the Civil Code[32] does not pose a problem of conflict with the CRPD. Establishing an invalidation provision... without even ensuring a definition of mental capacity' is 'a legislation that is somewhat less cautious.'[33]

Second, in the representation theory, 'it is necessary to coordinate with the protection of the other party regardless of whether the decision is made by the principal or the agent, and where the adjustment point is. It is one of the roles of the Civil Code to determine—and it is inevitable to discuss—this point when introducing a new legal system. However, in the recent discussions on SDM, this point [the protection of the other party] is mostly missed. It is unconscious and only the protection of the principal is emphasized.'[34] It is understood that the contrast with the fact that European countries, such as France, tend to attach importance to consideration for the security of transactions of the other party and a third party is the basis of awareness of the problem.

Third, in the theory of support, new issues have been presented regarding how to position the concept of 'support' that does not exist in the current Civil Code, and the effectiveness of legal acts by SDM.[35] The 'de facto adult guardianship' or 'informal arrangement'[36] chosen by most of the population is raised, as well

---

[31.] Japanese researchers argue that Japan's adult guardianship system conflicts with Article 12 of the CRPD both in legal system and practice. The typical ones: Teruaki Tayama (ed), *Adult Guardianship System and the Convention on the Rights of Persons with Disabilities* (Sanseido, 2012) 169; Makoto Arai, 'Convention on the Rights of Persons with Disabilities and Power of Attorney: Tiger at the Front Gate, Wolf at the Rear Gate' (2013) 28 (1 and 2) *Chiba University Law Studies* 53.

[32.] Refers to Article 3-2 of the Civil Code of Japan. It stipulates that if the person making a juridical act did not have mental capacity when manifesting the relevant intention, the juridical act is void. This provision was created in the 2017 civil code reform and came into force in April 2020.

[33.] Shimizu (n 29) 40–1.

[34.] Ibid 41–50.

[35.] Refers to Section 3.2 (7), 'Other Statutory Developments.' Peru in South America introduced a 'support' clause in their civil code in 2018; Keisuke Shimizu, 'Can the New Peruvian Law Protect the Rights of Persons with Disabilities? Based on the Trend of New Support System' (2021) 91 *Adult Guardianship Practices* 74–80, 77 (in Japanese).

[36.] There is a view that de facto guardianship or informal arrangement can be covered by the 'management of business' provision of the Civil Code (Article 697). Article 697 of the Civil Code stipulates: (1) A person who commences the management of business for another person without being obligated to do so (hereinafter in this Chapter referred to as 'Manager') must manage that business in accordance with the nature of the business, using the method that

as the issue that should be considered. The term 'de facto adult guardianship' means that relatives and nursing-home managers effectively support the person, regardless of the legal system, such as the adult guardianship system.[37]

f. Supported Decision-Making

Shoichi Sato (2016)[38] conducted a theoretical examination of SDM. Sato argues that SDM is based on the principle of presuming capacity for a person, and that a person has a decision-making capacity unless proven otherwise. For this reason, 'If you make a decision on your behalf, you are aware that the supporter does not have the capacity to support your decision-making, and the supporter has a responsibility to explain to others.'[39] As a result, SDM is prioritized and substituted decision-making is a last resort. This design is based on the MCA 2005 introduced by Suga and is a different approach from the current Civil Code based on the capacity doctrine. Based on this idea, SDM guidelines have been introduced since 2017, and in October 2020, the Guidelines for Adult Guardians Based on Supported Decision-Making were published, corresponding to Sato's views on SDM as its basics.[40]

Yasushi Kamiyama (2020)[41] advocates for SDM that confirms the CRPD based on the previous discussions of Suga and Sato. After analysis, Kamiyama presents three ways of thinking about SDM, namely: (i) 'The idea that since the CRPD excludes the possibility of all types of substituted decision-making, it must be completely transformed into a supported decision-making system (i.e.,

---

best conforms to the interests of that another person (the principal). (2) The Manager must engage in management of business in accordance with the intentions of the principal if the manager knows or is able to conjecture that intention. Fumie Suga, 'Reorganization of *Negotiorum Gestio* Theory for People with Inadequate Mental Capacity: An Attempt to Integrate Interpretation with the Adult Guardianship System Based on a Person-Centered Approach' in Takanobu Igarashi et al (eds), *The History and Future of Civil Law* (Seibundo, 2014) (in Japanese); There is the case law regarding the management of business: [A Supreme Court of Japan ruling on business management, Supreme Court of Japan, Civil Code Vol. 15, No. 10, page 2629 in Japanese on November 30, 1961].

[37.] The term 'de facto guardianship' is defined as 'partially or fully incompetent elder people are able to continue to maintain dignified lives, in a caring setting, without the need to resort to legal guardianship,' which 'includes both informal relationships, by people who based on kinship or other caring ties provide the care and decision-making, and formal relationships, by employees. paid workers, or other service providers, from various governmental and local agencies or organizations who provide care as part of their professional duty.' Israel Doron, 'From Guardianship to Long-Term Legal Care: Law and Caring for the Elderly' (2002) Doctoral dissertation, York University 178–225, 179.

[38.] Shoichi Sato, 'Is Decision-Making Support Available?' (2016) 2016 *Annual Report of the Philosophy of Law* 57, 71 (in Japanese).

[39.] Ibid 59.

[40.] When making important legal decisions (i.e., legal acts and relevant non-legal acts), the SDM guidelines for adult guardians allow adult guardians to go through the SDM process and shift to substituted decision-making only if SDM does not work. The guidelines admit that the term decision-making capacity, which is a presumption for SDM, is not based on the law in Japan but the guidelines.

[41.] Yasushi Kamiyama, 'Recent Policy Trends Regarding Supported Decision-Making in Japan' (2020) 72(4) [414] *The Doshisha Law Review* 445, 467 (in Japanese).

the stance of supported decision-making unification by the UN Committee),'
(ii) 'The direction in which substituted decision-making on behalf of a principal
is regarded as a type of supported decision-making by respecting the will of the
principal as the standard for decision-making (i.e., being close to a concept of
the 1st Government of Japan Report),'[42] (iii) 'Supported decision-making and
substituted decision-making are separated from the aspect of philosophy, and
with prioritization of the principle of supported decision-making, substituted
decision-making is used only as a last resort (i.e., the guardianship promotion
project is gradually moving in a direction that is compatible with this idea).'[43]
Kamiyama is in favor of the idea of (iii). Kamiyama's three divisions express
the differences in thinking about the SDM concept in Japan from the civil law
viewpoint. In view of (iii), the adult guardianship system and SDM can coexist
as independent law systems while prioritizing SDM. This is a civil law scholar's
unique view on SDM in Japan, which needs further discussion.

g. Future Developments

In his *Proposals for the Second-Term Basic Plan*, Arai (2021)[44] makes four key
points regarding future developments in adult guardianship: (i) He proposes
incorporating the functions of quasi-judicial institutions—specifically, notaries
and the Legal Affairs Bureau—into the regional collaboration network to enhance
community support systems. Notaries currently create voluntary guardianship
contracts at the request of principals as part of this network. Arai further suggests
that the Legal Affairs Bureau, which is responsible for registering voluntary
guardianship contracts by law, should also be given a monitoring role to ensure
that voluntary guardians petition the family court in a timely manner for the
appointment of voluntary guardian supervisors.(ii) He advocates for promoting SDM alongside substituted decision-making within the legal framework.
(iii) He recommends that teams comprising adult guardians and other individuals
involved with the principal should play a greater role in the principal's personal
protection. (iv) He proposes, as a measure against fraud, the establishment of
a registration system for voluntary guardianship contracts overseen by a core
agency, which would also monitor the invocation of such contracts within the
community. These proposals align with the future vision outlined in the Basic

---

[42.] Refers to Section 1.2.1 (2) b, 'Response by the Government of Japan.'

[43.] Kamiyama (n 41) 447–8.

[44.] Makoto Arai, 'The Adult Guardianship System Talks No. 15: III Enactment of the *Act on Promotion of the Adult Guardianship System*, 3 Basic Plan Interim Verification Report' (2021) 2124 *Periodicals* 60, 64 (in Japanese); Makoto Arai, *Formation and Development of the Adult Guardianship System* (Yuhikaku Publishing Co., Ltd., 2021) 220–4 (in Japanese).

Plan under the Promotion Act. Arai emphasizes that 'the Basic Plan is decided by the Ministerial Council of Japan and is a national project that must be realized.'[45]

In his keynote lecture *History, Current Status, and Future of the Adult Guardianship System in Japan* (2020),[46] delivered at the Seventeenth Annual Conference of JAGA in Tokyo on November 14, 2020, Tayama reflects on the two decades since the adult guardianship system's implementation in 2000 and introduces the concept of 'adult protection law.'[47] Drawing from German, Austrian, and Swiss civil laws, Tayama defines adult protection law as 'the collective legal regulations concerning the protection and care of adults with health problems or disabilities that prevent them from engaging in legal transactions without third-party assistance.' The essence of adult protection law, he notes, is to offer comprehensive legal care and protection for vulnerable adults without unduly restricting their human rights. In particular, Austria and Switzerland have incorporated adult protection law into their Civil Codes in ways that retain an independent and accessible character. Tayama argues that 'it is perhaps time for [Japan] to consider transforming the adult guardianship system into a generous [adult protection] system, with an emphasis on social welfare measures, rather than seeking to upgrade the guardianship system itself as a legally elaborate structure.'[48] His perspective, informed by recent developments in European legislation, suggests a future direction involving the transformation of Japan's guardianship system into a broader adult protection law—an alternative legal architecture distinct from the path envisaged by the Basic Plan.

h. Summary of Civil Law Scholars' Views and the Author's Stance

Previous research by Japanese civil law scholars on the adult guardianship system and related issues has been reviewed. In the existing deliberations by experts, the scope and responsibility of adult guardians for personal protection remain limited, while new perspectives have been introduced through comparative law studies, notably referencing the Mental Capacity Act 2005 (MCA 2005) of England and Wales. Although SDM guidelines have been published through the guardianship promotion project, academic critiques point out that Japan's response to the CRPD remains insufficient. Over the twenty-five years since the

---

[45.] Arai (n 44) 224.

[46.] Teruaki Tayama, 'History, Current Status, and Future of the Adult Guardianship System in Japan' (2020) 18 *Adult Guardianship Study* 18, 27 (in Japanese).

[47.] Ibid 27.

[48.] Ibid.

enforcement of the adult guardianship system, the legal challenges surrounding it have become increasingly clear.

Regarding future developments, civil law scholars offer two contrasting viewpoints: One group expects progress through the guardianship promotion project initiated by the Government of Japan, while another group proposes transforming the adult guardianship system into a broader adult protection system with greater emphasis on social welfare measures. The author's position in relation to these scholarly debates is outlined below:

(i)   This study is based on the premise that the Civil Code and relevant laws related to the adult guardianship system will continue to be maintained. More than twenty-five years after its enforcement, the adult guardianship system has established its normative framework. I therefore agree that the system is primarily intended for the property management of the principal, and that personal protection is to be conducted within the authority granted to adult guardians by the family courts (Hoshino and Uchida). Recognizing the role of the Civil Code, the fulfillment of welfare measures for vulnerable adults should be understood as a responsibility of the national government (Hoshino and Uchida).

(ii) It is desirable that SDM, rather than reliance on the adult guardianship system, be prioritized, in line with the SDM guidelines for adult guardians. This shift would lead to a framework characterized by 'large support' and 'small guardianship' (Kamiyama and Suga).[49]

(iii) The legislation of SDM should be considered in order to establish an advocacy system suited to Japan, while also addressing the risks of fraud and undue influence[50] faced by vulnerable adults. Legislation should reflect the principle that 'supported decision-making and substituted decision-making are philosophically distinct, and substituted decision-making is used only as a last resort' (Kamiyama). The adult guardianship system and SDM should thus coexist independently while complementing one another (Kamiyama).

[49.] If the use of the guardianship type in statutory guardianship is significantly reduced by prioritizing SDM, it could be considered that the revision of the Civil Code related to the adult guardianship system may not be always important. In such a case, the statutory guardianship type would be abolished in the statutory guardianship system from the viewpoint of conformity with the CRPD, as both Arai and Tayama opine.

[50.] The term 'undue influence' is characterized as occurring, where the quality of the interaction between the support person and the person being supported includes signs of fear, aggression, threat, deception, or manipulation (General Comment No. 1 by UN Committee on CRPD); 'Undue influence' is defined in the State of California, the US, as an 'excessive persuasion that causes another person to act or refrain from acting by overcoming that person's free will and results in inequity' (California Welfare and Institutions Code section 15610.70).

(2) Previous Research in Social Security Law

In Section 1.1.1 (1), it is recognized as necessary to develop complementary systems in the social security law to the adult guardianship system in ensuring personal protection. Therefore, we will review previous research on social security law regarding policies that would complement the adult guardianship system. The social security system supports the security of the people and the stability of their lives. It consists of social insurance (pension, health care, and long-term care (aged care)), public assistance, health care and public health, and social welfare, and supports people's lives for a lifetime.[51] The social security law is a general term for legislation that regulates legal relationships such as social insurance (pension, health care, and long-term care (aged care)), public assistance, health care and public health, and social welfare, which includes the social welfare law and legal advocacy.[52]

The social security law is the law of discipline in Japan based directly on 'Article 25 of the constitution of Japan…and provides benefits and burdens that are prerequisites for the purpose of establishing preconditions to enable the people to pursue their own lives.'[53] There are various theories about the legal basis of the social security law, such as 'right to life' in Article 25 of the constitution, social solidarity, and 'human dignity' in Article 13 of the constitution.[54] In this study, it is understood that all these theories are the legal basis of the social security law.

The challenges faced by adults with insufficient mental capacity are diverse and everyone has a right to enjoy support and protection when it is necessary. Complicated cases are often seen, such as a case where the principal has no relatives and no property and is abused or involved with antisocial forces. In such cases, it is difficult to resolve the challenges only with the adult guardianship system operated by the family courts. Therefore, involvement of the government, public agencies and civil society has become inevitable.[55]

[51.] Refers to the Ministry of Health, Labour, and Welfare of Japan, *What Is the Social Security System?* (Web Page, n/a) (in Japanese) <https://www.mhlw.go.jp/stf/newpage_21479.html>.

[52.] Yoshimi Kikuchi opines that the social security law is structured 'according to the difference in the content of benefits due to the nature of the security needs and is divided into three divisions: the income security law, which is a monetary benefit, the medical security law, which focuses on service benefits, and social service guarantee, which includes social welfare and legal advocacy.' Yoshimi Kikuchi, *Social Security Law* (Yuhikaku Publishing Co., Ltd., 2nd ed, 2014) 104 (in Japanese).

[53.] Ibid 101.

[54.] Ibid 113–16.

[55.] The part of the Yokohama Declaration relevant to Japan (which was made at the first World Congress of Adult Guardianship in Yokohama 2010 and partially revised at the Fifth World Congress in 2016) states that 'the system of the legal support and protection for adults should be available for everyone, and for this reason it is essential that the government publicly support the entire system' (underlined by the author). International Guardianship Network (IGN), *Yokohama Declaration* (Web Page, September 16, 2016) <https://www.international-guardianship.com/yokohama-declaration.htm>.

Under the circumstances, the deliberations by experts over the adult guardianship system are conducted by the Ministry of Health, Labour, and Welfare (Community Welfare and Services Division), which oversees the guardianship promotion project. In this project, 'advocacy support' is positioned at the core of the second term Basic Plan that was implemented in April 2022. The adult guardianship system is said to be positioned as part of the legal advocacy system under the social security law by scholars.[56] Therefore, the theories on the concept of legal advocacy in the Japanese context will be summarized, and the author's stance will be clarified after the theories on the relationship between the adult guardianship system and the social security law, and the community support that is the site of legal advocacy activities will be reviewed.

a. What Is Advocacy in the Japanese Context?

The term 'advocacy' is used diversely, which includes multi-functional meanings.[57] The concept of 'advocacy' is originally based on the act of a lawyer's proxy in the courts on behalf of a client. This concept applies to the field of social welfare, where a person who is socially disadvantaged cannot claim or remedy their rights or prevent their disadvantage by themselves. The concept now requires an advocacy activity in which a social or similar worker defends the person's rights.[58] The concept of advocacy was introduced in Japan in the 1960s and 1970s and it has been frequently used in the field of welfare since the 1990s. The term 'advocacy' is used in legislation.[59] In this way, the concept of advocacy has become prevalent in the field of social welfare, although its meaning is not defined by law but is left to the academic studies. The views of scholars on advocacy are summarized below.

Masateru Kawano (1999)[60] states that 'advocacy is the support activities of exercising rights, such as preventing abuse, assisting in the use of welfare services,

---

[56.] Keiko Matsushita, 'Advocacy by Adult Guardianship System: Establishment of the Significance and Role of Citizen Guardians' (2020) Doctoral dissertation, Kansai University 1, 96 (in Japanese).

[57.] Kimiyo Terada, 'A Discussion of How Advocacy Is Conceptualized in Social Welfare Research in Japan' (2016) 15(2) *Niigata Journal of Health and Welfare* 27, 34 (in Japanese); Williams and Field categorize advocacy into self-advocacy, legal advocacy, social advocacy, and systemic advocacy in the Australian context. Karen Williams and Sue Field, 'Advocacy and the Rights of the Vulnerable Older Person' (2021) 12 *Journal of Aging Law & Policy* 1, 37.

[58.] Miyo Akimoto, 'Support and Autonomy in Advocacy' (2004) 4 *Social Policy Research* 26–50, 27 (in Japanese); Atsushi Hirata, *Advocacy and Welfare Practice Activities: Re-Questioning Concepts and Systems* (Akashi Shoten, 2012) 11–29 (in Japanese).

[59.] For example, Article 1 of both the Elder Abuse Prevention Law and the Abuse Prevention Law for Persons with Disabilities uses the word '*kenri-yogo*' in Japanese (advocacy). According to the ordinance and regulations of the Ministry of Health, Labor and Welfare of Japan, 'Advocacy and the Adult Guardianship System' is stipulated in the national qualification examination subjects of certified social workers, care workers, and mental health workers.

[60.] Masateru Kawano, 'Basic Issues of "Welfare Advocacy in the Community"' (1999) 66(2) *Journal of Law and Politics* 55, 84 (in Japanese).

or managing property, from the standpoint of a person with insufficient mental capacity.'[61] The idea of advocacy is to 'respect the will of the person as much as possible in his/her self-determination, […] and therefore empowerment and self-advocacy are particularly important.'[62] The advocacy system can be viewed in a narrow or broad sense.[63] In a narrow sense, the advocacy system refers to the adult guardianship system and the community welfare advocacy program (currently, support program for self-reliance in daily life), in which adult guardians and daily-life support staff directly support adults with insufficient mental capacity. Advocacy in a broad sense includes, in addition to advocacy in a narrow sense, a comprehensive and specialized consultation desk and information provision, an auditing and self-inspection/third-party evaluation system, and a complaint resolution system.[64] Kawano's view on advocacy paves a way for discussion on the roles and scope of advocacy in the social security law studies, which takes influence on the disability law.[65] The discussion on advocacy is explored below.

Atsushi Hirata (2012)[66] asserts that advocacy is 'to support [a] person according to his/her will and preferences with respect to his/her legal rights based on the idea of enhancing the [person's] right to self-determination.'[67] Advocacy, in a narrow sense, is 'supporting self-determination ('supporting the self-determination process') and representing self-determination ('supporting the self-determination assertion stage')'[68] for adults with insufficient mental capacity. Advocacy, in a broad sense, is 'support for the realization of rights, such as acquisition of rights based on self-determination and restoration of rights ('supporting at the stage of realization of self-determination'),'[69] in addition to the two supports under advocacy in a narrow sense. The advocacy system in a narrow sense includes the adult guardianship system, support program for self-reliance in daily life, and various consultation support systems. Advocacy in a broad sense includes a

---

[61.] Ibid 58.

[62.] Ibid 59.

[63.] Ibid 64–6.

[64.] Kazuhiro Nishida follows Kawano's views on the advocacy in narrow and broad senses. Kazuhiro Nishida, 'Procedures for Advocating and Relieving Social Security Rights' in Japan Society for Social Security Law (ed), *Social Security Law in the 21st Century* (Lecture Book, Social Security Law, Volume 1) (Horitsu Bunka Sha, 2001) 167, 193 (in Japanese).

[65.] Masateru Kawano, 'Disability Law as a "New Social Law"' (2017) 1 *Disability Law* 9, 32 (in Japanese).

[66.] Hirata (n 58) 52; Atsushi Hirata, 'What Is Advocacy? Focusing on the Adult Guardianship System' (Lecture Paper at the Seminar on Social Welfare Sponsored by Public Interest Incorporated Foundation Tokyo 23-City on November 12, 2010) (in Japanese).

[67.] Hirata (n 58) 52.

[68.] Miyo Akimoto and Atsushi Hirata, *Social Welfare and Advocacy: Theory and Practice for Human Rights* (Yuhikaku Publishing Co., Ltd., 2015) 115 (in Japanese).

[69.] Ibid 116–18.

complaint resolution system, an ombudsperson system, and an abuse prevention system, in addition to the narrow-sense systems.[70]

Miyo Akimoto (2015)[71] states that advocacy is 'to support 'weak' individuals who are unable to enjoy freedom and benefits specified in the human image of the civil law (namely, 'strong' individuals)...Advocacy covers problems that have been considered in non-legal activities in addition to legal activities.'[72] Akimoto divides the advocacy system into two: (i) an adult guardianship system that directly supports vulnerable people and ensures accountability at the time of concluding a contract (social welfare law), and (ii) a consumer contract law that indirectly supports and protects vulnerable people, universal design, fraud prevention activities, and monitoring activities in the community.[73] Akimoto shows a unique composition of social welfare whereby vulnerable adults pursue well-being by choosing their own way of life by themselves. It combines advocacy in the 'world of law' (i.e., adult guardianship, social welfare law) and that in the 'world of facts' (i.e., information gathering, support program for self-reliance in daily life, etc.) which are supported by social workers.

b. Adult Guardianship System and Social Security Law

Theories on the relationship between the adult guardianship system and the social security law, which is mediated by the concept of advocacy, will be reviewed. Nobuyuki Iwama (2011)[74] describes what the point of contact between the adult guardianship system and social welfare brings about. Iwama addresses three points, namely: (i) Government responsibility as a safety;[75] (ii) Positioning the persons as the subject of the contract,[76] and (iii) Building an advocacy system in the community. Regarding (iii) above, a comprehensive advocacy system is being built in the community in which the local government, public agencies,

---

[70] Ibid.

[71] Akimoto and Hirata (n 68) (Akimoto-written part).

[72] Ibid 24–5.

[73] Ibid 81–9.

[74] Nobuyuki Iwama, 'Adult Guardianship System and Social Welfare: Exploring New Possibilities from the Point of Contact' (2011) 627 *The Journal of Ohara Institute for Social Research* 19, 29 (in Japanese).

[75] The responsibility of the Government and public agencies is stated in the abuse response program that is based on the Elder Abuse Prevention Law. There are cases in which the municipality supports the adult guardianship system, including the municipality's mayor lodging a petition.

[76] The social security system changes from a public measure method to a contract method, and the parties need to conclude a contract to have welfare services. The adult guardianship system can be used when those who lack mental capacity conclude a contract.

NPOs, practitioners, and citizens can participate. Iwama then discusses the role of social workers and the promotion of community-based welfare.[77]

In *Advocacy and Welfare Practice Activities*, Hirata (2012)[78] states that 'Article 858 (Respect for the Intention and Personal Consideration of the Adult Ward) of the Civil Code implies that the adult guardianship system is part of advocacy systems and stipulates two obligations to adult guardians, namely the obligation to respect the intention of the principal and the obligation to consider mental and physical condition and living circumstances of the principal. It is important to balance these two different obligations.' Hirata goes on to explain how adult guardians should balance these two obligations toward the principals.[79]

Toshiro Ishibashi (2014)[80] observes that '[the] adult guardianship system is closely related to the welfare and long-term care [aged care] systems, and it is premised that these are the systems that should complement one another. This interdisciplinary relationship, on the contrary, makes it difficult [for practitioners] to clearly understand the scope of duties, responsibilities, and obligations of adult guardians [in personal protection].'[81] Regarding legislation that complements the adult guardianship system, Ishibashi refers to the following list of laws and policies: the disability law (i.e., Basic Act for Persons with Disabilities, Act on Comprehensive Support for the Daily and Social Life of Persons with Disabilities, Act for the Mental Health and Welfare of Persons with Mental Disorders), the abuse prevention law (i.e., Elder Abuse Prevention Law, Abuse Prevention Law for Persons with Disabilities), subsidies related to the use of the adult guardianship system (the Social Welfare Act and relevant ordinances), and the support program for self-reliance in daily life (based on the Social Welfare Act).[82]

Civil law scholars address the relationship between the adult guardianship system and the social security law. For example, Kamiyama (2010)[83] states that '[the] Elder Abuse Prevention Law [Article 28] and the Abuse Prevention Law for Persons with Disabilities [Article 44] regard the adult guardianship system as one of the effective legal instruments to prevent abuse. [According to Article 32 of the Act on Social Welfare for the Elderly, Article 28 of the Act for the Welfare

---

[77.] Nobuyuki Iwama states that 'advocacy must guarantee efforts for realizing the way of life of the person to ensure that they live their own lives.' Iwama (n 74) 22.

[78.] Hirata (n 58).

[79.] Ibid 179–80.

[80.] Toshiro Ishibashi, 'Advocacy Services and the Social Security Law' in Akira Moriyama and Nobuyuki Koike (eds), *Realization of Citizen's Guardianship* (Nihon Kajo Publishing Co., Ltd., 2014) 231, 299 (in Japanese).

[81.] Ibid 256.

[82.] Ibid 258–88.

[83.] Yasushi Kamiyama, 'Introduction of the Public Adult Guardianship System in Japan: Referring to the German Operation Scheme' (2010) 641 *The Journal of Ohara Institute for Social Research* 44, 58 (in Japanese).

of Persons with Intellectual Disabilities, and Article 51-11-2 of the Act for the Mental Health and Welfare of Persons with Mental Disorders,] it is important that the right to petition for adult guardianship by a mayor of the municipality is regulated as the role of the municipality. Here, a scheme that attempts to realize a social welfare policy (i.e., prevention of abuse of vulnerable adults) is clearly seen in a form where the adult guardianship system under the Civil Code and the system under the social security law are interlinked.'[84] Kamiyama (2015)[85] also addresses 'adult guardianship as a social security law,' referring to passages of 'the advocacy function of the adult guardianship system' and 'cooperation with the social security law in the operational process [of the adult guardianship].'[86]

c. Community Support

Advocacy activities are implemented in a community to take care of vulnerable adults by law. Here, community support is focused on. One of the common goals of the social security law and policies is to realize a diverse society,[87] and to achieve this, the Government of Japan has adopted relevant policies to enhance the ability to solve community issues, strengthen communal ties, improve the comprehensive support system in the community, and encourage the utilization of skillful practitioners.[88] Therefore, advocacy should be observed in the context of where and how it is positioned in such policies.

Yoshimi Kikuchi (2019)[89] addresses 'the importance of supported decision-making in supporting the lives of persons in the community…and there is an aspect of the adult guardianship system that overlaps with the principles of a community-based general support center and a diverse society.'[90] Kikuchi states, 'Legal support, such as the adult guardianship system, should be positioned [not in the center

---

[84.] Ibid 54.

[85.] Yasushi Kamiyama, *Professional Guardian and Protection of Personal Affairs* (Civil Law Study Group, 3rd ed, 2015) (in Japanese).

[86.] Ibid 21–4.

[87.] A 'diverse society' refers to 'a society in which the community and various local actors participate, and the people are connected to other people and social resources across generations and fields for better living and purpose.' Ministry of Health, Labour, and Welfare of Japan, *Toward the Realization of a 'Diverse Society in Community'* (Web Page, February 7, 2017) (in Japanese) <https://www.mhlw.go.jp/stf/seisakunitsuite/bunya/0000184346.html>.

[88.] It can be understood that a diverse society demonstrates an image of a community where people help one another, where the value of equality is enhanced, and no discrimination is available due to a person's disability.

[89.] Yoshimi Kikuchi, *Supporting Social Security: Rethinking <Community>* (Iwanami Shoten Publishers, 2019) (in Japanese).

[90.] Ibid 193.

but] in one corner of the overall picture of 'community-based integrated care system' and a 'diverse society.'[91]

Atsushi Hirata (2012)[92] states that 'we need a "consultation support system" to prevent infringing on the person's rights and to restore and remedy the person's rights in the event of infringement.'[93] Jun Nishimura (2018)[94] asserts that 'since the social welfare basic structural reform around 2000 when a contract method was introduced...the welfare support law, which is indirect support through information provision, consultation support, skill development by practitioners, community planning, etc., has come to play an important role.'[95]

Policy measures, such as comprehensive consultation support, community development support, participation support, and multilayered support, were introduced in 2020 through the revision of the *Social Welfare Act* (Article 106-4-2).[96] In the article 'Social Security Law in the Light of Adult Guardianship and Advocacy,' Hiroshi Kawakubo (2020)[97] focuses on consultation support, concluding that 'the consultation support system, which is positioned as part of advocacy, empowers its nature in the community, and will expand the possibility of advocacy.'[98] There are various forms of consultation support, such as information provision, education and consultation, and consultation support in abuse cases, some of which are regulated by law and others are not. Because of these diverse forms, Kawakubo states that 'the legal evaluation [of consultation support] is a challenge.'[99]

d. Summary of Social Security Law Scholars' Views and the Author's Stance

Previous research by Japanese scholars in social security law and social welfare studies on advocacy, the adult guardianship system, and community support has

---

[91.] Ibid 194.

[92.] Hirata (n 58).

[93.] Ibid 208.

[94.] June Nishimura, 'Legal System of the Personal Social Services in Terms of Participation Support' (2018) 15(1) *Journal of Kanagawa University of Human Services* 1, 13 (in Japanese).

[95.] Ibid 13. June Nishimura states that 'consultation support does not always involve benefits. Initial consultation may lead to assistance planning, but in some cases, it may be limited to consultation assistance only.' Jun Nishimura, 'Legal Analysis of the Process of Social Service Provision: Tentative Study for Social Work Law' (2020) 14 *Annals of Public Policy* 119–35, 129 (in Japanese).

[96.] Refers to the Ministry of Health, Labour, and Welfare of Japan, *About the Multi-layered Support System Project* (Web Page, n/a) (in Japanese) <https://www.mhlw.go.jp/kyouseisyakaiportal/jigyou/>.

[97.] Hiroshi Kawakubo, 'Social Security Law in the Light of Adult Guardianship and Advocacy' (2020) 12 *Review of Social Security Law* 3, 22 (in Japanese).

[98.] Ibid 21.

[99.] Ibid.

been reviewed. Theories on advocacy are, to some extent, fluid and evolve over time; thus, there is no single established theory of advocacy from the perspectives of social security law and social welfare studies. Advocacy serves the function of building welfare systems, sharing the values and objectives of social security law with stakeholders, and connecting the law to practitioners' activities within communities.[100] The concept of advocacy enables expansion from the 'world of law' to the 'world of facts' (Akimoto), thereby bridging legal frameworks and practical realities.

The social security system in Japan has shifted from a public measure model to a contract-based model, allowing individuals to participate voluntarily through contracts based on their own will. The realization of a diverse society is affirmed in Article 1 of the Act on Promotion of the Adult Guardianship System, and the Basic Plan emphasizes 'advocacy support.' As a result, there is a strong likelihood that measures under the Social Welfare Act and the adult guardianship system—which share common objectives—will become increasingly functionally interlinked at the community level.

The author's position in relation to the scholarly viewpoints reviewed is as follows:

(i)   In this study, advocacy refers to 'support for persons with insufficient mental capacity to exercise their legal rights, according to their will and preferences, including preventing abuse, assisting in the use of welfare services, and managing property.'

(ii) The advocacy system, in a narrow sense, encompasses the adult guardianship system, SDM, abuse prevention law, and related programs such as support program for self-reliance in daily life and subsidies for expenses associated with adult guardianship use, all of which directly assist persons with insufficient mental capacity in accordance with the definition provided in (i). In a broader sense, the advocacy system includes consumer contract law, disability law, and complaint resolution mechanisms, which provide indirect support in addition to the direct measures.

(iii) A core agency could play a crucial role in adult guardianship and SDM for adults with insufficient mental capacity in the community. Building a multilayered and comprehensive community support system—through the collaboration of regional adult guardianship networks (centered around a core agency), community-based integrated care systems (including nursing care institutions), and local government initiatives

---

[100.] Hirata (n 58) 30–5.

addressing abuse—is considered an effective model for supporting a diverse society.

1.1.2 Function-Based Review

Next, the 'functions' needed to support and protect adults with insufficient mental capacity in the community will be sorted out. This study mainly targets older people with dementia and assumes a process in which their cognitive capacity gradually declines with aging. With the decline in their cognitive capacity, the following support and protection functions are required.

(a) The number of older people living alone increases with the aging of the population. For this reason, the number of areas where neighborhood associations and caregivers (i.e., care managers, helpers in aged care) watch over vulnerable people is increasing. Caregivers regularly visit older people who live alone, so they are aware of their current situation. Relevant institutions, such as the municipality (if necessary), are notified of such on-site information directly or via a community-based general support center.

(b) With aging of the principal, it is possible for the principal and/or its stake-holders to consult with the core agency in the community or community-based general support center about the principal's property management and personal protection, and confirm what kinds of support systems are available, and their terms and conditions of use. It is recommended that the principal discuss their plans for older age with their relatives or close friends at a 'life planning meeting'[101] to convey their personal wishes. When the principal's mental capacity is still intact, they can conclude a voluntary guardianship contract or a property management agency contract with a third party in preparation for a possible decline in cognitive capacity. In preparation for a future decline in cognitive capacity, it is possible to designate a relative (within two degrees) as an agent of the principal in the deposit account of a financial institution.[102]

[101.] Refers to the Ministry of Health, Labour, and Welfare of Japan, *Life Planning Meeting* (Web Page, n/a) (in Japanese) <https://www.mhlw.go.jp/stf/newpage_02783.html>.

[102.] Financial institutions in Japan started providing bank deposit services in which relatives (within two degrees) can function as agents for managing the principals' deposit accounts. This is a memorandum recently circulated among banks as the banking industrial guidelines for the agency of financial transactions: The Japanese Bankers' Association, *About the Way of Thinking about the Agency of Financial Transactions and Strengthening Cooperation between Banks and Local Governments/Social Welfare Institutions* (Web Page, February 18, 2021) (in Japanese) <https://www.zenginkyo.or.jp/news/2021/n021801/>.

(c)   If mild cognitive impairment occurs, it is recommended that the principal undergo an examination test for dementia. At this stage, the voluntary guardianship system may be used according to the relevant mental capacity of the principal. If there are no relatives or close friends to take care of the principal, the principal can apply for the council of social welfare's support program for self-reliance in daily life. It is extremely difficult to participate in the program because it is conducted with a limited budget under a strict qualification test, which tries to find out such information as whether the person can understand the contents of the support contract and what the financial condition of the person is like. Priority is given to older people who need public assistance.

(d)   The overwhelming majority of people receive informal arrangements from relatives or nursing-home managers when their mental capacity becomes insufficient. Informal arrangements are available to those under the care of relatives or nursing-home managers. If there are no relatives or are relatives but no intention of support, the principal may consult with the core agency. In some cases, the principal or mayor of the municipality may lodge a petition for adult guardianship. When using the adult guardianship system, the SDM Guidelines for Adult Guardians are applied, and the SDM process is implemented as a priority as much as possible while considering the will and preferences of the principal.

(e)   In the adult guardianship system, the conclusion of welfare service contracts should be based on personal protection. Daily life (i.e., purchase of daily necessities), identification, and personality matters are not subject to adult guardianship. In addition, the adult guardian does not have the legal authority to determine by himself/herself whereabout the residence of the principal or to give medical consent to doctors on behalf of the principal. The principal or the principal's stakeholders can consult with the adult guardian regarding the principal's residence and medical consent as a team. Regarding property management, deposits and savings can be managed by an adult guardian, but daily spending and identification activities, including wills, are outside the scope of the adult guardian's business. In principle, the principal manages daily spending, and if this is practically difficult, the principal is subjected to informal arrangement of relatives or the nursing-home manager.

(f)   If the person does not have any financial property, the core agency will notify the local government, and if it is deemed necessary by the local government's assessment, the procedure for the mayor's petition for adult guardianship may begin and subsidies for the guardianship fee be recognized. In a difficult case in which the principal is being abused or is a victim of antisocial forces, the local government may be notified by a core agency or a community-based general support center, which is the source of monitoring watch in a community, and the local government or police may intervene to protect the principal. The adult guardianship system is used to separate the principal from their adult children or relatives suspected of abusing the principal, and to change the principal's residence to independently support the principal.[103] Currently, the adult guardianship system and the abuse response program are simultaneously applied to such cases by the local government as an emergency response. Difficult cases,[104] for example, include a complicated background, such as one case for *hikikomori*,[105] a form of severe social withdrawal of the principal's adult children, and the other case for the principal who lives in a house filled with garbage or together with numerous pet dogs or cats.[106]

The above support and protection function flow is summarized in Table 1.1. This table corresponds to the scope of research in this study. The kinds of support and protection functions needed by a principal as their cognitive capacity declines can be understood from the table. The function column shows the functions of systems with legal and policy bases, such as the adult guardianship system and the abuse response program, and of systems with no legal and policy basis, such as informal arrangement. This function list is organized according to the main terms, and detailed functions may be required. The function of supporting and

---

[103] Refers to the response to an '80/50 problem' (or recently called a '90/60 problem'), where an unemployed son in his 50s (or 60s) is financially dependent on an older mother in her 80s (or 90s) who receives a pension.

[104] Difficult cases include five categories: financial problems, the need for living supports, family problems, service usage problems, and community and workplace problems, which are clarified by empirical studies. Noriharu Unuma and Kaoru Sekine, 'A Study of Difficult Cases in Adult Guardianship: Analyses the Contents and Support Methods through Corporate Guardianship by the Council of Social Welfare' (2022) 12 *Kogakkan University of Japanese Studies* 1, 28 (in Japanese).

[105] The term *'hikikomori'* in Japanese is 'characterized by adolescents and adults who become recluses in their parents' homes, unable to work or go to school for months or years.' Alan R. Teo and Albert C. Gaw, 'Hikikomori, a Japanese Culture-Bound Syndrome of Social Withdrawal? A Proposal for DSM-5' (2010) 198(6) *The Journal of Nervous and Mental Disease* 444, 449; The 2018 national survey estimated that 613,000 adults are in a state of severe social withdrawal, which is 1.45 per cent of the Japanese population aged 40 to 64.

[106] The knowledge of a member of staff of a public agency is referred to, who has been directly or indirectly involved in dealing with abuse cases for twenty years at the Adachi District Office in the Metropolitan Tokyo Government. Ichiro Watanabe, 'Aspects of the Adult Guardianship System from the Viewpoint of Local Governments–Citizen's Guardianship, Abuse Response, Support for the Elderly without Relatives, etc.' (2015) 3 *Quarterly Journal of Comparative Guardianship Law* 102, 131 (in Japanese); Ichiro Watanabe, 'Limitations of the Adult Guardianship System from the Safety Net Perspective: From Rescue to Preventive Advocacy' (2021) 15 *Quarterly Journal of Comparative Guardianship Law* 36, 63 (in Japanese).

protecting the principal is diverse, and the relevant institutions that provide this function, relevant legislation, and policies, are also diverse.[107]

Table 1.1: List of Main Functions to Support
and Protect the Principal

Status	Classification	Function	Directly Related System
Aging, single		Watching over	Watching over activity
Same as above		Consultation	Consultation support system
Same as above		Support planning	Life meeting, voluntary guardianship system/ delegation contract (notaries)
Same as above		Deposit account agent, etc.	Contracts with financial institutions, etc.
Mild cognitive impairment, insufficient mental capacity	Personal protection, property management	Informal arrangement	Support by relatives or the nursing-home manager, consultation support system
Mild cognitive impairment		Support for daily life	Support program for self-reliance in daily life, voluntary guardianship system/delegation contract
Insufficient mental capacity	Personal protection	Welfare service contract, etc.	Adult guardianship system/SDM guidelines
Same as above		Daily life and personal matters	Management by the principal, informal arrangement by relatives or the nursing-home manager

---

[107.] It is a challenge for a principal and its stakeholders to understand the overall picture in Table 1.1. Advanced directives or estate planning is recommended when a principal is healthy. Masayuki Tamaruya, 'Japanese Wealth Management and the Transformation of the Law of Trusts and Succession' (2019) 33 *Trust Law International* 147, 168.

Status	Classification	Function	Directly Related System
Same as above		Residence decision	Determined by the principal and stakeholders (the adult guardian) as a team
Same as above		Medical consent	Determined by the principal and stakeholders, medical guidelines[108]
Same as above	Property management	Management of deposits, real estate, etc.	Adult guardianship system/SDM guidelines
Same as above		Daily consumption, wills	Determined by the principal, informal arrangement by relatives or the nursing-home manager
A principal without financial property	Personal protection, public Assistance	Support by public agencies	Support program for self-reliance in daily life, adult guardianship system/SDM guidelines, welfare program
Difficult cases (abuse, etc.)	Abuse, victims of antisocial force etc.	Intervention by public agencies or police, etc.	Older people abuse prevention law, adult guardianship system/ SDM guidelines

Source: Made by the Author

1.1.3 Research Framework Based on Legal Advocacy

The purpose of this study is to explore the potential for adult support and protection legislation to form part of the broader legal framework encompassing the adult guardianship system, SDM, and elder abuse prevention for vulnerable adults,

---

108. Refers to the Ministry of Health, Labour, and Welfare of Japan, *Revised Guidelines for the Medical Supported Decision-Making Process in the Final Stages of Life* (Web Page, March 14, 2019) (in Japanese) <https://www.mhlw.go.jp/stf/houdou/0000197665.html>.

based on issues identified within Japan's adult guardianship system. A systematic review has been conducted on the adult guardianship system and related laws and policies, civil law theories concerning adult guardianship, social security law theories on advocacy, and the key functions necessary for supporting and protecting vulnerable adults. The author's theoretical stance with respect to civil law and social security law is clarified through this review. Consequently, the scope of the legal and policy frameworks, as well as the main functions needed to support and protect adults with impaired decision-making capacity, have been identified. Based on this systematic review, the research framework for the study is outlined below.

First, the subject matter of this study focuses primarily on legal acts involving the principal, applying an interdisciplinary approach based on civil law and social security law. Matters relating to legal affairs after the principal's death are excluded. With particular attention to international trends in legislation for supporting and protecting adults with impaired capacity—especially the legal reforms in Australia—this study seeks to develop a legislative theory for Japan through comparative legal analysis.

Second, this study covers legal and policy systems including the adult guardianship system, SDM frameworks, elder abuse prevention legislation, and related policies such as the 'Support Program for Self-Reliance in Daily Life' and the 'Community-Based Integrated Care System.' These legal and policy systems are collectively referred to as 'legal advocacy' in this study, focusing specifically on legal acts performed by or on behalf of the principal. Elder abuse prevention law is functionally linked to the adult guardianship system and is included in Table 1.1 (List of Main Functions to Support and Protect Vulnerable Adults) to illustrate this close relationship. In contrast, consumer contract law and trust law are excluded from the scope of this study, as they indirectly support vulnerable adults and require separate systematic analysis.

Third, this study proceeds on the assumption that the civil law and related laws concerning the adult guardianship system will remain largely unchanged. Emphasis is placed on the development of SDM, which respects the will and preferences of the principal. It is envisioned that SDM will emerge as an independent legal system coexisting with the adult guardianship framework. This study relies on the current guidelines issued by the Ministry of Health, Labour, and Welfare of Japan.

Fourth, although the COVID-19 pandemic has had extensive impacts on social life, the full extent of these effects remains unclear, and academic analysis is still insufficient. Accordingly, discussions related to the effects of COVID-19 are beyond the scope of this study.

1.2 Overview of the Legal Advocacy and Relevant Policy

1.2.1 Adult Guardianship System and the Promotion Act

(1) Adult Guardianship System in Japan

a. Statutory Guardianship System

Overview of Statutory Guardianship System

The number of adults with insufficient mental capacity who may have some troubles managing their property, such as real estate and money savings, and personal affairs, such as concluding a contract regarding aged care and admission to nursing home, is increasing.[109] Particularly, the number of older people with dementia increases as population ages, and it is estimated that there are approximately 6.0 million such people in Japan.[110] Even if the contract is disadvantageous to such people, they may conclude it without making careful consideration. In such cases, they may eventually suffer from their rash decisions. Supporting adults with insufficient mental capacity in a societal system is an urgent issue in a diverse society where they may cohabit with others. The adult guardianship system, with the aim to uphold such values as respect for self-determination, utilization of the remaining capacity of the principle, and normalization, came into effect on April 1, 2000. This was the enactment with the amendments to the Civil Code of Japan (hereinafter referred to as 'Civil Code') and some relevant legislation.[111] This system was implemented at the same time as the inauguration of the long-term care (aged care) insurance system. Therefore, both systems were called the two driving wheels of a car for older people's policy. It was expected that adult guardians would support the legal acts of principals to conclude contracts as the national welfare system changed from public measures to contracts. The adult guardianship system consists of two types of legal entities: the statutory guardianship system regulated by the Civil Code and the voluntary guardianship system regulated by the Act on Voluntary Guardianship Contract.

---

[109] This part is based on the previously published research note that analyzes the deliberations of experts in 2016–2021 on the adult guardianship system. Yukio Sakurai, 'Current Status and Issues of the Japan's Adult Guardianship System in the Promotion Act: Focused on the Deliberation Process of the Basic Plan' (2021) 30(1) *Yokohama Law Review* 397, 432 (in Japanese).

[110] Refers to the Ministry of Health, Labour, and Welfare, *Comprehensive Promotion of Dementia Measures* (Web Page, June 20, 2019) 4 (in Japanese) <https://www.mhlw.go.jp/content/12300000/000519620.pdf>.

[111] Four relevant legislations on the adult guardianship system in Japan, i.e., Act for Partial Revision of the Civil Code (Act No. 149 of 1999), Act on Voluntary Guardianship Contract (Act No. 150 of 1999), Act of Guardianship Registration (Act No. 152 of 1999), and Act on Coordination (Act No. 151 of 1999).

There are associated laws to regulate the adult guardianship registration system and the administrative procedures that support the systems.

The statutory guardianship system is divided into three types as stipulated in the Civil Code, namely 'guardianship,' 'curatorship,' and 'assistance,' according to the relevant mental capacity of the principal.[112] The 'guardian,' 'curator,' or 'assistant' who is appointed by the family court on petition (hereinafter referred to collectively as 'adult guardian') shall support and protect the principal with insufficient mental capacity. Support and protection should be done by adult guardians: (a) by acting on his or her behalf in performing legal acts, such as concluding contracts, (b) giving consent when the principal conducts a legal act by himself or herself, or (c) later revoking disadvantageous legal acts that the principal performed without consent of the adult guardian in his or her property management and personal affairs. The statutory guardianship system is a legal method based on a harmony between the values of respect for self-determination of the principal and the value of protection of the principal.[113] The three types of statutory guardianship are summarized in Table 1.2.

Before the current adult guardianship system was enacted in 2000, the Civil Code of Japan had an 'incompetence' and 'quasi-competence' system.[114] The incompetence/quasi-competence system was the legal instrument to regulate an adult with insufficient mental capacity. However, people saw the incompetence/ quasi-competence system punitively colored, such as depriving the rights of the individual in a uniform manner. Because the principal's administrative register states clearly that they are incompetent/quasi-competent persons. Consequently, people avoided using the system and the number of users was minimal.[115] Comparing with the old system, the current adult guardianship system has significantly improved.[116] The adult guardianship system is defined as 'respecting the will of the adult custodian and considering the physical and mental condition of the person and the situation of life' (Article 858 of the Civil Code).

[112.] This paragraph relies on the Ministry of Justice of Japan, *Adult Guardianship System and Adult Guardianship Registration System*.

[113.] The autonomy and right to self-determination of the principal are emphasized as values and the protection must be carried out as far as it is necessary. Ministry of Justice of Japan, Civil Affairs Bureau Counselor's Office (n 15) Appendix 1.

[114.] The legal terms 'incompetence' and 'quasi-competence' in English are referred to the article: Arai Makoto and Akira Homma, 'Guardianship for Adults in Japan: Legal Reforms and Advances in Practice' (2005) 24 *Australasian Journal on Ageing* 19–24, 20; before 1948 civil code reform, the incompetence/quasi-competence system was used mainly for preserving family property by proxy decision of the spouse on behalf of the principal.

[115.] Some 25,000 cases of the incompetence/quasi-incompetence system were registered on family register in the period from 1948 to 1997. This record shows that the incompetence/quasi-incompetence system was not used that much. Akiko Noda et al, *Q & A for the Realization of a Symbiotic Society* (Gyousei Corporation, 2008) 9 (in Japanese).

[116.] Teruaki Tayama, *Commentary on Adult Guardianship System* (Sanseido, 2nd ed, 2016) (in Japanese).

Table 1.2: Statutory Adult Guardianship System by Type

Type	Guardianship	Curatorship	Assistance
Target	Any person who constantly lacks the capacity to discern right and wrong due to mental disability (Article 7 of the Civil Code).	Any person whose capacity is extremely insufficient to appreciate right or wrong due to any mental disability (Article 11).	Any person who has insufficient capacity to appreciate right or wrong due to any mental disability (Article 15).
Those Who Can Make a Petition	The person in question, his/her spouse, any relative within the fourth degree of kinship, the guardian of a minor, the supervisor of the guardian of a minor, the curator, the supervisor of the curator, the assistant, the supervisor of the assistant, or a public prosecutor (Article 7); municipal mayor (Elder Welfare Act etc.; R-1).	The person in question, his/her spouse, any relative within the fourth degree of kinship, the guardian, the supervisor of the guardian, the assistant, the supervisor of the assistant, or a public prosecutor (Article 11); municipal mayor (Elder Welfare Act etc.; R-1).	The person in question, his/her spouse, any relative within the fourth degree of kinship, the guardian, the supervisor of the guardian, the curator, the supervisor of the curator, or a public prosecutor (Article 15); municipal mayor (Elder Welfare Act etc.; R-1).

Type	Guardianship	Curatorship	Assistance
Acts Requiring the Consent of Adult Guardians		Act of Paragraph 1, Article 13 of the Civil Code (R-2, R-3, R-4).	Within the scope of the petition, 'a specific law act' (Paragraph 1, Article 13) specified by a family court on trial. (R-1, R-2, R-4).
Acts That Can Be revoked	Acts other than acts related to daily life.	Same as above (R-2, R-3, R-4).	The same as above (R-2, R-4).
Scope of Power of Representation Given to Adult Guardians	All legal acts on property.	Within the scope of the petition, 'specific legal conduct' as the family court decides at the trial (R-1).	The same as left (R-1).

Source: Ministry of Justice of Japan[117]

Remarks: (R-1): The consent of the principal will be required if the petition is made by the person other than the principal to give a right of representation to a curator. The same is true when giving a right of consent and a right of representation to an assistant, or for the start of assistance.

(R-2): Article 13 (1) of the Civil Code states actions, such as debt, litigation, approval and abandonment of inheritance, and new construction, reconstruction, and extension construction.

(R-3): By trial in the family court, the scope of the right of consent and the right of revocation can be extended in addition to the acts prescribed in Article 13 (1) of the Civil Code.

(R-4): Activities related to daily life are excluded.

While the guardianship registration system of the Legal Affairs Bureau gives some consideration to secure commercial transactions with third parties. The

---

adult guardianship registration is a system that registers the contents of adult guardian authority and voluntary guardianship contracts, and to disclose registered information by issuing a document certifying the particulars recorded in a file of guardianship registration (i.e., a 'certificate of registered matters' or a 'certificate of no registration' according to its contents). Before concluding important contracts, contractors can confirm by registered information whether or not the parties have legal capacity to conclude the contracts.

Issues of Statutory Guardianship

When the statutory guardianship system was inaugurated, there were operational complaints, such as regarding the time it took from the petition for the guardianship to the family court to the appointment of an adult guardian.[118] There have been cases of adult guardians involved in illegal conducts due to a simple mistake, negligence, or some intention. The number of adult guardian misconduct cases reported to the courts in 2014 was 831, with total damages of approximately 5,670 million yen (US$39.4 million), the largest record available on the website.[119] Then, academic society and law/welfare professional associations published their own recommendations on improving the adult guardianship system.[120] At the tenth anniversary of the enforcement of the adult guardianship system (2010), the Ministry of Justice of Japan conducted a commissioned survey to verify the system.[121] There seemed to be some opinions to consider reforming the adult guardianship system.[122] However, the legislative measures regarding the adult guardianship system did not materialize until the Promotion Act in 2016, with the exception of the partial amendments to the Public Offices Election Act

---

[118.] The court data indicates a significant improvement: 35 per cent of the statutory guardianship cases in 2001 completed the appointment of the adult guardians within three months, but 87 per cent of the adult guardianship cases completed within three months in 2024. The Courts of Japan, *The Annual Overview of Adult Guardianship Cases* (Web Page, March 2025) (in Japanese) <https://www.courts.go.jp/toukei_siryou/siryo/kouken/index.html>.

[119.] Refers to the Courts of Japan, *The Cases of Fraud by Guardians, etc.* (Web Page, August 2, 2024) (in Japanese) <https://www.mhlw.go.jp/content/12000000/001281730.pdf>.

[120.] The Japan Adult Guardianship Law Corporate Association (JAGA) published recommendations for the proposal of amendments to the statutory guardianship system in 2008 and the voluntary guardianship system in 2012. The Japan Federation of Bar Association, Legal-Support Adult Guardian Center (Japan Federation of 'Shiho-Shoshi' Lawyers' Associations), and Japanese Association of Certified Social Workers independently published their own proposals on operational improvements and law revisions.

[121.] This study group (chair Akio Yamanome) published the report: Ministry of Justice of Japan, *Research Report: Analysis of the Current State of the Adult Guardianship System and Examination of Issues—Toward Smoother Use of the Adult Guardianship System* (Japan Institution of Business Law, 2010) (in Japanese).

[122.] A court judge states in his article that 'it is necessary for the adult guardianship system to clarify the parts that the courts should and can bear, and to have the civil society to take charge of the other parts.' Masato Kusano, 'Current Status and Future of the Adult Guardianship System from the Perspective of the Family Court' (2009) 47 *Japan Women's Bar Association Bulletin* 32–6, 35.

(Act No. 100 of 1950) in 2013.[123] Consequently, the adult guardianship system has been left to the family courts. The number of adult guardianship users has steadily grown since the implementation of the guardianship law in April 2000. The number of adult guardianship users in December 2021 was 239,933 cases (3.3 per cent year-on-year increase).[124] The annual increase, however, has been declining in recent years.[125] The number of adult guardianship users is thought to be 'significantly small compared to the number of elderly people with dementia'[126] and is estimated to be equivalent to approximately 2 per cent of potential users with insufficient mental capacity.[127] The remaining 98 per cent are estimated to be supported by relatives or nursing home managers.[128] The operational manner of the family courts has slightly changed with time.

Due to the operation of the family courts, 82.9 per cent of non-relatives, mostly lawyers, were appointed as adult guardians in December 2024. It is much higher than principals for which relatives were appointed, that is a significant change from the ratio of relative guardians in December 2001 (86.0 per cent).[129] In fact, the family courts have appointed mainly lawyers as adult guardians to administer property management of principals, which has made more burden on the family

---

[123] By the law revisions, principals with mental disabilities have the right to vote and are eligible to contest for elections announced after July 1, 2013. To ensure the fair implementation of elections, those who assist the voters to vote by proxy are limited to those who are engaged in the affairs related to the vote, and the obligational efforts to ensure fair implementation of absentee ballots, such as having witnesses present, have been established for absentee ballots in hospitals, nursing homes, etc. Ministry of Internal Affairs and Communications, *Adult Guardians' Voting Rights* (Web Page, May 2013) (in Japanese) <https://www.soumu.go.jp/senkyo/senkyo_s/news/touhyou/seinen/index.html>.

[124] The number of adult guardianship cases was 166,189 in 2012 (8.5 per cent year-on-year increase), 184,670 in 2014 (4.6 per cent year-on-year increase), 203,551 in 2016 (6.4 per cent year-on-year increase), 218,142 in 2018 (3.7 per cent year-on-year increase), 239,933 in 2021 (3.3 per cent year-on-year increase), and 253,941 in 2024 (1.8 per cent year-on-year increase).

[125] Ibid.

[126] Refers to the Ministry of Health, Labour, and Welfare of Japan, *Basic Plan for Promoting the Adult Guardianship System* (Web Page, March 24, 2017) 2 (in Japanese) <https://www.mhlw.go.jp/file/06-Seisakujouhou-12000000-Shakaiengokyoku-Shakai/keikaku1.pdf>.

[127] The ratio of adult guardianship users in Japan is estimated 2 to 3 per cent of the potential users, assuming that there is a total of 10 million people with insufficient mental capacity, such as 6 million older people with dementia, 0.7 million people with intellectual disabilities, 2.7 million people with mental disorders, and 0.5 million people with higher brain dysfunction. Regional Guardianship Promotion Project, *The Overview of the Adult Guardianship System* (Web Page, n/a) (in Japanese) <https://kouken-pj.org/about/>.

[128] Makoto Arai states that 'at least 1 per cent of the national population is a potential user of the adult guardianship system by international standard.' Makoto Arai, 'Enactment of the Act on Promotion of the Adult Guardian System and Prospects for the Adult Guardian System' 52 (in Japanese); Yasushi Kamiyama states that 'it seems controversial whether Japan assumes the use of more than 1.2 million guardians in the current situation.' Yasushi Kamiyama, 'The Issues Based on the Basic Plan for Promoting the Adult Guardianship System' (2018) 20 *Clinical Legal Research* 108 (in Japanese).

[129] Refers to the Courts of Japan, *The Annual Overview of Adult Guardianship Cases in FY2024* (Web Page, March 2025) (in Japanese); Yasushi Kamiyama states that the tendency to avoid appointing relatives as adult guardians and appoint professional guardians has increased after a decision made by the Hiroshima High Court on February 20, 2012 (page 141 of Law Times Report 1385). In this case, the high court admitted that the family court judge was liable for state compensation for failing to take appropriate supervisory measures to prevent further misappropriation by the adult guardian as a relative of the principal. Kamiyama (n 128) 111.

of the principal in guardianship fees and other aspects other than the fees.[130] Consequently, there is little progress in SDM and personal protection from a social welfare perspective.[131] Cases in which adult guardians embezzled the property of the principals were reported, and the credibility of the system was questioned.

The Regional Guardianship Promotion Project summarized the issues of the statutory guardianship system into eight items:[132] (i) The number of the adult guardianship system users is low,[133] (ii) It has become difficult for relatives of the principal to be appointed as adult guardians,[134] instead professional guardians[135] have been appointed in recent years,[136] (iii) The ratio of statutory 'guardianship type' users based on substituted decision-making to the total number of adult guardianship users is dominant,[137] (iv) It cannot be said that the appointment of community guardians[138] has been sufficient, (v) The need to respond to munic-

---

[130.] Shinya Saisho, 'Socialization of Care in View of the Socialization of Adult Guardianship: Impact of Occupational Professionalization on the Family' (2016) 28(2) *Family Sociology Research* 148–60, 148 (in Japanese); In contrast, there was a court decision in 2018 where a judicial scrivener appointed as an adult guardian was dismissed by the court because (1) the incomprehension of Article 858 (respect for the person's intention) of the Civil Code and (2) unreasonable refusal to explain to relatives made him unsuitable as an adult guardian. The dismissal decision No. 52 of the Nagoya High Court (March 28, 2017) was included in the Tokyo District Court Decision No. 26349 on January 22, 2018.

[131.] It is noted that for the operation of adult guardianship system, the viewpoint of property management was emphasized, and respect for the will of the principal and welfare viewpoint were insufficient in some cases. Ministry of Health, Labour, and Welfare of Japan, *Interim Verification Report on Basic Plan for Promoting Adult Guardianship System* (Expert Commission, March 17, 2020) 4 (in Japanese) <https://www.mhlw.go.jp/content/12201000/000609007.pdf>.

[132.] Refers to the 'Regional Guardianship Promotion Project,' which is joint research between the Division of Lifelong Learning Infrastructure Management, Graduate School of Education, the University of Tokyo, and the Regional Guardianship Promotion Center, *The Gist of the Adult Guardianship System* (Web Page, n/a) (in Japanese) <https://kouken-pj.org/about/>.

[133.] Approximately 97 to 98 per cent Japanese adults with insufficient mental capacity is estimated to live in informal arrangements. Regional Guardianship Promotion Project (n 127); Terry Carney states, '[1999 Japanese guardianship law] reforms underestimated the Japanese traditions of kinship and collective responsibility.' Terry Carney, 'Aged Capacity and Substitute Decision-Making in Australia and Japan' (2003) 2003/2004 *LAWASIA Journal* 1, 21; Israel Doron states that 'Japan and Israel are much more family and community oriented.... Both Sweden and Japan have preferred to base the alternatives to guardianship on a communal and cooperative approach.' Israel Doron, 'Elder Guardianship Kaleidoscope–A Comparative Perspective' (2002) 16(3) *International Journal of Law, Policy, and the Family* 368–98, 389.

[134.] The Japan Penal Code Article 244 regulates exemption from criminal acts by relatives. This provision is based on the idea that 'law does not enter into home.' If the relative is an adult guardian who looks after the principal, this rule does not apply [The Supreme Court of Japan ruling on a defendant's case of business embezzlement, Supreme Court of Japan, Penal Code Vol. 66, No. 10, page 981 on October 9, 2012]. Due to this case law, many relative guardians who violate law are revoked and relative guardians are replaced by professional guardians by the family courts. Toyohiro Sukimoto, 'Contemporary Challenges of Larceny Committed against Relatives' (2009) 78 *Seijo Jurisprudence* 95, 120 (in Japanese).

[135.] A 'professional guardian' refers to a person who has national qualification licenses, such as an attorney in law, a judicial scrivener, or licensed social worker, based on the relevant law, who has been appointed as an adult guardian.

[136.] Relative guardians in December 2024 were 17.1 per cent. The Courts of Japan (n 129).

[137.] Ibid. The breakdown by type was guardianship 179,373 (70.6 per cent), curatorship 54,916 (21.6 per cent), assistance 16,857 (6.6 per cent), and voluntary guardian 2,795 (1.3 per cent).

[138.] Third-party non-professional guardian appointed by the family court is called 'citizen guardian' in Japan, but the term 'community guardian' is used in this study.

ipal mayors' petition cases is significantly increasing,[139] (vi) Gap exist in each municipality's efforts toward the adult guardianship system, (vii) Fraudulent conducts by adult guardians cannot be eliminated,[140] and (viii) The increasing use of guardianship support trust system leads to less financial freedom of the principal.[141]

b. Voluntary Guardianship System

Voluntary Guardianship

The voluntary guardianship system involves the management of a principal's personal affairs and property by a voluntary guardian who is nominated by the principal while the principal has mental capacity. This is a legal method to prepare for a future when the mental capacity of the principal becomes insufficient. This system is regulated by the Act on Voluntary Guardianship Contract (Act No. 150 of 1999). This was newly introduced legal system in 2000.[142] As a popular procedure, a proxy contract between the principal and the nominee (the voluntary guardian) given the power of representation is prepared by a notary public.[143] The voluntary guardianship contract must be made in the form

---

[139.] It was established in 1999 that the mayor of a municipality can request a petition for adult guardianship (Article 32 of the *Elder Welfare Act*, Article 28 of the *Intellectually Handicapped Persons Welfare Act*, and Article 51–11 of the *Mental Health and Mental Disability Welfare Act*), when it is recognized that there is a particular need for the welfare of a person aged 65 and over (including one even under the age of 65, when it is deemed necessary), person with intellectual disabilities, and person with mental disabilities. The municipal mayor petition cases increased to be the largest in the annual guardianship petitions in 2020 and 2021. This is because 'a particular need for the welfare of a person aged 65 and over,' who has no relatives and close friends to look after and has no asset or enough money, increases in Japan.

[140.] The family courts introduced the safeguard measures, such as guardianship support trust system and appointment of an adult guardian's supervisor. Consequently, the misconduct cases that reported to the courts have been radically reduced, i.e., from the peak of the 831 misconduct cases with damage of 5,670 million yen (US$39.4 million) in 2014 to 184 misconduct cases with damage of 700 million yen (US$4.9 million) in 2023, but adult guardians' misconducts still happen. The Courts of Japan (n 119).

[141.] The 'guardianship support trust system' is a financial management system in which the guardians manage the financial payment within daily uses at deposits and savings and trust the money that is not usually used to the trust bank under the family court's supervision. This system was introduced in February 2012 and the cumulative trust and deposited property amount increased to approximately 1,014 billion yen (US$7.0 billion) as of December 2020. This system contributes to protection of financial assets of the principal but prevents from financial freedom of the principal. While 'the guardianship support deposit system' has been widely implemented in banks, which is a mechanism where the guardian manages the money necessary for payments among the person's property as savings and deposits the money that is not normally used in the guardianship support deposit account for security. The Courts of Japan, *About the Usage Status of Guardianship System Support Trusts, etc.* (January to December 2020) (Web Page, 2022) (in Japanese) <https://www.courts.go.jp/vc-files/courts/2021/20210528sintakugaikyou_R02.pdf>.

[142.] The legislative process, including the preliminary research by the legislative secretariat group, to conclude voluntary guardianship system in 1999 was summarized in the article: Makoto Arai, 'An Observation of the Voluntary Guardianship System–From Its Birth to the Future' (2009) 5 *Tsukuba Law Journal* 63, 74 (in Japanese); Makoto Arai addressed a reference statement on legislation of the adult guardianship system in the National Diet of Japan. House of the Representatives, the National Diet of Japan, *Minutes of the 20th Meeting of the Law Committee in the 145th National Diet* (Laws Committee, June 15, 1999) (in Japanese).

[143.] Relevant law and regulations for notary duties stipulate, 'A notary may not create any instrument with regard to matters that are in violation of laws and regulations, juridical acts that are void, or juridical acts that may be specified by the Ordinance of the Ministry of Justice of Japan (Article 3). When the mental capacity of the principal begins to decline, the voluntary guardian makes a petition with the family court to appoint the voluntary guardian's supervisor in adherence to the law (Article 4). The voluntary guardian then makes legal decisions, including signing contracts, on behalf of the principal under the supervision of the supervisor (Article 7). In some cases, the voluntary guardian can provide support specifically to the principal in personal protection and/or property management, according to the principal's own intentions on the contract. The guardianship registration system of the Legal Affairs Bureau, which is applied to the voluntary guardianship system, gives some consideration to secure commercial transactions with third parties.

Challenges of Voluntary Guardianship System

There are some challenges facing the voluntary guardianship system.[144] First, it is rare for a voluntary guardian to lodge a petition with the family court, in adherence to the law, to appoint a supervisor of the voluntary guardian. A voluntary guardian agreement, like a lasting power of attorney[145] (hereinafter referred to as 'LPA') and a supervisor nominated by the family court, is not always a single contract. In fact, a property management agreement, like an LPA, and a supervision agreement for personal affairs, including post-mortem affairs, are often concluded together as one package. In most popular cases in Japan, property management and supervision agreements are legally active when the mental capacity is sufficient. The voluntary guardian often keeps those agreements effective even after the mental capacity of the principal declines. In such a case, a petition with the family court indicates the decline in mental capacity of the principal is often not lodged.

---

rescinded on the grounds of limited capacity' (Article 26 of the *Notary Act*). Article 13 (1) of the *Regulation for Enforcement of the Notary Act* states that 'When a notary is to create or certify an instrument for a juridical act but there is doubt as to whether the juridical act is valid, whether the party has given due consideration to the juridical act, or whether the party has the capacity to do the juridical act, the notary must caution the persons concerned and have them provide the necessary explanations.' The Notification No. 634, March 13, 2000, Chief of Civil Affairs Bureau, the Ministry of Justice 'Regarding the handling of official affairs accompanying the enforcement of laws that partially amend the Civil Code' states, 'When there is a doubt about the principal's capacity to make decisions, a notary is requested to request the principal the submission of a medical certificate, etc. and save it, or create and save a document that records the points of the principal's situation, etc.'

[144.] Yasushi Sakai, 'The Actual Situation and Problems of the Voluntary Guardianship System from the Viewpoint of Notary Practice' (2010) 12 *Journal of Asian Cultures* 279, 295 (in Japanese).

[145.] An LPA is a legal document that lets the donor appoint one or more people known as attorneys to help him/ her make decisions or to make decisions on behalf. There are two types of LPA in the UK: 'health and welfare' and 'property and financial affairs.' While an enduring power of attorney (EPA) is a legal document that lets the donor appoint one or more people, known as attorneys, in register to help make decisions or to make decisions on their behalf about their property or money. GOV. UK, *Make, Register or End a Lasting Power of Attorney* (Web Page, n/a) <https://www.gov.uk/power-of-attorney>.

This may be due to four reasons. First, a voluntary guardian has little knowledge to do so in case the voluntary guardian is a relative of the principal. According to the Research survey by the Ministry of Justice of Japan on May 18, 2022, the respondents who answered no idea of the law provision to lodge a petition to the family court account for 24 per cent, and 92 per cent of these respondents were relatives of the principals.[146] Relatives of the principals account for 63 per cent of the voluntary guardians, while third-party practitioners account for 12 per cent and other institutions account for 15 per cent.[147]

Second, there is a legal interpretation of the Civil Code: It is the majority views of the civil law scholars in Japan regarding Article 111 (ground of termination of authority of agency) of the Civil Code that the authority of agency shall not be terminated without the respective items of the preceding paragraph upon the termination of the contract appointing him/her, even if the principal becomes incapacitated. This understanding comes from the older German civil code and its interpretation, which is different from that in common law jurisdictions.[148] This is one of the reasons a voluntary guardian does not always lodge a petition to the family court to appoint the supervisor because the contract is valid even after the principal becomes incapacitated and the voluntary guardian receives remuneration. A petition to the family court relies on the voluntary guardian's discretion because the principal with insufficient mental capacity cannot provide instructions to do so to the voluntary guardian. From the voluntary guardian's viewpoint, no incentive appears, at least for receiving remuneration, that the voluntary guardian must lodge a petition to the family court to appoint his/her supervisor.

Third, there is the issue of the principal's payment of remuneration to both the guardian and the guardian's supervisor. In statutory guardianship, the guardian's supervisor is not always appointed by the family court, and the principal basically pays remuneration to the guardian. The statutory guardian's remuneration is determined by the family court annually after the yearly service is complete, mainly considering the property of the principal and the guardian's workload. In contrast, the voluntary guardian's remuneration is concluded in the contract. There are some cases where the voluntary guardian's remuneration in the contract is set

---

[146.] Refers to the Ministry of Justice of Japan, 'Efforts to Promote the Adult Guardianship System: After November 2021' (Web Page, May 18, 2022) 1–28, 10–13 and 16–28 (in Japanese) <https://www.mhlw.go.jp/content/12000000/000938658.pdf>.

[147.] The number of respondents was 11,079 out of 80,000 contracting parties who concluded their contracts more than ten years ago (selected by the Ministry of Justice of Japan).

[148.] Takeshi Shimura, 'A Consideration on the Survival of Voluntary Agency Rights When the Person Is Incapacitated (Part 1)' (1996) 71(3) *Waseda Law Review* 1, 38 (in Japanese).

at a much higher rate than usual.[149] The principal pays such fees to the voluntary guardian and the supervisor (actually, the payment procedures are conducted by the voluntary guardian) until the principal dies. If a voluntary guardian is a relative of the principal, most contracts are based on no remuneration and the above-mentioned issue does not occur.

Fourth, there is the fundamental issue of who can be trusted to be responsible for the management of the property and personal affairs of the principal with insufficient mental capacity. Without this clarification, even if the law were properly reformed, the voluntary guardianship system would never work in practice.[150]

Discussion

The voluntary guardianship system is designed as a combination of an LPA and a safeguard for the principal by the voluntary guardian's supervisor appointed by the family court. This system is theoretically logical, but practically not workable.[151] Why are voluntary guardianship contracts not popular in Japan? One reason is regarding a systemic risk. In most cases, the voluntary guardian does not lodge a petition with the family court to appoint a supervisor to avoid safeguarding the principal. It can be assumed that this is a systemic risk associated with the voluntary guardianship system, where illegal conducts might happen. In fact, illegal conducts happened after the enforcement of the law in 2000.[152] The Bureau of Social Welfare and Public Health, Tokyo Metropolitan Government alerts the banner 'please be careful about malicious criminal acts related to voluntary guardianship system' on their website, which is cited by other websites, such as local governments, law firms, and NPOs. Recently, this alerting banner was deleted on the renewal of their website, but some trace of this remains on the

---

[149.] For example, an inappropriate voluntary guardianship case was reported where a judicial scrivener received 4 million yen (US$27,800) as remuneration for one and a half year in the voluntary guardianship in 2004. This case was found during the associations' in-house auditing to the members. Ministry of Health, Labour, and Welfare of Japan, *Expert Commission Meetings: The Minutes of the 4th Interim Verification Working Group Session* (Web Page, December 26, 2019) 14 (in Japanese) <https://www.mhlw.go.jp/stf/shingi2/0000212875.html>.

[150.] It is not so easy to find a trustworthy practitioner or institution other than relatives. A public agency which can function as a voluntary guardian with a reasonable remuneration would be a possible alternative entity if such an agency is available.

[151.] Trevor Ryan, an Australian researcher, analyzes possible reasons why voluntary guardianship are underutilized and finds out 'unsuitable social norms, a lack of awareness, excessive regulation, unresponsive doctrine, and entrenched judicial values.' He recommends promoting legal development based on 'imposition of formal legal norms and market mechanisms' replacing informal arrangement and administrative ordering. Trevor O. Ryan, 'Is Japan Ready for Enduring Powers? A Comparative Analysis of Enduring Powers Reform' (2014) 9(1) *Asian Journal of Comparative Law* 241–66, 243.

[152.] Refers to the Japan Federation of Bar Associations, *Recommendations for Improvement Regarding the Voluntary Guardianship System* (Web Page, July 16, 2009) (in Japanese) <https://www.nichibenren.or.jp/document/opinion/year/2009/090716_3.html>.

website.[153] This risk is responsible for the system's negative reputation among potential users.

Another reason is a unique mentality of the older Japanese people, which is pointed out by Japanese legal practitioners.[154] There is a tendency that the older Japanese people do not entrust property management to their family members or relatives when they are healthy. This tendency is due to a complex and nuanced psychological diagnosis of Japanese older women in particular.[155] Behind such a tendency, there may be a unique legal culture in Japan. One researcher wonders whether a legal culture of self-determining matters of a principal, contracting them with a voluntary guardian, will ever take root in Japan.[156] This remark may correspond to the well-known observation of what Takeyoshi Kawashima researched in his socio-legal studies in the 1960s. Namely, Japanese people have a unique legal consciousness on contracts and judicial resolutions, which differs from that in the Western countries.[157] Japan is a country with the rules of law, and the people generally respect the law system and social norms as ethical standards. The Japanese legal culture has changed for a half century; however, their change of legal culture is not adapted to the area of private autonomy for property management and personal affairs.

This issue needs more empirical data to clarify why the older Japanese people do not like to have voluntary guardianship. Nevertheless, the trend is confirmed by the data. The number of voluntary guardianship users who registered in the Legal Affairs Bureau by December 2021 was only 2,663 cases (1.1 per cent of all guardianship cases), although a total of approximately 250,000 voluntary guardianship contractors concluded the contracts drawn up by notary publics.[158]

[153.] For example, Higashiyamato City (rural part of Tokyo Metropolitan jurisdiction), *Please Be Careful about Malicious Criminal Acts Related to Voluntary Guardianship System* (Web Page, April 1, 2012) (in Japanese) <https://www.city.higashiyamato.lg.jp/index.cfm/32,29495,341,583,html>.

[154.] Legal practitioners in Yokohama opine two reasons by email correspondence with the author on March 25, 2022: The first is that, even in preparation for future risk of dementia, they have an ardent desire not to entrust property management to anyone (including relatives) while they are healthy. The second is that, if someone in their relatives is entrusted with property management, they do not want to be asked by other relatives why they entrust it to that person, that is, they do not want to be resented by others. As a result, most parties may develop dementia and file a petition for adult guardianship without any future allowance. Some other legal practitioners also agree with these views.

[155.] Ibid.

[156.] Tomoko Fukuda, 'Incapacity Planning Used by Revocable Living Trust: Proposal on Estate Planning for Incapacitated People' (2018) 47 *Bulletin of Graduate Studies of Law, Chuo University* 23–39, 38 (in Japanese) <https://core.ac.uk/download/pdf/229779078.pdf>.

[157.] Takeyoshi Kawashima's observation is known by law scholars in and outside Japan, but his essay is sometimes criticized by scholars due to insufficient evidence. Kawashima responded that this was just an essay. Takeyoshi Kawashima, *Legal Consciousness in Law in Japan* (Iwanami Shoten, Publishers, 1967) (in Japanese); Takeyoshi Kawashima, 'The Legal Consciousness of Contract in Japan' (translated by Charles R. Stevens) (1974) 7 *Law in Japan* 1, 21. <https://heinonline.org/HOL/LandingPage?handle=hein.journals/lij7&div=5&id=&page=>.

[158.] The breakdown of 250,000 contract cases is as follows: 70,000 cases within three and a half years after the conclusion of the contract, 100,000 cases three and a half to ten years after the conclusion of the contract, and 80,000

The most frequently occurring age among users was 70s.[159] This implies that most contracts do not develop to voluntary guardianship with the appointment of a supervisor by the family court but remain merely a property management agreement and a supervision agreement. It can be said that the voluntary guardianship system has not worked as intended by law.[160]

c. Risk–Benefit Comparison Analysis

It is recognized that the practice of the adult guardianship, including both statutory and voluntary guardianships, results in unexpected social risk.[161] Some risks may cause serious financial damages to principals and should not be overlooked.[162] The risks that may typically arise from the adult guardianship system are summarized as follows: First, there have been a number of incidents where adult guardians embezzled the proceeds from the principal's property. Second, there are no clear guidelines on how to respect the principal's intention as Article 858 of the Civil Code stipulates, which may consciously or unconsciously lead to a risk of misconduct by the adult guardian. Third, the voluntary guardian may not lodge a petition to the family court to appoint a supervisor for the adult guardian even if the principal's mental capacity declines. The voluntary guardian might maintain the agency contract to continue receiving remuneration and possibly misuse the authority to intercept the principal's property. The principal bears these three risks. Fourth, an adult guardian may be liable for unexpected compensation as a quasi-supervisor for damages to third parties caused by the principal.[163] The adult guardian bears this risk.

---

cases after ten years or more. Research Survey by the Ministry of Justice of Japan as of May 18, 2022. Ministry of Justice of Japan, 'Efforts to Promote the Adult Guardianship System: After November 2021.'

[159.] Ibid.

[160.] In Asia, Singapore is a country where LPAs are relatively accepted by the people. Namely, approximately a total of 135,000 LPAs, which is equivalent to 3.4 per cent of the national population of Singapore (Singapore nationalities and permanent residents with foreign passports), have been registered during the period between 2014 and 2021. The contracting parties ('donees') are mostly family members or relatives (96 per cent). Singapore Government promotes digitalization of LPAs in 2022 by reform of law. Office of the Public Guardian, Singapore, *Indicators of Activities* (Web Page, n/a) <https://www.msf.gov.sg/opg/Pages/Indicators-of-Activities.aspx>. This site is no longer available.

[161.] This part is a summary of the previously published article in Japanese by the author: Yukio Sakurai, 'A Risk Analysis on Japan's Adult Guardianship System Practice against Principals and Adult Guardians' (2017) 9 *Journal of Urban Social Studies* 175, 84 (in Japanese).

[162.] The term 'risk' refers to 'the effect of uncertainty on purpose, which can be expressed as a combination of social context, subject, including an individual and groups, the magnitude of impact and likelihood of impact.' Osamu Saito, 'Conceptual Framework and Analysis Method for Risk Trade-Off Analysis Part 1: Conceptual Framework for Risk Trade-Off Analysis' (2010) 20(2) *Journal of Japan Risk Research Journal* 97–106, 100–1 (in Japanese).

[163.] On March 1, 2016, the Supreme Court of Japan delivered a decision concerning the liability of caregivers for older individuals with dementia [Supreme Court of Japan, Decision on Claim for Damages, Civil Code Vol. 70, No. 3, p. 681 (March 1, 2016) (Hanrei Jiho No. 1647, p. 1), commonly referred to as the 'Central Japan Railway Case']. The Court held that 'the spouse of a person with dementia does not fall under the statutory supervisory

The adult guardianship system, however, secures the social benefits based on its legislative objectives as follows: (i) Ensuring smooth social transactions and day-to-day life of a principal by substituted decision-making for legal acts, including financial transactions and concluding the contract, of adults with insufficient mental capacity. (ii) Recovering the economic damages of a principal by revoking the contracts that would be financially damaging. (iii) Providing a voluntary guardianship agreement through a principal's own intention to prepare for the future when the principal's mental capacity declines, thereby recognizing the principal's right to self-determination.

In fact, there is no accumulation of quantitative case data for a risk–benefit comparison of the adult guardianship system; thus, it is not possible to quantify the probability of risk occurrence based on data. For this reason, only a conceptual comparison can be made. Apparently, the magnitude of influence of all risks cannot be said to be so large that it exceeds the total benefits of the adult guardianship system. Thus, in a general sense, it can be said that the adult guardianship system should be maintained, with possible amendments introduced to minimize social risks on legislation and practice. The clarifications in the policies can be concluded in this risk–benefit comparison analysis, (a) to take safeguards that will reduce each systemic risk as much as possible; and (b) to shift from informal arrangement to the adult guardianship system or the like to legally protect the principal, if the principal or relevant persons so wish.

(2) The CRPD and the General Comment No. 1

a. Adoption of the CRPD

Regarding the adult guardianship legislation, there were some developments in the international community.[164] The United Nations Convention on the Rights of Persons with Disabilities (hereinafter referred to as 'CRPD') was adopted on

---

obligation prescribed in Article 714, Paragraph (1) of the Civil Code.' However, it suggested that, where special circumstances exist—such as in the case of a spouse or adult guardian—a determination must be made based on an objective standard and considerations of equity as to whether the individual should be deemed to have a supervisory obligation. This judgment implies that an adult guardian who provides close support to the principal may, under certain conditions, be regarded as bearing such an obligation. Relatedly, the Tokyo High Court, in a decision dated October 29, 2015, found that a dementia nursing-home manager could be held liable under the theory of quasi-supervision. On this topic, Keisuke Shimizu offered an analysis in 'Reading and Understanding the Supreme Court Decision of the Central Japan Railway Case: Including the Perspective of Adult Guardianship' (2016) 6 *Adult Guardianship Practices* 84, 93 (in Japanese). Critical commentary was also provided by Shigeto Yonemura in 'Central Japan Railway Case: From a Civil Law Perspective' (2017) 7 *Social Security Studies* 191, 211 (in Japanese).

[164.] This part is an updated version of the previously published article in Japanese by the author: Yukio Sakurai, 'UN Convention on the Rights of Persons with Disabilities and Supported Decision-Making' (2017) 47 *The Graduate School Law Review, Nihon University* 276, 243 (in Japanese).

December 13, 2006, and came into effect on May 3, 2008.[165] Some 164 Parties have signed and 192 have ratified the CRPD as of May 2025.[166] The phrase 'Nothing about us without us,' emphasizing autonomy and right to self-determination of persons with disability, is a principle embodied in the CRPD. The purpose (Article 1) of the CRPD states that 'persons with disabilities include those who have long-term physical, mental, intellectual, or sensory impairments which in interaction with various barriers may hinder full and effective participation in society on an equal basis with others.'[167] Article 12 (equal recognition before the law) mentions that 'parties shall take appropriate measures to provide access by persons with disabilities to the support they may require in exercising their legal capacity.'[168] The CRPD stipulates measures to realize the rights of persons with disabilities, with the aim of ensuring their enjoyment of human rights and fundamental freedoms and promoting respect for their inherent dignity.[169]

The UN Committee on the Rights of Persons with Disabilities (hereinafter referred to as 'UN Committee') has a system of state review for examining government reports submitted by the state parties in accordance with Article 35 (reports of Parties).[170] The UN Committee has repeatedly recommended the state parties under review to shift from substituted decision-making to SDM.[171]

[165.] The CRPD has an *Optional Protocol* signed by ninety-four Parties and ratified by one hundred Parties as of February 2022, but the Government of Japan has not signed nor ratified it. The Optional Protocol of the CRPD stipulates an individual complaints mechanism for persons with disability, when they have their rights breached under the CRPD, to directly make complaints with the UN CRPD Committee.

[166.] Refers to the UN, *Convention on the Rights of Persons with Disabilities (CRPD)* (Web Page, May 6, 2022) <https://www.un.org/development/desa/disabilities/convention-on-the-rights-of-persons-with-disabilities. html#:~:text=Ratifications%2FAccessions%3A%20184>.

[167.] Theresia Degener, the former chair of the UN Committee, at a public lecture 'The Impact of the CRPD on the Legislation of Parties' held in Tokyo on December 4, 2019, stated that the general idea of Article 12 was based on the human rights model of disability.

[168.] The term 'legal capacity' does not exist in Japanese law, if dare described in the existing concept, that would be a concept that includes 'mental capacity' and 'capacity to act.' Teruaki Tayama, 'Ratification of the Convention on the Rights of Persons with Disabilities and the Adult Guardianship System' (2019) 30(1) *Geriatric Psychiatry Magazine* 27–33, 28 (in Japanese)'; A new publication: Mary Donnelly, Rosie Harding and Ezgi Tascioglu (eds), *Supporting Legal Capacity in Socio-Legal Context* (Hart Publishing, 2022).

[169.] Article 12 (4) and (5) of the CRPD stipulate the matters to be noted in detail when realizing Article 12 (1) to (3). Paragraph (4) includes the wording 'respect the rights, will and preferences of the person'; 'CRPD are described as centering on four key values: equality, autonomy, participation, and solidarity.' Eilionoir Flynn, *From Rhetoric to Action* (Cambridge University Press, 2013) 13. A similar view is addressed by Gerard Quinn and Theresia Degener, *Human Rights and Disabilities* (Office of the High Commissioner for Human Rights, UN, 2002) 1.

[170.] Article 35 of the CRPD stipulates that 'a Party shall report the comprehensive progress of domestic measures to the UN Committee within two years of the CRPD becoming effective in their country and submit a report at least every four years'; UN CRPD Committee has issued concluding observations that include the positive aspects of the member states. The first sixty-eight member states' positive aspects were based on 'law enactment or amendment' at 86.8 per cent and 'action plan' at 64.7 per cent according to analysis report by the Japan Council on Disabilities (May 2018).

[171.] Refers to the UN, *UN Treaty Body Data Base: Concluding Observations* (Web Page, February 2022) <https://tbinternet.ohchr.org/_layouts/15/treatybodyexternal/TBSearch.aspx?Lang=en&TreatyID=4&DocTypeID=5>.

Then, the UN General Comment No. 1, adopted on April 11, 2014,[172] notes that Article 12 implies a possible 'paradigm shift from substituted decision-making to supported decision-making (SDM)' in order to understand the principals' will and preferences and to implement their wishes.[173] From the perspective of the state parties (including Japan) that ratified the CRPD before the adoption of the General Comment No. 1, it was perceived that the interpretation of Article 12 of the CRPD was overwritten by the adoption of the General Comment No. 1.[174] Since then, however, some state parties have implemented or are considering legislation or reforms of the adult guardianship law.[175] What these state parties have in common is that they will legislate support measures or SDM system in order to replace the adult guardianship system and reduce the use of the adult guardianship.

b. Response by the Government of Japan

The Government of Japan signed the CRPD on September 28, 2007, and ratified it on January 20, 2014, after amending the relevant disability laws.[176] The Policy Committee for Persons with Disabilities[177] (hereinafter referred to as 'Policy Committee') in the Cabinet Office of Japan deliberated on the draft of the first

---

[172.] Paragraph 13, General Comment No. 1 states that 'legal capacity is the ability to hold rights and duties (legal standing) and to exercise those rights and duties (legal agency). It is the key to accessing meaningful participation in society. Mental capacity refers to the decision-making skills of a person, which naturally vary from one person to another and may be different for a given person depending on many factors, including environmental and social factors.' UN, Committee on the Rights of Persons with Disabilities, *General Comment No. 1* (Web Page, April 11, 2014) 6–8 <http://www.ohchr.org/EN/HRBodies/CRPD/Pages/GC.aspx>.

[173.] Article 12 of the CRPD does not have a clear statement of SDM but have a statement of the General Comment No. 1. Paul Skawron points out that 'the best interpretation should be preferred: one that requires the process of interpretation to be responsive to both truth and the detailed substantive rights found in the CRPD.' Paul Skowron, 'Giving Substance to the Best Interpretation of Will and Preferences' (2019) 62 *International Journal of Law and Psychiatry* 125, 134.

[174.] The General Comment No. 1 is previously criticized because of being 'regressive.' Adrian D. Ward, 'Abolition of All Guardianship and Mental Health Laws?' (Online, April 14, 2014) *Law Society of Scotland* <http://www.journalonline.co.uk/Magazine/59-4/1013832.aspx>.

[175.] Refers to Section 3.2, 'A Comparative Law Study in the International Context'; Volker Lipp remarks that guardianship and autonomy will become friends 'if we were to take the rights and requirements of the CRPD seriously and implement the concept of "supportive guardianship" in law and practice.' Volker Lipp and Julian O. Winn, 'Guardianship and Autonomy: Foes or Friends' (2011) 5 *Journal of International Aging and Policy* 41, 56.

[176.] In December 2009, the Government of Japan established the Headquarters for Promotion of Disability System Reform with the prime minister as the head; promoted reforms of domestic law system, including the legislations of the relevant laws, such as *Basic Law for Persons with Disabilities* (August 2011) and *Act to Comprehensively Support Daily Life and Social Life of Persons with Disabilities* (June 2012); and revised some acts, such as *Act on Promotion of Elimination of Discrimination on the Grounds of Disability* and *Act on Promotion of Employment of Persons with Disabilities* (June 2013). Cabinet Office of Japan, *CRPD* (Web Page, n/a) (in Japanese) <https://www8.cao.go.jp/shougai/un/kenri_jouyaku.html>.

[177.] The Policy Committee was established by law in the Cabinet Office in August 2011 to investigate and deliberate on the formulation or modification of the 'basic plan for persons with disabilities,' and to monitor and recommend the implementation status of the plan.

Government of Japan Report (hereinafter referred to as 'Japan Report') in 2015.[178] At the deliberations, the Policy Committee summarized the 'Points of Discussions'[179] and mainly examined three points concerning the adult guardianship system: (i) whether or not the adult guardianship system in Japan may conflict with Article 12 of the CRPD, (ii) whether or not the adult guardianship system may have the limitation of scope in supporting the principal, and (iii) whether or not the administrative burden on the family courts may be heavier with the adult guardianship operation.

Regarding the issue (i) above, there are views that Japan's adult guardianship system is most likely to conflict with Article 12 of the CRPD.[180] Nevertheless, the Ministry of Justice of Japan expressed the view that 'Japan's adult guardianship system does not conflict with Article 12.'[181] The first Japan Report is based on the Ministry of Justice's view and explains the relationship between the adult guardianship system in Japan and Article 12 in the legal text. In June 2016, the Government of Japan submitted the first Japan Report and the annex survey the 'Points of Discussion' to the UN Committee.[182] Following this submission, the Japan Federation of Bar Associations and other nine institutions for persons with disabilities submitted their own reports (parallel reports) to the UN Committee analyzing the frameworks and practices of the Japan laws related to the CRPD.[183]

[178.] The Policy Committee discussed the first draft Japan Report at the 26th to 28th sessions in the period of September 24 to December 18, 2015. The Policy Committee unanimously agreed to add the observation remarks, such as, 'The establishment of a social framework to assist decision making and the excise of legal capacity is urgently needed etc.' (Paragraph 83, underlined by the author) to the Japan Report, considering that Japan's Adult Guardianship System does not explicitly violate Article 12 of the CRPD, but Japan needs improvements to meet the value of Article 12 of the CRPD. UN Human Rights Treaty Bodies, *UN Treaty Body Data Base: CRPD/C/JPN/1* (Web Page, October 7, 2017) 18. <https://tbinternet.ohchr.org/_layouts/15/treatybodyexternal/Download.aspx?symbolno=CRPD%2fC%2fJPN%2f1&Lang=en>.

[179.] Refers to the Policy Committee, *The Points of Discussions—Issues Based on the Implementation Status of the Third Basic Plan for Persons with Disabilities* (Web Page, September 2015) (in Japanese) <https://www.mofa.go.jp/mofaj/files/000171084.pdf>.

[180.] There are Japanese researchers' majority views that Japan's adult guardianship system conflicts with Article 12 of the CRPD both in legal design and practice. The views are common that the statutory guardianship-type, in which the rights of the principal are automatically and uniformly restricted by the relevant capacity of the principal, accounts for about 75 per cent of the adult guardianship cases, has a high probability to violate Article 12 of the CRPD that respects the principal's rights and will and preferences. The typical ones: Tayama (n 31); Tayama (n 168) 27, 33; Arai (n 31); Yasushi Kamiyama, 'International Monitoring of the Convention on the Rights of Persons with Disabilities' (2015) 'Evaluation of the Adult Guardianship System' (2015) 2851 *Weekly Social Security* 48, 53 (all in Japanese).

[181.] Policy Committee (n 179) 1.

[182.] The UN Committee's state review of the Japan Report in 2020 was postponed to 2022 due to COVID-19 pandemic.

[183.] UN (n 171).

c. Enactment of the Promotion Act

Although the adult guardianship system is a legal instrument of supporting adults with insufficient mental capacity, it is underutilized.[184] Considering such a situation, the Act on the Promotion of the Adult Guardianship System[185] (Act No. 29 of 2016, hereinafter referred to as 'Promotion Act') was enacted on April 15, 2016 and came into effect on May 13, 2016.[186] The Promotion Act stipulates the legal frameworks for nationwide promotion of the adult guardianship system and establishes the Commission on Promotion of the Adult Guardianship System (hereinafter referred to as 'the Commission') to implement measures comprehensively and systematically for promoting the adult guardianship system.[187]

The structure of this Act[188] is as follows: The purpose of the Act states that 'supporting adults with insufficient mental capacity in a societal system is an urgent issue in an aging society and contributes to the diverse society where [such people] cohabit with others' (Article 1).[189] Considering such a situation as the adult guardianship system is underutilized, the basic principles (Article 3)[190] are mentioned and the responsibilities of the national and local governments, the effects of the relevant people, and the cooperation of relevant institutions are stipulated (Articles 4 to 8). The legal measures and the implementation status of these measures are stipulated

---

[184.] Refers to Article 1 (purpose) of the Promotion Act.

[185.] Refers to the commentary survey of the Acts: Yoshiguchi Oguchi et al, *Handbook of the Adult Guardianship Two Acts: Commentary on the Act on the Promotion of the Adult Guardianship System, the Civil Code and the Act on Revision of the Domestic Case Procedure* (Soseisha, 2016) (in Japanese).

[186.] At the deliberations in the National Diet, questions were raised regarding respect for the purpose of Article 12 of the CRPD and strengthening of supervision for adult guardians. House of Councillors adopted an 'Attachment Resolution' to ensure these two points. House of the Councillors, *Attachment Resolutions* (Web Page, April 5, 2016) (in Japanese) <https://www.sangiin.go.jp/japanese/gianjoho/ketsugi/190/f063_040503.pdf>; House of the Representatives, *The Reasons of Legislation* (Plenary Session of the 190th House of Representatives, March 24, 2016) <http://www.shugiin.go.jp/internet/itdb_annai.nsf/html/statics/housei/pdf/190hou20an.pdf/$File/190hou20an.pdf>.

[187.] House of the Representatives (n 186).

[188.] The bill was based on Japan's part of the Yokohama Declaration of the 2010 the first World Congress on Adult Guardianship in Yokohama. The Declaration recommends a system that the government supports the adult guardianship system in addition to the courts. The 'Yokohama Declaration' (the original version) refers to 2010 Adult Guardianship World Congress Organizing Committee (ed), *Autonomy and Protection in Adult Guardianship System* (Nippon Hyoron Sha Co., Ltd., 2012) (in Japanese).

[189.] Shoichi Ogano, 'The Role of Adult Guardianship System and Community Comprehensive Care: Community Symbiosis Society' (2020) 12 *Review of Social Security Law* 23, 48 (in Japanese).

[190.] The basic principles (Article 3) include respect for the values of the adult guardianship system (i.e., respect for the right to self-determination, emphasis on personal protection, and normalization), promotion of the adult guardianship system responding to the local demands, and the establishment of a regional collaboration network for the adult guardianship system. It was confirmed that a principle of 'utilization of the remaining capacity' mentioned as the value of the adult guardianship system at the reform of the Civil Code in 1999 was replaced by 'emphasis on personal protection' in the Promotion Act and the Basic Plan. It shows how important 'emphasis on personal protection' is in the Basic Plan.

(Articles 9 and 10). Eleven basic policies are shown (Article 11).[191] The Ministerial Committee on Promotion of the Adult Guardianship System (hereinafter referred to as 'Ministerial Committee'), headed by the Prime Minister, and the Commission on Promotion of the Adult Guardianship System (hereinafter referred to as 'the Commission'), organized by experts, are established (Article 13). The Basic Plan is to be established (Article 12). The Cabinet Office of Japan will play secretariat roles and cooperate with courts and ministries to promote measures related to adult guardianship (Article 13). It obliges the municipalities and prefectures to formulate their own basic plans and make efforts for necessary assistance (Articles 23 and 24).[192]

It is one of the 'promotion type of laws'[193] in Japan, and its legal character is a program style of regulation that clarifies an order for the conduct of the public agencies to take the policy but does not have specific legal enforcement over the conduct or procedure of an individual entity. This Act was originally based on *Komeito* (one of the leading coalition parties) lawmaker's draft legislation.

(3) The Basic Plan and the Interim Verification Report

a. The Basic Plan

The Commission comprised the members from the academia, the Supreme Court, disability associations, and local governments, and six extraordinary members from professional guardianship associations, the medical field (doctors), guardianship support agencies, and the editorial writing profession. The role of the Commission was to deliberate on the matters to be included in the Basic Plan for Promoting the Adult Guardianship System (Hereinafter referred to as 'Basic Plan') and report to the Ministerial Committee. How did the members of the Commission recognize the scope of deliberation?[194] The following three points can be derived by analyzing the statements that indicated the basic recognition of

---

[191.] Eleven items regarding the basic policies are listed in Article 11, the Promotion Act, which can be summarized as follows: (a) Examination of measures to promote curatorship and assistance, (b) Review of the legal system for restricting the rights due to the principal, (c) Examination of support for principals who have difficulty in making decisions regarding medical care, nursing care, etc., (d) Review of the scope of work of adult guardians after the death of principals, (e) Activation of the voluntary guardianship system, (f) Dissemination to the national public, (g) promotion according to the needs of community, (h) Securing huma resources who will be adult guardians in the community, (i) Supporting the activities of the adult guardianship implementing agency, (j) Enhancement and strengthening of the system in relevant agency, and (k) Ensuring close cooperation among relevant agencies.

[192.] In line with Ministry's guidelines, basic plans of municipalities and prefectures are placed under the existing 'municipal welfare plans' and 'prefectural plans for supporting community welfare,' which are stipulated by Articles 107 and 108 of *Social Welfare Act*. With these arrangements, the adult guardianship system is a part of the community welfare program in municipalities and prefectures.

[193.] Refers to the House of the Councillors, *Law [Window]—Basic Law* (Web Page, n/a) (in Japanese) <https://houseikyoku.sangiin.go.jp/column/column023.htm>; Kazunori Miyazaki, 'Structural Analysis of "Basic Laws"' (2017) 5 *Public Policy Shibayashi* 43, 57.

[194.] Sakurai (n 109).

the members in the minutes. (i) Improve the practices of the adult guardianship system under the current legal framework. (ii) Establish a regional collaboration network in communities for adult guardianship. (iii) Deliberate on the minimal items associated with the adult guardianship system. Beginning on September 23, 2016, the Commission held a total of sixteen deliberations and concluded the basic plan. After the approval of the Ministerial Committee, the Cabinet of Japan decided on the Basic Plan on March 24, 2017.

The Basic Plan has policy objectives that aim to improve the adult guardianship practices and enable users to realize their benefits. It may create a regional collaboration network for advocacy support of human rights, prevent fraud, and maintain social harmony by providing easy access to the core agency in the community.[195] The implementation plan for five years, covering until March 2022, was shown to the public. The Cabinet Office of Japan has informed the local governments of the Basic Plan, asking them to set up core agencies in communities and to formulate their own basic plan. The main points of the Basic Plan are summarized in Table 1.3.

A core agency is a focal point in a community that plays a leading role for advocacy in the Basic Plan to promote the adult guardianship system. The Promotion Act obliges the municipalities and prefectures to formulate their own basic plans within the regional welfare plans and make efforts for necessary assistance (Article 23 and 24 of the Promotion Act). This requires uniformly formulating core agencies nationwide with flexibility in scale and form. The authority of a core agency can be a choice either in a municipality or in a larger jurisdiction according to the needs of the adult guardianship system. As of October 2021, only 31.9 per cent of the 1,741 municipalities have established core agencies, while 16.7 per cent of the municipalities have the other existing agencies such as advocacy centers or adult guardianship support centers.[196] The situation reveals gaps between municipalities in regional collaboration networks centered on core agencies. Currently, three types of entities of core agencies are seen as: (a) directly managed by the municipalities (19.3 per cent), (b) outsourced to the Council of Social Welfare, NPOs, etc. (62.7 per cent), and (c) a combination of these two types (18.0 per cent).[197]

[195.] Refers to Section 5.2.1, 'Roles and Legal Status of a Core Agency for Community Support.'

[196.] Refers to the Ministry of Health, Labour, and Welfare of Japan, 'Results of a Survey on the Status of Measures Related to the Promotion of the Adult Guardianship System in October 2021 (Summary)' (Web Page, May 18, 2022) 1 (in Japanese) <https://www.mhlw.go.jp/content/12000000/000938666.pdf>.

[197.] Ibid.

Table 1.3: Main Points of the Basic Plan

(i) Improvement in systems and practices that enable users to realize benefits
• The appointment of guardians who emphasize not only property management but also SDM and personal protection.
• Examination of how a medical certificate can describe the contents of diagnosis based on the living situation of the person.
(ii) Creation of a regional collaboration network for advocacy support[198]
• Improvement in functions, such as (a) public relations of the system, (b) consultation on system usage, (c) promotion of system usage (matching), and (d) guardian support.
• Development of 'team' formation to watch over the principals, to coordinate the cooperation system of local professional organizations ('council'), and 'core agency (center).'
(iii) Thorough prevention of fraud and harmony with use
• Examination of new measures to coexist with and replace guardianship support trust system.

Source: Ministry of Health, Labour, and Welfare of Japan, *Basic Plan*[199]

b. The Interim Verification Report

In April 2018, the office for the promotion project was transferred from the Cabinet Office to the Ministry of Health, Labour, and Welfare of Japan. This was presumably because the Ministry may execute the Basic Plan to promote nationwide regional collaboration networks. The Ministry, on June 21, 2018, established the Ministerial Council on Promotion of the Adult Guardianship System, which comprises the Minister of Justice, the Minister of Health, Labour, and Welfare, and the Minister of Internal Affairs and Communications (hereinafter referred to as 'Ministerial Council'), and the Expert Commission on Promotion of the Adult Guardianship System (hereinafter referred to as 'Expert Commission'), which comprises experts from various fields. The role of the Ministerial Council and the Expert Commission is to examine the measures

---

[198.] The term 'advocacy support' is defined as 'support activities which have a common foundation for support and activities centered on the person, which are support for exercising their rights through supported decision-making and support for recovering from infringement of their rights in dealing with abuse and unfair property transactions, for adults with insufficient mental capacity to participate in the community and live independent lives.' Ministry of Health, Labour, and Welfare of Japan, *The Second Term Basic Plan for Promoting the Adult Guardianship System* (Web Page, 2022) (in Japanese) <https://www.mhlw.go.jp/stf/seisakunitsuite/bunya/0000202622_00017.html>.

[199.] Refers to the Ministry of Health, Labour, and Welfare of Japan, *Basic Plan for Promoting the Adult Guardianship System* (Web Page, March 24, 2017) (in Japanese) <https://www.mhlw.go.jp/file/06-Seisakujouhou-12000000-Shakaien-gokyoku-Shakai/keikaku1.pdf>.

stipulated in the Basic Plan and verify the progress of the project, based on Article 13-2 of the Promotion Act.

The six Expert Commission and four Interim Verification meetings were held from July 2018 to March 2020. The following three points can be derived from the remarks made by the Expert Commission members. First, the expert Commission stuck to the scope of the deliberations in the previous Commission and conducted a detailed examination of the Basic Plan.[200] Second, the members aired frank opinions during the deliberations.[201] Third, there was an opinion to broaden the scope of the deliberations to discuss a possible reform of the Civil Code and relevant laws.[202] The Expert Commission concluded the Interim Verification Report on the Basic Plan in March 2020.[203] Even after then, the Working Group for Supported Decision-Making published the 'Guidelines for Adult Guardians Based on Supported Decision-Making' in October 2020.[204] The Ministry started the basic virtual training program on SDM for municipality officers in December 2020.

(4) Measures and Theory for Updating the Adult Guardianship System in 2000–2025

The legislation, guidelines, and policy measures regarding the adult guardianship system implemented between April 2000 and March 2025 are summarized in Table 1.4. This table implies the updating process of Japan's adult guardianship system and its associated matters.

---

[200]. Many research surveys were submitted to the Expert Commission by the Supreme Court and ministries on requests. Ministry of Health, Labour, and Welfare of Japan, *Promotion of the Adult Guardianship System* (Web Page, n/a) (in Japanese) <https://www.mhlw.go.jp/stf/seisakunitsuite/bunya/0000202622.html>.

[201]. For example, a medical doctor member stated the actual situation in the hospital as follows: 'The guidelines are flooding the field, and when you look at the contents, you can see a lot of flapping across multiple departments of the Ministry of Health, Labour, and Welfare…The hospital is very confused now due to many relevant guidelines (November 20, 2019).' A member representing the disability institution aired their view on an issue regarding professional guardians. 'We are aware that there are many professional guardians who do not come to see principals and only get remuneration, and the remuneration for not doing anything. There are voices in community saying that they shouldn't have adult guardians (May 27, 2019).' Ministry of Health, Labour, and Welfare of Japan, *Expert Commission Meetings* (Web Page, February 2022) (in Japanese) <https://www.mhlw.go.jp/stf/shingi2/0000212875.html>.

[202]. One member wrote this view: Akio Yamanome, 'Interim Verification of the Basic Plan and the Future Prospects' (2020) 88 *Adult Guardianship Practices* 82–9, 89; Makoto Arai previously states that 'Japan's adult guardianship law is under pressure to undergo a drastic review.' Makoto Arai, 'Enactment of Act of Promotion of Adult Guardian System and Prospects for the Adult Guardian System' (2017) 1 *Disability Law* 51–76, 53 (in Japanese).

[203]. Refers to the Ministry of Health, Labour, and Welfare of Japan (n 131).

[204]. The guidelines encourage adult guardians to go through the additional process of SDM based on Article 858 of the Civil Code even in limited cases. An adult guardian is required to participate in SDM for legal acts of the principal that will have a significant impact on him/her (i.e., decision on the principal's residence, sale of the principal's assets, and gifts and expenses of the principal to a third party) and relevant non-legal acts. Ministry of Health, Labour, and Welfare of Japan, *Guidelines for Adult Guardians Based on Supported Decision-Making* (Web Page, October 30, 2020) (in Japanese) <https://www.mhlw.go.jp/stf/seisakunitsuite/bunya/0000202622.html>.

Table 1.4: Measures for Updating the Adult Guardianship
System in 2000–2025

Date	Contents	Decision Body
April 1, 2000	Enforcement of the Adult Guardianship System	
May 21, 2013 (enforced on June 30)	Promulgated the Act to Partially Revise the Public Offices Election Act, etc., for the Restoration of the Right to Vote for Principals[205] (Act No. 21 of 2013)	The 183rd National Diet
April 6, 2016 (enforced on October 13)	Promulgated the Act to Partially Revise the Civil Code and the Domestic Affairs Case Procedure Act to Facilitate the Work of the Adult Guardianship System[206] (Act No. 27 of 2016)	The 190th National Diet
April 15, 2016 (enforced on May 13, 2016)	Promulgated the Act on the Promotion of the Adult Guardianship System (Act No. 29 of 2016)	The 190th National Diet
May 13, 2016	Established the Ministerial Council and the Commission	Cabinet Office
March 24, 2017	The Cabinet of Japan decided on the Basic Plan for Promoting the Adult Guardianship System.	The Cabinet
March 31, 2017	Published the Guidelines of Supported Decision-Making for Using Disability Welfare Services, etc.[207]	Ministry of Health, Labour, and Welfare (MHLW)

[205.] Ministry of Internal Affairs and Communications (n 123).

[206.] The key points of the amendments to the Civil Code are: (i) adult guardians who have been nominated by a family court become possible to receive the transfer of the principal-addressed postal mails (postal transfer, Article 860–2 and Article 860–3 of the Civil Code), (ii) the contents and procedures of office work that an adult guardian can perform even after the death of an adult guardian (post-mortem office work, Article 873–2 of the Civil Code) are clarified. Along with these, the Domestic Affairs Case Procedure Law has been amended. The target of these amendments is limited to adult guardianship type and does not cover curatorship and assistant types. Ministry of Justice of Japan, *Act to Partially Revise the Civil Code and the Domestic Affairs Case Procedure Act* (Web Page, October 13, 2013) (in Japanese) <http://www.moj.go.jp/MINJI/minji07_00196.html>.

[207.] Refers to the Ministry of Health, Labour, and Welfare of Japan published the report at the Disabled Persons Group, Social Security Council in December 2015. The report states that guidelines should be created that summarize the definition and significance of SDM, standard processes, and points to keep in mind, and should be shared and disseminated among stakeholders, including those responsible for adult guardianship. Ministry of Health, Labour,

Date	Contents	Decision Body
December 1, 2017	Published the Working Paper to Review the Systems That Have Restrictions on the Rights of the Principals, etc. (the summary of discussion)[208]	MHLW
March 14, 2018	Revised Guidelines for the Medical Supported Decision-Making Process in the Final Stages of Life[209]	MHLW
April 1, 2018	The MHLW is responsible for the promotion project	MHLW
June 21, 2018	Established the Ministerial Council and the Expert Commission	MHLW
June 2018	Published the Guidelines of Supported Decision-Making for People with Dementia in Their Daily and Social Lives[210]	MHLW
April 1, 2019	Started to use the new formats of medical certificate form[211] in the adult guardianship system and personal information sheet[212]	The Courts

and Welfare of Japan, *Guidelines for Supported Decision When Using Disability Welfare Services* (Web Page, March 31, 2017) (in Japanese) <https://www.mhlw.go.jp/file/06-Seisakujouhou-12200000-Shakaiengokyokush-ougaihokenfukushibu/0000159854.pdf>.

[208.] This is the review policy of disqualification clauses summarized by the Commission. Cabinet Office, *Working Paper to Review the Systems That Have Restrictions on the Rights of the Principals, etc.—Summary of Discussion* (The Commission, December 11, 2017) (in Japanese) <http://www.moj.go.jp/content/001250073.pdf>.

[209.] Refers to the Ministry of Health, Labour, and Welfare of Japan, *Revised Guidelines for the Medical Supported Decision-Making Process in the Final Stages of Life* (Web Page, March 14, 2018) (in Japanese) <https://www.mhlw.go.jp/stf/houdou/0000197665.html>.

[210.] Refers to the Ministry of Health, Labour, and Welfare of Japan, *Guidelines of Supported Decision-Making for People with Dementia in Their Daily and Social Lives* (Web Page, June 2018) (in Japanese) <https://www.mhlw.go.jp/stf/seisakunitsuite/bunya/0000212395.html>.

[211.] About 5.5 per cent of the cases related to adult guardianship were appraised on psychological certificates in 2021; The doctor's medical certificate is often used in the petition procedures for adult guardianship. Thus, the format of the doctor's medical certificate was reviewed. Akiko Ota, 'Revision of Medical Certificate Format and Practical Status after Introduction of Personal Information Sheet' (2020) 90 *Adult Guardianship Practices* 3, 14. The Courts of Japan, *Medical Certificate Form and Its Guidelines* (Web Page, n/a) (in Japanese) <https://www.courts.go.jp/saiban/syurui/syurui_kazi/kazi_09_02/index.html>.

[212.] To properly protect the person's personality, a personal information sheet format was created for social workers and others; the sheet describes personal information, such as the characteristics of disabilities; it is attached to petitions. The national average as of December 2020 was 84.3 per cent for this sheet submission rate. The Courts of Japan, *Personal Information Sheet Form and Its Guidelines* (Web Page, n/a) (in Japanese) <https://www.courts.go.jp/saiban/syurui/syurui_kazi/kazi_09_02/index.html>.

Date	Contents	Decision Body
May 2019	Published the Guidelines for Hospitalization of Unrelated People and Support for People Who Have Difficulty in Making Medical Decisions[213]	Research Group,[214] MHLW
June 7, 2019 (enforced after June 14)	Promulgated the Act on the Development of Related Laws for Appropriate Measures to Restrict the Rights of Principals, etc. (Act No. 37 of 1989)[216]	The 198th National Diet[215]
June 18, 2019	Described the Promotion of the Adult Guardianship in the Outline to Promote Dementia Policy[217]	MHLW
December 11, 2019 (enforced March 1, 2021)	Promulgated the Act for Partial Revision of the Companies Act (Act No. 70 of 2019)[218]	Ministry of Justice

[213.] The adult guardian is legally not involved in the medical consent of the person by law, but if the person has no relatives or other close kin, the adult guardian may have to be involved in the medical consent in practice. This guideline was reported to the second Expert Commission on March 18, 2019. Ministry of Health, Labour, and Welfare, *Guidelines for Hospitalization of Unrelated People and Support for People Who Have Difficulty in Making Medical Decisions* (Web Page, May 2019) (in Japanese) <https://www.mhlw.go.jp/content/000516181.pdf>.

[214.] Refers to the 'Study on Understanding the Adult Guardianship System in the Medical Field and Understanding the Situation of the Roles That Hospitals Demand from Guarantors.' The principal investigator was Ryotaro Yamagata (Department of Social Medicine, Graduate School of Comprehensive Research, Yamanashi University).

[215.] The Attachment Resolutions were adopted by both the House of Representatives and the House of Councillors at the enactment of this law. ' The Attachment Resolutions comprise eleven items, including respect for the purpose of Article 12 of the CRPD, and request the government to understand the current problems with the participation of representing persons with disabilities, and take necessary measures when proposals or recommendations are made by the CRPD Committee.' House of the Councillors, the National Diet of Japan, *Attachment Resolutions* (Web Page, June 6, 2019) (in Japanese) <https://www.sangiin.go.jp/japanese/gianjoho/ketsugi/198/f063_060601.pdf>.

[216.] Refers to the Reference Survey No. 8 at the Third Interim Verification Working Group Meeting in the Experts Commission. For each system that has provisions (disqualification clauses) that uniformly exclude principals from qualifications, occupations, duties, etc., the situation, such as physical and mental disorders, is examined individually and practically, and it is necessary for each system to optimize the provisions for determining the presence or absence of various abilities (individual examination provisions), the necessary provisions for the procedures having been prepared in 187 Laws; Yasushi Kamiyama, 'Trends in Uniform Review of Disqualification Clauses for Adult Guardians, etc.' (2018) 72 [2975] *Weekly Social Security* 42, 47.

[217.] 'The promotion of the adult guardianship system' was described in (1) the Promotion of Dementia Barrier-Free of the Outline to Promote Dementia Policy Program. Cabinet Office, *The Outline to Promote Dementia Policy Program* (Web Page, June 18, 2019) 24 (in Japanese) <https://www.mhlw.go.jp/stf/seisakunitsuite/bunya/0000076236_00002.html>.

[218.] Refers to the Ministry of Justice of Japan, *Regarding the Law to Partially Revise the Companies Act* (Web Page, December 21, 2021) (in Japanese) <http://www.moj.go.jp/MINJI/minji07_00001.html>.

Date	Contents	Decision Body
March 24, 2020	Published the Interim Verification Report/Basic Plan	MHLW
April 1, 2020	Started to use the new Petition Form for the Adult Guardianship System[219]	The Courts
October 30, 2020	Published the Guidelines for Adult Guardians Based on Supported Decision-Making[220]	SDM Working Group, Expert Commission
December 22, 2021	The Expert Commission summarized 'The Matters to be included in the Second Term Basic Plan for Promoting the Adult Guardianship System (final summary)'[221]	MHLW
March 25, 2022	The Cabinet of Japan decided on the Second Term Basic Plan for Promoting the Adult Guardianship System.[222]	The Cabinet
June 7, 2022	The study group on the ideal adult guardianship system (chair Akio Yamanome) started deliberations on.[223]	Ministry of Justice
February 13, 2024	The study group reported their report outline to the Ministry of Justice	Minister of Justice
February 15, 2024	The Minister of Justice delivered an inquiry to the Legislative Council to reform the guardianship in the Civil Code.[224] The Legislative Council established the Civil Code (Adult Guardianship, etc.) Subcommittee.	Ministry of Justice

---

[219.] Refers to the Courts of Japan, *Petition Formats for Adult Guardianship* (Web Page, February 2022) (in Japanese) <https://www.courts.go.jp/saiban/syosiki/syosiki_kazisinpan/syosiki_01_01/index.html>.

[220.] Refers to the Ministry of Health, Labour, and Welfare of Japan (n 204).

[221.] The Ministry was allocated a system for promoting the adult guardianship 800 million yen (US$5.6 million) as a budget for the fiscal year 2020, 590 million yen (US$4.1 million) as a budget for the fiscal year 2021, and 950 million yen (US$6.6 million) as a budget for the fiscal year 2022.

[222.] Ministry of Health, Labour, and Welfare of Japan (n 198).

[223.] Refers to the Japan Institute of Business Law, *The Study Group on the Ideal Adult Guardianship System* (Web Page, June 2022) <https://www.shojihomu.or.jp/list/seinenkoken> (in Japanese).

[224.] Inquiry No. 126: In light of various circumstances surrounding the adult guardianship system, such as the aging of society, it seems necessary to review the adult guardianship system from the perspective of ensuring

Date	Contents	Decision Body
February 22, 2024	The study group on the ideal adult guardianship system issued the final report.[225]	Ministry of Justice
April 9, 2024	Legislative Council, Civil Code (Adult Guardianship, etc.) Subcommittee started deliberations on.[226]	Ministry of Justice
March 7, 2025	The Expert Commission issued the Interim Verification Report on the Second Term Basic Plan for Promoting the Adult Guardianship System.[227]	MHLW

Source: Made by the author

(5) The Issues of the Legislative Policy of Japan

A comparative analysis of Japan's legislative response to the adult guardianship system and those of other developed countries/regions reveals two major gaps: (a) Japan has pursued operational improvements within the existing legislative framework, while many other jurisdictions that have signed or ratified the CRPD have undertaken law reform or enacted new legislation to amend their adult guardianship systems.

(b) Japan continues to promote the adult guardianship system through the Promotion Act, whereas several countries have moved to restrict its use as a last resort, emphasizing SDM instead. Some jurisdictions have even abolished the terms 'guardian' and 'guardianship' in their legislation.[228]

These divergences can be further explained as follows.

---

that individuals who use the system can continue to live lives that are worthy of their dignity and to better protect their rights and interests. I would like the outline of such a review to be presented. The response of the Legislative Council to the Minister of Justice is expected in 2026.

[225.] The study group on the ideal adult guardianship system, 'The Final Report' (Web Page, February 22, 2024) (in Japanese) <https://www.moj.go.jp/content/001417182.pdf>.

[226.] Refers to the Ministry of Justice, *Legislative Council, Civil Code (Adult Guardianship, etc.) Subcommittee* (Web Page, April 2024) (in Japanese) <https://www.moj.go.jp/shingi1/housei02_003007_00008>.

[227.] Refers to the Ministry of Health, Labour, and Welfare, *Interim Verification Report on the Second Term Basic Plan for Promoting the Adult Guardianship System* (in Japanese) <https://www.mhlw.go.jp/content/12000000/001435369.pdf>.

[228.] Refers to Section 3.2, 'A Comparative Law Study in the International Context,' which notes that Switzerland and Austria have abolished the terms 'guardian' and 'guardianship' from their civil codes. The World Congress of Adult Guardianship has also renamed itself the World Congress on Adult Capacity (Edinburgh, June 2022) and, later, the World Congress on Adult Support and Care (Buenos Aires, August 2024), in alignment with the principles of the CRPD.

Regarding (a), at the inaugural meeting of the Commission on September 23, 2016, Chair Satoshi Omori[229] noted the existence of an agreement between the ruling coalition parties, the Liberal Democratic Party (LDP) and Komeito, not to amend the Civil Code under the framework of the Promotion Act. Although the rationale for this political decision was not publicly disclosed, the following factors likely influenced it: (i) Comprehensive legislative revision would require considerable time and resources,[230] while operational improvements were deemed urgently necessary.[231] (ii) Public debate on reforming the adult guardianship system had not matured, and amending the Civil Code and related laws might not yet receive broad public understanding.[232] (iii) Komeito, as a welfare-oriented political party, sought to demonstrate leadership by prioritizing improved personal protection within the existing legal framework.[233] Among these, (iii) appears to have been particularly influential.

Regarding (b), Japan's unique policy focus on promoting the adult guardianship system—unlike other developed countries—can be attributed to the following considerations in the context of a super-aged society: (i) The system remains underutilized, as acknowledged by the Promotion Act and Basic Plan, despite the growing population of older persons with dementia. (ii) With the increase in older people–only and single-person households,[234] it is increasingly difficult for family members to act as guardians, necessitating the development of regional support networks to assist individuals without familial support in accessing legal and welfare services.[235] (iii) The guardianship system in Japan has functioned

---

[229.] Emeritus professor at the University of Tokyo.

[230.] When the current adult guardianship system was enacted in December 1999, more than five years were spent to achieve the amendments to the Civil Code and the relevant legislation through full deliberation by the Legislative Council upon the request of the Minister of Justice. Ministry of Justice of Japan, Civil Affairs Bureau Counselor's Office (n 15).

[231.] Older people of the baby boom generation will be aged 75 and over in 2025 and Japan will have more populations aged 75 and over ('the year 2025 problem'). The older people with dementia will increase as the population ages. Japan needs some countermeasures as a public policy.

[232.] Academic societies and law/welfare associations deliberated and summarized the idea on the reform of law and regulations; however, the public has no idea of these views because little attention has been paid to the idea.

[233.] Komeito established the 'Adult Guardianship System Promotion Project Team' (chair Yoshinori Oguchi) in the party in December 2010 and made draft bill in 2012. Then, the lawmaker of Komeito submitted the Promotion bill to the National Diet. The chair Oguchi took office as Vice Minister of the Ministry of Health, Labour, and Welfare of Japan in 2018 to 2019 when the Expert Commission commenced deliberations.

[234.] The 57.8 per cent of households with persons aged 65 and over comprise households with single persons or households with a married older couple. The number of households with single persons, households with older single persons, and households with single parents are expected to increase. Households with single persons are expected to reach about 40 per cent in 2040. On the other hand, the number of households with couples and child continues to decrease. Ministry of Health, Labour, and Welfare of Japan, *Reference Survey No. 4 for Working Group* (Web Page, May 12, 2021) 5–6. <https://www.mhlw.go.jp/content/12000000/000777930.pdf>.

[235.] Tokiyo Shimizu, 'Current Status and Development of the Adult Guardianship System' (2019) 24(1) *International Public Policy Studies* 15–28, 22–3 (in Japanese); Aya Yamaguchi, 'Case Study on the Actual Condition and Function of the Community Support Network for Legal Support for the Elderly' (2022) 105 *Rikkyo Law Review* 208, 240 (in Japanese).

primarily to manage the finances of older persons,[236] who hold approximately 60 per cent of household financial assets—estimated at 2,230 trillion yen (US\$15.5 billion) as of December 2024—highlighting the need for a secure and reliable financial management framework.[237] (iv) The government promotes guardianship not only for financial protection but also for personal protection, in part due to the general unpopularity of LPAs among the Japanese public.[238]

Given these practical considerations, the Japanese government's promotion of the adult guardianship system appears understandable, especially in light of the current lack of viable alternatives for managing the affairs of those with diminished capacity. However, from a medium- to long-term perspective, Japan may need to explore legislative alternatives beyond the guardianship framework. As this study argues, the complex challenges faced by vulnerable adults call for a multifaceted response, integrating legal, policy, and community-based measures.

1.2.2 Supported Decision-Making

The support measures discussed in Sections 1.2.2 and 1.2.4 have been developed through amendments to social security legislation, such as the Social Welfare Act and various disability-related laws or guidelines. In contrast, healthcare decision-making in Section 1.2.3 is addressed primarily within the frameworks of medical law and medical ethics. While these measures may share similar objectives with the adult guardianship system—namely the support and protection of individuals with diminished capacity—their legal foundations and characteristics differ from those of the adult guardianship system.

(1) What Is Supported Decision-Making?

In this part, discussion is focused on SDM in a Japanese context. The concept of SDM differs in respect of definition, scope of the subject, and legal basis

---

[236.] The 58 per cent of reasons by motive to make a petition to the adult guardianship system is related to property management, such as management of saving accounts, sale of real estate, inheritance procedures, and insurance claim receipt. The Courts of Japan (n 129); In fact, at the workshop of the Fifth World Congress of Adult Guardianship in Seoul (October 26, 2018), Arai responded to an audience member's question thus 'I understand the significance of policies in developed countries that limit the adult guardianship system as a last resort and encourage…[greater] use [of] supported decision-making…In Japan, where the most appropriate property management for the elderly should be implemented, the introduction of supported decision-making in property management is premature.' Fifth World Congress on Adult Guardianship in Seoul, South Korea (Web Page, October 23–26, 2018) <http://wcag.gabia.io/wcag2018j/glance/parallel-dialogues/#tab-id-6>.

[237.] This is the highest record of the household financial assets in Japan. Bank of Japan, *Money Circulation in the Fourth Quarter of FY2024* (Web Page, May 2025) (in Japanese) <https://www.boj.or.jp/statistics/sj/sjexp.pdf>.

[238.] Approximately a total of 250,000 cases of LPAs have been concluded between contract parties (report by the Ministry of Justice of Japan on May 18, 2022) and 2,795 cases were registered as the voluntary guardianship by law, attached with a supervisor to the voluntary guardian nominated by the family courts, as of December 2024.

according to the country. For example, in the US and Australia, SDM as a legal device is regarded as an alternative to substituted decision-making, which is applied to the wider scope of subjects by law in some states while they have the guardianship system by their other law.[239] In Japan, SDM, which is attached to the guardianship system, is regarded as the standard of decision-making to understand the intentions of the principal, as Kamiyama addresses.[240] SDM is not always based on law but on a bilateral support agreement or the guidelines without enforcement. There is no unified view on SDM and each country or state applies the legislation or practices of SDM stipulated in their own policy. Some commonly shared international guidelines are Article 12 of the CRPD and General Comment No.1.[241]

(2) The SDM Guidelines

After the Government of Japan signed the CRPD in September 2007, the term 'supported decision-making' was inserted into disability laws, such as Article 23 of the Basic Act on Persons with Disabilities (revision in 2011, Act No. 84 of 1970) and Article 1-2, Article 42, and Article 51-22 of the Act on Comprehensive Support for the Daily and Social Life of Persons with Disabilities (revision in 2012, Act No. 123 of 2005).[242] No legislation however has defined what SDM should be or is like. Instead, further considerations of how to support decision-making for persons with disabilities have been carried out by three working groups by experts that were designated by the Ministry of Health, Labour, and Welfare of Japan by law.[243] The process of considerations was implemented after the Government of Japan ratified the CRPD on January 20, 2014. It was based on

---

[239.] Refers to Section 3.2 (5), 'U.S. Guardianship and Supported Decision-Making Acts'; Section 3.2 (6), 'Changes to Victoria and NSW State Acts in Australia'; Section 4.3.3 (2) c, 'Guidelines for Supported Decision-Making Practice'; and Section 4.5.1 (1), 'Australian Adult Support and Protection Legislation.'

[240.] Refers to Section 1.1.1 (1) f, 'Supported Decision-Making.' Yasushi Kamiyama presents three ways of thinking about SDM, namely: (i) 'The idea that since the CRPD excludes the possibility of all types of substituted decision-making, it must be completely transformed into a supported decision-making system,' (ii) 'The direction in which substituted decision-making on behalf of a principal is regarded as a type of supported decision-making by respecting the will of the principal as the standard for decision-making,' (iii) 'Supported decision-making and substituted decision-making are separated from the aspect of philosophy, and with prioritization of the principle of supported decision-making, substituted decision-making is used only as a last resort.'

[241.] Refers to Section 1.2.1 (2), 'The CRPD and the General Comment No. 1.'

[242.] The term 'supported decision-making' was additionally inserted into welfare laws without definitions, such as Article 21–5–17 of the Child Welfare Act (Act No. 164 of 1947) and Article 15–3 of the Act on Welfare of Mentally Retarded Persons (Act No. 37 of 1960).

[243.] Refers to Article 2 (Considerations) of Supplementary Provisions of the Act on Comprehensive Support for the Daily and Social Life of Persons with Disabilities. The law stipulates that approximately after three years of the enactment of this Act, the government of Japan shall take measures, if necessary, after due consideration of the matters pertaining to the provisions of the Act.

the decisions of the Social Security Council (Welfare Division)[244] regarding how to promote SDM and the adult guardianship system for people with disabilities on December 14, 2015.[245]

After deliberations by experts, three SDM guidelines were published step-by-step addressing nursing home managers, managers for older people with dementia, and adult guardians. These are 'SDM Guidelines for the Provision of Disabilities Welfare Services (March 2017),' 'SDM Guidelines for People with Dementia in Daily Life and Social Life (June 2018),' and 'Guidelines for Adult Guardians Based on SDM (October 2020).' The first two SDM guidelines are for nursing home managers regarding SDM activities for people with disabilities and people with dementia. These two operational guidelines cover SDM activities in general for people with disabilities and with dementia in their personal daily life and their social life at home or in nursing homes.

In contrast, the third SDM guidelines are addressed specifically for adult guardians who are requested to adopt SDM methods in their guardianship duties in legal acts and its associated personal acts in order to understand the will and preferences of their principals.[246] If SDM methods adopted by the adult guardians cannot be accepted by the principals due to the relevant capacity, then the adult guardians will be obliged to use substitute decision-making. The third SDM guidelines were deliberated and drafted by the working group under supervision of the Expert Commission by Promotion Act.

[244.] The 'Social Security Council' is one of the councils established by the Ministry of Health, Labour, and Welfare of Japan. This is an advisory body to the Minister of Health, Labour, and Welfare, which deliberates and investigates basic matters related to the social security system in general and the ideal form of various social security systems, and reports opinions. The 'Welfare Division' deliberates and investigates welfare policies.

[245.] The Social Security Council (Welfare Division) requested the Ministry to publish the SDM guidelines to make sure the definition, significance, standardized methods, and points to be reminded of SDM etc., to share them with the nursing home managers who support people with disabilities, and to provide the SDM training program with managers to improve their knowledge and skills of SDM. Ministry of Health, Labour, and Welfare of Japan, *The Social Security Council, Welfare Division the 79th Session Survey: About Review Three Years after the Enforcement of the Services and Support for Persons with Disabilities Act (Draft): 5. How to Support Decision-Making for Persons with Disabilities and Promote the Use of the Adult Guardianship System* (Web Page, December 2015) 16–17 (in Japanese) <https://www.mhlw.go.jp/file/05-Shingikai-12601000-Seisakutoukatsukan-Sanjikan-shitsu_Shakaihoshoutantou/0000106993.pdf>.

[246.] Yasushi Kamiyama states that 'clearly separating supported decision-making and proxy/substituted decision-making, approving the priority of supported decision-making as a rule, and showing room to accept proxy/substituted decision-making as a last resort at the minimum necessary cases only.' Yasushi Kamiyama, 'Recent Trends in Supported Decision-Making: Focusing on the Relationship with the Adult Guardianship System' (2020) 72(4) [414] *The Doshisha Law Review* 445, 467 (in Japanese).

(3) The Content of 'Guidelines for Adult Guardians Based on Supported Decision-Making'

a. Purpose of the Guidelines

The Civil Code of Japan stipulates that an adult guardian 'shall respect the intention of the adult ward and consider his/her mental and physical condition and living circumstances' (Articles 858, Paragraph 1 of Article 876-5, and Paragraph 1 of Article 876-10). In practice, an adult guardian may well exercise legal authority based on their own personal values without consideration for the principal's will and preferences and without contacting the principal's stakeholders. This may arise when the adult guardian assumes their position superior to that of the principal with insufficient mental capacity.[247] The Basic Plan includes a passage to 'clarify the role of an adult guardian as a decision-making supporter, along with general measures ensuring procedures and operational processes of supported decision-making.'[248] For users of adult guardianship to realize its benefits, it is essential for an adult guardian to carry out their duties based on the concept of SDM. The Expert Commission understands the need to formulate guidelines on how an adult guardian should apply SDM while discharging their duties.[249]

   In response to this need, a Supported Decision-Making Working Group (hereinafter referred to as 'SDM-WG') was established in May 2019 under the Expert Commission, which is made up of members of the Supreme Court, the Ministry of Health, Labour, and Welfare, and professional associations (i.e., the Japan Federation of Bar Association, the Legal-Support Adult Guardian Center (Japan Federation of 'Shiho-Shoshi' Lawyers' Associations), and the Japanese Association of Certified Social Workers).[250] Since then, the SDM-WG has deliberated on how to formulate the guidelines mainly from the perspective of the principal, conducted hearings for relevant associations that represent potential users, and completed the draft of the 'Guidelines for Adult Guardians Based on Supported Decision-Making' (hereinafter referred to as 'the Guidelines'). With some amendments after public reviews of the summary draft in June 2020, the Guidelines were published on October 30, 2020.

[247.] For example, even though a principal wants to live at their home in their community, an adult guardian may decide to put the principal in a nursing home without careful consideration, persuading the principal in the name of protection.

[248.] Refers to the Ministry of Health, Labour, and Welfare of Japan, *Basic Plan for Promoting the Adult Guardianship System* (Web Page, n/a) 25 (in Japanese).

[249.] Before the SDM-WG-made guidelines, Okayama prefecture's local guidelines are voluntarily created. Okayama Bar Association, *[Okayama Version] about Guidelines for Decision-Making Support for Adult Guardians (Okayama Decision-Making Support Project Team)* (Web Page, 2018/2021) (in Japanese) <https://www.okaben.or.jp/seinen_guideline.html>.

[250.] Refers to the Ministry of Health, Labor and Welfare of Japan (n 204) 1.

In the Guidelines, SDM is defined as 'activities for the principal to make decisions based on [the principal's] own values and preferences performed by supporters related to the principal, including an adult guardian, such as providing necessary information to the principal and drawing out the intentions and preferences of the principal, when there is a problem with the principal's mental capacity on a specific act.'[251] Since SDM is provided by an adult guardian as part of guardianship duties, situations in which an adult guardian is required to directly participate in decision-making support are in principle limited to such legal acts and relevant factual acts (i.e., decisions on the principal's residence, sale of the principal's assets, and gifts and expenses of the principal to a third party) that may have a significant impact on the principal.[252]

b. Seven Principles of the SDM Guidelines

The Guidelines clarify the 'seven principles,'[253] given below, regarding the procedures and operational processes of SDM, including substituted decision-making, that adult guardians should take into consideration. The Guidelines were drafted by the SDM-WG based on the Mental Capacity Act 2005 of England and Wales and the CRPD. The seven principles are composed of the five main principles (the first, second, third, fifth, and sixth principles), which are basically based on the MCA 2005, and the remaining two principles (the fourth and seventh principles), which are added to call attention to adult guardians who are not familiar with the idea of SDM capacity and SDM. The Guidelines also propose the reporting formats for each process.[254] Unlike the Expert Commission, the materials of SDM-WG's deliberations are undisclosed. It can be assumed that the policy intention of the guidelines can be in part clarified by referring to the published articles of an SDM-WG member.[255] Below, the seven principles and some comments are summarized.

[251.] Ibid 2.

[252.] Ibid.

[253.] The seven principles in the text are ones that were translated into English by the Japan Network for Supported Decision-Making <https://sdm-japan.net/>. The author received a permission to cite them from Toshihiko Mizushima on August 3, 2022.

[254.] Refers to the Ministry of Health, Labor and Welfare of Japan (n 204) [attachments].

[255.] Toshihiko Mizushima, 'Mission of the Guidelines for Adult Guardians Based on Supported Decision-Making' (2021) 142 *Social Welfare Research* 45, 54 (in Japanese); Toshihiko Mizushima, 'Issues and Responses to Practice the Guidelines for Adult Guardians Based on Supported Decision-Making' (2021) 92 *Adult Guardianship Practices* 23, 31 (in Japanese); Toshihiko Mizushima, 'Points of Supported Decision-Making Measures in the Second Term Basic Plan on for Promoting the Adult Guardianship System' (2022) 2022(2) *Law Plaza* 45, 49 (in Japanese).

> **First Principle**: Every person is presumed to have a decision-making capacity.

In the Guidelines, 'decision-making capacity' is defined as the capacity to make one's own decision with some support, and is composed of four elements: understanding information, memory retention, comparative examination, and expression of intention.[256] Decision-making capacity is not a concept stipulated by the law of Japan and is different from mental capacity (Article 3-2) and capacity to act (Section 3) stipulated in the Civil Code.

Regarding the first principle, views were expressed during the SDM-WG's deliberations that [the first principle] should be regarded as a matter of degree rather than [a question of] whether or not capacity exists, by reviewing each element of the principal's decision-making capacity. If an adult guardian makes a substituted decision on behalf of the principal because it is perceived that the principal lacks decision-making capacity, the principal may feel that their capacity has been denied. This perception of the principal's lack of decision-making capacity may arise from a lack of skill on the part of the supporter in fully understanding and interpreting the principal's will and preferences. [257] Assuming that a person more or less has a decision-making capacity, then when it is difficult for the supporter to understand the person's intention after all possible efforts, or when a serious influence that cannot be overlooked by the principal cannot be ruled out, it should be regarded as difficulty on the supporter's side. In a situation where it is necessary to decide such a pressing issue, it should be arranged such that the transition from SDM to substituted decision-making must be considered because of the difficulty on the supporter side.[258]

> **Second Principle**: The guardian must not move to substituted decision-making unless all practicable steps have been tried to help enable the person to make decisions for themselves.

The second principle is based on Paragraph 3, Article 1 of the Mental Capacity Act 2005 (hereinafter referred to as 'MCA 2005'). The SDM process includes preparing for the formation of a support team, explaining the purpose to the

---

[256.] Refers to the Ministry of Health, Labor and Welfare of Japan (n 204) 3.

[257.] Toshio Mizushima remarks that the SDM-WG understand that 'decision-making capacity is regarded as a total of the individual capacity of the principal and the decision-making support competence of the supporter.' Mizushima (n 255) 45–54, 46–7.

[258.] Ibid 47.

principal, and holding regular meetings with the principal. The purpose of this process is to support the formation and the expression of the intentions of the principal. The subject of SDM by an adult guardian is specifically limited to 'legal acts that may have a significant impact on the person and relevant factual acts.'[259] This is according to the guidelines based on the scope of responsibility of the adult guardian appointed by the family court as stipulated in the Civil Code.

> **Third Principle**: Even if a decision made by a person seems unreasonable at first glance by others, it should not be enough to judge that the person does not have decision-making capacity.

The third principle shows that the principal has the right to do stupid things.

> **Fourth Principle**: If the guardian and team members working for the person tried all practicable steps to help enable the person to make decisions by themselves and have significant difficulty confirming the person's will and decision, then substitute decision-making is to be considered. Still, even in such a case, the guardian shall act first based on the person's will, which is reasonably presumed on clear evidence (presumed will).

Regarding the fourth principle, if it is difficult to grasp the will and preferences of the principal despite all the decision-making support for a specific decision, and the decision-making cannot be postponed for legal protection, then the decision-making capacity of the principal should be reassessed. In the assessment for a specific decision-making situation, the supporter and the principal are examined respectively based on the following two points of view for each of the four elements of the decision-making capacity (i.e., understanding information, memory retention, comparative examination, and expression of intention): (i) if all the possibilities for SDM have been exhausted (assessment of the supporter's support competence) and (ii) whether it is difficult for the person to make a decision or confirm the decision (assessment of the principal's decision-making capacity). Since medical assessment of the principal is conducted to certify mental capacity conditions in a petition for adult guardianship, some member was of the opinion in the deliberations of the SDM-WG that 'the description of the decision-making capacity assessment of the principal should focus on the

---

[259.] Ibid.

functional assessment, following the MCA 2005 which requires both medical and functional assessments, and the SDM-WG members agreed [on] this view.'[260]

The guidelines attempt to estimate the principal's intention (i.e., best interpretation of the will and preferences of the principal) based on clear evidence. 'At the beginning of the SDM-WG deliberations, it was assumed that there would be five principles according to the model of the MCA 2005.... The fourth principle was then added in response to members' opinion that substituted decision-making in the principal's best interests should be…[a] last resort.'[261] This position was adopted because the SMD-WG members recognized that substituted decision-making in the principal's best interests would tend to lead to a paternalistic decision-making by the adult guardian.

In theory, the guardian shifts from SDM to substituted decision-making as a last resort under such conditions as mentioned above. In practice, however, how much effort the guardian spends to understand the will and preferences of the principal and when the guardian shifts from SDM to substituted decision-making can be assumed to be decided by the guardian in his/her discretion. Consequently, the border between SDM and substituted decision-making in this scheme tends to be ambiguous.

Fifth Principle: The guardian shall adopt a policy based on the best interests of the person, with the greatest possible respect for the person's beliefs, values, and preferences, when: (1) it is difficult even to presume the person's will, or (2) the person's presumed will or expressed wishes will have a significant impact that cannot be overlooked. For (2) significant impact, all three of the following conditions must be met: (i) The option is clearly disadvantageous to the person in comparison with other options available to the person. (ii) Once it occurs, the impact will be so serious that it will be difficult to recover. (iii) The likelihood of its occurrence will be highly certain.

Regarding the fifth principle, the idea is to consider other objective factors on the grounds that the best interests of the principal are respected as much as possible in every respect, namely their intention, feelings, and values. To avoid risk of harm while respecting the intention or presumed intention of the principal for legal protection, there are limited cases where substituted decision-making

---

[260.] Ibid 48.

[261.] Ibid 49. The term 'best interests' is a statutory principle stipulated in Section 4, the *Mental Capacity Act 2005*. It states that 'Any act done, or decision made for, or on behalf of, a person who lacks capacity must be done or made in his or her best interests.' British Medical Association (BMA), *Best Interests Decision-Making for Adults Who Lack Capacity: A Toolkit for Doctors Working in England and Wales* (BMA, 2024) <https://www.bma.org.uk/advice-and-support/ethics/adults-who-lack-capacity/best-interests-decision-making-for-adults-who-lack-capacity-toolkit> The term 'best interests' include both subjective and objective aspects. Masaru Nagawa, 'Supported Decision-Making, Adult Guardianship System, and Guidelines (Draft) (Special Feature: Concepts of Decision-Making Support for Persons with Disabilities and Its Application to Adult Guardianship)' (2016) 64 *Adult Guardian Practices* 36, 44 (in Japanese).

with outcomes may differ from the intentions, or be contrary to the intentions, of the principal. In such cases, these decisions shall be conducted by the adult guardian on their own responsibility. Consideration of the best interests of the principal is only allowed as a last resort.

Sixth Principle: Substituted decision-making based on the best interests of the person can only be made to the minimum extent necessary when the decision cannot be further postponed from the perspective of the legal protection of their rights, and no other measures are available.

Seventh Principle: Even once a substituted decision has been made, the guardian must return to Principle 1 and begin with a presumption of decision-making capacity in the next decision-making situation.

The sixth principle represents the least restrictive alternative. Regarding the seventh principle, 'this principle is added in formulating the guidelines together with the fourth principle in order to call attention to adult guardians who are not familiar with the idea   of decision-making capacity.'[262] Decision-making capacity is examined for each action and each situation, and when the need for SDM arises again, an adult guardian is required to return to the first principle and apply the SDM processes all over from scratch.

(4) Developments and Challenges of the SDM Guidelines

a. Developments

First, the project of the SDM guidelines is a positive development, namely to take necessary measures for nursing home managers, social workers, and adult guardians to guide SDM in the community support fields for people with disabilities and/or with dementia to respect the will and preferences of the principals. In Japan, there is a tendency to rely on guidelines instead of law particularly for a bioethical issue, such as medical care in the end-of-life situation. Norio Higuchi states that 'The guidelines are evaluated as useful and practical because they can be interpreted flexibly and can be easily changed.'[263] Like this view,

---

[262] Mizushima (n 255) 50.

[263] Norio Higuchi, 'Current Status and Challenges of End-of-Life Care Legal Issues' (2020) 2(5) *Geriatrics* 579–84, 581 (in Japanese).

a guiding principle of the SDM guidelines as a soft law would be practical and ethical regulation on SDM at the initial stages, because regulating SDM through a hard law at this stage might be unworkable when an SDM method has not yet been clearly fixed.[264] With this framework, improvement of guidelines based on practices on-site should be recommended. Second, the positive aspect of SDM guidelines is to require supporters, including adult guardians, to take necessary steps of SDM according to the seven principles and keep records in designated formats. Supporters and the principal's stakeholders as a team may review the process of SDM as to what they understand, how and why they decide so. These procedures may empower accountability of the supporters' activities to foster trust between the supporter and the principal.[265] Third, the SDM Guidelines may prioritize SDM rather than the substituted decision-making, even though it takes time for adult guardians to do so.

b. Challenges

There will be, however, some challenges to indefinitely maintain SDM guidelines, namely:

(i)   The guidelines can be applied with flexibility by users, but when a problem arises, the legal basis is ambiguous, and the responsibility is unclear. It is difficult to know which guidelines should be prioritized among multiple guidelines in related disciplines, including other guidelines regarding terminal care and health care.[266]

(ii) The risk of SDM practices concerns undue influence. Undue influence may happen when a supporter, by virtue of their superior or powerful position, tries to control a principal or to exercise improper persuasion.[267] Under the name of autonomy of the principal, a principal with insufficient mental capacity should ideally be assisted by their third-party supporter

---

[264] Yukio Sakurai, 'The Role of Soft Law in the Ageing Society of the Twenty-First Century' (2018) 13(1) *The International Journal of Interdisciplinary Global Studies* 1–10, 7.

[265] This opinion was addressed by lawyers under adult guardianship at the panel discussion of the SDM Guidelines online seminar, which was sponsored by the Legal-Support Adult Guardian Center in Tokyo on March 18, 2022.

[266] An Expert Commission member, a medical doctor stated the actual situation in the hospital as follows: 'The guidelines are flooding the field, and when you look at the contents, you can see a lot of flapping across multiple departments of the Ministry of Health, Labour, and Welfare…The hospital is very confused now due to many relevant guidelines.' Ministry of Health, Labour, and Welfare of Japan, *Expert Commission Meetings: The Minutes of the 2nd Interim Verification Working Group Session* (Web Page, November 20, 2019) (in Japanese) <https://www.mhlw.go.jp/stf/shingi2/0000212875.html>.

[267] Mary Joy Quinn, 'Undue Influence and Elder Abuse' (2002) 23(1) *Geriatric Nursing* 11–17, 15; Daniel A. Plotkin et al, 'Assessing Undue Influence' (2016) 44(3) *The Journal of the American Academy of Psychiatry and the Law* 344, 352.

to realize their will and preferences. In fact, however, the principal might be improperly influenced to engage in action that serves the interests of the third party.[268] In this regard, safeguards to protect against this risk are vital.[269] SDM guidelines struggle to provide such safeguards because of inability to provide workable means for their enforcement.[270] This is an ambiguity of the SDM function, scope, and legal status. In the middle to long-term, legislating SDM will be an issue, taking the CRPD requirements and the safeguards for SDM operational risk into consideration.[271]

In addition, SDM guidelines include some substantial issues as follows:

(iii)   The definition, standardization of methods, legal examination, safeguards for risk, human resources development and such for SDM are under development. The SDM guidelines for adult guardians fall short of the legal basis of the term 'supported decision-making capacity.'[272] Therefore, SDM is not yet a finished product able to be put into practical use in Japan at large. Review of SDM guidelines based on practices and experiences in support is required to improve the unified SDM definition, standardize

---

[268.] A case reported in a 2015 newsletter of the NPO 'Tokatsu Community Guardianship Association' (Chiba Prefecture) illustrates concerns regarding undue influence over older individuals with dementia. An older woman left a notarized will bequeathing all her property—valued at nearly US$1.4 million—exclusively to a social worker at her nursing home, as an expression of appreciation. Questions arose as to whether the will genuinely reflected her wishes or was influenced, wholly or partly, by the social worker. As there were no putative heirs withstanding to file a lawsuit, the social worker ultimately received the entire estate, despite breaching the internal rules of the nursing home and the social worker associations to which they belonged. Such circumstances, modeled on an actual incident, are highly likely to constitute a case of undue influence, particularly given that the woman, requiring the social worker's assistance, completed the notarized will at a notary public with two witnesses. Sakurai (n 264) 6–7.

[269.] Thomas F. Coleman states that 'for people with questionable capacity, [SDM] procedures should be developed to reduce or eliminate the risk of abuse or exploitation of seniors, people with disabilities, or other vulnerable adults' at 'Overview' in the report. Thomas F. Coleman, *Supported Decision-Making: My Transformation from a Curious Skeptic to an Enthusiastic Advocate* (Online, 2017) <https://tomcoleman.us/publications/sdm-essay-2017.pdf>.

[270.] In Germany, the first court of the Federal Constitutional Court decided that the federal legislature violated Article 3.3, Paragraph 2 of the Basic Law (Constitution) on December 16, 2021 [1BvR 1541/20] because the federal legislature did not legislate law to ensure that nobody with disability is at a disadvantage when allocating intensive care resources that are not available to all [in triage cases], and relied on the recommendations of the German Intensive Care Unit Interdisciplinary Association (DIVI), which were non-binding and not synonym for medical standards in specialized law. This decision shows that legislation must be conducted on such ethical issue as triage cases based on their constitution.

[271.] An idea of legislative framework that includes the protections offered by the Civil Code for vulnerable adults is vital and thus should be considered. Hayashi and Obara suggest that it is necessary to build a training system for practitioners as well as legislation in Japan to build a new support system with reference to English law and practice. Maho Hayashi and Naoyasu Obara, 'The Current Situation and Issues of Making Decisions for People Who Lack Capacity: Based on the Survey of Mental Capacity Act 2005' (2019) 60 *Memoirs of Beppu University* 89–101, 97; Japan Federation of Bar Associations, *Declaration Calling for the Establishment of a System for Comprehensive Supported Decision-Making* (Web Page, October 2, 2015) (in Japanese) <https://www.nichibenren. or.jp/document/civil_liberties/year/2015/2015_1.html>.

[272.] Refers to Section 5.2.2, 'Combined Models of Guardianship and Supported Decision-Making.'

SDM methods, and develop adequate safeguards for risk of the principals.[273] The guidelines should be unified into one representative set of guidelines to explicitly stipulate principles and due procedures.

(iv) Yasushi Kamiyama states that there are two views on the relationship between the guardianship and SDM in Japan: One is that the guardianship and SDM are independent of each other, and the other is that they are interlinked. In the former view, SDM is regarded as a 'legal system that will replace the adult guardianship system' to meet the requirements of Article 12 of the CRPD. In the latter view, SDM is regarded as a 'support method for substituted decision-making' to comply with Article 858 of the Civil Code.[274] Combining Article 12 of the CRPD and General Comment No. 1, SDM is regarded as a 'legal system' that will replace the adult guardianship system. In the SDM guidelines for nursing managers and managers of older people with dementia, however, SDM is regarded as a 'support method' of practicing Article 858 (Respect for the will of the adult ward and consideration for their personality) of the Civil Code.[275] In other words, 'SDM as a support method' is subordinated to Article 858 of the Civil Code. From policy and legal studies perspectives, it is questioned whether it is indeed necessary and enough to have the three SDM guidelines based on an idea of 'SDM as a support method.'

1.2.3 Healthcare Decision-Making

(1) Healthcare Decision-Making Framework in General

A healthcare decision-making framework offers a structured approach to guiding medical decisions, grounded in legal principles such as informed consent, ethical values like respect for individuals, and the protection of human rights. It provides a systematic methodology for resolving complex situations in which competing interests—such as patient autonomy, clinical judgment, and societal welfare—intersect. At its core, the framework upholds autonomy, ensuring that individuals retain the right to make informed

---

[273.] In the circular of the first SDM guidelines addressed to local governments on March 31, 2017, the Ministry of Health, Labour, and Welfare of Japan states that 'it is necessary to review the contents of the guidelines based on SDM practices.'

[274.] Refers to Section 1.2.1 (2), 'The CRPD and the General Comment No. 1.'

[275.] Yasushi Kamiyama basically supports the latter view but does not agree with the opinion that SDM is subordinated to the Civil Code. Kamiyama (n 41) 445–67, 447–8.

healthcare choices to the greatest extent possible.[276] This principle is balanced by beneficence and non-maleficence, which require healthcare providers to prioritize patient well-being and minimize harm.[277] The principle of justice further ensures equity in healthcare decisions, especially concerning resource allocation and access to care.[278]

From a jurisprudential perspective, a sound healthcare decision-making frame-work demands procedural mechanisms that guarantee fairness, inclusiveness, and legal certainty.[279] A critical component of this process is capacity assessment, recognizing that an individual's ability to make decisions varies depending on the complexity of the decision and the individual's personal circumstances. For individuals with diminished capacity, SDM mechanisms allow for participation to the greatest extent possible, often involving legally appointed representatives or trusted family members. This aligns with the concept of relational autonomy, which recognizes the interdependence of individuals and the importance of social relationships in shaping healthcare decisions.

When substitute decision-making is required, legal standards must be met—prioritizing either the patients previously expressed will and preferences or, in their absence, their best interests. The standard of best interests typically involves consideration of the patient's values, beliefs, and overall well-being.[280] These processes are governed by the principles of proportionality, transparency, and accountability, which aim to ensure that medical interventions are legally justi-fied, that decision-making is appropriately documented, and that fundamental human rights are respected.

The theoretical basis of healthcare decision-making frameworks draws on foundational legal and ethical doctrines. The ethics principles model—autonomy, beneficence, non-maleficence, and justice—serves as a flexible normative guide adaptable to various cultural and legal settings. Typically, a two-stage process is employed: first, evaluating medically appropriate options through clinical expertise; and second, conducting an ethics-legal analysis incorporating patient

---

[276] Tom Beauchamp and James Childress, 'Principles of Biomedical Ethics: Marking Its Fortieth Anniversary' (2019) 19(11) *The American Journal of Bioethics* 9–12 <https://doi.org/10.1080/15265161.2019.1665402>.

[277] Ibid.

[278] Ibid.

[279] Mary Donnelly, *Healthcare Decision-Making and the Law: Autonomy, Capacity, and Limits of the Liberalism* (Cambridge University Press, 2010); Matthé Scholten, 'Mental Capacity and Supported Decision-Making' in *Ethics in Psychiatry: European Contributions* (Springer, 2025) 27–51 <https://doi.org/10.1007/978-94-024-2274-0_3>.

[280] Kazuto Inaba, 'Healthcare Decision-Making: Patients, Families, and Representatives in the Terminal Stage' (2003) 2(2) *Medicine, Life, Ethics, and Society* Accessed March 27, 2025 (in Japanese) <https://www.med.osaka-u.ac.jp/pub/eth/OJ_files/OJ2-2/inaba.htm>.

values, statutory mandates, and broader societal considerations.[281] By integrating legal rigor with procedural safeguards, such frameworks ensure that medical decisions are not only clinically sound but also legally and ethically defensible.

Healthcare decision-making tools encompass both legal and non-legal instruments, which vary across countries depending on their healthcare policies and legislative foundations. Non-legal instruments may include government-issued guidelines or those developed by academic and professional medical communities.[282] While lacking binding legal authority in courts, such guidelines often inform clinical standards of care. Each country designs healthcare decision-making frameworks according to its unique needs and traditions, even when grounded in shared principles of clinical ethics. It is therefore essential that legal systems consider regional traditions and cultural values.[283]

Effective healthcare policy and decision-making benefit from cross-national collaboration and exchange of information. Balancing legal and ethical considerations is a shared global objective, with ethical norms often finding broader consensus internationally, while laws and guidelines remain jurisdiction specific. As medical technologies advance and social environments evolve, legal frameworks, clinical guidelines, and ethical standards must be continually updated to remain effective and relevant.

(2) Legal Relationship Between Doctors, Patients, and Family Members

This section explores the legal relationships between medical professionals, patients, and family members in the context of end-of-life medical care. It seeks to clarify key legal concepts in healthcare decision-making and consider policy directions for reform.

a. Doctor-Patient Relationship

The core purpose of clinical action is to act in the best interests of the patient. However, this is constrained by the subjective wishes, values, and preferences

---

[281] Stephanie L. Tang, 'When Providers and Families Cannot Agree: A New Look at Due Process for End-of-Life Care Disputes' (2023) 61(1) *Houston Law Review* <https://ssrn.com/abstract=4454895>.

[282] Yukio Sakurai. 'The Role of Law and Bioethics in Human Life and Death: Japanese Medical Law in End-of-Life Care' (2024) 25(1) *Australian Journal of Asian Law* 89–105 <https://ssrn.com/abstract=4964356>.

[283] Yukio Sakurai, 'The Political Process Involved in Formulating Healthcare Policy in Japan: With a Particular Focus on Advisory Councils, Interest Groups and Medical Officers' (2025) 15(1) *The Rest: Journal of Politics and Development* 82–96 <http://hdl.handle.net/10131/0002001605>.

of the patient, which must be balanced against the physician's professional judgment. The concept of medical legitimacy encapsulates this dual obligation: medical justification and informed consent.[284] In the US, medical justification draws from the principles' framework—autonomy, non-maleficence, beneficence, and justice. In Europe, it is grounded in principles such as autonomy, dignity, integrity, and vulnerability.

In U.S. medical law, informed consent is a foundational doctrine. Physicians are legally obligated to disclose diagnosis, treatment options, risks, and potential outcomes.[285] The landmark case *Canterbury v. Spence* (D.C. Cir. 1972)[286] emphasized that failure to secure informed consent violates the fiduciary duty owed by the physician to the patient—an important concept in American jurisprudence.[287] In civil law systems, the physician–patient relationship is typically understood as a quasi-agency contract, requiring medical care that conforms to prevailing standards.[288] Thus, regardless of jurisdiction, informed consent is a legal and ethical imperative. Its necessity is further affirmed in international human rights instruments such as the 2005 Universal Declaration on Bioethics and Human Rights,[289] which emphasizes the need to respect patient autonomy. While the core principles of informed consent and patient autonomy have been adopted globally—including in East Asia—their legislative incorporation and practical application vary widely depending on each country's legal infrastructure.[290]

End-of-life care introduces greater complexity into the doctor–patient relationship due to uncertain prognoses and treatment efficacy. Patients may experience fluctuations in decision-making capacity, requiring careful consideration of beneficence and respect for autonomy.[291] In Japan, Article 4-2(1) of the Medical Practitioners Act (1948), as amended in 2018, obliges doctors to align treatment

---

[284] Shigeki Nakayama, 'Consent and Intimate Relationships in Medical Care: From the Constitutional Perspective of "Respect for the Individual" (1)' (2024) 58(3) *Sendai Law Review* 269–96 (in Japanese) <http://hdl.handle.net/10965/0002000266>.

[285] Beauchamp and Childress (n 276).

[286] *Canterbury v. Spence* (1972) established the doctrine of informed consent, requiring medical doctors to disclose risks that a reasonable person would consider significant when making decisions about their medical care. JUSTIA, US Law *Canterbury v. Spence, No. 22099 (D.C. Cir. 1972)* (n.d.) <https://law.justia.com/cases/federal/appellate-courts/cadc/22099/22099.html>.

[287] Norio Higuchi, *Thinking about Medicine and Law* (Yuhikaku Publishing Co. Ltd., 2007) (in Japanese).

[288] Yutaka Teshima, *Introduction to Medical Law* (Yuhikaku Publishing Co. Ltd., 6th ed, 2022); Shigeto Yonemura, *Lectures on Medical Law* (Nippon Hyoron Sha Co., Ltd., 2016).

[289] UNESCO, *Universal Declaration on Bioethics and Human Rights of 2005* (2005) <https://www.unesco.org/en/legal-affairs/universal-declaration-bioethics-and-human-rights>.

[290] For example, Japan lacks explicit legislation concerning patient autonomy.

[291] Elissa Kolva, Barry Rosenfeld and Rebecca Saracino, 'Assessing the Decision-Making Capacity of Terminally Ill Patients with Cancer' (2018) 26(5) *The American Journal of Geriatric Psychiatry* 523–31 <https://doi.org/10.1016/j.jagp.2017.11.012>.

with the patient's wishes where possible. However, surveys by the MHLW reveal inconsistencies in how physicians interpret and apply this mandate. Many acknowledge the value of patient autonomy but hesitate to discuss advance decisions (ADs) in practice.[292]

International comparisons show that informed consent and communication obligations differ significantly. In the US, the 1990 Patient Self-Determination Act supports patient participation in medical decisions, including the use of ADs. All states have passed related laws. By contrast, Japan lacks legally binding provisions affirming patient rights in end-of-life care, partly due to an absence of court cases involving, for example, the withdrawal of life-sustaining treatment.[293] In addition to legal frameworks and medical ethics, traditional Japanese values—such as *toku* (virtue)—heavily influence medical decision-making. These emphasize social harmony and relational obligations over individual rights. A distinct legal framework tailored to Japanese cultural context is necessary. Such a system should balance the relational orientation of autonomy with the global legal standards for medical decision-making. While complex, this approach could support more effective legal evolution and policy adaptation across generations.

There has been a rise in patients or their family dissatisfaction leading to violence or harassment against healthcare professionals. Traditionally, patients respected healthcare professionals; however, now they openly express dissatisfaction, sometimes violently. A 2023 Fukuoka Medical Association survey identified unreasonable patient demands and harassment, which disrupts medical care and affects staff. Such behaviors in healthcare settings are referred to as 'patient harassment'. This is exacerbated by the COVID-19 pandemic, resulting from strained trust, reduced routine care, and grievances fueled by social media. Such harassment causes trauma among healthcare providers, leading to staffing shortages and criticism of hospital management. Addressing this requires collaboration among medical associations, authorities, and law enforcement.

b. Patient-Family Member Relationship

The relationship between patients and family members is shaped by cultural norms and societal expectations, which differ significantly across contexts.

[292.] Japan, MHLW, (2018) *61st Medical Division Meeting of the Social Security Council* Minutes for the Meeting held on April 11, 2018 (in Japanese) <https://www.mhlw.go.jp/stf/shingi2/0000212218_00001.html>.

[293.] A lawsuit is currently pending in Japan concerning the murder of a woman from Kyoto City with the incurable disease ALS by a medical doctor. This case may be worthy of discussion. Anri Asagumo, 'Relational Autonomy, the Right to Reject Treatment, and Advance Directives in Japan' (2022) 14 *Asian Bioethics Review* 57–69 <https://doi.org/10.1007/s41649-021-00191-1>.

Legally, this area falls under the domain of private autonomy, meaning state intervention is limited unless justified by overriding interests. In East Asia including Japan, family members often assume decision-making responsibilities, particularly when the patient lacks capacity. However, this arrangement can create tension between honoring the patient's autonomy and deferring to familial preferences—a dilemma especially prevalent in cultures that view family-oriented decision-making as a moral duty.[294]

In South Korea and Taiwan, legislation acknowledges the family's role in healthcare decision-making while also attempting to safeguard patient rights. Under South Korea's Act on Decisions on Life-Sustaining Treatment for Patients in Hospice and Palliative Care at the End of Life of 2016 (South Korea) (ELDA) family members may consent to the withdrawal of life-sustaining treatment if the patient's wishes are unknown or cannot be inferred. Similarly, Taiwan's Patient Right to Autonomy Act (PRAA) allows family decisions in the absence of ADs, provided they act in good faith and in the patient's best interests.

In contrast, Japanese law and policy lack clear provisions on family involvement in medical decisions.[295] While hospital ethics committees often mediate family–physician disputes, such mechanisms are informal and lack legal authority.[296] Family members frequently function as de facto proxies based on cultural and social expectations, despite the absence of a legal framework. This informal practice contrasts with the concept of 'ex lege representation,'[297] a legal mechanism through which certain individuals are authorized by law to act on behalf of another person without needing a court decision or voluntary designation.[298]

The current reliance on informal family representation in Japan reveals significant systemic deficiencies. Establishing a legal framework grounded in the concept of ex lege representation could enhance the legitimacy and transparency of family involvement in healthcare decision-making, while simultaneously offering greater protection for patients' rights. However, such a framework would also raise complex legal questions—such as how to identify which family

---

[294.] Sumytra Menon et al, *Some Unresolved Ethical Challenges in Healthcare Decision-Making: Navigating Family Involvement* (2020).

[295.] Nakayama (n 284).

[296.] Tsusnakuni Ikka, 'Reconsideration of Hospital Ethics Committee' (2013) 23(1) *Bioethics* 23–30 (in Japanese).

[297.] The term 'ex lege representation' was proposed by Adrian Ward in an email exchange. ELI, *European Commission's Public Consultation on the Initiative on the Cross-Border Protection of Vulnerable Adults: C. Inclusion of a Conflicts Rule on Ex Lege Powers of Representation* (2022) 17–18 <https://www.europeanlawinstitute.eu/fileadmin/user_upload/p_eli/Publications/ELI_Response_Protection_of_Adults.pdf>.

[298.] FL-EUR, *Questionnaire: Legal Protection and Empowerment of Vulnerable Adults* (n.d.) <https://fl-eur.eu/working_field_1__empowerment_and_protection/country-reports>.

member should hold decision-making authority and how to resolve intra-family conflicts—necessitating careful legal and procedural deliberation.

In practice, physicians often recognize a so-called key person among the patient's family or kin, irrespective of legal status or degree of relationship, who is regarded as the representative of the patient's interests. Once identified, physicians tend to communicate primarily with this key person—sometimes even more than with the patient—regarding treatment plans and scheduling, even in cases where the patient retains decision-making capacity. While this approach reflects a pragmatic solution commonly observed in clinical settings, it operates outside of any formal legal framework and may undermine the principle of patient autonomy.

c. Self-Determination, Supported Decision-Making, and Shared Decision-Making

Patient decision-making can take various forms, ranging from full autonomy to collaborative or supported arrangements. The most conventional model is autonomy-based self-decision-making, in which patients with sufficient capacity make independent healthcare choices. However, it is increasingly recognized that decision-making is shaped by various internal and external influences. One such influence is the concept of a 'nudge,' a behavioral policy tool that subtly guides choices without restricting freedom.[299] Scholars argue that when nudges significantly affect autonomy, they should be accompanied by safeguards.[300]

SDM emerges from a fusion of the vulnerability approach and a rights-based framework.[301] Here, third parties assist individuals who lack full decision-making capacity. In Japan, this model remains underdeveloped. The adult guardianship system focuses primarily on financial matters and provides little support for healthcare decision-making.[302] Advocacy organizations, NGOs, and some medical professionals have called for the expansion of SDM in healthcare.[303] The state of Victoria, Australia, offers a pioneering example: pilot programs train healthcare

---

[299] Rebecca Zeilstra, 'Nudging and the Safeguards of the Rule of Law' (2024) 25(5) *German Law Journal* 750–71 <https://doi.org/10.1017/glj.2024.30>.

[300] Ibid.

[301] Yukio Sakurai, 'Supported Decision-Making in the Japanese Context: Developments and Challenges' (2023) 3(1) *The Journal of Aging and Social Change* 151–69 <https://doi.org/10.18848/2576-5310/CGP/v13i01/151-169>.

[302] Makoto Arai, 'Japan Adult Guardianship Laws: Development and Reform Initiatives' in Lusina Ho and Rebecca Lee (eds), *Special Needs Financial Planning: A Comparative Perspective* (Cambridge University Press, 2019) S19–24.

[303] Asao Ogawa, 'End-of-Life Care for Dementia' (2019) 121 *Journal of Psychiatry* 289–97 (in Japanese).

professionals in SDM and establish legal protections for patient autonomy within community settings.[304]

Shared decision-making, meanwhile, has gained global attention as a means of promoting patient-centered care.[305] It aligns with ethical principles by fostering mutual respect and collaborative treatment planning. ACP has evolved from this approach. The concept of a fiduciary duty—a cornerstone of common law—better supports this model than the civil law concept of a quasi-agency contract. However, shared decision-making faces practical barriers: limited time, insufficient training, and a cultural hesitance to challenge medical authority.[306] Overcoming these challenges will require education, professional development, and institutional reforms.

Special considerations are needed for minors and persons with disabilities to ensure their rights are upheld within these decision-making frameworks.[307] Further research and practice-based innovation are essential. The appropriate decision-making model should reflect the patient's physical and mental condition, as well as their expressed wishes. In all cases, respect for patient autonomy must prevail, and undue influence must be prevented. Patient-centered approaches are particularly critical in both supported and shared decision-making scenarios.

d. Advance Decisions, Substituted Decisions, and the Best Interests Standard

Healthcare decisions may be categorized by their timing—whether made in advance or in reaction to an unfolding situation. ADs, such as living wills, are legal tools that allow individuals to articulate preferences for future medical treatment. These tools are designed to reduce uncertainty and prevent disputes by clarifying patient wishes beforehand. As discussed earlier, ADs are especially valuable for preserving autonomy in end-of-life care.

Nonetheless, cultural and legal challenges remain. Japanese legal systems are often modeled on Western legal ideologies, yet these frameworks may not

---

[304.] Shih-Ning Then and C. Bigby, 'Supported Decision-Making and the Disability Royal Commission: Research and Practice in Intellectual and Developmental Disabilities' (2024) 11(1) *Research and Practice in Intellectual and Developmental Disabilities* 86–106 <https://doi.org/10.1080/23297018.2024.2330961>.

[305.] Glyn Elwyn et al, 'Shared Decision Making: A Model for Clinical Practice' (2012) 27(10) *Journal of General Internal Medicine* 1361–7 <https://doi.org/10.1007/s11606-012-2077-6>.

[306.] Confucian familism weakens patient-clinician shared decision-making in end-of-life care of advanced cancer patients. Yuexi Yang et al, 'Confucian Familism and Shared Decision Making in End-of-Life Care for Patients with Advanced Cancers' (2022) 19 *International Journal of Environmental Research and Public Health* 10071 <https://doi.org/10.3390/ijerph191610071>.

[307.] Oluwaseun Rebecca Sobode et al, 'Shared Decision-Making in Adolescent Healthcare: A Literature Review of Ethical Considerations' (2024) 183 *European Journal of Pediatrics* 4195–203 <https://doi.org/10.1007/s00431-024-05687-0>.

be fully embraced by local populations, who maintain deeply rooted local customs and traditions. For instance, studies in Japan indicate that few individuals complete ADs.[308] Barriers include low legal awareness and cultural discomfort with discussing death.[309]

In the absence of ADs, families often make substitute decisions, which can lead to ethical dilemmas—particularly when social obligations conflict with the patient's best interests.[310] This ethical tension is well documented in the literature on medical ethics. In contrast, the Mental Capacity Act 2005 in England and Wales provides clearer procedures for substituted decision-making and emphasizes the standard of best interests, supported by statutory guidance.[311]

In Japan, the 'best interests' standard is often invoked by physicians but lacks explicit legal definition. This ambiguity may lead to inconsistent decision-making, reliance on institutional policies, or subjective professional judgment—all of which pose risks to patient autonomy and transparency.[312]

To address these issues, scholars advocate embedding ACP within routine care. Structured ACP initiatives not only uphold patient autonomy but also alleviate emotional burdens on families and medical professionals. International programs such as the U.S.-based Respecting Choices model provide useful templates. Legal reforms in Japan should also consider the development of culturally appropriate advance decision-making mechanisms, tailored to local contexts while ensuring consistency with human rights principles.

[308.] Sakurai (n 282). In Japan, there is a paucity of enduring powers of attorney for asset management, which bear resemblance to ADs for end-of-life medical care. Consequently, proactive preparations for end-of-life are not a prevalent phenomenon.

[309.] Beauchamp and Childress (n 276).

[310.] BunRong Kouy, 'On Taiwan Patient Right to Autonomy Act: How Family Stimulates Autonomy' (2019) 67 *Applied Ethics Review* 187–212.

[311.] Johnston Carolyn and Jane Liddle, 'The Mental Capacity Act 2005: A New Framework for Healthcare Decision Making' (2007) 33(2) *Journal of Medical Ethics* 94–7 <https://doi.org/10.1136/jme.2006.016972>.

[312.] Atsushi Asai, Taketoshi Okita and Seiji Bito, 'Discussions on Present Japanese Psychocultural-Social Tendencies as Obstacles to Clinical Shared Decision-Making in Japan' (2022) 14(2) *Asian Bioethics Review* 133–50 <https://doi.org/10.1007/s41649-021-00201-2>.

1.2.4 Elder Abuse Prevention Law and Relevant Policy

(1) Elder Abuse Prevention Act

a. Law Framework

With the aging of the population, elder abuse has become prevalent.[313] Although elder abuse is recognized as a social problem, the actual situation of abuse is not accurately understood, and effective countermeasures and prevention measures have not been explicitly established.[314] The issue of elder abuse was internationally taken up in the WHO Toronto Declaration on November 17, 2002 for its universal challenges and lack of legal framework.[315] Japan has responded to abuse of older people and persons with disabilities by offering public intervention and legislation aimed at preventing damage. The Act on the Prevention of Elder Abuse, Support for Caregiver of Elderly Persons and Other Related Matters (Act No. 124 of 2005, hereinafter referred to as 'Elder Abuse Prevention Act') was enacted, and afterward the Act on the Prevention of Abuse of Persons with Disabilities and Support for Caregivers (Act No. 79 of 2011, hereinafter referred to as 'Persons with Disabilities Abuse Prevention Act') was enacted.[316]

These two abuse prevention laws clarify the purpose of preventing abuse of older people and persons with disabilities (Article 1 of both laws) and ensure that 'caregivers' and 'care home staff members' (social workers) could be held liable for abuse (Article 2 of both laws). The elderly or older people refer to persons aged 65 or over (Article 2-1). The laws indicate the responsibilities of public and state authorities, including municipalities, in dealing with abuse by doing detections/responses. Namely, in the provisions of Article 6 (consultation, guidance, and advice) and below of the Elder Abuse Prevention Act, a municipality should provide consultations, guidance, and advice for older people and caregivers. When the municipality receives a report from older people or other relevant persons that he/she is subjected to abuse of older people by a caregiver, the municipality promptly confirms the safety of older people (Article 9: measures in case of receipt of a

---

[313.] This part is an updated version of the previously published article in Japanese by the author: Yukio Sakurai, 'Safeguarding Law for Vulnerable Adults at Risk of Harm: Focusing on Elder Abuse' (2020) 13 *Quarterly Journal of Comparative Guardianship Law* 3, 32 (in Japanese).

[314.] Naomi Kanai remarks that it is essential to consider abuse as a human right issue, not just a social problem. Naomi Kanai, 'Human Rights Violation in Private Area and Legal Regulation: Domestic Abuse and Enactment of Abuse Prevention Act' (2009) 30 *Journal of Political Science* 17–41, 35–8.

[315.] Yongjie Yon et al, 'Elder Abuse Prevalence in Community Settings: A Systematic Review and Meta-Analysis' (2017) 5(2) *Lancet Global Health* 147, 156.

[316.] These abuse prevention laws were enacted, following other two abuse-related laws: Act on the Prevention, etc. of Child Abuse (Act No. 82 of 2000) and Act on the Prevention of Spousal Violence and the Protection of Victims (Act No. 31 of 2001).

report, etc., of abuse). In addition to taking measures to confirm the facts related to the above, the municipality examines the response with the parties who collaborate with the relevant municipality (i.e., elder abuse response partners) pursuant to the provision of Article 16 (organizational system for collaboration and cooperation).[317]

Municipalities are subject to administrative supervision responsibility for abuse of older people, but the response in practice depends on the size of municipality, its financial situation, its personnel scale, presence of relevant institutions and experts related to abuse of older people, etc. These laws set out legal responsibility for relevant institutions to cooperate in dealing with abuse prevention. Both abuse prevention laws include the clause of 'promotion of adult guardianship system' (i.e., Article 28 of Elder Abuse Prevention Act and Article 44 of Persons with Disabilities Abuse Prevention Act) that prefectures/municipalities should take necessary supports to promote the adult guardianship system as one of possible abuse prevention measures.[318] While a regional collaboration network based on the Basic Plan of the adult guardianship is established, it can be positively considered that adult guardians need to familiar with measures based on the abuse prevention laws and refine such tasks as detecting and reporting abuse cases. Adult guardianship and elder abuse prevention will be closer interlinked with each other not only on a legal basis but also in practice through such activities.

b. Issues of Elder Abuse Prevention Act

It is worthwhile to recognize that Japan has developed abuse prevention legislation, but the issue is its methodology.[319] The associations of law professions have expressed their views on Japan's abuse prevention laws, questioning the effectiveness of the laws, because of the vagueness of legal responsibilities of the public agencies and practitioners, and stressing the need for law reform.[320]

[317.] Article 26 (research and studies) of the Elder Abuse Prevention Act stipulates that 'the State is to perform an analysis of elder abuse cases and conduct research and studies on methods for properly handling elder abuse, methods for properly taking care of elderly persons, and any other matters that contribute to the prevention of elder abuse, the protection of elderly persons who have been abused, and to the provision of support for caregivers.' Based on this Article, the annual survey of the responses to the abuse of older people by prefecture/municipality nationwide is published.

[318.] The adult guardianship system is often used by the municipality mayor to lodge a petition to the family court to appoint the adult guardian. This is mainly for cases where an older mother who is proven to be a victim of her adult child (normally a son), to help the older mother live independently on her pension away from her son. This is called an '80/50 problem' (or a '90/60 problem'), a typical financial abuse case in Japan, named after the situation where a son in his 50s (or 60s) financially depends on his older mother in her 80s (or 90s) who receives a pension. Watanabe (n 106).

[319.] Atsushi Hirata, 'Issues and Challenges in the Elderly Abuse Prevention Act' (2010) 1411 *Monthly Jurist* 116, 121 (in Japanese); Atsushi Hirata, 'How to Protect the Rights of the Elderly' (2021) October 2021 *Monthly Welfare* 33, 38 (in Japanese).

[320.] Refers to the Japan Federation of Bar Associations, *Opinion on Amendment of the Act on the Prevention of Elder Abuse, Support for Caregivers of Elderly Persons and Other Related Matters* (Web Page, September 26, 2010)

It is commonly pointed out that the abuse prevention laws in Japan may limit the definitions of abuse, narrowing the scope of abuse to circumscribed legal aspects. It can be said that this is in part due to some historical background of abuse research in Japan.[321] The Japan Academy for the Prevention of Elder Abuse, a multidisciplinary society that study elder abuse, has found a tendency of few research articles on 'abuse intervention and policies' in that research area while they have many articles on 'the actual situation of elder abuse prevention activities and the experience of nursing care staff for abuse.'[322] In addition, a financial exploitation and self-neglect, which are social issues in developed countries in global scale, are not explicitly defined as abuse in laws. Therefore, the definitions in abuse prevention laws in Japan partly differ from their definitions and scope in other countries/areas as well as the WHO.[323]

In fact, after legislation is passed, there is a tendency for elder abuse to slightly increase or not to so decrease statistically. The number of detected elder abuses by nursing home care workers was 1,123 in 2023 (versus 644 in 2019 and 621 in 2018) and the number of detected elder abuses by caregivers was 17,100 in 2023 (versus 16,928 in 2019 and 17,249 in 2018).[324] It can be said that despite the establishment of abuse prevention laws, Japan's current legal system makes the effective treatment and prevention of elder abuse challenges.[325] There is the need for a more accurate understanding of the actual situation of elder abuse, although the summary report of the detected elder abuse becomes available by

---

(in Japanese) <https://www.nichibenren.or.jp/document/opinion/year/2010/100916_2.html>; Japan Federation of 'Shiho-Shoshi' Lawyer's Associations and Adult Guardian Center Legal Support, *Proposals for Revision of the Act on the Prevention of Elder Abuse, Support for Caregivers of Elderly Persons and Other Related Matters* (Web Page, April 15, 2009) (in Japanese) <https://www.shiho-shoshi.or.jp/association/info_disclosure/opinion/3585/>.

[321] Katsuji Yamamoto states, referring to the historical background of abuse research in Japan, that (i) the definition of elder abuse in the US was not so precise to be adopted in legislation, (ii) it was unable to give a precise definition of elder abuse without enough empirical data, and (iii) a large-scale and detailed research survey and analysis of elder abuse has not been performed without a precise definition of elder abuse. Katsuji Yamamoto, 'Study on the Definition of Elder Person Abuse' (2014) 50(2) *The Japanese Journal of Law and Political Science* 61, 78 (in Japanese).

[322] This research is based on analysis of a total of seventy-two articles published in the journal of the said society in 2008–2017. Naoko Yamashita and Akemi Nakazawa, 'Analysis of Research Trends and Prevention of Elderly Abuse Prevention' (2019) 60 *Bulletin of Wayo Women's University* 153, 161 (in Japanese).

[323] Tadashi Wada et al, 'Detection of Elder Abuse in Japan Not Covered by the Elder Abuse Prevention Law in Comparison with WHO Definitions of Elder Abuse' (2022) 18(1) *Journal of the Japan Academy for the Prevention of Elder Abuse* 72, 86 (in Japanese).

[324] Refers to the Ministry of Health, Labour, and Welfare of Japan, *Elder Abuse Annual Survey in FY2023* (Web Page, December 2024) (in Japanese) <https://www.mhlw.go.jp/stf/newpage_48003.html>.

[325] The article suggests the possible existence of a 'gray zone' in elder abuse, which hints many suspects of abuse but are not certified. With a strict definition of elder abuse, the scale of elder abuse is underestimated, and thus grey zone is so important to understand the reality by a local government's initiative. Kyoko Nakamura, 'A Study about on the Definition of "Elder Abuse" and the Help of Our Country: Suggestion from a British Legal System' (Doctoral dissertation, Kumamoto Gakuen University, 2014) (in Japanese).

law.[326] In 2023, the Ministry of Health, Labour, and Welfare of Japan reported a total of 17,100 detected cases of elder abuse by caregivers including family members. Among these, 65.1 per cent involved physical abuse, 38.3 per cent psychological abuse, 19.4 per cent neglect, and 15.9 per cent economic abuse.[327]

It can be assumed that there are a lot of undetected but hidden or potential elder abuse cases behind the detected ones, which cannot be grasped in annual statistics. One research project recommends an idea to combine the summary report by law and the research project by local agency, including a 'gray zone' detection.[328] In the latter research, the activities for possible elder abuse will be carried out by local agency in a specific area for a certain period at random basis and to make data base in the local government for their response and prevention practices. The methodology of the research must be improved to achieve a more accurate understanding of the actual situation of abuse step-by-step without violating the human rights of the people concerned. Another research recommends an idea that the reporting obligation in law should be limited to practitioners working in a position that allows easy detection of abuse by nursing home care workers while imposing certain legal sanctions for any breach of that duty of practitioners, considering their legal responsibilities.[329] This idea may be from the U.S. elder abuse method of adult protection services with strict application of law and regulations.[330]

Elder abuse has been recognized as a serious problem in the twenty-first century.[331] The mechanism of abuse is complicated, and it can be understood that interdisciplinary studies on abuse is still premature. Conducting an international dialogue and comparative law studies of abuse status surveys among countries/ areas is essential, referring to acknowledgements of experience and wisdom

---

[326.] Article 26 (research and studies) of the Elder Abuse Prevention Act.

[327.] Ministry of Health, Labour, and Welfare of Japan (n 324).

[328.] Refers to the Ministry of Health, Labour, and Welfare of Japan, *Research Project on Factor Analysis of Elder Abuse and Establishment of Continuous Utilization and Feedback Methods of Survey Results* (Dementia Care Research Training Center Sendai, Online, March 2017) (in Japanese) <https://www.mhlw.go.jp/file/06-Seisaku-jouhou-12300000-Roukenkyoku/53_touhokuhukushikai.pdf>.

[329.] Norio Higuchi, 'Elder Abuse and Responsibilities of Professionals' (2018) 8 *Journal of Law and Political Science* 134, 102 (in Japanese).

[330.] Refers to Section 4.4.3 (a), 'Elder Abuse Legislation in Australia and England.'

[331.] A shocking incident occurred at *Tsukui Yamayurien*, a facility for people with intellectual disabilities in Kanagawa, on July 26, 2016, where a former caregiver working at the facility killed nineteen people with disabilities and injured twenty-seven people with disabilities/three facility staff. During the trial, many issues were debated even outside the court, including the quality of support, and SDM. Shoichi Sato, 'Social Exclusion for Persons with Disabilities' (2019) 85 *Sociology of Law* 58, 73 (in Japanese); Kazumi Ishiwata, 'Tsukui Yamayurien Incident and Supported-Decision Making: Community Life of People with Severe Disabilities' (2021) 17 *Journal of the Graduate of Toyo Eiwa University* 1, 12 (in Japanese).

of other countries/areas. In this sense, abuse is a global issue.[332] On the other hand, abuse is a local issue, where the responses to abuse cases and prevention measures by public agencies must be understood and accepted by people in the jurisdiction. In this regard, like the adult guardianship system, law and policy design and its operation should be considered to meet the mentality and lifestyle of people. It can be assumed necessary to discuss how to organize and effectively utilize the social resources of the jurisdiction, including municipality, core agencies, community-based general support centers and so on. Further discussion under the concept of legal advocacy, not as a mono policy of elder abuse, will be conducted in Chapter 5.[333]

(2) Relevant Policy in Community Support

a. Monitoring in the Community-Based Integrated Care System

Practitioners in community—such as welfare volunteers, aged care manager, helpers, and medical social workers—who regularly see older people are usually aware of changes in the elderly.[334] Based on the awareness of local welfare and other relevant officers, a system could be set up for reporting elder abuse to the community-based general support center, the municipality, and the police.[335] Through an immediate response system, issues in the local community could be quickly resolved.[336] This is however a post-treatment system that responds only after the damage due to elder abuse has happened and would not lead to prevention. Therefore, a step-by-step approach by the practitioners to monitor

---

[332.] WHO adopted a policy on *Ageing and Healthcare* at the 2016 General Assembly and is working with member countries and related institutions to deal with elder abuse. World Health Organization (WHO), *Elder Abuse* (Web Page, June 6, 2018) <https://www.who.int/news-room/fact-sheets/detail/elder-abuse>.

[333.] Refers to Section 5.2.1, 'Roles and Legal Status of a Core Agency for Community Support.'

[334.] 'Welfare volunteers' are persons commissioned by the Minister of Health, Labour and Welfare of Japan, who always stand in the position of residents, provide necessary assistance, and strive to promote social welfare in each region.' Welfare volunteers are prescribed in the *Commissioned Welfare Volunteers Act* (Act No. 198 of 1948). Ministry of Health, Labour and Welfare of Japan, *Welfare Volunteers and Child Welfare Volunteers* (Web Page, n/a) (in Japanese) <https://www.mhlw.go.jp/stf/seisakunitsuite/bunya/hukushi_kaigo/seikatsuhogo/minseiiin/index.html>.

[335.] A questionnaire survey in Kyoto finds that approximately 30 per cent of the care manager reports when they convince the existence of elder abuse and approximately 40 per cent of the care manager hesitates to report as they appreciate the feelings of the users and their family members. Mitsu Haruna, 'Present Situations on the Responses of Care Managers to the Case of Elder Abuse: Issues Extracted from a Questionnaire Survey at Care Managers and Community General Support Centers' (2020) 28 *Hanazono University Faculty of Sociology Research Bulletin* 11, 19 (in Japanese); According to a questionnaire survey to all the in-home care support agencies conducted in Kyoto city, approximately 80 per cent care managers handled cases of abuse or suspected abuse, and approximately 70 per cent felt signs of abuse when visiting the user's home. Mitsu Haruna, 'Practice of Abuse Discovery and Report of Care Manager' (2021) 29 *Hanazono University Faculty of Sociology Research Bulletin* 1, 8 (in Japanese).

[336.] This is the common view shared by the administrative officers in charge of elder abuse/the adult guardianship interviewed in August 2016 by the author in Tokyo, Kanagawa, Chiba, and Saitama prefecture offices; In fact, 29.6 per cent reporting of elder abuse at home to municipalities were carried out by aged care managers who regularly visited older people at home or in facilities in 2015. Ministry of Health, Labour and Welfare of Japan (n 328) 33.

community people would be considered most effective, particularly if it targets older people living alone in the community. In fact, some municipalities already carry out steady activities with ordinances approved by the local parliament.[337] Commercial corporations and shops that regularly contact older people in the community, such as a local bank, courier, or merchant, will also watch people and report the event to the support center. This function of commercial corporations and the like in the community is also encouraged by the Expert Commission's deliberation.[338]

There is a community-based general support center, which is a welfare agency mainly established by a municipality and is required to manage the health of older people in the community through a 'team approach' of three kinds of practitioners, namely public health nurses, social workers, and care support specialists.[339] The purpose of a community-based general support center is to comprehensively support the health care, aged care and any welfare of older people by providing such assistances based on the Paragraph 1, Article 115–46 of the Long-Term Care Insurance Act 1997. This center provides general information on the adult guardianship system to people in the community.[340]

b. Subsidies for Expenses Related to the Use of the Adult Guardianship System

After the revision of the Act on Social Welfare for the Elderly in 2012, Article 32-2 (improvement of the system related to guardianship, etc.) stipulates that the municipalities should implement 'training program' and make 'recommendations to the family courts of persons who can perform their duties properly and [provide] other necessary measures,' and prefectures should provide advice and the

---

[337] For example, the city of Kodaira (Tokyo) and the city of Nagareyama (Chiba) in the suburbs of the greater Tokyo adopted ordinances for watching over older people in 2019. Setagaya district (Tokyo) enacted on October 1, 2020, Ordinance for Hope to Live with Dementia in Setagaya District to deal with older people with dementia by medical care, aged care, and community-monitoring, based on deeper understandings of dementia in community; Tokyo Metropolitan Health and Welfare Bureau published a guidebook on *Watching the Elderly*. Arakawa district in Tokyo has been watching over older people as a district project since 2011. Tokyo Metropolitan Health and Welfare Bureau, *Guidebook on Watching the Elderly* (Web Page, January 2018) (in Japanese) <https://www.fukushihoken.metro.tokyo.lg.jp/kourei/koho/mimamoriguidebook.html>.

[338] Refers to the seventh Expert Commission meeting held on July 30, 2021.

[339] A 'community-based general support center' is an agency of the community-based integrated care system. Most centers are operated by corporations or NPOs in a delegation agreement with the municipality. Ministry of Health, Labour and Welfare of Japan, *Establishing 'The Community-Based Integrated Care System* (Web Page, n/a) <https://www.mhlw.go.jp/english/policy/care-welfare/care-welfare-elderly/dl/establish_e.pdf>.

[340] Keiichiro Harada defines community-based integrated care system as 'a care that can be conceptualized as a bundle of elements, such as medical care, long-term care (aged care), prevention, and life support, on the premise that a "residence" that meets the needs of a place of living is secured.' Keiichiro Harada, 'Legal Evaluation of Community-Based Integrated Care System' (Special Feature: Reexamination of Laws and Policies Supporting Social Security: 1st Social Security Law Forum) (2019) 10 *Social Security Law Research* 91–118, 117 (in Japanese); Peipei Song and Wei Tang, 'The Community-Based Integrated Care System in Japan: Health Care and Nursing Care Challenges Posed by Super-Aged Society' (2019) 13(3) *Bioscience Trends* 279, 281.

other assistance' to the municipalities. Under this law, the municipalities have developed activities to inform people of the adult guardianship system by holding seminars and training programs for community guardians while subsidizing the NPO agencies that host them. The number of community guardians appointed was 331 cases (1 per cent of the adult guardians) in December 2024.[341] Some municipalities have set up support agencies, such as 'adult guardianship center,' and most municipalities subsidize the petition expenses lodged of the mayors of municipalities and/or remuneration for the adult guardianship.[342] There are some local parliaments to issue ordinances to clarify their subsidies and support project to the adult guardianship system. Statistics indicate that the number of petitions to the adult guardianship system by municipality mayors is increasing. In December 2024, there were 9,980 petition requests by municipal mayors, accounting for 23.9 per cent of the total number of petition requests—a 3.9 per cent increase compared to the previous year. The highest number of petitions was from municipal mayors, followed by petitions from principals (23.5 per cent) and adult children of principals (19.3 per cent).[343] The number of older people with insufficient mental capacity and living alone without property or close relatives is increasing. Thus, financial assistance should be provided for such economically disadvantaged people using this program, who are assumed to be potential users of the adult guardianship system in personal protection.

[341.] A total of 18,000 have participated in the community guardian training program until April 2021, and a total of 1,577 have been appointed as community guardians by the family courts, 2,199 work for guardianship NPO staff, and 2,820 work for Support Program for Self-Reliance in Daily Life (The research by the Ministry of Health, Labour, and Welfare as of October 1, 2021). There is room to consider how to utilize these trained human resources that are not fully used. The Courts of Japan, *Overview of Adult Guardianship-Related Cases in FY2024* (in Japanese); In order to activate community guardians, institutional supports would be important, such as support of the guardian implementing agency, dissemination and enlightenment of the system, guardianship remuneration, support considering the life stage of the community guardian, and protecting community guardians' privacy. Nobuko Nagano and Atsushi Ozawa, 'The Situation and Problems of the Guardianship Activities of Citizen Guardians: A Qualitative Analysis of Open-Ended Statements in the Questionnaire' (2021) 62(1) *Japanese Journal of Social Welfare* 52, 68.

[342.] These are subsidy systems to support low-income older people who need to use the adult guardianship system. The subsidy is granted by the municipalities based on a regional support project grant to be shared by the national government and the local governments (i.e., prefectures and designated municipalities). A typical service-receiving aid would be a long-term care insurance service for older people who have severe dementia and no relatives to provide support. In such a case, the expenses required for petition for the adult guardianship system (e.g., petition and registration fees, certificate cost) and a part of the remuneration for adult guardians would be subsidized upon approval within the budget. In April 2024, approximately 98 per cent of the municipalities (1,741) offered subsidies to older people and persons with disabilities to cover the petition expenses and remuneration of guardians. Ministry of Health, Labour and Welfare of Japan, *FY2024 Survey Results on the Status of Measures to Promote the Use of the Adult Guardianship System (Summary)* (Web Page, December 2024) (in Japanese) <https://www.mhlw.go.jp/content/001029500.pdf>.

[343.] Courts of Japan (n 341).

c. Support Program for Self-Reliance in Daily Life

Current Status of the Support Program

The previous project, Community Welfare Advocacy, was inaugurated in October 1999 based on Article 2-3 (xii) of the Social Welfare Act.[344] This is a social welfare system that supports people with insufficient metal capacity to use simple welfare services and manage their finance arrangements for daily use. In 2009, the project was renamed Support Program for Self-reliance in Daily Life (hereinafter referred to as 'support program'). The users are usually requested to pay a fee of 1,200 yen (US$8.3) per service from their pockets twice a month on average unless otherwise decided.[345] The number of users of the support program was 56,550 (National Council of Social Welfare) as of March 2023. This is based on the national treasury subsidy project financially shared by the national and local governments (i.e., prefectures and designated cities) at a ratio of 50:50. The purpose of the support program is to support adults with insufficient mental capacity by assisting them in use of welfare services or the like so that they may live independent lives in communities. The support program includes assistance, such as help with welfare services, complaint solution systems, administrative procedures for residence renovation or rental, and monetary deposits and withdrawals. The entities in charge of this support program are 1,596 Councils of Social Welfare under the supervision of forty-seven prefecture-based Councils of Social Welfare over Japan and 4,016 specialists (full-time or part-time) and 15,388 support staff (part-time) work for this support program.[346] This support program selects applicants that meet two conditions: (i) persons with insufficient mental capacity; (ii) persons qualified to understand the contract related to the assistance service program. Consequently, the users are limited to persons with mild cognitive impairment (MCI) who can understand the contract. The qualifications are verified by each Council of Social Welfare, to which the fund is granted by the local government.

[344.] Article 2-3 (xii) of the Social Welfare Act stipulates 'the appropriate use of welfare services, free of charge or at low cost.'

[345.] Refers to the National Council of Social Welfare of Japan, *Action Report No. 246 (15 August 2022): Survey Results on the FY 2022 Support Program for Self-Reliance in Daily Life* (Web Page, March 2023) (in Japanese) <https://www.shakyo.or.jp/ActionReport/2023/v248-0815.pdf>.

[346.] Ibid. The Social Welfare Councils are regulated by Article 109 of the Social Welfare Act to provide welfare service over Japan. Most of expenditures incurred in this program is mainly for human resources who provide assistances.

Issues of the Support Program

Regarding the administrative process of making the support program, the empirical analysis on the community welfare advocacy project during the inauguration period, which focuses on the executive documents to clarify the decision-making process in the Ministry, finds conflicting logics between 'the needs of people with insufficient mental capacity' and 'the feasibility to expand the support program nationwide.'[347] Another policy analysis, which focuses on the provisions of laws and regulations of the program, finds 'no substantial improvements of relevant program has been made although the necessity of improvement was frequently recalled' by users and its stakeholders.[348] In the welfare administration, it is hard to say that this support program emphasizes on advocacy of vulnerable adults with insufficient mental capacity as a policy.[349]

Currently, there are positive and negative opinions on the support program. The positive one is mainly expressed by welfare practitioners, who stress that this support program provides a welfare service to meet the needs of adults with insufficient mental capacity, and the support program is easy to access with little personal and financial resistance to the principal or its family. Thus, more grants should be offered to promote the support program on a larger scale of application.[350] The negative view is advocated by a civil law scholar, who thinks that persons with mildly insufficient mental capacity should use the 'assistance' or 'curatorship' type of the adult guardianship system rather than the welfare measures.[351] The latter opinion theoretically makes sense, but in fact, 59.0 per cent of the users who newly joined this support program in July 2020 were receiving public financial assistance—i.e., more than half of new users had no choice but to use this program due to their disadvantaged financial eligibility. Due to their disadvantaged financial eligibility, some users who have developed dementia

---

[347] Hiroya Noda, 'Logics and Issues Related to the Design of Community Welfare Advocacy Projects During the Project Formation Period' (2022) 70 *Bulletin of the Faculty of Education and Welfare, Aichi Prefectural University* 35–48, 47 (in Japanese).

[348] Hiroya Noda, 'Development and Characteristics of Support Program for Using Welfare Services in Services for Independence in Daily Living Program' (2022) 13 *Bulletin of the Graduate School of Human Development* 47–59, 58 (in Japanese).

[349] Ibid.

[350] This comment was stated at the Expert Commission and has been included in the Interim Verification Report. Ministry of Health, Labour, and Welfare of Japan, *Interim Verification Report on Basic Plan for Promoting Adult Guardianship System* (Web Page, March 17, 2020) 16 (in Japanese) <https://www.mhlw.go.jp/stf/shingi2/0000212875.html>.

[351] This opinion, which is expressed by a civil law scholar at the Commission's session (October 9, 2019), points out that the border of the scope is vague between the support program and the adult guardianship system. This aspect may happen due to the conflicting logics in the program as Hiroya Noda remarks. Afterward, the civil law scholar has changed mind to accept the support program to see it with the adult guardianship in a reasonable balance (April 21, 2021).

cannot apply for a petition to the adult guardianship system and stay at the support program. The border of both programs is a systemic issue.

Since the growth of the number of the support program users has slowed down for few years, it is understood that this support program has almost reached the limit of institutional capacity, and the appropriate utilization of social resources has become an issue.[352] However, if they try to increase the institutional capacity rapidly, they are exposed to the risk of misconducts of the supporters. In fact, the monitoring system at prefecture-based Councils of Social Welfare is also said to be full of capacity, and the issue is to expand the capacity of human resources for monitoring. The support program resources must be properly distributed to those in need of support, on the one hand, and it must be monitored and supervised so that misconducts of the supporter due to deterioration of the support program do not occur, on the other hand. It is understood that the projection of the support program service demands nationwide has not been researched yet, and this support program is practically implemented as much as the grants are available. Most of the expenditures in this program is mainly for human resources who provide assistances.

It can be concluded that this support program needs a drastic review in the respects of the border between this support program and the adult guardianship system, and the scale of subsidies and human resources needed for the support program, including prefecture-based Councils of Social Welfare monitoring capacity.[353]

1.3 Summary: Legal Advocacy to Meet People's Multiple Needs

A systematic review is conducted on the adult guardianship system and relevant laws and policies, theories of civil law relating to adult guardianship, theories of social security law concerning legal advocacy, and the key functions necessary to support and protect vulnerable adults. The author's theoretical stance within the domains of civil law and social security law is made explicit. Through this analytical structure, the scope of the legal and policy systems—as well as the primary functions involved in supporting and protecting adults with diminished

---

[352.] Atsushi Hirata, 'Current Status and Issues of Support Program for Self-Reliance in Daily Life Projects from the Perspective of Advocacy' (2021) 2021 *Advocacy and Abuse Prevention* 28, 31 (in Japanese).

[353.] Regarding the border between the support program for self-reliance in daily life and adult guardianship system, the Akashi City, Hyogo prefecture utilizes their own assessment sheet with citizens in the department to deal with both program and system. Yoshinori Kayama, 'About the Usefulness of the Assessment Sheet Devised by Akashi City: To Distinguish between the Adult Guardianship System and the Support Program for Self-Reliance in Daily Life' (2022) 805 *Hougaku Seminar* 61, 67 (in Japanese).

mental capacity—are clarified. Based on this comprehensive review, the research framework of this study is presented below.

First, this study focuses on legal acts that involve the principal during their lifetime; it applies an interdisciplinary approach grounded in both civil law and social security law. Legal affairs that arise after the death of the principal fall outside the scope of this research. The study aims to develop legislative theory for the support and protection of vulnerable adults in Japan, informed by comparative legal analysis, with particular emphasis on recent legal reforms in Australia. Second, the analysis encompasses a range of legal and policy systems, including the adult guardianship system, SDM, elder abuse prevention law, and related social policies—namely the 'Support Program for Self-Reliance in Daily Life' and the 'Community-Based Integrated Care System.' Third, the study proceeds on the assumption that the current civil law and associated statutes governing adult guardianship in Japan will remain unchanged in the near term. The focus is placed on the development of SDM as an independent legal mechanism that can coexist with the existing guardianship framework. The envisioned legal structure for SDM is grounded in the existing guidelines issued by Japan's Ministry of Health, Labour, and Welfare. Fourth, the study does not address the impact of the COVID-19 pandemic on the adult guardianship system, as this lies outside its scope.

In this context, the adult guardianship system, SDM, elder abuse prevention law, and the aforementioned policies are reviewed. At present, legal protection for adults with limited decision-making capacity in Japan is primarily provided through statutory guardianship as defined in the Civil Code. However, in practice, many individuals rely on informal arrangements. SDM has been introduced in certain social welfare laws, and relevant guidelines have been published for stakeholders such as care home administrators, social workers specializing in dementia care, and legal guardians. Although law and policies for prevention of elder abuse have been adopted, there is currently no clear coordination or integration among the various related laws. Consequently, it remains difficult for individuals—particularly potential users and their families—to grasp the full structure of legal advocacy systems. From a user perspective, the current framework does not offer a sufficient range of options for community-based legal and social support. An additional issue concerns how the legal and policy systems can be adapted to meet the needs of adults with limited capacity who lack familial, or social support, have no financial resources, or are at risk of abuse by relatives or acquaintances. As this study highlights, Japan faces significant challenges in designing and implementing an effective legal and policy framework for the support and protection of vulnerable adults.

CHAPTER 2

Vulnerability Approach and Autonomy

This chapter explores the conceptual and theoretical foundations necessary for developing adult support and protection legislation. It examines the intersection of vulnerability and autonomy, incorporating both the vulnerability approach, which emphasizes the need for legal and policy protections for those at risk of harm, and the capability approach, which highlights the importance of respecting individual autonomy and diverse abilities. The chapter also introduces the concept of relational autonomy and considers international trends—including the influence of the Convention on the Rights of Persons with Disabilities (CRPD)—that support the integration of guardianship, supported decision-making (SDM), and elder abuse prevention into a unified and rights-based legal framework.

2.1 Vulnerable Adults

This section examines how aging issues are being addressed globally and in Japan, and identifies the value of researching issues related to older adults through the lens of the vulnerability approach.

2.1.1 The Aging of Population

(1) Global Trend

An aging society refers to one in which the demographic ratio of older people aged 60 or 65 and over is considerably higher compared to past available records.[1] An explicit definition of the age range considered to be older people has not been established. According to the United Nations (UN), the elderly comprise the population aged 60 and over, while in developed countries, including Japan, the World Health Organization (hereinafter referred to as 'WHO') consider the

---

[1] In Japan, the population is categorized as an 'ageing society' when the aging ratio is between 7 and 14 per cent, an 'aged society' when the aging ratio is between 14 and 21 per cent, and a 'super-aged society' when the aging ratio is over 21 per cent. Aging ratio refers to per centage of population aged 65 and over out of the national population.

elderly to fall within the range of age 65 and over. Nevertheless, the global trend of aging is apparent.[2] By area, Asia and Europe are aging the most rapidly, while Africa is experiencing far less aging. The UN understands the global trend of aging and how aging will affect countries/areas in the future. The UN predicts that 'in the coming decades many countries are likely to face fiscal and political pressures in relation to public systems for health care, pensions, and social protection for a growing older population.'[3] Each country/area is responsible for coping with the challenges of aging while the UN has been debating a possible convention on the rights of older persons.[4]

A serious problem faced worldwide is the rapid increase of older people with dementia in proportion to the aging population.[5] Dementia is referred to as 'a syndrome in which there is deterioration in memory, thinking, behavior, and the ability to perform everyday activities.'[6] According to the WHO, over 50 million people have dementia worldwide, and the number of these people will almost triple by 2050.[7] Dementia is one of the major causes of disability and dependency among older people. It has a physical, psychological, social, and economic impact, not only on people with dementia but also on their caregivers, relatives, and society at large.[8] Importance must be given to not only the medical model but also the social model of dementia. Namely, it should break down the prejudice against dementia and foster tolerance to accept people with dementia in the community. For this reason, a movement of people with dementia themselves to express their own opinions about facilities and services has just begun.[9]

---

[2] There were 703 million persons aged 65 years or over in the world in 2019 and the number of older persons is projected to 1.5 billion in 2050. Globally, the share of the population aged 65 years or over will increase from 9 per cent in 2019 to 16 per cent by 2050. By 2050, one in six people in the world will be aged 65 years or over and one in four persons living in Europe and Northern America will be aged 65 or over. UN, *World Population Ageing 2019: Highlights* (Online, 2019) <https://www.un.org/en/development/desa/population/publications/pdf/ageing/WorldPopulationAgeing2019-Highlights.pdf>.

[3] Refers to the UN, *Ageing* (Web Page, 2019) <https://www.un.org/en/global-issues/ageing>.

[4] Israel Doron and Itai Apter, 'The Debate Around the Need for an International Convention on the Rights of Older Persons' (2010) 50(5) *Gerontologist* 586, 593.

[5] Refers to the Alzheimer's Disease International, *World Alzheimer Report 2021* (Web Page, September 21, 2021) <https://www.alzint.org/resource/world-alzheimer-report-2021/>.

[6] Refers to the WHO, *Dementia* (Web Page, January 27, 2021) <https://www.who.int/news-room/facts-in-pictures/detail/dementia>.

[7] Ibid.

[8] Care ethics of social workers is one of the key factors in caring for older people with dementia, particularly in self-neglect cases. Angelika Thelin, 'Care Ethics for Supported Decision-Making. A Narrative Policy Analysis Regarding Social Work in Cases of Dementia and Self-Neglect' (2021) 15(2) *Ethics and Social Welfare* 167, 184.

[9] Some not-for-profit organizations (NPOs) or associations in Japan support older people with dementia and those who support people with dementia. Yukio Sakurai, 'Social Design Concepts on Dementia and Japan's Adult Guardianship System' (2017) 8 *Social Design Review* 142–7, 143–4.

(2) Japan Trend

Japan is becoming the most aged society in the world. In fact, the proportion of Japan's population aged 65 and over was 29.1 per cent in September 2021.[10] The breakdown of 29.1 per cent by gender was 26.0 per cent for male and 32.0 per cent for female. It is expected to rise to 38.4 per cent by 2065.[11] Thus, Japan has become a super-aged society,[12] and the population is even aging further. The details are as follows: The number of people with dementia and mild cognitive impairment (hereinafter referred to as 'MCI') is increasing in proportion to the aging population. Out of 36.40 million older people in September 2021, 6.00 million had dementia and 4.00 million had MCI. By 2025, the number of older people is expected to rise to 36.57 million, of which 7.30 million are forecast to have dementia and another 5.89 million are expected to be afflicted with MCI.[13] In September 2021, the number of older people aged 75 and over was 18.80 million (15.0 per cent), and it is expected to rise to 21.80 million in 2025 (17.8 per cent).[14] By 2025, the baby boom generation will surpass 75 years of age, and Japan will face an extraordinarily super-aged society just four years later. At that time, Japan is predicted to have approximately 12.6 million people with insufficient mental capacity.[15] That would account for one-third of Japan's older population, who would constitute more or less 10 per cent of the total population. This serious issue caused by the demographic change is called 'the 2025 problem' in Japan.[16]

Such an extraordinarily aged environment would significantly alter the Japanese society. Mental capacity is required for people to be accorded the right to legally engage in day-to-day activities. As the number of older people with dementia increases, various incidents related to dementia are expected to increase. Such

---

[10] Refers to the Ministry of Internal Affairs and Communications of Japan, *News Release* (Web Page, September 19, 2021) (in Japanese) <https://www.stat.go.jp/data/topics/topi1210.html>.

[11] Refers to the Cabinet Office of Japan, *Annual Report on the Ageing Society 2021 [Summary]* (Web Page, 2022) 3 <https://www8.cao.go.jp/kourei/english/annualreport/2021/pdf/2021.pdf>.

[12] Italy (23.6 per cent aging ratio), Portugal (23.1 per cent), and Finland (23.0 per cent) follow Japan as the most aged countries in 2021. Ministry of Internal Affairs and Communications of Japan (n 10).

[13] Refers to the Cabinet Office of Japan, *Estimating the Number of the Elderly with Dementia (Figure 1–2–11), Annual Report on the Ageing Society FY 2018* (Web Page, 2019) (in Japanese) <https://www8.cao.go.jp/kourei/whitepaper/w-2017/html/gaiyou/s1_2_3.html>.

[14] Refers to the Ministry of Internal Affairs and Communications of Japan (n 10).

[15] Japan's population is projected to have a total of 12.6 million people with insufficient mental capacity in 2025, comprising 7.3 million older people with dementia and 5.3 million people with intellectual/mental impairments and higher brain dysfunction.

[16] Takao Komine, 'Thinking About the 2025 Problem—Part 1: Population Change and the 2025 Problem' (Online, November 7, 2016) (Speech delivered at the International Institute for Population Sciences held in Tokyo, 2015) <https://npi.or.jp/en/research/2016/11/07130823.html>.

incidents include aimless wandering by older people, sudden disappearance of older people,[17] increased cases of traffic accidents involving older people,[18] and elder abuse. Elder abuse is referred to as 'a single, or repeated act, or lack of appropriate action, occurring within any relationship, where there is an expectation of trust that causes harm or distress to an older person.'[19] It can be of various forms: physical, psychological/emotional, sexual, and financial—or a form that simply reflects intentional or unintentional neglect.[20]

An extraordinarily aged environment in Japan would have indirect effects on the society in a broader sense. For example, it would lead to changes in people's lifestyle, such as employment, consumption, and community in a 100-year life.[21] It would increase financial burdens on the social welfare systems, including health care, aged care,[22] and public pensions. Thus, the social systems, including the law frameworks, will be reconsidered to adjust to the reality.[23] While we have an assumption in the Civil Code that humans have capacity and autonomy, it is also assumed that humans behave as rationally as possible.[24] In this sense, humans without full capacity and autonomy are regarded as an exception, i.e., as those who fall short of mental capacity must be placed under the supervision of others, such as guardians, by law (Articles 7, 11, and 15 of the Civil Code). This legal system faces a challenge in an aged society where the number of older people with dementia is sharply increasing. Such people will constitute approximately 10 per cent of the total population in 2025 as mentioned before. They should no longer be regarded as a minority and an exception in the Civil Code but should be included as citizens. It can, therefore, be argued that

---

[17] Regarding sudden disappearance of older people, 19.2 per cent (i.e., 16,927 out of 87,962) of all missing persons in Japan who were reported to the National Police Agency in 2018 presumably had dementia. National Police Agency, *The Situation of the Missing Citizens in 2018* (Web Page, June 2019) 3 (in Japanese) <https://www.npa.go.jp/safetylife/seianki/fumei/H29yukuehumeisha.pdf>.

[18] Refers to the Cabinet Office of Japan, 'FY2017 Situation of Traffic Accidents and Current Situation of Measures for Traffic Safety: Promotion of Traffic Safety for the Elderly' in *White Paper on Traffic Safety in Japan 2018* (Web Page, 2019) <https://www8.cao.go.jp/koutu/taisaku/h30kou_haku/english/pdf/1-t1.pdf>.

[19] Refers to the WHO, *The Toronto Declaration on the Global Prevention of Elder Abuse* (Web Page, November 17, 2002) <https://eapon.ca/wp-content/uploads/2021/09/toronto_declaration_en.pdf>.

[20] Ibid.

[21] The 100-year life planning is advocated by this book: Lynda Gratton and Andrew Scot, *The 100-Year Life: Living and Working in an Age of Longevity* (Bloomsbury Business; Reprint ed., 2017).

[22] In this study, the term 'aged care' is used, although alternative terms are also available, such as 'elderly care' and 'long-term care,' which takes after the name of the law: *Long-Term Care Insurance Act* (Act No. 123 of December 17, 1997).

[23] The Great East Japan Earthquake in March 2011 highlighted the issues of a super-aging society in natural disasters, particularly the need for a community-based support system. Naoko Muramatsu and Hiroko Akiyama, 'Japan: Super-Aging Society Preparing for the Future' (2011) 51(4) *The Gerontologist* 425, 432.

[24] Martha Albertson Fineman criticizes that the prototype of the legal subject ignores vulnerability and dependency. Martha Albertson Fineman, 'Vulnerability and Inevitable Inequality' (2017) 4 *Oslo Law Review* 133–49, 148–9.

this is the time that the legal status of adults with insufficient mental capacity and the relevant law system were reconsidered.[25] In other words, the legal status of adults with insufficient mental capacity should be explored from a broader perspective than the Civil Code of Japan (hereinafter referred to as 'Civil Code') framework and relevant laws.

2.1.2 Older People and Vulnerable Adults

(1) Age of Older People

The elderly refers to people aged 65 and over in Japan, but in some countries/ areas or international agencies, the term refers to people aged 60 and over as mentioned before. There is no internationally standardized definition of the elderly.[26] In fact, laws indicating the age of the elderly in Japan are not unified. For example, age 55 is stipulated in the Ordinance for Enforcement of the Act on Stabilization of Employment of Elderly Persons (Article 1, Ordinance of Ministry of Labour of Japan No. 24 of 1971), age 60 in the Act on Securement of Stable Supply of Elderly Persons' Housing (Article 52, Act No. 26 of 2001), age 65 in the Act on Assurance of Medical care for Elderly People (Article 32, Act No. 80 of 1982), and age 70 in the Road Traffic Act (Article 5(4) and 74, Act No. 105 of 1960).

Under such circumstances, a joint working group of the Japan Gerontologi-cal Society/the Japan Geriatrics Society decided in 2017 to categorize people aged 65 to 74 as 'the associate elderly'; people aged 75 to 89 as 'the elderly'; and people aged 90 and over as 'the super elderly.'[27] The same working group expressed the opinion that older people should be people aged 75 and over. In contrast, the Age Discrimination Act of 1975 indicates in the US that it prohibits discrimination based on age in programs and activities receiving federal financial assistance.[28] This federal law has had a significant impact on the elimination of

---

[25] For example, Hiroshi Kobayashi, a welfare practitioner, proposes a conceptual model to consider a vulnerable adult as a human standard rather than a healthy adult, which, he assumes, better suits the society. The transfor-mation of the human model is said to be a shift of perception from a 'strong individual' to a 'weak individual' based model. Hiroshi Kobayashi, 'Creating a Place for Supported Decision-Making through the Transformation of Human Image' 64 *Adult Guardianship Practices* (2016) 21, 28 (in Japanese).

[26] This is the article to discuss what the legal age is by chronological, biological, and subjective age: Alexander A. Boni-Saenz, 'Legal Age' (2022) 63(2/3) *Boston College Law Review* 521, 569. <https://lawdigitalcommons. bc.edu/bclr/>.

[27] A Joint Working Group of the Japan Gerontological Society and the Japan Geriatrics Society, *Recommendations from the Japan Gerontological Society/the Japan Geriatrics Society Definition Study Working Group (Overview) on the Definition and Classification of the Elderly* (Online, January 5, 2017) (in Japanese) <https://www.jpn-geriat-soc.or.jp/proposal/pdf/definition_01.pdf>.

[28] Refers to the U.S. Department of Labor, *Age Discrimination* (Web Page, n/a) <https://www.dol.gov/general/ topic/discrimination/agedisc>.

age discrimination. The elimination of age discrimination is gradually occurring in Japan. It can, therefore, be understood that the definition of the elderly is set as a statistical or analytical convenience.

The older people's health status and property possessions vary widely among individuals, and it is difficult to place older people aged 65 and over in one group. The elderly used to refer to those who had reached retirement, but now this retirement term can last 25 to 35 years in a 100-year life. For this reason, Lawrence A. Frolik points out that it is necessary to divide older people into three age groups, namely age 65 to 74, age 75 to 84, and age 85 and over.[29] This is because the lives of older people in each group vary, and the required legal actions also differ. This observation generally coincides with the working group's opinion.

(2) Characteristics of Older People

Some older people may be victims as well as perpetrators in crimes. Japan's National Police Agency reported 20,987 cases of 'special fraud'[30] in 2024, such as remittance fraud and non-remittance fraud, which amounted to a loss of 72,150 million yen (US$501 million) by victims. Among these cases, 55.6 per cent of the victims of special fraud were older people, and the average damage per case was 3.44 million yen (US$24,000). These totals comprise only fraud reported to the police and do not represent the total amount of financial fraud damage that occurred. On the other hand, the ratio of criminal cases in which older people are perpetrators or victims has been flat or slightly increasing,[31] although the number of crimes in Japan has been decreasing.

Some differences are seen in older people's behaviors by country for unknown reasons.[32] Ninety per cent of these crimes in which older people are perpetrators include shoplifting, stealing food and drinks, and so on. The motive for the crime

---

[29.] Lawrence A. Frolik, 'The Developing Field of Elder Law Redux: Ten Years After' (2002) 10 *The Elder Law Journal* 1, 14.

[30.] The term 'special fraud' is used by the National Police Agency of Japan; it is classified into remittance fraud—including the 'hey it's me' fraud, billing fraud, advance-fee loan fraud, and refund fraud—and non-remittance fraud—including misuse of electronic money. The National Police Agency of Japan, *About Recognition of Special Fraud and Arrest Status FY 2024* (Web Page, 2025) (in Japanese) <https://www.npa.go.jp/news/release/2024/20240226001.html#:~:text=%E5%A0%B1%E9%81%93%E7%99%BA%E8%A1%A8%E8%B3%87%E6%96%99%E3%81%AE%E6%A6%82%E8%A6%81,4%EF%BC%85%EF%BC%89%E3%81%A8E3%81%AA%E3%81%A3%E3%81%9F%E3%80%82>.

[31.] Refers to the National Police Agency of Japan, 'Crimes by the Elderly' in *The National Police Agency's Crime Situation in 2018* (Web Page, August 2019) (in Japanese) <https://www.npa.go.jp/toukei/seianki/H30/h30keihou-hantoukeisiryou.pdf>.

[32.] Japanese researchers pointed out that the increase in crime by older people is a unique situation in Japan and this phenomenon is not seen in any other country. Tatsuya Ota, 'Measures and Prevention of Elderly Crime: Focusing on the Characteristics of Elderly Criminals and Police Responses' (Keynote Speech delivered at Forum on Actual Conditions and Countermeasures for Elderly Crimes, Tokyo, December 2, 2013) (in Japanese); Mayu Kawakami,

is assumed to stem from economic hardship and greed. Among the perpetrators are older people who repeat these crimes. In addition, some older people engage in repeated nuisance behaviors, such as stalking young women or excessively raising consumer complaints.[33] It can be inferred that not only economic distress and greed elicit these behaviors but also psychological factors unique to older people. Psychological factors of older people have not been well elucidated academically.[34] They may comprise social factors, such as community withdrawal, depersonalization, and loneliness; neurological factors, such as the tendency to run away due to stress; and psychiatric factors, such as failure of brain inhibitory functions.[35] Multiple factors can be assumed to be interrelated and influential.[36]

In recent years, traffic accidents caused by older drivers have become problematic in Japan. Mental and physical factors, including dementia and diminished physical capacity, are assumed to be causes of accidents involving older driving cars. Some observations indicate that the number of older falling victim to consumer and financial damage is not decreasing.[37] The lifespan of people is stretching to the age of 100, and the expansion of older people's period of life is creating new social issues, including financial fraud and financial exploitation.[38]

The definition and scope of financial exploitation are not so clear enough because there are multiple definitions as well as multiple dimensions of financial exploitation in the international context.[39] In addition, the opinions of

---

'Characteristics of Elderly Offenders in Japan: In Comparison with Study on Criminality of Elderly Offenders in the United States' (2018) 47 *Graduate School Annual Report* 131, 149 (in Japanese).

[33] Statistics show that stalkers aged 60 and over account for about 12.3 per cent of annual perpetrators. The National Police Agency of Japan, *Responding to Stalker Cases and Spousal Violence Cases in 2024* (Web Page, June 5, 2025) (in Japanese) <https://www.npa.go.jp/bureau/safetylife/stalker/R6_STDVRP_CA_kouhoushiryou.pdf>.

[34] Regarding personality changes in older people, many aspects have not been clarified yet, and it can be said that it is a theme that needs further examination in the future. Hiroaki Enomoto, 'Psychology of the Elderly' (2006) 70 *Japanese Journal of Research on Household Economics* 28–37, 29 (in Japanese).

[35] Lut Tamam, Mehtap Bican and Necla Keskin, 'Impulse Control Disorders in Elderly Patients' (2014) 55(4) *Comprehensive Psychiatry* 1022, 1028 <https://www.ncbi.nlm.nih.gov/pubmed/24405774>.

[36] The behavioral patterns of older people with dementia need to be clarified by brain science and psychology. From the interviews by the author of the greater Tokyo prefectural offices, such as Tokyo, Kanagawa, Chiba, and Saitama, in August 2015.

[37] Hikaru Oba et al, 'The Economic Burden of Dementia: Evidence from a Survey of Households of People with Dementia and Their Caregivers' (2021) 18 *International Journal of Environmental Research and Public Health* 2717, 2727.

[38] Akira Murata suggests that some measures should be introduced to protect the interests of the elderly, such as a financial literacy test for the elderly when concluding the contract and a voice/video recording to conclude the contract. Akira Murata, 'Thinking about Mental Capacity: Attention to be Paid to Defining Mental Capacity' (2016) 66(3) *Meijyo Law Review* 183, 227 (in Japanese); Jingjin Shao et al, 'Why are Older Adults Victims of Fraud? Current Knowledge and Prospects Regarding Older Adults' Vulnerability to Fraud' (2019) 31(3) *Journal of Elder Abuse and Neglect* 225, 243.

[39] Stephen Deane, *Elder Financial Exploitation: Why It is A Concern, What Regulators are Doing about It, and Looking Ahead* (U.S. Securities and Exchange Commission/Office of the Investor Advocate, Online, 2018) 1 and 7–12 <https://www.sec.gov/files/elder-financial-exploitation.pdf>; Yukio Sakurai, 'Challenges of Property

experts are still divided on the definitive scope of financial exploitation.[40] This is mainly due to lack of statistics to grasp the details of financial exploitation. It is, however, well known that cognitive decline is a key factor that makes the elderly more susceptible to financial exploitation.[41] A neurological research shows that patients with mild cognitive impairment perform worse than healthy controls in financial decision-making and in several domains of financial ability. Conversely, financial decision-making is relatively preserved in the sample of patients with Parkinson's disease and stroke.[42] Commercial banks and banking industry groups are developing various ideas to deal with older customers. Financial abuse, which is financial exploitation in a narrow sense, covers the exploitation of a principal's property by family members or close friends.[43] The limited scope of the law system makes it difficult for an impartial third party to grasp the facts in relation to protection of privacy and personal information of the principal.[44]

The characteristics of older people have traditionally included diminished mental and physical capacity due to aging; thus, 'protection' for vulnerable older people who may be easily damaged has become a public policy. The 'autonomy' that respects self-determination of older people as an independent personality must be emphasized by the Constitution. It can be assumed that adding 'self-discipline' may be beneficial to control risk for misconduct, crimes, and nuisances by older people living as members of the community. The characteristics of older people

---

Management for Older Adults in Japan: Focusing on Financial Exploitation and Informal Arrangement' (2022) 12(2) *The Journal of Aging and Social Change* 1, 18 <https://doi.org/10.18848/2576-5310/CGP/v12i02/1-18>.

[40.] There is a view that financial exploitation 'may occur in different psychological contexts (no awareness, consent, implied consent) and may co-occur with other types of financial exploitation.' Stacey Wood and Peter A. Lichtenberg, 'Financial Capacity and Financial Exploitation of Older Adults: Research Findings, Policy Recommendations and Clinical Implications' (2017) 40(1) *Clinical Gerontologist* 3–13, 3.

[41.] Deane (n 39) 2 and 13–15; It is explained that 'we find that decreasing cognition is associated with higher scam susceptibility scores and is predictive of fraud victimization.' Keith Jacks Gamble et al, 'The Causes and Consequences of Financial Fraud Among Older Americans' (Boston College Center for Retirement Research, Online, 2014) <http://crr.bc.edu/wp-content/uploads/2014/11/wp_2014-13.pdf>; it is explained that 'age-related changes in decision-making capacity can directly influence financial competence and financial exploitation risk in older adulthood.' R. Nathan Spreng et al, 'Aging and Financial Exploitation Risk' in Ronan M. Factora (ed), *Aging and Money* (Springer, 2021) 55–73.

[42.] Financial ability is defined as 'the capacity to manage money and financial assets in ways that meet a person's needs, and that are consistent with their values and self-interest.' Laura Danesin et al, 'Financial Decision-Making in Neurological Patients' (2022) 12 *Brain Science* 529 <https://doi.org/10.3390/brainsci12050529>.

[43.] 'The older parent–adult child dynamic is multifaceted and complex, as old resentments and sensitivities about intra-familial fairness mix with new obligations and concerns about parental vulnerability to exploitation and harm (of which adult children may also be a source).' Margaret Isabel Hall, 'Law and Dementia: Family Context and the Experience of Dementia in Old Age' in Beverley Clough and Jonathan Herring (eds), *Disability, Care and Family Law* (Routledge, 2021) 203–29.

[44.] Louise Kyle (from the Australian NGO Senior Rights Victoria) points out that '[t]here is no one pathway to reform that will reduce the risk and prevalence of financial abuse in assets for care situations.' Louise Kyle, 'Out of the Shadows: A Discussion on Law Reform for the Prevention of Financial Abuse of Older People' (2013) 7 *Elder Law Review* 1–32, 25.

however, are assumed to vary depending on various factors, such as personality, age, gender, and economy.[45] Diminishing capacity occurs after a certain age or with dementia. In other words, it can be understood that the three values of 'autonomy,' 'protection,' and 'self-discipline' should remain prevalent among older people. Balance should be maintained among the three values, though they compete against one another sometimes in accordance with changes with age and mental/physical capacity.

(3) Chief Focus on Older People with Dementia

In addition to older people, there are other types of vulnerable people in society, such as those with intellectual and mental disabilities, physical disabilities, and higher brain dysfunction, as the law of Japan defines persons with disabilities.[46] Each group has its inherent characteristics in their diagnosis and requires support to meet a broad range of needs. Thus, it is considered inappropriate to view vulnerable people as one category. Moreover, there is an emerging concept of 'persons aging with disability,' which represents a new field of study.[47] Although it is important to acknowledge this concept, it complicates the research. Considering these factors, vulnerable adults in this study do not belong to a specific group, but the chief focus is on 'elderly people living with dementia,' considering their growing population and its social impacts.[48]

According to some Japanese experts of social welfare studies, an adult who is suspected to have dementia tends to refuse seeing doctors, and when the adult is most likely to have dementia, relatives tend to doubt the diagnosis.[49] Thus, the practitioner in charge struggles with convincing them to see doctors. The reason for this, according to experts, is that the principal and their relatives have a strong desire for the principal to stay healthy and tend to refuse the

---

[45.] Fusako Seki (ed), 'Human Characteristics of the Elderly' in *Theory and Practice of Elder Law* (Chuokeizai-Sha Holdings, Inc., 2025) 50, 83 (in Japanese); Fusako Seki, 'Overview of the Elder Law' (2019) 35 Social Security Law 5, 19 (in Japanese); Fusako Seki and Norio Higuchi, *Elder Law: Legal Basics for a Super-Aged Society* (Tokyo University Press, 2019) (in Japanese).

[46.] Article 2 of the Basic Act for Persons with Disabilities (Act No. 84 of 1970) defines (i) Person with disabilities and (ii) Social barriers to meet social model of disabilities. Japan Law Translation, *Basic Act for Persons with Disabilities*.

[47.] The term 'persons ageing with disability' refers to individuals who experience the onset of disability in early life or mid-life and who continue to experience disability over the life course as ages. This definition contrasts with those who "age into disability," whose impairments emerge later in life, by emphasizing lifelong disability that precedes older age. Michelle Putnam et al, 'Understanding Ageing with Disability' in Michelle Putnam and Christine Bigby (eds), *Handbook on Ageing with Disabilities* (Routledge, 2021) 22.

[48.] Iracema Leroi et al, 'Dementia in "Super-aged" Japan: Challenges and Solutions' (2018) 8(4) *Neurodegenerative Disease Management* <https://doi.org/10.2217/nmt-2018-0007>.

[49.] These are comments expressed by Shinich Okada at the panel session in the 65th Autumn Conference of the Japan Society for the Study of Social Welfare held at Tokyo Metropolitan University on October 21, 2017.

fact.[50] People often resist acknowledging the diagnosis of dementia and may avoid undergoing dementia tests.[51] In other words, people generally tend to ignore help that could be beneficial—to the extent that although it may be reasonable to see things from the viewpoint of experts, there is a tendency among people to refuse an unwelcome fact, even if there are legal justifications. Considering the complexity of older people with dementia and its stakeholders, how shall we see the legal status of adults with insufficient mental capacity?

2.2 Vulnerability and Safeguarding

2.2.1 Introduction

The purpose of this section is to clarify the theoretical foundation for adult support and protection, with a focus on the vulnerability approach and related considerations.[52] A conceptual discussion will be presented on an alternative legal framework based on the vulnerability approach. In common law jurisdictions, this perspective supports the idea of safeguarding law, where vulnerable adults or adults at risk of harm must be protected by law and public policy from abuse. Within this context, the adult guardianship system, SDM, and elder abuse prevention measures can be understood as components of an integrated legislative framework, referred to in this study as 'adult support and protection legislation.'

An adult support and protection legislative framework is assumed to be essential for fulfilling the state's responsibilities in an aging society. This section attempts to conceptualize adult support and protection through the lens of safeguarding laws, thereby laying the groundwork for future research to further develop and refine this legal concept. The following three questions will be examined: (i) What does the vulnerability approach reveal about alternative legislative policies and laws that better align with societal realities, and how do safeguarding laws function to protect adults in common law jurisdictions? (ii) How do relevant

---

[50.] Issho Matsumoto (a dementia doctor) addresses that most relatives do not want to acknowledge that his/her family member has dementia because he/she unconsciously perceives the condition as a stigma and therefore refuses to accept it. Matsumoto suggests that the relatives had better naturally accept dementia, rather than the negative image of dementia. Issho Matsumoto, 'Psychosomatic Disorder Caused by Refusal of Family Member's Dementia: Notice the Screams of Mind and Body' (Column in *The Asahi Shimbun* newspaper on August 16, 2019) (in Japanese) <https://nakamaaru.asahi.com/article/14865543>.

[51.] Yukimichi Imai (a dementia doctor) explains how to take the patient to see doctors, based on a tendency that people will not easily acknowledge the diagnosis of dementia. Yukimichi Imai, *Dementia Net Column No. 7: Dementia Patients Refuse to See Doctor's–How to Take Them to Doctor's* (Web Page, February 2, 2013) (in Japanese) <https://info.ninchisho.net/column/psychiatry_007>.

[52.] This chapter is an updated version of the previously published article by the author: Yukio Sakurai, 'Vulnerability Approach and Adult Support and Protection: Based on Safeguarding Law for Adults at Risk' (2021) 11(1) *The Journal of Aging and Social Change* 19, 34 <https://doi.org/10.18848/2576-5310/CGP/v11i01/19-34>.

considerations—such as the capability approach and concepts of autonomy, including relational autonomy—affect the protection of adults? (iii) How essential will the development of adult support and protection legislation be for Japan?

2.2.2 Vulnerability

A concept of vulnerability may offer some suggestions on the legal status of adults with insufficient mental capacity. Vulnerability is referred to as 'the quality of being weak and easily hurt physically or emotionally.'[53] The concept of vulnerability is used in various academic fields, including philosophy, ethics, ecology, geography, physics, studies of risk, and social sciences.[54] There is, however, no interdisciplinary unified concept.[55] Each field has its own definition, and it is challenging to explicitly define vulnerability in each academic field.[56] According to Jonathan Herring,

> P is vulnerable if the following three factors are present: 1. P faces a risk of harm. 2. P does not have the resources to be able to avoid the risk of harm materializing. 3. P would not be able to adequately respond to the harm if the risk materialized.[57]

Discussion of vulnerability has been explored by Martha Albertson Fineman in social sciences. Fineman's main points in her publications can be summarized as follows: The vulnerability theory challenges the concept of vulnerability as a dominant, static, and individualized legal subject, and argue for the recognition of the human condition, which is finite and fragile, as well as socially and

---

[53.] Refers to the Oxford Learner's Dictionaries, *Vulnerability* (Web Page, February 2022) <https://www.oxford-learnersdictionaries.com/definition/english/vulnerability>.

[54.] In history, the concept of vulnerability stems from philosophical discussions by Hannah Arendt (1958) and Emanuel Levinas (1969); natural sciences, including ecology, geography, and risk studies in the 1970s; and social sciences, particularly development studies by Amartya Sen (1982). Marja-Liisa Honkasalo, 'Vulnerability and Inquiring into Relationality' (2018) 43(3) *Suomen Antropologi (Journal of the Finnish Anthropological Society)* 1–21, 3–4; A study on vulnerability in bioethics: Wendy Rogers, Catriona Mackenzie and Susan Dodds, 'Why Bioethics Needs a Concept of Vulnerability' (2012) 5(2) *International Journal of Feminist Approaches to Bioethics* 11, 38.

[55.] The term 'frailty,' which is similar to vulnerability, is defined as 'a clinically recognizable state of increased vulnerability resulting from ageing-associated decline in reserve and function across multiple physiologic systems.' Qian-Lie Xue, 'The Frailty Syndrome: Definition and Natural History' (2011) 27(1) *Clinics in Geriatric Medicine* 1, 15.

[56.] Jeffrey Alwang, Paul B. Siegel and Steen L. Jorgensen, *Vulnerability: A View from Different Disciplines* (Social Protection Discussion Papers and Notes 23304, The World Bank, 2001); Shitangsu Kumar Paul, 'Vulnerability Concepts and Its Application in Various Fields: A Review on Geographical Perspective' (2013) 8 *Journal of Life and Earth Science* 63, 81.

[57.] Jonathan Herring, *Vulnerable Adults and the Law* (Oxford University Publishing: Kindle, 2016) 857/7258.

materially dynamic.[58] The term 'vulnerable' describes a universal, inevitable, enduring aspect of the human condition that should be at the heart of the concept of social and state responsibility.[59] Human beings are vulnerable to inescapable interrelationships and interdependencies.[60] The human vulnerability and dependency across the life course rely on other individuals, the family, and the state and its institutions.[61] The vulnerability approach is ultimately centered on the role and function of the state or governing authority as it uses law to construct and maintain the social institutions and relationships that govern everyday life.[62] The vulnerability approach to social justice recognizes that the relationship between the individual and the society is synergetic and thus ongoing.[63]

Fineman's views have been reviewed by scholars in various respects. Some typical comments on Fineman's views can be categorized as follows:

(i)   Analysis of risk and assets of vulnerable adults: Understanding social vulnerability involves examining both the risks and the assets of vulnerable adults, thereby informing the development of social policy and the field of planning gerontology.[64]

(ii)   Responsibility of the state or the public: Fineman focuses on the social processes that generate vulnerability and the responsibility of the state and its institutions in reducing the risks and consequences of vulnerability.[65] A vulnerability analysis emphasizes interdependence within social institutions and the need for public responsibility for the shared vulnerability.[66]

(iii) Unifying aspects to the social model: A vulnerability theory and recognition of universal vulnerability provide an important unifying aspect

---

[58.] Martha Albertson Fineman, 'Introducing Vulnerability' in Martha Albertson Fineman and Jonathan W. Fineman (eds), *Vulnerability and the Legal Organization of Work* (Routledge, 2017) 12.

[59.] Martha Albertson Fineman, 'The Vulnerable Subject: Anchoring Equality in the Human Condition' (2008) 20(1) *Yale Journal of Law & Feminism* 1–23, 8.

[60.] Martha Albertson Fineman, '"Elderly" as Vulnerable: Rethinking the Nature of Individual and Societal Responsibility' (2012) 20 *Elder Law Journal* 71–112, 71.

[61.] Ibid 111.

[62.] Martha Albertson Fineman, 'Populations, Pandemics, and Politics' (2021) 21(3) *International Journal of Discrimination and the Law* 184, 190.

[63.] Martha Albertson Fineman, 'Beyond Equality and Discrimination' (2020) 73 *SMU Law Review Forum* 51–62, 61–2.

[64.] Diego Sanchez-Gonzalez and Carmen Egea-Jimenez, 'Social Vulnerability Approach to Investigate the Social and Environmental Disadvantages: Its Application in the Study of Elderly People' (Online, 2011) 17 (69) *Papeles de Población* <http://www.scielo.org.mx/scielo.php?script=sci_arttext&pid=S1405-74252011000300006>.

[65.] Elina Virokannas, Suvi Liuski and Marjo Kuronen, 'The Contested Concept of Vulnerability: A Literature Review' (2018) 23(2) *European Journal of Social Work* 327–39, 337.

[66.] Titti Mattsson and Mirjam Katzin, 'Vulnerability and Ageing' in Ann Numhauser-Henning (ed), *Elder Law: Evolving European Perspectives* (Monograph Book, 2017) 159; Titti Mattsson and Lottie Giertz, 'Vulnerability, Law, and Dementia: An Interdisciplinary Discussion of Legislation and Practice' (2020) 21(1) *Theoretical Inquiries in Law* 139, 159.

to the social model of disability and see to it that societal structures and institutions have impact.[67]

(iv)   Personal responsibility: The interest in the concept of vulnerability is increasing in part because the liberal ethics of bearing personal responsibility for life's vicissitudes is losing salience for increasing numbers of people.[68]

(v)   Useful for setting broad policy goals: Fineman's observations on vulnerable approach are better appreciated from the perspective of law study in a sense that vulnerability theory can be useful in setting broad policy goals (e.g., ensuring that all people have adequate income or adequate health care), but the vulnerability approach is less helpful in choosing policy interventions to achieve its goal.[69]

The comments are thus categorized as analysis of risk and assets of vulnerable adults, responsibility of the state and the public, unifying aspects to the social model, personal responsibility, and useful for setting broad policy goals. Vulnerability implies principles, such as 'the movement from formal equality to substantive equality, and the role [that] institutions play in mitigating vulnerability through a more active state.'[70] It can be assumed that the category (v) addresses a potential limitation of vulnerability in policymaking by virtue of its ambiguous nature; however, this does not negate the importance of vulnerability.[71] It is essential to recognize the limits of the concept of vulnerability, to apply it appropriately within its scope, and to avoid extending it beyond its intended boundaries.

The notion of vulnerability is based on the understanding that people are more or less vulnerable. Vulnerability suggests reliance or dependency on others, particularly in the cases of older people and persons with disabilities who heavily rely on others. The notion of vulnerability is certainly general but vague. It is a simple and understandable concept that defines human nature and 'the inescapable interrelation and interdependence that mark human existence.'[72] Such

---

[67] Tom Shakespeare, 'The Social Model of Disability' in Lennard J. Davis (ed), *The Disability Studies Reader* (Routledge, 2010) 266, 273; Beverley Clough, 'Disability and Vulnerability: Challenging the Capacity/Incapacity Binary' (2017) 16(3) *Social Policy and Society* 469, 481.

[68] Terry Carney, 'Vulnerability: False Hope for Vulnerable Social Security Clients?' (2018) 41(3) *The University of New South Wales Law Journal* 783–817, 784.

[69] Nina A. Kohn, 'Vulnerability Theory and the Role of Government' (2014) 26 *Yale Journal of Law and Feminism* 1–27, 26.

[70] Teresa Somes, 'Identifying Vulnerability: The Argument for Law Reform for Failed Family Accommodation Arrangements' (Online, 2020) 12(1) *Elder Law Review* <https://www.westernsydney.edu.au/__data/assets/pdf_file/0003/1633044/JANUARY_2020_SOMES_Family_Agreements.pdf>.

[71] Nina A. Kohn states that 'although Fineman's theory of vulnerability theory cannot be used as a prescriptive tool, vulnerability may be a useful construct around which to structure social welfare policy.' Kohn (n 69) 25–7.

[72] Fineman (n 60) 71.

a general implication may include the idea that humans do not always have full capacity and autonomy. Therefore, humans do not always behave as rationally as possible, regardless of whether they have the relevant mental capacity. It can be assumed that the idea mentioned here may suit better with the reality in an aged society than the Civil Code based on the capacity doctrine.[73]

2.2.3 Vulnerability Approach

From the vulnerability approach, a general view is derived that vulnerable adults at risk of harm must be protected by law and public policy. Jonathan Herring acknowledges that 'the elderly has a fundamental human right to protection from abuse and the state has an obligation to put in place law and public policy to combat elder abuse.'[74] This view may clarify people's perception of the vulnerability approach, based on the fact that 'vulnerability is a human characteristic, regardless of the relevant mental capacity of the principal.'[75] It may hint at a possible reformation of the relevant mental capacity doctrine in the Civil Code to the vulnerability approach or retain the combination of the mental capacity doctrine and vulnerable approach in the future. This is on a legal foundation based on the combination of civil law (i.e., guardianship on the capacity doctrine) and the social security law (abuse prevention on the vulnerable approach). The vulnerability approach encourages respect for human rights, in particular equality as a universal value, affecting law and public policy. 'Fineman's vulnerability theory presents a promising theoretical lens that offer particular concern with the lived experience of each individual and also preserves universal scope.'[76] As Fineman points out, 'vulnerability can be embraced by people wanting to remove stigma from a designated group.'[77]

The notion of vulnerability is general but vague; thus, vulnerability alone is not enough for academic research and the construction of appropriate policy

---

[73.] A different interpretation of vulnerability is possible. Davis and Aldieri state that 'vulnerability, as an existential as opposed to a political description, is a limited rubric under which to organize against neoliberal forces.' Benjamin P. Davis and Eric Aldieri, 'Precarity and Resistance: A Critique of Martha Fineman's Vulnerability Theory' (Online, 2021) *Hypatia* 1, 17 <https://doi.org/10.1017/hyp.2021.25>.

[74.] Jonathan Herring, 'Elder Abuse: A Human Rights Agenda for the Future' in Israel Doron and Ann M. Soden (eds), *Beyond Elder Law: New Directions in Law and Aging* (Springer Science & Business Media, 2012) 175.

[75.] The similar argument to the vulnerability approach is advocated in Australia. Lise Barry and Susannah Sage-Jacobson, 'Human Rights, Older People and Decision Making in Australia' (2015) 9 *Elder Law Review* 1–21, 1.

[76.] Andrew Pilliar, 'Filling the Normative Hole at the Centre of Access to Justice: Toward a Person-Centred Conception' (2022) 55(1) *UBC Law Review* 149, 203 <https://ssrn.com/abstract=4100809>.

[77.] Fineman (n 60) 112; Daniel Bedford, 'Introduction: Vulnerability Refigured' in Daniel Bedford and Jonathan Herring (eds), *Embracing Vulnerability, The Challenges, and Implications for Law* (Routledge, 2020) 93–5.

instruments.[78] Combining vulnerability with a rights-based approach may result in a greater understanding.[79] One legal concept derived from combination of vulnerability with a rights-based approach is 'supported decision-making.' SDM is an effective method by which vulnerable adults can decide to live their own lives with third-party support. It is 'the provision of support which enables people with cognitive disabilities to exercise their legal decision-making rights (also called legal capacity).'[80] SDM is not just a method of providing welfare to vulnerable adults but can be defined and organized as a legal instrument based on a rights-based approach.[81]

Responding to the needs of vulnerable adults can be challenging. The legal system on adult guardianship has come to be considered as lacking in flexibility. Thus, the adult guardianship system has become undervalued for vulnerable adults with insufficient mental capacity. A key element in this critique is the role of Article 12 (equal recognition before the law) of the Convention on the Rights of Persons with Disabilities (hereinafter referred to as 'CRPD') adopted by the UN in 2006. The CRPD is ratified by 192 UN member countries/areas as of May 2025. According to Article 12 and General Comment No. 1 (adopted April 11, 2014) of the UN CRPD Committee, people are encouraged to use SDM rather than substituted decision-making. Because SDM is supposed to respect the will and preferences of the principal. In other words, the autonomy and right to self-determination of the principal should be respected.[82] This is based on a human rights model. Autonomy and rights to self-determination are at the center of human rights and have been regarded as a universal value in international human rights law.[83]

[78.] Kohn (n 69) 26; Margaret Hall points out a similar view that 'theorizing, and then identifying vulnerability allows us to focus explicitly, and therefore carefully, on the identification of situations or contexts in which vulnerability justifies a social response.' Margaret Isabel Hall 'Mental Capacity in the (Civil) Law: Capacity, Autonomy and Vulnerability' (2012) 58(1) *McGill Law Journal* 1–35, 33.

[79.] A 'rights-based approach' refers to 'a framework that integrates the norms, principles, standards and goals of the international human rights system into the plans and processes of development.' Boesen Jakob Kirkemann and Tomas Martin, *Applying a Rights-based Approach: An Inspirational Guide for Civil Society* (The Danish Institute for Human Rights, 2007) 9.

[80.] Refers to the Victorian Office of Public Advocacy (Victorian OPA), *Supported Decision-Making in Victoria* (Victorian OPA Report, Online, October 2020) 6 <https://www.publicadvocate.vic.gov.au/your-rights/your-healthcare/your-supported-medical-decisions>.

[81.] Refers to Section 1.2.2 (4), 'Developments and Challenges of the SDM Guidelines' and Section 5.2.3 (1) b, 'Legal Status of SDM Law'; Robert M. Gordon, 'The Emergence of Assisted (Supported) Decision-Making in the Canadian Law of Adult Guardianship and Substitute Decision-Making' (2000) 23(1) *International Journal of Law and Psychiatry* 61, 77 <https://doi.org/10.1016/S0160-2527(99)00034-5>.

[82.] The CRPD is the human rights treaty to have a comprehensive national surveillance mechanism and the treaty to systematize a human rights model for disability. Theresia Degener, 'A Human Rights Model of Disability' in Peter Blanck and Eilionóir Flynn (eds), *Routledge Handbook of Disability Law and Human Rights* (Routledge, 2016) 31–49.

[83.] Maria Isolina Dabove, 'Autonomy, Self-Determination, and Human Rights: Legal Safeguards in Argentina to Prevent Elder Abuse and Neglect' (2018) 32 *International Journal of Law, Policy and The Family* 80, 92; Stephen Hopgood, Jack Snyder and Leslie Vinjamuri, *Human Rights Futures* (Cambridge University Press, Reprint, 2018).

This UN CRPD Committee's view was assumed to be difficult to accept when it was made public due to wide discrepancies between the UN CRPD Committee's view and the legislation of member countries/areas. It is, however, gradually being accepted. Some UN member countries have accepted this idea and have even partly amended their civil code or relevant laws or enacted new legislation. Namely, the civil code was partly amended in Switzerland (2013), Austria (2017), Peru (2018), and Germany (2021), and the new act was legislated in Ireland (2015) and the state of Victoria (2019) in Australia. In addition, the US, which has signed but not ratified the CRPD, has accepted the proposition of this Article 12.[84] Some U.S. states have taken relevant actions, including Texas (2015) and Delaware (2016). The American Bar Association (hereinafter referred to as 'ABA') made an institutional resolution in August 2017,[85] recommending the introduction of SDM system into state laws, and some states followed the recommendations.[86] It is understood that the move to legislate SDM into the statute is in progress in developed countries under the influence of the CRPD. In this sense, it can be assumed that SDM is an example of the integration of the concept of vulnerability with a rights-based approach, reflecting a general trend.

2.2.4 Safeguarding Laws for Adult at Risk

With SDM, the risk of the supporter unduly influencing the principal's intention consciously or unconsciously may arise.[87] Since a person's mind is not visible, the question is how a third party can perceive the existence of harm that would be difficult for people other than the relevant parties to understand. Therefore, SDM requires safeguarding measures in its nature, which should be monitored by third parties. In legislation, safeguarding provisions to eliminate the risk of manipulation must be incorporated into the law.[88] Safeguards provisions may protect persons by promptly intervening to the extent required by the public authorities if the persons are in danger of harm.[89] Safeguards are not only sub-

---

[84] Arlene S. Kanter, 'Let us Try Again: Why the United States Should Ratify the United Nations Convention on the Rights of People with Disabilities' (2019) 35 *Touro Law Review* 301, 343.

[85] Refers to the American Bar Association (ABA), *Resolution 113: American Bar Association Adopted by The House of Delegates* (Web Page, August 14–15, 2017) <https://health.ucdavis.edu/mindinstitute/centers/cedd/pdf/sdm-aba-resolution.pdf>.

[86] Refers to Section 3.2 (5), 'U.S. Guardianship and Supported Decision-Making Acts.'

[87] Mary Joy Quinn, 'Undue Influence and Elder Abuse' (2002) 23 (1) *Geriatric Nursing* 11, 17.

[88] Refers to Section 1.2.2 (4), 'Developments and Challenges of the SDM Guidelines.' This is because safeguards on guidelines are not enforceable to any party, and it can be assumed to be powerless and not useful for protection of principals' interests. This comment is applicable to the 'SDM guidelines for adult guardians.'

[89] Gerard Quinn, 'Personhood & Legal Capacity Perspectives on the Paradigm Shift of Article 12 CRPD' (Conference Paper, Conference on Disability and Legal Capacity under the CRPD held in Harvard Law School, February 20, 2010).

ject to SDM but also to any protection of vulnerable adults that is based on the vulnerability approach. With regard to safeguards or safeguarding, it is seen as an idea of safeguarding law or policy that vulnerable adults or adults at risk of harm must be protected by law and public policy from abuse.[90] This idea consists in the fact that 'the elderly have fundamental human rights to protection from abuse' and 'the state has an obligation to put in place law and public policy to combat abuse.'[91]

In general, vulnerability, adults at risk of harm, and safeguarding law or policy are seen in common law jurisdictions, and they are, in fact, differently made into legislation or policy by each individual country. Previous studies on comparative law analysis in common law jurisdictions were focused on adult safeguarding laws in England, Scotland, Ireland, the US, Canada (the province of British Columbia), and Australia (the state of Victoria).[92] The definitions of 'vulnerable adult,' 'at-risk adult,' or 'adult at risk' in safeguarding law or policy report of the adult protection systems have a certain diversity according to country. These definitions are summarized in Table 2.1.

---

[90] Safeguard guidelines of social workers for people with dementia in England and Wales based on laws and policies: Jeremy Dixon et al, 'Safeguarding People Living with Dementia: How Social Workers Can Use Supported Decision-Making Strategies to Support the Human Rights of Individuals during Adult Safeguarding Enquiries' (2021) 52(3) *The British Journal of Social Work* 1307, 1324; Michael Mandelstam, *Safeguarding Vulnerable Adults and the Law* (Jessica Kingsley Publishers, 2008).

[91] Herring (n 74) 175.

[92] Lorna Montgomery et al, 'Implications of Divergences in Adult Protection Legislation' (2016) 18(3) *Journal of Adult Protection* 1, 16; Wayne Michael Martin et al, 'Towards Compliance with CRPD Art. 12 in Capacity/Incapacity Legislation Across the UK' (The Essex Autonomy Project—Three Jurisdictions Report, 2016); Sarah Donnelly et al, *Adult Safeguarding Legislation and Policy Rapid Realist Literature Review* (Health Service Executive, National Safeguarding Office and Trigraph Limited, 2017); Sarah Donnelly and Marita O'Brien, 'Adult Safeguarding Legislation—The Key to Addressing Dualism of Agency and Structure? An Exploration of How Irish Social Workers Protect Adults at Risk in the Absence of Adult Safeguarding Legislation' (Online, 2022) 52(6) *The British Journal of Social Work* 3677–96 <https://doi.org/10.1093/bjsw/bcac003>.

Table 2.1: Definitions of 'Vulnerable Adults' or 'Adults at Risk' by Country

State/Act	Definitions
England, Care Act 2014	Section 42(1) Enquiry by local authority in Safeguarding adults at risk of abuse or neglect: This section applies where a local authority has reasonable cause to suspect that an adult in its area (whether or not ordinarily resident there)—(a) has needs for care and support (whether or not the authority is meeting any of those needs), (b) is experiencing, or is at risk of, abuse or neglect, and (c) as a result of those needs is unable to protect himself or herself against the abuse or neglect or the risk of it.
Wales, Social Services and Well-Being (Wales) Act 2014	Section 126(1) Adults at risk: An 'adult at risk', for the purposes of this Part, is an adult who—(a) is experiencing or is at risk of abuse or neglect, (b) has needs for care and support (whether the authority is meeting any of those needs), and (c) because of those needs is unable to protect himself or herself against the abuse or neglect or the risk of it.
Scotland, Adult Support and Protection (Scotland) Act 2007	Section 3(1) Adults at risk: 'Adults at risk' are adults who—(a) are unable to safeguard their own well-being, property, rights or other interests, (b) are at risk of harm, and (c) because they are affected by disability, mental disorder, illness or physical or mental infirmity, are more vulnerable to being harmed than adults who are not so affected.
Ireland, Safeguarding Vulnerable Persons at Risk of Abuse[93]	National Policy and Procedures Page 10: People with disabilities and older people may be particularly vulnerable due to: diminished social skills; dependence on others for personal and intimate care; capacity to report; sensory difficulties; isolation; power differentials.

[93.] Refers to the Health Service Executive, *Safeguarding Vulnerable Persons at Risk of Abuse* (National Policy and Procedures, December 2014); Department of Social Protection, Safeguarding Vulnerable Adults (Web Page, May 30, 2022) <https://www.gov.ie/en/publication/3f6bc5-safeguarding-vulnerable-adults/>.

State/Act	Definitions
Singapore, Vulnerable Adults Act 2018[94]	Section 2: 'vulnerable adult' means an individual who—(a) is 18 years of age or older; and (b) is, by reason of mental or physical infirmity, disability or incapacity, incapable of protecting himself or herself from abuse, neglect, or self-neglect.
Canada, The Province of British Columbia, Adult Guardianship Act 1996 Chapter 6	Section 44: The purpose of this Part is to provide for support and assistance for adults who are abused or neglected and who are unable to seek support and assistance because of (a) physical restraint, (b) a physical handicap that limits their ability to seek help, or (c) an illness, disease, injury, or other condition that affects their ability to make decisions about the abuse or neglect.
The US, Texas Human Resources Code Chapter 48, 2005. Investigations and protective services for older and Disabled person	§ 48.002. Definitions: (5) 'Protective services' means the services furnished by the department or by a protective services agency to an older or disabled person who has been determined to be in a state of abuse, neglect, or exploitation. (1) 'Elderly person' means a person 65 years of age or older. (8) 'Disabled person' means a person with a mental, physical, or developmental disability that substantially impairs the person's ability to provide adequately for the person's care or protection and who is: (A) 18 years of age or older.
Australia, Elder Abuse—A National Legal Response (ALRC Report 131)[95]	Recommendation 14–3: Adult safeguarding laws should define 'at-risk adults' to mean people aged 18 years and over who: (a) have care and support needs; (b) are being abused, or neglected, or are at risk of abuse or neglect; and (c) are unable to protect themselves from abuse or neglect because of their care and support needs.

Source: Made by the author

[94.] Wing-Cheong Chan, 'Holding the Therapeutic State at Bay? Balancing Autonomy and Protection in Singapore's Vulnerable Adults Act' (Online, 2020) 12(1) *Elder Law Review* <https://www.westernsydney.edu.au/__data/assets/pdf_file/0019/1633033/JANUARY_20_2020_WING_CHAN_SINGAPORES_VAA_Article_for_Elder_Law_Review.pdf>.

[95.] Refers to the ALRC, *Elder Abuse—A National Legal Response* (ALRC Report 131, 2017).

In contrast, some common principles are seen in the adult protection system in common law jurisdictions: namely, the adult guardianship and elder abuse legislations are closely related like the two sides of a coin. For example, in England, the same national judicial and administrative agencies—i.e., the Court of Protection and the Office of the Public Guardian—that administer the adult guardianship under the Mental Capacity Act 2005 (hereinafter referred to as 'MCA 2005') are responsible for 'care and support' for adults at risk of harm. This is based on Section 42(1)(a) of the *Care Act 2014*.[96]

In Australia, guardianship law reform in the states and special territories, including elder abuse legislation, is in progress.[97] In the state of South Australia, elder abuse is addressed by a neighboring agency of guardianship, i.e., the Adult Safeguarding Unit. The state of New South Wales (NSW) newly established an Aging and Disability Commissioner and launched a similar public policy to combat elder abuse. Which public agency is responsible for both guardianship and elder abuse is subject to the relevant state and special territory in Australia, and it should be noted that guardianship is regarded as one of the legal instruments for dealing with elder abuse. Based on the values of the CRPD, the international tendency is to restrict the use of the guardianship system and encourage the use of SDM.

From these perspectives, it can be understood that the guardianship system, SDM, and safeguards against elder abuse are regarded as one package of legislation and are embodied in public policy. This is, in fact, because the victims of elder abuse are vulnerable adults that include some people with healthy mental capacity and others with insufficient mental capacity. Adults with insufficient mental capacity are at higher risk of becoming victims by elder abuse. In addition, in cases of financial exploitation, the victim of the abuse is likely to hide the damage and events from relevant agencies, including the police, because the perpetrator is perhaps a relative or a close acquaintance of the principal.[98] It is estimated that the elder abuse rate is higher than the official report because there are many cases where the victims do not have the physical or mental capacity to report the abuse to the relevant authority, or psychologically hesitate to report

---

[96.] The MCA 2005 stipulates that 'incapacity' to make a particular decision must meet two requirements: (i) the principal is unable to understand, retain or use the information relevant to the decision; (ii) their inability to do so is 'because of an impairment of the mind.' Jonathan Herring and Jesse Wall, 'Autonomy, Capacity and Vulnerable Adults: Filling the Gaps in the *Mental Capacity Act*' (2015) 35(4) *Legal Studies* 698–719, 701; Peter Bartlett, 'At the Interface Between Paradigms: English Mental Capacity Law and the CRPD' (2020) 11 *Frontiers in Psychiatry* 881, 894.

[97.] Refers to Section 4.4.3, 'Discussion on Elder Abuse Legislation.'

[98.] From the interview of Victorian State Trustees Limited (VCAT satellite office) by the author on March 3, 2017; Lewis Melanie, 'Financial Elder Abuse in a Victorian Context: Now and into the Future' (Conference Paper at the fourth National Conference on Elder Abuse held in Melbourne on February 24–25, 2016).

it due to a complicated mental characteristic unique to vulnerable adults even though they have the physical or mental capacity.[99]

2.3 Adult Support and Protection

2.3.1 Capability Approach and Autonomy

(1) Capability Approach

The vulnerability approach and safeguarding law or policy have been discussed. The balancing of competing values and principles is essential, but it is difficult to implement in practice. Based on such balancing with vulnerability, two more ideas will be discussed. One is the capability approach, and the other is autonomy. Amartya Sen's capability approach is basically different from vulnerability approach on a basic level.[100]

Sen's main arguments in his publications can be summarized as follows. The capability approach is grounded in the need to assess welfare not solely in terms of income or utility,[101] but in terms of what individuals are effectively able to be and do—that is, their *substantive freedoms*. It emphasizes the diverse needs, circumstances, and values of individuals, focusing on both potential actions (what a person is capable of doing) and actual achievements (what a person ends up doing), which Sen refers to collectively as *functionings*. According to Sen, human *capabilities* are defined in relation to these functionings and consist of the various combinations of valued functionings that a person has the real opportunity to achieve.[102]

Functionings represent different aspects of a person's well-being, including both basic and complex activities and states.[103] These range from the most elementary—such as being adequately nourished, avoiding preventable disease, or living in safety—to more advanced and often socially dependent aspects, such as participating in cultural life, engaging in meaningful work, or enjoying

---

[99.] Yukio Sakurai, 'Challenges of Property Management for Older Adults in Japan: Focusing on Financial Exploitation and Informal Arrangement' (2022) 12(2) *The Journal of Aging and Social Change* 1, 18.

[100.] Abrahim H. Khan states that Sen's capability approach is based on an Indian religion and philosophy '*dharma*' (a spiritualized secularism rendered in English as 'religion'). Abrahim H. Khan, 'Postulating an Affinity: Amartya Sen on Capability and Tagore' (2012) 19(1) *Annals of Neurosciences* 3–7, 6.

[101.] Amartya K. Sen, 'Human Rights and Capabilities' (2005) 6(2) *Journal of Human Development* 151, 166.

[102.] Amartya K. Sen, *The Idea of Justice* (Penguin Books Ltd, 2009) 236.

[103.] Amartya K. Sen, 'Capability and Well-Being' in Martha C. Nussbaum and Amartya Sen (eds), *Quality of Life* (Oxford University Press, 1992) 30–53, 31.

self-respect and social inclusion.[104] In this framework, capabilities are not just theoretical options but must reflect genuine freedom and access; they are shaped by a variety of factors including personal characteristics (such as age, gender, and physical or mental health), social arrangements (including legal rights, institutional structures, and economic policies), and environmental conditions.[105]

Sen's approach is distinctive in that it allows both well-being and freedom to be evaluated in terms of the capability to achieve *functionings* that individuals have reason to value. Importantly, this avoids imposing a fixed metric of welfare across all people and contexts. Within this approach, poverty is redefined not merely as a lack of material resources but as a deprivation of basic capabilities— such as the capability to live a long and healthy life, to receive an education, or to participate equally in society.[106] Thus, poverty is seen as a multidimensional problem, requiring policy responses that go beyond income redistribution and address broader inequalities in capability.

Moreover, Sen emphasizes that what individuals are able to do (*capabilities*) and what they actually do (*functionings*) will naturally differ across persons, reflecting individual preferences, goals, and circumstances. This variation is not only natural but desirable, as it reflects the diversity of human lives and aspirations. For instance, in the case of persons with disabilities, what matters is not simply their autonomous ability to function but also what they can accomplish with reasonable and just support from others. In this light, freedom is not merely the absence of interference but the presence of real opportunities to live a life one has reason to value.

Ultimately, the evaluation of human well-being in the capability approach includes the achievements realized through one's abilities, the freedom to choose among different life paths, and the autonomy to determine and revise one's goals. This notion of freedom is central: It includes not only the freedom to act and to achieve specific outcomes but also the freedom to reflect critically on one's values and to pursue changes in life's direction based on such reflection.

Le Galès and Bungener argue that

> adopting the capability approach directs attention not to who gives care and why
> or for what result, in the sense of what final result, but on how one gives care,

---

[104] Ibid.

[105] Ibid 33.

[106] Amartya K. Sen, 'Well-Being, Capability, and Public Policy' (1994) 53(7/9) *Journal of Economists and Annuals of Economics* 333–47, 334.

according to what ways things are done, what specific modes of accompaniment are used and for what reasons or motivations.[107]

This perspective places particular emphasis on the process by which individuals are supported in exercising their freedom to choose and to pursue a life they have reason to value. The capability approach is thus especially valued for its attention to individual autonomy, self-determination, and freedom not only to select an outcome but also to determine the path toward that outcome. It respects the diversity of individuals by recognizing differences in needs, preferences, and contexts, and by affirming the importance of enabling each person to reflect on and shape a way of life that aligns with their own characteristics and values.

The capability approach has been discussed by many researchers in a broader sense,[108] including Martha C. Nussbaum,[109] and discussion is still ongoing and application of the capability approach is attempted to a broad area.[110] For example, in the recent discussion on Article 19 (living independently and being included in the community) of the CRPD, it is advocated that 'we have sought to ground the right to live independently in the community in the capability approach as it can serve as the ethical framework and foundations that can justify such a right.'[111]

Capabilities are formed through the combination of internal and external conditions.[112] Namely, the internal conditions encompass individual, often biological characteristics while the external factors encompass both the physical and social environments. It can be assumed that this discussion may correspond to a human rights model and a social model in people with disabilities. It could

---

[107.] Catherine Le Galès and Martine Bungener, 'The Family Accompaniment of Persons with Dementia Seen Through the Lens of the Capability Approach' (2019) 18(1) *Dementia* 55–79, 74.

[108.] An overview article regarding the capability approach: Ryuhei Yoshida, 'Review of Capability Approach: For Limitation and the Future' (2020) 57 *Hokusei Review, the School of Social Welfare* 13, 23 (in Japanese); Martha C. Nussbaum, *Creating Capabilities: The Human Development Approach* (The Belknap Press of Harvard University Press, 2013).

[109.] Martha Nussbaum argues political philosophy in a broad sense and shows her list of central human capabilities, which includes ten items. The approach in her discussion differs from that of Sen. Martha C. Nussbaum, *Frontiers of Justice: Disability, Nationality, Species Membership* (Harvard University Press, 2006).

[110.] For example, a survey to analyze the diversification of welfare service users in Japan, referring to Sen's capability approach: Miyo Akimoto, *Social Welfare Users and Human Rights: Diversification of User Image and Guarantee of Human Rights* (Yuhikaku Publishing Co., Ltd., 2010) (in Japanese).

[111.] Mary Donnelly states that 'the CRPD has a good deal in common with the capabilities approach which broadens the lens of engagement and recognises that external factors can impede or enhance individual agency.' Mary Donnelly, 'Dementia: A Legal Overview' in Charles Foster, Jonathan Herring and Israel Doron (eds), *The Law and Ethics of Dementia* (Hart Publishing, 2014) 271–83, 277; This right was conceptualized as a capability, and it was shown that it is grounded in the two values of freedom and dignity. Emma Wynne Bannister and Sridhar Venkatapuram, 'Grounding the Right to Live in the Community (CRPD Article 19) in the Capabilities Approach to Social Justice' (2020) 69 *International Journal of Law and Psychiatry* 6.

[112.] Deneulin Séverine and Lila Shahani, *An Introduction to the Human Development and Capability Approach: Freedom and Agency* (Earthscan, 2009).

therefore be understood that the notion of capability may provide some answer to the question of what freedom is like or what human rights are like.[113] This implies a sense that each person seeks an autonomous way of life, based on the notion of capability, with individual freedom and human rights, even the person has various constraints, such as social, physical, mental, and financial. In this sense, the capability approach may give us some ethical guidelines in contemporary society.

(2) Autonomy

a. Individual Autonomy

Autonomy is close to right to self-determination. Self-determination is said to identify 'external, structural (social and political) conditions for individual autonomy, specifically in freedom conditions and opportunity conditions.'[114] Catriona Mackenzie defines that self-determination is to have 'the freedom and opportunity to make and enact choices of practical import to one's life, that is, choices of what to value, who to be, and what to do.'[115] Some psychologists state that the notion of autonomy is 'regulation by the self.'[116] Gerald Dworkin asserts that individual autonomy is 'a second-order capacity of person to reflect critically upon their first-order preferences, desires, wishes, and so forth and the capacity to accept or attempt to change these in light of higher-order preferences and values.'[117] Koji Sato argues, in part citing Robert Young (1986),[118] that individual autonomy implies two aspects: the freedom to act without external constraints and individual self-determination in accordance with a chosen plan of life.[119] Considering these views on individual autonomy, it can be seen that the scope of autonomy may be broader

---

[113.] This is the paper on the capability approach and human rights: Polly Vizard, Sakiko Fukuda-Parr and Diane Elson, 'Introduction: The Capability Approach and Human Rights' (2011) 12(1) *Journal of Human Development and Capabilities* 1, 12.

[114.] Catriona Mackenzie, 'Three Dimensions of Autonomy: A Relational Analysis' in Andrea Veltman and Mark Piper (eds), *Autonomy, Oppression, and Gender* (Oxford University Press, 2014) 15–41, 25.

[115.] Ibid. Catriona Mackenzie remarks that 'the promotion of autonomy is a matter of social justice.' Catriona Mackenzie, 'Relational Autonomy, Normative Authority and Perfectionism' (2008) 39 *Journal of Social Philosophy* 512–33, 530.

[116.] Richard M. Ryan and Edward L. Deci, 'Self-Regulation and the Problem of Human Autonomy: Does Psychology Need Choice, Self-Determination, and Will?' (2006) 74(6) *Journal of Personality* 1557–85, 1557.

[117.] Gerald Dworkin (ed), 'The Nature of Autonomy' in *The Theory and Practice of Autonomy* (Cambridge University Press, 1988) 3–20, 20; Gerald Dworkin, 'The Nature of Autonomy' 2 *Nordic Journal of Studies in Educational Policy* (2015, an unchanged republishing) Article: 28479.

[118.] Robert Young, *Personal Autonomy: Beyond Negative and Positive Liberty* (Routledge, 1986).

[119.] Koji Sato, 'The Meaning of "Self-Determination" in the Constitutional Studies' (1990) [1989] *Legal Philosophy Annual Report* 76–99, 86–87 (in Japanese).

than that of self-determination, and both autonomy and self-determination are regarded as universal values.[120]

In history, the notion of individual autonomy has been argued and developed by Immanuel Kant and Kantian scholars, including John Rawls,[121] on the one hand, by John Stuart Mill and utilitarian liberal philosophy scholars, on the other hand. Kantian scholars emphasize on the moral and ethics of internal motives of human being based on a human-centered approach,[122] while Mill does not use the term autonomy but respects 'the principle of individual liberty on the utilitarian bias that it is through liberty that huma individuality develop.'[123] Mary Donnelly remarks, based on Mill's insight, that 'a view of autonomy as empowerment provides a better way of thinking about autonomy than the traditional liberal view of autonomy as non-interference.'[124]

From a feminist point of view, there are some arguments by Fineman against individual autonomy.[125] Fineman criticizes the autonomy myth, which she believes has caused the US to fail in effective public policymaking.[126] Thus, Fineman wants to introduce the U.S. public debate the alternative term of 'dependency' and 'substantive equality.' Fineman raises an argument on 'vulnerability' to ask for state responsibility to protect vulnerable people. In this regard, it can be understood that vulnerability is used as a conflicting concept against individual autonomy, since the 'vulnerable theory [as an universal one] asserts that agency or [individual] autonomy should always be understood as particular, partial, and contextual.'[127] Daniel Bedford comments that vulnerability has been positioned as 'the other of the ideal of autonomy.'[128] Christine Straehle states that the 'nor-

---

[120]. Hirohide Takikawa remarks that self-determination comprises three values, namely (i) an instrumental value: self-determination, which entrusts the decision to the individual, is the most efficient means and tool for achieving the well-being of each individual; (ii) a growth value: a person can grow by self-determination; and (iii) a symbolic value: there are occasions when it makes sense that the decision is made by the person by himself/herself. Self-determination does not always demand self-responsibility because of exemptional cases, such as incapacity and no intention/negligence. Hirohide Takikawa, 'Between Self-Decision and Self-Responsibility: A Philosophy of Law Consideration' (2001) *Law Seminar* 32, 35 (in Japanese).

[121]. John Rawls, *A Theory Justice* [tr Takashi Kawamoto et al] (Kinokuniya Bookstore, 2nd ed., 2010) (in Japanese).

[122]. For example, Hiroyuki Hasuo, 'The Structure of "Autonomy" in Kant's Moral Philosophy: New Possibilities through Practice of "Duty of Love"' (2010) 6 *Civilization Structure Theory* 15, 34 (in Japanese).

[123]. Mary Donnelly, *Healthcare Decision-Making and the Law—Autonomy, Capacity and the Limits of Liberalism* (Cambridge University Press (Kindle), 2010) 914 and 1484.

[124]. Ibid 1485. Mary Donnelly also states that the MCA 2005 is based on the traditional liberal view as non-interference.

[125]. Other viewpoints than feminist can be seen as 'receptivity, dependency, and social and clinical psychology.' Tom O'shea, 'Critics of Autonomy' (Essex Autonomy Project: Green Paper Report, 2012) 1, 26.

[126]. Martha Albertson Fineman, *The Autonomy Myth: A Theory of Dependency* (The New Press, 2004).

[127]. Fineman (n 58) 8.

[128]. Bedford (n 77).

mative and moral question behind vulnerability-based theories is a concern for individual autonomy and the conditions of individual agency.'[129]

Considering the views above, it can be understood that individual autonomy is no doubt valuable, and sometimes may conflict with other values, including vulnerability. As Sato remarks, the idea of individual autonomy closely relates to the value of the community and thus is reasonably restricted by public welfare.[130] The question then is what public welfare is like. Here, it can be said that public welfare is 'a device that coordinates conflicts between rights and conflicts between the public interest and rights'[131] or 'the ultimate philosophy of domestic law'[132] that people in the community must respect and it should be deliberately clarified case by case in a democratic process.

b. Relational Autonomy

The notion of autonomy includes a different approach—relational autonomy.[133] Relational autonomy is often advocated in the field of bioethics, specifically with the principal's family members or relatives when medical treatment or serious physical operations are determined to be necessary.[134] Relational autonomy, however, is not limited to bioethics; it can be applied to a general field.[135] In fact, Jonathan Herring states that 'to be autonomous is not to be isolated and free of responsibility, but to be in a network of relationship, with their dependant

---

[129] Christine Straehle, 'Introduction: Vulnerability, Autonomy, and Applied Ethics' in Christine Straehle (ed), *Vulnerability, Autonomy and Applied Ethics* (Routledge, 2017) 1–18.

[130] Sato (n 119) 90–2.

[131] Keigo Obayashi remarks that 'Public welfare can function in various ways according to the situation, and it may function as a basis for restricting rights, or it may also serve as a criterion for judgment to the constitution.' Keigo Obayashi, 'What Is Public Welfare: Public Welfare as the Standard' (2022) 807 *Hougaku Seminar* 39–44, 44 (in Japanese).

[132] Tomoo Odaka, *The Ultimate in Law* (Yuhikaku Publishing Co., Ltd., 2nd ed., 1965) 228 (in Japanese).

[133] Hisao Ikeya states that 'A view of universal vulnerability prompts us to change the mainstream view of "individual autonomy" into one of "relative autonomy."' Hisao Ikeya, 'Bioethics and Vulnerability' (2016) 10 *The Bulletin of Ryotokuji University* 105, 128 (in Japanese).

[134] Catriona Mckenzie remarks that 'Relational theories of autonomy seem to have had greatest traction outside the discipline, or in sub-discipline, such as bioethics, applied ethics, and political philosophy where there is a (relatively) larger proportion of women.' Catriona McKenzie, 'Feminist Innovation in Philosophy: Relational Autonomy and Social Justice' (2019) 72 *Women's Studies International Forum* <https://doi.org/10.1016/j.wsif.2018.05.003>; Carlos Gómez-Vírseda et al review fifty articles regarding 'relational autonomy' in the bioethics. C. Gómez-Vírseda et al, 'Relational Autonomy: What Does it Mean and How Is It Used in End-of-Life Care? A Systematic Review of Argument-based Ethics Literature' (2019) *BMC Medical Ethics* 76, 91.

[135] Shotaro Tahara remarks that individual autonomy is often criticized in contemporary debates, because it underestimates or denies such things as love, friendship, and interdependence, which most people consider valuable.' Then, the concept of relational autonomy is discussed. Shotaro Tahara, 'What Should Autonomous Agents Be Like? From the Individualistic to the Substantive Conception' (2017) 5 *Waseda Rilas Journal* 193, 203 (in Japanese).

responsibilities.'[136] Jonathan Herring also states that 'our decisions are rarely "ours" but are the results of consultation and discussion. They are made in the context of our relationships, reflecting the obligations we owe to those around us. This does not require us to abandon autonomy, but to rethink it in a deeply relational way.'[137]

The notion of relational autonomy may imply a greater understanding of human relationships involving the principal, including health care and aged care.[138] Jonathan Herring states that 'dependency on others is an aspect of humanity'[139] and 'vulnerabilities, care and identities become mutual and interdependent'[140] with the notion of relational autonomy. 'The emphasis on caring relationships acknowledges that it is a huge simplification to separate people into carers and those cared for. In the caring relationships we are all in there merging of interests and selves.'[141] In relation to people with dementia, Terry Carney states that

> it is here that richer concepts of relational autonomy and vulnerability prove their worth in helping to understand the ethical, social and legal issues in dementia care—searching out and promoting relational harmonies while remaining vigilant to correct disharmonies such as abuse and neglect, or even the 'pathogenic' vulnerability manufactured by poor legal processes.[142]

[136.] Jonathan Herring, 'Relational Autonomy and Rape' in S. Day Sclater, F. Ebtehaj, E. Jackson and M. Richards (eds), *Regulating Autonomy* (Oxford Legal Studies Research Paper No. 12, Hart, 2010) 13.

[137.] Jonathan Herring, *Vulnerable Adults and the Law* (Oxford University Press (Kindle), 2016) 1998.

[138.] Healthcare decision-making is one of the issues often discussed with relational autonomy, as addressed in 'Introduction.' Sumytra Menon et al, 'Some Unresolved Ethical Challenges in Healthcare Decision-making: Navigating Family Involvement' (2020) 12(1) *Asian Bioethics Review* 27, 36; Tatsuya Morita et al, 'Relational Autonomy in Advanced Care Planning' (2020) 30(5) *Palliative Care* 399, 402 (in Japanese).

[139.] Jonathan Herring, 'The Disability Critique of Care' (2014) 8 *Elder Law Review*, Article 2, 12; Jonathan Herring states that 'people are understood as relational, interconnected, and interdependent. The law's job is to uphold and maintain relationships and protect people from the abuses that can occur within them.' Jonathan Herring, *Relational Autonomy and Family Law* (Springer Science & Business Media, 2014) 13.

[140.] Herring (n 139) 15.

[141.] Jonathan Herring, 'Ethics of Care and Disability Rights: Complementary or Contradictory?' in Loraine Gelsthorpe, Perveez Mody and Brian Sloan (eds), *Spaces of Care* (Hart Publishing, 2020) 180; From action theory of philosophy viewpoint, an interactive uncontrollability of care is discussed, which implies that the matter is not so simple. Seisuke Hayakawa, 'Caring and Vulnerable Agency' (2014) 3 *Studies on Action Theory* 1, 10; Jun Nishimura, 'Ethics of Care and Social Security Law: for the Conversion from the Benefit-Centered Law to the Support-Centered Law' (2021) 18(1) *Journal of Kanagawa University of Human Services* 9, 18 (in Japanese).

[142.] Terry Carney, 'People with Dementia and Other Cognitive Disabilities: Relationally Vulnerable or a Source of Agency and Care?' (Sydney Law School Research Paper No. 20/17) (Online, 2020) 12(1) *Elder Law Review* <https://ssrn.com/abstract=3561294>.

The notion of relational autonomy may imply why people are motivated to care for other people in need. This may be because people recognize their mutual vulnerability and need for care for others.[143]

Relational autonomy is rooted in feminist studies and is proposed with the purpose of criticizing the concept of individualist autonomy and proposing a different approach. Considering independent relationships of humans in family, community, and society, the notion of relational autonomy is assumed to be crucial in practice. This is because one's pattern of human conduct and decision-making is largely influenced by family, community, and society.[144] This general tendency illustrates one characteristic of humans living in a community.[145] This relational autonomy, however, does not refer to a strictly defined concept of autonomy in theory, but to a loosely organized research trend that shares a research policy of incorporating relationships with others into autonomous research.[146] It is assumed that this tendency may hint that the notion of relational autonomy has something imperfect to be a general theory.

The point of discussion is how to demonstrate the notion of relational autonomy in a legal framework.[147] The important decision-making areas that the principal should be able to freely execute without excessive interference must be considered, namely voting, marriage, life or death decisions, and matters of creed or belief. The principal's own decision must be respected as an individual autonomous decision, which is a basic principle of human rights. If the principal has little ability to decide on an important issue for some reason, then relational autonomy as support approach should prevail as an alternative to individual autonomy.[148] Even in such a case, relational autonomy needs to be carefully examined by a third party as a witness to determine whether or not it is unduly affected from others.[149] In the other important decision-making areas besides the above-mentioned

---

[143.] Refers to Section 4.3.3 (3), 'What are the Common Values in Australian Law Reforms?' and Section 4.5.1 (3) e, 'Empowering Dimension.' Regarding autonomy, Paragraph 1.37 of the ALRC Report 124 states that 'This Inquiry has been informed by autonomy in the sense of "empowerment", not just "non-interference". This involves seeing an individual in relation to others, in a "relational" or "social" sense and understanding that connects with respect for the family as the "natural and fundamental group unit of society" that is entitled to protection by State Parties.' It can be assumed that ALRC Report 124 is based on the notion of relational autonomy.

[144.] Joan Braun, 'Legal Interventions to Protect Vulnerable Adults: Can Relational Autonomy Provide a New Way Forward?' (Online, 2020) 12(2) *Elder Law Review* <https://www.westernsydney.edu.au/__data/assets/pdf_file/0017/1714220/PEER_REVIEWED_BRAUN_Article.pdf>.

[145.] Refers to Section 2.1.2 (2), 'Characteristics of the Elderly.' We have discussed self-discipline, in addition to autonomy and protection as the values of older people.

[146.] Shotaro Tahara, 'Substantive Conceptions of Autonomy: An Approach Based on Shared Characteristics' (2022) 1 *Bulletin of the Faculty of Humanities, Ibaraki University. Studies in Social Sciences* 55–76, 63 (in Japanese).

[147.] Hiroshi Ohe, 'Rights and Relationships' (1999) 53 *St. Paul's Review of Law and Politics* 149, 178 (in Japanese).

[148.] Megan S. Wright, 'Dementia, Autonomy, and Supported Healthcare Decision Making' (Pennsylvania State Law Research Paper No. 05-2019) (2020) 79 *Maryland Law Review* 257, 324.

[149.] Lucy Series remarks that 'the MCA 2005 was built upon two conflicting premises: one is that autonomy is a function of a person's individual psychological makeup, the other is that the idea of autonomy sometimes can be

ones, relational autonomy can be utilized according to some ethical guidelines to safeguard the principal's interests. This is because human relationships with others, including relatives, are not always as good as the principal likes but may be harmful to the principal in the worst case.[150] It can be said that the weak point in relational autonomy must be ambiguity whether having risk for undue or harmful influence of the principal for some reason, and the principal with intellectual/ mental disability may not identify risk by himself/herself.

Catriona Mackenzie remarks that 'autonomy and capabilities must be central to an ethics of vulnerability,' which is 'both universal and context specific, both inherent to the human condition yet always already shaped by social and political relationship and institutions.'[151] This understanding leads her to further state that

> *non-paternalistic forms of protection recognize vulnerable persons or social groups as equal citizens, but as citizens who may need targeted forms of assistance to convert resources into functionings and hence...reach the threshold level of capabilities to enable them to full equal citizenship. Such forms of assistance thus foster and promote autonomy.[152]*

In other words, it can be assumed that paternalistic interventions would amplify relationships of domination and inequality among citizens of a community or a relationship between a community and citizens, without considering the individual circumstances of the targeted citizens.

Theoretically, it is essential to seek an appropriate balance between *autonomy* and *vulnerability*, a normative aspiration broadly shared across ethical and legal discourses, including among vulnerable adults themselves. *Autonomy*, traditionally understood as the capacity for self-governance or independent decision-making, is often invoked as a foundational value in liberal democratic societies. However, this ideal becomes complex when applied to individuals whose decision-making capacities may be compromised or shaped by dependency, disability, or aging.

---

affected by their external circumstances. A narrow "support" approach is taken as necessary in the MCA, whilst the CRPD offers refreshing ways of thinking how relationships can foster relational autonomy in the legal capacity.' Lucy Series, 'Relationships, Autonomy and Legal Capacity: Mental Capacity and Support Paradigms' (2015) 40 *International Journal of Law and Psychiatry* 80, 91.

[150] Jaime Tabitha Lindsey, 'Protecting and Empowering Vulnerable Adults: Mental Capacity Law in Practice' (doctoral dissertation, University of Birmingham, 2018) 1–341, 41.

[151] Catriona Mackenzie remarks that 'the notion of situational vulnerability focuses attention on aspects of a person's interpersonal, social, political, economic, or environmental situation. The notion of pathogenic vulnerability draws attention to the way that situational vulnerabilities can give rise to compounded capability deficits or corrosive disadvantage and...to the way that badly designed social policy responses to vulnerability can cause or compound major capability failure.' Catriona Mackenzie, 'The Importance of Relational Autonomy and Capabilities for an Ethics of Vulnerability' in Catriona Mackenzie, Wendy Rogers and Susan Dodds (eds), *Vulnerability: New Essays in Ethics and Feminist Philosophy (Studies in Feminist Philosophy)* (Oxford University Press, 2013) 54–6.

[152] Ibid 55.

Conversely, *vulnerability* reflects the susceptibility to harm, often resulting from structural inequalities, relational dependencies, or situational constraints.

The challenge, then, lies in reconciling these two concepts—autonomy and vulnerability—within law and policy. Approaches to achieving this balance are not uniform; they differ according to legal traditions, policy priorities, cultural understandings of personhood, and the specific populations considered 'vulnerable.' For instance, the needs and risks faced by older adults with cognitive decline may differ substantially from those of individuals with intellectual disabilities or those experiencing social exclusion.

A promising theoretical development lies in *relational autonomy*, which reframes autonomy not as isolated self-determination, but as fundamentally shaped by interpersonal relationships and social contexts. Under this model, promoting autonomy entails acknowledging the social conditions that enable or constrain decision-making. This view helps explain why 'the obligation to promote autonomy is not only consistent with but also central to the normative obligations involved in responding to vulnerability.'[153] In such an understanding, *autonomy* and *vulnerability* are no longer seen as opposing principles, but as potentially integrated within a holistic ethical framework.

Janet Delgado defines *relational autonomy* as 'the capacity to make decisions as a person constituted and embedded in social relationships.'[154] This conceptualization highlights the role of mutual trust and social embeddedness—such as ties to family, close friends, cultural norms, and community networks—in supporting decision-making capacity. These social supports may, in certain contexts, foster an environment where a constructive balance between autonomy and vulnerability can be achieved.[155]

However, such an ideal balance is not universally attainable. Relational autonomy depends on the presence of supportive, respectful, and non-coercive relationships, which are not guaranteed in all settings. Moreover, societal structures may reinforce certain vulnerabilities rather than mitigate them. Therefore,

---

[153.] Ibid 56.

[154.] Janet Delgado, 'Re-thinking Relational Autonomy: Challenging the Triumph of Autonomy through Vulnerability' (2019) 5 *Bioethics Update* 50–65, 60–1 and 63; Margaret Isabel Hall sets out her approach of vulnerability and relational autonomy as legal concepts for guardianship and advanced planning. Margaret Isabel Hall, 'Relational Autonomy, Vulnerability theory, Older Adults and the Law: Making It Real' (2020) 12 *Elder Law Review* <https://www.westernsydney.edu.au/__data/assets/pdf_file/0003/1633026/January_2020_Elder_Law_Review_MI_Hall_ESSAY.pdf>.

[155.] Refers to Section 4.3.3 (2) d, 'Non-remuneration Policy' and Section 4.5.1 (1) d, 'What Aspects of Supported Decision-Making Require Further Research.' This may be part of the reasons why Australian guardianship and SDM largely rely on relatives or close friends of principals, or public guardians/advocates as guardians/administrators and supporters without remuneration; The article analyzes what and how guardians take the processes to understanding the will and preferences of principals, focusing on their personal factors. Alice L. Holmes et al, 'Integrity in Guardianship Decision Making: Applying the Will and Preferences Paradigm' (Online, 2022) *Journal of the American Medical Directors Association* 1, 8 <https://doi.org/10.1016/j.jamda.2022.01.050>.

while relational autonomy offers a valuable supplement to overly individualistic models of autonomy, it is not yet a fully established or operationalized general theory. Rather, it remains an evolving framework with both normative potential and practical limitations, particularly in contexts where social support is weak or compromised.[156]

2.3.2 Notion of Adult Support and Protection

As human rights awareness has become more widespread and the principle of equal recognition before the law, embodied in Article 12 of the CRPD, has gained international acceptance, discrimination against persons with disabilities is no longer tolerated. Mary Donnelly notes that 'the legal communications explored show that…it was only with the advent of human rights that the normative focus shifted to the legal system.'[157] Furthermore, legislation aimed at adults with insufficient mental capacity, including older individuals with dementia, is now required to uphold the principle of equality. It is hoped that adults with insufficient mental capacity will be able to live alongside others in society, recognizing that anyone may experience diminished capacity in the future. Legislation addressing serious social issues such as dementia, adult guardianship, SDM, and safeguards against elder abuse should be viewed not as isolated legal instruments, but as components of a complementary legal framework.

In common law jurisdictions, elder abuse policies are referred to by different legislative terms: 'safeguarding'[158] in England, Wales, Ireland, and Australian states; 'adult support and protection'[159] in Scotland; 'adult protection'[160] in Canadian provinces; and 'adult protective services (APS)'[161] in U.S. states and local

---

[156.] Any complicated conceptual argument, such as those related to vulnerability and autonomy, can be simplified, but it might carry the risk of unconsciously deviating from reality. For example, Paul Skowron raises a question about 'Judges in England and Wales tell[ing] three contradictory stories about the relationship between autonomy and mental capacity.' Paul Skowron states that 'any reform attempting to remake the law around that one concept can be expected to fail.' He argues on how logically judges in England and Wales utilize the terms 'autonomy' and 'mental capacity' in a specific case, which resulted in the three contradictory stories related to the same terms. Therefore, he analogically opines that one concept cannot unify the law and people must accept 'complexity.' Paul Skowron, 'The Relationship between Autonomy and Adult Mental Capacity in the Law of England and Wales' (2019) 27(1) *Medical Law Review* 32, 58.

[157.] Mary Donnelly, 'Changing Values and Growing Expectations' (2017) 70(1) *Current Legal Problems* 305–36, 335.

[158.] Safeguarding is 'a term we use to describe how we protect adults or children from abuse or neglect.' UK Gov., *Policy Paper SD8: Office of the Public Guardian Safeguarding Policy* (Web Page, January 11, 2022) <https://www.gov.uk/government/publications/safeguarding-policy-protecting-vulnerable-adults/sd8-opgs-safeguarding-policy>.

[159.] 'All adults at risk of harm have right to be safe and protected.' Scottish Government, *Social Care: Adult Support and Protection* (Web Page, n/a) <https://www.gov.scot/policies/social-care/adult-support-and-protection/>.

[160.] Robert M. Gordon, 'Adult Protection Legislation in Canada: Models, Issues, and Problems' (2001) 24(2–3) *International Journal of Law and Psychiatry* 117, 134.

[161.] Holly Ramsey-Klawsnik, 'Understanding and Working with Adult Protective Services' (Online, May 2018) <https://www.advancingstates.org/hcbs/article/understanding-and-working-adult-protective-services>; Adult Protective

governments. Similarly, some European countries, including Switzerland and Austria, amended their civil codes in 2013 and 2017, respectively, abolishing the terminology of 'guardian' and 'guardianship' and renaming these sections as 'adult protection law.'[162] These changes explicitly reflect a shift from traditional guardianship models to frameworks aimed at protection. In Austria, the *Erwachsenenschutzrecht* (adult protection law)[163] is also positioned as a legal instrument for preventing elder abuse, aligning with the human rights approach seen in common law jurisdictions. Thus, despite differences in legal traditions, both common law and civil law jurisdictions have coincidentally adopted similar legislative concepts centered around 'adult protection.'

In light of these common legal developments and the foundation of legal advocacy discussed in Chapter 1,[164] the systems of adult guardianship, SDM, and safeguards against elder abuse can be understood as forming a complementary framework for adult protection. In this study, this collective framework is referred to as 'adult support and protection legislation.'[165] It is emphasized that such legislation, mainly developed in common law jurisdictions, reflects a human rights-based approach to safeguarding vulnerable adults.

The legal transformations observed in some developed countries represent a shift from traditional guardianship law toward the development of adult support and protection legislation. As noted by Teruaki Tayama in Chapter 1,[166] this trend suggests the potential for future civil law reform in Japan, moving from a guardianship-centered system to an adult protection model. Building upon this perspective, the next chapter will review country-specific legal developments, focusing on the concept of adult support and protection.

Services (APS), Law Enforcement, and the Courts are the systems charged with addressing the abuse, but there is no uniformity in their roles and little coordination between the system providers. Georgia J. Anetzberger and Morgan R. Thurston, 'Addressing Guardianship Abuse: The Roles of Adult Protective Services, Law Enforcement, and the Courts' (Conference paper at the Fourth National Guardianship Summit in New York on May 10–14, 2021).

[162.] Refers to Section 3.2 (2), 'Switzerland Adult Protection Law' and Section 3.2 (3), 'Austrian Adult Protection Law.'

[163.] Refers to the Austrian Federal Ministry of Justice, *The New Adult Protection Law* (Brochure in English, 2018) <https://www.bmj.gv.at/dam/jcr:e74fdd3a-19a3-4489-9918-cf2c1d0c720c/justiz_kurzbroschuere_erwschg_en_v2.pdf>.

[164.] Refers to Section 1.1.3, 'Research Framework Based on Legal Advocacy.'

[165.] Shih-Ning Then, 'Evolution and Innovation in Guardianship Laws: Assisted Decision-Making' (2013) 35 *Sydney Law Review* 133–66, 145–7; Lise Barry and Susannah Sage-Jacobson, 'Human Rights, Older People and Decision Making in Australia' (2015) 9 *Elder Law Review* 1–21, 1.

[166.] Refers to Section 1.1.1 (1) g, 'Future Developments.'

2.4 Summary: A Good Balance of Vulnerability and Autonomy

As Japan's population continues to age, the proportion of adults with diminished mental capacity—including those living with dementia—is steadily increasing. In 2025, this group constitutes approximately 10 per cent of the national population. Given this demographic shift, such individuals can no longer be treated as a marginal minority or legal exception under the Civil Code; rather, they must be fully recognized as citizens with rights and entitlements. The concept of vulnerability offers important insights into the legal status of adults with insufficient mental capacity. From the vulnerability approach, a normative view emerges that adults at risk of harm must be afforded legal and policy protection, particularly from abuse and neglect. This approach underpins the idea of safeguarding law, in which the state bears a responsibility to uphold the human rights of vulnerable adults by implementing appropriate legislative and policy frameworks. It reframes vulnerability not as a personal deficiency but as a condition that demands a structural, rights-based response.

In contrast, the capability approach emphasizes individual autonomy by focusing on a person's capacity and freedom to make decisions according to their own values and preferences. It recognizes the diversity of individuals and promotes respect for their agency. While autonomy is a foundational value in modern liberal democracies, it may be justifiably limited when balanced against broader public interests. In sensitive situations such as end-of-life decision-making, the concept of relational autonomy—which takes into account the social context of the individual, including the influence of family and close relationships—can offer a more nuanced understanding of autonomy. Although the vulnerability and capability approach both aim to safeguard human rights, they do so from different philosophical standpoints—one universal and protective, and the other individual and empowering. Therefore, both frameworks are valuable for analyzing key legal and ethical challenges in supporting adults with diminished capacity. Theoretical balance between these two perspectives is essential. When autonomy is understood in relational terms, a more equitable and context-sensitive balance between autonomy and vulnerability can be achieved. Relational autonomy, although not yet an established doctrine, holds promise in addressing the limitations of a strictly individualistic conception of autonomy.

In alignment with the values and obligations enshrined in the CRPD, there is a growing international consensus in favor of restricting the use of guardianship and promoting SDM. Across various legal traditions—both common law and civil law jurisdictions—countries are converging on similar legislative terminology such as 'adult protection.' These developments suggest that adult guardianship, SDM, and elder abuse prevention measures should not be treated as separate legal mechanisms, but rather as integrated elements of a comprehensive legal framework tailored to the needs of persons with cognitive impairments. This study refers to such an integrated legal framework as adult support and protection legislation. While the concept has its origins in common law jurisdictions—particularly those that emphasize a human rights-based approach to safeguarding—its principles are increasingly influencing reforms in civil law countries as well. The observed legal transformations across various developed nations reflect a shared commitment to building cohesive systems of support for vulnerable adults. Accordingly, the next chapter will undertake a comparative analysis of legislative developments in select jurisdictions.

CHAPTER 3

Adult Support and Protection
in the International Context

This chapter examines the emerging legislative trends in adult support and protection across Europe and common law jurisdictions. By analyzing key legal instruments, such as the 2000 Hague Convention and subsequent national reforms, the chapter identifies common principles—respect for autonomy, the adoption of supported decision-making (SDM), the use of less restrictive alternatives, and the balance between state duties and individual rights. These shared elements form the foundation for defining a comprehensive adult support and protection legislative framework.

3.1 Introduction

This chapter reviews adult support and protection legislation in the international context.[1] For this purpose, the chapter examines the research question: 'How do developed countries/areas cope with the adult guardianship system, SDM, and safeguards against elder abuse, and what are the implications of a legal concept of adult support and protection legislation?'

There is a Japanese civil law scholar's unique view that, referring to the German and the Switzerland civil laws, adult protection law is defined as 'the collective legal regulations, including the protection and care of adults with health problems or disabilities that prevent them from engaging in legal transactions without the assistance of a third party.'[2] There is no clear legal definition of adult support

---

[1] This chapter is an updated version of the previously published article by the author: 'The Ageing and Adult Protection Legislative System: A Comparative Law Study' (2019) 9(1) *The International Journal of Aging and Social Change* 53, 69 <https://doi.org/10.18848/2576-5310/CGP/v09i01/53-69>.

[2] Teruaki Tayama, 'History, Current Status, and Future of the Adult Guardianship System in Japan' (2020) (Keynote Speech at the 17th Annual Academic Conference of Japan Adult Guardianship Law Corporate Association (JAGA) held in Tokyo on November 14, 2020) 18 *Adult Guardianship Study* 18, 27 (in Japanese).

and protection.[3] To clarify the definition of adult support and protection, reform of laws and legislation related to adult support and protection will be reviewed.

It can be assumed that legislation related to adult support and protection being developed in Europe, Australia, Canada, and the US may share some common characteristics that constitute the legal framework. In this chapter, such common characteristics will be clarified by reviewing the legislations concerned. The scope of countries/areas to be examined is considered in the following manner. Japan is regarded as having the most advanced adult guardianship system and responses to abuse and abuse prevention legislation in Asia; for this reason, other Asian countries are not referenced. Developed countries outside Asia are cited, however, considering the geographic balance of the countries in question, Canada has not been included, but the US and Australia have been included in this chapter. Below, comparative law studies of the 2000 Protection of Adults Convention and the following developments and the relevant policies and reforms to adult support and protection legislation in developed countries, such as Switzerland, Austria, Scotland, the US, and Australia will be reviewed.

3.2 A Comparative Law Study in the International Context

(1) 2000 Protection of Adults Convention and the Following Developments

a. 2000 Protection of Adults Convention

The Convention on International Protection of Adults, now called The Hague Convention of 13 January 2000 on the International Protection of Adults (here-inafter referred to as '2000 Protection of Adults Convention'), was adopted in 2000 by the Hague Conference on Private International Law.[4] This Conference was based on the recent tendency for mobility, particularly of older people to live in foreign countries. The 2000 Protection of Adults Convention 'applies to the protection in international situations of adults who, because of an impairment or insufficiency of their personal faculties, are not able to protect their interests'

[3.] No common methods nor definition of the terms regarding 'adult safeguarding' are established among countries, such as Scotland, England, Northern Ireland, Canada, and Australia. This implication can be applied to the adult support and protection. Sarah Donnelly et al, *Adult Safeguarding Legislation and Policy Rapid Realist Literature Review* (Health Service Executive, National Safeguarding Office and Trigraph Limited, 2017) 176; Lorna Montgomery et al, 'Implications of Divergences in Adult Protection Legislation' (2016) 18(3) *Journal of Adult Protection* 1, 16.

[4.] Refers to the Hague Conference on International Private Law (HCCH), *The Hague Convention of 13 January 2000 on the International Protection of Adults* (Web Page, January 13, 2000) <https://www.hcch.net/en/instruments/conventions/full-text/?cid=71>.

(Paragraph 1, Article 1). It regulates the judicial or administrative authorities of the contracting state in which the adults, i.e., those who have reached age 18 (Paragraph 1, Article 2), have their habitual residence, regulates jurisdiction over the protection of the adult person and property (Paragraph 1, Article 5), regulates subordinate jurisdiction to the state of which the adult is a national (Article 7), and further regulates subordinate jurisdiction over where property of the adult is situated (Article 9).

It is understood that EU countries, which have eliminated border restrictions, have largely set the provisions of international private law within the EU, where citizens can freely mobilize and choose their residences. There are concerns about gaps in the protection of vulnerable adults in Europe, particularly for person and property due to the diversity of legal systems and limited accessions to the key international instrument.[5] The 2000 Protection of Adults Convention was adopted to adjust those gaps in the protection of vulnerable adults in Europe, particularly in cross-border situations.[6] However, the Convention has entered into force in fourteen European countries.[7] Therefore, this convention is accepted in a limited area.

b. Policies in Europe

In Europe, there are developments related to the protection of vulnerable adults. The Convention for the Protection of Human Rights and Fundamental Freedoms was adopted by the Council of Europe (1950). The judicial function of the European Court of Human Rights (ECHR) is centered around human rights protection. Under this umbrella, the Recommendation Rec (1999) 4 on Principles concerning the Legal Protection of Incapable Adults was adopted by the Council of Europe (the Committee of Ministers on 23 February 1999, at the 660th meeting of the Ministers' Deputies).[8] This is the recommendations on principles concerning the

---

[5.] Refers to the European Parliament, *Legislative Train-Protection of Vulnerable Adults* (Web Page, November 20, 2019) <https://www.europarl.europa.eu/legislative-train/theme-area-of-justice-and-fundamental-rights/file-protection-of-vulnerable-adults>.

[6.] The European Notarial Network open website with support from the European Commission for citizens on protective measures for the vulnerable and minors in twenty-two European countries that have civil law notarial system. European Notarial Network, *The Vulnerable in Europe* (Web Page, August 2022) <https://www.notariesofeurope.eu/en/citizens/vulnerables-in-europe/>.

[7.] The fourteen European countries are Austria, Belgium, Cyprus, Czech Republic, Estonia, Finland, France, Germany, Greece, Latvia, Monaco, Portugal, Switzerland, and the UK. Other five countries who have signed but have not ratified are Ireland, Italy, Luxemburg, the Netherlands, and Poland. Overheid.nl, *Verdrag Inzake de Internationale Bescherming van Volwassenen (Convention on the International Protection of Adults)* (Web Page, August 2022) <https://verdragenbank.overheid.nl/en/Verdrag/Details/009250>.

[8.] Refers to the Council of Europe, *Explanatory Memorandum/Recommendation Rec (1999) 4 on Principles Concerning the Legal Protection of Incapable Adults* (Web Page, February 23, 1999) <https://rm.coe.int/09000016805e302a>.

legal protection of incapable adults. The recommendation includes key principles, such as 'Principle 5—Necessity and subsidiarity,'[9] and indicates that 'any legislation addressing the problem of incapable adults should give a prominent place to these principles.' Then, the Recommendation CM/Rec (2009)11 of the Committee of Ministers to Member States on Principles concerning Continuing Power of Attorney and Advance Directives for Incapacity was adopted by the Council of Europe (the Committee of Ministers on 9 December 2009 at the 1073rd meeting of the Ministers' Deputies).[10] This is the recommendation of voluntary measures with respect to the principle of self-determination. Further studies regarding the principles of continuing powers of attorney, advance directives, and so on are ongoing. For example, a Scottish researcher Adrian D. Ward issued *Enabling Citizens to Plan for Incapacity*[11] in the Council of Europe.

In the EU, Article 25 (the rights of older people) and Article 26 (integration of persons with disabilities) of the Charter of Fundamental Rights of the European Union (2000/C 364/01) recognize and respect human rights of older people and persons with disabilities. In addition, the European Parliament under the EU created the research project 'Protect Vulnerable Adults—European Added Value Assessment'[12] and is considering the development of adult protection policies for vulnerable adults.[13] In December 2020, a European NGO, Alzheimer Europe published a report entitled *Legal Capacity and Decision Making: The Ethical Implications of Lack of Legal Capacity on the Lives of People with*

[9.] The 'principle of subsidiary' ensures that in deciding whether a measure is necessary, account should be taken of any less-formal arrangements that might be made or used, and of any assistance that might be provided by family members, public authorities, or other means. The principle of subsidiarity can be said to refer to the least restrictive alternative. Council of Europe, *Principles Concerning the Legal Protection of Incapable Adults* (Web Page, February 23, 1999) <https://rm.coe.int/09000016805e302a>; Teruaki Tayama, *Commentary on Adult Guardianship System* (Sanseido, 2nd ed, 2016) 57 and 136 (in Japanese).

[10.] Refers to the Council of Europe, *Recommendation CM/Rec (2009) 11 and Explanatory Memorandum: Principles Concerning Continuing Powers of Attorney and Advance Directives for Incapacity* (Web Page, December 9, 2009) <https://rm.coe.int/CoERMPublicCommonSearchServices/DisplayDCTMContent?documentId=090000168070965f>.

[11.] Adrian D. Ward, *Enabling Citizens to Plan for Incapacity* (Council of Europe, Online, 2017) <https://rm.coe.int/cdcj-2017-2e-final-rapport-vs-21-06-2018/16808b64ae>.

[12.] Refers to the European Parliamentary Research Service (EPRS), *Protection of Vulnerable Adults—European Added Value Assessment* (EPRS, Online, November 11, 2016) <https://doi.org/10.2861/664256>.

[13.] A vulnerable adult is defined 'a person who has reached the age of 18 years and who, by reason of an impairment or insufficiency of his or her personal faculties, is not in a position to protect his or her interests (personal affairs and/or personal property, whether temporarily or permanently)' in the resolution of European Parliament. European Parliament, *Resolution of 1 June 2017 with Recommendations to the Commission on the Protection of Vulnerable Adults* (Web Page, June 1, 2017) <https://www.europarl.europa.eu/doceo/document/TA-8-2017-0235_EN.html?redirect>.

Dementia[14] of a study funded under an operating grant from the EU's Health Program (2014–2020).[15]

Some content of the report is cited as follows:[16]

> *We believe that such [an effective and fair] system should also incorporate substitute decision-making to the extent that this is necessary, proportionate, and carry out in an ethical manner. We therefore promote the combined supported decision-making model developed by Scholten and Gather.[17] This incorporates substitute decision-making, if deemed necessary.*

This model combines SDM with competence assessment, which will be discussed further in Chapter 5.[18] Below, the legislation of individual countries is reviewed, bearing the European regional legislative and policy frameworks in mind.

(2) Switzerland Adult Protection Law

The CRPD was adopted in 2006 and, as of January 2022, 164 state parties have signed, and 192 state parties have ratified or accepted it.[19] There has been a move to amend domestic law to establish an effective relationship between the CRPD and the adult guardianship system. The enactment of the Law on the Protection of Adults, based on Switzerland's amendments to its civil code in January 2013, could be taken as a case of adult protection legislation. Switzerland's adult protection law provides the following six main points:[20] (i) Make decisions using

---

[14.] Refers to the Alzheimer Europe, *Legal Capacity and Decision Making: The Ethical Implications of Lack of Legal Capacity on the Lives of People with Dementia* (Dementia in Europe Ethics Report 2000) (Alzheimer Europe, December 2020) <https://www.alzheimer-europe.org/resources/publications/2020-alzheimer-europe-report-legal-capacity-and-decision-making-ethical>.

[15.] Alzheimer Europe is 'a non-profit non-governmental organization (NGO) that aims to be a voice of people with dementia and their carers, which make dementia a European priority, promote a rights-based approach to dementia, support dementia research, and strengthen the European dementia movement.' Alzheimer Europe (Web Page, June 2022)<https://www.alzheimer-europe.org/resources/publications/annual-and-financial-report-2020>.

[16.] Alzheimer Europe, *Legal Capacity and Decision Making: The Ethical Implications of Lack of Legal Capacity on the Lives of People with Dementia: Summary Report* (Web Page, December 2020) 5 <https://www.alzheimer-europe.org/sites/default/files/2021-11/Alzheimer%20Europe%20summary%20on%202020%20Report%20Legal%20capacity%20and%20decision%20making%20summary.pdf>; Alzheimer Europe (n 14) 22–3.

[17.] Scholten and Gather predict 'adverse consequences of CRPD Article 12 for the persons with mental disabilities' and propose the combined SDM model. Matthé Scholten and J. Gather, 'Adverse Consequences of Article 12 of the UN Convention on the Rights of Persons with Disabilities for Persons with Mental Disabilities and an Alternative Way Forward' (2018) 44 *Journal of Medical Ethics* 226, 233.

[18.] Refers to Section 5.2.2, 'Combined Models of Guardianship and Supported Decision-Making.'

[19.] Refers to the UN, *Convention on the Rights of Persons with Disabilities (CRPD)* (Web Page, May 6, 2022) <https://www.un.org/development/desa/disabilities/convention-on-the-rights-of-persons-with-disabilities.html#:~:text=Ratifications%2FAccessions%3A%20184https://>.

[20.] Ingeborg Schwenzer and Tomie Keller, 'A New Law for the Protection of Adults' in Bill Atkin (ed), *The International Survey of Family Law* (Jordan Publishing Limited, 2013) 375, 386.

tailor-made measures for an adult who needs assistance; (ii) as much as possible, do not limit the human rights of the individual; (iii) prohibit the use of negative terms such as 'adult guardianship'; (iv) establish the Child and Adult Protection Authority (CAPA) in the cantons; (v) recognize the right of a proxy for a spouse or a registered partner to consult with a doctor about medical treatment for the principal; and (vi) approve advance directive of terminal medical care and the preparation of a living will in advance, before mental capacity becomes insufficient, to respect right to self-determination of an adult by himself/herself. Amendments to the civil code in Switzerland abolished the framework of the traditional adult guardianship system that restricted the principal's ability.[21] The current adult protection system in Switzerland can be assumed to be an advanced legislative system that theoretically respects autonomy, right to self-determination, and normalization.[22] In practice, it is essential for the public agencies, Child and Adult Protection Authority ('CAPA') in the cantons to carefully implement measures to protect vulnerable people to reflect the aim of the law in a more professional and interdisciplinary way.[23]

(3) Austrian Adult Protection Law

a. Adult Protection Law

A move to establish a part of adult protection legislation that theoretically respects autonomy, right to self-determination and support rather than representation is also seen in Austria.[24] Austria amended its civil code and enacted the Adult Protection Law in March 2017, which came into force in

---

[21.] Ibid.

[22.] Philippe Meier, 'The Swiss 2013 Guardianship Law Reform—A Presentation and A First Assessment in the Light of the Convention on the Rights of Persons with Disabilities' (Online, 2016) 10 *Elder Law Review* <https://www.westernsydney.edu.au/__data/assets/pdf_file/0018/1161513/The_Swiss_2013_Guardianship_Law_Reform_-_Philippe_Meier.pdf>.

[23.] A critical view on the CAPA operation for minors in Zurich: Martina Koch, Esteban Piñeiro and Nathalie Pasche, '"Wir sind ein Dienst, keine Behörde." Multiple institutionelle Logiken in einem Schweizer Jugendamt—Ein ethnografisches Fallbeispiel aus der street-level bureaucracy' ('We Are a Service, Not an Authority': Multiple Institutional Logics in a Swiss Youth Welfare Office. An Ethnographic Case Study from Street-Level Bureaucracy) (2019) 20(2) *Forum: Qualitative Sozialforschung* Article 21.

[24.] Hitomi Aoki summarizes the principles of the Austrian Adult Protection Law: (i) respect of autonomy and priority on support (ii) support rather than representation, (iii) maintenance of representation, (iv) impact of personal intention on the appointment of an agency, and (v) duties of the Adult Protection Association. Hitomi Aoki, 'From Representation to Support: A Consideration of Austrian Law Reform (1)' (2019) 26(1) *Toin Law Review* 53–81, 58–61 (in Japanese).

July 2018. Four types of legal measures defined by the Adult Protection Law are as follows:[25]

(i) Enduring Power of Attorney[26] (hereinafter referred to as 'EPA'; *Vorsorgevollmacht*): It is necessary for an adult to have full capacity to conclude an EPA with or without the involvement of an adult protection association and to register it at the Central Austrian Representation Register (*Österreichisches Zentrales Vertretungsregister*, ÖZVV). An EPA takes effect when an adult cannot decide by himself/herself, and this fact is registered in the Central Austrian Representation Register. The court can only be involved in limited cases: (1) if the adult and the attorney disagree regarding medical treatment, (2) if the residence of the adult shall be relocated abroad, and (3) if the adult has ordered in the EPA that the court should approve the attorneys' decisions about important economic matters.

(ii) Elective Representation of Adults (*Gewählte Erwachsenenvertretung*, newly introduced as a special form of EPA): Even if an adult has no longer full capacity, he/she can conclude an elective representation agreement to appoint a representative out of his/her relatives or close friends. It is necessary for an adult to understand the consequences of appointing a representative, at least in broad terms, and act accordingly. This scheme requires entry in the register and is subject to supervision of the courts. The adoption of this scheme results is based on a decision taken by the individual represented, and it is valid indefinitely. This scheme is considered after the Representation Agreement available in the British Columbia province of Canada.[27]

(iii) Statutory Representation of Adults (*Gesetzliche Erwachsenenvertretung*, newly introduced due to abolition of EPA of relatives): Statutory representation of adults should be applied to all matters that an adult cannot handle by himself/herself, particularly all medical and nursing care matters as

---

[25.] Refers to the Austrian Federal Ministry of Justice, *The New Adult Protection Law* (Brochure in English, 2018) <https://www.bmj.gv.at/dam/jcr:e74fdd3a-19a3-4489-9918-cf2c1d0c720c/justiz_kurzbroschuere_erwschg_en_v2.pdf>; Michael Ludwig Ganner, 'The New Austrian Adult Protection Law of 2018.' (2020) 41 JULGAR 175–98. <https://julgar.pt/wp-content/uploads/2020/05/JULGAR41-08-MG.pdf>; Tomoko Fukuda, 'Implications of Austrian New Adult Guardianship System' in Akihisa Shibuya et al. (eds), *Practice and Promotion of Adult Guardianship and Civil Trust* (Nihon Kajo Publishing Co., Ltd., 2021) 465–77 (in Japanese).

[26.] An EPA is a legal document that lets the donor appoint one or more people, known as attorneys, in register to help make decisions or to make decisions on their behalf about their property or money.

[27.] The *Representation Agreement Act 1996* is the first Canadian legislation in the British Columbia province to establish a comprehensive framework for SDM. See British Columbia, *Incapacity Planning* (Web Page, n/a) <https://www2.gov.bc.ca/gov/content/health/managing-your-health/incapacity-planning>; Canadian Centre for Elder Law (CCEL), *Study Paper on Inclusive Investing: Respecting the Rights of Vulnerable Investors through Supported Decision-Making* (Canadian Centre for Elder Law, May 5, 2021) 73–7 <https://ssrn.com/abstract=3855139>.

well as financial matters. This scheme requires entry in the register and is subject to supervision of the courts. The representation authority is reviewed after three years when in principle it expires unless otherwise necessary.

(iv)   Court-Appointed Representation of Adults (*Gerichtliche Erwachsenen-vertretung*, newly introduced due to abolition of the guardianship system): Court-appointed representation of adult is supposed to govern adult representation by a third party as a last resort for some specific matters, such as important property management as well as for all medical and nursing care matters. The law does not permit a court-appointed representative to manage all a person's affairs. The representation scheme ceases to apply when the specific matter has been dealt with, or after three years, whichever is sooner.

b. Clearing and Registration

Under the adult protection law, some administrative procedures have been implemented by Adult Protection Associations (*VertretungsNetz*),[28] a group of NPOs that mainly provide a mandatory 'clearing' function ordered by the Federal Ministry of Justice of Austria. Adult Protection Associations (*VertretungsNetz*) are associations in Austria which advocate the federal rights of people with mental illness or intellectual impairment.[29] The 'clearing' function offers several benefits for the Ministry of Justice and the users.[30] First, the applicants may consult with the Adult Protection Associations more informally than with the courts. Second, the 'clearing' function led to a six-per cent decrease in number of court-appointed representation petitions in 2018/2019 compared to the previous year. Third, 'clearing' has replaced court-appointed representation with less restrictive measures, i.e., elective representation or statutory representation. The statistics show that 47 per cent of the applicants replaced measures in the first year 2018/2019. Fourth, the replacement by 'clearing' may contribute to administrative and financial rationalization of the courts. The brochure *The New Adult Protection Law* indicates the background of the Law reform is due to some systemic problems in the previous system that an

---

[28.] The Adult Protection Associations (*VertretungsNetz*) operate twenty-nine offices in Austrian federal states except Vorarlberg. Approximately 700 employees work for the Associations and 295 employees work for court-appointed representatives or carry out clearing for adult protection. The Associations, as a not-for-profit entity, provide public services to people. The Federal Ministry of Justice provides subsidy equivalent to 90 per cent of the administrative expenses of the Associations. A manager of the Associations has contributed to the law reform study group as a member, which was organized by Peter Barth, the Federal Ministry of Justice (i.e., Peter Barth, 'Reform of the Austrian Sachwalter Law' (Conference material at the 4th WCAG2016 held in Berlin on September 14–17, 2016)). From the interview of the Adult Protection Associations by the author in Vienna on September 17, 2019.

[29.] Hitomi Aoki, 'Function of the Subsidiarity Principle in the Adult Guardianship System' (2016) 8 *Bulletin of Waseda University Institute of Advanced Study* 5–25, 19–21 (in Japanese).

[30.] From the interview of Michael Ludwig Ganner by the author in Innsbruck on September 18, 2019.

increase of guardianship cases leads to the shortage of quality guardians and no attractive alternative measures available than guardianship.[31]

Any of the above four legal measures must be recorded in the Central Austrian Representation Register that is in the custody of the civil law notaries. The total number of Austrian adult protection registrations as in August 2019 was 177,162, which was equivalent to 2.0 per cent of the national population of Austria (i.e., approximately 8.6 million) and could be assumed to be so high.[32] According to an empirical research analysis, carried out using a questionnaire survey in 2019, both 'clearing' and the national register system were appreciated by the stakeholders, such as courts, associations, lawyers/notaries, and adult guardians.[33] Thus, those outsourcing methods to the Adult Protection Associations and the Notaries by law can contribute to positive results of the adult protection law. As a rule, lawyers or the Notaries can act as representatives for a maximum of fifteen principals with mental or intellectual disabilities. The idea of the Austrian adult protection law can be considered reasonable for meeting the value of the CRPD, involving in the Adult Protection Associations and the Notaries. The issue is how other persons than experts of adult protection will understand the adult protection law scheme, including medical practitioners, schoolteachers, church officials, local politicians, who may influence people in a daily life.[34]

(4) Scottish Mental Health Law Review

a. Independent Review of Mental Health Law

Scotland is in the process of reviewing the laws and policies related to mental health, capacity, and adult protection under the name 'Independent Review of Mental Health Law' (hereinafter referred to as 'Independent Review').[35] On March 19, 2019, the Scottish Government announced an overarching review of the mental health legislative framework and commissioned the Scottish Mental

---

[31.] Refers to the Austrian Federal Ministry of Justice, *The New Adult Protection Law* (Brochure in English, 2018) 2–3.

[32.] According to the Austrian Chamber of Civil Law Notaries as of August 31, 2019, the breakdown of the 177, 162 Austrian adult protection registers was as follows: EPA (142,937), Elective Representation (1,812), Statutory Representation (9,114), Court-Appoint Representation (6,374), Interim Representation (2,642), Positive Adult Representative available (13,528), Negative Adult Representative available (224), and Preliminary Objection (531).

[33.] Michael Ludwig Ganner, *Umfrage zum Erwachsenenschutzgesetzin* (Adult Protection Law Survey) (University of Innsbruck, Online, December 2, 2019) (in German) <https://www.uibk.ac.at/rtf/>.

[34.] From the interview of Michael Ludwig Ganner by the author in Innsbruck on September 18, 2019.

[35.] Scottish Parliament, *Mental Health and Adults with Incapacity Law in Scotland—What Next?* (Web Page, June 13, 2021) <https://spice-spotlight.scot/2021/06/23/mental-health-and-adults-with-incapacity-law-in-scotland-what-next/>.

Health Law Review (hereinafter referred to as 'Scottish Review').[36] The intention of the Government of Scotland is mentioned in the 'terms of reference' to the Scottish Review.[37] The work of the Scottish Review is due in September 2022, with a final report and recommendations to be submitted to the Minister for Mental Wellbeing and Social Care (Scotland).

The principal aim of the review is 'to improve the rights and protections of persons who may be subject to the existing provisions of mental health, incapacity or adult support and protection legislation as a consequence of having a mental disorder and remove barriers to those caring for their health and welfare.'[38] For this principal aim, comprehensive reform is necessitated by the decision of the Cabinet of Scotland that deliberations are important to renovate the current system and come up with a more comprehensive package that will include such measures as mental health care, aged care, advance directives, and medical decision-making in intensive care situations.[39] Two review processes are ongoing under an umbrella of the Independent Review, namely the one is that the Government of Scotland reviews 'aspects of mental health legislation to strengthen rights and protections of people who are impacted by the legislation and to ensure it reflects people's rights under the UN CRPD and the European Convention on Human Rights,'[40] and the other is that a Joint Working Group of the Law Society of Scotland reviews law reform proposals.[41]

The scope of mental health law as an umbrella term refers to the key legislation to be reviewed, namely the Mental Health (Care and Treatment) (Scotland) Act 2003 (hereinafter referred to as '2003 Act'), the Adults with Incapacity (Scotland) Act 2000[42] (hereinafter referred to as 'AWIA'), and the Adult Support and Protection (Scotland) Act 2007 (hereinafter referred to as 'ASPA'). In Scotland,

---

[36] Law Society of Scotland, *Mental Health: A Blueprint for Reform* (Web Page, December 12, 2022) <https://www. lawscot.org.uk/members/journal/issues/vol-67-issue-12/mental-health-a-blueprint-for-reform/#:~:text=The%20 Review%20argues%20that%20the,rights%20of%20a%20particular%20group>.

[37] Refers to the Scottish Government, *Review of Mental Health Law in Scotland* (Web Page, May 2020) <https:// consult.gov.scot/mental-health-law-secretariat/review-of-mental-health-law-in-scotland/>.

[38] Ibid.

[39] Refers to the Scottish Government, *Mental Health Strategy: 2017–2027* (Web Page, March 30, 2017) <https:// www.gov.scot/publications/mental-health-strategy-2017-2027/>.

[40] Scottish Parliament (n 35).

[41] From email correspondence between Adrian D. Ward and the author on July 27, 2021; Law Society of Scotland, *Reforms Must Ensure that the Law Does Not Discriminate Against People Who Do Not Have a Diagnosed Mental Illness* (Web Page, June 6, 2022) <https://www.lawscot.org.uk/news-and-events/law-society-news/ mental-health-law-review-response/>.

[42] Section 1(6) of the AWI stipulates 'incapable' means incapable of—(a) acting; or (b) making decisions; or (c) communicating decisions; or (d) understanding decisions; or (e) retaining the memory of decisions, as mentioned in any provision of this Act, by reason of mental disorder or of inability to communicate because of physical disability; but a person shall not fall within definition by reason only of a lack of deficiency in a faculty of

the safeguarding of vulnerable adults at risk is established by these three legisla-tions.[43] The purpose of each law is summarized as follows:[44] (a) the purpose of the 2003 Act has historically been (at least since 1960) to authorize and regulate compulsory care and treatment for mental disorder, where the person's ability to make a treatment decision is compromised by the mental disorder; (b) the purpose of the AWIA is to allow people whose impairments mean they cannot safely take actions or make decisions involving their finance, welfare or medical treatment to have this done for them; (c) the purpose of the ASPA is to provide a set of short-term measures to protect people who, because of impairment or circumstances, may be vulnerable to abuse.[45]

The Scottish Review is chaired by John Scott QC who was appointed by the Government of Scotland in May 2019. The chair John Scott states in the In-terim Report July 2021 that 'the human rights-based approach we have adopted means that mental health law should in future have a significantly wide scope, and that has an important impact on the principles which should govern the legislation.'[46] The Health and Social Care Alliance (hereinafter referred to as 'the ALLIANCE') is established as the national third sector intermediary for a range of health and social care organizations.[47] The ALLIANCE has a mem-bership of over 3,000 various types of health and social care organizations and is a working partner of the Government of Scotland under the Memorandum of Understanding. This partnership between the Government and Scotland and the ALLIANCE means that the Scottish Review is based on the participation of the civil society at large.

Following deliberations lasting less than three years, which commenced in May 2019, the Study Group published its primary conclusions in March 2022 and sought public feedback. In May of the same year, the Study Group issued a further call for public commentary on advance directives, independent advocacy, and the intersection of criminal and mental health law (forensic

---

communication if that lack or deficiency can be made good by human or mechanical aid (whether of an interpretive nature or otherwise); and 'incapacity' shall be constructed accordingly.

[43] The British Association for Counselling and Psychotherapy (BACP) report states that 'there are several pieces of legislation [in Scotland], which are particularly relevant to people who may be vulnerable by reason of mental illness, incapacity, infirmity, or disability.' Adrian D. Ward et al, *Safeguarding Vulnerable Adults in Scotland* (British Association for Counselling and Psychotherapy (BACP), 2018) 7.

[44] Refers to the Scottish Mental Health Law Review, *Interim Report July 2021*, 15–16.

[45] Ailsa Stewart remarks that the intervention orders of the ASPA have been used 'sparingly and only where serious harm has been perpetrated.' Ailsa E. Stewart, 'The Implementation of Adult Support and Protection (Scotland) Act (2007)' (Doctoral dissertation, University of Glasgow, 2016).

[46] Refers to the Scottish Mental Health Law Review (n 44) 13; The author confirmed with John Scott at the panel of the WCAC2022 in Edinburg (June 6, 2022) that it has not been decided whether the mental health law review would lead to a unified legislation, gradual revision of individual laws, or simultaneous revision of multiple laws.

[47] Refers to the ALLIANCE, *ALLIANCE* (Web Page, February 2022) <https://www.alliance-scotland.org.uk/>.

issues).[48] After consolidating all responses, the Study Group finalized its final report and submitted it to the Minister of Mental Welfare and Social Services on 30 September 2022. The Report is a comprehensive document, spanning approximately 900 pages and containing 200 proposals.[49] Following its submission to the Government of Scotland, the process of law reform and/or legislation will proceed in the Parliament of Scotland. In response, the Government of Scotland announced the establishment of a new Mental Health and Capacity Reform Programme to coordinate and promote further changes and improvements over time, in line with the ambitions set out in the Report.[50]

b. Review of the *Adults with Incapacity (Scotland) Act 2000*

Prior to the Mental Health Independent Review, the Government of Scotland conducted a review of the AWIA in 2018.[51] The proposed amendments to the AWIA sought to address emerging social needs that had arisen since its implementation, particularly in light of the Convention on the Rights of Persons with Disabilities (CRPD) and relevant case law from the European Court of Human Rights (ECHR). These amendments aimed at establishing a more holistic system of support that respects the will and preferences of adults over the age of 16, in a manner that is non-discriminatory and consistent with human rights principles.

The key reform proposals outlined in January 2018 included the following:[52]

(i)   Strengthening the statutory principles to reflect the need for support in exercising legal capacity;

(ii)   Encouraging the use of powers of attorney;

(iii) Introducing a graded guardianship system (grades 1 to 3);[53]

---

[48] Refers to the Scottish Mental Health Law Review, *Consultation June 2022 – Additional Proposals* (Web Page, 2022) <https://consult.gov.scot/mental-health-law-secretariat/forensic-proposals/>.

[49] Scottish Mental Health Law Review, *Final Report* (Web Page, September 30, 2022) <https://webarchive.nrscotland.gov.uk/20230327160310/https://www.mentalhealthlawreview.scot/>.

[50] Scottish Government, *Scottish Mental Health Law Review: Our Response* (Web Page, June 28, 2023) <https://www.gov.scot/publications/scottish-mental-health-law-review-response/>.

[51] Refers to the Government of Scotland, *Adults with Incapacity (Scotland) Act 2000: Proposals for Reform* (Web Page, January 13, 2018) <https://www.gov.scot/publications/adults-incapacity-scotland-act-2000-proposals-reform/pages/2/>.

[52] Ibid.

[53] Refers to the Government of Scotland (n 51) 27. The proposal in legal revision 'graded guardianship,' which aims to classify guardianship into grades 1–3, was originally proposed by the Office of the Public Guardian. Grade 1–3 seems to be similar to the statutory guardianship types in Japan, i.e., assistance, curatorship, and guardianship.

(iv)   Establishing a dedicated judicial forum for AWIA-related cases;

(v)   Creating a short-term placement order;

(vi)   Introducing the right of appeal against residential placements or restrictions within placements; and

(vii) Amending the authorization process for medical treatment.

The Scottish Government invited public consultation from January to April 2018 and received 317 written submissions (253 of which were made publicly available online) from individuals and institutions.[54] Based on these responses and subsequent survey findings, the working committee determined that further deliberation was necessary, with a view to comprehensive law reform.[55] This constituted a political decision, and as a result, the AWIA review was incorporated into the broader Independent Review.

Currently, Scotland's adult protection framework allows for public intervention on behalf of adults at risk of harm, not merely as a rescue mechanism.[56] The legislation provides for three types of protection orders—assessment, removal, and banning—which must be granted by a sheriff during a court hearing, based on the civil standard of proof (balance of probabilities). Ongoing discussions are expected to focus on how best to balance state responsibility with individual rights, particularly in the context of the Adult Support and Protection (Scotland) Act 2007 (ASPA) improvement plan (2019–2022) and its upcoming review.[57] The Scottish Review appears to envision the mental health legislation as a central framework, articulating core principles with broad applicability and close inter-linkages to the AWIA and ASPA, thereby facilitating a comprehensive system of adult support and protection. Accordingly, it may be said that the integration of adult guardianship, SDM, and adult protection is being gradually pursued under the Scottish Review. Nonetheless, it is anticipated that the complete legislative

---

[54.] Laura Gilman, *Adults with Incapacity* (The Scottish Parliament, SPICe Briefing, January 2022) 22–5.

[55.] Adrian D. Ward comments that a review of the 2003 Act will substantially broaden the scope of review and is likely to have some delay for completion. Adrian D. Ward, 'Scottish Government Review Extended and Delayed' (39 Essex Chamber, *Mental Capacity Report: Scotland Issue 93*, April 2019) <https://www.39essex.com/sites/default/files/Mental-Capacity-Report-April-2019-Scotland.pdf>.

[56.] Kathryn Jane Mackay, 'Adult Support and Protection (Scotland) Act 2007: Reflections on Developing Practice and Present-Day Challenges' (2017) 19(4) *Journal of Adult Protection* 187–98, 193; Fiona Sherwood-Johnson, 'Constructions of Vulnerability in Comparative Perspective: Scottish Protection Policies and the Trouble with "Adults at Risk"' (2013) 28(7) *Disability and Society* 908, 921; Jill Stavert, 'Supported Decision-Making and Paradigm Shifts: Word Play or Real Change?' (2021) 11 *Frontier in Psychiatry* 1, 9.

[57.] Refers to the Government of Scotland, *Adult Support and Protection: Improvement Plan 2019–2022* (Web Page, October 2, 2019) <https://www.gov.scot/publications/adult-support-protection-improvement-plan-2019-2022/pages/7/>.

reform process will span at least a decade.[58] The AWIA reform is expected to take place within 2025.[59]

(5) U.S. Guardianship and Supported Decision-Making Acts

a. Guardianship Law

In the US, adult guardianship and SDM are legislated in the states. This is in part because the Uniform Law Commission (hereinafter referred to as 'ULC'), which is known as the National Conference of Commissioners on Uniform State Laws and was established in 1892, drafted and released the Uniform Guardianship and Protective Proceedings Act (hereinafter referred to as 'UGPPA') in 1997. The UGPPA was updated to the Uniform Adult Guardianship and Protective Proceedings Jurisdiction Act (hereinafter referred to as 'UAGPPJA') in 2007 and to the Uniform Guardianship, Conservatorship, and Other Protective Arrangements Act[60] (hereinafter referred to as 'UGCOPAA') in 2017. These uniform acts have been endorsed by the National Guardianship Association (hereinafter referred to as 'NGA')[61] and the American Bar Association (hereinafter referred to as 'ABA'). Thus, each state lagging in legal development of adult guardianship law needed to address this issue. Since the release of the UGPPA, fifty states have completed legislation of the adult guardianship laws and are currently in the process of reforming the guardianship laws to meet the needs of citizens. Some seven states enacted the guardianship laws, following the UGPPA.[62] All but four states adopted the UAGPPJA, the four states that have not adopted the UAGPPJA are Florida, Kansas, Michigan, and Texas.[63] Two states, Maine (2018) and Washington (2019), enacted the guardianship laws, following the

---

[58.] Adrian D. Ward states that 'human rights must be translated into law, and law into practice.' Adrian D. Ward, 'Adult Incapacity Law: Visions for the Future Drawn from the Unfinished Story of a New Subject with A Long History' (2020) 26 *International Journal of Mental Health and Capacity Law* 13–34, 13.

[59.] Scottish Government, *Adults with Incapacity Amendment Act: Consultation Analysis Summary* (Web Page, January 27, 2025) <https://www.gov.scot/publications/adults-incapacity-amendment-act-summary-analysis-response-consultation/>.

[60.] Refers to the Uniform Law Commission (ULC), *Guardianship, Conservatorship, and Other Protective Arrangements Act* (Web Page, n/a) <https://www.uniformlaws.org/committees/community-home?CommunityKey=2eba8 654-8871-4905-ad38-aabbd573911c>.

[61.] Refers to the National Guardianship Association (NGA), *Homepage* (Web Page, n/a) <https://www.guardianship.org/>.

[62.] Refers to the ULC (n 60).

[63.] Refers to the ABA, *2021 Adult Guardianship Legislation Summary* (Online, December 2021) <https://www.americanbar.org/content/dam/aba/administrative/law_aging/2021-guardianship-leg-summry.pdf>.

UGCOPAA.[64] The unification of the guardianship law in the US cannot work as intended but is moving forward.

The guardianship system, however, has been criticized by researchers in the US mainly for its paternalistic characteristics.[65] The guardianship law has evolved through technical solutions, such as procedural safeguards at guardianship hearings and the least restrictive alternative principle advocated in the 1980s.[66] Alternatives to avoid guardianship have also been developed, such as durable power of attorney, trust, direct deposit and automatic payment, and system of representative payees to receive pension.[67] In fact, the guardianship activities have been handled by the state courts and the public remains unaware of what happens on-site during guardianship hearings. In recent years, given media reports of misconduct of adult guardians and excessive guardianship interventions,[68] voices have been raised calling for a court improvement program in guardianship or reform of the guardianship law, particularly to prevent misconduct of adult guardians.[69]

A bill for the Guardianship Accountability Act of 2021 was tabled in the federal Senate in September 2021 to require 'the Elder justice Coordinating Council to create a National Online Resource Center on guardianship for the publication of resources and data relating to court-determined adult guardianships' and

---

[64.] Weisbord and Horton states that disparity is seen in law development between the guardianship/SDM, as is modernized, and testamentary capacity, as is behind time, in the state of California, focusing on the legal system's treatment of individuals with disabilities in testamentary capacity claims. Reid K. Weisbord and David Horton, 'The Future of Testamentary Capacity' (Online, 2021) *Washington and Lee Law Review*, Forthcoming, Rutgers Law School Research Paper <https://ssrn.com/abstract=3964342>.

[65.] 'The fourteenth century English law principle *parens patriae*, which existed in the colonial time that the state played a role as a parent of the state, grew unexamined into the state law. By this principle, the state is allowed by law to protect through the court people who do not protect their interests by themselves. The state courts delegate this responsibility to guardians and supervise their activities. This mechanism may function paternalistic to principles.' Erica Wood, 'Recharging Adult Guardianship Reform: Six Current Paths Forward' (2016) 1(1) *Journal of Aging, Longevity, Law, and Policy* 8–53, 8–9 and 23; Nobuhito Yoshinaka, 'Origins of the Thought of Parens Patriae' (2006) 30(1) *Hiroshima Law Review* 29, 51 (in Japanese).

[66.] Roger B. Sherman, 'Guardianship: Time for a Reassessment' (1980) 49(3) *Fordham Law Review* 350, 378; Shirli Werner and Rachel Chabany, 'Guardianship Law Versus Supported Decision-Making Policies: Perceptions of Persons with Intellectual or Psychiatric Disabilities and Parents' (2015) 86(5) *The American Journal of Orthopsychiatry* 486, 499.

[67.] Alternatives to full guardianship are summarized in Table 1 of the article: Kahli Zietlow et al, 'Guardianship: A Medicolegal Review for Clinicians' (Online, 2022) 70(11) *Journal of the American Geriatrics Society* 3070–79 <https://doi.org/10.1111/jgs.17797>; Lawrence A. Frolik, 'How to Avoid Guardianship for Your Clients and Yourself!' (Social Science Research Network Electronic Paper Collection, Online, 2013) <https://papers.ssrn.com/sol3/papers.cfm?abstract_id=2314589>; David Godfrey, 'Using Alternatives to Guardianship to Defend Against or Terminate Guardianship' (Online, 2021) <https://www.americanbar.org/groups/law_aging/resources/guardianship_law_practice/>.

[68.] For example, the film *I Care a Lot* features crime cases of adult guardians and received a lot of attention in 2020; Nina A. Kohn, 'Britney Spears' Case Has Shown Why Guardianship Laws Need to Change' (*The Guardian*, August 18, 2021) <https://www.theguardian.com/commentisfree/2021/aug/18/britney-spears-case-guardianship-laws>; Lisa Zammiello, 'Don't You Know That Your Law Is Toxic? Britney Spears and Abusive Guardianship: A Revisionary Approach to the Uniform Probate Code, California Probate Code, and Texas Estates Code to Ensure Equitable Outcomes' (2021) 13(2) *Estate Planning & Community Property Law Journal* 587, 631.

[69.] David Godfrey states that 'a Court Improvement Program is needed in the adult guardianship as the Child Welfare Court did in 1993.' David Godfrey, 'Challenges in Guardianship and Guardianship Abuse' (2021) 42(4) *Bifocal* 84, 86.

'the state programs related to overseeing the administration of court-appointed guardian arrangements.'[70] These measures are to facilitate access to resources and data related to the adult guardianship determined by the court as well as administrative monitoring of adult guardians in order to strengthen supervision. The ABA adopted an institutional resolution to invest in a court improvement program on August 3, 2020.[71] Some other proposals appear in academic research, such as uniform guidance to court judges on the 'incapacitated' and a mandatory review process for adult guardianship. At the Fourth National Guardianship Summit in May 2021, twenty-two recommendations to improve and reform the adult guardianship system in the US were adopted.[72] This summit conference is held every ten years, which is sponsored by the National Guardianship Network (NGN), which comprises thirteen national guardianship related organizations. The recommendations include rights-based guardianships, SDM, limited guardianship and protective arrangements (in the UGCOPAA), rethinking guardianship monitoring and addressing abuse, addressing fiduciary responsibilities and tensions, and guardianship court improvement programs.[73] These issues require states to reconsider legislative and administrative improvements in guardianship to properly protect principals' interests.[74]

b. Supported Decision-Making Legislation

SDM based on the mutual agreement between the principal and the supporter is encouraged as an alternative to guardianship from the perspective of autonomy.[75]

[70.] Refers to the Congress Gov, 'S.2881—Guardianship Accountability Act of 2021' (Web Page, September 28, 2021) <https://www.congress.gov/bill/117th-congress/senate-bill/2881/actions>.

[71.] Refers to the ABA, *ABA House Concludes Historic Meeting After Adopting Robust List of New Policies* (Web Page, August 4, 2020) <https://www.americanbar.org/news/abanews/aba-news-archives/2020/08/annual-meeting-house-actions/>.

[72.] Refers to the Syracuse University, College of Law, *The Fourth National Guardianship Summit/2021: Maximizing Autonomy and Ensuring Accountability* (Web Page, May 10–14, 2021) <http://law.syr.edu/academics/conferences-symposia/the-fourth-national-guardianship-summit-autonomy-and-accountability>.

[73.] Nina A. Kohn and David English, 'Protective Orders and Limited Guardianships: Legal Tools for Sidelining Plenary Guardianship' (Conference paper at the Fourth National Guardianship Summit 2021 in New York, May 10–14, 2021).

[74.] Annemarie M. Kelly et al states that the U.S. guardianship system is 'rife with fairness and inefficiencies,' reviewing 50-State guardianship laws. Annemarie M. Kelly et al, 'A 50-State Review of Guardianship Laws: Specific Concerns for Special Needs Planning' (2021) 75(1) *Journal of Financial Service Professionals* 59, 79.

[75.] Leslie Salzman, 'Rethinking Guardianship (Again): Substituted Decision-Making as a Violation of the Integration Mandate of Title II of the Americans with Disabilities Act' (2009) 282 *Cardozo Working Paper* 156, 220; Leslie Salzman, 'Guardianship for Persons with Mental Illness — A Legal and Appropriate Alternative?' (2011) 4(2) *St. Louis University Journal of Health Law & Policy* 279, 330; Nina A. Kohn, Jeremy A. Blumenthal and Amy T. Campbell, 'Supported Decision-Making: A Viable Alternative to Guardianship?' (2013) 117(4) *Penn State Law Review* 1111, 1157; ABA, Commission on Law and Aging, *Supporting Decision Making Across the Age Spectrum* (Online, 2020) <https://www.americanbar.org/groups/law_aging/resources/guardianship_law_practice/>.

The case law *Ross v. Hatch*, Circuit Court for the City of Newport News, August 2, 2013, became a symbolic court decision for the value of SDM.[76] The move has progressed to include SDM in legislation in the US. Two U.S. states have enacted laws on SDM at the earlier stage. The first was the Supported Decision-Making Agreement Act (Texas State Act, Chapter 1357), which came into effect in September 2015.[77] While the Texas state law governs SDM agreement, the Delaware state law covers the overall SDM framework, including SDM agreements.[78]

The second was Title 16, Health and Safety, Individuals with Disabilities, Chapter 94A. Supported Decision-Making (Delaware State Act, Chapter 94A), which was enacted in Delaware in 2016.[79] Article 9402A(a) (1) of the Delaware State Act states that the purpose of the act is to 'provide an assistance in gathering and assessing information, making informed decisions, and communicating decisions to adults who do not require a guardian or substituted decision maker for such activities, but who would benefit from decision-making assistance.' In other words, the Delaware state law does not regard SDM as an instrument to completely replace the adult guardianship system but can accept the co-use of an EPA or many adults in the preliminary stage of petition to the adult guardianship system. If the legal capacity of the principal is insufficient, then either an EPA or the adult guardianship system would be adopted instead of SDM. For this reason, it was inferred that legislation could be made in 2016 when a uniform method of SDM was not yet fully established in detail. Article 9404 stipulates that adults are presumed to have the capacity to be self-sustaining and prescribes that the mental capacity of an adult should not be determined solely through a method of communication. Article 9406 prohibits the unjust intimidation of principles by supporters and decision-making by supporters without the principals' consent.

In August 2017, the ABA introduced an institutional resolution recommending that each state incorporate the provisions on SDM in the state law and that

---

[76.] This is the case that the court decided to accept SDM treatment (as an alternative of the guardianship) to Margaret Jenny Hatch, a woman with Down syndrome, respecting her wishes to do so. Jonathan Martinis, Jason Harris, Dean Fox and Peter Blanck, 'State Guardianship Laws and Supported Decision-Making in the United States After Ross and Ross v. Hatch: Analysis and Implications for Research, Policy, Education, and Advocacy' (Online, July 2021) *Journal of Disability Policy Studies* <https://doi.org/10.1177/10442073211028586>; Takeshi Shimura, 'Underlying the Self-Decision Support Principle as an Alternative to the Adult Guardianship System in the United States (1): Seeking Suggestions from American Case Law, Enactment, and Theory to Japanese Law' (2021) 93 *Adult Guardianship Practices* 88, 96 (in Japanese).

[77.] Gabrielle Bechyne, 'Supported Decision-Making Agreements in Texas' (2020) 13(31) *Estate Planning and Community Property Law Journal* 311, 351.

[78.] There is a publication that synthesizes the published literature on the use of SDM in the US, describing the policy, procedure, and practice approaches of SDM. L. VanPuymbrouck, *Supported Decision-Making in the United States: A White Paper* (The Council on Quality and Leadership Report, 2017).

[79.] This paragraph refers to the previously published article: Yukio Sakurai, 'An Essay on the Adult Protection System in Japan: Referring to Delaware State Law and the Revision of European Law' (2018) 8 *Quarterly Journal of Comparative Guardianship Law* 3, 21 (in Japanese).

the courts consider SDM as a less restrictive alternative to guardianship.[80] The National Center of State Courts, with cooperation of ABA, provides the online training program of SDM with free of charge.[81] For this reason, SDM legislation has developed and is expected to develop even more in the U.S. states.[82] In fact, twelve states—Columbia (2018), Wisconsin (2018), Alaska (2018), Indiana (2019), Nevada (2019), North Dakota (2019), Rhode Island (2019), Louisiana (2020), Colorado (2021), Oklahoma (2021), Virginia (2021), and Montana (2012)—have statutorily recognized SDM.[83] In addition, another five states—including Missouri, Tennessee, Utah, and Washington—have recognized SDM in other ways, including as a less restrictive option than guardianship and affirming the rights of people to continue to make their decisions whenever possible.[84]

Critical views appeared against the development of legislation on SDM. Nina A. Kohn pointed out that the U.S. SDM found 'the wide gap between the concept of SDM and its actual implementation in the state legislation.'[85] This opinion requests states to reconsider the legislative and administrative improvements in SDM and its safeguard measures, in addition to the guardianship law and administration as mentioned before.[86] On the other hand, Andrew Peterson et al. propose a 'three-step model' that specifies the necessary conditions of SDM for individuals with dynamic impairments: identifying domains for support; identifying kinds of support; and reaching a mutually

---

[80.] Refers to the ABA, *Resolution 113: American Bar Association Adopted by The House of Delegates* (Web Page, August 14–15, 2017) <https://health.ucdavis.edu/mindinstitute/centers/cedd/pdf/sdm-aba-resolution.pdf>; ABA, *Least Restrictive Alternative References in State Guardianship Statutes* (Web Page, June 23, 2018) <https://www.americanbar.org/content/dam/aba/publications/judicial_division/2018-model-code-statealj.pdf>.

[81.] The presentation indicates that 'there is no one-size-fits-all approach to supported decision-making…. every person's supported decision-making should be tailor-made to address the specific wants and needs of the person.' The National Center for State Courts, *Finding the Right Fit: Decision-Making Supports and Guardianship* (Web Page, 2019) 25 <http://www.supporteddecisionmaking.org/legal-resource/finding-right-fit-decision-making-supports-and-guardianship-online-course>.

[82.] Rachel Mattingly Phillips, 'Model Language for Supported Decision-Making Statutes' (2020) 98 *Washington University Law Review* 615, 644.

[83.] Refers to the ABA (n 63) 14.

[84.] Ibid. The Arc of Northern Virginia conducted the pilot project of SDM and issued the report (2021). The Arc of Northern Virginia and The Burton Blatt Institute at Syracuse University (BBI), '*I Learned that I Have a Voice in My Future' Summary, Findings, and Recommendations of The Virginia Supported Decision-Making Pilot Project* (The Arc of Northern Virginia and The Burton Blatt Institute at Syracuse University (BBI), Online, January 31, 2021) <https://bbi.syr.edu/wp-content/uploads/application/pdf/2021_virginia_SDM_pilot_project.pdf>.

[85.] Nina A. Kohn points out her observations of the 'wide gap between the U.S. SDM legislations and its actual implementations, and proposes four measures, including to construct[ion] of public system for support, as an alternative, person-centered approach to SDM.' Nina A. Kohn, 'Legislating Supported Decision-Making' (2021) 7 *Harvard Journal on Legislation* 313–56, 353–5.

[86.] Kristin Booth Glen states, 'Supported decision-making (SDM) for persons with intellectual and developmental disabilities (I/DD) has been part of legal scholarly discourse for more than a decade, but has, at least in the United States, entered the "real world" of practice only recently.' This remark demonstrates that the SDM practice has not been done enough in the US. This article addresses the experience and lessons of the SDM pilot project conducted in New York. Kristin Booth Glen, 'Supported Decision Making from Theory to Practice: Further Reflections on An Intentional Pilot Project' (2020) 13(1) *Albany Government Law Review* 24018.

acceptable and formal agreement.[87] Such a model and its code of conduct for SDM will be of help for a supporter to better deal with an individual's needs for impairment.

c. Adult Protective Services

Adult Protective Services (hereinafter referred to as 'APS') have been developed through legislation in each state of the US as a safeguard against abuse.[88] APS programs are established based on the reform of welfare state law, such as Senate Bill (SB) 2199, which was enforced in January 1999 in the state of California, and APS funding that has been annually budgeted.[89] Older people aged 65 and over and dependent adults aged 18 to 64 are protected in APS program. APS is usually located in country welfare agencies.[90] With the implementation of SB 2199 in California state, the definition of mandatory reporting in the APS program has expanded, and APS agencies are requested to operate a 24-hour response system. APS programs are established over the U.S. states to combat elder abuse by law; however, elder abuse has not been resolved yet. The North American Securities Administrators Association (NASAA) adopted the NASAA Model Act to Protect Vulnerable Adults from Financial Exploitation in 2016, and thirty-three states adopted this model Act, in whole or in part, as of February 2022.[91]

[87.] Andrew Peterson, Jason Karlawish and Emily Largent, 'Supported Decision-Making with People at the Margins of Autonomy' (Online, 2020) *The American Journal of Bioethics* 1, 15. <https://doi.org/10.1080/15265161.2020.1863507>.

[88.] Refers to the National Adult Protective Services Association (NAPSA), *Adult Protective Services Recommended Minimum Program Standards* (NAPSA, Online, 2013) <http://www.napsa-now.org/wp-content/uploads/2014/04/Recommended-Program-Standards.pdf>; National Adult Protective Services Association (NAPSA), *National Policy and Advocacy* (Web Page, n/a) <https://www.napsa-now.org/policy-advocacy/national-policy/>; Jason Burnett et al, 'Addressing Senior Financial Abuse: Adult Protective Services and Other Community Resources' in Ronan M. Factora (ed), *Aging and Money: Reducing Risk of Financial Exploitation and Protecting Financial Resources* (Springer, 2nd ed., 2021); This is an empirical APS analysis in the state of Ohio: Kenneth J. Steinman and Georgia J. Anetzberger, 'Measuring the Diverse Characteristics of County Adult Protective Services Programs' (2022) 34(3) *Journal of Elder Abuse & Neglect* 153, 173.

[89.] Refers to the APS, Research and Development Division, 'Early Impact of SB 2199 on the Adult Protective Services Program' (Online, 2000) <https://www.cdss.ca.gov/research/res/pdf/dapreports/APS-SB2199.pdf>; Nina Santo, 'Breaking the Silence: Strategies for Combating Elder Abuse in California' (Online, 2000) 31 *McGeorge Law Review* 801–38, 818 <https://scholarlycommons.pacific.edu/mlr/vol31/iss3/11>.

[90.] There is a difference of philosophy of service and community responsiveness between APS and Public Guardian Offices in most countries of states in the U.S. Diane Kaljian, 'Public Guardian and Collaboration in Three Countries: Models of Adult Protective Services' (Online, 2016) <https://mackcenter.berkeley.edu/sites/default/files/aas-2016-05-06/AAS/TOC-AAS-3.pdf>; Stephanie Chamberlain et al, 'Going It Alone: A Scoping Review of Unbefriended Older Adults' (2018) 37(1) *Canadian Journal on Aging (La Vevue Canadienne du Vieillissement)* 1, 11 <https://doi.org/10.1017/S0714980817000563>.

[91.] FINRA, *Addressing and Reporting Financial Exploitation of Senior and Vulnerable Investors* (Web Page, June 2023). <https://www.finra.org/sites/default/files/2023-05/NASAA-SEC-FINRA-Training-Senior-Investor-Protection-June2023.pdf>.

In October 2017, the Federal government adopted the Elder Abuse Prevention and Prosecution Act, which governs investigations into elder abuse, including financial exploitation, and encourages positive judicial responses.[92] This federal legislation is part of the APS advocated by the US, although it is said that enormous financial exploitation damages have been occurring, it is still not possible to grasp the actual damage amounts involving older people.[93] This law was implemented against the fact that responses to elder abuse by the courts were not as positive as responses by the police and other public agencies. The Financial Exploitation Prevention Act came into effect in September 2021 in the state of Michigan.[94]

In order to secure the interests of the aging population with insufficient mental capacity in the US, the implementation of multiple potential benefits for special needs planning, including financial planning, is emphasized, when older people are still healthy. It is recommended that U.S. courts and legislatures urgently analyze guardianship matters and leverage other less restrictive types of estate planning tools to serve persons with special needs.[95] The approach to promoting SDM and elder abuse legislation in parallel seems to be similar to Australia's public policy, which is discussed next.

(6) Changes to Victoria and NSW State Acts in Australia

a. State Level

In the state of Victoria, the Guardianship and Administration Act 2019 was enacted in May 2019 and came into force in March 2020. This is the first replacement of the Guardianship and Administration Act 1986 in thirty-three years. This legislation was in response to the request of the Attorney-General of Victoria in May 2009 that the Victorian Law Reform Commission[96] (hereinafter referred

---

[92.] Atsuko Harada (the National Diet Library of Japan), 'American Law on the Prevention of Elderly Abuse: Elderly Abuse Prevention and Prosecution Law 2017' (June 2018) 276 *Foreign Legislation* 1, 20 (in Japanese).

[93.] Kevin E. Hansen et al, 'Criminal and Adult Protection Financial Exploitation Laws in the United States: How Do the Statutes Measure Up to Existing Research?' (2016) 42(3) *Mitchell Hamline Law Review*, Article 3.

[94.] Refers to the Department of Attorney General, Government of Michigan, *New Protections in Place for Vulnerable Adults as Financial Exploitation Prevention Act Goes into Effect Sunday* (Web Page September 25, 2021) <https://www.michigan.gov/ag/0,4534,7-359-92297_47203-569109--,00.html>.

[95.] Annemarie M. Kelly et al, 'Implementing Guardianship Policies in Special Needs Planning: Five Potential Positives' (2020) 74(5) *Journal of Financial Service Professionals* 49, 63; Emily S. Taylor Poppe, 'Surprised by the Inevitable: A National Survey of Estate Planning Utilization' (2020) 53 *University of California Davis Law Review* 2511, 2560.

[96.] The Victorian Law Reform Commission (VLRC) is 'a central law reform agency in Victoria,' which was established by the *Victorian Law Reform Commission Act 2000*. 'The Attorney-General said in May 2000 that the charter of the VLRC would be "to facilitate community-wide debate of law reform issues and to assist members of Parliament in identifying key areas of law reform. The aim is to place Victoria at the cutting edge in law reform

to as 'VLRC') amend the Victorian Act 1986. After deliberations by experts, the VLRC submitted a report, *Guardianship: Final Report No. 24*[97] (hereinafter referred to as 'VLRC Report 24'), to the state Attorney-General in April 2012. The VLRC Report 24 proposed reform proposals that included 440 items. Some proposals have been incorporated into the two other laws, the Powers of Attorney Act 2014 and the Victoria Medical Treatment Planning and Decision Act 2016. The main changes of the Victorian 2019 Act to the 1986 Act are as follows:

(i)   The primary objective is to protect and promote the human rights and dignity of persons with disability by adhering to the CRPD and recognizing the need to support persons with disability to make, participate in and implement decisions that affect their lives (section 7: primary object, Victorian 2019 Act).

(ii)   A person is presumed to have decision-making capacity unless there is evidence to the contrary (section 5(2): meaning of decision-making capacity). SDM is incorporated into the law system to respect the will and preferences of the principal, and supportive guardians and supportive administrators are appointed by the tribunal (part 4: supportive guardianship orders and supportive administration orders).

(iii) The appointment of adult guardians by the tribunal is only a last resort (section 30: VCAT may make a guardianship order or administration order), and in principle, a hearing of all candidates for the roles of supportive guardians and supportive administrators is conducted to set up tailor-made assistance in response to the request of the principal (section 85).

In the state of New South Wales (NSW), an amendment project of the Adult Guardianship Act 1987 is underway. The NSW Law Reform Commission[98] (hereinafter referred to as 'NSW LRC') consulted with the Attorney-General of NSW in 2016 about undertaking a review of the 1987 Act. The report, *Report 145: Review of the Guardianship Act 1987*[99] (hereinafter referred to as 'NSW LRC Report 145'), was submitted in February 2018. Afterward, the NSW LRC Report

---

in Australia.''' Victorian Law Reform Commission (VLRC), *Our Story* (Web Page, n/a) <https://www.lawreform. vic.gov.au/about-us/our-story/>.

[97.] Refers to the VLRC Report 24 and 'Project Timeline' starting from the announcement of the guardianship review (June 19, 2009) till the VLRC Report 24 publication date (April 12, 2012). VLRC, *Guardianship* (Web Page, April 12, 2012) <https://www.lawreform.vic.gov.au/project/guardianship/>.

[98.] 'The NSW Law Reform Commission is an independent statutory body constituted under the Law Reform Commission Act 1967 (NSW). We provide expert law reform advice to Government on matters that the Attorney General refers to us.' NSW Law Reform Commission, *About Us: What We Do* (Web Page, September 2024) <https://lawreform.nsw.gov.au/about-us/what-we-do.html>.

[99.] NSW Law Reform Commission, *NSW LRC Report 145: Review of the Guardianship Act 1987* (Web Page, May 2018) <https://lawreform.nsw.gov.au/documents/Current-projects/Guardianship/Report/Report%20145.pdf>.

145 was partially revised to reflect public comments, and the final report was tabled to the state parliaments in August 2018. The main points of possible amendment proposals regarding this report are as follows:

(i)   The revised law will be renamed Assisted Decision-Making Act. If the principal is aged 18 or older and desires assisted decision-making by an appropriate supporter, the principal may make a personal support agreement with the supporter.

(ii)   The tribunal may appoint a supporter by a tribunal support order as a last resort, and the supporter can assist the principal in decision-making. The Act cannot enforce change to any informal arrangements if they are made with the consent of the principal and the supporter.

(iii) Supporters carry out decision-making support in accordance with decision support agreements or tribunal orders, and when providing an assistance, supporters are obliged to observe the general principles of the Act.

It can be understood that the NSW LRC Report 145 proposes a more advanced institutional design in line with the CRPD than the VLRC Report 24. That is, the paternalistic aspect of adult guardianship is undesirable, and a policy has been introduced to prioritize respect for autonomy and right to self-determination.

b. National Level

At the national level, the Australian Law Reform Commission[100] (hereinafter referred to as 'ALRC') report, *Equality, Capacity and Disability in Commonwealth Laws: Final Report No. 124* (hereinafter referred to as 'ALRC report 124') was published and tabled in the national parliament in 2014.[101] This is a national guardianship law reform report, which has mainly examined the 'ability to excise legal capacity' and 'equal recognition before the law of people with disability' in the CRPD, and provides the four National Decision-Making Principles.[102] In

---

[100] The Australian Law Reform Commission (ALRC) is 'an advisory body to the Attorney-General by law and is regarded as an independent organization with the mission of professional deliberations on law amendments.' Rosalind F. Croucher, 'Law Reform Agencies and Government—Independence, Survival and Effective Law Reform' (2018) 43(1) *University of Western Australia Law Review* 78, 91.

[101] The 'terms of reference' of ALRC Report 124 includes 'how maximizing individual autonomy and independence could be modelled in Commonwealth laws and legal frameworks.' Australian Law Reform Commission (ALRC), *Equality, Capacity and Disability in Commonwealth Laws: Final Report* (ALRC Report 124, 2014) <https://www.alrc.gov.au/publication/equality-capacity-and-disability-in-commonwealth-laws-alrc-report-124/>.

[102] Bruce Alston, a member of ALRC then, examines how the National Decision-Making Principles may be used by communities, policymakers, and governments to promote legal changes to ensure that individuals with disability have an equal right to make decisions for themselves. Bruce Alston, 'Towards Supported Decision-Making: Article 12 of the Convention on the Rights of Persons with Disabilities and Guardianship Law Reform' (2017) 35 *Law in Context* 21, 43.

addition, the ALRC also published the report, *Elder Abuse—A National Legal Response Final Report*[103] (hereinafter referred to as 'ALRC Report 131') in June 2017 to ensure that the national statutory policy on prevention of elder abuse is observed. Then, the National Disability Advocacy Program Decision Support Pilot was launched in 2018, funded by the Commonwealth Department of Social Service.[104] The Serious Incident Response Scheme (hereinafter referred to as 'SIRS') was implemented on April 1, 2022, as an initiative to help prevent and reduce the risk and occurrence of incidents of abuse and neglect in residential aged care services subsidized by the Australian Government.[105] It can be said that Australia has promoted legislation or law reform project regarding the guardianship, SDM, and abuse prevention at the state level, particularly in Victoria and NSW, and at the national level.

(7) Other Statutory Developments

Three countries of Ireland, Peru, and Germany have advanced statutory developments in adult protection, of which developments are sketched as follows:

(a)   In Ireland, the Assisted Decision-Making (Capacity) Act (2015) replaced the Ward of Court system for adults. The Irish adult protection system is that (i) assisted decision-making by the mutual agreement is used under the supervision of the Office of the Public Guardian (OPG), (ii) a co-decision-making option is introduced, (iii) a decision-making representative, which replaced the adult guardian, is appointed by the court as a last resort under the supervision of the OPG, and (iv) an EPA is available. This project is called the 'Decision Support Service' (DDS) conducted by the DDS (director: Áine Flynn) under the supervision of the Mental Health Commission (MHC).[106] The new framework of (i) to (iv) above

---

[103.] ALRC, *Elder Abuse—A National Legal Response (ALRC Report 131)* (Web Page, June 14, 2017) <https://www.alrc.gov.au/publication/elder-abuse-a-national-legal-response-alrc-report-131/>.

[104.] Refers to the Australian Government, Department of Social Services, *National Disability Advocacy Program* (Web Page, September 29, 2020) <https://www.dss.gov.au/our-responsibilities/disability-and-carers/program-services/for-people-with-disability/national-disability-advocacy-program-ndap>; John Chesterman and Lois Bedson, *Decision Time: Activating the Rights of Adults with Cognitive Disability* (Victorian OPA Report, March 1, 2021) 22 <https://www.publicadvocate.vic.gov.au/opa-s-work/research/141-decision-time>.

[105.] Refers to the Department of Health and Aged Care (Australian Government), *Serious Incident Response Scheme (SIRS)* (Web Page, May 31, 2022) <https://www.health.gov.au/initiatives-and-programs/serious-incident-response-scheme-sirs>; The article states that 'the SIRS may lead to the prioritization of reporting over action.' Lise Barry and Patrick Hughes, 'The New Serious Incident Response Scheme and the Responsive Regulation of Abuse in Aged Care' (2022) 29(1) *Journal of Law and Medicine* 465–80, 480.

[106.] Refers to the Mental Health Commission (MHC), *The Decision Support Service* (Web Page, n/a) <https://decisionsupportservice.ie/>; The MHC, *MHC 2019 – 2022 Strategy: 'Protecting People's Rights'* <https://www.mhcirl.ie/sites/default/files/2021-01/MHC_Strategy_2019-2022.pdf>.

was implemented in Autumn 2022 after the Assisted Decision-Making (Capacity) (Amendment) Bill 2022 passed through the parliament. It is noted that 'the commencement of assisted decision-making provides an opportunity to redefine the provision, practices, and priorities of health-care in Ireland to enable improved patient-centered care.'[107] Monitoring its operation on-site is important after the implementation of the systems in Autumn 2022.

(b)   In Peru, the Peruvian Civil Code was partially amended in September 2018. Article 3(2) of the Peruvian Civil Code states that 'persons with disabilities have equal ability to act in all aspects of life,' following the values of Article 12 of the CRPD. The amendment added a new term 'support (*apoyo*)' provision (Article 659B of the Peruvian Civil Code) that is largely used for vulnerable adults, while maintaining the substituted decision-making for those in a coma. In principle, the 'support' does not have any power of representation in a legal sense and is regarded as an assistance to vulnerable adults.[108] The 'safeguards (*salvaguar-dias*)' (Article 45B of the Peruvian Civil Code) should cope with an abuse of law or an undue influence, but its measures are not addressed clearly.[109] The amendment to Peruvian civil code shows a possibility to incorporate the concept of support in the civil code, although the support does not have any power of legal representation. Monitoring is important as to how the support functions in practice. The Peruvian Civil Code reform may impact Latin American countries' legislation that has adapted to a stricter interpretation according to the mandates

---

[107.] Relevant articles regarding the law: Mary Donnelly and Caoimhe Gleeson, 'The Assisted Decision-Making (Capacity) Act 2015 in the Courts: Hearing the Voice of the Relevant Person' (2024) 8(2) *Irish Judicial Studies Journal* 47–66 <https://cora.ucc.ie/items/69a9bead-a5e0-455a-ba1a-92971f37e418>; Éidín Ní Shé et al. 'What Bothers Me Most Is the Disparity between the Choices that People Have or Don't Have: A Qualitative Study on the Health Systems Responsiveness to Implementing the Assisted Decision-Making (Capacity) Act in Ireland' (2020) 17(9) *International Journal of Environmental Research and Public Health* 3294, 3307; A different view is seen in the article: Mary Donnelly, 'Deciding in Dementia: The Possibilities and Limits of Supported Decision-Making' (Online, 2019) 66 *International Journal of Law and Psychiatry* 101466 <https://doi.org/10.1016/j.ijlp.2019.101466>; Ruth Uster and Tadhg Stapleton, 'Overview of the Assisted Decision-Making (Capacity) Act (2015): Implications and Opportunities for Occupational Therapy' (2018) 46(2) *Irish Journal of Occupational Therapy* 130, 140; Satoshi Taniguchi, 'A Study on An "Advance Healthcare Directive" in Ireland's Assisted Decision-Making (Capacity) Act 2015' (2020) 63(1) *The Economic Journal of Takasaki City University of Economics* 41, 71 (in Japanese); John Lombard and Hope Davidson, 'The Older Person's Experience of Autonomy in Healthcare Decision-Making in Ireland: The Relationship between Law, Policy, and Practice' (2022) 22(4) *Medical Law International* 1, 25 <https://doi.org/10.1177/09685332221109239>.

[108.] Antonio Martinez-Pujalte, 'Legal Capacity and Supported Decision-Making: Lessons from Some Recent Legal Reforms' (Online, 2019) 8(1) *Laws* 4 <https://doi.org/10.3390/laws8010004>; Renato Constantino, 'The Flag of Imagination: Peru's New Reform on Legal Capacity for Persons with Intellectual and Psychosocial Disabilities and the Need for New Understandings in Private Law' (2020) 14 *The Age of Human Rights Journal* 155, 180; Alberto Vásquez Encalada, Kimber Bialik and Kaitlin Stober, 'Supported Decision Making in South America: Analysis of Three Countries' Experiences' 18(10) *International Journal of Environmental Research and Public Health* 5204.

[109.] Keisuke Shimizu, 'Can the New Peruvian Law Protect the Rights of Persons with Disabilities? Based on the Trend of New Support System' (2021) 91 *Adult Guardianship Practices* 74–80, 77 (in Japanese).

derived from the CRPD in Argentina (2014), Costa Rica (2016), and Colombia (2019).[110]

(c)   In Germany, there are two systems for supporting and protecting vulnerable adults. One is the statutory care law (*Betreuung*) system, and the other is enduring power of attorney. The current guardianship and care law was enacted in September 1990 and enforced in 1992, which separated 'the guardianship law system for minors' and 'the care lawsy stem for adults.' The care law was implemented in parallel with the Aged (Long-Term) Care Insurance Law (1994), reviewing the adult protection in the German Civil Code.[111] The care law was designed to consider self-determination of the principal and to avoid restrictions of human rights of the principal without necessity, and establishes the legal principles, such as the principles of necessity and of subsidiarity. Considering the requirements of the CRPD, the German federal government established the research project, the 'Court-appointed Legal representatives/*Betreuer* in Germany: Quality in Legal Care' (2015–2017).[112] The intention of the German federal government was to review the care law system and its practices and to prepare the reform of the care law to meet the requirements of the CRPD and relevant case law in Germany and Europe.

The new law was prepared based on this research project and the bill on the reform of guardianship and care law passed the federal parliament on May 4, 2021. The new law in the German Civil Code will come into force in January 2023. Some new provisions are seen in the new law, namely, the mutual representation of spouses in health care affairs; this is a proxy right which is limited to emergency representation and no obligation to exercise (Article 1858), a detailed catalog of acts with the court permission obligations (Articles 1848–1854); the scope of the court involvement and control becomes broader and more roles of assistance of the Care Associations to principals are organized (Article 10 etc. of the Care Organization Law).[113] The new law also places greater emphasis on

---

[110] Nicolás Espejo Yaksic, 'Legal Capacity, Disability and Human Rights: Changes and Challenges' (Oxford Human Rights Hub Blog, Online, July 9, 2020) <https://ohrh.law.ox.ac.uk/legal-capacity-disability-and-human-rights-changes-and-challenges/>.

[111] Kazuichiro Iwashi, 'Autonomy and Protection of the Elderly in Germany' (2013) 85(7) [1061] *The Horitsu Jiho* 26, 32. (in Japanese)

[112] In 2015, the Federal Ministry of Justice and Consumer Protection commissioned a research project regarding the CRPD Committee's criticism to the German Law of the care law based on Article 12, the CRPD. The research project was concerned with questions: how the Law of the care law is implemented in practice; what the guiding principles for quality standards are; whether structural quality deficits exist, and if so, what the possible causes for these deficits are. Dagmar Brosey, 'Court-Appointed Legal representatives (Betreuer) in Germany: Quality Requirements and their Implementation' (Conference paper at the fifth WCAG2018 held in Seoul on October 23–25, 2018).

[113] Michael Ludwig Ganner [translated by Teruaki Tayama], 'Annotation of the German New Care Act' (2021) 15 *Quarterly Journal of Comparative Guardianship Law* 3, 12 (in Japanese); Dagmar Brosey, 'Aspects of the Reform

the contribution of carers and related associations in providing personal affairs support to principals.

3.3 Analysis of Adult Support and Protection Legislation

3.3.1 Differences

The way to develop a statutory system to support and protect vulnerable adults may vary by country or state. The European continental countries, in general, have amended their civil codes to incorporate the concept of adult support and protection into the revised provisions. This has been done in Switzerland, Ireland, and Austria. In these countries, the leading players in legal reform are the parliaments, which are supported by the governments. Particularly in Austria, the Federal Ministry of Justice held the law reform study team meetings, which included persons with disabilities and practitioners, for three and a half years before concluding a report.[114]

Australia has developed its own unique adult guardianship legislation. Australian states have adopted their own system that splits adult guardianship roles between the guardian and the administrator or financial manager (hereinafter referred to as 'administrator'). Each Australian state has established a tribunal, the Office of the Public Advocate or the Public Guardian, and a public trustee or a state trustees company limited. With amendments to the guardianship law for the first time in over thirty years, the Australian States of Victoria and NSW have legislated or will legislate SDM. Australia will consider legislation of elder abuse at the national or state level to develop its own adult protection system. Scotland aims to come up with a comprehensive mental health law package that will include such measures as mental health care, aged care, advance directives, and medical decision-making in intensive care situations. The legislative reforms of both Australia and Scotland, like those of European continental countries, are implemented by parliaments and supported by the Law Reform Commission or Mental Health Law Review, which is an independent law expert group.

In the US, the states of Texas and Delaware have legislated SDM. The ULC updated the uniform act (UGCOPAA) in 2017, and the ABA made an institutional resolution to recommend to each state to incorporate SDM into the

---

of the German Legislation of Betreuung: Support and representation of adults regarding to legal capacity in the German Law Reform' (American Bar Association (ABA), *Voice of Experience*, October 27, 2021) <https://www.americanbar.org/groups/senior_lawyers/publications/voice_of_experience/2021/voice-of-experience-october-2021/reform-aspects-of-betreuung/>.

[114.] From the interview of the Adult Protection Associations by the author in Vienna on September 17, 2019.

state law. Some states have followed this recommendation.[115] Since the 1980s, lawyers' associations in the US have created a field of law known as elder law. In addition to property management for older people and protection of their personal affairs, elder law has some overlap with adult protection service law.[116] The main public opinion leaders of the reform of the adult guardianship system in the US are mainly lawyers' associations over the states represented by the ULC, NGA, ABA, and the like, and the state parliaments referred to the views of these associations. One characteristic of the US is that lawyers' associations play a significant role in the transformation of the legal system in this field, and the courts use cases to provide direction.

The adoption of reformed law or legislation differs by country, and how close to the requirements of the General Comments No.1 and Article 12 the CRPD the said reformed law or legislation is placed also differs by country. Namely, reform of the civil code has been achieved in Switzerland, Austria, Peru, and Germany while legislation was made in some states of the US and Australia, and Ireland. The CRPD Committee reviews each state party's report to examine how the state meets the requirements of the CRPD and comments on it. The Victorian Act 2019 in Australia may be the closest to the CRPD's requirements in a sense that the law includes SDM and prioritizes SDM rather than substituted decision-making. Guardianship state law reform such as the Victorian Act 2019 and the national elder abuse prevention policy are being carried out in parallel in Australia. This legislation and policy are expected to provide a unique adult support and protection system that will expand within Australia. For this reason, the development concerning adult guardianship, SDM, and elder abuse prevention in Australia will be reviewed in the next chapter in greater detail, with a focus on the legislative framework and values of the law and policy.

3.3.2 Commonalities

From a legal system viewpoint, the continental Europe and Japan share the civil code jurisdictions, while the US and Australia share common law jurisdictions. Even though no two legal systems are exactly the same, comparing one country's law with another will be possible to some extent from a legal perspective.

[115.] Refers to Section 3.2 (5), 'U.S. Guardianship and Supported Decision-Making Acts.'

[116.] Nina A. Kohn, 'Elder Rights: The Next Civil Rights Movement' (2012) 21(2) *Temple Political and Civil Rights Law Review* 321, 328; Nina A. Kohn, 'A Civil Rights Approach to Elder Law' in Israel Doron and Ann Soden (eds), *Beyond Elder Law* (Springer, 2012) 19–34.

Referring to legislative developments of the above countries and states, some commonality can be found as below.

First, respect for human rights, particularly a principal's autonomy and right to self-determination, is found in all the legislation or reform policy reports.[117] This is indicated in each country's or state's comments mentioned in this chapter. The phrase *nothing about us without us*, emphasizing autonomy and right to self-determination of persons with disability, is a principle embodied in the CRPD.[118] In this sense, it is a symbolic change that the term 'guardianship' has been abolished, and the name Adult Protection Law is used in Switzerland and Austria. The NSW Law Reform Commission (Australia) proposes the same renaming: Assisted Decision-Making Act. It can be assumed that these legislations were influenced by the CRPD's human-rights approach.[119]

Second, legal developments are found to some extent in legislation of the above countries or states. Article 12 of the CRPD—equal recognition before the law—mentions that 'parties shall take appropriate measures to provide access by persons with disabilities to the support they may require in exercising their legal capacity.' UN General Comment No. 1 (2014)[120] acknowledges that Article 12 implies a possible paradigm shift from substituted decision-making to SDM. This shift ensures that the principal's will and preferences are understood, and their wishes implemented. No country or state has reached a perfect paradigm shift as recommended by the UN. The above countries and states, however, have developed their own legislative systems or reform policy reports, which were considered in light of their own sociocultural background to balance the systems with the existing law systems.

Third, some common principles can be found in the legislation and reform reports of the above countries and states as follows: (i) the provision of necessary support tailored to individual circumstances, with the aim of minimizing restrictions on the principal's human rights. The principle of necessity requires that no protective measure should be implemented unless it is essential, taking into account the specific circumstances of each case; (ii) the adoption of less

---

[117.] Australian Attorney-General's Office shows that 'rights to self-determination entail the entitlement of peoples to have control over their destiny and to be treated respectfully, which include peoples being free to pursue their economic, social, and cultural development.' Attorney-General's Office, *Rights to Self-Determination* (Web Page, n/a) <https://www.ag.gov.au/rights-and-protections/human-rights-and-anti-discrimination/human-rights-scrutiny/public-sector-guidance-sheets/right-self-determination>.

[118.] The phrase, *nothing about us without us* was used to show the common thoughts of all persons with disabilities in the process to formulate the CRPD in the UN. UN, *International Day of Disabled Persons 2004* (Web Page, December 3, 2004) <https://www.un.org/development/desa/disabilities/international-day-of-persons-with-disabilities-3-december/international-day-of-disabled-persons-2004-nothing-about-us-without-us.html>.

[119.] Shih-Ning Then, 'Evolution and Innovation in Guardianship Laws: Assisted Decision-Making' (2013) 35 *Sydney Law Review* 133–66, 145–7.

[120.] Refers to the UN, the CRPD Committee, *General Comment No. 1* (Web Page, April 11, 2014) 6–8. <http://www.ohchr.org/EN/HRBodies/CRPD/Pages/GC.aspx>.

restrictive alternatives should be prioritized. Guardianship legislation stipulates that any person exercising powers under such legislation must promote outcomes that represent the least restrictive means of enabling persons with disabilities to enjoy freedom of decision and action.'

Point (i) may follow the *principle of necessity* which was adopted in the Council of Europe.[121] It is, for example, indicated in the Scottish reform report, which states that 'enhanced principles within the legislation [are] to reflect the *need* for an adult to have support for the exercise of legal capacity.'[122] The Victorian 2019 Act explicitly states, in section 38 (power of guardian), that 'the power to sign and do anything…is *necessary* to give effect to any power or duty vested in the guardian.' This principle is presumed to follow the VLRC Report 24 (2012), which states that 'people with impaired decision-making ability should be provided with the support *necessary* for them to make, participate in and implement decisions that affect their lives (VLRC Report 24 Recommendation 21(c): new general principles).' In fact, in the Victorian guardianship practice, the representation authority is usually reviewed after one to three years of self-revocation term, which in principle expires unless otherwise necessary. This principle can be said to coincide with the 'support' principle, which states that 'persons who require support in decision-making must be provided with access to the support *necessary* for them to make, communicate and participate in decisions that affect their lives,' as one of the National Decision-Making Principles in the ALRC Report 124 (Paragraphs 3.18 to 3.27). It can be assumed that the principle of necessity is adopted not only to minimize restriction of a principal's human rights but also to minimize administrative and financial burdens on relevant public agencies, including the tribunal.

Point (ii) may follow the *principle of subsidiarity* (*least restrictive alternative*) which was adopted in Council of Europe.[123] It is, for example, emphasized in the Swiss reform, which stresses that Switzerland's adult protection law 'as much as possible, do not limit the human rights of the individual.' The Victorian 2019 Act, section 4(1)(c) states as a general principle that 'powers, functions and duties under this Act should be exercised, carried out and performed in a way which is…*the least restrictive* of the ability of a person with a disability to decide and act as is possible in the circumstances.'[124] Article 9402A(b)(3) of the US's Delaware state act also states that 'all adults should receive the most effective

---

[121.] Refers to Section 3.2 (1), '2000 Protection of Adults Convention and the Following Developments,' i.e., '*Principle 5—Necessity and subsidiarity*' Council of Europe, *Principles Concerning the Legal Protection of Incapable Adults.*

[122.] Refers to the Government of Scotland (n 51) 10.

[123.] Refers to Section 3.2 (1), '2000 Protection of Adults Convention and the Following Developments.'

[124.] A previous law of the state of Victoria (Australia), *Guardianship and Administration Act 1986* Part 1—preliminary 4. Objects of Act (2), states that 'this Act is to be exercised or performed so that—(a) the means which is the *least restrictive* of a person's freedom of decision and action as is possible in the circumstances is adopted.'

yet *least restrictive and intrusive* form of support, assistance, or protection when they are unable to care for themselves or manage their affairs alone.' These two principles are assumed to be the basics shared by legislation, reform policy reports and current laws of the above countries and states.

Fourth, there is a balance between state responsibility and citizen rights. There used to be a tendency for limited state responsibility and more citizen rights in the conventional family system. As the population ages and the traditional family system partly breaks down, problems related to vulnerable adults have increased and sometimes become social problems. State or local authorities, including police intervention, are required in the case of abuse. In this sense, an intervention must be implemented in a reasonable way so as not to violate the sound life of people and to ensure clear, evidence-based procedures of why and how the intervention has been justified by law.

After all, an adult support and protection legislative system can be said to refer to a comprehensive package of laws for legal advocacy that aims to protect vulnerable adults through the least restrictive measures, as long as is necessary, by taking their will and preferences into consideration. In other words, an adult support and protection legislative system offers necessary support according to individual characteristics, minimizes restriction of a principal's rights, and takes less restrictive alternative measures.

3.4 Summary: Adult Support and Protection Is Defined

This section sought to identify the common characteristics that constitute emerging legal frameworks for supporting and protecting vulnerable adults across Europe and common law jurisdictions. It reviewed the 2000 Hague Convention on the International Protection of Adults and subsequent legislative developments in countries such as Switzerland, Austria, Scotland, the US, and Australia. While notable differences exist—reflecting each country's unique socio-legal context—it is natural that statutory approaches vary across jurisdictions.

Despite these differences, several key commonalities have emerged. First is a consistent emphasis on respect for human rights, particularly the autonomy and right to self-determination of the individual (the principal). Second, there is a broad acceptance of Article 12 of the CRPD, which affirms equal recognition before the law. UN General Comment No. 1 (2014) further suggests a paradigm shift from substituted decision-making to SDM, which seeks to respect and implement the principal's will and preferences. Third, the principles of necessity and the use of less restrictive alternatives are reflected in both legislation and reform policy documents across the reviewed jurisdictions. These principles ensure that any intervention is proportionate and tailored to individual circumstances. Fourth, there is a discernible balance in each country between state responsibility and the rights of citizens, recognizing both the protective role of the state and the autonomy of the individual.

From this comparative analysis, adult support and protection legislation may be defined as a comprehensive legal advocacy framework aimed at safeguarding vulnerable adults through the least restrictive means necessary, with a focus on respecting their individual will and preferences. Such a system provides personalized support, limits unnecessary constraints on legal capacity, and ensures interventions are guided by the principle of least restriction.

CHAPTER 4

Adult Support and Protection
in the Australian Context

This chapter examines recent legal reforms in Australia concerning adult guardianship, supported decision-making, and elder abuse prevention.[1] It focuses on legislative developments in the states of Victoria and New South Wales and explores how these reforms reflect the values of the Convention on the Rights of Persons with Disabilities (CRPD). The chapter highlights the emergence of a comprehensive adult support and protection system in Australia, analyzing its theoretical basis and institutional design. It also discusses the implications of Australia's legislative approach for other countries facing similar aging-related legal challenges.

4.1 Introduction

Chapter 4 examines recent legislative developments in the States of Victoria and New South Wales (hereinafter referred to as 'NSW') in the Commonwealth of Australia (hereinafter referred to as 'Australia') concerning guardianship law reforms and national elder abuse policy. It outlines the legal content, policy objectives, and key features of these legislative changes and assesses their significance from the perspective of adult support and protection.

Victoria and NSW, as leading states in guardianship reform, are undertaking their first major revisions in over thirty years to incorporate supported decision-making into their laws. Concurrently, Australia is advancing elder abuse legislation under a national policy framework—collectively referred to here as the 'Australian legislative project.' Analyzing this project helps clarify the legal meaning and purpose of adult support and protection legislation. Furthermore, the Australian

---

[1.] This chapter is an updated version of the previously published articles by the author: Yukio Sakurai, 'Australian Adult Support and Protection for Vulnerable Adults: Through Law Reforms of Guardianship and Elder Abuse Legislation (Part I)' (2020) 25(2) *Yokohama Journal of Social Sciences* 119, 139 <https://doi.org/10.18880/00013445>, Yukio Sakurai, 'Australian Adult Support and Protection for Vulnerable Adults: Through Law Reforms of Guardianship and Elder Abuse Legislation (Part II)' (2021) 25(4) *Yokohama Journal of Social Sciences* 97, 119 <https://doi.org/10.18880/00013705>.

experience may offer valuable insights for countries such as Japan in developing laws and policies related to adult guardianship, supported decision-making, and elder abuse prevention.

In 2009, John Brayley, then Public Advocate of South Australia, articulated foundational ideas for an adult support and protection paradigm. He emphasized that this model focuses on vulnerability rather than incapacity, enabling broader access to assistance; promotes teamwork, partnership, and local accountability; and offers multi-sectoral responses akin to domestic violence strategies.[2] Brayley also proposed a 'stepped approach to substituted and supported decision-making,' graphically mapping these concepts along axes of care/protection and autonomy/self-determination.[3]

The adult support and protection system is conceptualized as a legal framework comprising multiple laws aimed at protecting vulnerable adults through the least restrictive measures, with attention to their will and preferences.[4] It includes adult guardianship, supported decision-making, and elder abuse safeguards, forming a package of legal advocacy tools rather than a single statute.[5] Research methods for this chapter include literature review and expert interviews.[6] Due to limited Japanese-language scholarship on Australian guardianship law, this study relies primarily on Australian and international sources, with reference to key Japanese works such as Suga (2007), Nishida (2015), the Japan Federation of Bar Associations (2015), and Sugita (2021).[7]

[2.] The author partially changed the text to Italic letters for an emphasis. John Brayley, 'Supported Decision-making in Australia' (Conference Paper, Victorian Office of the Public Advocate held in Melbourne on December 14, 2009) 16–17.

[3.] Ibid 5–7; John Brayley, 'Developing a Model of Practice for Supported Decision Making' (Office of the Public Advocate, South Australia. In collaboration with the Julia Farr MS McLeod Benevolent Fund, 2011) 11–13.

[4.] Refers to Section 3.3.2, 'Commonalities.'

[5.] The term 'vulnerable adults' is used in this study as the object of adult support and protection legislation, although the object is defined by each relevant law.

[6.] The author conducted interview with experts in Melbourne (Victoria) on March 1 to 3, 2017, and March 4 to 12, 2019. The subjects of the survey were the Victorian Civil and Administrative Tribunal (VCAT), the Office of the Public Advocate (OPA), State Trustees Limited (STL) headquarters and VCAT satellite offices, the Melbourne Central Police, and the Department of Health and Human Services; the Social Equity Research Institute, the Senior Rights Victoria and COTA Victoria; University of Melbourne, Monash University, La Trobe University, the University of Sydney, and Queensland University of Technology who joined the Australian Adult Guardianship and Administration Council conference (AGAC2019) in Canberra on March 13 to 15, 2019. The author joined a supported decision-making facilitation training (two weeks), conducted by Cher Nicholson in Adelaide (South Australia) in February 23 to March 4, 2016.

[7.] Fumie Suga, 'Australia's Adult Guardianship System—from a Comparative Law Perspective' (2007) 20 *Adult Guardianship Practices* 106, 117. (in Japanese); Kazuhiro Nishida, 'Trends in Welfare Legislation on Guardianship and Responsibility and Role of Public: Based on Australian Law' (2015) 2636 *Weekly Social Security* 46, 51 (in Japanese); Japan Federation of Bar Associations, 'Supported Decision-Making (SDM) Model in the South Australia' (Human Rights Convention/Symposium No. 58 the Second Subcommittee: Survey No. 2, Online, October 1, 2015) (in Japanese) <https://www.nichibenren.or.jp/document/symposium/jinken_taikai.html>; Hiroko Sugita, 'A Study on the Supported Decision-Making System for the Elderly with Dementia (2): Focusing on the South Australian Legal System' (2021) 179 *The Graduate School Law Review* 71–98, 94 (in Japanese).

The chapter addresses the following three research questions: (i) What new legislation and draft amendments are being enacted in Victoria and proposed by the NSW Law Reform Commission, and how can they be interpreted legally? (ii) What national policy proposals on elder abuse are being developed by the Australian Law Reform Commission, and what is their legal significance? (iii) From the perspective of adult support and protection legislation, how does the Australian legislative project inform possible legislative developments in Japan through comparative analysis?

4.2 Australian Guardianship Laws

4.2.1 Australian Law and Its Guardianship

The Australia comprises six states and two territories with self-governing powers, i.e., NSW, Queensland, South Australia, Tasmania, Victoria, Western Australia, the Australian Capital Territory, and the Northern Territory.[8] These states and special territories have their own constitutions, parliaments, governments, and laws. These parliaments are permitted to pass laws related to any matter that is not controlled by the Commonwealth under sections 51 and 52 of the Australian Constitution.[9]

Australia has the common law system, and the sources of the laws include legislation made by parliament and case laws developed by the judiciary. Under such a legal structure, the guardianship system is defined by the legislation of each state and special territory. The guardianship system in Australia has uniformity. Namely, each state and special territory has three main Acts: Guardianship Act, Powers of Attorney Act, and Civil and Administrative Tribunal Act. Each state and special territory has three main public agencies: Office of the Public Advocate or Office of the Public Guardian, Civil and Administrative Tribunal, and a State or Public Trustee, which may work for the guardianship system. The summary of relevant legislation and public agencies is provided in Tables 4.1 and 4.2.

[8.] Refers to the Parliament of Australia, *The Constitution* (Web Page, May 2022) <https://www.aph.gov.au/About_Parliament/ House_of_Representatives/Powers_practice_and_procedure/00_-_Infosheets/Infosheet_13_-_The_Constitution>.

[9.] Refers to the Parliament of Australia, *Making Laws* (Web Page, May 2022) <https://www.aph.gov.au/About_Parliament/ House_of_Representatives/Powers_practice_and_procedure/00_-_Infosheets/Infosheet_7_-_Making_laws>.

Table 4.1: Relevant Legislation by Jurisdiction

Jurisdiction	Guardianship and administration	Powers of Attorney	Civil and Administrative Tribunal
Australian Capital Territory (ACT)	Guardianship and Management of Property Act 1991	Powers of Attorney Act 2006	ACT Civil and Administrative Tribunal Act 2008
Northern Territory (NT)	Guardianship of Adults Act 2016	Powers of Attorney Act 1992	Northern Territory Civil and Administrative Tribunal Act 2014
New South Wales (NSW)	Guardianship Act 1987	Powers of Attorney Act 2003	Civil and Administrative Tribunal Act 2013
Queensland	Guardianship and Administration Act 2000[10]	Powers of Attorney Act 1998	Queensland Civil and Administrative Tribunal Act 2009
South Australia (SA)	Guardianship and Administration Act 1993	Powers of Attorney Act and Agency 1984	South Australian Civil and Administrative Tribunal Act 2013
Tasmania	Guardianship and Administration Act 1995, Wills Act 2008	Powers of Attorney Act 2000	Guardianship and Administration Regulations 2017
Victoria	Guardianship and Administration Act 2019	Powers of Attorney Act 2014	Victorian Civil and Administrative Tribunal Act 1998
Western Australia (WA)	Guardianship and Administration Act 1990	Powers of Attorney Act 1990	State Administrative Tribunal Act 2004

---

[10]. Changes to guardianship laws and new enduring power of attorney and advance health directive forms commenced based on the Act on November 30, 2020. Queensland Government, *Changes to Guardianship Laws and Forms* (Web Page, November 30, 2020) <https://www.qld.gov.au/law/legal-mediation-and-justice-of-the-peace/power-of-attorney-and-making-decisions-for-others/guardianship-changes>.

Source: Partly modified by the author based on Sue Field, Karen Williams
and Carolyn Sappideen, *Elder Law: A Guide to Working with Older
Australians* (the Federation Express, 2018) 15

Table 4.2: Guardianship and Trustee Agencies by Jurisdiction

Jurisdiction	*Guardianship Agency*	*Trustee Agency*
ACT	The Public Trustee and Guardian (R-1)	The Public Trustee and Guardian (R-1)
NT	Office of the Public Guardian	Public Trustee Community Services Division
NSW	Office of the Public Guardian (R-2)	NSW Trustee and Guardian (R-2)
Queensland	Office of the Public Guardian Office of the Public Advocate (R-3)	The Public Trustee
SA	Office of the Public Advocate	The Public Trustee
Tasmania	Office of the Public Guardian	The Public Trustee
Victoria	Office of the Public Advocate	State Trustees Limited (R-4)
WA	Office of the Public Advocate	Public Trust Office

Source: Partly modified by the author based on Sue Field, Karen Williams
and Carolyn Sappideen, *Elder Law: A Guide to Working with
Older Australians* (the Federation Express, 2018) 15

*Remarks: (R-1) The agency merged with both offices of public guardian
and public trustee on April 1, 2016. (R-2) The administration department
of both institutions has been shared since 2009. (R-3) The Public
Advocate in Queensland works on behalf of adults with impaired
decision-making capacity but does not advocate directly on behalf of
individuals. (R-4) State Trustees Limited in Victoria is a 100 per cent state-
owned corporation, and the other trustee agencies that belong to each
state's treasury institution.*

As seen in Table 4.2, the States of Victoria and NSW enacted the Guardianship and Administration Act 1986[11] and the Guardianship Act 1987 and offered guardianship models in Australia. Regarding guardianship laws, both states have played leading roles in Australia.[12] Namely, Victoria took the lead by providing basic structures of guardianship. Within a few years after the enactment of legislation in 1986, other Australian states and special territories followed by creating guardianship tribunals together with associated public advocates, or the more restricted form, public guardians.[13] Arrangements made by financial management agencies were also adopted. NSW took the lead by enacting substituted consent for medical treatment in the 'Part 5 Medical and Dental Treatment' of the Guardianship Act 1987 (NSW).[14]

Modern guardianship and administration law was established by states and special territories over Australia between 1986 and 2000 based on above two Acts.[15] It is understood that the legislation and policies of these two states in guardianship may generally represent the basic stances of Australian legislation at large, and other states and territories followed their lead. Therefore, the analysis provided in this chapter will focus on these two states, Victoria and NSW, as representatives of Australian guardianship models. In the States of Victoria and NSW, draft amendments to the guardianship state laws were made for the first time in over thirty years.[16] In Victoria, the bill passed the state parliament in May 2019, and the Guardianship and Administration Act 2019 came into force in March 2020. A national statutory policy regarding elder abuse was tabled in June 2017 at the federal parliament aiming at legislating elder abuse at the national

---

[11.] The original name of the law was the *Guardianship and Administration Board Act 1985*, which came into force in 1987, and was renamed the *Guardianship and Administration Act 1986* in 1998 by the *Tribunals and Licensing Authorities (Miscellaneous Amendments) Act 1998* section 115. Nick O'Neill and Carmelle Peisah, 'Chapter 5—The Development of Modern Guardianship and Administration' in Nick O'Neill and Carmelle Peisah (eds), *Capacity and the Law* (Sydney University Press, 2011) 7.

[12.] Victoria's adult guardianship system was known as the 'Victorian model,' based on the 'one-stop-shop' concept. Victoria and NSW were in a rivalry relation with each other to make guardianship models. Terry Carney and David Tait, *The Adult Guardianship: Experiment Tribunals and Popular Justice* (The Federation Press, 1997) 18 and 23.

[13.] Guardianship in Australia includes two main duties conducted by two independent entities, namely the guardian and/or the administrator/financial manager nominated separately by tribunal orders. The guardian takes care of the principal's personal affairs, and the administrator or financial manager manages the principal's finances. Therefore, an administration in this Chapter as a duty of the administrator or financial manager refers to financial management of the principal.

[14.] Part 5 explored discussion: Ben White et al, 'The Legal Role of Medical Professionals in Decisions to Withhold or Withdraw Life-sustaining Treatment: Part 1 (New South Wales)' (2011) 18(3) *Journal of Law and Medicine* 498–522, 508.

[15.] The main issue in the 1980s was how to accommodate people with intellectual disabilities in communities with deinstitutionalization of psychiatric hospitals. Steve Bottomley, 'Mental Health Law Reform and Psychiatric Deinstitutionalization: The Issues in New South Wales' (1987) 10 *International Journal of Law and Psychiatry* 369, 362.

[16.] Refers to the Reference Survey: The Way Law Reform Reports are Processed in Australia. This survey summarizes how the law reform reports are processed in legislation, which is addressed by Terry Carney. The author received the permission from Terry Carney to include it in this study by email correspondence on July 20, 2021.

or state level. This process of amendments to state laws and national legislation policy was a response to social-environmental changes that are happening across Australia as follows:

First, Australia is seen as a steady rise in the aging of the population.[17] There is a rapid increase in the number of older people who suffer from dementia.[18] Adults with intellectual disabilities previously comprised adults with insufficient mental capacity, but mostly now consist of older people with dementia. People with higher brain dysfunction and those with mental disabilities are also increasing.[19] Australian state and special territory governments are now requested to respond to those who have various disabilities, including insufficient mental capacity.

Second, national legislation that respects the autonomy and right to self-determination of a person with disabilities is required. This is for legislative acceptance of the UN CRPD, which was ratified by Australia with a declaration of reservation in July 2008.[20] National legislation must follow the values of the CRPD.[21] In practice, supported decision-making activities recommended by the CRPD and its General Comment No.1 to realize the will and preferences of persons with disabilities are gradually being implemented in the community.[22]

[17.] The proportion of the population aged 65 and over in Australia was 15.6 per cent (2019) and is expected to rise 23.0 per cent (2055). Thirty per cent of older people aged 85 and over suffer from dementia. The current population of Australia is approximately 25 million. ALRC, *Elder Abuse—A National Legal Response Final Report* (ALRC Report 131, 2017) 18 <https://www.alrc.gov.au/publications/elder-abuse-report>.

[18.] There is an estimate of 472,000 Australians living with dementia in 2021, and the number of people with dementia is expected to increase to 590,000 by 2028 and 1,076,000 by 2058. (2018 commissioned research undertaken by the National Centre for Social and Economic Modelling (NATSEM), University of Canberra. Dementia Australia, *Dementia Statistics* (Web Page, January 2021) <https://www.dementia.org.au/statistics>; Craig Sinclair et al, *Supporting Decision-Making: A Guide for People Living with Dementia, Family Members and Carers* (Cognitive Decline Partnership Centre, 2018).

[19.] Refers to the New South Wales Law Reform Commission (NSW LRC), *Review of the Guardianship Act 1987* (NSW LRC Report 145, 2018) xxii.

[20.] The Government of Australia declared its understanding of several points at the ratification of the CRPD on July 17, 2008, including that the Convention fully allows supported or substituted decision-making arrangements, which provide for decisions to be made on behalf of a person, only when such arrangements are necessary, that is, as a last resort and subject to safeguards. UN, *Treaty Collection: Australia: 15. Convention on the Rights of Persons with Disabilities* (Web Page, n/a) <https://treaties.un.org/pages/ViewDetails.aspx?src=TREATY&mtdsg_no=IV-15&chapter=4#EndDec>.

[21.] Anita Smith, 'Developments in Australian Incapacity Legislation' (2018) 145 *PRECEDENT* 4, 8; see Article 3 (general principles) of the CRPD, such as respect for inherent dignity, individual autonomy including the freedom to make one's own choices, and independence of persons; non-discrimination; full and effective participation and inclusion in society, and so on. UN, *Convention on Rights of Persons with Disabilities (CRPD)*.

[22.] Australia has many practices of supported decision-making, which have explored discussion for research, such as legal capacity, autonomy, dignity of risk, and elder abuse. Piers Gooding, 'Supported Decision Making: A Rights-based Disability Concept and Its Implications for Mental Health Law' (2012) 20(3) *Psychiatry, Psychology and Law* 431, 451; Typical articles on supported decision-making in Australia: Michelle Browning, Christine Bigby and Jacinta Douglas, 'Supported Decision Making: Understanding How Its Conceptual Link to Legal Capacity Is Influencing the Development of Practice' (2014) 1(1) *Research and Practice in Intellectual and Developmental Disabilities* 34, 45; Anna Arstein-Kerslake et al, 'Future Direction is Supported Decision-Making' (Online 2017) 37(1) *Disability Studies Quarterly* <https://dsq-sds.org/article/id/360/>; Terry Carney, 'Supported Decision-Making in Australia: Meeting the Challenge of Moving from Capacity to Capacity-Building?' (2017) 35(2) *Disability, Rights and Law Reform in Australia* 44, 63.

The consciousness and mindset of supporters who stand by persons with disabilities are now changing.

Third, the Australian society has become multicultural due to the acceptance of immigrants with diverse languages and cultures, particularly since the 1970s. Acceptance and maintenance of diversity, including older people, must be considered, which may influence advocacy activities in the community.

4.2.2 Victorian State Act

(1) Guardianship Legislation

The Guardianship and Administration Act 2019 (Act No. 13 of 2019) was enacted in May 2019 and came into force in March 2020 in the state of Victoria. The earlier legislation, the Guardianship and Administration Act 1986 (hereinafter referred to as 'Victorian Act 1986')[23] and the Powers of Attorney Act 2014 (hereinafter referred to as 'PoA Act 2014'), will be reviewed. The Victorian Act 1986 and the PoA Act 2014 are the essential laws to prescribe the legal frameworks of the adult guardianship system.[24] The main points are summarized as follows:[25]

(a)   The guardianship system is mainly divided into two types: guardianship for personal affairs of the principal and an administration for the financial management of the principal.[26] The Victorian Civil and Administrative Tribunal (hereinafter referred to as 'VCAT') appoints the guardian and/ or the administrator separately (sections 22 and 46 of the Victorian Act 1986).[27] They are responsible for personal affairs (the guardian) and financial management (the administrator) of the principal. VCAT may appoint multiple guardians or administrators. VCAT may appoint administrators to

---

[23.] The Victorian Act 1986 was drafted based on the designs proposed in the 'Cocks Report,' which was the legislative report submitted in 1982 by the Victorian Minister's Committee on Rights & Protective Legislation for Intellectually Handicapped Persons headed by Errol Cocks. Victoria. Minister's Committee on Rights & Protective Legislation for Intellectually Handicapped Persons and Errol Cocks, *Report of The Minister's Committee on Rights & Protective Legislation for Intellectually Handicapped Persons* (Victorian State Government, 1982) <https://www.vgls.vic.gov.au/client/en_AU/VGLS-public/search/results?qu=Cocks%2C+E.+%28Errol%29&ps=300>.

[24.] Section 3(1) (definitions) of the Victorian Act 1986 states that the term 'disability' includes physical ability. The Japan's statutory guardianship system is not subject to people with physical disabilities.

[25.] The main features are summarized by the author based on the relevant Acts and website information on the guardianship law and policy, such as the Office of the Public Advocate (OPA). Victorian OPA, *Guardianship and Administration* (Web Page, 2019) <https://www.publicadvocate.vic.gov.au/guardianship-administration>.

[26.] The 'represented person' in law refers to 'the principal' in this study.

[27.] The emergence of the tribunal-based guardianship system was first in Tasmania in 1963. 'The *Mental Health Act 1963 (Tas.)* established both a Guardianship Board, with power to regulate its own proceedings, and a Mental Health Review Tribunal.' Nick O'Neill and Carmelle Peisah, 'Chapter 5—The Development of Modern Guardianship and Administration' in Nick O'Neill and Carmelle Peisah (eds), *Capacity and the Law 2021 Edition* (Online, December 14, 2021) 3 <http://austlii.community/foswiki/Books/CapacityAndTheLaw/WebHome>.

have joint and several powers but ensuring that they act jointly on major financial transactions. Additionally, VCAT might appoint administrators with different powers, for example, one administrator may have powers to engage in specific litigation for the principal, whereas the other managers have powers to engage in his or her usual financial responsibilities.[28]

(b) A guardian is not entitled to any remuneration for acting that role.[29] A relative or friend of the principal is usually appointed as the guardian. If the relative or friend is not eligible for appointment, VCAT may appoint a Public Advocate as the adult guardian (section 23). The Public Advocate may further assign his/her duties to either an advocate guardian who belongs to the Office of the Public Advocate (hereinafter referred to as 'OPA'), or a community guardian who is an individual or a not-for-profit organization (hereinafter referred to as 'NPO') that has participated in an adult guardianship training program (section 18).[30]

(c) Among relatives, friends, solicitors, accountants, the State Trustees Limited (hereinafter referred to as 'STL'), and professional financial manager, an administrator should be appointed by VCAT as a person appropriate for the principal in financial management (section 47). The Public Advocate is not appointed as an administrator. The administrator conducts financial processes, such as banking affairs, payments, sales of assets, and makes legal decisions that are in the best interest of the principal (section 48). An administrator is not entitled to any remuneration for acting that role, but the remuneration of a professional administrator is entitled to be approved by the VCAT (section 47A).

(d) The *PoA Act 2014* establishes a general power of attorney (PoA) and an enduring power of attorney (hereinafter referred to as 'EPA'). An EPA is a legal document that lets the donor appoint one or more people, known as attorneys, to help make decisions or to make decisions on their behalf about their property or money. The designated third party by PoA or EPA makes decisions concerning the principal. A PoA loses its legal effect if the mental capacity of the principal is lost. In an EPA, a proxy can be made

---

[28.] The VCAT can appoint a guardian or administrator who has the power to undertake legal proceedings in the name of and on behalf of the principal, and in relation to personal or financial matters named in the order. Victorian OPA, *Litigation Guardian* (Web Page, n/a) <https://www.publicadvocate.vic.gov.au/guardianship-and-administration/litigation-guardian>.

[29.] Non-remuneration policy for guardians and administrators is adopted in the Victorian Act 1986 based on the Cocks Report 1982. This is 'to avoid the conflict associated with payment,' as remarked by Terry Carney in email correspondence on December 6, 2021. Due to this policy, paid workers or corporations receiving remuneration are basically not eligible to be appointed guardians or administrators except for those who are accepted by section 94A. This policy is adopted in jurisdictions all over Australia.

[30.] Eleven community guardians involved with fifteen guardianship matters in the state of Victoria between 2020 and 2021. Victoria, Office of Public Advocacy (OPA), *Annual Report 2020–2021* (Victorian OPA Report, Online, 2021) 19 <https://www.publicadvocate.vic.gov.au/opa-s-work/our-organisation/annual-reports/opa-annual-reports/359-opa-annual-report-2020-2021>.

for decision by a designated third party even if the principal loses his/her mental capacity. It is widely encouraged by those who are over the age of 18, i.e., citizens who can understand the meaning and impact of an EPA. An EPA is not required to register at any authority.[31] An EPA is common in common law jurisdictions, including the UK, the US, and Canada. The PoA Act 2014 introduces the 'supportive attorney' appointment, which is regarded as a milestone with proceeding to supported decision-making.[32]

(2) Public Agencies

The state of Victoria has three public agencies as the component that are involved in guardianship as follows:

(a)   The Office of the Public Advocate[33] (hereinafter referred to as 'OPA') was established within the Department of Justice and Community Safety of the state of Victoria, based on the Victorian Act 1986. The director-general of Victorian OPA, the Public Advocate, is an individual who is appointed by the Governor in Council, who holds office for seven years (schedule 3 cl 1(1) of the Victorian Act 1986). The Public Advocate is independent of the state government and is responsible for directly reporting to the state parliament (schedule 3 cl 1(5)). The main roles of the Victorian OPA are as follows: advice and consultation service; research and policy planning in advocacy for persons with disabilities; education; public relations; seminar activities; and operating volunteer programs, including the community visitor program (sections 15 and 16).

(b)   The Victorian Civil and Administrative Tribunal (VCAT) was established in 1998 based on the Victorian Civil and Administrative Tribunal Act 1998 (hereinafter referred to as 'VCAT Act 1998'). It became an independent institute from the state courts system by the *Courts Services Victoria Act 2014*. VCAT has a total of six offices in the state of Victoria. (Through COVID-19 pandemic, their style of operation changed to a hybrid

---

[31.] A mandatory registration scheme for enduring power of attorney relating to financial matters is a possible measure to prevent financial exploitation but has not been materialized yet. Australian Government, Attorney-General's Department, *National Register of Enduring Powers of Attorney: Public Consultation Paper* (Attorney-General's Department, April 2021) <https://www.ag.gov.au/rights-and-protections/publications/national-register-epoa-public-consultation-paper-and-submission-template>.

[32.] A 'supportive attorney' is a person under Part 7 of the *PoA Act 2014* to support a person with disability to excise his/her rights in making and giving effect to decisions related to any personal, financial, or other matter specified in the appointment. A supportive attorney is not entitled to any remuneration (section 84 and 90 (2) of *PoA Act 2014*); John Chesterman, 'Supported Decision-Making' in Sue Field, Karen Williams and Carolyn Sappideen (eds), *Elder Law: A Guide to Working with Older Australians* (The Federation Press, 2018) 103–4.

[33.] The Victorian OPA has 122 paid employees with an annual income of A$15.6 million (US$10.0 million), which breaks down into A$12.4 million (US$7.9 million) by output appropriation (the state budget) and A$3.2 million (US$2.0 million) by the grants. Victorian OPA (n 30) 60–2.

approach, combining online and in-person hearings.) VCAT deals with civil disputes, such as residential tenancies, guardianship, civil claims, planning and environment, and Owners Corporation. A total of 75,290 cases were lodged between 2020 and 2021, of which some 14,169 cases (18.8 per cent) were the guardianship cases as a part of the human rights division.[34] The President and Vice Presidents (a total ten judicial members) of the VCAT are judges, but the other 191 VCAT members who decide guardianship cases are practitioners with relevant human rights experience in legal practice or community members with practical experience.[35] They have hearings at the VCAT with the applicants and their related citizens, including relatives, friends, nursing home practitioners, and interpreters within thirty days after receiving the applications.[36] A VCAT member issues an order for the guardianship with a one to three years self-revocation term and judges whether or not to renew the order at the rehearing when the term is over.[37] The VCAT 'must act fairly and according to the substantial merits of the case in all proceedings' (section 97 of the VCAT Act 1998) while the VCAT allows the members be flexible in their decision-making processes (section 98).[38] Emphasis is placed on *the principle of necessity*

---

[34] There were 17,452 major applications and activities in the VCAT guardianship list between 2020 and 2021. The break down by section showed 5,473 guardianship/administration orders, 6,917 reassessment orders, 3,268 advice to the administrator, 548 PoAs, and 1,246 the others. The number of PoA applications was as small as some 3 per cent but the cases of complicated PoAs increased. Victorian Civil and Administrative Tribunal (VCAT), *Annual Report 2020–21* (Online, 2021) <https://www.vcat.vic.gov.au/about-vcat/annual-reports-and-strategic-plan> 49 and 81.

[35] The VCAT has a total of 201 members, including ten judicial members (president/vice presidents), and 263 staff in office as of June 2021 and one VCAT member holds hearings and issues an order to the applicants. VCAT (n 34), 120; in the state of NSW, three members who are composed of a lawyer in attorney, a welfare practitioner, and a community representative conduct hearing. Interview of VCAT by the author on March 6, 2019; 'tribunal members usually sit as a single member or multi-disciplinary panels of three and come from various disciplines, including law, medicine, finance, social work and welfare.' Robyn Carroll and Anita Smith, 'Mediation in Guardianship Proceedings for the Elderly: An Australian Perspective' (2010) 28(1) *The Windsor Yearbook of Access to Justice* 53–80, 63.

[36] The author attended four hearing sessions at VCAT with permission on am March 12, 2019. Hearings are set in forty-five-minute increments seven times a day for one member, and a hearing may even end in less time. The conversations at each session are recorded for evidence. An interpreter is frequently arranged by the VCAT to interpret English into an applicant's mother tongue and vice versa if an applicant does not understand English. The VCAT cases are published in a web-database with privacy considerations. AustLii, *Victorian Civil and Administrative Tribunal* (Web Page, n/a) <http://www.austlii.edu.au/cgi-bin/viewdb/au/cases/vic/VCAT/>.

[37] In empirical test data, tribunal members in the State of Queensland largely rely on medical evidence in capacity assessment of principals and the preference for evidence of incapacity in personal/financial capacity decisions is seen. Sam Boyle, 'Determining Capacity: How Beneficence Can Operate in an Autonomy-Focused Legal Regime' (2018) 26(1) *The Elder Law Journal* 35, 63; VCAT cases between 2001 and 2016 are analyzes: Joanne Watson et al, 'The Impact of the United Nations Convention on the Rights of Persons with Disabilities (CRPD) on Victorian Guardianship Practice' (Online, 2020) *Disability and Rehabilitation* <https://doi.org/10.1080/0963 8288.2020.1836680>.

[38] Section 98(1) of the VCAT Act 1998 stipulates that 'The Tribunal—(a) is bound by the rules of natural justice; (b) is not bound by the rules of evidence or any practices or procedures applicable to courts of record, except to the extent that it adopts those rules, practices or procedures; (c) may inform itself on any matter as it sees fit; (d) must conduct each proceeding with as little formality and technicality, and determine each proceeding with as much speed, as the requirements of this Act and the enabling enactment and a proper consideration of the matters before it permit.'

and the *less restrictive alternative*.[39] In case of dispute on an EPA, relevant people can lodge a petition to the VCAT to settle a dispute, although an EPA is not required to register at public agencies by law.[40]

(c)   The State Trustees Limited (hereinafter referred to as 'STL'), a state-run financial management company in the state of Victoria, provides financial management services with fees.[41] STL provides various management services with citizens, including wills, PoA/EPA, estates, and personal financial administration.[42] If the relative or friend of the principal is not a qualified person, the VCAT may appoint an STL as the administrator with or without fees (section 47A).[43] STL assists the VCAT by contract on reviewing and providing the financial reports which the administrators must submit annually to the VCAT.[44] STL has a satellite office in the VCAT headquarter and its manager is in charge of any business transaction between the TSL and VCAT, including financial exploitation claims.[45] It seems that there is room for the STL to improve their services to respond to the needs of clients by carefully taking their will and preferences into consideration.[46]

---

[39] For example, there was the case that VCAT withdrew a guardianship order with 'an emphasis on exploring less restrictive options, promoting AC's best interests, and giving effect to his wishes.' AC (Guardianship) [2009] VCAT 753 (May 8, 2009).

[40] The Supreme Court or VCAT may order an attorney under an EPA to compensate the principal a loss caused by an attorney contravening any provision of the Power of Attorney Act 2014 (section 77). There was the case that the NSW Civil and Administrative Tribunal reviewed the EPA and revoked it, then issued an order to appoint the other person as a public guardian. QBU [2008] NSWGT 18 (July 4, 2008); See these articles regarding the misuse or abuse of PoAs: Nola M. Ries, 'When Powers of Attorney Go Wrong: Preventing Financial Abuse of Older People by Enduring Attorneys' (2018) 148 *Precedent* 9, 13; This is the article to analyze damage and countermeasures related to CPAs in five European countries.

[41] The STL is 100 per cent owned by the Victorian state treasurer and the policy of the STL is determined by the board members who are appointed by the Victorian Minister of Treasure. STL has 506 employees with an income AS$72.2 million (US$46.1 million), and AS$21.0 (US$13.4 million, approximately 29.0 per cent of the income) is 'community service agreement income,' which is a state subsidy. This state subsidy is based on the statutory agreement regulated by section 21 of the State Trustees (State Own Company) Act 1994. Victoria State Trustees Limited, *Annual Report 2021* (Online, 2021) <https://www.statetrustees.com.au/about-us/our-governance/annual-reports> 25 and 44.

[42] The STL has about 9,000 personal financial administration clients and about 6,700 PoA contracts clients. STL takes care of 220,000 wills and 31,000 estates. STL, *Homepage* (Web Page, March 2021) <https://www.statetrustees.com.au/>.

[43] If the principal cannot pay fees, VCAT may appeal that the principal does not have to pay fees to the STL, and the fees are paid from the state budget on behalf of the principal (from the interview of the VCAT on March 6, 2019, by the author). There is a case that the tribunal appoints a state trustee as the administrator because of potential conflict of interest between the principal and the son. *SA (Guardianship) [2008] VCAT 2345 (17 November 2008)*.

[44] From the interview of STL VCAT satellite office by the author on March 3, 2017.

[45] The STL suggests the clients who suffer from fraudulent damage or financial exploitation to claim to the VCAT (from the interview of the STL VCAT satellite office by the author on March 6, 2019).

[46] The client complaints against the STL have been increasing over the years, which resulted in a Victorian ombudsman investigation to determine the reason. The findings were reported in June 2019, which pointed out thirty problem cases involving in the STL and proposed fourteen recommendations to the STL and the Victorian State

(3) Dispute Response Mechanism

VCAT has adopted a dispute response mechanism known as alternative dispute resolution (hereinafter referred to as 'ADR'). Four measures can be processed through VCAT: complaint resolution; mediation; Fast Track Mediation and Hearing service (hereinafter referred to as 'FTMH'); and appeals to the Supreme Court.[47]

(a)   Any member of the public or group of people, including companies or public agencies, can make a complaint through the VCAT.[48] VCAT takes a three-tier approach (i.e., frontline resolution, investigation, internal interview) to resolve complaints. In fact, VCAT received 313 complaints about VCAT people or processes between July 2020 and June 2021 and provided a response within ten business days of receiving the complaint of these cases.[49]

(b)   VCAT advocates mediation as the preferred option for resolving disputes. Mediation provides an alternative to hearing as a way of resolving a dispute. Mediation is more informal, less stressful for those involved, and can lead to better outcomes—people may feel empowered by the process. VCAT expanded the reach of the FTMH in 2017. If the amount in dispute is between A\$500 and A\$10,000 (US\$319 and US\$6,390), parties may be invited to attend a mediation—an opportunity to resolve the dispute by talking through the issues with the other people involved. It is assisted by an accredited mediator from the Dispute Settlement Centre of Victoria (hereinafter referred to as 'DSCV') or the VCAT.[50] If the dispute is not resolved at mediation, the dispute goes to a VCAT hearing within a few hours. At the hearing, a VCAT member decides the case. There are no hearing fees necessary for this same-day service. Between July 2020 and June 2021, VCAT assessed 1,695 cases as being suitable for the FTMH (online video). About 46 per cent of the cases out of the mediation and

---

Government for improvements. Victorian Ombudsman, *Investigation into State Trustees* (Web Page, June 29, 2019) <https://www.ombudsman.vic.gov.au/our-impact/investigation-reports/investigation-into-state-trustees/>.

[47.] It is emphasized that the persons with disabilities must be included in any process of ADR so that the principals' wishes are considered in the resolution of the dispute. Law Institute Victoria, *ONE–VCAT: President's Review of the Victorian Civil and Administrative Tribunal* (VCAT Report, 2009).

[48.] Alternatively, people may complain with the Victorian Ombudsman. VCAT, *Complaints Policy* (Web Page, n/a) <https://www.vcat.vic.gov.au/about-vcat/feedback-and-complaints/complaints-policy>.

[49.] Twenty complaints out of a total 313 complaints were fully or partially upheld because the allegations were substantiated. VCAT (n 34) 126.

[50.] The Victorian Government supports the FTMH program with A\$6.26 million (US\$4.0 million) over four years to the DSCV.

compulsory conference conducted for 2,725 cases were settled.[51] Mediation and the FTMH, however, are not often used in the guardianship cases because of its characteristics.[52]

(c)   If the VCAT is satisfied on reasonable ground that there is an immediate risk of harm to the health, welfare or property of a proposed principal if the order was not made, the VCAT may prioritize a case in the guardianship and administration list.[53] The VCAT may apply two different processes, namely the VCAT makes an urgent guardianship order or urgent administration order (valid for twenty-one days) to parties concerned without hearing,[54] or has a hearing to facilitate the process. These are in the process of guardianship and administration list and a VCAT member issues an order.[55] These cases are mostly disputed between older mothers and their sons. In such family dispute cases, it is assumed by the statistics that the VCAT hearing would be appropriate, keeping people's sentiments and privacy in mind. VCAT decisions can be appealed to the Supreme Court only on the question of law—that is, where a party believes the judge or tribunal member made a legal error. Between July 2020 and June 2021, the total number of appeals lodged was seventy-six, and only three of these appeals were granted and upheld by the Supreme Court.[56]

(4) Victorian Unique Legislations

The state of Victoria has unique legislation to regulate the charter of human rights, a medical treatment/medical treatment decision, and voluntary assisted dying as follows:

[51.] Refers to the VCAT (n 34) 53.

[52.] A VCAT member comments on the mediation system in practice by email (August 12, 2021) that 'only when there is a compensation application against an attorney and the principal is deceased, VCAT members would generally mediate in a guardianship matter.' Robyn Carroll and Anita Smith, 'Mediation in Guardianship Proceedings for the Elderly: An Australian Perspective' (2010) 28(1) *The Windsor Yearbook of Access to Justice* 53, 80.

[53.] Refers to the Victorian Act 2019 section 36(2), which stipulates that the 'risk of harm' is abuse, exploitation, neglect, and self-neglect.

[54.] Ibid.

[55.] The STL report in 2016 indicates that approximately 15 per cent of the financial exploitation cases employing hearing through the VCAT could recover the financial damage. The 2014–2015 dispute results were reported by the Victorian STL: 26 per cent investigation has not progressed due to personal death, etc.; 39 per cent insufficient evidence; 20 per cent has not chosen legal procedure; 15 per cent has recovered damages by using legal procedure. Lewis Melanie, 'Financial Elder Abuse in a Victorian Context: Now and into the Future' (Conference Paper at the fourth National Conference on Elder Abuse held in Melbourne on February 24–25, 2016).

[56.] Refers to the VCAT (n 34) 99. This appeal is based on section 148 of the *Victorian Civil and Administrative Tribunal Act 1998*.

(a)   The Charter of Human Rights and Responsibilities Act 2006 is a law that
      sets out the basic rights, freedom, and responsibilities of people in the
      state of Victoria, in which twenty fundamental human rights are listed.[57] It
      regulates the relationship between the government and the people it serves.
      The Constitution in Australia does not state a bill of rights. Human rights
      are protected by case laws and statute laws. This Act is a comprehensive
      law that empowers human rights in the state of Victoria; however, some
      critiques are addressed with lack of some rights. Some rights are not in-
      cluded in the Charter after the debates in the state parliament, such as the
      right to life and the right to self-determination because 'the Charter only
      includes human rights that had extraordinarily strong, certainly at least
      majority community support.'[58]

(b)   VCAT can grant the authority of medical consent for or refuse medical
      treatment to the third party after hearings, and usually nominates a person
      other than the guardian or administrator.[59] The Victorian Medical Treatment
      Planning and Decisions Act 2016 was enacted in 2016 and came into force
      on March 12, 2018.[60] In this law, a medical support person is to support
      the principal by communicating information on the principal's medical
      treatment, including when the principal does not have a decision-making
      capacity. However, a medical support person does not have the power to
      make a principal's medical treatment decision (section 32). The medical
      treatment decision-maker, not a medical support person, who is appointed
      by the principal or the VCAT has the power to make the principal's med-
      ical treatment decisions (section 55).[61] The Act 2016 makes it possible
      for Victorians to create legally binding advance care directives to make
      an instructional directive about treatment a person consents to or refuses,
      or a values directive about a person's views and values (section 6). In

---

[57.] Refers to the Victorian Equal Opportunity and Human Rights Commission, *Victoria's Charter of Human Rights and Responsibilities* (Web Page, n/a) <https://www.humanrights.vic.gov.au/legal-and-policy/victorias-human-rights-laws/the-charter/>.

[58.] George Williams, 'The Victorian Charter of Human Rights and Responsibilities: Origins and Scope' (2006) 30(3) *Melbourne University Law Review* 880, 905.

[59.] The tribunals of the states and special territories except the Northern Territory have powers to provide consent for or refuse medical treatment on behalf of a person with a disability by trial. Sue Field, Karen Williams and Carolyn Sappideen, *Elder Law: A Guide to Working with Older Australians* (The Federation Press, 2018) 27.

[60.] Futoshi Iwata, 'The Role of the Law in the Medical Care and Care of the Elderly in Australia: Focusing on the Recent Amendments to Victoria State Law' (2019) 80(1) *Comparative Law Research* 42, 55 (in Japanese).

[61.] It is complicated that legally recognized multiple support schemes for people with disabilities by law are seen in the state of Victoria, in addition to a guardian/administrator and a supportive guardian/administrator (the *Guardianship and Administration Act 2019*), i.e., a medical support person, a medical treatment decision-maker (the *Medical Treatment Planning and Decisions Act 2016*), a supportive attorney (the *Powers of Attorney Act 2014*), a plan nominee or correspondence nominee (*The National Disability Insurance Scheme Act 2013*), and a nominated person (the *Mental Health Act 2014*).

practice, there are statutory and non-statutory advance care directives, which still makes the situation complex.[62]

(c)   The Voluntary Assisted Dying Act 2017 was enacted on November 29, 2017, and came into force on June 9, 2019.[63] The law was drafted, as a model law in the U.S. state of Oregon, with comprehensive safeguards and rigorous protections.[64] Voluntary assisted dying is available to Victorians who are over the age of 18, who have lived in Victoria for at least twelve months, and who have decision-making capacity.[65] It is only for people who are suffering from an incurable, advanced and progressive disease, illness or medical condition, who are experiencing intolerable suffering. The condition must be assessed by two medical practitioners to be expected to cause death within six months. The Voluntary Assisted Dying Review Board independently monitors and reviews all activities under the law. Since the enforcement of the Act in June 2019 till June 2021, it was reported that a total of 331 people died from taking the prescribed medication.[66]

(5) Victorian Interdisciplinary Research and Practices

Victorian interdisciplinary research and practices are seen in the state of Victoria to support people with disability or diagnoses as follows:

(a)   The practice framework of La Trobe University provides an evidence-based guide for engaging in effective support for decision-making with people with disability. 'The framework outlines the steps, principles, and strategies

---

[62.] The recent research survey shows that 60 per cent of people with dementia had some form of advanced care planning documentation and only half of the cases in which advanced care planning was documented included an advanced care directive completed by the person themselves. Jamie Bryant et al, 'Advance Care Planning Participation by People with Dementia: A Cross-Sectional Survey and Medical' (2021) *BMJ Supportive and Palliative Care* 1, 5.

[63.] The Voluntary Assisted Dying Act 2019 (WA) was enacted in the state of Western Australia. Takako Minami, 'Characterization of the Voluntary Assisted Dying Legislation in the Australian State of Victoria' (2018) 28(1) *Bioethics* 40, 48 (in Japanese); Takako Minami, 'Issues Surrounding Voluntary Assisted Dying Laws in Australia' (2021) 34 *Journal of Australian Studies* 14, 29 (in Japanese); Ben White et al, 'Does the Voluntary Assisted Dying Act 2017 (Vic) Reflect Its Stated Policy Goals?' (2020) 43(2) *UNSW Law Journal* 417, 451; Nola M. Ries and Elise Mansfield, 'Supported Decision-Making: A Good Idea in Principle but We Need to Consider Supporting Decisions about Voluntary Assisted Dying' in Daniel J. Fleming and David J. Carter (eds), *Voluntary Assisted Dying: Law? Health? Justice?* (ANU Press, 2022) 49, 73.

[64.] From the interview of the Victorian Department of Health and Human Services by the author on March 12, 2019.

[65.] Refers to the Health Vic., *Voluntary Assisted Dying* (Web Page, October 24, 2021) <https://www2.health.vic.gov.au/hospitals-and-health-services/patient-care/end-of-life-care/voluntary-assisted-dying>.

[66.] It was reported that 836 people have been assessed for eligibility to access a voluntary assisted dying, 674 permit applications have been made, 597 permits have been issued, and 331 people have died since June 2019. Victorian Voluntary Assisted Dying Review Board, *Voluntary Assisted Dying Report of Operations (January to June 2021)* (Victoria State Government, December 14, 2021) <https://www.health.vic.gov.au/voluntary-assisted-dying/voluntary-assisted-dying-review-board>.

involved in support for decision-making. It focuses on understanding the will and preferences of people with cognitive disabilities and guides those who provide support including families, support workers, guardians, and health professionals.'[67]

(b) Lisa Brophy presents findings from an interdisciplinary supported decision-making project, investigating the facilitators for people living with diagnoses, including severe depression;[68]

(c) The National Disability Services (NDS) developed a checklist to quantify and operationalize 'at risk' adults for disability service providers and organizations. This checklist is useful for local governments and the relevant agencies;[69]

(d) A study of collaboration of healthcare staff and lawyers reveals that 'the Community Health Service (hereinafter referred to as 'CHS') staff regarding the integration of a lawyer into their CHS.' It is confirmed by research data that 'these CHS staff were aware of the potential impacts of elder abuse and supported embedding a lawyer in the health service.' Such a CHS staff and lawyer collaboration model can be assumed to be an applied method to be useful to start with community whenever they are possible.[70]

(e) A research program by Monash University in the State of Victoria, known as the Protecting Elders' Assets Study (PEAS), examines rural and multicultural responses to intra-familial and inter-generational asset management in the State of Victoria.[71] This research implies gaps of behavior in asset management among older Victorians according to their cultural backgrounds. It establishes the fact that Australians with roots in non-English speaking countries, such as Vietnamese Australians, do not use EPAs as much as Australians with English-speaking ancestry do. It can be said that, generally, people with Asian origins do not use EPAs.

(f) The dignity of risk, i.e., the principle of allowing an individual the dignity afforded by risk-taking, with subsequent enhancement of personal growth

---

[67] Jacinta Douglas and Christine Bigby, 'Development of an Evidence-based Practice Framework to Guide Decision Making Support for People with Cognitive Impairment' (2020) 42(3) *Disability and Rehabilitation* 434, 441.

[68] Lisa Brophy et al, 'Community Treatment Orders and Supported Decision-Making' (2019) 10 *Frontiers in Psychiatry* Article 414.

[69] Emily Moir et al, 'Best Practice for Estimating Elder Abuse Prevalence in Australia: Moving Towards the Dynamic Concept of "Adults at Risk" and Away from Arbitrary Age Cut-Offs' (2017) 29(2) *Current Issues in Criminal Justice* 181, 190.

[70] Virginia J. Lewis et al, 'Addressing Elder Abuse Through Integrating Law into Health: What Do Allied Health Professionals at a Community Health Service in Melbourne, Australia, Think?' (2019) 17 *Australasian Journal of Ageing* 1, 6.

[71] C. King et al, 'For Love or Money: Intergenerational Management of Older Victorians' Assets, Protecting Elders' Assets Study' (Monash University, Eastern Health Clinical School, 2011) <https://www.eapu.com.au/uploads/research_resources/VIC-For_Love_or_Money_JUN_2011-Monash.pdf>.

and quality of life or risk enablement[72] is being discussed as a process of positively taking risk within established safeguards.[73] By this method, people with disability would keep consumer choice and control over activities. This is a significant development in risk and welfare studies that is to be researched further to seek a possibility to overcome certain risk factors by advocating the risk.

(6) Main Characteristics and Summary of the Victorian Act 1986

Viewing the above, the main characteristics of the Victorian guardianship system can be summarized as the following six points:[74] (i) The roles of the guardian, administrator, and medical support person/medical treatment decision-maker are legally separated;[75] (ii) emphasis is placed on *the principle of necessity* and the *less restrictive alternative* in the adult guardianship system; (iii) VCAT as the tribunal, not the courts, make a judgement on the adult guardianship by hearings and issues orders; (iv) OPA provides various public supports for the guardianship in policy reviewing that contributes to the community; (v) a state-run financial management company, STL provides financial management services with fees; and (vi) collaboration of practitioners, institutions, and NPOs in communities are ongoing. Please refer to Table 4.3 as the summary of the Victorian Act 1986.

[72.] The 'risk enablement' refers to a way of supporting people with a cognitive impairment, such as intellectual disabilities, traumatic brain injury or dementia, to participate in activities that involve risk. La Trobe University (Victoria), *Enabling Risk* (Web Page, n/a) <http://www.enablingriskresource.com.au/>.

[73.] The 'dignity of risk' refers to 'the principle of allowing an individual the dignity afforded by risk-taking, with subsequence of personal growth and quality of life.' Joseph E. Ibrahim raises a dilemma case whether or not an older person with dementia is fit to drive, conflicting interests between the person with dementia and the community in a short video. Joseph E. Ibrahim and Marie-Claire Davis, 'Impediments to Applying the "Dignity of Risk" Principle in Residential Aged Care Services' (2013) 32(3) *Australasian Journal on Ageing* 188–93, 189; Victorian Equal Opportunity and Human Rights Commission, *Rights and Risk* (Victorian Equal Opportunity and Human Rights Commission, 2014) 14; Marta H. Woolford et al, 'Applying Dignity of Risk Principles to Improve Quality of Life for Vulnerable Persons' (2020) 35(1) *International Journal of Geriatric Psychiatry* 122, 130.

[74.] The five principles of the Australian guardianship law are seen: (a) presumption of capacity, (b) the least restrictive option taken by the decision-maker, (c) respect for autonomy, (d) inclusion as a valued member of the community, and (e) the adult's welfare and interests. Lindy Willmott et al, 'Guardianship and Health Decisions in China and Australia: A Comparative Analysis' (2017) 12(2) *Asian Journal of Comparative Law* 371, 400.

[75.] It is viewed that such divisions of the roles and duties by the adult guardian, the administrator, and medical support person/medical treatment decision maker may make sense to the principal because of cross-checking and balancing the function of one another. In this sense, they say that the worst case is where the adult guardian can do everything to the principal without any accountability. From the interview of Victorian OPA by the author on March 5, 2019.

Table 4.3: Victorian Act 1986

Items	Comments
Adult Guardianship System	Divided into two types: adult guardianship and financial management or administration which are responsible for personal affairs and financial management of the represented person.
Adult Guardian	A friend or relative familiar with the represented person is usually appointed. If the friend or relative is not a qualified person, VCAT may appoint a public advocate (an advocate guardian).
Administrator	Among friends, relatives, staff solicitor, accountant, state trustees, and professional financial manager, an administrator shall be appointed by VCAT as a person appropriate for the represented person in financial management.
Remuneration	A guardian or an administrator is not entitled to any remuneration for acting that role, but the remuneration of a professional administrator is entitled to be approved by the VCAT.
Enduring Power of Attorney (EPA)	EPA is widely encouraged for those who are over the age of 18, that can understand the meaning and impact of an EPA.
Office of Public Advocate (OPA)	Victorian OPA has been established within the Department of Justice and Community Safety of Victoria. The main roles of OPA are as follows: advice and consultation services; research and policy planning in advocacy for persons with disabilities; education; public relations; seminar activities; and operating volunteer programs, including the community visitor program.[76]

---

[76] 'Community Visitors,' which are Victorian Governor in Council appointees, are appointed for a three-year term, and have significant powers of entry and inspection to Victorian accommodation facilities for people with disability or mental illness in their local area. They visit unannounced, monitor, and write a report on adequacy of the services provided. Victorian OPA, *Community Visitors* (Web Page, n/a) <https://www.publicadvocate.vic. gov.au/opa-volunteers/community-visitors>; Terry Carney states this is one of 'advocacy solutions as a way of

Items	*Comments*
Victorian Civil and Administrative Tribunal (VCAT)	A total of six offices in Victoria. VCAT primarily deals with disputes concerning human rights affairs including adult guardianship. The staff consists of an expert who has a long experience in adult guardianship and administration.
Medical Treatment Planning and Decisions Act 2016	A medical decision-making system based on an advanced care directive came into force on March 12, 2018. *Voluntary Assisted Dying Act 2017* was introduced and came into force on June 19, 2019.

Source: Made by the author

4.2.3 NSW State Act: Summary

Please refer to Table 4.4 as the summary of the NSW State Act (the Guardianship Act 1987).[77]

Table 4.4: NSW State Act 1987

Items	*Comments*
Adult Guardianship System	Mainly divided into two types: guardianship and financial management. The Guardianship Act 1987 is the key legislation in NSW which protects the rights of people with impaired decision-making capacity.

---

solving the conundrum how to regulate or influence that private marketplace in a practical way.' Terry Carney, 'The Limits and the Social Legacy of Guardianship in Australia' (1898) 18(4) *Federal Law Review* 231–66, 265.

[77.] The scope of a person with disability is defined in a broader sense in Article 3(2), the Guardianship Act 1987: '(a) who is intellectually, physically, psychologically, or sensorily disabled, (b) who is of advanced age, (c) who is a mentally ill person within the meaning of the Mental Health Act 2007, or (d) who is otherwise disabled, and who, by virtue of that fact, is restricted in one or more major life activities to such an extent that he or she requires supervision or social habilitation.'

Items	*Comments*
Adult Guardian	A guardian is a substitute decision-maker appointed by NCAT or the Supreme Court with authority to make health and lifestyle decisions. A person is not eligible to be appointed as a guardian, who provides the services for fees to the person, such as medical service, accommodation, and any other services to support the person making the appointment.
Financial Manager	A financial manager shall be appointed as a person appropriate for the represented person in financial management among friends, relatives, staff solicitor, accountant, NSW Trustee and Guardian, and professional financial manager.
Enduring Power of Attorney (EPA)	EPA is widely encouraged for those who are over the age of 18, that can understand the meaning and impact of an EPA.
Office of NSW Public Guardian (OPG)	OPG promotes the rights and interests of people with disabilities through the practice of guardianship, advocacy, and education. PG is a statutory official appointed by the Guardianship Division of the NSW Civil and Administrative Tribunal (NCAT) or the Supreme Court under the Guardianship Act 1987.
NSW Civil and Administrative Tribunal (NCAT)	NCAT exercises a protective jurisdiction under the Guardianship Act 1987. Its purpose is to protect and promote the rights and welfare of adults with impaired decision-making capacity.
Medical Treatment Guidelines	Guardianship Act 1987 (section 33) regulates medical treatments. The Medical Treatment Guidelines (April 2016) offers further details.

Source: Made by the author

4.3 Victoria and NSW State Acts Incorporating Supported Decision-Making

4.3.1 Amendments to Victoria State Act and After

(1) Amendments to Victoria State Act

In the State of Victoria, the Guardianship and Administration Act 2019[78] (hereinafter referred to as 'Victorian Act 2019') was enacted in May 2019 and came into force in March 2020. The Victorian Act 2019, which superseded the Victorian Act 1986, can be summarized as follows:

(i)   The Victorian Act 2019 indicates that 'a person is presumed to have decision-making capacity unless there is evidence to the contrary' (section 5(2)) and recognizes that 'a person has capacity to make a decision in relation to a matter (decision-making capacity)' (section 5(1)).[79]

(ii) The purpose of the Victorian Act 2019 is 'to promote the personal and social wellbeing of a person' (section 4). For that reason, 'the will and preferences of a person with a disability should direct, as far as practicable, decisions made for that person' (section 8).

(iii) Even when some support is needed for the principal, it is not always the case that the supportive guardian and the supportive administrator are appointed by the Victorian Civil and Administrative Tribunal (VCAT). If a close relative plays such a role properly, there is no need to change (section 31).

(iv) The appointment of adult guardians will be limited by the VCAT as a last resort. Thus, the adult guardian and the administrator must respect the will and preferences of the principal, substitute the principal's decision as far as necessary, and explain the substituted decision so that the principal can understand the content (sections 41 and 46).

(v)   Supported decision-making is incorporated into the legislative system (sections 79 to 98, Part 4—supportive guardianship orders and supportive administration orders). The principal can appoint a supportive attorney who has the legal authority to make supportive decisions on personal affairs or financial management (Part 7—Power of Attorney Appointments, Power of

---

[78.] Victorian Act 2019, Section 3(1) (definitions) stipulates that the 'disability' in relation to a person means neurological impairment, intellectual impairment, mental disorder, brain injury, physical disability, or dementia.

[79.] Similarly, the England and Wales law, the Mental Capacity Act 2005 (MCA 2005) stipulates that 'A person must be assumed to have capacity unless it is established that he lacks capacity' (section 1(2)).

Attorney Act 2014). In addition, on behalf of the principal, the VCAT may designate the supportive guardian and supportive administrator (section 87). A supportive guardian and a supportive administrator are not entitled to any remuneration for acting in that role (section 95).

(vi) If an adult guardian or an administrator performs an illegal act, such as financial fraud or financial exploitation, the provisions to impose penalties are stipulated (sections 188 and 189), and a warranty for damages is included in the law (sections 181 and 185).

(2) Number of Tribunal Orders in 2023–2024

The number of applicants for the guardianship list in the State of Victoria from July 2023 to June 2024 was 6,316 applications, i.e., 3,174 for guardians and 3,142 for administrators. There were 3,615 tribunal orders, i.e., 1,559 for guardians and 2,056 for administrators.[80] In the State of NSW, the number of applications was 9,331, i.e., 5,453 for guardians and 3,878 for administrators. There were 5,665 tribunal orders, i.e., 3,015 for guardians and 2,650 for administrators. The difference between the number of applications to the guardianship list and that of the tribunal orders was assumed to be the number of reassessing applications after the end of the guardianship term. Regarding the breakdown between the public or private guardians and administrators in tribunal orders (public: Public Advocate or Public Guardian, etc.; private: relatives, friends, professionals, etc.), in the state of Victoria, the guardians' public–private ratio was 32:68, the administrators' public–private ratio was 44:56. In the state of NSW, the guardians' public–private ratio was 43:57 and the administrators' public–private ratio was 48:52. The ratios of the public and private of the guardians and administrators in both states are more or less 45:55, except for the Victorian administrators' one.[81]

The number of tribunal orders across Australia between July 2023 and June 2024 was 20,499.[82] It should be noted that the number of guardianship list tribunal orders includes cases where the same applicants applied for both guardians and administrators. If there is a 50 per cent overlap between guardians and administrators for cases where the same applicants applied, the number of tribunal orders per year could be estimated approximately at 13,700 on a different applicant basis. The

---

[80.] Refers to the Australian Guardianship and Administration Council (AGAC), *Australian Adult Guardianship Orders 2023/24* (Web Page, February 2025) Report on adult guardianship and administration/financial management applications and new orders. <https://www.agac.org.au/assets/images/AGAC-Guardianship_orders_Report-2023-2024_2025-03-03-021515.pdf>.

[81.] Ibid.

[82.] Ibid. There are no statistics indicating the number of contracted EPAs in Australia because document is not required by law to be registered at public agencies.

number of guardianship orders in 2024 was approximately 38,800 in Japan,[83] which has a population five times greater than Australia's. With an Australian population scale, the number of orders in Australia and Japan would be adjusted to 13,700 and 7,760 respectively. It is therefore understood that the guardianship system is used considerably more in Australia than in Japan (approximately 1.8 times).[84]

As demonstrated by the findings from the two aforementioned states, the guardianship system in Australia relies predominantly on unpaid relatives and friends, who serve as private guardians in approximately 55 per cent of all cases. In instances where no suitable candidate is available or where concerns arise regarding a potential guardian's suitability or conflicts of interest, the Civil and Administrative Tribunal appoints a public body—such as the Public Advocate or a Property Administrator—to assume guardianship responsibilities. These public appointments account for roughly 45 per cent of cases.

By contrast, the appointment of supportive guardians or supportive administrators under the Guardianship and Administration Act 2019 in Victoria remains limited. The number of appointments made by the Victorian Civil and Administrative Tribunal (VCAT) was modest: 22 supportive guardians and 24 supportive administrators in 2019–2020, 18 and 30 in 2020–2021, 28 and 37 in 2021–2022, 33 and 45 in 2022–2023, and 9 and 40 in 2023–2024 respectively. Notably, all supportive guardians that were appointed to date have been family members, and no appointments of the Public Advocate in a supportive role have been recorded.[85]

These figures suggest that the current practice may diverge, at least in part, from the original intent of the legislation, which aimed to institutionalize supported decision-making as a viable alternative to substituted decision-making. The implementation of supported decision-making in Victoria thus remains in its early stages of development.

---

[83] Refers to the Courts of Japan, *The Annual Overview of Adult Guardianship Cases in FY2024* (Web Page, March 2025) 2 (in Japanese) <https://www.courts.go.jp/toukei_siryou/siryo/kouken/index.html>

[84] The AGAC statistics remarks that the number of Australian tribunal orders include some temporary and emergency ones that should be excluded for comparison but could not be done due to a technical reason. For this reason, Australian figure may appear larger, but this does not deny the trend that the guardianship system is used more in Australia than in Japan.

[85] This assertion is supported by data obtained from the Victorian Civil and Administrative Tribunal (VCAT) on November 3, 2022, February 23, 2023, and April 30, 2025. According to the then Public Advocate, Dr Colleen Pearce, the guardianship application form was downloaded 12,097 times in 2021–2022, whereas the supported decision-making application form was downloaded only eighty-eight times. This disparity led to the conclusion that awareness and promotion of supported decision-making remain insufficient (Melbourne, February 23, 2023). As of April 30, 2025, the Office of the Public Advocate (OPA) has updated its policy to no longer accept appointments under supportive guardianships, stating that it does not provide consent for the purposes of section 88(1) of the Guardianship and Administration Act 2019 (Vic).

4.3.2 Draft Amendments to NSW State Act

In the State of NSW, the draft amendment to the Guardianship Act 1987 was tabled in the NSW state parliament in August 2018 but the consideration of its implementation has been deferred. The main points of the proposal for amendments to the state law can be summarized as follows:

(i) The draft amendments propose to dispel substituted decision-making in the adult guardianship system to minimize possible restrictions on the rights of the principal. Instead, it will introduce supported decision-making to respect the principal's will and preferences.

(ii) The revised law will be renamed the Assisted Decision-Making Act. If the principal is age 18 or older and desires assisted decision-making by an appropriate supporter, the principal may make a personal support agreement with the supporter. The supporter must not be age 16 or younger, the Public Trustee or the Public Advocate, or subject to bankruptcy or possessing a criminal record if financial management is the subject of support. Personal agreements prepared in a predetermined formal and witness procedures are necessary.

(iii) Each official name is to be renamed as follows: The Public Guardian to the Public Representative, the Office of the Public Guardian to the Office of Public Advocate; the Guardian Division of the NSW Civil and Tribunal to the Assisted Decision-Making Division of the NSW Civil and Administrative Tribunal; and the NSW Trustee and Guardian to the NSW Trustee. Consequently, the term guardian is entirely deleted. The duties of the Office of the Public Advocate cover assistance for supportive decision-making, problem-solving, information provision, aid and support, abuse, and neglect.

(iv) The principal shall be deemed to have decision-making ability. The supporter carries out decision-making support following the support agreement or a tribunal order. When assisting, the supporter is obliged to observe the general principles of the revised Act. A person should not be prohibited from appointment as a supporter on the basis that they will receive financial remuneration for their appointment.

(v) The tribunal may appoint a supporter by a tribunal support order if required, and the supporter may assist the principal in decision-making. In addition to the principal, a public representative, the Office of the Public Advocate, or any other person who is involved in the life and welfare of the principal may also make this application to the tribunal. The Act has no enforcement to change informal arrangements if they are implemented with the consent of the principal and the supporter.

(vi)   The mental capacity of the principal is lost, and the substituted decision-making for the principal is required as a last resort, the tribunal may issue a representation-order to the representative. If the principal has an EPA with a third party, then the agreement becomes effective and the designated third party will take the substituted decision-making in line with the EPA.[86]

4.3.3 Comments on Amendments to Victoria and NSW State Acts

(1) Comparisons Between Amendments to Victoria and NSW State Acts

The main comparisons between the amendments to Victoria and NSW State Acts are summarized in Table 4.5.[87]

Table 4.5: Comparisons between Amendments
to Victoria and NSW State Acts

Guardianship and Administration	Victoria	NSW	Remarks
Legislation	Guardianship and Administration Act (Enacted in May 2019)	Assisted Decision-Making Act (Under consideration)	NSW will rename the Act.
Purpose	To promote personal and social well-being of the person.	To respect the will and preferences of the person.	NSW directly follows CRPD.

[86.] The state of Queensland (Australia) implemented the new guardianship law which includes the improved enduring power of attorney and advanced health directive forms as of November 30, 2020. The Queensland Cabinet and Ministerial Directory, *Guardianship Reforms Improve Safeguards for Vulnerable Queenslanders* (Web Page, November 30, 2020) <https://statements.qld.gov.au/statements/91064>.

[87.] The Guardianship and Administration bill 2014 did not pass the state parliament in 2014, and the bill 2018 passed in May 2019. Both bill contents had no considerable changes, and it was assumed that the necessity of amendments to the guardianship law was well understood in 2019 as the ageing of the population has progressed. It was also influenced by the ALRC Report 124 (2014) that indicated the national guideline principles for the guardianship. In fact, there were no objections in the parliament debates. The session on 19 December 2018 was a turning point to the conclusion of the bill in the parliament. The process of the parliament debates for the bill 2018: See Parliament of Victoria, *Parliamentary Debates (HANSARD) in Legislative Assembly, Fifty-Eighth Parliament, First Session (Wednesday, 7 March 2018 and Thursday, 29 March 2018) and in Legislative Assembly, Fifty-Ninth Parliament, First Session (Wednesday, 19 December 2018 and Tuesday, 28 May 2019)* (Web Page, n/a) <https://www.parliament.vic.gov.au/hansard/daily-hansard>.

Guardianship and Administration	Victoria	NSW	Remarks
Decision-Making Capacity/Ability	A person is presumed to have a decision-making capacity unless there is evidence to the contrary.	A person shall be deemed to have a decision-making ability if some criteria is fulfilled.	The same.
Supportive Guardian and Supportive Administrator or Supporters	A person or Tribunal may designate a supportive guardian and a supportive administrator.	A person may enter into a personal support agreement with a supporter, or Tribunal may appoint a supporter by order.	The same.
Remuneration	A supportive guardian and a supportive administrator are not entitled to any remuneration for acting in that role.	A person should not be prohibited from appointment as a supporter on the basis that they will receive financial remuneration for their appointment.	Victoria does not accept supporters receiving remuneration. NSW accepts exceptions.
Informal Arrangements	No need to change informal arrangements if they work well.	The Act has no enforcement to change informal arrangements if they are implemented with the consent of a person and a supporter.	The same.
Tribunal	Tribunals may limit guardianship appointments by hearings as possible.	Tribunal may appoint a supporter by an order who may assist a person in decision-making.	Almost the same.

Guardianship and Administration	Victoria	NSW	Remarks
Office of the Public Advocate	Office of the Public Advocate	Office of the Public Advocate (To be renamed)	The same.
Substituted Decision-Making When the Mental Capacity Is Lost	Tribunal may issue an order to an adult guardian and an administrator, or EPA becomes effective.	Tribunal may issue a representation order to a representative, or EPA becomes effective.	Almost the same.

Source: Made by the author

(2) Victoria Act 2019 Versus NSW LRC Report 145

a. Purpose of Act/Report

The Victorian Act 2019 reflects the values of the CRPD.[88] It respects the will and preferences of the principal, and understands the policy to implement the values of the CRPD. It also tries to fuse the values of the CRPD with the existing guardianship system. NSW LRC Report 145 proposes a more advanced institutional design in line with the values of the CRPD compared to those of the State of Victoria. In particular, the report suggests that the paternalistic aspect of the guardianship system is undesirable. A policy will be introduced to prioritize respect for autonomy and the right to self-determination more, even if the protection of the principal may be somewhat lessened.[89] Overall, it is assumed that autonomy is the right to self-determination of the principal to be directly respected in the NSW LRC Report 145.

---

[88] Paragraph 27 of General Comment No. 1 (Corrigendum issued on January 26, 2018) for the CRPD stipulates some points that 'Substituted decision-making regimes can take many different forms, including plenary guardianship, judicial interdiction, and partial guardianship. However, these regimes have certain common characteristics: they can be defined as systems where: (a) legal capacity is removed from a person, even if this is in respect of a single decision; (b) a substitute decision maker can be appointed by someone other than the person concerned, and this can be done against his or her will; or (c) any decision made by a substitute decision maker is based on what is believed to be in the objective "best interests" of the person concerned, as opposed to being based on the person's own will and preferences.' UN, Committee on the Rights of Persons with Disabilities, *General Comment No. 1* (Web Page, partly amended 2018/2014) <https://documents.un.org/doc/undoc/gen/g18/119/05/pdf/g1811905.pdf.

[89] Refers to the Sydney Health Law, 'NSW Law Reform Commission Recommends Far-Reaching Reform of Guardianship Legislation' (Web Page, February 21, 2018) <https://sydneyhealthlaw.com/tag/assisted-decision-making/>.

The purpose of the Victorian Act 2019 is 'to promote the social and personal wellbeing of the person.' It can be considered a compromise between 'best interests' as a current criterion and 'the will and preferences' as the CRPD requires for the principal.[90] Supported decision-making is incorporated into the legal system, and a supportive guardian and a supportive administrator have a role in this. An adult guardian and an administrator can conduct substituted decision-making only in cases that it is deemed necessary. They must fulfill accountability to the principal and are obliged to report the contents of the substituted decision-making to the VCAT annually in writing. As a system, substituted decision-making is regarded as a last resort, narrowing down opportunities for substituted decision-making, instead of urging supported decision-making as an alternative. This policy seems to indicate that the Victorian Act 2019 corresponds to the challenges of the State of Victoria as well as the CRPD.[91]

The purpose of the NSW LRC Report 145 is 'to respect the will and preferences of the principal,' to implement and to ensure the will and preferences of the principal. Renaming of various terms intends to design a new system that is entirely different from the current guardianship system. The report also intends to use the terms, 'supporter' and 'representative,' following the ALRC Report 124 (2014).[92] The revised law is to be called the Assisted Decision-Making Act rather than the Guardianship Act 1987. It pushes forward 'assisted decision-making' as a new legal concept. If the mental capacity of the principal is lost and substituted decision-making for the principal is required as a last resort, the tribunal may issue a representation order to the representative. The revised law is thus intended to supersede the Guardianship Act 1987.

b. Capacity and Capacity Assessment

Regarding 'mental capacity' of a person, 'capacity is not a unitary concept but rather refers to specific decisions, tasks, or domains…. Capacity is also issue

---

[90.] It is called a strategic compromise. From the interview of Victorian OPA by the author on March 5, 2019.

[91.] Based on the interviews of the Australian experts by the author on March 1 to 3, 2017, the challenges of the state of Victoria can be summarized in the four points: (i) Rapid and appropriate responses by the Victorian OPA and VCAT to the adult guardianship cases are increasing in number and have become more complicated. (ii) Revise the law for improving legal system to meet the international human rights requirements. (iii) Realization of supported decision-making. (iv) Combat elder abuse, particularly responding to adults at risk for undue influence and financial exploitation. Yukio Sakurai, 'Adult Guardianship System in Australia and Its Recent Discussion Points' (2018) 7 *Quarterly Journal of Comparative Guardianship Law* 30, 41 (in Japanese).

[92.] The ALRC Report 124 in Chapter 4: Supported Decision-Making in Commonwealth Laws provides a Commonwealth decision-making model based on the positions of 'supporters' and 'representatives.' Australian Law Reform Commission (ALRC), *Equality, Capacity and Disability in Commonwealth Laws Final Report* (ALRC Report 124, 2014) 91–118; The terms of 'supporters' and 'representatives' are carefully selected and used. Rosalind Croucher, 'Confronting Words: Driving a New Legal Lexicon of Disability' (2017) 35 *Law Context: A Socio-Legal Journal* 15, 20.

specific.'[93] The Victorian Act 2019 and the NSW LRC Report 145 share the key legal concept 'decision-making capacity' and its capacity assessment procedures. The Victorian Act 2019 section 5(1) stipulates the definition of decision-making capacity that

> *a person has capacity to make a decision in relation to a matter (decision-making*
> *capacity) if the person is able—(a) to understand the information and the effect*
> *of the decision; and (b) to retain that information to the extent necessary to make*
> *the decision; and (c) to use or weigh that information as part of the process*
> *of making the decision; and (d) to communicate the decision and the person's*
> *views and needs as to the decision in some way, including by speech, gesture*
> *or other means.*

The NSW LRC Report 145 recommends 'a new definition of decision-making ability that is consistent with…the Capacity Toolkit and the recommendations of the VLRC [the Victorian Act 2019].'[94] This means that the Victorian Act 2019 and the NSW LRC Report 145 share the same legal concept 'decision-making capacity' on the same ground.

With regard to 'capacity assessment' procedures, the NSW *Capacity Toolkit,* as guidelines on capacity, includes 'capacity assessment principles' (section 3).[95] The 'capacity assessment principles' are composed of six principles to be applied when assessing a person's capacity. These are as follows: (i) Always presume a person has capacity; (ii) Capacity is decision specific; (iii) Do not assume a person lacks capacity based on appearance; (iv) Assess the person's decision-making ability—not the decision they make; (v) Respect a person's privacy; and (vi) Substitute decision-making is a last resort. These principles aim to support and protect vulnerable adults and help them make the most of their decision-making ability.[96] In the State of Victoria, these principles are shared with the capacity

---

[93] This is acknowledged in *Gibbons and Wright* case [*GIBBONS v. WRIGHT* [1954] Hight Court of Australia 91 CLR 423, April 23, 1954] where the High Court said: 'The mental capacity required by law in respect of any instrument is relative to the particular transaction which is being affected by means of the instrument and may be described as the capacity to understand the nature of the transaction when it is explained.' Nick O'Neill and Carmelle Peisah, 'Chapter 1—What Is Capacity?' in Nick O'Neill and Carmelle Peisah (eds), *Capacity and the Law 2021 Edition* (Online, 2021) <http://austlii.community/foswiki/Books/CapacityAndTheLaw/WebHome>.

[94] Refers to the NSW LRC Report 145, Paragraph 6.12.

[95] Refers to the NSW Government, Communities and Justice, *Capacity Toolkit* (Web Page, November 27, 2024) <https://dcj.nsw.gov.au/resources/capacity-toolkit.html>.

[96] Hilary Brown points out that the standard of mental capacity in MCA 2005 (England and Wales) is based on a cognitive, linear model of decision-making and the emotional factors of the principals are not taken into consideration. The emotional factors include their personal history, their relationship history or family dynamics. This discussion can be applied to the Australian capacity assessment. Hilary Brown, 'The Role of Emotion in Decision-Making' (2011) 13(4) *The Journal of Adult Protection* 194, 202.

guidelines *The LIV Capacity Guidelines and Toolkit* published by the Law Institute Victoria and reflected in the Victorian Act 2019 (section 5).[97]

c. Guidelines for Supported Decision-Making Practice

The guidelines for supported decision-making are shown in the capacity guidelines *The LIV Capacity Guidelines and Toolkit* in the state of Victoria. It seems that there are some points to be clarified when supporters practice supported decision-making on site.[98] In fact, reviewing the supported decision-making pilot programs in Australia from 2010 to 2015, it was tentatively concluded that 'some form of authority may facilitate the role of supporters, help to engage others in a person's life, and integrate decision making support across all life domains.'[99] The Victorian Act 2019 does not state any operational details about the scope of supported decision-making. For example, a Canadian report points out that the use of supported decision-making should be limited to a certain area.[100] This report suggests the eligible scope of supported decision-making practice by type of disability but no such report is seen in Australia.[101] A challenge is how to properly implement supported decision-making and to deal with risks for possible undue influence and illegal acts accompanying supported decision-making.[102] In addition, VCAT is requested to have hearings with principals as much as possible.

[97.] Refers to the Law Institute Victoria, *The LIV Capacity Guidelines and Toolkit* (Online, Concise edition: November 2020) <https://www.liv.asn.au/download.aspx?DocumentVersionKey=3e89e8a7-cead-4efb-ba1e-d3682848213a&srsltid=AfmBOooDA0enVC5wigC07oiG5W03ef8EV5m4suhrJPTL5x7qgxaVShTU>.

[98.] Supported decision-making has been widely practiced on sites in Australia. Jan Killeen, *Supported Decision-Making: Learning from Australia* (Rights for Persons with Cognitive Disabilities: Learning from Australia, 2016).

[99.] Australian people have learnt the lesson from SDM pilot programs since 2010 that 'it may be that workable models of delivering decision making support need to straddle civil society and the law.' Christine Bigby et al, 'Delivering Decision Making Support to People with Cognitive Disability—What Has Been Learned from Pilot Programs in Australia from 2010 to 2015' (2017) 52 *Australian Journal of Social Issues* 222–40, 222 and 236.

[100.] A report from Ontario, Canada, notes that supported decision-making is relatively suitable for persons with intellectual or developmental disabilities, but less appropriate for those with psychiatric or social psychological disabilities. It further suggests that older individuals with dementia should rely on informal arrangements for a period before substituted decision-making proceedings commence. See Krista James and Laura Watts, *Understanding the Lived Experiences of Supported Decision-Making in Canada: Legal Capacity, Decision-Making and Guardianship* (Web Page, Study Paper, Canadian Center for Elder Law, commissioned by the Law Commission of Ontario, March 2014) <https://www.bcli.org/project/understanding-lived-experience-supported-decision-making>. In British Columbia, the Representation Agreement has provided a workable framework for individuals with intellectual and developmental disabilities but has proven less effective for persons with dementia. See Mary Donnelly, 'Deciding in Dementia: The Possibilities and Limits of Supported Decision-Making' (2019) 60 *International Journal of Law and Psychiatry* <https://doi.org/10.1016/j.ijlp.2019.101466>.

[101.] An article appears to point out that it is essential for health and legal practitioners to make 'an understanding of these inter-professional differences in perceived roles of providing decision-making support' for people with dementia. Craig Sinclair et al, 'Professionals' Views and Experiences in Supporting Decision-Making Involvement for People Living with Dementia' (2021) 20(1) *Dementia* 84, 105.

[102.] A principal with insufficient mental capacity may be assisted by a supported decision-maker for the principal's will and preferences, but in fact, the principal might be forced to engage in an action that serves the interest of the supported decision-maker. Mary Joy Quinn, 'Undue Influence and Elder Abuse' (2002) 23(1) *Geriatric Nursing* 11, 17.

VCAT has been able to conduct most hearings by either having the principal at the hearing or being satisfied that he or she is unable or unwilling to attend.[103]

In NSW, the *Capacity Toolkit* guidelines have been prepared like the case in the state of Victoria. Assisted decision-making is a challenge to administer. The challenges are the same as these in the State of Victoria, i.e., to properly implement supported decision-making and avoid possible undue influence and illegal acts accompanying assisted decision-making.[104] Personal support agreements are not required to be registered with public agencies. It is thus unclear to what degree public agencies will be involved in the event of a dispute or misbehavior related to an assisted decision-making contract.

d. Non-remuneration Policy

The Victorian Act 2019 does not recognize remuneration for acting in SDM (section 95). The Victorian Act 2019 expects principals' supportive guardians and supportive administrators to be relatives, friends, or public advocates, but not legal/welfare practitioners.[105] This non-remuneration policy is established in the Victorian Act 1986 based on the Cocks Report 1982[106] and has been applied to other jurisdictions over Australia because this is in order to avoid the conflict of interest associated with payment.[107] The Victorian Act 2019 recognizes that principals' supportive guardians and supportive administrators are supporters for 'decision-making' of the principals, there does not often arise a situation

---

[103.] A member of the VCAT comments that 'Since COVID-19 pandemic, VCAT has implemented new administrative processes by telephone or video conference to ensure that [they] can capture the principal's will and preference in the hearing.' From email correspondence of a VCAT member by the author on August 12, 2021.

[104.] Kathy Pryor states that financial exploitation is often referred to as undue influence, which is so difficult to address legislatively. Kathy Pryor, 'Averting Financial Exploitation and Undue Influence through Legislation' (2016) 31(2) *Age in Action* 1, 6.

[105.] The VLRC Report 24 (2012), Paragraph 8.89 states that 'supporter arrangements are designed for close, personal relationship, which cannot be replaced by professional appointments.'

[106.] 'The Cocks Report 1982' is the final report made by the Victorian Minister's Committee on Rights & Protective Legislation for Intellectually Handicapped Persons headed by Errol Cocks. Victoria. Minister's Committee on Rights & Protective Legislation for Intellectually Handicapped Persons and Errol Cocks, *Report of The Minister's Committee on Rights & Protective Legislation for Intellectually Handicapped Persons* (Victorian State Government, 1982).

[107.] This view was addressed by Terry Carney in email correspondence on December 6, 2021; Cocks and Duffy define advocacy as: 'functioning (speaking, acting, writing) with minimum conflict of interest on behalf of the sincerely perceived interests of a person or group, in order to promote, protect and defend the welfare of, and justice for, either individuals or groups, in a fashion which strives to be emphatic and vigorous,' referring to the article: Wolf Wolfensberger, *Social Advocacies on behalf of Devalued and Disadvantaged People* (Workshop provided at Adelaide, 1992). They propose five principles for advocacy: '(i) Advocacy is on the side of the disadvantaged person/people. (ii) Advocacy is concerned with genuine life needs. (iii) Advocacy strives to minimize conflicts of interest. (iv) Advocacy engages in vigorous action. (v) Advocacy has fidelity to disadvantaged people.' They review the term advocacy with 'its emphasis on minimum conflict of interest and its focus on action.' This approach may lead to non-remuneration policy to avoid paid social workers due to potential conflict of interest by payment. Errol Cocks and Gordon Duffy, *The Nature and Purposes of Advocacy for People with Disabilities* (Edith Cowan University Publications, 1993) 42 and 121 <https://ro.ecu.edu.au/ecuworks/7172>.

where they need to have specialist skills.[108] Principals' supportive guardians and supportive administrators must have sufficient skills to seek advice or arrange care by specialists. Staff in the Office of the Public Advocate (OPA) are people with a social welfare background, such as a social worker, lawyer, or nurse etc., which assist supportive guardians and supportive administrators to know where to seek such advice and how to evaluate that advice in making their decisions.

In contrast, the NSW LRC Report 145 recommends that 'a person should not be prohibited from appointment as a supporter on the basis that they will receive financial remuneration for their appointment' (paragraph 7.50 (2)). The issue of remuneration for supporters in SDM suggests the difference between the Victorian and NSW law reform policies in 'who will act as supporters and for what purpose.' Namely, the Victorian Act 2019 adopts the design that relatives, friends, or public advocates should act as supporters for decision-making of the principals, and the NSW LRC Report 145 basically follows the same design as Victoria's but allowing some exceptional cases to appoint paid workers or corporations receiving remuneration if they are deemed necessary.[109]

e. Summary

In summary, the State of Victorian is advanced in practice to implement supported decision-making by law, appointing supportive attorneys by principals or appointing supportive guardians/supportive administrators on their behalf by tribunal orders. Monitoring VCAT as the tribunal operation in the Victorian Act 2019 will be attention after the enforcement in March 2020. NSW-proposed law is more advanced than the Victorian Act 2019 with hopes that the purpose of the law follows the CRPD. The supported decision-making concept is more incorporated into the law reform plan. In addition, its renaming of the Assisted Decision-Making Act gives an innovative image to NSW citizens who listen to and see this naming. This system will be entirely renewed from the current NSW guardianship system, which has a flexibility of the non-remuneration policy to involve legal/welfare practitioners receiving remuneration as supporters if it is necessary. It is, however, uncertain whether the NSW LRC Report 145 proposals will be accepted by the NSW parliament. It is subject to change in the NSW State parliament debates and drafting bill.[110]

---

[108] From email correspondence of a VCAT member with the author on September 2, 2021. She points out: 'a supportive guardian or a guardian is strictly a supporter of decision-making or decision-maker for the principal.'

[109] The NSW LRC Report 145 policy allows an alternative to appoint paid a worker or corporation as an exceptional case where no family member, friend, public advocate is prepared to act as a supporter of the principal.

[110] This was Terry Carney's remarks in the AGAC2019 conference in Canberra on March 15, 2019.

(3) What Are the Common Values in Australian Law Reforms?

What are the values that are considered common in two law reforms? It is presumed by Australian scholars, including Terry Carney, that these are mentioned as the National Decision-Making Principles addressed in the ALRC Report 124.[111] The ALRC Report 124 is the national guardianship law reform report, which has mainly examined the 'ability to excise legal capacity' and 'equal recognition before the law of people with disability' that the CRPD requires, and provides the four National Decision-Making Principles (Paragraph 3.4). Namely, Principle 1: *The equal right to make decisions* (i.e., all adults have an equal right to make decisions that affect their lives and to have these decisions respected.), Principle 2: *Support* (i.e., persons who require support in decision-making must be provided with access to the support necessary for them to make, communicate and participate in decisions that affect their lives.), Principle 3: *Will, preferences and rights* (i.e., the will, preferences and rights of persons who may require decision-making support must direct decisions that affect their lives.), and Principle 4: *Safeguards* (i.e., laws and legal frameworks must contain appropriate and effective safeguards concerning interventions for persons who may require decision-making support, including to prevent abuse and undue influence.). In addition, the ALRC Report 124 provides five Framing Principles for guiding the recommendations for reform: *dignity; equality; autonomy; inclusion and participation;* and *accountability* (Paragraph 1.34 to 1.39).[112]

The ALRC considers an overall framework of these principles and guidelines as the template for the specific reforms in national and state/special territory levels (Paragraph 3.7). Stakeholders have supported these principles which are reflected in a Commonwealth decision-making model that is developed in the ALRC Report 124 (Paragraph 1.51 to 1.116). These principles and the ALRC Report 124 are known in Australia and cited in administrative and judicial documents, parliamentary debates, and academic articles. In fact, the four National Decision-Making Principles

---

[111.] From the interview and email correspondence to Victorian OPA and Terry Carney on March 5, 14, and afterward, 2019 by the author; Terry Carney et al, 'Realising "Will, Preferences and Rights": Reconciling Differences on Best Practice Support for Decision-Making?' (Online, 2019) *Griffith Law Review* <https://doi.org/10.1080/10383441 .2019.1690741>; Bruce Alston, a member of ALRC then, states that 'the [National Decision-Making] Principles can be a catalyst for facilitating important law reform over following decades.' Bruce Alston, 'Towards Supported Decision-Making: Article 12 of the Convention on the Rights of Persons with Disabilities and Guardianship Law Reform' (2017) 35 *Law in Context* 21–43, 1 and 27–31.

[112.] Regarding autonomy, Paragraph 1.37, the ALRC Report 124 states that 'This Inquiry has been informed by autonomy in the sense of "empowerment", not just "non-interference". This involves seeing an individual in relation to others, in a "relational" or "social" sense and understanding that connects with respect for the family as the "natural and fundamental group unit of Society" that is entitled to protection by States Parties.' It can be assumed that ALRC Report 124 is based on the notion of relational autonomy, although 'Terms and Reference' of ALRC report 124 includes 'how maximizing "individual autonomy" and "independence" could be modelled in Commonwealth laws and legal frameworks.'

are used for the policy guideline document for aged care providers in Australia.[113] Furthermore, the ALRC Report 124 has become known by international agencies because the Australian national government submitted their combined second and third reports to the UN Committee on September 6, 2018.[114] These reports explained a recommendation addressed by the ALRC Report 124 that 'a Commonwealth decision-making model be introduced into relevant laws and legal frameworks that encourage supported decision-making.'[115]

The Victorian Act 2019 and the NSW LRC Report 145 have been produced through a democratic process by the state Law Reform Commission and the state parliament. Both referred to the public opinions expressed by the Office of the Public Advocate or the Guardian, relevant public agencies, NPOs, experts, and civil society. It is recognized that people in Australia respect the consensus-making process through democratic procedures, even though it takes time to make law and public policy concerning the guardianship system.[116] These law reforms follow four National Decision-Making Principles, and five Framing Principles addressed in the ALRC Report 124.

4.4 Legislation for Elder Abuse

4.4.1 Background of Elder Abuse Legislation

In Australia, as in other developed countries, elder abuse occurs frequently. Elder abuse only came to the fore in the late 1980s. Since then, it has gradually become more prevalent after numbers of publications and research projects on the topic.[117]

[113.] Craig Sinclair, Sue Field and Meredith Blake, *Supported Decision-Making in Aged Care: A Policy Development Guideline for Aged Care Providers in Australia* (Cognitive Decline Partnership Centre, 2nd ed, 2018); Meredith Blake et al, 'Supported Decision-Making for People with Dementia: An Examination of Four Australian Guardianship Law' (2021) 28(2) *Journal of law and Medicine* 389–420, 405–16.

[114.] Refers to the UN, *Combined Second and Third Periodic Reports submitted by Australia under Article 35 of the Convention, due in 2018* (Web Page, February 5, 2019) <https://tbinternet.ohchr.org/_layouts/15/treatybodyexternal/Download.aspx?symbolno=CRPD/C/AUS/2-3&Lang=en>.

[115.] Refers to the ALRC Report 124, Paragraph 146.

[116.] 'It is from such small steps that sufficient incremental knowledge ultimately accrues, and apparently worthy social policies are refined over time.' Terry Carney, 'Supported Decision-making in Australia: Meeting the Challenge of Moving from Capacity to Capacity-Building?' 35(2) *Disability, Rights and Law Reform in Australia* (2017) 63; Ronald McCallum, a well-known blind law scholar in Australia, states that 'Australia's moves in these legal fields have been rather slow, nevertheless in time most, if not all, jurisdictions will most likely adopt to varying degrees the paradigm change ushered by article 12.' Ronald McCallum, *Research Report: The United Nations Convention on the Rights of Persons with Disabilities: An Assessment of Australia's Level of Compliance* (Royal Commission into Violence, Abuse, Neglect and Exploitation of People with Disability, October 2020) 55.

[117.] Regarding domestic violence, the research project team in the state of Victoria reported recommendations in 2014. Delanie Woodlock et al, *Voices Against Violence Paper One: Summary Report and Recommendations* (Women with Disabilities Victoria, Victorian Office of the Public Advocate, and Domestic Violence Resource Centre Victoria, 2014).

However, there is no comprehensive legislation to combat elder abuse in Australia. Instead, the Aged Care (Security and Protection) Act 2007 was enacted to amend the Aged Care Act 1997, a national law, inserting an additional Article 63-1AA.[118] This Article states that 'responsibilities relating to alleged and suspected assaults' require mandatory reporting of incidents of elder abuse occurring in institutional aged care settings.[119] The object of the Aged Care Act 1997 (Article 2-1) is 'to provide funding of aged care services and to promote a high quality of care and accommodation for the recipients of aged care services.' Therefore, adult protection against elder abuse is not central but is regarded as a matter associated with aged care activity, and the definition of elder abuse is not included in the Act.

Elder abuse has become more visible than before after some media and research reports of the last few years concerning the issue. Elder abuse is one of the major social problems in Australia.[120] Elder abuse often goes unreported because the perpetrators are frequently the adult children of the victims; this may contribute to the reluctance of older people to seek help.[121] It is assumed that elder abuse is a complex, multidimensional, and often hidden form of abuse, and requires a multi-faceted response.[122] The current problem of elder abuse is left to the treatment in each state, special territory, and local government in Australia, but these entities cannot fully tackle elder abuse problems.

In fact, the number of calls to the NPO, Seniors Rights Victoria's advice call service related to elder abuse from the period July 2012 to June 2019 increased every year. The proportions of calls concerning financial abuse and social abuse particularly increased, with 6.12 per cent increase in financial abuse and 4.21 per cent increase in social abuse.[123] Research in the state of Victoria indicates that

---

[118.] Rae Kaspiew, Rachel Carson and Helen Rhoades, Elder Abuse: Understanding Issues, Frameworks and Responses (Research Report No. 35, Australian Institute of Family Studies, 2016/Correction November 2, 2018) 22; Susan Kurrle and Gerard Naughtin, 'An Overview of Elder Abuse and Neglect in Australia' (2008) 20(2) Journal of Elder Abuse & Neglect 108, 125.

[119.] Krista James, Legal Definitions of Elder Abuse and Neglect (Department of Justice Canada, 2019) 57–62.

[120.] A case for elder abuse in an aged care setting. Yvette Maker and Bernadette McSherry, 'Regulating Restraint Use in Mental Health and Aged Care Settings: Lessons from the Oakden Scandal' (2019) 44(1) Alternative Law Review 29, 36.

[121.] Between 5 per cent and 14 per cent of older Australians experience elder abuse in any given year, and the prevalence of neglect may be higher. Briony Dow et al, 'Elder Abuse in Australia' in Mala Kapur Shankardass (ed), International Handbook of Elder Abuse and Mistreatment (Springer, 2020) 559–74; Almost 60 per cent perpetrators of elder abuse incidents is a family member. National Council of Aging, Gets the Facts on Elder Abuse (Web Page, February 21, 2022) <https://www.ncoa.org/article/get-the-facts-on-elder-abuse>.

[122.] A systematic review of the literature reveals that elder abuse is a multifactorial phenomenon and various risk factors are involved, such as age, sex, marital status, educational level, income, family arrangement, family relationship, social support, solitude, mental disorder, depression, dependence on others for activities of daily living (ADL) and instrumental activities of daily living (IADL), and others. Maria Angélica Bezerra dos Santos et al, 'Factors Associated with Elder Abuse: A Systematic Review of the Literature' (2020) 25 Ciência & Saúde Coletiva 2153–75, 2173.

[123.] Melanie Joosten et al, Seven Years of Elder Abuse Data in Victoria (2012–2019) (National Ageing Research Institute in Partnership with Seniors Rights Victoria, August 2020) 35.

elder abuse prevalence rates among the principals in the guardianship were estimated to be 13 per cent in 2013–2014 and 21 per cent in 2016–2017. Research
shows that women who have experienced elder abuse are at a higher rate than
men, and older people with dementia or intellectual disability are more likely to
have experienced elder abuse than those with other disabilities.[124] It is crucial
to grasp the actual situation of damage related to financial exploitation and to
inform the public of the necessity of protecting vulnerable adults, particularly
older people with dementia.[125] It also shows an upward trend of the elder abuse
prevalence rate among the principals in the guardianship.[126]

Considering the lack of legislation and public policy that prevents to and
responds elder abuse in states and special territories, there is a view that a collaborative national strategy, incorporating a right-based approach to the review
and reform of state and special territory laws, is essential.[127] For this reason, the
responsible entity in question was upgraded from the state and special territory
to the Commonwealth. Officially, the Attorney-General for Australia announced
an inquiry into the Australia Law Reform Commission (hereinafter referred to as
'ALRC') on 'protecting the rights of older Australians from abuse' on February
23, 2016.[128]

The inquiry includes a matter concerning 'relevant international obligations
relating to the rights of older people under United Nations (UN) human rights
conventions to which Australia is a party.'[129] A new national legislative policy
has been discussed. After debates by experts over a few years, amendments
through public comments review were devised. Then, the report *Elder Abuse—A
National Legal response*[130] (ALRC Report No. 131, 2017, hereinafter referred to
as 'ALRC Report 131') was tabled in the Commonwealth parliament on June 14,

---

[124.] Lois Bedson, John Chesterman and Michael Woods, 'The Prevalence of Elder Abuse Among Adult Guardianship Clients' (2018) 18 *Macquarie Law Journal* 15–34, 25.

[125.] Natalia Wuth, 'Enduring Powers of Attorney with Limited Remedies—It's Time to Face the Facts!' (2013) 7 *Elder Law Review* 1, 30.

[126.] Ben Chen, 'Elder Financial Abuse: Capacity Law and Economics' (2020) 106 *Cornell Law Review* 1457, 1538.

[127.] John Chesterman proposes five key reform imperatives: reducing reliance on substitute decision-making, facilitating complaints, funded advocacy, on-site monitoring, and investigation of concerns. John Chesterman, 'The Future of Adult Guardianship in Federal Australia' (2013) 66(1) *Australian Social Work* 26, 38; Wendy Lacey, 'Neglectful to the Point of Cruelty? Elder Abuse and the Rights of Older Persons in Australia' (2014) 36 *Sydney Law Review* 99, 130; Stephen Duckett and Anika Stobart, 'From Rationing to Rights: Creating a Universal Entitlement to Aged Care' (2021) 54(2) *The Australian Economic Review* 257, 265.

[128.] Refers to the Australian Law Reform Commission (ALRC), *Terms of Reference: Protecting the Rights of Older Australians from Abuse* (Web Page, February 23, 2016) <https://www.alrc.gov.au/inquiry/elder-abuse-2/terms-of-reference-19/>.

[129.] Ibid.

[130.] Refers to the ALRC (n 17).

2017. This report was released at a symposium on elder abuse held in Melbourne on the World Elder Abuse Awareness Day (June 15) in 2017.

4.4.2 ALRC Report 131 and the Responses

(1) ALRC Report 131

a. Legislative Policy to Combat Elder Abuse

The ALRC Report 131 clarifies the Australian national legislative policy to combat elder abuse. The Report considers elder abuse a serious social problem in Australia. Elder abuse is defined as 'a single, or repeated act, or lack of appropriate action, occurring within any relationship where there is an expectation of trust, which causes harm or distress to an older person' (paragraph 2.25/paragraph 2.45 of ALRC Report 131).[131] Five types of abuse are stated in the Report: psychological or emotional abuse, financial abuse, physical abuse, neglect, and sexual abuse (paragraph 2.46 to 2.60).

The ALRC Report 131 takes into consideration relevant international obligations relating to the rights of older people under the UN conventions. The United Nations Principles for Older Persons was adopted by the General Assembly resolution 46/91 of December 16, 1991.[132] This resolution recommended the UN Parties to incorporate the following five principles into their national programs: *Interdependence, Participation, Care, Self-fulfillment,* and *Dignity.*[133] Paragraph 11.18 of the ALRC Report 131 refers to the resolution of the UN Principles for Older Persons regarding the *dignity and autonomy* (paragraph 2.84 to 2.87) of older people

The ALRC Report 131 is based on two key framing principles, namely *dignity and autonomy* and *protection and safeguarding* (paragraph 2.83 to 2.99). *Dignity and autonomy* refer to 'the principle that all Australians have rights, which do not diminish with age, to live dignified, self-determined lives, free from exploitation, violence and abuse.' *Protection and safeguarding* are 'the principle that laws and legal frameworks should provide appropriate protections and safeguards

---

[131.] Refers to the WHO, *The Toronto Declaration on the Global Prevention of Elder Abuse* (Web Page, November 17, 2002) <https://eapon.ca/wp-content/uploads/2021/09/toronto_declaration_en.pdf>; WHO, *Elder Abuse* (Web Page, June 6, 2018) <https://www.who.int/news-room/fact-sheets/detail/elder-abuse>.

[132.] Refers to the UN, Human Rights Office of the High Commissioner, *United Nations Principles for Older Persons Adopted by General Assembly Resolution 46/91* (Web Page, December 16, 1991) <https://www.ohchr.org/en/instruments-mechanisms/instruments/united-nations-principles-older-persons> <https://www.ohchr.org/en/professionalinterest/pages/olderpersons.aspx>.

[133.] Alan Gutterman, 'Convention on Human Rights of Older Persons' (Online, 2021) <https://ssrn.com/abstract=3876618>.

for older Australians, while minimizing interference with the rights and references of the person.' The policy stresses that the *dignity and autonomy* of older
people, in addition to their *protection and safeguarding*, should be considered
in a balanced manner.

A number of key terms are summarized in the Terminology of the ALRC Report 131, such as 'supported and substitute decision-making,' 'supporters and
representatives,' 'will, preferences and rights' standard, 'national decision-making
principles,' and 'legal capacity' (paragraph 2.100 to 2.119). These key terms are
clarified and discussed in the ALRC Report 124, a national law reform report on
the guardianship system. Thus, it can be understood that the policy to combat
elder abuse and the reforms of the guardianship law are positioned back-to-back.
This close relationship between the two ALRC Reports 124 and 133 in the
national policy is addressed in the 'Terms of Reference' and is also advocated
by the former President of the ALRC, Rosalind F. Croucher, who published the
ALRC Reports 124 and 131.[134]

b. Countermeasures to Cope with Elder Abuse

The ALRC Report 131 offers twelve countermeasures to cope with elder abuse,
namely (1) a national plan to combat elder abuse, (2) aged care, (3) enduring
appointment, (4) family agreements,[135] (5) superannuation, (6) wills, (7) banking, (8) guardianship and administration, (9) health and the national disability
insurance scheme (NDIS), (10) social security, (11) criminal justice responses,
and (12) safeguarding adults at risk. The scope of the countermeasures against
elder abuse is broader and comprehensive. These are the ALRC's response 'with
a set of recommendations—traversing laws and legal frameworks across Commonwealth, state and territory laws—aimed at achieving a nationally consistent
response to elder abuse' (paragraph 1.20). It includes incorporating elder abuse
programs in school and community education and conducting academic research
on elder abuse in a scientific way to elucidate the actual situation. Captioned

---

[134.] Rosalind F. Croucher highlights how deeply the ALRC members debated on elder abuse based on the guardianship reform report. Rosalind F. Croucher, 'Modelling Supported Decision Making in Commonwealth Laws—The
ALRC's 2014 Report and Making It Work' (Conference Paper, AGAC conference held in Sydney on October
18, 2016) 11–20.

[135.] The 'family agreements' are discussed at Chapter 6 of the ALRC Report 131. Family agreements between a
principal and their relatives are not typically put in writing, and the relatives take care of the principals in exchange
for the principals' property transfer. Such agreements are fragile, and the principals' interests are not guaranteed
by law. The Australian Law Reform Commission (ALRC) recommends that disputes within families should be
under the jurisdiction of the tribunal, but access to the tribunal is another challenge for vulnerable adults. ALRC
(n 17) 203–30.

'Safeguarding Adult at Risk,'[136] Chapter 14 of the ALRC Report 131 proposes establishing the first adult safeguarding law in Australia.[137] It quotes Jonathan Herring's remark: 'older people have a fundamental human right to protection from abuse. That obliges the state to put in place legal and social structures to combat elder abuse' (paragraph 14.12).[138] This acknowledgment in part comes from the vulnerability approach, where a general view is to be derived that vulnerable adults at risk of harm must be protected by the law and public policy.[139] A review of current state-based measures to reduce elder abuse shows that considerable gaps exist between the elder abuse measures required by law and those practically provided by public agencies.

It may be assumed that the gaps exist among public agencies in part because Australia adopts a three-tier administrative system, such as national, state, and special territory, and local government. Recognizing that elder abuse occurs within the ranks of the current administrative system, a national elder abuse legislation framework is needed to fill the gaps (paragraph 14.36).[140] Paragraph 14.37 of the ALRC Report 131 states that the ALRC recommends 'the introduction of adult safeguarding law throughout Australia as an important measure filling the gap.' This will provide a uniform standard policy throughout Australia. Daily responses to elder abuse will then be provided by local governments by each state and special territory law under the uniform national legislative policy.[141] The ALRC Report 131 acknowledges the lack of statutory role of safeguarding and supporting adults at risk of harm and thus proposes necessary institutional steps to improve this challenge.

In the ALRC's view, support and protection to adults at risk of harm should be provided by state and special territory safeguarding agencies (paragraph 14.40).

[136.] 'Safeguarding is protecting the welfare and human rights of people that are, in some way, connected your charity or its work—particularly people that may be at risk of abuse, neglect or exploitation.' Australian Government (ACNC), *Governance Toolkit: Safeguarding Vulnerable People* (Web Page, n/a) <https://www.acnc.gov.au/for-charities/manage-your-charity/governance-hub/governance-toolkit/governance-toolkit-safeguarding-vulnerable-people>.

[137.] Refers to the Australian research focusing on the adult safeguarding comparison analysis in common law jurisdictions: John Chesterman, *Responding to Violence, Abuse, Exploitation and Neglect: Improving Our Protection of At-risk Adults* (Report for Winston Churchill Memorial Trust of Australia, 2013).

[138.] Jonathan Herring, 'Elder Abuse: A Human Rights Agenda for the Future' in Israel Doron and Ann M. Soden (eds), *Beyond Elder Law: New Directions in Law and Aging* (Springer Science and Business Media, 2012) 175.

[139.] Refers to Section 2.3.2, 'Vulnerability Approach.'

[140.] Refers to a *Closing the Gaps* report co-author Wendy Lacey's remarks: 'State-based frameworks presently contain a number of significant flaws: there is no dedicated agency with statutorily mandated responsibility to investigate cases of elder abuse, coordinate interagency responses and seek intervention orders where necessary; referral services between agencies can provide partial solutions in cases of elder abuse, but do not encourage a multi-disciplinary and multi-agency response in complex cases.' Wendy Lacey, 'Neglectful to the Point of Cruelty? Elder Abuse and the Rights of Older Persons in Australia' (2014) 36 *Sydney Law Review* 99–130, 105.

[141.] There is an article asking, 'if the reforms are implemented, what will the implications for lawyers in philosophical and practical terms?' Margaret Castles, 'A Critical Commentary on the 2017 ALRC Elder Abuse Report: Looking for an Ethical Baseline for Lawyers' (2018) 18 *Macquarie Law Journal* 115, 130.

Safeguarding agencies should have a statutory duty to make inquiries where they have reasonable grounds to suspect that a person is an at-risk adult (recommendation 14-3).[142] The first step of an inquiry should be to contact the at-risk adult. If a safeguarding agency has reasonable grounds to conclude that a person is an at-risk adult, the agency may take necessary actions with the adult's consent (recommendation 14-5).[143] Responding effectively to elder abuse may often require the cooperation and expertise of people from multiple disciplines and multiple agencies (paragraph 14.132).[144] Adult safeguarding agencies should lead and coordinate this work. The ALRC Report 131 recommends that adult safeguarding agencies should provide a clear point of accountability within the government (paragraph 14.138).

The ALRC concludes that the consent of an adult at risk must be secured before safeguarding agencies can investigate, or take any other action, in relation to the abuse or neglect of the adult (recommendation 14-4). This is due to the respect to the autonomy of an adult at risk. An adult safeguarding agency sometimes may seek court orders to prevent someone suspected of abuse from contacting an at-risk adult, and in particularly emergency cases, the safety of the at-risk adult needs to be secured, even against their wishes.[145] The ALRC Report 131 suggest that in limited cases it may be appropriate to act without their consent (paragraph 14.102).[146] This may apply to only whose who need such care and support and cannot protect themselves (recommendation 14-4).[147] This is a rescue model which is only activated in limited cases where law regulates. An adult safeguarding agency must determine whether the intervention

---

[142.] 'At-risk adult' is defined in the Report as people aged 18 or over who: (a) have care and support needs; (b) are being abused or neglected or are at risk of abuse or neglect; and (c) are unable to protect themselves from abuse or neglect because of their care and support needs.

[143.] The actions that can be taken by a safeguarding agency include: (a) coordinate legal, medical, and other services for the adult; (b) meet with relevant government agencies and other bodies and professionals to prepare a plan to stop the abuse and support the adult; (c) report the abuse to the police; (d) apply for a court order; or (e) decide to take no further action.

[144.] Rae Kaspiew, Rachel Carson and Helen Rhoades, Elder Abuse: Understanding Issues, Frameworks and Responses (Research Report No. 35, Australian Institute of Family Studies, 2016/Correction November 2, 2018) 43–44.

[145.] Rosalind F. Croucher and Julie MacKenzie, 'Framing Law Reform to Address Elder Abuse' (2018) 18 *Macquarie Law Journal* 5–14, 14.

[146.] The ALRC Report 124 states in the footnote that 'this is reflected in the "will, preferences and rights guidelines" in the ALRC Report 124 in relation to the "representative decision-making"' (ALRC Report 124, 77); Dunn et al states that 'First, protective interventions would need to reduce the risk of the "vulnerable adult" being denied the ability to make a free choice, being abused, or being unable to give complete, coherent, and accurate evidence. Second, these interventions would need to engage meaningfully with that person's subjective experience of his/her vulnerability such that any intervention does not impinge negatively on his/her self-identity, or his/her perceived ability to lead a meaningful life. Only if these two criteria were met would a protective intervention in the life of an autonomous adult be ethically defensible.' Michael C. Dunn et al, 'To Empower or to Protect? Constructing the "Vulnerable Adult" in English Law and Public Policy' (2008) 28(2) *Legal Studies* 234–53, 248.

[147.] The ALRC Report 131 (recommendation 14-4) states that 'consent is not required: (a) in serious cases of physical abuse, sexual abuse, or neglect; (b) if the safeguarding agency cannot contact the adult, despite extensive efforts to do so; or (c) if the adult lacks legal capacity to give consent in the circumstances.'

is done, when and how it is done. This mission clarifies a logical reason why adult safeguarding agencies should provide a clear point of accountability within the government.

(2) Responses to the ALRC Report 131

a. National Response

In response to the ALRC Report 131, Age Discrimination Commissioner Dr. Kay Patterson made a keynote speech, titled 'Elder Abuse is Everybody's Business,' at the Aged Rights Advocacy Service World Elder Abuse Awareness Day Conference held in Adelaide on June 15, 2018.[148] Later, the Prime Minister of Australia Scot Morrison announced on September 18, 2018, that the Royal Commission into Aged Care Quality and Safety (hereinafter referred to as 'Royal Commission') was introduced by the Letters Patent December 6, 2018.[149] The Royal Commission was established by the Governor-General of the Commonwealth on October 8, 2018. The Royal Commission organized a national campaign, at which they held hearings and accepted submissions regarding elder abuse in Australia. The Royal Commission has received a total of 10,102 submissions and 6,729 telephone calls by July 31, 2020. On March 1, 2021, the Royal Commission then published and tabled in Parliament a *Final Report—Care, Dignity and Respect* to summarize the activities and propose 148 wide-ranging recommendations, including a new Aged Care Act.[150] The report calls for fundamental reform of aged care system. It says that 'a philosophical shift is required that places the people receiving care at the center of quality and safety regulation. This means a new system empowering them and respecting their rights.'[151]

Following the above activity, the Attorney-General of Australia conducted public consultation in April to June 2021 regarding 'A mandatory national registration

---

[148]. Kay Patterson stressed that 'the multidimensional nature of elder abuse, and the expectations of individuals affected by elder abuse, require multi-disciplinary responses. We need more collaborations and partnerships to make the most of everyone's expertise and plug the gaps in services and supports.' This speech clarifies the main points of the measures to reduce elder abuse. The Australian Human Rights Commission's Age Discrimination Commissioner Kay Patterson, 'Elder Abuse Is Everybody's Business' (Speech delivered at the Aged Rights Advocacy Service World Elder Abuse Awareness Day Conference held in Adelaide on June 15, 2018).

[149]. Refers to the Royal Commission, *Letters Patent—6 December 2018* (Web Page, December 6, 2018) <https://www.royalcommission.gov.au/aged-care/letters-patent>.

[150]. Refers to the Royal Commission, *Final Report—Care, Dignity and Respect* (Web Page, March 1, 2021) <https://www.royalcommission.gov.au/aged-care/final-report>..

[151]. Refers to the Royal Commission, *Final Report—Care, Dignity and Respect* [Volume 1: Summary and Recommendations] 21 <https://www.royalcommission.gov.au/aged-care/final-report>.

scheme for enduring powers of attorney relating to financial matters.'[152] This action is to comply with the recommendation of the ALRC Report 131 (recommendation 5.3) and will consider policy design of a mandatory national online register of EPAs to be adopted in the future so as to reduce the financial abuse of older Australians.[153] The policy design of a national register includes a digitalization of EPAs.[154] In the background, numerous cases of financial exploitations are estimated to happen with misconducts of EPAs in Australia.[155]

Similarly, the Serious Incident Response Scheme (hereinafter referred to as 'SIRS') was implemented on April 1, 2022, as an initiative to help prevent and reduce the risk and occurrence of incidents of abuse and neglect in residential aged care services subsidized by the Australian Government.[156] The SIRS was proposed by the ALRC Report 131 (recommendation 4.4) and reconfirmed by the Royal Commission 2021 report. The SIRS complement existing provider obligations under the Aged Care Act by establishing responsibilities for providers to prevent and manage incidents, to use incident data to drive quality improvement and to report serious incidents. The Department of Health and Aged Care conducted public consultation in June to August 2022 regarding the SIRS framework, namely, responsibility to manage and prevent incidents, responsibility to notify reportable incidents, scope of reportable incidents, and reporting timeframe and priorities. These two policies are still under the process of establishment.

Regarding the national budget and policy, the national government had an annual budget of approximately A\$15 million (US\$9.6 million) related to the elder abuse policy measures since the 2016 fiscal year. This budget was then increased to A\$22 million (US\$14.1 million) in the 2018–2019 fiscal year. On March 19, 2019, the Commonwealth Attorney-General launched the *National Plan to Respond to the Abuse of Older Australians (Elder Abuse) 2019–2023*[157] (hereinafter referred to as 'National Plan'). Developed in collaboration with

---

[152.] Refers to the Commonwealth Attorney-General's Department, *National Register of Enduring Powers of Attorney* (Web Page, April 2022) <https://www.ag.gov.au/rights-and-protections/consultations/national-register-enduring-powers-attorney>.

[153.] Trevor Ryan, 'Developments in Enduring Powers of Attorney Law in Australia' in Lusina Ho and Rebecca Lee (eds) *Special Needs Financial Planning: A Comparative Perspective* (Cambridge University Press, 2019) 179–211, https:// doi.org/10.1017/9781108646925.007; Rieneke Stelma-Roorda, 'The Misuse or Abuse of Continuing Powers of Attorney: What Are Appropriate Safeguards?' (2021) 00 *International Journal of Law, Policy and The Family* 1, 25, https://doi.org/10.1093/lawfam/ebab022.

[154.] The digitalization of lasting powers of attorney is implemented in Singapore by the reform of the Singapore MCA 2021.

[155.] Anita Smith, 'Tribunal Update: Compensation Where Loss Caused by Actions of An Attorney Using Power of Attorney' (2019) 12 *Elder Law Review* <*https://classic.austlii.edu.au/au/journals/ElderLawRw/2019/17.html*>.

[156.] Refers to the Department of Health and Aged Care (Australian Government), *Serious Incident Response Scheme (SIRS)* (Web Page, May 31, 2022) <https://www.health.gov.au/initiatives-and-programs/serious-incident-response-scheme-sirs>.

[157.] Refers to the Council of Attorney-General, *National Plan to Respond to the Abuse of Older Australians (Elder Abuse) 2019–2023* (Attorney-General's Department, July 8, 2019) <https://www.ag.gov.au/rights-and-protections/ publications/national-plan-respond-abuse-older-australians-elder-abuse-2019-2023>.

state and special territory governments, the National Plan provides an overview of the issues that all governments need to act on as a priority. The five key priority areas are included in the National Plan: 1) enhancing our understanding, 2) improving community awareness and access to information, 3) strengthening service responses, 4) planning for future decision-making, and 5) strengthening safeguards for vulnerable older adults.[158]

Developments of Elder Abuse Prevention since 2023

Since 2023, significant developments have occurred in Australia's legal and policy landscape concerning elder abuse prevention, particularly through reforms addressing coercive control. A major shift was marked by the release of the *National Principles to Address Coercive Control in Family and Domestic Violence* in September 2023,[159] which expanded the scope beyond intimate partner violence to include broader familial and caregiving relationships—thereby acknowledging the relevance of coercive control in the abuse of older people. Complementing this, the Federal Government released educational materials, including a factsheet specifically addressing how coercive control affects older individuals.

In line with the existing National Plan, the government is in the process of formulating the *National Plan to End the Abuse and Mistreatment of Older People 2024–2034*.[160] The draft National Plan outlines a ten-year strategy supported by two five-year action plans, aiming to end rather than merely respond to elder abuse. It adopts a human rights-based, cross-portfolio approach to address systemic issues and aligns with broader national efforts like the Plan to End Violence Against Women and Children. The plan commits to ongoing monitoring, evaluation, and public reporting of progress. It provides a strategic framework to coordinate efforts across governments, sectors, and communities. An accompanying Program Logic clarifies how actions will lead to measurable outcomes over time.

[158.] Refers to the Commonwealth Attorney-General's Department, *Protecting the Rights of Older Australians* (Web Page, n/a) <https://www.ag.gov.au/rights-and-protections/protecting-rights-older-australians#national-plan-to-respond-to-the-abuse-of-older-australians>.

[159.] Refers to the Commonwealth Attorney-General's Department, *The National Principles to Address Coercive Control in Family and Domestic Violence* (Web Page, March 5, 2024) <https://www.ag.gov.au/families-and-marriage/publications/national-principles-address-coercive-control-family-and-domestic-violence>.

[160.] Refers to the Council of Attorney-General, *Consultation draft of the National Plan to End the Abuse and Mistreatment of Older People 2024-2034* (Attorney-General's Department, February 17, 2025) <https://consultations.ag.gov.au/families-and-marriage/eamop/>.

b. Response by State

State of South Australia

There has been a remarkable progress in elder abuse legislation in the state of South Australia. The 2011 Wendy Lacey co-author report *Closing the Gaps*[161] was presented to the state parliament, and legislation of an Act on adult guardianship was considered to combat elder abuse. Consequently, the *Office of the Aging (Adult Safeguarding) Amendment Act 2018* was enacted in November 2018 to amend the *Office for the Ageing Act 1995*. The Act was planned to be implemented step by step. At the first stage, older people aged 65 and over and indigenous older people aged 50 and over became subject to the law in 2019.[162] The target of the Act was expected to expand gradually for three years.

In the South Australian state elder abuse legislation, all political parties supported the bill, but a debate took place between the Ruling and Opposition parties on the public agency that should be responsible for elder abuse. The Office of the Public Advocate in charge of the guardianship was a candidate for the agency responsible for elder abuse. It was then concluded that the adoption of this proposal should be dropped.[163] If elder abuse duties were added to the Office of the Public Advocate's existing duties, it was understood that the governance of the Office would have become difficult, presumably due to a possible conflict of interest within the agency. Therefore, the responsibility was given to a new agency, the Adult Safeguarding Unit (ASU). This decision corresponds to the ALRC Report 131 recommendation.[164] The ASU is located

---

[161] Wendy Lacey, Nicholas Procter and Kay Price, *Closing the Gaps: Enhancing South Australia's Response to the Abuse of Vulnerable Older People* (Office of the Public Advocate in collaboration with the University of South Australia, 2011); Wendy Lacey et al published another report based on interview surveys of relevant agencies: Wendy Lacey et al, *Prevalence of elder abuse in South Australia: Final Report: Current Data Collection Practices of Key Agencies* (University of South Australia, Department of Health and Ageing (SA), 2017).

[162] This is due to shorter lifetime expectancy of indigenous people. According to Census of population in 2016, just 5 per cent of indigenous people were aged 65 and over compared with 16 per cent of the non-indigenous population in Australia. Australian Institute of Health and Welfare (AIHW), *Older Australian at A Glance* (Web Page, September 10, 2018) <https://www.aihw.gov.au/reports/older-people/older-australia-at-a-glance/contents/summary>.

[163] Stephan G. Wade, the Minister for Health and Wellbeing, stated that 'the government has chosen to establish the adult safeguarding unit as a function of the new office for ageing well primarily because it enables coordination with the continuum of responses to elder abuse that unit already provides, including statewide policy development, awareness raising, including across culturally and linguistically diverse groups, workforce training and other policy initiatives.' South Australia, SA Parliamentary Debates (Legislative Council), HANSARD–10–24770 (Web Page, October 23, 2018) 1723–24 <https://hansardsearch.parliament.sa.gov.au/daily/uh/2018-10-23/25>.

[164] The ALRC Report 131 states that 'the states and territories decide which of their agencies might perform this role, or whether a new agency needs to be created' (Paragraph 14–50); John Chesterman remarks that 'new agencies could be created if particular jurisdictions took the view that such an initiative would provide better responses.' John Chesterman, 'The Abuse of Older Australians (Elder Abuse): Reform Activity and Imperatives' (2019) 73(3) *Australian Social Work* 381, 389.

at the Office for Well Aging and has a focus on safeguarding the rights of adults at risk of abuse.

State of NSW

Similarly, in the state of New South Wales (NSW), an Ageing and Disability Commission was established in July 2019 by the NSW Ageing and Disability Commissioner Act 2019 to better protect vulnerable adults.[165] The Ageing and Disability Commission is an independent agency of the NSW Government.[166] The role is 'to better protect older people and adults with disability from abuse, neglect and exploitation from someone they know living in their home or community, and promote their fundamental human rights.'[167] The activities of the ASU in the state of South Australia and those of the Ageing and Disability Commission in the state of NSW have begun, and the results can be expected to affect future national legislation on elder abuse and legislation in other states and special territories. The point to note is how effectively the ASU and the Ageing and Disability Commission will conduct their broad investigative powers by law, considering conflicting objectives between safeguarding and self-autonomy of vulnerable adults.[168]

State of Victoria

In the state of Victoria, the Victorian Act 2019 states that the functions of the Public Advocate include the protection of persons with disabilities from abuse (section 5).[169] The Public Advocate, however, does not have enough power and personnel to do so. The Victorian OPA recommends that

> *state and special territory governments amend their guardianship legislation*
> *in order to give public advocates and public guardians the broad power to*

---

[165] Lenny Roth, 'Adult Safeguarding Laws: Reviewing the Proposal for NSW Ageing and Disability Commissioner' in *NSW Parliamentary Research Service E-brief Issue 3/2019* (NSW Parliamentary Research Service, Online, March 2019) <https://www.parliament.nsw.gov.au/researchpapers/Documents/Adult%20safeguarding%20laws.pdf>.

[166] People recognize 'an urgent need for an effective, integrated framework and independent lead agency for responding to the abuse and neglect of all vulnerable adults in NSW.' New South Wales Ombudsman, *Abuse and Neglect of Vulnerable Adults in NSW—the Need for Action* (Web Page, November 2, 2018) 21. <https://www.ombo.nsw.gov.au/reports/report-to-parliament/abuse-and-neglect-of-vulnerable-adults-in-nsw-the-need-for-action-2-november-2018>.

[167] Refers to the NSW Government, Ageing and Disability Commission, *Who We Are* (Web Page, November 23, 2020) <https://ageingdisabilitycommission.nsw.gov.au/about-us/who-we-are.html>.

[168] For example, the *Ageing and Disability Commissioner Act 2019* No. 7, section 12 stipulates that 'The Commissioner has the following functions—(a) to deal with allegations of abuse, neglect and exploitation of adults with disability and older adults, whether on the basis of a report made to the Commissioner or at the Commissioner's own initiative, including by referring matters to appropriate persons or bodies and by conducting investigations.'

[169] The Public Advocate 'may investigate any complaint or allegation that a person is under inappropriate guardianship, is being exploited or abused or is in need of guardianship (section 16(1)g).'

investigate, via complaints or on their own motion, the abuse, neglect and ex-
ploitation of adults with apparent impaired decision-making ability, where this
apparent impaired ability is likely to be more than temporary.[170]

It has not been concluded in the state parliament when and where the adult safeguarding body will be formed and placed in the State of Victoria.[171] It can be assumed that the state parliament might hesitate to establish the adult safeguarding body, which has powers to intervene into the self-autonomy in civil society, because it may appear a dilemma between the freedom of people and protection by public intervention.

Developments of Elder Abuse Prevention Since 2023

Since 2023, significant developments have occurred in Australia's legal and policy landscape concerning elder abuse prevention at the state level, particularly through reforms addressing coercive control.[172] Queensland and NSW have enacted standalone criminal offences for coercive control. Queensland's approach is notably inclusive, with its 2024 legislation extending protection to domestic, family, and informal care relationships. The accompanying reforms include targeted public awareness strategies, a communication framework identifying older people as a priority group, and changes to civil protection laws. In contrast, the NSW Act, commencing in July 2024, criminalizes coercive control only within intimate partner relationships. Although civil protection provisions in NSW have broadened to include coercive conduct, the exclusion of non-partner family relationships risks marginalizing older victim-survivors.

Other jurisdictions are progressing more cautiously. South Australia has proposed criminalization limited to intimate partners and does not specifically address older people in its consultation materials. Western Australia has expressed intent to criminalize coercive control and has acknowledged the abuse of older people in its policy discourse, forming a taskforce to guide future reforms. The Northern Territory has amended its civil regime to recognize coercive control but has yet to introduce a criminal offence. No substantial reforms have been made in Tasmania, Victoria, or the Australian Capital Territory.

[170.] John Chesterman and Lois Bedson (Victorian OPA), *Decision Time* (Victorian OPA Report, 2021) 61–62; Office of Public Advocate, *Line of Sight: Refocusing Victoria's Adult Safeguarding Laws and Practices* (OPA, 2022) <https://www.publicadvocate.vic.gov.au/opa-s-work/research/503-line-of-sight-refocussing-victoria-s-adult-safeguarding-laws-and-practices>.

[171.] John Chesterman, 'The Future of Adult Safeguarding in Australia' (2019) 54(4) *Australian Journal of Social Sciences* 360–70, 367

[172.] Recent developments in legislation and policy for elder abuse by states are addressed at: Leanne Collingburn and Deni Jokovic-Wroe, *Update on Elder Abuse and Coercive Control in Australia* (Web Page, June 13, 2024) <https://www.hopgoodganim.com.au/news-insights/update-on-elder-abuse-and-coercive-control-in-australia/>.

As elder abuse is expected to rise, a key concern is the risk of excluding older people when coercive control laws focus narrowly on intimate partners. Queensland's broader legislative model offers a more inclusive framework, while the upcoming 2026 review of the NSW Act presents a crucial opportunity to reassess and potentially expand the scope of protections. Moving forward, holistic reform efforts must involve sectorwide education, sustained funding, and robust monitoring mechanisms to ensure elder abuse—including coercive control—is comprehensively addressed across Australia.

4.4.3 Discussion on Elder Abuse Legislation

(a) Elder Abuse Legislation in Australia and England

It is particularly interesting to see in the ALRC Report 131 that (3) enduring appointment, (8) guardianship and administration, and (12) safeguarding adults at risk are listed as the instruments of safeguards to combat elder abuse. Legal devices for the adult guardianship, supported decision-making, and safeguards against elder abuse are interrelated.[173] Amendments to the adult guardianship system in state laws and the national legislative policy of elder abuse are on-going in parallel and are expected to provide a unique Australian adult support and protection legislative system. The Australian elder abuse legislation mainly draw from England's elder abuse safeguard measures, as can be seen in the ALRC Report 131, to take care of older people from the viewpoint of human rights protection.[174]

In England, the Care Act 2014 was enacted, which regulates 'safeguarding adults at risk of abuse or neglect' (sections 42 to 47 of the Act).[175] The Act replaces the term 'vulnerable adult' with 'adult at risk' and regulates that a local authority should provide 'care and support' with an adult at risk to promote that individual's well-being (sections 42 and 1).[176] According to the UK Government,

---

[173] Terry Carney and Shih-Ning Then, 'Combating Elder Abuse: Any Role for Supported-Decision-Making, Adult Guardianship or Other Laws?' in Mala Kapur Shankardass (ed), *Combating Elder Abuse in Australia and India* (Nova Science, 2021).

[174] From the interviews of Victorian OPA and the Senior Rights Melbourne by the author on March 2–3, 2017.

[175] The guidance for elder abuse was published in 2000 and 2015 before and after the legislation of the *Care Act 2014*. Department of Health of UK, *No Secrets: Guidance on Developing and Implementing Multi-Agency Policies and Procedures to Protect Vulnerable Adults from Abuse* (Department of Health of UK, 2nd ed, 2015).

[176] The *Care Act 2014* replaces the term 'vulnerable adults' with 'adults at risk' to underscore that the emphasis should be on the circumstances adults find themselves, rather than on an individual's impairment.' It implies more attention to social model of people with disabilities. Sarah Donnelly et al, *Adult Safeguarding Legislation and Policy Rapid Realist Literature Review* (Health Service Executive, National Safeguarding Office and Trigraph Limited, 2017) 25; Bridget Penhale et al, 'The *Care Act 2014*: A New Legal Framework for Safeguarding Adults in Civil Society' (2017) 19(4) *The Journal of Adult Protection* 169, 174.

adults at risk of harm can be abused by a wide range of people, including family members, practitioners, paid care workers, other adults at risk, volunteers, other service users, neighbors, friends and associates, people who deliberately take advantage of vulnerable people, strangers, and people who see an opportunity to abuse.[177] Section 43(1) of the Act states that 'each local authority must establish a Safeguarding Adults Board (an 'SAB') for its area.' An SAB comprises the local authority, National Health Service (NHS), the police, and so on, who may play an important role in adult safeguarding activities in the community. An SAB has the primary responsibility to deal with an abuse case in the community in cooperation with other agencies by making a safeguarding adults at risk referral (SAAR) or vice versa.

In this regard, the public agencies engaged in adult safeguarding for abuse, on a SAAR basis, are the Office of the Public Guardian (hereinafter referred to as 'OPG') and the Court of Protection. The OPG is a public agency established under the Ministry of Justice in 2007, a year before the enforcement of the Mental Capacity Act 2005[178] (hereinafter referred to as 'MCA 2005'). The OPG, originally in charge of guardianship, finds suspected abuse of adults at risk of harm based on the authority of the public guardian as a public body with legal power, also in cooperation with other public agencies, including local authority.[179] The purpose of the OPG is to protect adults at risk of harm by receiving investigative reports, recognizing abuse, and managing the findings. The OPG supervises people, reports to other public agencies, such as local authority, the police, and the Forced Marriage Unit,[180] and shares information when it is necessary.

[177.] Refers to the GOV. UK, *Policy Paper SD8: Office of the Public Guardian Safeguarding Policy* (Web Page, n/a) <https://www.gov.uk/government/publications/safeguarding-policy-protecting-vulnerable-adults/sd8-opgs-safeguarding-policy>; in Japan, elder abuse by third parties other than 'caregivers' at home and 'care home staff members' in nursing home is not covered by the Elder Abuse Prevention Act. If empirical data often indicate elder abuse by third parties other than caregivers at home and care home staff members in nursing home, it may be worth considering a possible amendment to the laws to clarify that third parties could be held liable for abuse.

[178.] The *Mental Capacity (Amendment) Act 2019* amends the *Mental Capacity Act 2005* to replace the deprivation of liberty safeguards (DoLS) with the liberty protection safeguards (LPS). The new law came into effective in November 2020. GOV. UK, *Mental Capacity (Amendment) Act 2019: Liberty Protection Safeguards (LPS)* (Web Page, December 17, 2021) <https://www.gov.uk/government/collections/mental-capacity-amendment-act-2019-liberty-protection-safeguards-lps>; Lucy Series, 'Comment: *Mental Capacity (Amendment) Act 2019 (UK)*' (Online, 2020) 12(Part 1) *The Elder Law Review* <https://www.westernsydney.edu.au/elr/elder_law/elder_law_review_elr/elder_law_review_vol_12_part_1>.

[179.] David Reid et al, 'Form and Function: Views from Members of Adult Protection Committees in England and Wales' (2009) 11(4) *The Journal of Adult Protection* 20, 29.

[180.] A forced marriage is recognized in the U.K. as 'a form of domestic or child abuse and a serious abuse of human rights.' The Forced Marriage Unit (FMU) is a joint Foreign and Commonwealth Office and Home Office unit that enforces the government's forced marriage policy and undertakes outreach and casework. GOV. UK, Law and the Justice System, *Forced Marriage* (Web Page, May 24, 2019) <https://www.gov.uk/guidance/forced-marriage>.

It can be assumed that the legal devices for the adult guardianship, supported decision-making, and safeguards against elder abuse in England are interrelated to some extent. It is also presumed that England's elder abuse legislation has a background with a purpose intended for broad and social correspondence, including school and community education. This may correspond to 'the emphasis should be on the circumstances adults find themselves, rather than on an individual's impairment.'[181] This seems to emphasize a preventive model rather than a reactive model. A preventive model is presumably based on a method aimed at diminishing possible root causes of the problem by taking proactive measures, including social, legal, and systemic ones.[182] This preventive method is different from the U.S. elder abuse method of adult protection services. In the US, most of the elder abuse programs take place at the state level. People or agencies that notice suspicious behavior related to elder abuse inform the police and deal with strict application of law and regulations.[183] It can be said that Australian elder abuse policy is consistent with the character of Australian's multicultural society and draws more England's elder abuse legislation than U.S. method, which refers to a preventive approach rather than a reactive approach.[184] The *National Plan to End the Abuse and Mistreatment of Older People 2024–2034* is a comprehensive strategy that aims to address the issue of elder abuse on a multidimensional level within the Commonwealth.

(b) Elder Abuse Responses of Australian States

Following the ALRC Report 131, the activities of the ASU in the state of South Australia and those of the Ageing and Disability Commission in the state of NSW have begun by the state initiatives.[185] Since 2023, Australian states have taken divergent approaches to addressing coercive control in elder abuse prevention, with the state of Queensland enacting inclusive legislation that extends protections beyond intimate partner relationships to encompass family and informal care

---

[181.] Refers to the previous remarks [871]. Sarah Donnelly et al (n 176) 25.

[182.] Two approaches addressing elder abuse are comparatively discussed between the US and Japan, i.e., a reactive approach (the US) and a preventive approach (Japan). Bryan A. Liang and Fusako Seki, 'Protecting the Elderly: Policy Lessons from an Analysis of Japan and USA Approaches' (2009) 18(2) *Yokohama Law Review* 1, 37.

[183.] The three main federal APS statutes in the US are 'Title VII (Vulnerable Elder Rights Protection Activities) of the *Older Americans Act* (OAA), the *Violence against Women Act*, and the *Elder Justice Act* (EJA) portion of the *Affordable Care Act* (ACA).' Marshall B. Kapp, 'Future Directions in Public Policy Relating to Elder Abuse' in XinQi Dong (ed), *Elder Abuse* (Springer, 2017) 695.

[184.] From the interviews of Victorian OPA and the Senior Rights Melbourne by the author on March 2–3, 2017.

[185.] The February 2022 report addresses that 'Australia needs national consistency in power of attorney (PoA), a national PoA register to verify PoA documents, and a place to report suspected abuse in each state.' National Seniors Australia, *Scams and Financial Abuse Update: Snapshots from National Seniors Australia* (National Seniors Australia, 2022) 19.

dynamics, while the state of NSW has adopted a narrower framework limited to intimate partnerships. For these reforms to constitute long-term improvements to the prevention of and response to elder abuse, extensive community education and adequate funding are essential, so that the relevant policy and legislative system could be continued and scale up in national level.[186] The elder abuse policy requires 'nuanced consideration of many and varied factors, including the nature of relationships of care and support, cultural values, and the role of civil society.'[187] According to the legal system of Australia, the procedure on legal reforms of each state and special territory under the umbrella of the Commonwealth is first informally negotiated between the national government and the state and special territory government.[188] Second, the national and the state and special territory parliaments will deliberate on the bills. For this reason, it is expected that a considerable amount of time will be required for these legislations to be completed.[189] A strong and unified initiative over the national and state and special territory levels is vital if the legislations are to address the scourge of elder abuse.[190] It can be said that combating elder abuse is an important Australian national project.

4.5 Australian Principal Values and the Implications

4.5.1 Discussion on Australian Adult Support and Protection

(1) Australian Adult Support and Protection Legislation

a. Policy Objectives

The policy objectives of the Australian legislative project can be summarized as follow: First, the framework of the guardianship system established over thirty years ago has been or would be changed. Supported decision-making has been or would be incorporated into the legislation that was recommended by the UN

[186.] Chesterman (n 164) 387.

[187.] Terry Carney, 'Combating Elder Abuse: Any Role for Supported-Decision-Making, Adult Guardianship or Other Laws?' in Mala Kapur Shankardass (ed), *Combating Elder Abuse in Australia and India* (Nova Science Publishers, 2020) 1–20, 15.

[188.] The institutional mechanism to adjust interests between national and state/territory is reported. Jun Ashida (National Diet Library of Japan), 'Australian Intergovernmental Council: Method of Federal and State Government Coordination' (2018) 277 *Foreign Legislation* 77, 91 (in Japanese).

[189.] From the interview of Victorian OPA by the author on March 2–3, 2017.

[190.] An article to focus on lawyers' responsibilities by using screening tools for older clients: Nola M. Ries, 'Elder Abuse and Lawyers' Ethical Responsibilities: Incorporating Screening into Practice' (2018) 21(1) *Legal Ethics* 23, 45; Dow et al (n 121).

CRPD.[191] Second, personal protection, autonomy and right to self-determination were clarified and prioritized, even if they may somewhat change the balance of protection and autonomy.[192] Third, informal arrangements by relatives or close kin are kept as they are without forcing any changes unless problems arise. And fourth, to propose personal protection measures in a broader area. These measures include a policy to formulate treatment and safeguards through regulations of commercial banks and other financial institutions as well as school and community education.

In the two Australian States of Victoria and NSW, the guardianship system and supported decision-making are incorporated int the state legislation. Legal devices for guardianship, supported decision-making, and safeguards against elder abuse are interrelated. Amendments to the adult guardianship system in the state Acts and the national legislative policy of elder abuse are ongoing in parallel and are expected to provide a unique Australian legislative system. The adult support and protection system refers to an offer of necessary sustenance, according to individual characteristics, that minimizes restrictions on a principal's rights. This system is considered to take less restrictive alternative measures. A person-centered approach is emphasized according to the relevant mental capacity of the principal, unlike a traditional guardianship system that uniformly restricts rights.

If the adult support and protection system is considered as a comprehensive legal system, the amendments to the state laws and national legislative policy covered in this chapter are an example of legislation of the adult support and protection.[193] The values enshrined in the CRPD, international human rights law, and rising human rights awareness make up the background of the adult support and protection system.[194] The Australian legislative project has been under discussion at the Law Reform Commission of each state and national government in response to rising human rights laws and awareness. This movement is a positive response to an aging society and will be of relevance to other countries, including Japan.

[191.] McCallum (n 116) 46–55.

[192.] ALRC Report 131, Paragraph 1.19 states that 'the autonomy of older people should not be afforded less respect than the autonomy of others. However, in limited cases, where there is particularly serious abuse of vulnerable people, protection should be given additional weight.'

[193.] Reviewing sixty-seven international law reform reports on the guardianship, nine reports were found to have recommendations to enact supported decision-making, including five reports in Australia, two reports in Canada, one report in the UK, and one Uniform Law in the US. Shih-Ning Then et al, 'Supporting Decision-making of Adults with Cognitive Disabilities: The Role of Law Reform Agencies—Recommendations, Rationales and Influence' (2018) 61 *International Journal of Law and Psychiatry* 64, 75.

[194.] 'Law reform initiatives must think beyond the limits of existing domestic laws to imagine different and interconnected legal, social, cultural and political responses to disability.' Fleur Beaupert, Linda Steele and Piers Gooding, 'Introduction to Disability, Rights and Law Reform in Australia: Pushing Beyond Legal Futures' in Fleur Beaupert, Linda Steele, and Piers Gooding (eds), *Disability, Rights and Law Reform in Australia* (The Federation Press, 2017) 14.

b. Unique Institutional Design

In the meantime, some unique institutional designs that support the Australian adult support and protection system need to be understood.[195] First, Australia has the Public Advocate or the Public Guardian in each jurisdiction. This office, a part of the State Department of Justice, implements a legal support system and deals with human rights policy issues at large. Second, Australia has a tribunal system. The tribunal is independent of the courts and is engaged in prompt and straightforward dispute solution for tenancy, family, civil, and human rights issues. Third, Australia has a state-run or public financial management institution, State Trustees Limited or Public Trustee.[196] State Trustees Limited or Public Trustee is appointed with fees when there is no person suitable to serve as an administrator for a principal with insufficient mental capacity, or when more professional financial management skill is required.[197] Fourth, Australia has many NPOs that operate in communities based on a charity, grant, or welfare funding system. This concept of institutional agencies mentioned above may enable the smooth implementation of the guardianship in practice.

Figure 4.1 is an illustration of the relevant agencies and their interrelations with people in the community who apply to participate in the Victorian adult support and protection and the Public Advocate tasked with responding to these people. This is an attempt to show a conceptual illustration, simplifying the mechanism and interrelations between relevant agencies and people in community.[198] The Australian adult support and protection system is a costly design because personnel expenses and operational expenses of public agencies related to adult guardianship are almost fixed. As far as Australia is concerned, the

---

[195] Terry Carney remarks that public agencies 'offer a responsive and personalized service rather than bureaucratic and impersonal service to which they may be predisposed by virtue of the prior history (and operating "culture") of such institutions.' Terry Carney, 'Challenges to the Australian Guardianship and Administration Model' (2003) 2 *Elder Law Review* <http://classic.austlii.edu.au/au/journals/ElderLawRw/2003/8.html>.

[196] The history of public trustees started in Australia at the colonial days in 1880s, following the development in New Zealand, which influenced England to establish public trustees: E. J. Trevelyan et al, 'The Public Trustee in India, New Zealand, Australia, and England' (1916) 16(2) *Journal of the Society of Comparative Legislation* 110–39, 126–30.

[197] In the state of Victoria, five types of public guardianship are utilized, centered on three types of public agencies. Namely, the tribunal is involved in the dispute of the EPA, the Public Advocate office associated NPOs/individuals are involved in SDM/guardianship for personal support, the STL is involved in SDM/guardianship for property management, and NPOs/individuals are independently involved in SDM/guardianship. See Suga-classified public guardianship types: (i) judicial direct intervention type, (ii) administrative direct control (public guardianship) type, (iii) public sector type, (iv) private organization formation (corporate guardianship) type, and (v) individual type. Fumie Suga, *The Doctrine of Autonomous Support in the English Adult Guardianship System: Towards a Society Pursuing the Best Interests* (Minerva Shobo, 2010) 258 (in Japanese).

[198] Hiroko Sugita advocates an idea to build an advocacy network for older people with dementia in collaboration with medical care, aged care, and the judiciary using the existing community-based integrated care system, and to provide support centered on advance directives created by the principals, referring to the state of South Australia's laws and policy. Hiroko Sugita, 'A Study on the Supported Decision-Making System for the Elderly with Dementia (2): Focusing on the South Australian Legal System' (2021) 179 *The Graduate School Law Review* 71–98, 94 (in Japanese).

national population scale is relatively small, at approximately 25 million, and thus these institutional agencies can be run. The national productivity and the living standard are relatively high to pay for the institutional burden. But it is unlikely that this institutional design will be applied in the exact same way to any other country, including Japan.[199] This is because there will be financial challenges in maintaining the institutional agencies in any country with a higher population scale, such as Japan. Therefore, when importing the concept of the Australian institutional agencies to another country, it is vital to revise its instrumental design to minimize the financial burden.

c. Uncertainties on SDM Development

There are some uncertainties as to how supported decision-making model is to be developed. In the process of legislation, further consideration should be given to the supported decision-making model.[200] For example, what supported decision-making model will be most effective to older people with dementia?[201] Mary Donnelly remarks that 'After almost two decades in operation, it would appear that, in spite of its success for adults with intellectual/development disabilities, the Representation Agreement Act 2000[202] in British Columbia (Canada) has not delivered a workable framework for people with dementia.'[203] Craig Sinclair proposed 'a spectrum model of supported decision-making which incorporates both a formal framework for "supporters" and recourse to a

---

[199.] From the interview by the author of a Japanese lawyer in attorney, a leading member of the Japan Adult Guardianship Law Corporation Association (JAGA) at the World Congress of Adult Guardianship (WCAG) in Seoul, South Korea on October 25, 2018.

[200.] Malcolm Parker, 'Getting the Balance Right: Conceptual Considerations Concerning Legal Capacity and Supported Decision-Making' (2016) 13(3) *Journal of Bioethical Inquiry* 381, 393.

[201.] Craig Sinclair et al implemented the interdisciplinary project 'Supported Decision-Making in Dementia Care across three states in Australia (2016–19).' Through legal, policy and empirical social science research in the project, they have produced a policy guideline for aged care providers, a consumer guidebook, and other resources. The University of Sydney, *Supported Decision-Making* (Web Page, n/a) <https://cdpc.sydney.edu.au/research/planning-decision-making-and-risk/supported-decision-making/>; A woman living with dementia (age 54) of the project issues a short essay: Theresa Flavin, 'Supported Decision Making for People Living with Dementia' (2020) 19(1) *Dementia* 95, 97.

[202.] The Representation Agreement Act 1996 is the first Canadian legislation in the British Columbia province to establish a comprehensive framework for supported decision-making. See British Columbia, *Incapacity Planning* (Web Page, n/a) <https://www2.gov.bc.ca/gov/content/health/managing-your-health/incapacity-planning>; Canadian Centre for Elder Law (CCEL), *Study Paper on Inclusive Investing: Respecting the Rights of Vulnerable Investors through Supported Decision-Making* (Canadian Centre for Elder Law, May 5, 2021) 73–7 <https://ssrn.com/abstract=3855139>.

[203.] A tendency is seen to move straight to substituted decision-making in dementia cases because it is easier and convenient to supporters. Mary Donnelly, 'Deciding in Dementia: The Possibilities and Limits of Supported Decision-Making' (Online, 2019) 60 *International Journal of Law and Psychiatry* <https://doi.org/10.1016/j.ijlp.2019.101466>.

"representatives" role as a last resort.'[204] Based on the interviews and analysis of cases of dementia across three states in Australia, this model is considered to cope with the characteristics of dementia, which is 'a condition resulting in gradual and progressive decline, but with [an] unpredictable course.'[205] It can be assumed necessary to accumulate practical issues associated with implementing supported decision-making, and to make systematic efforts to establish counter-measures and safeguards. Possible undue influence and a supporter's misconduct may be the problems.[206] Undue influence may happen by a supporter using a superior position to control a principal or to exercise improper persuasion.[207] Under the principle of autonomy, a principal with insufficient mental capacity might be assisted through supported decision-making activity by a third party in the principal's best interests. But, in fact, the principal might be forced to engage in action that serves the interest of a third party.

Figure 4.1: Illustration of the Victorian Adult Support and Protection Framework

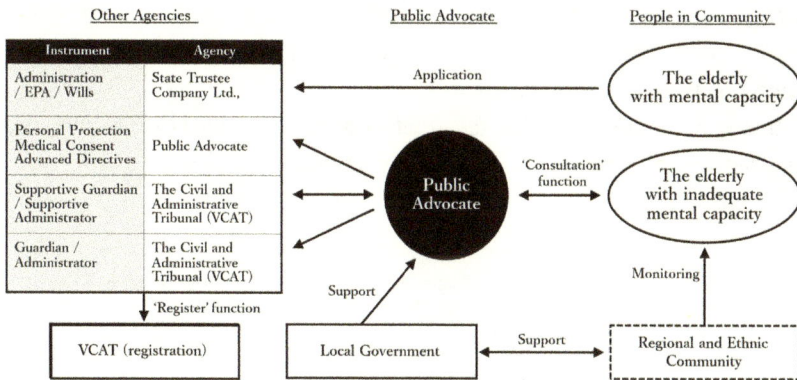

Source: Made by the Author

[204.] Craig Sinclair et al, '"A Real Bucket of Worms": Views of People Living with Dementia and Family Members on Supported Decision-Making' (2019) 16 *Journal of Bioethical Inquiry* 587–608, 605; Terry Carney and Shih-Ning Then, 'Support for Decision-Making for People Age with a Cognitive Impairment' in Michelle Putnam and Christine Bigby (eds), *Handbook Ageing and Disability* (Routledge, 2021) 186–95.

[205.] Sinclair et al (n 204) 605.

[206.] Fiona R. Burns, 'Elders and Testamentary Undue Influence in Australia' (2005) 28(1) *UNSW Law Journal* 145, 185.

[207.] Mary Joy Quinn, 'Undue Influence and Elder Abuse' (2002) 23(1) *Geriatric Nursing* 11–17, 15.

d. What Aspects of Supported Decision-Making Require Further Research

There is room necessary for further research on supported decision-making (SDM), particularly regarding the principal's autonomy and self-determination. It is important for the state of NSW-proposed Assisted Decision-Making Act to respect the will and preferences of the principal when examining measures to properly determine them.[208] This is because the meaning of the will and preferences and practice implications are, in fact, sometimes disputed and poorly understood by practitioners.[209] These measures to determine them may need a nuanced understanding of the will and preferences of the principal.[210] These measures also may include how to incorporate opinions of relatives and acquaintances surrounding the principal in decision-making process.[211] The guidelines, such as the code of practice or toolkits for SDM, would be essential.[212] It is important to train professionals to lead and coordinate supporters' activities. This professional human resource system may correspond to how to guide SDM practices on site and how to solve any technical problems related to SDM in communities. If such a professional is called a 'supported decision-making counselor,' some consideration is needed specifically as to the qualification requirements and training course methods that this counselor should have.

In England and Wales, when the Mental Capacity Act 2005 (MCA 2005) was enacted, an independent mental capacity advocate (hereinafter referred to as

---

[208.] Karen Strickland et al, 'Supported Decision-Making to Assist Older Persons Experiencing Elder Abuse: An Integrative Review' (2021) 28(4) *Collegian* 447, 455; Malcolm Parker, 'Getting the Balance Right: Conceptual Considerations Concerning Legal Capacity and Supported Decision-Making' (2016) 13(3) *Journal of Bioethical Inquiry* 381, 393.

[209.] Carney et al (n 111).

[210.] A recent research survey finds that 'the highly individualized and contextually dependent nature of SDM has implications for SDM practice.' Michelle Browning, Christine Bigby and Jacinta Douglas, 'A Process of Decision-Making Support: Exploring Supported Decision-Making Practice in Canada' (Online, 2020) 46(2) *Journal of Intellectual & Developmental Disability* 138–49 <https://doi.org/10.3109/13668250.2020.1789269>; Another article analyzes what and how guardians take the processes to understanding the will and preferences of principals, focusing on their personal factors. Alice L. Holmes et al, 'Integrity in Guardianship Decision Making: Applying the Will and Preferences Paradigm' (Online, 2022) 23(7) *Journal of the American Medical Directors Association* 1, 8 <https://doi.org/10.1016/j.jamda.2022.01.050>.

[211.] The model of ASSET (South Australia) is effective in such a case: if a decision-maker (a principal) with disability wishes to independently live in an apartment by his/herself, but the parents disagree. A team may help his/her wishes come true under the condition that every team member agrees with the decision-makers wishes. This model is based on mutual agreements among all team members to respect the decision-makers wishes. It is understood that this model tries to avoid any misunderstanding among team members. The ASSET model is applied to people with disabilities in Japan, but it is being used on a small scale and further development may be expected. Piers Gooding, 'Supported Decision Making: A Rights-Based Disability Concept and Its Implications for Mental Health Law' (2012) 20(3) *Psychiatry, Psychology and Law* 431, 451.

[212.] Peterson et al proposes 'three-step model for implementing supported decision-making,' which comprises (i) identify domains where support is needed and desired, (ii) identify kinds of support that are (or will be) needed and desired, and (iii) establish a supported decision-making agreement. Andrew Peterson, Janson Karlawish and Emily Largent, 'Supported Decision Making with People at the Margins of Autonomy' (Online, 2020) 21(11) *The American Journal of Bioethics* 1, 15 <https://doi.org/10.1080/15265161.2020.1863507>.

'IMCA') system based on the MCA 2005 was introduced.[213] The main tasks of an IMCA are support for an important legal decision, such as making decision about where they live and about serious medical treatment options. An IMCA may perform as a supporter of the principal who has lost their mental capacity when there is no suitable supporter like a relative or an acquaintance. The Office of the Public Advocate (OPA) in states and special territories of Australia or a relevant public agency may support practical activities of SDM.[214] This will be a challenge in Japan, where there is no public agency or profession like the OPA or an IMCA who supports decision-making practices and helps to solve technical problems in communities, accessing to personal information of principals.

The aspects of supported decision-making that need further research are an empirical analysis of practices on site and 'social change and policy amendment' in addition to the regulatory reform of SDM, particularly support mechanisms and networks in community.[215] Regarding the former issue, based on interviews with parents who act supporters to their adult children with an intellectual disability, Shih-Ning Then et al note a challenge at moving from support for decision-making to substituted decision-making. Namely, Then et al demonstrate that the additional 'considerations of risk and future opportunities for the principal proved to be more nuanced factors taken into account by supporters who shifted into a substituted decision-maker role, and this is not well accounted for in their legal frameworks.'[216] Regarding the latter issue, as Christine Bigby and Jacinta Douglas point out, supported decision-making must incorporate 'mechanism that proactively reach out to find, encourage and nurture supporters for the many people who do not have strong existing support networks.'[217] It is supposed that the support mechanisms and networks in community would be part

---

[213.] Refers to the Social Care Institute for Excellence (UK), *Independent Mental Capacity Advocate (IMCA)* (Web Page, January 2010) <https://www.scie.org.uk/mca/imca>.

[214.] Gerard Quinn proposed the 'Office of Public Support' as a moral agency of the person in 2016. Gerard Quinn, 'Reflecting Will and Preference in Decision Making' (2016) (Conference Paper, Australian Guardianship and Administration Council (AGAC) Conference held in Sydney on October 17–18, 2016) 31.

[215.] Interviews research survey in England suggests that 'as a range of SDM techniques have been developed in practice, paradoxically, it appears that decisions become more complex and the supports available to people with disabilities reduce, particularly for more difficult decisions, such as finances, healthcare, and legal matters.' Harding and Taşcıoğlu have pointed out the importance of supports of multi-domains, including social change and policy amendment in addition to regulatory reform. Rosie Harding and Ezgi Taşcıoğlu, 'Supported Decision-Making from Theory to Practice: Implementing the Right to Enjoy Legal Capacity' (2018) 8(2) *Societies* 25–42, 39–40.

[216.] Shih-Ning Then et al, 'Moving from Support for Decision-Making to Substitute Decision-Making: Legal Frameworks and Perspectives of Supporters of Adults with Intellectual Disabilities' (2022) 37(3) *Law in Context* <https://doi.org/10.26826/law-in-context.v37i3.174>.

[217.] Christine Bigby and Jacinta Douglas, 'Supported Decision Making' in Roger J. Stancliffe, Michael L. Wehmeyer, Karrie A. Shogren and Brian H. Abery (eds), *Choice, Preference, and Disability: Promoting Self-Determination Across the Lifespan* (Springer, 2020) 45–66, 61.

of the foundation where supporters can deal with various types of disabilities, including intellectual/mental disabilities, higher brain dysfunction, and dementia. It is therefore required to specifically consider how to support people who do not have effective mechanisms and networks in remote areas.[218] An idea would be a combination service of weekly patrol around the principals' residences and daily online communication by social workers.

(2) The National Disability Insurance Scheme

a. What Is the NDIS?

The national Disability Insurance Scheme[219] (hereinafter referred to as 'NDIS') is not central in this study. Considering the significant role of the NDIS, it must be appropriate to take it up as long as the NDIS is systematically involved in the guardianship. The NDIS is a major program designed as a national insurance system by law, the National Disability Insurance Scheme Act 2013 (Act No. 131 of 2017). It provides support and services under the supervision of the nominees as an option to people with disabilities.[220] The NDIS is designed to empower people with disabilities and facilitate their choice and control (section 3(1)). It started the post-trial roll-out in 2016 and completed over Australia in 2020. The intention was for the NDIS and the guardianship to play their respective roles in the legislative process. Namely, the NDIS participants are people less than the age of 65 who have permanent and significant disabilities (approximately a total of 500,000 persons in Australia) and receive support and services as early intervention.[221] While vulnerable adults with insufficient mental capacity, regardless of age or reason, can lodge to the tribunal for the guardianship list.

---

[218] Ilan Wiesel et al, 'The Temporalities of Supported Decision-Making by People with Cognitive Disability' (2020) 23(7) *Social and Cultural Geography*. 934–52 <https://doi.org/10.1080/14649365.2020.1829689>

[219] Terry Carney states that the NDIS will be the second largest national government program after Medicare at A$21.5 billion (US$13.7 billion) annually in the full implementation. Terry Carney et al, 'National Disability Insurance Scheme Plan Decision-Making: Or When Tailor-Made Case Planning Met Taylorism & the Algorithms?' (2019) 42(3) *Melbourne University Law Review* 1–37, 3.

[220] Sue Olney and Helen Dickinson, 'Australia's New National Disability Insurance Scheme: Implications for Policy and Practice' (2019) 2(3) *Policy Design and Practice* 275, 290.

[221] Section 17A (Principles relating to the participation of people with disability) of the *National Disability Insurance Scheme Act 2013* stipulates: (1) People with disability are assumed, so far as is reasonable in the circumstances, to have capacity to determine their own best interests and make decisions that affect their own lives. (2) People with disability will be supported in their dealings and communications with the Agency so that their capacity to exercise choice and control is maximized. Australian Government, *National Disability Insurance Scheme Act 2013*.

b. Relationship Between the NDIS and the Guardianship

The current Australian trend in the relationship between the NDIS and the guardianship can be summarized as follows: First, regarding the domestic legislation of the CRPD requirements, states and special territories have been trying to deal with disability policy, the guardianship, and safeguards against elder abuse in a unified manner across Australia. In other words, national standardization has been occurring in response to public policy and laws to some extent. Second, common goals behind the NDIS and the guardianship reform include autonomy, right to self-determination, and consumer choice.[222] These common goals are thought to be in line with the values of the CRPD. Third, the guardianship, supported decision-making, and the NDIS are positioned as legal instruments to prevent elder abuse, and each legal system and policy must complement the other. To put together the above three points, it could be said that the NDIS is packaged with social welfare policy, guardianship, supported decision-making, and safeguards against elder abuse.

Some NDIS participants have wanted to nominate their guardians (mainly public advocates) as the nominees in the state of Victoria, as the Annual Report 2020–2021 of Victorian OPA states.[223] There has been a trend that the new guardianship orders in which the represented person (the principal) was a participant in the NDIS were increasing in number and the percentage of the all eligible matters involving NDIS.[224] The reasons why this happens is not so clear, presumably due to the eligibility of the NDIS nominee candidates or the like.[225] The decision by the NDIS participants should be respected as consumer choice, but from the

---

[222.] John Chesterman emphasizes on 'consumer choice' or 'consumer directed care' to meet individual needs even in adult protection programs. John Chesterman, 'Modernising Adult Protection in an Age of Choice' (2014) 73(4) *Australian Journal of Public Administration* 517–24, 519; John Chesterman, 'Supported Decision-Making' in Sue Field, Karen Williams and Carolyn Sappideen (eds), *Elder Law: A Guide to Working with Older Australians* (The Federation Press, 2018) 105; John Chesterman, 'Adult Guardianship and Its Alternatives in Australia' in Claire Spivakovsky, Kate Seear and Adrian Carter (eds) *Critical Perspectives on Coercive Interventions* (Routledge, 2018) 225–35; John Chesterman, 'The Future of Adult Safeguarding in Australia' (2019) 54(4) *Australian Journal of Social Sciences* 360–70, 362–3.

[223.] Refers to the Victorian OPA, *Annual Report 2020–21:* 'Continuing NDIS Impact' 17; Australian Government's view: 'There is a presumption that a guardian should be appointed nominee where their responsibilities are comparable to the duties of a nominee.' NDIS, *Guardians and Nominees Explained* (Web Page, November 5, 2019) <https://www.ndis.gov.au/understanding/families-and-carers/guardians-and-nominees-explained>. Furthermore, the June 2025 OPA report confirmed this trend. OPA, *Multiple Appointments* (Web Page, June 30, 2025) <https://www.publicadvocate.vic.gov.au/opa-s-work/research/808-multiple-appointments>.

[224.] Ibid [Victorian OPA]. It has increased as follows: 20.0 per cent (83 out of 415) in 2017–2018, 58.6 per cent (284 out of 485) in 2018–2019, 72.6 per cent (369 out of 508) in 2019–2020, and 82.0 per cent (521 out of 635) in 2020–2021.

[225.] Some jurisdictions, such as Queensland, Victoria, and Western Australia, have also experienced increased demand for public guardianship services resulting from decision-making needs related to the NDIS.' Victorian OPA, *Decision Time* (Web Page, March 1, 2021) 54 <https://www.publicadvocate.vic.gov.au/opa-s-work/research/141-decision-time>.

viewpoint of the principles of the Victorian Act 2019, backlash by the NDIS participants has apparently led to an increase in the number of guardians over the last three years.[226] It is unpredictable what the situation will be like. Namely, how will the NDIS and the guardianship, including the Victorian Act 2019, be reconciled in practice? Further observations will be important.[227]

Furthermore, then Victorian Public Advocate, Colleen Pearce, published a discussion paper titled *Manipulation and Personal Autonomy* on September 24, 2024 for a roundtable discussion at Victorian OPA.[228] The paper focuses on examining and describing forms of targeted manipulation employed by NDIS-funded organizations and workers to exploit NDIS participants. It was subsequently made publicly available, highlighting problematic practices.

Australia is a Commonwealth that inherited English law, and Australia's legal and administrative structure differs from Japan's. The simplification of the Australian guardianship system remains within the scope of common law, administrative law jurisdictions, including the management of public agencies related to the guardianship. The NDIS is a part of social welfare law, and its administration is performed through public agencies and private service providers in communities.[229] Thus, administrative law and common law are mutually involved in jurisdictions. It can be understood that both the guardianship and the NDIS function within a similar domain and are ultimately heading toward the same goals. The difference between them is that the NDIS is a national insurance system run by tax, based on both national and state laws, while the guardianship is a state or special territory law system. Due to efforts to standardize the guardianship system at the state and special territory level under the national policy, it is expected that the difference among states and special territories of the guardianship system will not be so large. It could therefore be understood that the guardianship and the NDIS are to be placed to mutually complement each other in the legal domain, although some competing phenomenon happens in some States as mentioned above.

[226.] It may include the number of petitions to the tribunal asking for adding the nominee duties to the guardians because the guardians without such an authorization cannot be engaged in the nominee. A NDIS nominee, in contrast of a guardian, can sign any service contract based on the NDIS and manage the budget associated with NDIS planning. Emiko Kiguchi, Masaru Nagawa and Yukio Sakurai, 'Australian Guardianship and National Disability Insurance Scheme: Focusing on Supported Decision-Making Practices in the States of Victoria and New South Wales' (2020) 33 *Journal of Australian Studies* 1–14, 9 (in Japanese).

[227.] The NDIS faces challenges: 'it ultimately falls short in fully embracing the obligations of Article 12 and the notions of autonomy and personhood underlying it.' Emily Cukalevski, 'Supporting Choice and Control—An Analysis of the Approach Taken to Legal Capacity in Australia's National Disability Insurance Scheme' (2019) 8(2) *Disability Human Rights Law* 1–19, 1.

[228.] Victorian Office of Public Advocate (OPA), *Manipulation and Personal Autonomy* (Web Page, September 24, 2024) <https://www.publicadvocate.vic.gov.au/opa-s-work/research/745-manipulation-and-personal-autonomy>.

[229.] The NDIS aims to better link between the community and people with disabilities by relevant interactivities. Productivity Commission, *Disability Care and Support, Report No. 54* (Productivity Commission, 2011) 2.

(3) Standardization of Legislation and Policy on Guardianship, Supported Decision-Making, and Elder Abuse Prevention in Australia

In Australia, the regulation of guardianship, supported decision-making, and the prevention of elder abuse primarily falls under the jurisdiction of state and territory governments. Consequently, legislative and policy developments in these areas have largely occurred at the subnational level. These three domains—guardianship, supported decision-making, and elder abuse prevention—are closely interconnected and align with broader national frameworks, including aged care, the National Disability Insurance Scheme (NDIS), human rights, education, and healthcare. Nevertheless, as this paper has shown, significant inconsistencies persist across jurisdictions. This fragmentation is further compounded by confusion between national and state-level systems, particularly evident in the implementation of the NDIS in Victoria. These challenges underscore the pressing need for stronger national leadership to promote greater uniformity in legislation and policy across Australia.

In response to these challenges, the federal government has initiated steps toward national coordination. The Royal Commission into Violence, Abuse, Neglect and Exploitation of People with Disability, established in April 2019, convened roundtable discussions on guardianship, supported decision-making, and elder abuse prevention on May 31 and June 1, 2022. These meetings brought together representatives from the Commonwealth, state and territory governments, and civil society organizations, fostering substantive dialogue. A record of proceedings was compiled,[230] and a summary report was published in October 2022.[231] To further address the lack of standardization in supported decision-making practices, the Royal Commission commissioned a team of academic experts to produce a comprehensive 400-page report.[232] This document outlines core principles, methodologies, evaluation criteria, professional training standards, and the role of volunteers in supported decision-making. Both the roundtable

---

[230.] Royal Commission into Violence, Abuse, Neglect and Exploitation of People with Disability, *Supported Decision-Making and Guardianship—Proposals for Reform Roundtable* (Web Page, June 3, 2022). <https://disability.royalcommission.gov.au/publications/supported-decision-making-and-guardianship-proposals-reform-roundtable>.

[231.] Royal Commission, *Roundtable—Supported Decision-Making and Guardianship—Summary Report* (October 21, 2022) <https://disability.royalcommission.gov.au/publications/roundtable-supported-decision-making-and-guardianship-summary-report-auslan>.

[232.] Christine Bigby et al, *Diversity, Dignity, Equity and Best Practice: A Framework for Supported Decision-Making* (Royal Commission into Violence, Abuse, Neglect and Exploitation of People with Disability, January 24, 2023) <https://disability.royalcommission.gov.au/publications/diversity-dignity-equity-and-best-practice-framework-supported-decision-making>.

summary and the expert report were incorporated into the Royal Commission's final report, released on September 28, 2023.[233]

These coordinated efforts are expected to lay the groundwork for greater harmonization of legislation and policy across Australia. It is anticipated that guardianship, supported decision-making, and elder abuse prevention measures will become increasingly standardized at the national level. In the long term, these developments may culminate in the establishment of a unified federal statute—potentially an Australian Adult Support and Protection Act.

Achieving this goal, however, will require sustained and collaborative efforts by both the Commonwealth and state and territory governments to implement the recommendations outlined in the Royal Commission's final report. Australian scholars emphasize the critical role of the Commonwealth Government in initiating and driving the practical implementation of these recommendations.[234]

(4) Theoretical Framework

A theoretical analysis of the guardianship law reforms and national legislation policy of elder abuse in Australia is shown in accordance with a multidimensional model of elder law. The multidimensional model of elder law was advocated by Israel Doron in 2003/2009 as 'an efficient comparison tool in international and comparative law.'[235] The purpose of the model is to clarify elder law system through mapping, as shown in Figure 4.2, and to make a comparative law study in the international context.[236] It is assumed that this model can be applied to the adult support and protection law, because the adult support and protection law is listed as part of elder law in the publications and both laws share the same values.[237]

[233.] Royal Commission, *Publications—Final Report* (Web Page, September 28, 2023) <https://disability.royalcommission.gov.au/publications/final-report>. The final report contains 222 recommendations for amending legislation, policies, structures and practices.

[234.] Shih-Ning Then and Christine Bigby, 'Supported Decision-Making and the Disability Royal Commission, Research and Practice in Intellectual and Developmental Disabilities' (2024) 11(1) *Research and Practice in Intellectual and Developmental Disabilities* 86–106 <https://doi.org/10.1080/23297018.2024.2330961>; John Chesterman, 'Adult Safeguarding in Australia after the Disability Royal Commission, Research and Practice in Intellectual and Developmental Disabilities' (2024) 11(1) *Research and Practice in Intellectual and Developmental Disabilities* 53–62 <https://doi.org/10.1080/23297018.2024.2316291>.

[235.] This model was originally introduced in the article in 2003 without consideration of supported decision-making before the CRPD was adopted in the UN. Israel Doron, 'A Multi-Dimensional Model of Elder Law: An Israeli Example' (2003) 28(3) *Ageing International* 242–59, 256; Israel Doron (ed), 'A Multi-Dimensional Model of Elder Law' in *Theories on Law and Ageing* (Springer, 2009) 59–74.

[236.] Israel Doron proposes that 'the model can be used to examine any legal system or to analyze its various laws by observing how these correspond to each of the model's suggested dimensions.' Doron (n 235) 255.

[237.] LawrenceFrolik and Alison Barnes, *Elder Law: Cases and Materials* (LexisNexsis, 6th ed, 2015); Sue Field, Karen Williams and Carolyn Sappideen, *Elder Law: A Guide to Working with Older Australians* (The Federation Press, 2018).

Hence, the Australian adult support and protection legislation system, comprising guardianship state law reforms and national legislation policy of elder abuse, is reviewed in line with this model. Some comments on each dimension are provided as follows:

a. Legal Principles Dimension

With such an understanding that a multidimensional model of elder law can be applied to the adult support and protection law, the legal principles dimension comprises the values that are common in elder law as well as the adult support and protection law. The values that are common in the reforms of Australian two state guardianship laws refer to the four principles included in the 'National Decision-Making Principles' addressed in the ALRC Report 124, as discussed at 4.3.3(3) 'What are the Common Values?' It has been also confirmed, at 4.4.2(1) 'ALRC Report 131,' that the reforms of the Australian two state guardianship laws and the national legislative policy for elder abuse are positioned back-to-back and share the same values. Therefore, the Australian adult support and protection legislation system based on the Australian guardianship laws and the national policy for elder abuse is commonly based on the 'National Decision-Making Principles.' These Principles are principle 1, *the equal right to make decisions*; principle 2, *support*; principle 3, will, preferences and rights; and principle 4, *safeguards*. The ALRC Report 124 also identifies five framing principles to guide the recommendations for reform, namely *dignity*, *equality*, *autonomy*, *inclusion and participation*, and *accountability*. There has been widespread support by stakeholders for these principles, which are reflected in a Commonwealth decision-making model developed in the ALRC Report 124. The said principles may correspond to the values of the CRPD.[238]

b. Protective Dimension

By law, the adult guardianship system provides, as a last resort, substituted decision-making as a *protective* measure to principals with insufficient mental capacity. A public agency provides *protective* intervention to vulnerable adults at risk of harm from elder abuse. Both are legal instruments to *protect* vulnerable adults and are based on the vulnerability approach, bearing in mind that the least restrictive measures should be taken. This is in order to avoid excess paternalism, which may violate the human rights of the principal. Public agencies are involved in the activities and include the Office of the Public Advocate or

---

[238.] Refers to Section 4.3.3 (3), 'What Are the Common Values?'

the Public Guardian, the tribunal, public trustee, and relevant agencies related to elder abuse.

c. Supportive Dimension

Supported decision-making and relevant measures are offered through law, such as the Victorian Act 2019, to principals with insufficient mental capacity or to vulnerable adults. These *supportive* measures are implemented on an agreement basis, by tribunal order, an EPA, or through informal arrangements if the principal is satisfied with the support. Public agencies are not always involved in supported decision-making activities, instead relatives, friends of principals or NPOs may be more involved. Public agencies include the Office of the Public Advocate or the Public Guardian, the tribunal, public trustee, and relevant agencies related to elder abuse.

Figure 4.2: The Multidimensional Model of Elder Law

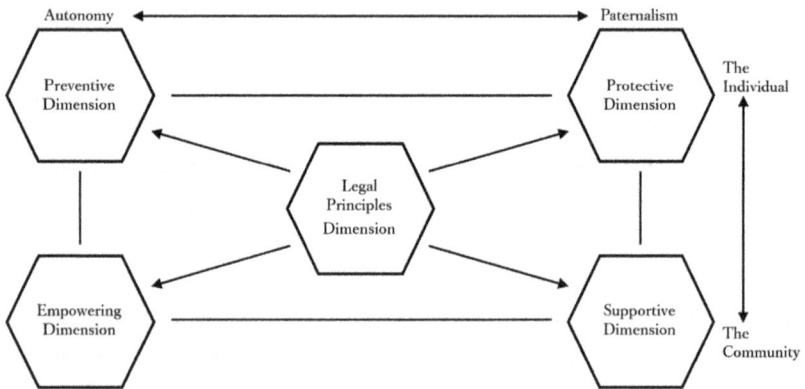

Source: Israel Doron, models in 2003/2009

d. Preventive Dimension

Supported decision-making and advanced planning measures for assets and healthcare treatment, as well as an EPA and the guardianship system, provide *preventive* measures for vulnerable adults at risk of harm. The harm includes, among others, abuse and financial exploitation. It is desirable for adults to use these *preventive* measures of their own accord. Public agencies—such as the Public Advocate or the Public Guardian, the tribunal, public trustee, and relevant agencies related to elder abuse—provide some *preventive* guidelines and pay careful attention to possible misconducts by supporters, guardians, or relevant persons. These guidelines ensure that the autonomy and self-determination of the principal are respected.

e. Empowering Dimension

Vulnerable adults should be encouraged and *empowered* to use supported decision-making and relevant planning measures of their own accord, as well as an EPA. The purpose is to respect their autonomy and self-determination more than preventive dimension, focusing on his/her uniqueness as an individual. ALRC Report 124 considers an approach to autonomy as *empowerment* of people with disability (Paragraph 1.38). This implies that ALRC Report 124 is based on the notion of individual autonomy and relational autonomy.[239] The dignity of risk is being discussed as a process of positively taking risk within established safeguards.[240] By this method, people with disabilities seek *empowerment* to overcome certain risk factors. Even in dispute cases, the principals and relevant persons may use alternative dispute resolution (ADR) provided by the tribunal outside the courts or relevant measures. For example, in the State of Victoria, four measures are available through VCAT.[241] It is understood that people may choose the solution that best suits their circumstances.

f. Summary

The Australian adult support and protection system could be illustrated as a legal architecture in accordance with the multidimensional model. The multidimensional model comprises four dimensions—*protective, supportive, preventive,* and *empowering*—and a legal principles dimension at the center to connect with each of the four other dimensions. The value indicator matrix is set horizontally between autonomy and paternalism and vertically between the individual and the community. Legal instruments, such as guardianship, EPA, supported decision-making, ADR, and safeguards against elder abuse, and the relevant public agencies are placed in mapping within the four dimensions. Those are based on

---

[239] Refers to Section 2.4.1 (2) b, 'Relational Autonomy.' Regarding autonomy, Paragraph 1.37 of the ALRC Report 124 states that 'This Inquiry has been informed by autonomy in the sense of "empowerment", not just "non-interference". This involves seeing an individual in relation to others, in a "relational" or "social" sense and understanding that connects with respect for the family as the "natural and fundamental group unit of society" that is entitled to protection by State Parties.'

[240] Refers to Section 4.2.2 (5), 'Victorian Interdisciplinary Research and Practices.'

[241] Refers to Section 4.2.2 (3), 'Dispute Response Mechanism.'

the foundation of the National Decision-Making Principles, that corresponds to the legal principles dimension.

It is noteworthy how the four dimensions are kept in a reasonable balance by the legal principles dimension at the center to connect with each of the four other dimensions. Advocacy refers to any action by an individual or a corporation, or any public policy to empower vulnerable adults on minimum conflict of interest between people or between people and society.[242] Implementing advocacy to empower vulnerable adults may contribute to improving four dimensions to keep in a reasonable balance. It can be concluded through the model analysis that the Australian adult support and protection system is theoretically a comprehensive and well-designed legal architecture aimed to cover the possible needs of adults in various aspects. This legal architecture, however, is still under construction and needs more time to reach the final product. There is likely to be variation in effectiveness between jurisdictions. The paramount importance would be a balance between autonomy and protection to be assigned case by case,[243] but 'in particular emergency cases, the safety of the at-risk adult needs to be secured, even against their wishes.'[244]

4.5.2 Implications from Australian Legislative Project

The Australian legislative project suggests several implications, which can be summarized as follows:

(a)   The Australian law reforms and legislation increasingly reflect the values of the CRPD within the legal system.[245] This development is underpinned by the broader rise of international human rights law and a growing awareness of human rights. In Australia, individuals are presumed to have decision-making capacity unless proven otherwise, and state and special territory governments have sought to reduce reliance on adult guardianship as a last resort. Emphasis is placed on the principles of necessity and the use of less restrictive alternatives within supported decision-making and

---

[242.] Errol Cocks and Gordon Duffy, *The Nature and Purposes of Advocacy for People with Disabilities* (Edith Cowan University Publications, 1993) 121 <https://ro.ecu.edu.au/ecuworks/7172>.

[243.] Terry Carney remarks 'shifting (and delicate) balance points to be found between competing ethical principles (such as autonomy and protection), adequate accountability and freedom from undue regulation, and "workability" (fidelity of practice to intended objectives)' Terry Carney, 'Searching for Workable Alternatives to Guardianship for Vulnerable Populations?' (2015) 1(1) *Ethics, Medicine and Public Health* 113, 119.

[244.] Refers to Section 4.4.2 (1), ALRC Report 131.' The ALRC Report 131 addresses the importance of protection of vulnerable adults at risk in emergency cases.

[245.] It is mentioned as 'A Human Rights Approach' in the article: Shih-Ning Then, 'Evolution and Innovation in Guardianship Laws: Assisted Decision-Making' (2013) 35 *Sydney Law Review* 133–66, 145–7.

guardianship systems. Legal frameworks for adult guardianship, supported decision-making, and safeguards against elder abuse are closely interrelated.

(b) Australian guardianship law reforms aim to legislate and strengthen supported decision-making (SDM). Victoria, for instance, has introduced new SDM mechanisms such as supportive guardians and supportive administrators, alongside supportive attorneys and medical treatment supporters, to uphold the will and preferences of principals. These roles are legally distinct from those of guardians, administrators, and medical treatment decision-makers. Notably, the Guardianship and Administration Act 2019 (Victoria) adopts a non-remuneration policy for guardians, administrators, supportive guardians and supportive administrators, in order to avoid conflicts of interest, with exceptions made for certain professional administration cases. Paid workers and corporations are generally excluded from being appointed to these supportive roles.

(c) Australia has established specialized public agencies at the state and special territory levels, including the Offices of the Public Advocate or Public Guardian, tribunals, and public trustees or State Trustees Limited. The Offices of the Public Advocate or Public Guardian provide diverse community-based support and policy review functions for guardianship. Tribunals, rather than courts, adjudicate guardianship matters and issue relevant orders following hearings. Public Trustees offer financial management services for persons with disabilities and older individuals, often filling gaps that private financial institutions—primarily motivated by profit—may not adequately address. This public agency model offers useful reference points for other countries, including Japan.

(d) The availability of dispute resolution mechanisms through tribunals is a notable feature for users. In Victoria, the Victorian Civil and Administrative Tribunal (VCAT) offers four pathways according to the nature of the dispute: complaint resolution, mediation, Fast Track Mediation and Hearing (FTMH), and appeals to the Supreme Court. VCAT is responsible for appointing supportive guardians and administrators after hearings, with provisions for reassessment if circumstances materially change. Parties may seek a rehearing before a more senior VCAT member within specified time limits or appeal to the Supreme Court on points of law (though the latter option is limited).

(e) Australia has a vibrant network of NPOs that operate at the community level, funded by charitable donations, grants, or welfare programs.[246] These NPOs provide critical services in adult guardianship, supported

---

[246.] For example, the Community Legal Centres (CLCs) Australia, non-profit community-based organizations, provide support to 170 community legal centers across Australia (Web Page, 2019) <https://clcs.org.au/findlegalhelp>.

decision-making, and prevention of elder abuse, often in collaboration with local governments and public agencies. The role of ethnic community organizations, regardless of their size, is particularly important in ensuring culturally and linguistically appropriate support.

Gooding and Carney observe that Australia has adopted a 'reformist and incrementalist' approach to issues of legal capacity, equality, and disability, in alignment with global standards.[247] Australia's approach illustrates a process of gradual yet steady progress, characterized by engagement with civil society through democratic processes. While significant steps have been taken, including the standardization of legal measures across Australia, it is recognized that the legislative project remains ongoing. Continued attention must therefore be directed toward future developments in laws and policies concerning adult support and protection at the national, state and special territory, and local government levels, as well as within civil society.

4.6 Summary: Implications from Australian Legislative Project Are Clarified

This chapter has examined the amendments to guardianship legislation in the Australian states of Victoria and New South Wales (NSW), along with national legislative policies addressing elder abuse—collectively referred to as the Australian legislative project. In both states, the guardianship system and supported decision-making have been, or are in the process of being, positioned as key legal safeguards to prevent elder abuse. In May 2019, Victoria enacted integrated legislation combining supported decision-making with the adult guardianship system. In NSW, the Law Reform Commission submitted a reform report to the state Parliament in August 2018. These legislative developments are consistent with the 'Commonwealth Decision-Making Model' proposed in the Australian Law Reform Commission (ALRC) Report No. 124 (2014), designed to reflect the principles of Article 12 of the Convention on the Rights of Persons with Disabilities (CRPD). Building upon this, the ALRC issued Report No. 131 in 2017, which specifically addressed elder abuse and advocated guardianship and supported decision-making as protective measures. Following this, states such

---

[247.] Piers Michael Gooding and Terry Carney, 'Australia: Lessons from a Reformist Path to Supported Decision-Making' in Michael Bach and Nicolás Espejo Yaksic (eds), *Legal Capacity, Disability and Human Rights: Towards A Comprehensive Approach* (Supreme Court of Mexico, Human Rights Division, Online, 2021) 255–76 <https://ssrn.com/abstract=3928342> <https://doi.org/10.1017/9781839704284.015>; Shigeaki Tanaka, *Contemporary Jurisprudence* (Yuhikaku Publishing Co., Ltd., 2011) 442 (in Japanese).

as South Australia and NSW established elder abuse response agencies under their respective state laws.

These legislative efforts represent Australia's ongoing attempt to harmonize domestic law with the values of the CRPD. Despite some recognition that existing guardianship laws may still conflict with Article 12, the current reforms promote supported decision-making as the preferred model, while restricting substituted decision-making to a last-resort measure. Supported decision-making is thus presented as a legal framework that honors and implements the will and preferences of the principal. This direction reflects a positive attitude within the Australian Government toward international human rights law. Indeed, Australia's national legal and policy approaches to Article 12 were formally accepted by the UN Committee during a review in October 2019. Australia's adult support and protection system is also characterized by unique institutional designs. These include three central public agencies in each state or territory: the Office of the Public Advocate (or Public Guardian), a tribunal, and either a public trustee or State Trustees Limited. If adult support and protection legislation is understood as a comprehensive legal framework, then the state-level reforms and national elder abuse policy initiatives cited in this chapter represent an important legislative model. This model provides a proactive legal response to the challenges of an aging society and offers valuable lessons for other countries, including Japan.

A theoretical analysis of the Australian legislative project reveals that it aligns with a multidimensional elder law model. The legal framework is based on the National Decision-Making Principles outlined in ALRC Report No. 124, which include: (1) the equal right to make decisions; (2) access to necessary support; (3) respect for will, preferences, and rights; and (4) provision of appropriate safeguards. Through this lens, the Australian adult support and protection system can be understood as a well-structured and comprehensive legal architecture that addresses the diverse needs of adults with impaired decision-making capacity. However, this legal structure remains under development and requires further refinement to reach its full potential. The Australian legislative project provides several key implications for public policy and legal reform in adult guardianship, supported decision-making, and elder abuse prevention. These implications include: (a) alignment of law reform with CRPD values; (b) a legislative focus on supported decision-making; (c) the establishment of public agencies such as the Public Advocate or Guardian, tribunals, and public trustees; (d) the importance of accessible dispute resolution through tribunals; and (e) the significant role of nonprofit organizations operating within communities, often supported through charitable, grant-based, or welfare funding schemes.

The Idea of Adult Support
and Protection in Japan

This chapter examines the possibilities for establishing an adult support and protection legislative framework in Japan. Drawing on principles from Australia's legal reforms and international human rights standards, it explores the roles of community-based agencies, the integration of supported decision-making (SDM), and the design of a legal model grounded in both autonomy and protection. The chapter also proposes a modified multidimensional model tailored to Japan's social context, while reflecting on its potential relevance in a global setting.

5.1 Introduction

The implications of Australia's legislation of guardianship and administration as well as elder abuse addressed in Chapter 4 are of help in consideration of Japan's adult support and protection legislative system.[1] Such implications include respect for the values of the Convention on the Rights of Persons with Disabilities (CRPD), legislation of SDM, roles of public agencies, a dispute response mechanism of the tribunal, and roles of not-for-profit organizations (NPOs) in communities.[2] In order to consider how these implications of Australia's legislation and policies are applied to Japan's legislation, it is important to establish the common ground for discussion on law comparison between Japan and Australia. Because a simple application of these implications of Australia's legislation and policies to Japan's legislation would not be realistic, considering the gaps between the law systems and policies of Japan and Australia. For this purpose, two essential legal devices, which have not been explicitly framed in Japan, must be considered to adapt them to Japan's adult support and protection

---

[1] Refers to Section 4.5.2, 'Implications from Australian Legislative Project.'

[2] Ibid.

legislation. Then, further discussion on adult support and protection legislation based on guardianship law comparison explores in this chapter.[3]

One such device has to do with the roles and legal status of a core agency. A core agency is a focal point in a community that plays a central role for advocacy in line with the Basic Plan.[4] In this study, a core agency is positioned as a multifunctional agency to work for legal advocacy in community support, in addition to the role that is stipulated in the Basic Plan to promote the adult guardianship system. A core agency has the potential to empower the role in community support if people in the community want to do so. The other device has to do with the legal status and basic principles of SDM.[5] It must be clarified how SDM can be placed and framed in Japan's legislation in the middle and long term such that the values of the CRPD are respected. Both a core agency and SDM are essential legal devices that can be used to frame Japan's adult support and protection legislative system. For this reason, some implications from law comparison studies on other countries besides Australia are considered, in addition to the implications of Australia's legislation.[6] Upon consideration of both a core agency and SDM, Japan's adult support and protection framework and its values will be reviewed.

5.2 Considerations for a Core Agency and Supported Decision-Making

5.2.1 Roles and Legal Status of a Core Agency for Community Support

(1) Roles of a Core Agency

a. A Core Agency in the Basic Plan

A core agency is a focal point in a community that currently plays a central role for advocacy support in line with the Basic Plan to promote the adult guardianship system.[7] The Act on Promotion of the Adult Guardianship System 2016 (Act No. 29 of 2016, hereinafter referred to as 'Promotion Act') obliges the 1,741 municipalities and 47 prefectures to formulate their own basic plans within

---

[3.] This part is an updated version of the previously published article by the author: Yukio Sakurai, 'The Idea of Adult Support and Protection Legislation in Japan: Multiple Options for Vulnerable Adults to Make Their Own Choices' (2021) 12(1) *The Journal of Aging & Social Change* 31, 47 <https://doi.org/10.18848/2576-5310/CGP/v12i01/31-47>.

[4.] Refers to Section 1.2.1 (2) c, 'Enactment of the Promotion Act.'

[5.] Refers to Section 1.2.2, 'Supported Decision-Making.'

[6.] Refers to Section 3.2, 'A Comparative Law Study in the International Context.'

[7.] Refers to Section 1.2.1 (2) c, 'Enactment of the Promotion Act.'

the regional welfare plans under the national Basic Plan and make efforts for necessary assistance (Article 23 and 24 of the Promotion Act). This requires uniformly formulating core agencies nationwide with flexibility in scale and form. The authority of a core agency can be a choice either in a municipality or in a larger jurisdiction according to the needs of the adult guardianship system.

As of April 1, 2024, 68.2 per cent of Japan's 1,741 municipalities had established core agencies, and an additional 10.3 per cent plan to do so by FY2027.[8] Thus, by FY2027, a total of 78.5 per cent of municipalities are expected to have core agencies in place. Among them, the majority (75.6 per cent) have core agencies operating within their own jurisdictions, while 17.9 per cent operate across broader regional jurisdictions.[9] Currently, there are three types of core agency arrangements: (a) those directly managed by the municipality (29.0 per cent); (b) those outsourced to Councils of Social Welfare, NPOs, or similar entities (53.7 per cent); and (c) hybrid models combining both approaches (17.4 per cent).[10]

The current situation reveals an 11.5 per cent disparity among municipalities in establishing regional collaboration networks centered on core agencies, despite the Basic Plan's goal of creating a nationwide network. To address these gaps— particularly in smaller municipalities—several measures may be considered. One approach is to reform existing institutions, such as advocacy centers, adult guardianship support centers, or community-based general support centers, to incorporate core agency functions. Alternatively, prefectural governments could establish public guardian agencies and delegate the operation of core agencies to municipalities where such functions are deemed necessary.[11]

b. A Core Agency in Japan's Adult Support and Protection

It is important to consider the multiple roles of a core agency in the community to deal with Japan's adult support and protection legislative system. This idea would enable core agencies to implement legal advocacy transactions with people in the community. It can be called a 'community support.'[12] Once it is established, a core agency is accessible to vulnerable adults with insufficient mental capacity, the family court, and the municipality in the jurisdiction. It is a policy design that civil society, the family court, and the municipality should maintain

---

[8.] Refers to the Ministry of Health, Labour, and Welfare of Japan, 'Results of A Survey on the Status of Measures Related to the Promotion of the Adult Guardianship System in April 2024 (Summary)' (Web Page, January 2025) (in Japanese) <https://www.mhlw.go.jp/content/000973040.pdf>.

[9.] Ibid.

[10.] Ibid.

[11.] Refers to Section 5.2.1 (2) b, 'An Idea of Public Guardian Agency.'

[12.] Refers to Section 1.1.1 (2) c, 'Community Support.'

a triangle relationship through the central coordination of a core agency.[13] This is the foundation of the regional collaboration network. A core agency has three main roles (given below) of community support, according to the Basic Plan,[14] and each role should be explored with relevant considerations.

(i)   Role of a control tower to design the overall concept of community support for legal advocacy and manage and coordinate promotion of the adult support and protection system.

(ii) Role of a secretariat to supervise the 'local council' in the community for community support.

(iii) Role of management to provide 'data-professional consideration and analysis' in the community.

Point (i) is the main function of a core agency, primarily in accordance with the Basic Plan to promote the adult guardianship system. A core agency should have the control tower roles not only for the promotion of the adult guardianship system but also for community support in adult support and protection.[15] The community support function of a core agency in adult support and protection will contribute to various respects, including the promotion of local advocacy measures available, monitoring local advocacy activities in the community, sharing local advocacy information among parties concerned, and reporting to the authorities.

Point (ii) implies that a core agency should provide community support with people, formulating the 'local council' meeting comprising relevant local experts when it is deemed necessary. The local council is a collegial body that promotes a system for voluntary cooperation by strengthening the relationship among practitioners' associations and related institutions in each jurisdiction.[16] In the local council meeting, legal, welfare, and relevant experts may provide necessary support to the 'team.' To properly demonstrate the roles of community support, relevant experts, such as legal and welfare practitioners, will have to collaborate and share a platform to discuss advocacy issues in the community and produce solutions. This collaboration between legal and welfare practitioners can be made even on individual basis, not limited to the local council meeting, but on

---

[13.] Refers to the Ministry of Health, Labour, and Welfare of Japan, 'Regarding the Basic Plan for Promoting the Adult Guardianship System' (Web Page, March 24, 2017) 13 (in Japanese) <https://www.mhlw.go.jp/file/06-Seisakujouhou-12000000-Shakaiengokyoku-Shakai/keikaku1.pdf>.

[14.] Ibid.

[15.] Refers to the Ministry of Health, Labour, and Welfare of Japan, *Chapter 2: Roles of Core Agencies* (Web Page, n/a) 14 (in Japanese) <https://www.mhlw.go.jp/content/000503191.pdf>.

[16.] Ibid 15.

the ground of a core agency.[17] This is in order to support and protect vulnerable people in the community, such as information exchange, providing consultation and advice, relay or dual appointment of the supporter for SDM activities or the adult guardian.

Point (iii) includes data collection and analysis projects in the jurisdiction.[18] Through the day-to-day duties of a core agency, relevant information on adult support and protection becomes available to the core agency, which can be analyzed in due course. Such data can be consolidated on a broader scale by community, municipality, prefecture, and country. The consolidated data and analysis will be worthwhile for fact-finding and policymaking, which will cover relevant information on informal arrangements and SDM cases. The situation of these people is not known by third parties and potential risks of abuse of principals are expected. If a core agency can watch informal arrangements and SDM cases directly or indirectly in a community and collect information on informal arrangements and SDM cases with the consents of principals, then some transparency can be established in the community and safeguards to abuse risks will be provided to some extent.[19]

Artificial intelligence (AI) may support such data consolidation and analysis in the near future. Big data analysis conducted with subsidy from the Ministry of Health, Labour, and Welfare of Japan or its related institution could be useful for monitoring any scientific progress in adult support and protection.[20] This data collection and analysis project would contribute to not only business efficiency of core agencies but also related fields, such as dementia studies and its international co-research. It is therefore essential that core agencies keep personal information strictly confidential to maintain privacy, including possible technical protection to cyber-attack, in accordance with the relevant laws and regulations.[21]

---

[17] How relevant institutions may share their duties in the community is determined according to the social resources and support needs available in the community, and the organization and function of community support are specified based on the basic plan and welfare plan prepared by each prefecture and municipality. In response to such local government's plans, citizens are expected to participate in advocacy activities such as social workers, community guardians, and welfare supporters in the community.

[18] Refers to the Ministry of Health, Labour, and Welfare of Japan (n 15) 14.

[19] Legislative design is discussed in '5.2.3 A Preliminary Idea of Supported Decision-Making Legislation,' which covers informal arrangements and SDM cases. It is noted in '1.3.1 (1) Adult Guardianship System in Japan' that Japan has many elderly people with informal arrangements.

[20] It could be an idea that a department or an institution 'core agency support center' be established as a central control office under the supervision of Ministry of Health, Labour, and Welfare of Japan in order to take care of data processing, analysis, and feeding back to policymaking.

[21] There are general guidelines for municipalities to work on effective data utilization services. Ministry of Internal Affairs and Communications of Japan, Information Distribution Administration Bureau, *Guidebook for Data Utilization in Local Governments Version. 2.0* (Web Page, May 2019) (in Japanese) <https://www.soumu.go.jp/main_content/000620312.pdf>.

C. Additional Delegation to a Core Agency

In the state of Victoria (Australia), the Victorian Civil and Administrative Tribunal (VCAT) refers investigations to the Office of the Public Advocate (OPA) under the Victorian Civil and Administrative Tribunal Act 1998 (section 94 to 96, Division 6—Referral to experts) to assist in determining guardianship and administration applications. In 2020–2021, VCAT referred 425 cases of investigations to the Victorian OPA mainly for the reasons of 'evidence of need for order (53.0 per cent),' 'evidence of capacity or disability (27.1 per cent)' and 'conflicts between individuals (19.6 per cent)' and the Victorian OPA reported back to the VCAT.[22] According to Victorian OPA, almost one third of these investigations completed in 2020–2021 resulted in VCAT applications being withdrawn or dismissed, reducing the number of the public guardianship cases.[23]

In Japan, investigations are basically carried out by the family court investigators in compliance with Article 58 (Investigation of facts by family court investigators) of the Domestic Relations Case Procedure Act (Act No. 52 of May 25, 2011). According to Article 62 (Commissioned investigation, etc.) of the same Act, it can be understood that the family court can commission the necessary investigations directly to a core agency or indirectly to a core agency via local government to request the necessary investigation reports.[24] The practical detail must be clarified on site, but a core agency may contribute to the family courts as an outsourced investigator by law.

When the specific authority of the local government is additionally delegated to the core agency, the core agency will be engaged in such additional duties on top of its normal duties. It can be assumed that each municipality may decide what specific authority of the municipality it delegates to the core agency in due course, according to the local needs in the jurisdiction. It should be noted that the scope of outsourcing by a municipality is limited by law, such that Article 72 of the Attorney Act (Act No. 205 of June 10, 1949) and Article 73 of the Judicial Scrivener Act (Act No. 197, 1950) prohibit unqualified persons from performing certain professional legal tasks. Such duties cannot be outsourced by a municipality to a core agency.

[22.] Refers to the Victorian Office of the Public Advocate (Victorian OPA), *Annual Report 2020–2021* (Victorian OPA Report, 2021) 21 <https://www.publicadvocate.vic.gov.au/opa-s-work/our-organisation/annual-reports/opa-annual-reports/359-opa-annual-report-2020-2021>.

[23.] Ibid 22.

[24.] Article 62 (Commissioned investigation, etc.) of the *Domestic Relations Case Procedure Act* stipulates that 'the family court may commission the necessary investigations to government agencies, public offices or other persons deemed appropriate, and…request the necessary reports.'

One idea of such additional delegation would be a 'clearing' function, which is addressed at the Austrian law reform in Chapter 3.[25] A core agency with a clearing function would consult with an applicant seeking to petition to the family court for adult guardianship, examine whether the adult guardianship system would suit the principal, and, if the system is deemed unsuitable, suggest that the applicant does not make a petition for adult guardianship but instead should use a less restrictive and more suitable alternative measure. This 'clearing' function would help people in the community make the best law or policy measure selection while reducing any burden on the family courts.[26]

The other idea of additional delegation would be a municipal mayor's petition for the adult guardianship system.[27] This system, pursuant to Article 32 of the Act on Social Welfare for the Elderly (Act No. 133 of 1963), is an administrative process prescribed by law. If the clerical work concerning the request by the mayor of a municipality is referred to in the preparation of draft documents, and the preparatory actions themselves are performed by the municipal staff and the applicant is the mayor of the municipality, then the municipality will be able to outsource a part of the clerical work to a core agency through a delegation agreement.

(2) Legal Status of a Core Agency

a. A Core Agency as a Quasi-public Institution

A core agency is not always a public entity. Thus, the legal entity of a core agency is not always the same as that of an Office of the Public Advocate (OPA) or Office of the Public Guardian (OPG), which is the public entity under the Attorney-General of the state or special territory in Australia.[28] A core agency, however, must share personal information with the family court as a duty. Thus, a core agency must be either a public entity under the municipality's supervision or a private entity that has a delegation agreement with the municipality to carry out public duties. In other words, the core agency must functionally work as a public agency for public duties and keep any personal information strictly confidential with the family court and the municipality, regardless of its legal entity. Therefore, a core agency is regarded as a quasi-public institution with an obligation of accountability to the public.

[25.] Refers to Section 3.2 (3), 'Austrian Adult Protection Law.' In Austria, the Adult Protection Associations (*VertretungsNetz*) oversee clearing, delegating from the Federal Ministry of Justice.

[26.] Ibid.

[27.] Refers to Section 1.2.1 (1), 'Adult Guardianship System and the Promotion Act.'

[28.] Refers to Section 4.2.2 (2), 'Public Agencies.'

b. An Idea of Public Guardian Agency

To cope with difficult cases of the guardianship in which the principal is being abused or is a victim of antisocial forces, there is an opinion for a local government to establish a public guardian agency to directly take care of these vulnerable people, not through an NPO or a welfare corporation receiving subsidy. This is the administrative direct control (public guardianship) type among the Suga-classified public guardianship types.[29] This idea is assumed to be eligible by a local government's discretion within the current law framework.[30] If such a public guardian agency is established in an area where principals are frequently abused or are victims of antisocial forces, the public guardian agency may act as a public guardian, being appointed by the family court upon the mayor's petition, for these vulnerable people. A public guardian should collaborate with the core agency in the community, the police, and the municipality who is in charge of abuse and social welfare assistance. It can be assumed that candidate areas where a public guardian agency is established may be limited to specific areas of large cities, such as Tokyo, Osaka, and Nagoya where difficult cases frequently happen far beyond the national average. The roles of a core agency may be further empowered with such collaboration of a public guardian agency.

(3) Characteristics of a Core Agency

a. A Core Agency as a Multifunctional Shop

From a user's viewpoint, a core agency should explicitly provide information on community support, such as support for monitoring watch, informal arrangements, welfare assistance, SDM, and adult guardianship with people in the community. Thus, a core agency is a kind of multifunctional shop that serves more than the adult guardianship system. In this respect, a core agency differs from the existing 'guardianship support center' or the like, which is a mono-functional agency that provides assistance to the adult guardianship system.

[29.] Suga-classified five public guardianship types: (i) judicial direct intervention type, (ii) administrative direct control (public guardianship) type, (iii) public sector type, (iv) private organization formation (corporate guardianship) type, and (v) individual type. Fumie Suga, *The Doctrine of Autonomous Support in the English Adult Guardianship System: Towards a Society Pursuing the Best Interests* (Minerva Shobo, 2010) 258 (in Japanese).

[30.] Makoto Arai states that 'I am proposing that local governments may establish "public guardians" and I think it possible to establish them within the current law system' at the 11th Expert Commission meeting. Ministry of Health, Labour, and Welfare of Japan, *Expert Commission Meetings: The Minutes of the 11th Session* (Web Page, October 25, 2021) 20 (in Japanese) <https://www.mhlw.go.jp/stf/shingi2/0000212875.html>.

b. Collaboration Between a Core Agency and a Community-Based General Support Center

A core agency also differs from a 'community-based general support center' (hereinafter referred to as 'general support center') in such respects as purpose, human resources, and the law, which is an agency of the community-based integrated care system in the welfare policy. Most general support centers are operated by welfare corporations or NPOs in a delegation agreement with the municipality.[31] A general support center is a welfare agency mainly established by a municipality and is required to manage the health of older people in the community through a 'team approach' of three kinds of practitioners, namely public health nurses, licensed social workers, and care support specialists.[32] The purpose of a general support center is to comprehensively support the health care, aged care (long-term care), and any welfare of older people by providing such assistances based on the Paragraph 1, Article 115–46 of the Long-Term Care Insurance Act 1997. Through the amendments to the Social Welfare Act in 2020, the methods of a general support center are renewed to offer 'consultation assistance' in welfare measures to people with disabilities in the community.[33] A general support center has a relationship with the municipality but not with the family court. Therefore, the judicial relationship with the family court and legal practitioners in a community is another characteristic of a core agency.[34]

As a core agency and a general support center may 'aim at realizing a diverse society where people cohabit in [the] community,' they can collaborate with each other to develop community support system.[35] It can be assumed that a possible merger of or sharing of office by these two agencies in the community would be a choice if there is no obstacle with the subsidy system in each proper scheme and no conflict of interests.[36] Such collaboration of these two agencies can be assumed to be eligible on a prefecture and/or a municipality basis if this plan is properly authorized and incorporated in the basic plan

---

[31.] Refers to the Ministry of Health, Labour, and Welfare of Japan, *Establishing 'the Community-Based Integrated Care System'* (Web Page, n/a) <https://www.mhlw.go.jp/english/policy/care-welfare/care-welfare-elderly/dl/establish_e.pdf>.

[32.] Ibid.

[33.] Article 4 (community-based welfare) was added to the *Social Welfare Act 2020*, which states that the 'promotion of community-based welfare must be carried out with the aim of realizing a community where residents can participate and coexist while mutually respecting personality and individuality.'

[34.] Michihiro Osawa, 'Cooperation of the Judiciary, Welfare Administration, and the Private in Adult Guardianship System Utilization Promotion' (2020) 15 *The Study of Social Well-Being and Development, Nihon Fukushi University Graduate Schools* 21, 32 (in Japanese).

[35.] Refers to the Ministry of Health, Labour, and Welfare of Japan (n 31).

[36.] From the online interview of an Expert Commission member by the author on September 7, 2020.

and the welfare plan of the prefecture and/or the municipality.[37] This attempt will contribute to establish 'one-stop shop' with multiple functions to support and protect vulnerable adults in community to meet the users' convenience to access.[38]

(4) Contributions of Civil Society for Community Support

a. Participation and Assistance of Civil Society

At this stage, adult support and protection is an imaginary legal architecture and will only materialize if relevant legislation, law reforms and policies are enacted with the people's consent in a democratic process. The significant momentum needed to implement a new regime is people's participation in and support of the architecture.[39] Participation means that people take part in community activities to assist one another in the spirit of mutual aid.[40] Indeed, it is a challenge to get people to participate in and assist the architecture. It can, however, be assumed that people's as well as civil society's understanding of relevant law and public policy of adult support and protection are vital for realizing consumer choice[41] and people's voluntary participation in the system.

Legal systems are enforced equally across the country based on uniform standards. This approach ensures that the minimum requirements for the values needed by older people and people with disabilities remain diverse. This approach is far from the achievement based on the underlying value of adult support and protection legislation. For this reason, voluntary activities rooted in community characteristics by civil society should be activated.[42] Support

---

[37.] 'Municipal welfare plans' and 'prefectural plans for supporting community welfare' are regulated by Articles 107 and 108 of the Social Welfare Act of Japan.

[38.] An effort is being made to move from field-specific, application-oriented support toward a more comprehensive framework that prioritizes preventive measures. Masaki Harada, 'Comprehensive Support System and Community–Based Welfare Plan: Conversion to Community–Based Welfare Administration' (Conference paper at Japan Community Welfare Society 2017 Public Research Forum, 2018); Shoichi Ogano, 'The Role of Adult Guardianship System and Community Comprehensive Care: Community Symbiosis Society' (2020) 12 *Review of Social Security Law* 23, 48 (in Japanese).

[39.] Wataru Omori, 'Significance and Promotion Measures of Participatory Administration' (2019) 11 *Journal of Urban Social Studies* 1, 13 (in Japanese).

[40.] People's participation is advocated: Yu Nagata, 'Progress and Issues of "Participation of Citizens" in Social Welfare' (2015) 123 *Social Welfare Studies* 19–27, 26 (in Japanese); Jun Nishimura, 'Legal System of the Personal Social Services in Terms of Participation Support' (2018) 15(1) *Journal of Kanagawa University of Human Services* 1, 13 (in Japanese).

[41.] John Chesterman emphasizes 'consumer choice' or 'consumer directed care' to meet individual needs even in adult protection programs. John Chesterman, 'Modernising Adult Protection in an Age of Choice' (2014) 73(4) *Australian Journal of Public Administration* 517–24, 519; John Chesterman, 'The Future of Adult Safeguarding in Australia' (2019) 54(4) *Australian Journal of Social Sciences* 360–70, 362–3.

[42.] Consequently, the border between voluntary activities and the social security law sphere becomes ambiguous. It is believed that the first step toward the realization of an inclusive society will be for the national and local

by public agencies is essential to the system because they are key players in the architecture, even to intervene in the private autonomy area by law when necessary. Municipalities should support civil society by providing preferential benefits, administrative guidelines, and training opportunities to people. Then, the Ministry of Health, Labour, and Welfare of Japan may consolidate the local activities, analyze the performance and data, and decide on the national policy and the guidelines.

Civil society should be able to take leadership in such multi-agency mechanisms which comprise the core agency, the municipality, the court, and the government of Japan. In a modern democracy, any legislation and policy can be enacted and implemented with people's participation and assistance. Moreover, people's understanding is crucial not only for the government to provide subsidies or grants for the policy but also for people to positively participate, with fees or no fees, to support vulnerable adults at risk of harm. In this sense, people are required to participate in the political and social process. In other words, the participation and assistance of civil society is essential to the conduct of social activities in a community, such as acting as a monitor, community supported decision-maker, staff of a welfare NPO, community guardian, staff of a public trustee (to be established).[43] In addition, it is also essential to activate judicial social work and ensure judicial access of vulnerable adults through the intermediary of core agencies in a regional collaboration network based on the Basic Plan.[44]

b. Registration for Informal Arrangement with a Core Agency

Informal arrangement has been discussed in Chapters 1 and 4.[45] In Asia, the family is a social unit, and even if the legal system is not in place, it is customary for people to help each other based on their kinship.[46] The research program known as the Protecting Elders' Assets Study (PEAS) by Monash university examines

---

governments to properly demonstrate their responsibility to secure financial resources, secure and train human resources, and then seek the cooperation of local people. Toshiro Ishibashi, 'The Community Comprehensive Care System, Mutual-Aid Society and the Academic Sphere of Social Security Law' (2019) 68 *Bulletin of the Faculty of Education Kumamoto University* 163, 171 (in Japanese); Toshiro Ishibashi et al, 'Development of a System to Support the Elderly, People with Disability, and People Living in Poverty in the Community' (2019) 26(1) *Administration* 1, 48 (in Japanese).

[43] These are articles that address civil society assistance available in Japan and Australia: Kohei Tsuchiya, 'Citizen Guardian and Welfare Administration' (2016) 29(2) *Chuo Gakuin University Law Review* 211, 235. (in Japanese); Jenny Onyx, Sue Kenny and Kevin Brown, 'Active Citizenship: An Empirical Investigation' (2012) 11(1) *Social Policy and Society* 55, 66.

[44] Ryo Hamano, 'Access to Justice in a Super Aging Society: Structure and Reform' (2020) 103 *Rikkyo Law Review* 129, 184 (in Japanese).

[45] Refers to Section 1.1.2, 'Function-Based Review' and Section 4.3.3 (1), 'Comparisons Between Amendments to Victoria and NSW State Acts.'

[46] Stella Quah, *Families in Asia* (Routledge, 2nd ed, 2008).

rural and multi-cultural responses to intra-familial and inter-generational asset management in the state of Victoria.[47] This research implies there are behavioral gaps among older Victorians regarding asset management, influenced by their cultural backgrounds. It shows the fact that Australians of non-English-speaking origins, such as Vietnamese Australians, do not use EPAs as their English-speaking counterparts do. It can be said that people of Asian origin tend to rely more on kinship than on EPAs. In Asia, EPAs have become common in Singapore. Approximately 3.4 per cent of the population, comprising Singapore nationals and permanent residents, have created LPAs through initiatives by Singapore Government, with most involving relatives as the counterparty (i.e., 96 per cent).[48] This behavioral pattern may be related to national culture and a tendency that shows how much people rely on law and their kinship.

In Japan, most adults who do not use the adult guardianship system, including voluntary guardianship, rely instead on informal arrangements with relatives, close friends, or nursing home managers for personal affairs and property management.[49] In fact, the number of adult guardianship users is estimated to be only about 2 to 3 per cent of the potential users with insufficient mental capacity, while the remaining 97 to 98 per cent people are estimated to be supported through informal arrangements.[50] Those who are in informal arrangements may face a risk for abuse, particularly financial abuse, or financial exploitation. Elder abuse is regulated by the elder abuse prevention laws, and annual statistics report the number of elder abuse cases. However, these statistics do not capture the whole picture but only recognize the limited number of elder abuse cases reported by public agencies.[51]

In Australia, informal arrangement is recognized as no need to change informal means if they work well (section 31, the Victorian Act 2019).[52] Informal arrange-

---

[47.] Christopher King et al, 'For Love or Money: Intergenerational Management of Older Victorians' Assets, Protecting Elders' Assets Study' (Monash University, Eastern Health Clinical School, 2011) <https://www.eapu.com.au/uploads/research_resources/VIC-For_Love_or_Money_JUN_2011-Monash.pdf>.

[48.] Office of the Public Guardian, Singapore, 'Indicators of Activities' <https://www.msf.gov.sg/opg/Pages/Indicators-of-Activities.aspx>. This site is no longer available.

[49.] Carry and Singer take up three different types of support model: a 'legalistic model (guardianship),' a 'welfare model,' and a 'developmental model' to deal with people with intellectual disabilities and discuss which is the best model among them. Informal arrangement is the third type of a development support model. Terry Carney and Peter Singer, 'Ethical and Legal Issues in Guardianship Options for Intellectually Disadvantaged People' (Australian Government Publishing Service, Human Rights Commission 3 Monograph Series No. 2, 1986) 1–124, 113–17.

[50.] Refers to Section 1.2.1, 'Adult Guardianship System and the Promotion Act.'

[51.] The number of elder abuse cases by nursing home care workers was 595 in 2020 (versus 644 in 2019 and 621 in 2018) and the number of elder abuse cases by caregivers was 17,281 in 2020 (versus 16,928 in 2019 and 17,249 in 2018). Ministry of Health, Labour, and Welfare of Japan, 'Elderly Abuse Annual Survey in FY2020' (in Japanese) <https://www.mhlw.go.jp/stf/houdou/0000196989_00008.html>.

[52.] Refers to Section 4.3.3 (1), 'Comparisons between Amendments to Victoria and NSW State Acts.'

ments, including family agreements,[53] are common among Australians, but they also use EPAs, SDM, or guardianship as necessary. Australia is a contract-based society and even family members use SDM or guardianship with a self-revocation term of one year or less for crucial decisions involving the principal. In contrast, most Japanese people simply rely on informal arrangement and do not use a law system such as guardianship, because Japan's adult guardianship system does not recognize guardianship with a self-revocation term of one year or less.

It can be recommended that guardianship with a self-revocation term of with one year or less should be introduced in Japan and that stakeholders, including principals and their relatives or nursing-home managers, should register any informal arrangement with the core agency by their own accord. Adults with insufficient mental capacity who have no relatives or close friends and have no financial assets may consult with the core agency to seek measures for his/her support, including welfare assistance of the municipality, and the core agency may give them advice accordingly.[54]

c. Alternatives to Guardianship

Alternatives to guardianship are developing in a unique way.[55] First, the municipality provides older adults with seminars to encourage them to keep personal notes regarding their property, a wish list for healthcare treatment and aged care, and a wish list of their end-of-life processes. While these personal notes have no binding legal effect as advanced directives, they are useful as a reference to family members or relatives to understand what and how they should support the older adult at the appropriate time. These personal notes are called 'ending notes' in Japan.[56] Ending notes are regarded as part of informal arrangements as an alternative to guardianship. These notes were originally created as simple planning notes as to how to end older people's life. These notes have developed to include supplementary personal notes regarding their creed, property management, healthcare treatment, aged care, end-of-life process, and even post-mortem affairs, considering users' needs. As a background, Japan has no legislation to regulate a

---

[53.] Family agreements are not typically put in writing between the principals and their relatives, and the relatives take care of the principals in exchange for the principals' property transfer or the like. Such agreements are fragile, and the principals' interests are not guaranteed by law. The ALRC recommends that the tribunal be given jurisdiction over disputes within families, but an access to the tribunal is another challenge for vulnerable adults. Australian Law Reform Commission (ALRC), 'Elder Abuse—A National Legal Response Final Report' (ALRC Report No. 131, 2017) 203–30 <https://www.alrc.gov.au/publications/elder-abuse-report>.

[54.] Refers to Section 5.2.3 (1), 'Main Contents of SDM Law.'

[55.] Refers to Section 3.2 (5), 'U.S. Guardianship and Supported Decision-Making Acts.' Alternatives to guardianship in the US are mentioned.

[56.] Refers to the Nara City, 'Nara City-Version Ending Notes Will be Distributed Free of Charge' (Web Page, *Japan NEWS*, May 27, 2021) <https://re-how.net/all/1113919/>.

third party's medical consent, advanced directives, and voluntary assisted dying, which are legislated in the state of Victoria.[57] Instead, the relevant guidelines guide medical practitioners to deal with such sensitive issues as a form of soft law and case law on passive euthanasia serves as a guideline.[58] Norio Higuchi states that 'since the law is regarded as formalistic, uniformly applied, and inflexible in Japan in general term, this [death with dignity] act if enacted may not help the development of medical ethics in the end-of-life situation.'[59] Property management is assumed to be handled in the same manner as these sensitive issues.[60]

Second, financial institutions in Japan started from few years ago to provide bank deposit services in which relatives (within two degrees) can register as an agent for managing the principals' deposit accounts.[61] Recently, they started providing financial support of property management in their internet banking with adult guardians who take care of adults with insufficient mental capacity.[62] Older Japanese people owns approximately 60 per cent of the national household financial assets in Japan, which is worth a total of 2,230 trillion yen (US$15.5 billion) as of December 2024.[63] The report of the Dai-ichi Life Economic Research Institute estimates the financial assets held by older adults with dementia is projected to increase from 143 trillion yen (US$1.0 trillion) in 2017 to 215 trillion yen (US$1.49 trillion) in 2030.[64] If these amounts are left in banks, the deposits will be frozen and transferred to the national treasury. Financial institutions, including banking corporations, can contribute to older adults and its stakeholders through their service provisions.

Another alternative is for older adults to settle a family trust for succession planning purposes.[65] Special needs trust, adopted in the US and Singapore, is also worth considering. If a social business to look after vulnerable adults becomes successful, such an industry would generate much employment in Japan.

[57.] Refers to Section 4.2.2 (4), 'Victorian Unique Legislations.'

[58.] Refers to Section 1.2.1 (4), 'Measures and Theory for Updating the Adult Guardianship System in 2000–2025.'

[59.] Norio Higuchi, 'Legal Issues on Medical Interventions in Terminally Ill Patients' (2015) 25(1) *Medical Care and Society* 21–34, 34 (in Japanese); Norio Higuchi, 'Current Status and Challenges of End-of-Life Care Legal Issues' (2020) 2(5) *Geriatrics* 579, 584 (in Japanese).

[60.] The guidelines are flexibly used, but have no binding power to any people, and can give no legal power in case of dispute.

[61.] Refers to Section 1.1.2, 'Function-Based Review.' Sumitomo Mitsui Banking Corporation (SMBC), *Agent Nomination Procedure* (Web Page, n/a) (in Japanese) <https://www.smbc.co.jp/kojin/otetsuduki/sonota/dairi/>.

[62.] Refers to the Sumitomo Mitsui Banking Corporation (SMBC), *Adult Guardianship System SMBC Support Service* (Web Page, July 2022) (in Japanese) <https://www.smbc.co.jp/news/pdf/j20220727_02.pdf>.

[63.] Refers to the Bank of Japan, *Money Circulation in the First Quarter of FY2022* (Web Page, June 2022) (in Japanese) <https://www.boj.or.jp/statistics/sj/sjexp.pdf>.

[64.] Refers to the Dai-ichi Life Economic Research Institute, *Economic Trends* (Web Page, 2018) (in Japanese) <https://www.dlri.co.jp/pdf/macro/2018/hoshi180828.pdf>.

[65.] All measures need safeguards of the principals' interests. Masayuki Tamaruya, 'Japanese Wealth Management and the Transformation of the Law of Trusts and Succession' (2019) 33 *Trust Law International* 147, 168.

Social business and social responsibilities related to adult support and protection legislation and values of community support would be important.[66] This is based on people's compassion and benevolence to support and protect vulnerable adults by their own initiatives even without state control.[67]

5.2.2 Combined Models of Guardianship and Supported Decision-Making

SDM will be reviewed in this section. The status of SDM in Japan has been mentioned in Chapter 1, as follows:[68] (i) The term SDM was additionally inserted into some disability/welfare laws after the Government of Japan signed the CRPD in September 2007. The term SDM was additionally inserted into disability/welfare laws. The establishment and practice of SDM methods that respect the individual's will and preferences were expected. However, no welfare legislation has defined what SDM should be or is like. (ii) The Ministry of Health, Labour, and Welfare of Japan has published three SDM guidelines for nursing managers, for managers of older people with dementia, and for adult guardians.[69] (iii) The main contents of SDM guidelines for adult guardians, particularly seven principles, were reviewed. (iv) The pros and cons of SDM guidelines were examined.

(1) Combined Models of Guardianship and SDM in Australia, Europe, and Japan

Article 12 of the CRPD combined with its General Comment No. 1 recommends that state parties should proceed with a paradigm shift from substituted decision-making to SDM in order to respect the 'rights, will and preferences of the principals.'[70] Since then, state parties of the UN have considered how

---

[66.] For example, financial institutions, particularly small-and-medium-sized banks in Japan, will become surplus, and an unemployment risk will arise from radical rationalization. In such a case, one idea would be to establish a public agency on local basis that specializes in financial management for older people or people with disabilities, like the Victorian State Trustees Limited (STL) that is wholly owned by the state of Victoria in Australia. Such public corporation may employ personnel with financial business experience, but their salary level would be considerably less. The other idea is that small-and-medium-sized banks may participate in the financial management and welfare business for older people through their subsidiary corporations based on the recent amendments to the *Banking Act* (November 2021).

[67.] Jonathan Herring's statement that 'in the caring relationships we are all in, there is a merging of interests and selves' underscores the importance of the notion of relational autonomy. It reflects the belief that people possess empathy and an ethic of care toward vulnerable adults who are at risk of harm..

[68.] Refers to Section 1.2.2, 'Supported Decision-Making.'

[69.] The three SDM guidelines refer to the 'SDM Guidelines for the Provision of Disabilities Welfare Services (March 2017),' 'SDM Guidelines for People with Dementia in Daily Life and Social Life (June 2018),' and 'Guidelines for Adult Guardians Based on SDM (October 2020).'

[70.] Refers to Section 1.2.1 (2), 'The CRPD and the General Comment No. 1.'

to accommodate the values of the CRPD in their laws and policies. They have adopted different models by way of law reforms, legislation, or establishing guidelines. Some states, such as Switzerland and Austria, renamed their adult protection law and no longer use the term 'guardian/guardianship.'[71]

This part reviews three types of combined models of guardianship and SDM in Australia, Europe, and Japan.[72] This is in order to clarify how they integrate guardianship and SDM into their laws, policies, or reports and compare similarities and differences between models. With this conceptual comparison, the stance of the Government of Japan regarding SDM will be reconfirmed. Australian law is examined because the implications of Australia's legislation of guardianship and administration as well as elder abuse, which are addressed in Chapter 4,[73] are of help in consideration of Japan's adult support and protection legislative system. The reason Europe, and not the US, is taken up is because Europe includes civil law and common law systems, Australia follows common law, and Japan has in place the civil law system, and Europe's legal systems can be balanced among the three models. Below, the three combined models of guardianship and SDM in Australia, Europe, and Japan are examined.[74]

a. Victorian Model

The state of Victoria has the most advanced guardianship laws and policies in Australia.[75] The legislation, Guardianship and Administration Act 2019 (Victoria) (hereinafter referred to as 'Victorian Act 2019'), incorporates SDM in supportive guardian and supportive administrator system while keeping the guardianship system as a last resort. The Victorian Act 2019 was enacted in May 2019 and came into force in March 2020. It will be sometimes referred to as the 'Victorian model.' For legislative acceptance of the CRPD, which was ratified by Australia with a declaration of reservation in July 2008,[76] uniform national legislation that respects the autonomy and right to self-determination of persons with disabilities

---

[71.] Refers to Section 3.2 (2), 'Switzerland Adult Protection Law' and Section 3.2 (3), 'Austrian Adult Protection Law.'

[72.] This part is an updated version of the previously published article by the author: Yukio Sakurai 'The Idea of Adult Support and Protection Legislation in Japan: Multiple Options for Vulnerable Adults to Make Their Own Choices' (2021) 12(1) *The Journal of Aging & Social Change* 31, 47 <https://doi.org/10.18848/2576-5310/CGP/v12i01/31-47>.

[73.] Refers to Section 4.5.2, 'Implications from Australian Legislative Project.'

[74.] Refers to Section 3.2 (7), 'Other Statutory Developments.' In addition to three types of combined models of guardianship and SDM in Australia, Europe, and Japan, Peruvian model is eligible, which incorporates 'support' function in their civil code while maintaining the status quo of adult guardianship, and needs further study for comparison.

[75.] Refers to Section 4.2.1, 'Australian Laws and its Guardianship.'

[76.] The Government of Australia declared its understanding of several points at the ratification of the CRPD on July 17, 2008, including that the CRPD allows substituted decision-making arrangements, which provide for decisions to be made on behalf of a person, only when such arrangements are necessary, that is, as a last resort and subject to

is required.[77] Legislative projects in Australian states and special territories are being carried out to improve the domestic legislation in compliance with the values of the CRPD. Legislative projects in Australian states and special territories other than the state of Victoria are still ongoing.

They recognize that the current guardianship law may be partially in conflict with Article 12 of the CRPD. Consequently, their legislative reforms would be designed to position substituted decision-making as a last resort and, instead, encourage SDM.[78] Thus, SDM is positioned as a legal system that will replace substituted decision-making with limitations. Substituted decision-making will be used only when the tribunals acknowledge with evidence that the principal has no capacity to make decisions. Australians are said to think highly of relationships with others, known as 'mateship.'[79] Rather than relying on lawyers to protect their interests, they help each other in community or within the same group of relatives and cultural backgrounds and utilize public institutions when necessary.

The summary of the Victorian Act 2019 is in part cited from Chapter 4[80] as follows:

(i)   The Victorian Act 2019 indicates that 'a person is presumed to have decision-making capacity unless there is evidence to the contrary' (section 5(2)) and recognizes that 'a person has capacity to make a decision in relation to a matter (decision-making capacity)' (section 5(1)).

(ii)   The purpose of the Victorian Act 2019 is 'to promote the personal and social wellbeing of a person' (section 4). For that reason, 'the will and preferences of a person with a disability should direct, as far as practicable, decisions made for that person' (section 8).

(iii)   Even when some support is needed for the principal, it is not always the case that the supportive guardian and the supportive administrator are appointed by the Victorian Civil and Administrative Tribunal (VCAT). If a close relative plays such a role properly, there is no need to change (section 31).

---

safeguards. UN, *Treaty Collection: Australia: 15. Convention on the Rights of Persons with Disabilities* (Web Page, February 2022) <https://treaties.un.org/pages/ViewDetails.aspx?src=TREATY&mtdsg_no=IV-15&chapter=4#EndDec>.

[77.] John Chesterman, 'The Future of Adult Guardianship in Federal Australia' (2013) 66(1) *Australian Social Work* 26, 38.

[78.] Australian welfare practitioners have practiced SDM in pilot programs since 2010. This article summarizes the results of these SDM pilot practices conducted between 2010 and 2015. Christine Bigby et al, 'Delivering Decision Making Support to People with Cognitive Disability—What Has Been Learned from Pilot Programs in Australia from 2010 to 2015' (2017) 52 *Australian Journal of Social Issues* 222, 240.

[79.] 'An Australian code of conduct that emphasizes egalitarianism and fellowship.' Merriam-Webster, *Mateship* (Web Page, n/a) <https://www.merriam-webster.com/dictionary/mateship>.

[80.] Refers to Section 4.3.1, 'Amendments to Victorian State Act.'

(iv)   The appointment of adult guardians will be limited by the VCAT as a last
        resort. Thus, the adult guardian and the administrator must respect the will
        and preferences of the principal, substitute the principal's decision as far
        as necessary, and explain the substituted decision so that the principal can
        understand the content (sections 41 and 46).

(v)   SDM is incorporated into the legislative system (sections 79 to 98, Part 4—
        supportive guardianship orders and supportive administration orders). The
        principal can appoint a supportive attorney who has the legal authority to
        make supportive decisions on personal affairs or financial management
        (Part 7—Power of Attorney Appointments, Power of Attorney Act 2014). In
        addition, on behalf of the principal, the VCAT may appoint the supportive
        guardian and supportive administrator (section 87). A supportive guardian
        and a supportive administrator are not entitled to any remuneration for
        acting in that role (section 95).

b. Alzheimer Europe Model

There is no unified guardianship and SDM laws and policies in Europe except for
some EU Recommendations to member countries on adult protection.[81] European
countries individually consider where and how they accommodate the values of
the CRPD in their laws and policies. Currently, the Mental Capacity Act 2005
(England and Wales) and the Assisted Decision-Making (Capacity) Act 2015
(Ireland) incorporate SDM in the respective country laws, and other European
countries still consider where and how to accommodate SDM.

As stated in Chapter 3,[82] a European NGO, Alzheimer Europe, published a
report in December 2020, entitled *Legal Capacity and Decision Making: The
Ethical Implications of Lack of Legal Capacity on the Lives of People with Dementia* (hereinafter referred to as 'Alzheimer Europe 2020 report'),[83] of a study
funded under an operating grant from the EU's Health Program (2014–2020). The
Alzheimer Europe 2020 report was drafted by European interdisciplinary experts
in the working group, which proposes the combined SDM model developed by
Scholten and Gather (2018).[84] This model combines SDM with competence

---

[81] Refers to Section 3.2 (1), '2000 Protection of Adults Convention and the Following Developments.'

[82] Ibid.

[83] Refers to the Alzheimer Europe, *Legal Capacity and Decision Making: The Ethical Implications of Lack of Legal Capacity on the Lives of People with Dementia* (Alzheimer Europe, December 2020) <https://www.alzhei-mer-europe.org/resources/publications/2020-alzheimer-europe-report-legal-capacity-and-decision-making-ethical>.

[84] Scholten and Gather predict 'adverse consequences of CRPD Article 12 for the persons with mental disabilities' and propose the combined supported decision-making model. Matthé Scholten and Jakov Gather, 'Adverse Con-sequences of Article 12 of the UN Convention on the Rights of Persons with Disabilities for Persons with Mental Disabilities and an Alternative Way Forward' (2018) 44 *Journal of Medical Ethics* 226, 233.

assessment 'is based on the view that it is sometimes permissible to deny people the right to make their decisions but that this should only be the case for people whose functional decision-making capacity is substantially impaired and if all resources of SDM have been exhausted.'[85]

The combined SDM model has not been legislated in a specific law or policy of any European country. This model has ethical implications based on the understanding that 'the main role of ethics is to question the most important practices and procedures and to open the way to finding better solutions ('Preface' of the Alzheimer Europe 2020 report).'[86] Thus, it is worthwhile to consider the model as an ethical framework for guardianship and SDM in Europe, regardless of whether or not it falls into civil law or common law jurisdiction. Here, it is called the 'Alzheimer Europe model.'

The Alzheimer Europe model comprises the following six steps addressed in the Alzheimer Europe 2020 report,[87] namely: (i) presumption of decision-making capacity, (ii) rebuttal of this presumption, (iii) assessment of decision-making capacity, (iv) supported decision-making, (v) monitoring, and (vi) substitute decision-making as a last resort. This model, which agrees with the CRPD's general principles of equality and non-discrimination,[88] promotes autonomy of people with dementia, on the one hand, and supports and protects these vulnerable people due to insufficient mental capacity against abuse and undue influence, on the other hand.[89] This model can be materialized by law reform, legislation, or guidelines, according to the European country's legislative intention.

c. Japanese Model

As discussed in Chapter 1,[90] Japan promotes the adult guardianship system by establishing a regional collaboration network and improving guardianship practices, unlike in other developed countries, while providing guidelines for implementing SDM. Here, we refer to this Japanese system as the 'Japanese model.'

---

[85] Refers to the Alzheimer Europe (n 83) 22.

[86] Ibid.

[87] Ibid.

[88] Refers to the Alzheimer Europe (n 83) 15; Matthé Scholten, Jakov Gather and Jochen Vollmann, 'Equality in the Informed Consent Process: Competence to Consent, Substitute Decision Making, and Discrimination of Persons with Mental Disorders' (2021) 46(1) *Journal of Medicine and Philosophy* 108, 136.

[89] Scholten, Gather and Vollmann (n 88); Matthé Scholten, 'Mental Capacity and Supported Decision-Making,' in Hanfried Helmchen, Norman Sartorius and Jakov Gather (eds), *Ethics in Psychiatry: European Contributions* (Springer Netherlands, 2025) 27–51; This is a clinical and ethical studies' review article in Italy: Marina Gasparini et al, 'The Evaluation of Capacity in Dementia: Ethical Constraints and Best Practice. A Systematic Review' (2021) 57(3) *Ann Ist Super Sanità* 212, 225.

[90] Refers to Section 1.2.1, 'Adult Guardianship System and the Promotion Act.'

In Japan, the adult guardianship system is underutilized. The Japanese model includes the voluntary guardianship system, which is similar to a lasting power of attorney (LPA) involving the voluntary guardian's supervisor to be appointed by the family courts, but few people use this system. In most cases, relatives or nursing-home managers of the principal provide informal arrangements for the principals. It is apparent that Japanese older adults largely rely on family and relatives or nursing home managers. Principals in informal arrangements do not receive legal protections provided by the adult guardianship system, where the risk of abuse may exist. Elder abuse is regulated by the elder abuse prevention law, and the annual statistics show how many elder abuses happen, although it does not capture the whole picture as only a few cases of elder abuse are reported.[91]

The guidelines encourage adult guardians to go through the process of SDM based on Article 858 of the Civil Code even in limited cases. Namely, an adult guardian is required to participate in SDM for legal acts of the principal that will have a significant impact on the principal (i.e., decisions on the principal's residence, sale of the principal's assets, and gifts and expenses of the principal to a third party) and incidental factual acts.[92] An online training program on the basic SDM practice has started for the staff of municipalities and core agencies since December 2020.

In Japan, there is a tendency to rely on guidelines instead of law particularly for a bioethical issue.[93] Positive aspects of guidelines are seen as non-rigid, flexible, and easy to amend as far as it is necessary. A guiding principle of the SDM guidelines as a soft law would be practical and ethical regulation on SDM at the initial stages, because regulating SDM through a hard law at this stage might be unworkable when an SDM method has not yet been clearly fixed.[94] On the other hand, issues of the SDM guidelines have been discussed in Chapter 1,[95] namely vague legal effects, little or no effective safeguards, no standardized SDM practices, and SDM as a support method rather than a legal system. The relationship between guardianship and SDM is indicated by the SDM guidelines for adult guardians. The SDM guidelines suggest that the adult guardians should practice

---

[91.] Refers to Section 1.2.3 (1), 'Elder Abuse Prevention Act.' The number of elder abuse cases by nursing home care workers was 595 in 2020, and the number of elder abuse cases by caregivers was 17,281 in 2020. Ministry of Health, Labour, and Welfare of Japan (n 51).

[92.] Refers to the Ministry of Health, Labour, and Welfare of Japan, *Guidelines for Adult Guardians Based on Supported Decision-Making* (Online, October 30, 2020) (in Japanese) <https://www.mhlw.go.jp/content/000750502.pdf>.

[93.] Norio Higuchi, 'Legal Issues on Medical Interventions in Terminally Ill Patients' (2015) 25(1) *Medical Care and Society* 21–34, 34 (in Japanese); Norio Higuchi, 'Current Status and Challenges of End-of-Life Care Legal Issues' (2020) 2(5) *Geriatrics* 579, 584 (in Japanese).

[94.] Yukio Sakurai, 'The Role of Soft Law in the Ageing Society of the Twenty-First Century' (2018) 13(1) *The International Journal of Interdisciplinary Global Studies* 1–10, 7.

[95.] Refers to Section 1.2.2 (4), 'Developments and Challenges of the SDM Guidelines.'

SDM with principals as a priority, only opting for substituted decision-making if SDM does not function. However, this suggestion is based on the guidelines without enforcement and thus it is unclear how much said guidelines will be respected and implemented by the adult guardians on site. In this sense, the adult guardians have discretion whether or not to follow the guidelines, which cannot guarantee equality to give the same standardized SDM and guardianship services to the principals. Furthermore, the issues of the SDM guidelines may cause a certain risk for undue influence of the adult guardians to the principals. Therefore, the guidelines can be useful for the time being, but legislation will be an option for the equality of operation and for protection of rights of the principals.

(2) Comparison of the Three Models

a. Similarities

Underlying Principles and Values

A similarity can be seen in the principles and values of the three models, all of which combine guardianship and SDM to deal with adults with insufficient mental capacity. The Victorian model has as its background the Victorian Law Reform Commission (VLRC) report, *Guardianship: Final Report No. 24* (VLRC Report 24) at the state level, and the Australian Law Reform Commission (ALRC) report, *Equality, Capacity and Disability in Commonwealth Laws: Final Report No. 124* (ALRC Report 124) at the national level. The former state report proposed reform proposals that included 440 items in 2012 before General Comment No. 1 was adopted by the UN Committee. The latter national report mainly examined in 2014 'equal recognition before the law' and 'legal capacity' in Article 12 of the CRPD and provides the four National Decision-Making Principles, viz.: *the equal right to make decisions; Support; Will, preferences and rights;* and *safeguards.*[96] The Victorian model is based on above state and national reform reports, including these National Decision-Making Principles.[97]

The Alzheimer Europe model is based on the combined SDM model developed by Scholten and Gather in their bioethics studies (2018).[98] The Alzheimer Europe 2020 report emphasized non-discrimination, respect for individual autonomy, and the values of the CRPD, including reasonable accommodation.[99] The

---

[96.] Refers to Section 4.3.3 (3), 'What Are the Common Values?'

[97.] Ibid.

[98.] Matthé Scholten and Jakov Gather (n 84).

[99.] Refers to the Alzheimer Europe (n 83) 22.

Alzheimer Europe model is based on these principles and values of the report. The Japanese model is based on the Promotion Act and the Basic Plan, which emphasize the values of the adult guardianship system, viz.: respect for the right to self-determination, emphasis on personal protection, and normalization in order to attain a diverse society where people cohabit in the community.[100] All these principles and values of the three models, including the Japanese model, are positive and share a similar purpose of respecting the will and preferences of vulnerable people.

The Notion of Decision-Making Capacity

Another similarity is seen in the legal concept of decision-making capacity. It is important to note that the presumption of decision-making capacity is shared by the Victorian and Alzheimer Europe models, such that, according to the Victorian Act 2019, 'a person is assumed to have decision-making capacity unless there is evidence to the contrary.' The presumption of decision-making capacity is adopted in common law jurisdictions, but this legal concept can be used in civil law jurisdictions as the Alzheimer Europe model suggests. With the assumption of decision-making capacity, SDM of the principal with third party assistance can make sense.

In the Japanese model, the guardianship system adopts the capacity doctrine in the Civil Code, although the SDM guidelines for adult guardians include the term 'decision-making capacity' and suggest that the adult guardians should adopt SDM in decision-making process of principals and apply substituted decision-making as a last resort. The SDM guidelines state that

> decision-making capacity is not a concept stipulated by law and is different from mental capacity and capacity to act [in the Civil Code]. The SDM guidelines adopt the idea that decision-making capacity is not an alternative to having or not having but varies according to the presence or absence and degree of support.[101]

[100.] A 'diverse society' refers to a society in which the community and various local actors participate, and the people are connected to other people and social resources across generations and fields for better living and purpose. Ministry of Health, Labour, and Welfare, *Toward the Realization of a 'Diverse Society in Community'* (Web Page, February 7, 2017) (in Japanese) <https://www.mhlw.go.jp/stf/newpage_00506.html>.

[101.] It is understood that the SDM Guidelines were drafted by the SDM-WG largely based on the *Mental Capacity Act 2005* (MCA 2005) of England and Wales and the CRPD. Ministry of Health, Labour, and Welfare of Japan (n 92) 3 (in Japanese); There is a view that 'presumption of patient's will' in healthcare system be recognized by a civil law scholar. Shoichi Ogano, 'Development of Adult Guardianship Systems in Japan' (2013) 50(5) *Nihon Ronen Igakkai Zasshi (Journal of the Japan Geriatrics Society)* 638–40, 640 (in Japanese).

In this respect, the SDM guidelines for adult guardians seem to require additional duties on the Civil Code of Japan. Consequently, all three models more or less adopt the legal concept of decision-making capacity.

Family Reliance by Short-Term Guardianship or Informal Arrangement

In Victoria, informal arrangements are similarly prevalent. However, the legal framework actively supports family-based caregiving through enduring powers of attorney and short-term guardianship appointments by relatives or close friends without remuneration. The Victorian Law Reform Commission's (VLRC) 2012 *Guardianship Final Report 24* emphasized that supporter arrangements should build upon existing close personal relationships, not professional replacements. Despite informal family agreements being legally fragile, Victorians make more strategic use of formal legal tools when necessary, balancing familial support with legal protections.

In Japan, the use of the adult guardianship system remains limited, with only 2 per cent to 3 per cent of individuals with cognitive impairments utilizing formal guardianship services. The overwhelming majority rely on informal arrangements, typically managed by family members. This heavy reliance on family increases the risk of elder abuse, particularly financial exploitation, a phenomenon underreported despite the existence of an elder abuse prevention law.[102] The reluctance to engage with the formal guardianship system stems partly from its cost—85 per cent of court-appointed guardians are paid professionals— and from cultural preferences to avoid interference by outsiders. Economic considerations also play a significant role, as welfare activities by non-family members are uncommon unless compensation is provided. Japan could enhance its guardianship system by introducing a limited, short-term guardianship model that would allow family reliance to coexist with legal safeguards. Such a model would enable individuals to engage with the formal system for critical decisions without fully relinquishing family autonomy.

b. Differences

Legal Basis of SDM

The purpose of the three models is the same as mentioned above, which is respecting the will and preferences of principals, but their bases are different. The Victorian model is enshrined in the Victorian Act 2019 while the Japanese model is based on a combination of existing guardianship laws and separate SDM

[102.] Ministry of Health, Labour, and Welfare (MHLW) of Japan (n 51).

guidelines. The Alzheimer Europe model is an ethical framework based on the Alzheimer Europe 2020 report and can be materialized by law reforms, legislation, or establish guidelines, according to the individual country's legislative intention.

SDM as a Legal System or a Support Method

The difference between the three types of models lies in where and how they accommodate SDM in their laws and policies. The Victorian model accommodates SDM in the supportive guardian and supportive administrator system of the Victorian Act 2019. The principal can appoint a supportive attorney who has the legal authority to make supportive decisions on personal affairs or financial management (Part 7—Power of Attorney Appointments, Power of Attorney Act 2014). In addition, on behalf of the principal, the tribunals may appoint the supportive guardian and/or supportive administrator, with appointment of an adult guardian as a last resort. Many people use enduring power of attorneys (EPAs). The Alzheimer Europe model comprises the six steps in the guardianship and SDM framework as mentioned before, which is similar to the Victorian model.[103] Both Victorian and Alzheimer Europe models share a similar combined mechanism of SDM and guardianship. In the Victorian and Alzheimer Europe's models, SDM is positioned as a 'legal system' that will in part replace substituted decision-making. In other words, SDM and guardianship are theoretically independent, and SDM is prioritized over guardianship.

The Japanese model applies SDM guidelines to change the way that adult guardians are encouraged to go about discharging their responsibilities. Yasushi Kamiyama states that there are two theoretical views on the relationship between the adult guardianship and SDM in Japan: one is that guardianship and SDM are independent, and the other is that they are interlinked.[104] In the former view, SDM is regarded as a 'legal system' that will replace the adult guardianship system. In the latter view, SDM is regarded as a 'support method' for substituted decision-making. As far as the guidelines for adult guardians are concerned, SDM is regarded as a 'support method' to Article 858 (respect for the will of the adult ward and consideration for their personality) of the Civil Code. In other words, SDM as a support method is not theoretically independent but is subordinated to Article 858 of the Civil Code under the SDM guidelines.

[103.] Refers to Section 3.2 (1), '2000 Protection of Adults Convention and the Following Developments'; From email correspondence of John Chesterman and the author on June 21, 2021.

[104.] Yasushi Kamiyama, 'Recent Policy Trends Regarding Supported Decision-Making in Japan' (2020) 72(4) [414] *The Doshisha Law Review* 445–67, 447–8 (in Japanese).

Non-remuneration Policy or Paid Guardian

Another difference between the Victorian and Japanese models is that the Victorian model does not recognize remuneration for acting in SDM or guardianship except for cases involving Victorian State Trustees Ltd (STL) and other professional administrators (section 175, Victorian Act 2019).[105] The Victorian model expects principals' supportive guardians and supportive administrators or guardians and administrators to be relatives, friends, or public advocates, but not legal/welfare practitioners receiving remuneration. This non-remuneration policy is established in the Victorian Act 1986 based on the Cocks Report 1982[106] and has been applied to other jurisdictions over Australia. This principle is in order to avoid the conflict of interest associated with payment.[107] The Victorian model recognizes that principals' supportive guardians and supportive administrators or guardians and administrators are 'supporters for decision-making' or 'decision-makers' of the principals, there does not often arise a situation where they need to have specialist skills.[108] Instead, principals' supportive guardians and supportive administrators or guardians and administrators must have sufficient skills to seek advice or arrange care by specialists. Staff in the Office of the Public Advocate (OPA) are people with a social welfare background, such as a social worker, lawyer, or nurse etc., which assist supportive guardians or guardians to know where to seek such advice and how to evaluate that advice in making their decisions.

The Japanese model largely relies on remuneration for acting guardians, which is decided by the family courts case by case and paid by the principal. In fact, the ratio of non-relative guardian cases in December 2024 was approximately 83 per cent, with most non-relative guardians and legal/welfare practitioners receiving remuneration.[109] The Alzheimer Europe model does not deal with remuneration, thus allowing for individual European countries. The issue of remuneration suggests the difference between the Victorian and Japanese models in 'who will act as supporters or guardians and for what purpose.' Namely, the Victorian model adopts relatives, friends, public advocates or STL/professional administrators as supporters for decision-making or decision-makers of the

---

[105.] Refers to Section 4.3.3 (2) d, 'Non-remuneration Policy.'

[106.] The Cocks Report 1982 is the final report made by the Victorian Minister's Committee on Rights & Protective Legislation for Intellectually Handicapped Persons headed by Errol Cocks. Victoria. Minister's Committee on Rights & Protective Legislation for Intellectually Handicapped Persons and Errol Cocks, *Report of The Minister's Committee on Rights & Protective Legislation for Intellectually Handicapped Persons* (Victorian State Government, 1982).

[107.] This view was addressed by Terry Carney in email correspondence on December 6, 2021.

[108.] From email correspondence of a VCAT member with the author on September 2, 2021.

[109.] Refers to the Courts of Japan, *The Annual Overview of Adult Guardianship Cases in FY2024* (Web Page, March 2025) (in Japanese) <https://www.courts.go.jp/toukei_siryou/siryo/kouken/index.html>.

principals. The Japanese model adopts mainly legal/welfare practitioners as adult guardians receiving remuneration. Without remuneration, it is anticipated that legal/welfare practitioners will not accept guardianship in Japan.

c. Discussion

By examining the three types of models, we have reviewed how countries go for a combination of guardianship and SDM to deal with adults with insufficient mental capacity. The comparison of the three types of models is summarized by an item in Table 5.1. It can be understood that these three types of models imply a possible legislative development of the combined model of guardianship and SDM laws and policies. There is a diversity of laws and policies in countries or reports that share the same values of the CRPD and democratic procedures. The difference between the Japanese model and the Victorian and Alzheimer Europe's models can be assumed to be based on how they prioritize the requirements of Article 12 of the CRPD, including an understanding whether or not the current guardianship law meets these requirements, and how seriously they understand the necessity to legislate or reform law. In fact, the Basic Plan, Japan's adult guardianship promotion policy, does not refer to the CRPD.[110] In contrast, the Alzheimer Europe 2020 report agrees with the CRPD's general principles of equality and non-discrimination.[111] The ALRC Report 124, 2014, which demonstrates the basic principles of guardianship and SDM in Australia, is based on the Terms of Reference referring to the CRPD.[112]

As mentioned in Chapter 1,[113] the Ministry of Justice of Japan expresses the view that Japan's adult guardianship system does not conflict with Article 12 of the CRPD. Based on this understanding, the deliberations of the Expert Commission are being carried out to maintain the status quo of the adult guardianship laws. It appears that the understanding of the Ministry of Justice of Japan makes the Japanese model less developed in legislation or the relevant law reform. It is therefore anticipated that the UN Committee review of the Japan Report in August 2022 might trigger a fundamental review of the Japanese model.[114] It can be concluded that the Japanese model has room for

---

[110.] Japan Federation of Bar Associations, 'Written Opinion on Items to be Included in the Draft Basic Plan for Promoting the Adult Guardianship System' (Web Page, January 19, 2017) 1 (in Japanese), chrome-extension:// efaidnbmnnnibpcajpcglclefindmkaj/https://www.nichibenren.or.jp/library/pdf/document/opinion/2017/170119_2.pdf.

[111.] Refers to Section 5.2.2 (1) b, 'Alzheimer Europe Model.'

[112.] ALRC, ALRC Report 124, 2014, 5.

[113.] Refers to Section 1.2.1 (2), 'The CRPD and the General Comment No. 1.'

[114.] Osamu Nagase, 'The First Review of the Japan Report and Parallel Reports' (2021) 461 *New Normalization* (in Japanese) <https://www.dinf.ne.jp/d/2/424.html>.

legislative improvements, particularly due to the SDM guidelines without enforcement nor judicial norms for dispute solutions, comparing with the Victorian and Alzheimer Europe's models.

Effective reform must acknowledge the invisible yet powerful influence of cultural norms and strive to create systems that are both legally sound and socially resonant. Understanding the nuanced behavioral patterns underlying guardianship practices is essential, not only for domestic reforms but also for meaningful comparative legal studies. Cultural and linguistic barriers often obscure deeper insights, making it crucial to explore these factors explicitly. In adapting guardianship laws for aging societies, the key lies in harmonizing the values of familial support and individual autonomy to foster legal systems that reflect and support the lived realities of their people. Moving forward, Japanese society would benefit from fostering public discourse on these value conflicts, particularly among younger and postwar generations. Promoting conversations about autonomy, dignity, and the appropriate scope of legal interventions could help reshape societal expectations and enhance the guardianship system's responsiveness to the needs of an aging population.

Table 5.1: Comparison of the Three Types of Models

	Japanese Model	Alzheimer Europe Model	Victorian Model
Basis of the Statutory Guardianship Law, Policy, or Report	The Civil Code, Promotion Act, and the Basic Plan	Alzheimer Europe 2020 Report	Victorian Act 2019 (incorporating supported decision-making)
Status of the statutory guardianship	To promote guardianship for advocacy support	Guardianship as a last resort	Guardianship as a last resort
Principles and Values	Values of Promotion Act: Self-determination, personal protection, normalization	Non-discrimination, respect for autonomy, and values of the CRPD	National Decision-Making Principles in the ALRC Report 124

	Japanese Model	Alzheimer Europe Model	Victorian Model
Capacity	Capacity doctrine (Civil Code), presumption of decision-making capacity (SDM guidelines)	Presumption of decision-making capacity	Presumption of decision-making capacity
Guardians	Legal/welfare practitioners, welfare corporations/ NPOs, or relatives	–	Guardians: Relatives, friends, or public advocates Administrators: Relatives, friends, or Victorian STL and other professionals
Remuneration	The family courts decide yearly remuneration ex. post case by case	–	No remuneration except for cases involving Victorian STL and other professional administrators
Lasting or Enduring Power of Attorney or Voluntary Guardianship	Voluntary Guardianship System based on the Act on Voluntary Guardianship Contract 1999	LPA/EPA based on individual European state law or common law	EPA based on the Power of Attorney Act 2014
Basis of SDM Law, Policy, or Report	Guidelines, the welfare laws, or Article 858 of the Civil Code	Alzheimer Europe 2020 Report	Victorian Act 2019 (incorporating supported decision-making)

	Japanese Model	Alzheimer Europe Model	Victorian Model
The Purpose of SDM	To respect the will and preferences of a person	To respect the will and preferences of a person	To promote the social and personal wellbeing of a person
The Role of SDM	A support method based on the welfare laws or Article 858 of the Civil Code	A legal system that will in part replace substituted decision-making	A legal system that will in part replace substituted decision-making
Supporter	Nursing-home manager, social worker, and adult guardian	Any supporter appointed by the mutual agreement	Supportive guardian and/ or supportive administrator appointed by the tribunals or by the mutual agreement, supportive attorney appointed by the mutual agreement

Source: Made by the author

5.2.3 A Preliminary Idea of Supported Decision-Making Legislation

(1) Main Contents of SDM Law

a. Scope of SDM Law: Legal Acts and Its Associated Non-legal Acts for Personal Protection

In order to explore the discussion for Japan's adult support and protection, how SDM will be placed and framed in Japan's legislation must be clarified in the middle to long-term. SDM will be potentially an important legal instrument as an alternative to the adult guardianship system to protect the human rights of these people.[115] On the same time, SDM must be secured by safeguards because

---

[115] Nina A. Kohn, Jeremy A. Blumenthal and Amy T. Campbell, 'Supported Decision-Making: A Viable Alternative to Guardianship?' (2013) 117(4) *Pennsylvania State Law Review* 1111, 1157; Thomas F. Coleman, *Supported*

SDM might be involved in undue influence due to its characteristic.[116] Given the existence of many vulnerable adults, including older people with dementia, and some challenges to indefinitely maintain SDM guidelines as discussed in Chapter 1,[117] it is time the Government of Japan considered legislation on SDM that would respond to the needs of principals.[118] After reviewing process of the SDM guidelines as a soft law, it will be possible for Japan to legislate SDM to match the advanced model, such as the Victorian model or Alzheimer Europe model.

With regard to the scope of SDM law, it specifically focuses on SDM for legal acts of the principal that will have a significant impact on the principal (i.e., decision on the principal's residence, sale of the principal's assets, and gifts and expenses of the principal to a third party) and its associated non-legal activities.[119] Therefore, it can be assumed that the scope of SDM legislation at the initial stage will be narrowed to the legal acts and its associated non-legal activities, as the SDM guidelines for adult guardians define. In addition, the scope of SDM legislation at the initial stage will be further narrowed to the 'personal protection' (i.e., excluding property management) in an agreement between the principal and the supporter. This is because the remaining area, including property management and welfare activities, needs further consideration to legislate and maintain the guidelines on them.[120] With an assumption that the scope of SDM legislation is narrowed to the legal acts and its associated non-legal activities, and is further narrowed to the personal protection, one preliminary idea of SDM legislation framework will be proposed below.

b. Legal Status of SDM Law

SDM in a Specific Law

The legal status of SDM will be regulated by either a specific law or the Civil Code, according to the relevant legislation policy in the National Diet of Japan.

Decision-Making: My Transformation from a Curious Skeptic to an Enthusiastic Advocate (Online, 2017) <https://tomcoleman.us/publications/sdm-essay-2017.pdf>.

[116.] Yasushi Kamiyama states that in the process of narrowing down the options presented to the principal, there should be 'some kind of supporter-inducing element (paternalism element)' potentially available, regardless of whether it is intentional or not. Kamiyama (n 104) 460–3 (in Japanese).

[117.] Refers to Section 1.2.2 (4), 'Developments and Challenges of the SDM Guidelines.'

[118.] Japan Federation of Bar Associations published the 2015 Declaration to call for the establishment of a comprehensive SDM system, including legislation. Japan Federation of Bar Associations, *Declaration Calling for the Establishment of a Comprehensive System for Supported Decision-Making* (Web Page, October 2, 2015) (in Japanese) <https://www.nichibenren.or.jp/document/civil_liberties/year/2015/2015_1.html>.

[119.] The scope of SDM in this study is the same as stipulated in the SDM guidelines for adult guardians.

[120.] To secure protection of the principal from undue influence risk, safeguarding measures must be established by law attached with a judicial or public supervision for SDM activities in property management.

In the process of legislation of SDM, it will be feasible to have a combination of the law (i.e., a specific law or the Civil Code) and the guidelines to regulate SDM. Discussion goes on in this study with the assumption that the Civil Code and relevant laws concerning the adult guardianship system will stay status quo, as is set out in Introduction.[121] Therefore, an idea of a specific law regulating SDM will be mentioned.

SDM can be based on a mutual agreement between a principal and a supporter.[122] In this scheme, a principal needs the capacity to understand the contents of the agreement in order to conclude it. An SDM agreement between the principal and the supporter given the power of support for SDM is prepared and notarized by a notary public.[123] An adult may participate in an SDM agreement with the relevant conditions that are separately determined. A notary public will assess the capacity of the principal as in voluntary guardianship. Discussions concerning the effective capacity in which SDM could be legally accepted will be carefully examined after accumulating empirical data on site.

Consequently, this may narrow the scope of the principals who can participate in the SDM scheme due to capacity assessment by the notary public. People with mild cognitive impairment (MCI) are assumed to be potential users of SDM law.[124] Nevertheless, at an initial stage, it could be acceptable to carefully implement and supervise practice based on an SDM. With the agreement, supporters can assist principals to make decisions and communicate these decisions on behalf of the principals, but this must not be called substituted decision-making for the principals.

[121.] Refers to Introduction, Section 2 (2), 'Methodology.'

[122.] Refers to Section 3.2 (5), 'U.S. Guardianship and Supported Decision-Making Acts.' *TITLE 16, Health and Safety, Individuals with Disabilities, CHAPTER 94A Supported Decision-Making* in the state of Delaware.

[123.] A notary public system in Japan has a uniqueness. A notary is appointed by the Ministry of Justice of Japan under Article 11 of the *Notary Act* (Act No. 53 of 1908) among qualified legal professions who have more than 30 years of work experience under Article 13. The notary examinations under Article 12 of the law are repealed by Supplementary Provisions 2, *Notary Personnel Capacity Rules* (the Ministry of Legal Affairs Ordinance No. 10 of 1949) and the number of notary personnel capacity is fixed in the attached Table of the Rules: 688. The actual number of appointments is less than the notary personnel capacity. (In contrast, there were 9,355 notaries in Germany even as of 2004.) Notaries, who are subject to the supervision of the Minister of Justice of Japan and affiliated with each Legal Affairs Bureau, are treated as quasi-civil servants. Notaries are not in a position to directly indemnify them for business mistakes. In the event of a misconduct that causes significant damage to the user, the *State Redress Act* (Act No. 125 of 1947) provides a way for the user to claim damages against the state. In the event of a misconduct of notary that causes great damage to the user, the Ministry of Justice of Japan can request the notary public suspension of business or resignation (Articles 79, 80, and 81). Japan Federation of Bar Associations, *German Notary System Survey Report* (Japan Federation of Bar Associations, Consumer Affairs Committee, 2004) (in Japanese).

[124.] Out of 36.17 million older people in September 2020, 6 million had dementia and 4 million had MCI. By 2025, the population of older people is expected to rise to 36.57 million, and 7.30 million of those are forecast to have dementia and another 5.89 million are expected to be afflicted with MCI. Some of the older people with MCI will develop dementia. Cabinet Office of Japan, *Estimating the Number of the Elderly with Dementia (Figure 1–2–11), Annual Report on the Ageing Society FY 2018* (Web Page, 2019) (in Japanese) <https://www8.cao.go.jp/kourei/whitepaper/w-2017/html/gaiyou/s1_2_3.html>.

One of the key issues of SDM is finding the right supporter. It will be ideal if the supporter is one who knows the principal well, can properly support the principal in line with the agreement, and will have no conflict of interest in dealing with the principal, such as relatives or close friends. A pair of law and welfare practitioners as co-supporters would be preferable if they trust each other.[125] This combination will be a type of support to the principal, sharing knowledge and skill in a good balance, although the remuneration becomes double. This SDM scheme will not require any judicial involvement of the courts but will require public involvement through core agencies. It proposes to provide support and protection for vulnerable[126] adults whose SDM agreement is registered at a core agency at the principal's approval. SDM law is envisaged to establish a mechanism that provides a certain level of support and protection for the principal and the principal's stakeholders, even in an informal arrangement where the principal is supported by relatives or a nursing-home manager.

Target of SDM Law

For the basic principles, the target of SDM is defined as vulnerable adults who do not need an adult guardian or other substitute decision-maker for their activities, but who will benefit from SDM. SDM will thus be in place mainly for people with MCI who may not need the adult guardianship system and can understand the contract. Therefore, SDM and the adult guardianship system can theoretically coexist without any legal conflict between them.[127] SDM should include the implications from Australia with respect to its purpose and basic principles. The Victorian State Act 2019, for example, has the purpose to 'promote the personal and social wellbeing of a person' (section 4) and a basic principle that is based on a 'presumption of decision-making capacity' (section 5). 'An adult has the capacity to make decisions in relation to a matter if the adult can fulfill some specific conditions that are separately determined.' 'Adults are presumed to have decision-making capacity unless there is evidence to the contrary' (section 5(2)).

[125.] For example, some members of the Elder Law Society Japan exercise guardianship with a combination of legal/welfare practitioners in Yokohama, Japan. Elder Law Society Japan (Web Page, n/a) (in Japanese) <https://elderlawjapan.jp/>.

[126.] 'Vulnerable' means a state in which one is at risk in terms of social and physical conditions, and to require support and protection from a third party in daily life. This includes not only adults with insufficient mental capacity, such as older people with dementia, but also those who cannot manage their daily lives by themselves due to physical disabilities, brain dysfunction, alcoholism, drug addiction, and the likes. This is because SDM is based on the vulnerability approach as addressed in Section 2.3.2, 'Vulnerability Approach.'

[127.] Refers to Section 3.2 (5), 'U.S. Guardianship and Supported Decision-Making Acts.' Delaware State Act (2016) provides the legal status of 'supported decision-making agreements' for the target of SDM, namely 'adults who would benefit from decision-making assistance.' If the capacity of the principal becomes insufficient, either the enduring power of attorney (EPA) or the adult guardianship system will prevail.

c. Characteristics of SDM Law

Considering the characteristics of the relevant legal devices, such as welfare assistance, SDM, and the adult guardianship system, people's understanding of legal devices and their participation in the policy will be essential as consumer choice. It can be assumed that SDM has no legal enforcement but provides preferential benefits to people in the community, asking for their participation in the policy through their own initiatives. In other words, SDM needs to be a legal device for people in the community to understand its purpose, methods, and legal effects in accordance with the SDM agreement. In this sense, SDM legislation must be a part of a collaboration agreement type of law between people in the community and the municipality.[128] The municipality can include such private areas under its administrative control if the people consent. Therefore, it can be assumed that individualism or privacy may voluntarily permit some social norms by law in exchange for the user's consent.[129] Considering such a legal function in the context of individualism or privacy, SDM will be proposed as a framework that can adapt to the diversity and changing environment of people in a super-aged society.

d. Summary: Main Contents of SDM Law

The main contents of the SDM law that have been discussed are summarized below.[130]

(i)   The core agency, regardless of whether it is a public or private entity, should be established in the community as directed by the Basic Plan. It

---

[128.] 'Collaboration' refers to 'a collaborative effort to coordinate, plan and execute activities [in order] to achieve a common aim or goal by those who include two or more supporters (including professional and non-professional supporters) and sometimes clients belonging to different professions, institutions and disciplines.'(translated into English by the author) Masafumi Nakamura, Asuka Okada and Chizuko Fujita, 'Review on "Cooperation" and "Collaboration" in the Field of Clinical Psychology: Focusing on the Differences in the Definitions and Concepts' (2013) 7 *Journal of Graduate School of Human Science, Kagoshima Jyunshin University* 1, 13 (in Japanese); Madoka Miwa, 'The Concept of "Partnership" from a Legal Perspective' (2015) 8 *Academia Social Sciences* 99, 114 (in Japanese).

[129.] The relationship between a core agency and people in the community can be seen similarly in the Pacte Civil de Solidarité (PaCS) in France. The PaCS has established a 'give and take' relationship between couples in marriage in fact and the local government, making use of the PaCS in an area where privacy and individualism should dominate. Michihiro Tanaka, 'Commentary on the French Civil Code: Family Law (5)' (2012) 62(4) *Journal of Law and Politics* 173, 195 (in Japanese); Noriko Sato, 'Adoption du Pacs et Transformation de la Relation Intime Comme Lutte Symbolique' (Adoption of the PaCS and Transformation of the Intimate Relationship as a Symbolic Struggle) (2004) 112 *Philosophy* 1, 12 (in Japanese).

[130.] Refers to the 'Draft Bill on Supported Decision-Making for Vulnerable Adults' in Japanese and English in the previously published article by the author: Yukio Sakurai, 'An Essay on the Adult Protection System in Japan: Referring to Delaware State Law and the Revision of European Law' (2018) 8 *Quarterly Comparative Guardianship Law* 3, 21 (in Japanese).

should be responsible for multiple functions stipulated in the Basic Plan, including confidentiality involving individual information and privacy. Some public functions may be delegated to the core agency based on ordinances or regulations created by the relevant local parliament or government.

(ii) The scope of SDM legislation at the initial stage will be narrowed to the legal acts and its associated non-legal activities, as the SDM guidelines for adult guardians define, and be further narrowed to the personal protection only (i.e., excluding property management) in an agreement between the principal and the supporter. This is because the remaining area, including property management and welfare activities, needs further consideration to legislate and maintain the guidelines on them.

(iii) To simplify this discussion, an idea of a specific law regulating SDM will be mentioned. In such a case, SDM can be based on a mutual agreement between a principal and a supporter.[131] In this scheme, a principal needs the capacity to understand the contents of the agreement in order to conclude it.

(iv) Principals and supporters in the community are recommended to conclude an SDM agreement prepared by a notary public and register it at the core agency. Stakeholders, including principals and supporters, may consult with the core agency and the core agency may give advice, forming a local council meeting comprising relevant local experts if necessary.[132]

(v) It is recommended that people in the community register any informal arrangement with the core agency. Stakeholders, including principals and their relatives or nursing-home managers, may consult with the core agency and the core agency may give advice accordingly.

(vi) The target of SDM is defined as vulnerable adults who do not need an adult guardian or other substitute decision-maker for their activities, but who will benefit from SDM. SDM and the adult guardianship system can theoretically coexist without any legal conflict between them.

(vii) SDM legislation must be a part of a collaboration agreement type of law between people in the community and the municipality, based on people's voluntary participation in the policy. It can be assumed that individualism

---

[131.] Refers to Section 3.2 (5), 'U.S. Guardianship and Supported Decision-Making Acts.' *TITLE 16, Health and Safety, Individuals with Disabilities, CHAPTER 94A Supported Decision-Making* in the state of Delaware.

[132.] Regardless of before or after the commencement of adult guardianship, the practitioners' institutions and related associations in each community should cooperate with each other so that legal and welfare practitioners' institutions and related associations can provide necessary support to the 'team.' This is a local committee that promotes the system in which each practitioners' institution and each related association cooperate voluntarily. For the functions and roles of the 'regional collaboration network' to be properly demonstrated and developed, local parties, such as practitioners' institutions, should collaborate and formulate a place for series of discussions regarding the examination, coordination, and resolution of community issues. The core agency serves as the secretariat and are responsible for monitoring the community activities. Ministry of Health, Labour, and Welfare of Japan (n 15) 15.

or privacy may voluntarily permit some social norms by law in exchange for the user's consent.

(2) Issues of SDM Legislation

Five issues need to be reformed for empowering SDM legislation in the future.

First, the roles of the core agency will be extended to 'monitoring and supervision' in addition to providing 'consultation and advice' if the municipality delegates any specific authority by an ordinance or a regulation. An ordinance or a regulation created by the local parliament or municipality would be an important justification to empower the role of the core agency based on the consensus of the local people in the jurisdiction. The monitoring and supervisory function of the core agency is expected to prevent fraudulent acts by supporters and adult guardians in the jurisdiction, and to effectively respond to the unlikely event of fraudulent acts. In such a case, the power of the core agency will be expanded to some extent, which may, in turn, restrict the freedom of community people. Thus, the governance of the core agency must be improved to ensure accountability, transparency, and social responsibilities for the stakeholders.[133] Any performance inspection by a third party, such as ad hoc auditing and community monitoring, should be implemented by the municipality or its delegates.

Second, the idea of establishing a public guardian agency at the prefectural level is worth considering. A public guardian agency established by a prefecture should have local offices to delegate municipalities to run core agencies. These core agencies are public-run entities to ensure accountability, transparency, and a sense of social responsibilities on the part of stakeholders. A public guardian agency and public-run core agencies will directly take care of principles, as far as no conflict of interest is recognized, when the family courts nominate as an adult guardian upon a municipal mayor's petition for the adult guardianship system. This style of management would empower community support for vulnerable adults and contribute to expanding and strengthening core agency networks particularly in large cities where difficult cases, including abuse, are frequently found.

Third, when SDM is legislated to cover legal acts and their associated non-legal activities for personal protection only, the societal impacts of the legislation will not be that great. Theoretically, empowering societal influence at the next stage of SDM legislation could expand the scope of support and protection for vulnerable adults. For example, if the scope of SDM legislation covers the whole

---

[133.] Terry Carney et al, 'Paternalism to Empowerment: All in the Eye of the Beholder?' (Online, 2021) 38(3) *Disability and Society* 1–21, 2–3 <https://doi.org/10.1080/09687599.2021.1941781>.

legal activities, including property management, then further consideration for safeguarding the principal's interests will be required. Safeguarding measures may include regulations of supporter's fiduciary obligation, and a code of practice to give guidance to the supporter's procedures in detail.[134] Any performance inspection by a third party, such as ad hoc auditing and community monitoring, should be implemented by the municipality or its delegates. The importance would be practices on site in the SDM pilot projects where issues of SDM for property management are clarified by examining empirical data. The SDM pilot project, including that of Toyota city, must be promoted.[135] The subsequent section will provide a detailed discussion of this project.

Fourth, the Ministry of Health, Labour, and Welfare of Japan inaugurated online SDM training sessions in December 2020 to provide officers and staff at municipalities and core agencies with basic knowledge and skills about SDM. Such training sessions are important for sharing knowledge and skills with relevant parties, including stakeholders such as medical care, aged care, financial institutions, etc., and improving the level of understanding of SDM throughout Japan. As mentioned in Chapter 4,[136] 'supported decision-making counselors' will be trained through a national qualification system because day-to-day assistance from knowledgeable and skilled professionals will be important to cope with various types of cases.[137] The SDM training programs should be improved to offer necessary skills and knowledge at a higher level based on the analysis of data on practice at the SDM pilot projects.[138] For a future review, the SDM law should be re-examined, including the legal framework and methods of SDM, after three years of the enforcement of the law. The re-examination will provide an opportunity to improve the legal framework and practice of SDM with the policymakers, lawmakers, and practitioners in due course.

Fifth, it would be decided in the future whether SDM will be incorporated into the Civil Code or the other laws of Japan. In such a case, judicial involvement of

---

[134.] The Mental Capacity Act 2005 has the 'Code of Practice' giving guidance for decision in detail under the MCA 2005. The Code of Practice can be updated flexibly to meet the needs of people and show the best practice. GOV. UK, *Code of Practice* (Web Page, October 14, 2020) <https://www.gov.uk/government/publications/mental-capacity-act-code-of-practice>.

[135.] Toyota City (Aichi prefecture), *The Promotion of Advocacy Support and Supported Decision-Making in the Toyota City* (Web Page, June 2, 2021) (in Japanese) <https://www.mhlw.go.jp/content/12000000/000790684.pdf>.

[136.] Refers to Section 4.5.1 (1), Australian Adult Support and Protection Legislation.'

[137.] One of the impressive things in the supported decision-making facilitation training program (eight-day course), conducted by Cher Nicholson (ASSET SA) in Adelaide (South Australia) on February 23 to March 4, 2016, was that professional practitioners voluntarily taught social workers and helpers on site in the community. That human relationship is essential for social workers to maintain the quality of advocacy activities.

[138.] The commissioned research on how to organize the decision-making support system, focusing on information technology: The Japan Research Institute Limited, *Research Report on Contact-Building by Using Information Technology to Support Decision-Making of Older People* (Commissioned by the Ministry of Health, Labour, and Welfare of Japan in 2020) (Web Page, April 9, 2021) (in Japanese) <https://www.jri.co.jp/page.jsp?id=38656>.

the family courts or their alternative is perhaps required to appoint supporters. A question then will be raised whether or not the family courts are suitable to appoint supporters to vulnerable adults for personal protection, considering that personal protection includes welfare of support that are not familiar with the family courts. The tribunal system and its members' background in the state of Victoria (Australia) would be of reference.[139] Reorganization of the family courts and their associated institutions or reform of the judicial institution system is required to deal with the SDM business, including appointment, monitoring and supervision, and dismissal of supporters. Amendments to the Civil Code at the legislative debates in the National Diet of Japan after the full deliberations by the Legislative Council as ordered by the Minister of Justice of Japan are necessary. The project may bring a possibility, as a legislative policy, to transform the adult guardianship system to adult protection law, as Teruaki Tayama suggests in Chapter 1,[140] or to stay status quo based on the capacity doctrine. In any case, the legal status of 'decision-making capacity,' which comes from the common law and stays at the SDM guidelines, and the capacity doctrine, which stays in the Civil Code of Japan, will be issues. Namely, it must be deliberated on how to accommodate the legal concept 'decision-making capacity' in the Civil Code where the capacity doctrine stays as a basic principle.

(3) SDM Model Project in Toyota City

Practices in the SDM model projects are important, where potential issues of SDM for property management and personal protection are systematically clarified.[141] Several local governments participate in the SDM model projects such as Nagano prefecture, Yao City of Osaka prefecture, and Toyota city of Aichi prefecture. They implement their unique projects according to the local needs of advocacy activities. Below, we focus on the Toyota City project 2023–2025.[142]

- Due to the characteristics of Toyota City, which has developed as an automobile corporate-based industrial town, many citizens start living in Toyota City when they get a job there. There are many retired citizens

---

[139.] In the state of Victoria (Australia), the tribunal members with practitioners' background issue the supportive guardian and supportive administrator orders. This mechanism based on practitioners' experience leads to an administrative arrangement rather than a judicial decision.

[140.] Refers to Section 1.1.1 (1) g, 'Future Developments.'

[141.] This section refers to the published article: Yukio Sakurai, 'Supported Decision-Making in the Japanese Context: Developments and Challenges' (2023) 13(1) *The Journal of Aging and Social Change* 151, 169.

[142.] Toyota City, 'Trial of Local Life Supported Decision-Making Project in Toyota City' (2023) (in Japanese) <https://www.mhlw.go.jp/content/12000000/001036950.pdf>.

who live alone with no relatives (Toyota City has an estimated 6,000 to 6,500 older adults with disability). With the increase in the number of single older adults living with no relatives in Toyota City, greater advocacy measures other than the adult guardianship and current welfare systems are needed to protect their rights.

- The key point of the Toyota City project is that both 'service providers,' who provide life-based services such as financial management, and 'decision-making followers,' who support the principal's decision-making, are involved in the support system.

- In addition, it is assumed that the 'Advocacy Support Committee' will respond (such as by dispatching specialists who consistently consider issues from the principal's viewpoint) when periodically checking financial management and providing crucial decision-making support for the principal.

The SDM-Japan[143] is involved in the Toyota City project. SDM-Japan is developing an SDM method suitable for Japanese people. Their missions in the Toyota City project are to formulate SDM practices based on the theory of SDM and establish evaluation methods of SDM activities for supervision and improvement. Mizushima states that

> *in order to enhance the effectiveness of this project, in addition to decision-making followers who are involved in the principal on a regular basis, two mechanisms are essential. First, an independent advocate. This is an expert whose role is to independently understand a principal's intentions, preferences, and values in a particular setting. Second, when the principal conflicts with others, it is necessary to set up a forum for discussion to mitigate the conflict. It is inevitable that opinions may differ between the principal and those who are involved and a conflict arises. It is necessary to create an organization to coordinate this conflict and a mechanism to avoid abuse of the relationship and suppression of the opinion of the principal. This organization will be a tripartite collegial body composed of relevant parties, professionals, and citizens who make non-binding recommendations in case of mutual disagreement between the principal and the supporters.[144]*

Mizushima also remarks that

[143.] SDM-Japan promotes an SDM model originally learnt from Cher Nicholson <https://assetsa.wordpress.com/> of the state of South Australia and modified to the Japanese context, and the Scotland-based Talking Mats <https://www.talkingmats.com/>.

[144.] From an online interview of Toshihiko Mizushima by the author.

the evaluation method of the quality of SDM is essential for succession by others or the next generation. Currently, evaluation methods have not been sufficiently established. If a framework for evaluation methods for SDM is established, it will be possible to adopt the methods at local governments to formulate the SDM methods over Japan.[145]

Another advocate, Toru Morichi[146] is of the opinion that

SDM in Japan still has a long way to go. It is assumed essential to consider both aspects of SDM: one aspect that develops a universal SDM model, referring to SDM models of other developed countries such as Australia; the other aspect that creates a Japanese SDM model, taking people's behavioral patterns such as family reliance into consideration. Rather than separating SDM and substituted decision-making based on capacity assessment of a person, it can be assumed appropriate to deal with these two types of decision-making [based on the vulnerability approach] in practice. What is needed is not to establish a single definitive SDM approach, but to create multiple SDM methods that match a variety of needs on site.

In fact, the Japan Federation of Bar Associations issued a draft SDM bill on April 12, 2023 (Japan Federation of Bar Association 2023), proposing that as the SDM bill aims to realize autonomy of principals, the focus will be on SDM for vulnerable adults. As an extension of SDM, substituted decision-making is recognized as a last resort in cases where decisions cannot be made by the principal even with support. Voluntary guardianship and statutory guardianship under the current Civil Code are to be regulated by SDM laws.

Starting with the Toyota City project, Japan's SDM will have opportunities to operate on a small scale, and it will likely be reviewed and improved with support from stakeholders including SDM-Japan and the Ministry. A step-by-step approach would gradually lead to the formulation of the social norms that may encourage the use of SDM through guidelines and legislation, with adult guardianship to be used only as a last resort. In such a situation, SDM may coexist with and complement the adult guardianship system, both of which will prevent vulnerable adults from abuse. By reviewing the SDM guidelines as a soft law, it will be possible for Japan to legislate SDM to match the advanced SDM models.

[145.] Ibid.

[146.] From an email correspondence between Toru Morichi and the author on April 5, 2023. Morichi is the Secretary-General of SDM-Japan and Assistant Professor at the Faculty of Human Sciences, University of Tsukuba, Japan.

(4) Review of the Second Term Basic Plan
and the Study Group

The second term Basic Plan expands the scope of deliberations of the Expert Commission under the concept of 'advocacy support.' Based on this understanding, the issues of the Expert Commission deliberations will be examined. First, the direction to make the Basic Plan that fits the users' perspectives has been reiterated in the deliberations. In order to formulate an effective Basic Plan that fits the users' perspectives, it is important to hear the opinions of adults with insufficient mental capacity and their relevant institutions and ensure their opinions to be reflected in the Basic Plan.[147] Of those with insufficient mental capacities, older people with dementia have the largest in number, but it is practically hard to grasp their actual situations and their opinions. The phrase *Nothing about us without us*, emphasizing autonomy and the right to self-determination of people with disability, is a principle embodied in the CRPD. With this phrase, it would be an idea for the Ministry of Health, Labour, and Welfare of Japan to conduct nationwide research of older people with dementia and their supporters.[148] Such large-scale research surveys and their analyses would give some suggestions on how to better focus the discussion.

Second, it is essential to consider the legal relationship between the adult guardianship system and Article 12 (equal recognition before the law) of the CRPD. Developed countries, which understand the necessity to legislate or reform laws to meet the requirements of the CRPD, encourage the use of SDM as an alternative to the adult guardianship system and make policies to reduce the use of the adult guardianship, positioning it as a last resort. The attachment resolutions of the National Diet of Japan adopted in 2016 and 2019[149] require the Government of Japan to implement policies that meet the requirements of Article 12 of the CRPD. The review of the Japan Report by the UN CRPD Committee was conducted in August 2022.[150] The Expert Commission is requested

---

[147.] Fumie Imura points out the importance of listening to the 'voices' of those who have difficulties in making autonomous decisions and suggests reforming the system into one that respects the subjective efforts of its users and tries to involve them in the decision-making process. Fumie Imura, 'Reviewing the Adult Guardianship System from the Standpoint of its Users' (2016) 4 *Bulletin of Rikkyo University Community Welfare Research Institute* 149, 169.

[148.] There is a questionnaire survey report of 2,000 relatives who support older people with dementia. According to this survey, 6.4 per cent respondents are the users of the adult guardianship system and 55.4 per cent respondents answer that, '[they] know about the adult guardianship system, but [they] do not want to use it.' Mizuho Information & Research Institute, Inc., 'Survey Results on Management Support of Deposits and Savings, Property for People with Dementia' (Web Page, May 19, 2017) (in Japanese) <https://www.mizuho-ir.co.jp/company/release/2017/ninchisho0519.html>.

[149.] Refers to the Attachment Resolutions in 2016 and 2019. House of the Councillors, *Attachment Resolutions* (Web Page, April 5, 2016) (in Japanese); House of the Councillors, the National Diet of Japan, *Attachment Resolutions* (Web Page, June 6, 2019) (in Japanese) <https://www.mizuho-rt.co.jp/company/release/2017/page_0007/index.html>.

[150.] The review session was held by the UN CRPD Committee (Geneva) on August 22 and 23, 2022.

to deliberate on the issues to be raised by the UN CRPD Committee concerning the adult guardianship system and Article 12 of the CRPD and its relevant issues together with the Policy Committee.[151] It is recommended to consider the legal status and the issues of SDM, based on the international consensus views on SDM and the CRPD.[152]

The Ministry of Justice of Japan delegated the study group (Chair Akio Yamanome) to deliberate on the ideal adult guardianship system on June 7, 2022.[153] This study group was formed based on the policy of 'reviewing the adult guardianship system' mentioned in the second term Basic Plan. This implies that the Ministry of Justice of Japan is considering amendments to the Civil Code and relevant laws related to the adult guardianship system later.[154]

As for points of discussion of the adult guardianship system, there are two different opinions of civil law scholars: One opinion is to expect the progress of the guardianship promotion project initiated by the Government of Japan, and the other opinion is to consider transforming the adult guardianship system into a generous (adult protection) system with an emphasis on social welfare measures.[155] In the second term Basic Plan, these two opinions have become closer and almost synchronized into one direction through five-year deliberations of the experts under the concept of advocacy support that demonstrates 'comprehensive support measures including adult guardianship system.'[156] To clarify the policy direction easy to understand for people, it is recommended that the Government of Japan should promote transforming the adult guardianship system into the adult support and protection law.

Second, the study group should deliberate on the issues from a broader and long-term perspective. Namely, one is to clarify what roles the adult guardianship

---

[151.] The Policy Committee submitted their updated observation report to the UN Committee before the Japan report review in August 2022, including their remarks toward Article 12, the CRPD. Cabinet Office of Japan, *Policy Committee* (Web Page, 66th Session Survey No. 6, June 14, 2022) <https://www8.cao.go.jp/shougai/suishin/seisaku_iinkai/index.html>.

[152.] Emiko Kiguchi states that the legal interpretation of SDM has been divided into these two, i.e., 'supported decision-making as an alternative to the adult guardianship system' and 'decision-making support from the perspective of operating the adult guardianship system.' The idea of community-based welfare policy has not been unified, which causes confusion on-site. Emiko Kiguchi, 'Trends in Domestic Debates over Decision Support' (2017) 9 *Welfare and Social Development Research* 5, 12.

[153.] Refers to the Japan Institute of Business Law, *The Study Group on the Ideal Adult Guardianship System* (Web Page, 2022) (in Japanese) <https://www.shojihomu.or.jp/list/seinenkoken>.

[154.] This is a preliminary study by researchers, practitioners, and disability associations for law reform. Amendments to the Civil Code at the legislative debates in the National Diet of Japan after the full deliberations by the Legislative Council as ordered by the Minister of Justice of Japan are necessary. The recent news reports possible amendments to the Civil Code in FY2026 (*Yahoo News*, August 12, 2022).

[155.] Refers to Section 1.1.1 (1) g, 'Future Developments.'

[156.] Refers to the Ministry of Health, Labour, and Welfare of Japan, *The Second Term Basic Plan for Promoting the Adult Guardianship System* (Web Page, 2022) 4 (in Japanese) <https://www.mhlw.go.jp/stf/seisakunitsuite/bunya/0000202622_00017.html>.

system will play in legal advocacy to comply with the requirements of the CRPD, including the recommendations to be issued by the UN CRPD Committee later. This discussion includes the legal relationship between the capacity doctrine and the notion of decision-making capacity. The other is to consider how the Ministry of Justice, which oversees legislative policy of the Civil Code and relevant laws, will coproduce the legislative policy with the Ministry of Health, Labour, and Welfare, which is charge of the second term Basic Plan.[157] This discussion includes how advocacy support is organized in community support, including welfare and elder abuse prevention measures.

Based on these two essential points of discussion, further deliberations on what measures would be introduced and improved in the adult guardianship system should be conducted, such as an introduction of limited guardianship for a temporary use, replacement of the adult guardian requested by the principal, and remuneration policy.[158] These three measures are practical topics for operation in the short and middle term but cannot be said essential in the long term.

The Study Group concluded on February 13, 2024, that amendments to the Civil Code provisions on adult guardianship were inevitable, as the system would become more functional through the introduction of the three proposed measures mentioned above, while maintaining the existing framework.[159] After an extended deliberative process, including discussions within the Study Group, the Ministry of Justice resolved to initiate reform of the adult guardianship system under the Civil Code. On February 15, 2024, the minister of justice formally submitted an inquiry to the 199th Legislative Council for their proposals, with a response expected by 2026.[160] In response, the Legislative Council established the Civil Code (Adult Guardianship, etc.) Subcommittee, chaired by Akio Yamanome, which began its deliberations on April 9, 2024.

Following the Ministry of Justice's initiative, it is anticipated that the Ministry of Health, Labour, and Welfare will also pursue reforms to the social welfare system related to guardianship, in parallel with the ongoing discussions of the Expert Commission on operational improvements. In other words, legislative

---

[157.] Yasushi Kamiyama, 'Memorandum on the Medium to Long-Term Issues of Adult Guardianship: Toward Revision of Adult Guardianship Law' in Nobuhiro Oka et al (eds), *Development in the Civil Code and Trust Law in an Aged Society* (NIPPON HYORON SHA CO., LTD., 2022) (in Japanese).

[158.] Japan Institute of Business Law (n 153).

[159.] Ibid.

[160.] Inquiry No. 126: In view of the various circumstances surrounding the adult guardianship system, including the aging of society, it appears necessary to undertake a review of the system from the perspective of ensuring that individuals who rely on it can continue to lead lives consistent with their dignity, while better safeguarding their rights and interests. I request that an outline for such a review be presented. Legislative Council, *Civil Code (Adult Guardianship, etc.) Subcommittee* (Web Page, 2025) (in Japanese) <https://www.moj.go.jp/shingi1/housei02_003007_00008.html>

reform, operational reform, and social welfare system reform related to guardian-ship are expected to proceed concurrently in the coming years. This coordinated approach suggests a potential move toward a more comprehensive restructuring of the adult guardianship system and its related social welfare framework.

However, it is widely anticipated that the forthcoming reforms will be modest in scope and unlikely to incorporate more progressive models, such as an adult support and protection system. Moreover, coordinating reforms across multiple systems governed by two separate ministries presents significant challenges in ensuring coherence and balance. This difficulty arises from the bureaucratic structure of the Japanese government, which lacks mechanisms for effectively managing cross-ministerial issues. As a result, legislative reform is likely to focus on addressing issues that have emerged over the past twenty-five years, rather than anticipating and preparing for future challenges. In this sense, the reform appears retrospective rather than forward-looking, and the revised system may already be outdated by the time it is implemented. This reflects a broader tendency within bureaucratic processes to prioritize incremental adjustments over structural innovation—often to the detriment of citizens, who ultimately bear the consequences as end users of the system. A more fundamental review of the relevant systems will likely become inevitable in the future, when another opportunity arises to consider reform from a different, more forward-looking perspective.

(5) Step-by-Step Approach

Legislation on the development of SDM may require the step-by-step approach addressed in Table 5.2. In these Options, Japan is positioned at 'Option A—The current legal framework with an enhanced focus on SDM guidelines' and is anticipated to proceed to 'Option B—Functional approach to legal capacity, where some law and policy recognize the role of SDM in practice.' It will be a challenge for Japan to jump from Option A to 'Option C—Phased-in fully inclusive SDM in the guardianship and welfare laws to recognize the role of SDM' because SDM is not a complete legal system and requires further review in practice. Namely, review of SDM guidelines based on practices and experiences in support is required to improve the unified SDM definition, standardize SDM methods, and develop adequate safeguards for risk of the principals.[161]

[161.] Refers to Section 1.2.2 (4), 'Developments and Challenges of the SDM Guidelines.'

Table 5.2: Step-by-Step Approach

• Option A—The current legal framework with an enhanced focus on SDM guidelines: This will not change the capacity doctrine of the Civil Code, but will introduce SDM guidelines, information resources, and training to maximize provision of SDM to meet the requirements necessary for the exercise of legal capacity within the current framework of the welfare laws and the Civil Code. SDM guidelines for adult guardians suggest that the adult guardians should practice SDM with principals as a priority, only opting for substituted decision-making if SDM does not function.
• Option B—Functional approach to legal capacity, where some law and policy recognize the role of SDM in practice: This will establish consistent functional assessments for legal capacity, mainly for dementia tests, across main statutes in decision-making capacity and recognize SDM, making it possible for people to exercise legal capacity on that basis. Some laws, regulations, ordinances, policy and guidelines will be developed to support SDM implementation. Review of SDM guidelines based on practices and experiences in support is required to improve the unified SDM definition, standardize SDM methods, and develop adequate safeguards for risk of the principals.
• Option C—Phased-in fully inclusive SDM in the guardianship and welfare laws to recognize the role of SDM: A comprehensive approach to legally recognize SDM in a specific law or in the Civil Code with supports as required, will be adopted. Policy, guidelines, training, and community support systems will also be developed. The legal status of 'decision-making capacity' and the capacity doctrine in the Civil Code will be one of the issues to be deliberated on by the Legislative Council.

Source: Made by the author[162]

The SDM guidelines as a soft law would be practical and ethical regulation on SDM at the initial stage because regulating SDM through a hard law might

---

[162.] These are created by the author, referring to the report: Michael Bach and Lana Kerzner, *Supported Decision Making: A Roadmap for Reform in Newfoundland & Labrador Final Report* (A Legal Capacity Research Report from IRIS—Institute for Research and Development on Inclusion and Society, 2020) 43–6.

be unworkable when an SDM method has not yet been clearly fixed.[163] This process would gradually formulate the social norms that may encourage the use of SDM through guidelines and legislation, with the adult guardianship to be used only as a last resort. In such a law system, SDM may coexist with and complement the adult guardianship system, and both devices may prevent vulnerable adults from abuse. The legislative process and experiences in the state of Victoria (Australia), which took a decade to legislate the guardianship law that incorporates SDM on it, while practicing SDM projects in communities would be of reference to Japan. In particular, the process of accumulating empirical research on SDM, which has been conducted by universities and NPOs in various parts of Australia since around 2010, forms a social consensus and reaches legislation.[164] Bach and Kerzner state that 'this re-balancing [of autonomy and safeguarding] will not be accomplished without substantial legislative and institutional reform in legal capacity law, adult protection law and mental health law.'[165] Indeed, legislation or law reform is vital to pave a way forward for Japan's adult support and protection.

5.3 The Idea of Adult Support and Protection in Japan

5.3.1 Illustration of Adult Support and Protection Legislation and Framework

(1) Adult Support and Protection Legislation

The legislation and policy framework of adult support and protection for vulnerable adults is summarized in Table 5.3. It is understood that an adult support and protection framework in Japan refers to a combination of laws and policies that comprise multi-laws, such as the adult guardianship system, SDM, abuse prevention law, relevant policy measures for adults with insufficient mental capacity. The importance is that the framework of the laws and policies are

---

[163.] Yukio Sakurai, 'The Role of Soft Law in the Ageing Society of the Twenty-First Century' (2018) 13(1) *The International Journal of Interdisciplinary Global Studies* 1–10, 7.

[164.] This is the reason Gooding and Carney address that Australia has adopted 'a *reformist* and *incrementalist* reform approach to legal capacity, equality and disability,' following global standards. Piers Michael Gooding and Terry Carney AO, 'Australia: Lessons from a Reformist Path to Supported Decision-Making' in Michael Bach and Nicolás Espejo Yaksic (eds), *Legal Capacity, Disability and Human Rights: Towards A Comprehensive Approach* (Supreme Court of Mexico, Human Rights Division, 2021); Shigeaki Tanaka, *Contemporary Jurisprudence* (Yuhikaku Publishing Co., Ltd., 2011) 442 (in Japanese)

[165.] Michael Bach and Lana Kerzner, *A New Paradigm for Protecting Autonomy, and the Right to Legal Capacity: Advancing Substantive Equality for Persons with Disabilities through Law, Policy and Practice* (The Report commissioned by The Law Commission of Ontario, 2010) 183.

explained with people in the community support centered by a core agency for consumer choice of vulnerable adults and are utilized as safety protection for vulnerable adults.

As a fundamental principle, it is essential that a comprehensive package of adult support and protection measures be provided so that people may make their own decisions (*principle of presumption of decision-making capacity*) when choosing whatever is suitable and necessary (*principle of necessity*). These measures should aim at protecting vulnerable adults by including the least restrictive measures (*the least restrictive alternative*) as much as possible, taking the will and preferences of the adults into consideration (*respect for an adult's will and preferences*). It is also important to strike a balance between state responsibility and people's rights (*self-determination*). State responsibility, including police power, should exist if clear evidence-based procedures are provided and the human rights of people are not violated.

Table 5.3: Legislation and Policy of Adult Support and Protection

First, there are five laws related to the adult guardianship system enacted in Japan.
- Act for the Partial Revision of the Civil Code, Act No. 149 of 1999.
- Act on Voluntary Guardianship Contract, Act No. 150 of 1999.
- Act on Coordination, Act No. 151 of 1999.
- Act of Guardianship Registration, Act No. 152 of 1999.
- Act on Promotion of the Adult Guardian System, Act No. 29 of 2016.

Second, we have the SDM guidelines and an idea on SDM legislation.

- The Guidelines for Supported Decision-Making for Nursing-Home Managers, Managers for the Elderly with Dementia, and Adult Guardians, which will be unified into single guidelines.
- One Preliminary Idea on SDM Legislation.

Third, we have two laws related to elder abuse and abuse of people with disabilities.

- Act on the Prevention of Elder Abuse, Support for Caregivers of Elderly Persons and Other Related Matters, Act No. 124 of November 9, 2005.
- Act on the Prevention of Abuse of Persons with Disabilities and Support for Caregivers, Act No. 79 of June 24, 2011.

> Fourth, we have three public policy measures for adults with insufficient mental capacity.
>
> • 'Subsidies for Expenses Related to Use of the Adult Guardianship System' is granted by the local government.
> • 'Voluntary Watch Service' conducted by volunteers based on an ordinance or local regulation.
>
> Fifth, relevant legal advocacy policies in the social security law.
>
> • 'Support Program for Self-Reliance in Daily Life' conducted by the Councils of Social Welfare.
>
> Fifth, relevant legal advocacy policies in the social security law.

Source: Summarized by the Author

(2) Adult Support and Protection Framework

Figure 5.1 is an illustration of the relevant agencies and their interrelations with people in the community who apply to participate in adult support and protection and the core agency tasked with responding to these people. This is an attempt to show a conceptual illustration, simplifying the mechanism and interrelations between relevant agencies and people in the community. Some comments on this illustration follow.

Figure 5.1: Illustration of the Japan's Adult Support and Protection Framework

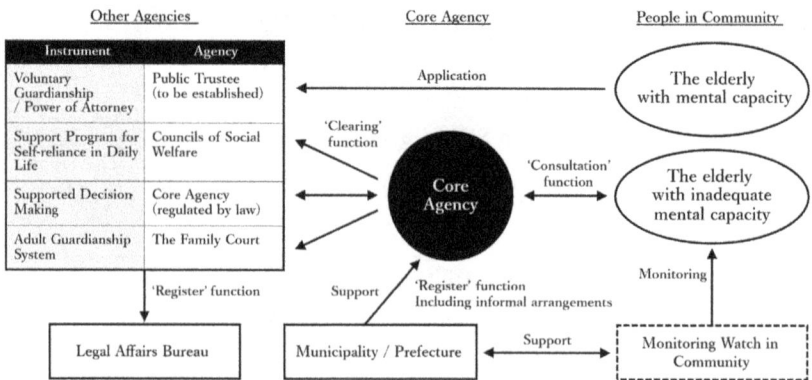

Source: Made by the Author

First, a core agency will offer 'clearing' function in a community to sort the guardianship applicants before petitioning.[166] This is an attempt to make a fair distribution of relevant people to less restrictive support measures that best suits the situation among the multi-optional laws and policies in community support and consequently reduce the number of the adult guardianship users rather than to promote the adult guardianship system. This policy may meet the international standard to use adult guardianship as a last resort and, instead, encourages the use of SDM or less restrictive support measures while reducing or not increasing the office and financial burden of the family courts.

Second, as illustrated in Figure 5.1, a public trustee is a public corporation, which is not available now in Japan but can be established by the government in the future, that takes care of financial management for some fees.[167] People may conclude a lasting power of attorney (LPA) more easily since a public trustee may be regarded as a corporate voluntary guardian if the principal has no conflict of interests with the public trustee. These functions of the public trustee will contribute to the value of autonomy and right to self-determination of people in financial management and estate planning. As long as a public trustee is available in the community, a shortage of adult guardian candidates in financial management will not occur. A public trustee will be able to assist the family court with office work, including evaluating and reporting the annual reports of adult guardians to the family court, by a delegation agreement if the relevant law permits.

Third, people in the community may consult with the core agency and other relevant agencies to choose the measure that best suits the situation among the multi-optional laws and policies in community support.[168] Even people in informal arrangement may consult with such agencies for consultation and advice, registering at a core agency.[169] As a core agency and a community-based general support center may aim at realizing a diverse society where people cohabit in [the] community, they should collaborate to develop community support system.[170] Even in dispute cases, the principal and relevant persons may use alternative dispute resolution (ADR) provided by the core agency or a corresponding agency outside the court. The core agency and other relevant agencies may provide an opportunity for local employment and the development of relevant social businesses throughout Japan. Civil society should function as a positive force

---

[166.] Refers to Section 5.2.1 (1) c, 'Additional Delegation of a Core Agency.'

[167.] Refers to Section 4.5.2, 'Implications from Australian Legislative Project.'

[168.] Refers to Section 5.2.1 (1), 'Roles of a Core Agency.'

[169.] Refers to Section 5.2.3 (1) b, 'Legal Status of SDM Law.'

[170.] Refers to Section 5.2.1 (3), 'Characteristics of a Core Agency.'

within the community. One proposed approach is the creation of a 'cooperative society' in each region, in which community members actively participate and collaborate to enhance individual autonomy through mutual consultation.[171] The key challenge lies in establishing effective mechanisms for such community-based consultations.

Fourth, welfare measures are not prepared enough for advocacy support so that they need reconsideration. There are contemporary issues that cannot be solved by the existing legal measures of social security law (i.e., community-based integrated care system, support program for self-reliance in daily life, etc.), and revisions of current legal measures and other legal measures that address contemporary issues should be examined. These measures are not only within the framework of advocacy in a broad sense[172] (i.e., an auditing and self-inspection/ third-party evaluation system, and a complaint resolution system) but also within the scope of human rights institutions (i.e., the ombudsman,[173] A national human rights institution[174]). This is the issue for studying in the future.

This section examines contemporary issues emerging within local communities. In certain cases—such as when an older individual living alone dies without an identifiable next of kin or designated party responsible for burial—the municipality in which the death occurs assumes legal responsibility for funeral arrangements, pursuant to relevant laws and regulations.[175] Funeral costs are initially covered by the deceased's estate; if the estate is insufficient, the municipality provides temporary financial assistance.

Currently, strict legal protections of individual privacy and personal information benefit citizens but pose significant challenges for municipal authorities.[176]

---

[171] Keiji Shimada, 'Participation and Coproduction' (2016) 42(457) *Monthly Review of Local Government* 1–36, 31–3 (in Japanese).

[172] Refers to Section 1.1.1 (2) a, 'What Is Advocacy in the Japanese Context?'

[173] The scope of ombudsman institutions varies, encompassing oversight of parliaments, central and local administrations, and, in some cases, the judiciary. They provide an alternative avenue for addressing complaints or grievances without resorting to the courts. Kiyohide Yamatani, 'A Reconsideration of the Ombudsman System in Administrative Control Theory' (2021) 173 *Public Administration Review Quarterly* 37, 49 (in Japanese).

[174] A national human rights institution that advocates for human rights and allows individuals in the community to file claims directly would be a desirable model. Theresia Degener, the former chair of the UN CRPD Committee, made a proposal at a public lecture in Tokyo (December 9, 2019), urging Japan to establish a national human rights authority, an independent body from the Government, in accordance with the *Paris Principles*. United Nations, Human Rights Office of the High Commissioner, *Principles Relating to the Status of National Institutions (The Paris Principles)* (Web Page, December 20, 1993) <https://www.ohchr.org/EN/ProfessionalInterest/Pages/StatusOfNationalInstitutions.aspx>.

[175] Article 9 of the Act Concerning Graveyards, Burials, etc. (Law No. 48 of May 31, 1948) stipulates that the municipal authority in whose jurisdiction the death occurs is responsible for handling unidentified or unclaimed bodies. In addition, the Act on the Treatment of Persons Who Contracted Disease or Died While Traveling (Act No. 93 of 1899) serves as the legal basis for municipal governments, such as city halls, to allocate public funds for this purpose.

[176] In a YouTube video <https://www.youtube.com/watch?v=CiliJOfbPkE&t=36s> (in Japanese), the director of Yokosuka City addressed this fact in an interview.

Municipalities often struggle to identify deceased older individuals and their potential stakeholders during investigations of solitary deaths. In the past, it was relatively easy to obtain such information through home telephone directories or local telephone offices. However, with the shift from home telephones to personalized mobile phones and email, such information is no longer publicly accessible to third parties, including municipal authorities. In response to these challenges, some municipalities have proactively developed public support measures aimed at assisting older adults without familial or social support networks.

For example, Yokosuka City offers two services aimed at supporting end-of-life preparation.[177] The first, the Ending Plan Support Program, involves municipal staff visiting older adults living alone to provide guidance on funeral planning in collaboration with funeral enterprises and, if desired, assistance in drafting a living will.[178] This service is limited to older residents living alone or in similarly vulnerable situations. The second, My End-of-Life Registration, enables all citizens to register their end-of-life preferences with Yokosuka City Hall in advance.[179] In the event of an emergency, this information may be shared with hospitals, fire departments, police, welfare offices, or individuals designated by the registrant.

Similarly, the local assembly of Yamato City has enacted an ordinance mandating municipal support for older residents in preparing for end-of-life arrangements.[180] These localized initiatives may help promote autonomous end-of-life planning, protect against undue influence, and warrant further legislative and empirical analysis.[181] They also suggest that older adults should recognize the need to take proactive steps toward end-of-life preparations well in advance, while they are

---

[177.] In the YouTube video (n 176), the director of Yokosuka City explained that since 2000, the city has increasingly managed posthumous affairs for individuals with known identities but without relatives or willing acquaintances. In response, the municipality began encouraging elderly residents living alone to make advance arrangements for their own funerals, supported by voluntary collaborations with funeral service providers.

[178.] Yokosuka City, 'Yokosuka City Ending Plan Support Business' (2023) (in Japanese) <https://www.city.yokosuka.kanagawa.jp/2610/syuukatusien/endingplan-support.html>.

[179.] Yokosuka City, 'My End-of-Life Registration' (2024) (in Japanese) <https://www.city.yokosuka.kanagawa.jp/2610/syuukatusien/syuukatutouroku.html>.

[180.] As outlined in Ordinance Article 3 (Basic Principles), the municipality's stance toward citizens is clearly defined.: 'End-of-life support shall be provided in accordance with the following principles: (1) Creating an environment in which citizens can actively engage in end-of-life planning; (2) Accurately identifying citizens' needs regarding end-of-life planning and implementing appropriate measures; (3) Respecting and deepening understanding of each citizen's approach to end-of-life planning. Respecting and deepening understanding of each citizen's approach to end-of-life planning.' Yamato City, 'Yamato City End-of-Life Support Ordinance' (2021) (in Japanese) <https://www.city.yamato.lg.jp/gyosei/soshik/60/ohitorisama/2517.html>.

[181.] One potential solution is to amend Article 9 of Act (n 175) to make the municipality of the deceased's registered residence—rather than where the death occurred—responsible for managing unidentified or unclaimed bodies. According to the director of Yokosuka City, retroactive measures could then be implemented to address related issues by municipalities.

still in good health. These implications can be linked to the policy measures outlined in Figure 4.2 for each jurisdiction.

5.3.2 Function-based Review of Transactions in a Community

(1) People in a Community Applying to Participate in the Process

For people in a community to take advantage of the laws and policies for the support and protection of vulnerable adults at risk of harm, the application process, outlined in Step 1 to Step 8 by category, must be followed.[182]

Step 1: Vulnerable adults in the community are under the supervision of welfare practitioners monitoring activities.

Welfare practitioners in the community, such as local welfare officers, aged care managers, helpers, and social workers, who frequently meet with older people are said to easily grasp changes in the life of older people. Based on the awareness of local welfare and other relevant officers, a system can be set up for reporting to the local aged care support center, the core agency, the municipality, the consumer service center, and the police, according to the problem in question.[183]

Step 2: People in the community contact the core agency for consultation.

The applicant, i.e., the principal as well as the principal's stakeholders, needs to have some records of the principal's daily behavior, particularly what is out of the ordinary, and how and when this behavior appears. With these personal records of the principal, the applicant's consultation process with the core agency will progress more smoothly. Upon consultation, the applicant will be informed about the policy measures and legal instruments that are available, and which among them would best suit the principal.[184] In preparation for a future decline in cognitive capacity, it is possible for the principal to designate a relative (within two degrees) as an agent of himself/herself in the deposit account of a financial institution.[185] If the principal is suspected to have dementia or other mental illness, the core agency will suggest that the principal see a doctor at the earliest convenience. For further consideration, if necessary, the applicant will have to obtain a medical report from a doctor certifying the mental capacity of the principal, but this is not obligatory at this stage.

---

[182] Refers to Section 5.3.1 (2), 'Adult Support and Protection Framework.'

[183] Refers to Section 1.2.4 (2) (a), 'Monitoring in the Community-Based Integrated Care System.'

[184] Refers to Section 5.2.1 (1) a, 'Roles of a Core Agency.'

[185] Refers to Section 1.1.2, 'Function-Based Review.'

Step 3: The applicant's registration at the core agency.

If the applicant will not apply to take advantage of any policy or legal instrument but desires to maintain contact with the core agency for further consultation, it is recommended that the applicant registers either a copy of the supported decision-making agreement, if available, or provides relevant information on an informal arrangement to the core agency.[186] Telephone or online communication with the core agency will be possible once it is registered.

Step 4: The applicant is interested in a welfare program.

If the applicant desires to apply to be a part of the 'support program for self-reliance in daily life' or other alternative welfare programs, the applicant will need to contact the office of the social welfare council located nearest to the principal's residence for procedures.[187] However, the approval of the office of the social welfare council will be subject to an assessment process by the council.

Step 5: The applicant is interested in supported decision-making.

If the applicant applies to participate in supported decision-making, the applicant will have to make a supported decision-making agreement in a notary deed in line with the relevant law or guidelines.[188] The core agency will assist the applicant by providing a standard agreement format, and the applicant will make their own agreement with the advice of the core agency. If necessary, the applicant will consult with a lawyer or another expert. After a notary has completed the agreement, the applicant will be suggested to register a copy of the agreement at the core agency.[189] When the agreement is registered, the applicant will be advised by the core agency to participate in seminars and training programs related to supported decision-making that are sponsored by the municipality.

Step 6: The applicant is interested in the voluntary guardianship system.

If the applicant desires to apply to the notary public for voluntary guardianship, the applicant will contact the notary public with the support of the core agency to conclude the voluntary guardianship contracts.[190] The applicant can consult on the standard format of the agreements and relevant matters on voluntary guardianship with the core agency. The most important point other than the contracts is who will be a voluntary guardian to suit the principal among candidates, such as relatives or third-party practitioners.

---

[186] Refers to Section 5.2.3 (1) b, 'Legal Status.'

[187] Refers to Section 1.2.4 (2) (c), 'Support Program for Self-Reliance in Daily Life.'

[188] Refers to Section 5.2.3 (1) b, 'Legal Status.'

[189] Ibid.

[190] Refers to Section 1.2.1 (1) b, 'Voluntary Guardianship System.'

Step 7: The applicant is interested in the adult guardianship system.

(a)   If the core agency, after their assessment, does not agree with the adult
      guardianship application, the core agency will advise the applicant to use
      a less restrictive alternative measure, such as supported decision-making
      or relevant welfare measure.[191] If the applicant wants to apply to the
      family court for adult guardianship, and the core agency agrees with the
      proceeding, the applicant will have to obtain a medical doctor's report
      certifying that the principal has a mental disability or the like.[192]

(b)   The applicant will prepare a personal information sheet to be filled by
      the social worker who takes care of the principal, considering the mental
      capacity and lifestyle of the principal.[193] At the next step, the applicant will
      organize petition documents and lodge a petition at the family court.[194]
      The core agency will assist the applicant in preparing such documents
      before the petition is lodged. After this is done, a hearing might be held
      at the family court. During the hearing, the principal will be accompanied
      by the principal's stakeholders. Evidence required by the family court will
      need to be shown. The hearing will possibly confirm who or what entity
      will act as a guardian and the duties of the guardian.

(c)   Once the principal's adult guardian is appointed by the family court, the
      adult guardian will have their duties stipulated by the principal.[195] The
      statement of the family court to appoint the adult guardian will be regis-
      tered with the Legal Affairs Bureau by the family court. The registrar will
      disclose the registration information by issuing a registration certificate
      at the Legal Affairs Bureau over Japan.

(d)   The adult guardianship will continue unless otherwise revoked by the
      family court or the principal dies. The guardian's position will be cancelled
      only if the guardian fails to fulfill the guardianship duties provided in the
      Civil Code, or misconduct is confirmed. The principal and the principal's

---

[191.] Refers to Section 5.2.1 (1), 'Roles of a Core Agency.'

[192.] The medical doctor's report includes the following items in line with the official format: (i) medical diagnosis; (ii) opinion about mental capacity of the principal; (iii) basis for judgment in various respects; (iv) signature of the doctor and the name of the hospital. The Courts of Japan, *Medical Certificate Form and Its Guidelines* (Web Page, February 2022) (in Japanese) <https://www.courts.go.jp/saiban/syurui/syurui_kazi/kazi_09_02/index.html>.

[193.] Refers to the Courts of Japan, *Personal Information Sheet Form and Its Guidelines* (Web Page, n/a) (in Japanese) <https://www.courts.go.jp/saiban/syurui/syurui_kazi/kazi_09_02/index.html>.

[194.] Refers to the Courts of Japan, *Petition Formats for Adult Guardianship* (Web Page, n/a) (in Japanese) <https://www.courts.go.jp/saiban/syosiki/syosiki_kazisinpan/syosiki_01_01/index.html>.

[195.] The main duties of the adult guardian are: (i) preparing a guardian financial management plan and filing this plan with the court within sixty days of signing letters of guardianship. (ii) assessing and releasing confidential records of the principal. (iii) visiting the principal to ensure that their personal needs are met. (iv) deciding on an appropriate living environment. (v) reporting annual guardian activities by documents to the family court.

stakeholders or even the guardian may consult with the core agency regarding the guardian's activities for advice if necessary.

Step 8: The applicant is in trouble or abused.
In case of older consumer trouble, elder abuse or financial exploitation, the
principal or the principal's stakeholders should contact the public agency or the
police in charge of elder abuse.[196] But if the principal or the stakeholders do not
want to do so, they can contact the core agency to arrange a consultation. The
core agency will then contact the public agency in charge of elder abuse to consult about how to deal with the case.[197] If it is an emergency case, the principal
or the principal's stakeholders should directly contact the public agency or the
police for an emergency rescue by phone.

(2) Core Agency Responding to People in a Community for Support

The core agency as a multi-functional shop should respond to the application
steps of people in a community in (1) above with the following Response 1 to
Response 8 in community support.[198]

Response 1: Watching people in the community.
The core agency can quickly resolve issues in the community through an
immediate response system for reporting abuse or the like to the public
agency.[199] This is, however, a post-treatment response system after the
damage must have happened and will not lead to safeguards. In the future,
a core agency will have to carry out welfare functions in addition to legal
advocacy and collaborate with the local older care management center on
its initiative.

Response 2: Responding to people in the community upon consultation.
The core agency may respond case by case to the principal and stakeholders,
including supporters, relatives, and nursing-home managers, on policy measures

---

[196.] 'The main factors identified as reasons elder abuse happens are related to the nature of the issue (the inherent
complexity of elder abuse, pervasive ageism, insufficient awareness and doubts about prevalence estimates, and
the intractability of the issue), the policy environment (the restricted ability in the field of elder abuse to capitalise
on policy windows and processes), and the capabilities of the proponents of prevention of elder abuse (disagree-
ments over the nature of the problem and solutions, challenges in individual and organisational leadership, and an
absence of alliances with other issues).' Christopher Mikton et al, 'Factors Shaping the Global Political Priority of
Addressing Elder Abuse: A Qualitative Policy Analysis' (Online, July 8, 2022) 3(8) *The Lancet Healthy Longevity*
E531–9 <https://doi.org/10.1016/S2666-7568(22)00143-X>.

[197.] Refers to Section 5.3.2 (3), 'Dispute Response Mechanism.'

[198.] Refers to Section 5.3.1 (2), 'Adult Support and Protection Framework.'

[199.] Refers to Section 1.2.4 (2) (a), 'Monitoring in the Community-based Integrated Care System.'

and legal instruments that are available and assumed to best suit the principal.[200] If the principal is suspected to have dementia or other mental illness but the stakeholders cannot say for sure, the core agency will suggest that the principal and the principal's stakeholders see a doctor for a dementia test or mental illness as soon as possible.

Response 3: Keeping contact with people in the community.
The core agency will register the principal and the stakeholders for a supported decision-making agreement or an informal arrangement and maintain contact for further advice.[201] Telephone or online communication between the principal/the stakeholders and the core agency will be possible once the relevant information is registered. The core agency will monitor the situation of the principals in their jurisdiction by telephone or face-to-face meeting if the principal or the principal's stakeholders may consent.

Response 4: Advice on welfare programs.
The core agency will advise potential users of the 'support program for self-reliance in daily life' or other welfare programs of the necessary procedures and the location of the council of social welfare.[202] The core agency will provide advice to the user from a third party's perspective. By the dignity of risk as a process of positively taking risk within established safeguards, people with disability seek a possibility to overcome certain risk factors by advocating the risk.[203]

Response 5: Advice on supported decision-making agreement.
The core agency will show the principal and the stakeholders a standard SDM agreement format so that they can make their own agreement accordingly, and then register a copy at the core agency.[204] If the applicant has no candidate among relatives and close friends who can act as a supporter, the core agency will introduce some candidates from third parties or NPOs that are listed in the core agency.[205] After the agreement in the notary deed is concluded by a notary public, the core agency will monitor SDM activities and provide advice or training program for SDM practice when requested by the principal or supporter.

Response 6: Advice on voluntary guardianship.

[200.] Refers to Section 5.2.1 (1) a, 'Roles of a Core Agency.'

[201.] Refers to Section 5.2.3 (1) b, 'Legal Status.'

[202.] Refers to Section 1.2.4 (2) (c), 'Support Program for Self-Reliance in Daily Life.'

[203.] Refers to Section 4.2.2 (5), 'Victorian Interdisciplinary Research and Practices.'

[204.] Refers to Section 5.2.3 (1) b, 'Legal Status.'

[205.] Refers to Section 5.2.1 (1) a, 'Roles of a Core Agency.'

The core agency will support the applicant in their procedures with the notary public for voluntary guardianship.[206] The core agency will provide the principal with necessary information on the voluntary guardianship contract, including the merits and demerits of voluntary guardianship and points to carefully consider prior to the procedures. If the applicant has no candidate among their relatives and close friends who can act as a voluntary guardian, the core agency will introduce some candidates from third parties or NPOs that are listed in the core agency.[207] After conclusion of the contract in the notary deed by the notary public, the core agency will monitor activities of the voluntary guardian and provide advice at the request of the voluntary guardian, the principal or the principal's relative.

Response 7: Advice on the adult guardianship system.
The core agency will support the applicant's petition to the family court as a third party. The core agency will monitor activities of the adult guardian and provide advice at the request of the guardian, the principal or the principal's stakeholders. There is a subsidy for expenses (e.g., lodging fees, registration fees, certificate cost) to support low-income older people who need to use the adult guardianship system.[208] The subsidy is granted by the local government based on a regional support project. The core agency will support application for the grant to the municipality if it is deemed necessary. After the adult guardian is appointed, the core agency will advise any enquiry available from the principal, the principal's stakeholders, or the adult guardian.

Response 8: Response to trouble or abuse.
The core agency, after it has been contacted by the principal or the principal's stakeholders, will contact the local government or relevant agency, including the police in charge of elder abuse, to consult on how to deal with elder abuse cases.[209] As the prompt reaction is sometimes required to respond elder abuse, 24 hour's emergency contact service by telephone will be vital. If there is an urgent and pressing need – such as someone badly neglected or at high risk of abuse or exploitation, an emergency rescue support system should urgently function in a community by the relevant agencies, including the core agency to take necessary steps.

[206.] Refers to Section 1.2.1 (1) b, 'Voluntary Guardianship System.'

[207.] Refers to Section 5.2.1 (1) a, 'Roles of a Core Agency.'

[208.] Refers to Section 1.2.4 (2) (b), 'Subsidies for Expenses Related to the Use of the Adult Guardianship System.'

[209.] Refers to Section 1.2.4 (1), 'Elder Abuse Prevention Act.'

(3) Dispute Response Mechanism

How should a dispute between a principal and the principal's stakeholders be resolved? If the core agency can set up a dispute response mechanism, like the Victorian Civil and Administrative Tribunal (VCAT) in the state of Victoria, Australia,[210] for consultation, complaint resolution, mediation, and sending appeals to the family court or reports to the police, the principal and stakeholders may contact the core agency for consultation. Then, the core agency will suggest the solution that will best suit the applicant. Even a mere comment or a complaint expressed by people in the community should be recorded by the core agency as a possible suggestion. Such casual communication between people in the community and the core agency will be important in order to build trust and a sense of care.

For mediation,[211] the issue of who would be the mediator would arise. There are two ideas. One, the mediator can be selected from the members of the local council on an ad hoc basis. The core agency will conclude an agreement with any existing certified ADR institution overseen by an attorney or judicial scrivener. The other idea is that the core agency can apply directly to the ADR certification system.[212] Whether an ad hoc or a permanent mediation formula is used, it is important for the core agency to demonstrate sympathy with people in the community and keep all relevant information strictly confidential. It is important for a party in the dispute not to feel that the core agency may side with the other party. In case of any legal issue, the services of a lawyer may be required, and a suitable mediator needs to be arranged. Therefore, skill training and experience are important in mediation.[213] The core agency should keep records of dispute cases, mediations, and analyses so that such data can be consolidated. If the principal or the principal's stakeholders feel that the dispute cannot be resolved

---

[210.] Refers to Section 4.2.2 (3), 'Dispute Response Mechanism.'

[211.] The number of mediation filings in FY2020 in Japan was 1,027, and the number of the acceptances was 1,023. The number of resolution cases was 381. Most of the resolution cases were due to settlement and mediation. Out of the cases settled at dispute resolution centers nationwide in FY2020, 59.6 per cent of cases involved financial damage to the tune of less than 1 million yen (US$ 6,944), and 40.4 per cent to the tune of 1 million yen or more. Japan Federation of Bar Associations, *Statistical Annual Report of Arbitration ADR in FY2020* (Online, September 2021) (in Japanese) <https://www.nichibenren.or.jp/document/statistics/adr_statistical_yearbook.html>.

[212.] This is based on the stipulation in the *Act on Promotion of Use of Alternative Dispute Resolution* (Act No. 151 of 2004) to have a permanent ADR unit within the core agency. The principal or the stakeholders will participate in mediation to resolve the issue.

[213.] From the interview of Ann Soden, an elder law clinic practitioner in Montreal, Canada, by the author on May 6, 2019. Ann Soden has been an elder law mediator for sixteen years, looking after older people who have lost their property management rights due to mismanagement by adult guardians, courts, etc. She noted that a mechanical use of the existing legal system cannot solve older people's disputes effectively. The Elder Law Clinic holds a family conference where people, family members, welfare/medical/legal practitioners, civil servants etc. meet to discuss how to guarantee the rights of older people.

by mediation, they can appeal to the family court or report the issue to the police if it is considered a criminal case. A consultation with a lawyer may be important.

5.3.3 Values of Adult Support and Protection to Global Application

With the legislation and operational mechanisms now clarified, the discussion shifts to the normative framework that underpins adult support and protection. The value framework relevant to adult support and protection legislation is illustrated in Figure 5.2. This represents a modified version of the multidimensional model of elder law (hereafter referred to as the 'modified model'), adapted by the author from the original model developed by Israel Doron. The following section provides commentary on the key principles, indicators, and dimensions incorporated in this model.

Figure 5.2: The Modified Multidimensional Model of Elder Law

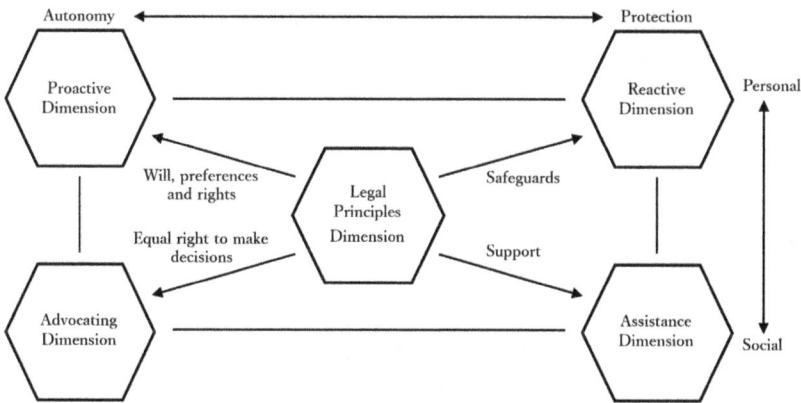

Source: Partly modified by the author based on the Model of Doron 2003/2009[214]

(1) Principal Values of the Legal Principles Dimension

As was reviewed in Chapter 1,[215] the adult guardianship system in Japan upholds respect to right to self-determination, emphasis on personal protection, and normalization in statutory guardianship, and autonomy and right to self-determination

---

[214.] This is an open model that anyone can comment and modify by his/her own responsibility, which was confirmed by Israel Doron in his online lecture at the Elder Law Society Japan meeting held on February 26, 2022. The multidimensional model of elder law was originally introduced in the article in 2003 with some amendments afterward. Israel Doron (ed), 'A Multi-Dimensional Model of Elder Law: An Israeli Example' (2003) 28(3) *Ageing International* 242, 259; Israel Doron, 'A Multi-Dimensional Model of Elder Law' in *Theories on Law and Ageing* (Springer, 2009) 59–74.

[215.] Refers to Section 1.2.1, 'Adult Guardianship System and the Promotion Act.'

in voluntary guardianship as its principal values. The Promotion Act was implemented with the following key values: *support, diverse society* (Article 1), *equality, dignity of an individual*, and *will and preferences* (Article 3). The Basic Plan, which is based on the Promotion Act, has policy objectives aimed at improving systems and practices that enable the users to realize benefits, create a regional collaboration network for the advocacy of human rights, prevent fraud, and maintain social harmony through easy access to the core agency in the community. The second term Basic Plan, which was inaugurated in April 2022, emphasizes 'advocacy support' as the main principle in a community support system. The term 'advocacy support' is defined as

> *support activities which have a common foundation for support and activities centered on the person, which are support for exercising their rights through supported decision-making and support for recovering from infringement of their rights in dealing with abuse and unfair property transactions, for adults with insufficient mental capacity to participate in the community and live independent lives.*[216]

The legal principles dimension in Australia refers to the four principles already discussed in Chapter 4,[217] namely: principle 1, *equal right to make decisions*; principle 2, *support*; principle 3, *will, preferences and rights*; and principle 4, *safeguards*. These principles are as suggested by the 'National Decision-Making Principles' addressed in the ALRC Report 124.[218] The ALRC Report 124 also states five framing principles to guide recommendations for reform, namely: *dignity, equality, autonomy, inclusion and participation*, and *accountability*. There has been wide support by stakeholders for these principles, which are reflected in a Commonwealth decision-making model developed in the Report. The said values have been adopted in Australia, which may correspond to the universal values stipulated in Article 12 (equal recognition before the law) of the CRPD.[219]

It can be observed from the examples of both Japan and Australia that international consensus has almost reached on the CRPD, which 192 states/ areas have ratified as of May 2025. The Australian National Decision-Making Principles clearly reflect some principal values—namely principle 1, *the equal*

[216.] Refers to the Ministry of Health, Labour, and Welfare of Japan, *The Second Term Basic Plan for Promoting the Adult Guardianship System* (Web Page, 2022) (in Japanese) <https://www.mhlw.go.jp/stf/seisakunitsuite/bunya/0000202622_00017.html>.

[217.] Refers to Section 4.5.1 (3), 'Theoretical Framework.'

[218.] Refers to the ALRC Report 124, 2014, 12.

[219.] From the interviews of Terry Carney and Victorian OPA by the author on March 14 and March 5, 2019.

right to make decisions; principle 2, *support*; principle 3, *will, preferences and rights*; and principle 4, *safeguards*—that could be applied to the legal principles dimension of other countries, including Japan.

(2) Indicators' Matrix

What does it mean to have the indicators' matrix of *autonomy* and *protection* on a horizontal level and that of *personal* and *social* on a vertical level? First, the indicators' matrix of *autonomy* and *protection* on a horizontal level is reviewed. The necessity of protection for vulnerable adults or adults at risk of harm has been discussed in Chapter 2;[220] there is a general view that 'vulnerable adults at risk of harm must be protected by law and public policy from abuse.'[221] This general view may change people's perceptions of the 'vulnerability approach' as a criterion for the adult protection system—since vulnerability is a human characteristic regardless of mental capacity—and, instead, encourage respect for human rights as a universal value that affects the law and public policy. Thus, there is the need to have legal safeguards as a reactive dimension to *protect* vulnerable adults or adults at risk of harm. *Autonomy* and *right to self-determination*, two universal values that need to be respected, have also been discussed in Chapter 2.[222] The capability approach is valued for its respect for individual autonomy and right to self-determination and the freedom given to the person to choose a process. This notion respects the diversity of people and gives them the opportunity to think about a way of life that suits their individual characteristics. This idea, as a *proactive* dimension, leads further to respect for a person's will and preferences, and promotes the right to *individual autonomy*. The vulnerable approach and autonomy, which have been discussed in Chapter 2,[223] are the foundation of the indicator's matrix of *autonomy* and *protection* on a horizontal level.

Second, now the indicators' matrix of *personal* and *social* on a vertical level is reviewed. The discussions so far have focused on the internal motives of human beings because humans have been the main player in modern philosophical studies. This is due to *personal* value. We live in an aged society with diverse people and cultures. It has been pointed out in Chapter 2[224] that, regarding human relations around a person, the notion of *relational autonomy* is assumed to be particularly important in practice because one's pattern of human conduct and decision-making is largely influenced by one's family, community, and society.

[220.] Refers to Section 2.3.2, 'Vulnerability Approach.'

[221.] Ibid.

[222.] Refers to Section 2.3.1, 'Capability Approach and Autonomy.'

[223.] Refers to Section 2.2.3, 'Vulnerability Approach' and Section 2.3.1, 'Capability Approach and Autonomy.'

[224.] Refers to Section 2.3.1, 'Capability Approach and Autonomy.'

This suggests that *the social* aspect must be considered in addition to *personal*. For example, a diverse society is considered as the objective by Article 1 (purpose) of the Promotion Act. This shows the importance of interdependent relationship between various agencies, such as people, institutions, government, and other relevant players, with mutual assistance on an equal footing.[225] The *social* aspect includes not only an equal and horizontal transactions between the parties in private autonomy but also an imbalanced relationship between the parties where vertical intervention by public agencies to private autonomy as necessary is designed by law, as is discussed on the consumer contract law in Chapter 1.[226] As an *assistance* dimension, this marrying of the *social* with the *personal* aspects leads to support for vulnerable adults or adults at risk of harm, legislative and policy measures in *reactive* and *proactive* dimensions are utilized to support and protect their interests according to their personal needs, and, as an *advocating* dimension, vigorously emphasizes not only their right to make decisions but also protection of their safety.

(3) Four Dimensions

a. Reactive Dimension

The term *reactive* refers to a response to properly reacting to a vulnerable adult when he/she is identified or deserved as a suspect.[227] Depending on the awareness of commissioned welfare volunteers, social workers, and helpers, a *reactive* system for reporting concerns to the community-based general support center, the municipality, and the police may be eligible. For this, an immediate response system is needed to quickly resolve issues in the local community. By law, the adult guardianship system provides protective measures to principals with insufficient mental capacity. The municipality intervenes in abuse cases for vulnerable adults at risk of harm with the assistance of a core agency. The community support for watching activities in the community and the adult guardianship system are *reactive* legal instruments, based on the vulnerability approach, which act as *safeguards* to protect vulnerable adults.[228] They also ensure that the least restrictive alternative measures are taken. This is to avoid excess paternalism, which may violate the human rights of the principal. Agencies involved in the activities

---

[225.] Ibid.

[226.] Refers to Section 1.1.1 (1) d, 'Research on the Mental Capacity Act 2005 (England and Wales)' for the discussion on the consumer contract law.

[227.] The term 'reactive' refers to 'reacting to events or situations rather than acting first to change or prevent something.' Cambridge Dictionary (Web Page, n/a) <https://dictionary.cambridge.org/ja/dictionary/english/reactive>.

[228.] Refers to Section 1.2.4 (2) (a), 'Monitoring in the Community-based Integrated Care System.'

include the core agency, the family court, a public trustee (to be established), and other relevant agencies concerned with elder abuse, giving careful attention to misconduct by supporters and other relevant persons.

b. Proactive Dimension

The term *proactive* refers to a response not only to properly react to a vulnerable adult when he/she is identified or deserved a suspect but also to prevent its risk by some measures.[229] Day-to-day voluntary activities to monitor the community are basic and *proactive* and are based on the idea of an ordinance or local regulation. SDM and other relevant instruments, as well as the lasting power of attorney and the adult guardianship system, provide *proactive* measures, such as estate planning and/or protection of the interests, to vulnerable adults at risk of abuse. Abuse includes financial exploitation, involving family members, relatives, or close friends of the principal. It is desirable that the adults use these *proactive* measures at their own accord, including estate planning and advanced directive measures. In preparation for a future decline in cognitive capacity, it is possible for older people to designate a relative (within two degrees) as an agent of himself/herself in the deposit account of a financial institution.[230] This is to ensure that the autonomy and self-determination of the principal, as well as their *will, preferences, and rights*, are respected. Agencies, such as the core agency, the family court, the public trustee (to be established), and other relevant agencies concerned with elder abuse, give careful attention to misconduct by supporters and other relevant persons. The core agency may serve as 'consultation and advice' activities to the community people, which may contribute to *proactive* effects.

c. Assistance Dimension

The term *assistance* refers to any kind of support by relatives or third parties, whom they are assumed appropriate to vulnerable adults.[231] Support programs for self-reliance in daily life conducted by the social welfare council and other welfare programs may *support* the principal by providing them with *assistance* in using welfare and other related services in community support. This is to ensure that

---

[229.] The term 'proactive' refers to 'taking action by causing change and not only reacting to change when it happens.' (Web Page, n/a) <https://dictionary.cambridge.org/ja/dictionary/english/proactive>.

[230.] Refers to Section 1.1.2, 'Function-based Review.' Financial institutions in Japan provide bank deposit services in which relatives (within two degrees) can function as agents for managing the principals' deposit accounts.

[231.] The term 'assistance' refers to 'help, especially money or resources that are given to people, countries, etc. when they have experienced a difficult situation.' (Web Page, n/a) <https://dictionary.cambridge.org/ja/dictionary/english/assistance>.

the principal may live independently in the community as possible. SDM and relevant measures are offered through some guidelines or legislation, such as the preliminary idea of SDM legislation that is advocated in this chapter.[232] They are offered to principals with insufficient mental capacity or vulnerable adults on an agreement basis, or through informal arrangements if the principal is satisfied with the *assistance*. Agencies, such as the core agency, the family court, the public trustee (to be established), and other relevant ones, provide community support with people in the community. They are not always involved in SDM activities but indirectly can assist it. The core agency serves as 'consultation and advice' to the community people. The local government may establish its own public guardian agency, if it is necessary, directly to take care of vulnerable adults in difficult cases.[233]

d. Advocating Dimension

The term *advocacy* refers to any action by an individual or a corporation, or any public policy to empower vulnerable adults on minimum conflict of interest between people or between people and society.[234] Vulnerable adults should be *advocated* for and empowered to use, of their own accord, SDM and other relevant measures, including an LPA. It is desirable that adults use these *self-advocating* measures at their own accord, including estate planning and advanced directive measures. This is to respect the autonomy and right to self-determination of the principal by *advocating* the *equal right to making decisions,* focusing on his/ her uniqueness as an individual. By the dignity of risk as a process of positively taking risk within established safeguards, people with disability seek the possibility to overcome certain risk factors by *advocating* the risk.[235] It is reminded that ALRC Report 124 considers an approach to autonomy as empowerment of people with disability (Paragraph 1.38). It can be assumed that ALRC Report 124 includes the notion of relational autonomy.[236] Even in dispute cases, the principal and stakeholders may use ADR provided by the core agency or another relevant agency besides the court, which refers to the section on the response system in

---

[232.] Refers to Section 5.2.3, 'A Preliminary Idea of Supported Decision-Making Legislation.'

[233.] Refers to Section 5.2.1 (1), 'Roles of a Core Agency.'

[234.] Errol Cocks and Gordon Duffy, *The Nature and Purposes of Advocacy for People with Disabilities* (Edith Cowan University Publications, 1993) 121 <https://ro.ecu.edu.au/ecuworks/7172>.

[235.] Refers to Section 4.2.2 (5), 'Victorian Interdisciplinary Research and Practices.'

[236.] Refers to Section 2.4.1 (2) b, 'Relational Autonomy.' Regarding 'autonomy,' Paragraph 1.37 of the ALRC Report 124 states that 'this Inquiry has been informed by autonomy in the sense of "empowerment", not just "non-interference". This involves seeing an individual in relation to others, in a "relational" or "social" sense and understanding that connects with respect for the family as the "natural and fundamental group unit of society" that is entitled to protection by State Parties.'

the state of Victoria, Australia.[237] People may choose the solution that best suits their circumstances in community support. The core agency may be empowered to serve as 'monitoring and supervision' activities, in addition to 'consultation and advice,' to the community people if any delegation agreement is concluded.[238] An idea of establishment of a public guardian agency by a prefecture which delegates municipalities to run core agencies is worth considering.

(4) Japanese Identity and Global Application

The value framework of Japan's adult support and protection legislation and policy system, based on the modified multidimensional model, has been described. There is a view regarding two culturally distinct principles of autonomy: 'the Western principle of autonomy demands self-determination, assumes a subjective conception of the good, and promotes the value of individual independence, whereas the East Asian principle of autonomy requires family-determination, presupposes an objective conception of the good, and upholds the value of harmonious dependence.'[239] Although this may be a stereotypical argument contrasting Western and East Asian principles of autonomy, it reflects part of the truth regarding the different approaches to autonomy in the two jurisdictions.[240]

Given the divergence in traditions and local customs between West and East Asia, it is possible that measures adopted in West Asia may not always be well received or applicable in the East Asian context. There is a growing trend in East Asia toward a preference for human relationships over legal documents. This is evidenced by the relatively low uptake of adult guardianship systems, both statutory and enduring powers of attorney. This suggests that a separate set of considerations may be required in East Asia, distinct from those typically applied in the West.

It is essential to consider the cognitive processes and behavioral patterns of individuals to identify effective methods of communication. This aspect presents a significant challenge. Although the distinctive thoughts and behavioral patterns of East Asians are typically perceived as a subjective impression, the underlying mechanisms remain inadequately elucidated within academic disciplines such as medicine, anthropology and psychology. These characteristics are typically grouped under the umbrella term 'culture.' Prior research has discussed people's

---

[237.] Refers to Section 4.2.2 (3), 'Dispute Response Mechanism.'

[238.] Ibid.

[239.] Ruiping Fan, 'Self-Determination vs. Family-Determination: Two Incommensurable Principles of Autonomy' (1997) 11(3/4) *Bioethics* 309–22, 309.

[240.] Emiko Ochiai, 'Why Does the "Japanese-style Welfare Regime" Remain Familial? 4. Comments on the Report' (2015) 27(1) *Japanese Journal of Family Sociology* 61, 68 (in Japanese).

'legal consciousness' in general terms, but specific legal policies derived from this understanding have yet to be established.[241]

From the Japanese perspective, it would be ideal to establish an adult support and protection framework rooted in Japanese identity. How can such a goal be achieved? Japanese society must consider how the relationship between vulnerability and autonomy should be balanced in the Japanese context, adopting measures informed by the advocacy dimension of the modified multidimensional model while taking into account the Japanese principle of autonomy.

In other words, Japanese people should determine, by their own accord, whether informal arrangements, legal and policy measures, or a combination of the two, would best suit their needs. They must also consider which law and policy measures should be adopted, to what extent vulnerable adults should be protected, and to what extent their individual autonomy should be secured. Through such deliberations, the Japanese principle of autonomy can be clarified.[242] In any case, the balancing point between vulnerability and autonomy in Japan will remain a central issue for discussion. It can be said that no single general principle exists regarding this balance; rather, each case must be examined individually, considering the specific person and the specific situation. Another important point of discussion concerns how relational autonomy can complement individual autonomy in the Japanese context.[243]

It is natural that legislative developments differ among countries. During the opening address at the Fourth World Congress on Adult Guardianship in Berlin in 2016, Adrian D. Ward of Scotland stated: 'We should not start with a concept which is at best one answer, and an uncertain one, until we have formulated the question, and the destination for which—for each individual—we may want to find the most appropriate vehicle.'[244] The important perspective

---

[241.] Yukio Sakurai, 'Adaptation of Law and Policy in an Aged Society: Guardianship Law and People's Behavioral Pattern' (2023) 13(2) *The Rest: The Journal of Politics and Development* 144–54.

[242.] Hang Wu Tang, a scholar in Singapore, raises a question whether the Singapore's *Mental Capacity Act 2008*, respecting individual autonomy, suits Singaporeans, considering their local culture, namely 'the family functions as the primary unit of care for persons who lack capacity and vulnerable persons.' The article reviews the process of how Singapore's *Mental Capacity Act 2008* was adapted and fine-tuned to operate in a jurisdiction with different culture conditions, religions, familial norms, and social institutions. Hang Wu Tang states that 'adult guardianship law is a particularly complex and challenging area of law to transport from a foreign jurisdiction because it operates at the crossroads of familial, social, cultural, and religious context.' Hang Wu Tang, 'Singapore's Adult Guardianship Law and the Role of the Family in Medical Decision-Making' (2022) 36(1) *International Journal of Law, Policy and the Family* 1–21, 3.

[243.] Refers to Section 2.3.1 (2) b, 'Relational Autonomy.'

[244.] Adrian D. Ward, 'Legal Protection of Adults—An International Comparison' (Opening Address to the Fourth World Congress on Adult Guardianship held at Erkner near Berlin on September 14–17, 2016) 16(10) *The Journal* <https://www.lawscot.org.uk/members/journal/issues/vol-61-issue-10/legal-protection-of-adults-an-international-comparison/>.

is not the law itself as a vehicle, but rather the establishment of an effective legal framework that citizens find satisfactory in practice. This perspective, initially applied to adult guardianship law, can also be extended to adult support and protection legislation. Behind every piece of legislation lies a value framework—often invisible—that must suit the specific needs of the people it serves.

In this chapter, the universal values embedded in the Australian framework and the CRPD framework have been discussed in relation to Japan's adult support and protection framework. From the perspective of value frameworks in both Japan and Australia, it can be observed that international consensus on legal principles has been nearly achieved through the CRPD, representing a set of universal values. In this regard, it can be said that Japan's adult support and protection legislative system is based on a combination of these universal values, as stipulated in the Australian and CRPD frameworks, and legal and policy measures adapted to the specific needs of Japanese society. Therefore, while the focus of discussion within the modified multidimensional model, particularly regarding support and protection measures in community support, is on Japan, the essence of the discussion is relevant for global application, sharing the universal values.

5.4 Summary: Japan's Adult Support and Protection Legislation Framework

Chapter 5 examined the potential development of Japan's adult support and protection legislative framework, drawing on the legal principles and policy implications from the Australian case discussed in Chapter 4.

First, the chapter reviewed the role and legal status of a core agency—a community-based institution intended to promote the adult guardianship system. The proposal suggests expanding its function to encompass adult support and protection more broadly. Such an agency should be accessible to older adults with impaired decision-making capacity, the family court, and municipal author-ities. Regardless of its organizational form, the core agency should function as a public institution, maintaining strict confidentiality in information-sharing with the court and local governments. Aggregated data collected by the agency could contribute to evidence-based policymaking, especially in addressing informal arrangements and SDM cases. From the user's perspective, the core agency should serve as a multifunctional support center, clearly offering accessible information on available community-based services, including monitoring networks, welfare support, informal arrangements, SDM, and guardianship services.

Second, the chapter compared legal models in Australia, Europe, and Japan, focusing on the integration of guardianship and SDM in responding to the needs of adults with reduced capacity. While each country shares the values enshrined in the CRPD and adheres to democratic processes, legislative and policy responses diverge. Compared with the more advanced Victorian and Alzheimer Europe models, the Japanese model shows room for improvement. In particular, Japan lacks sufficient safeguards for SDM, which is susceptible to undue influence. This divergence may stem from differing interpretations of CRPD Article 12. Japan's Ministry of Justice maintains that its guardianship system does not conflict with the CRPD, a view that may explain the absence of significant legislative reform in this area.

Third, the chapter proposed a preliminary legal concept for SDM in Japan, envisioning it as a standalone statute applied to relevant parties without legal compulsion. Instead, the law could offer incentives for voluntary participation in community-based support systems. Agreements—formal or informal—would be voluntarily registered with the core agency. The agency's role could evolve from simply offering consultation services to also conducting monitoring and supervision if delegated such authority by local governments. This study highlights the importance of revising SDM guidelines to incorporate accumulated practice-based knowledge, with the aim of clarifying the legal definition of SDM, standardizing operational methods, and developing appropriate safeguards—drawing on the experience of Victoria's decade-long implementation.

Fourth, the chapter presented a conceptual design for an adult support and protection framework in Japan and discussed the principles underpinning relevant legislation and policy. It emphasized the functional interactions between the core agency and community members, arguing that meaningful civic participation is critical for effective community-based support. The active involvement of civil society is therefore essential to institutionalizing this framework.

Fifth, the chapter articulated a value-based framework for Japan's adult support and protection system, using a modified multidimensional model. This model comprises four operational dimensions—reactive, proactive, assistance, and advocacy—anchored by a central axis of legal principles. These dimensions are mapped onto two intersecting axes: autonomy versus protection (horizontal), and personal versus social (vertical). The vulnerability approach serves as the normative foundation of this model. Accordingly, Japan's legislative and policy framework is understood as an integration of universal values—such as those reflected in the CRPD and Australian legal reform—and context-specific legal and policy measures that respond to Japan's unique socio-cultural landscape. While the framework is focused on Japan, its foundational principles may have broader relevance in addressing global challenges in adult protection.

Conclusion

This study has explored the potential for adult support and protection legislation to function as an integrated legal framework encompassing adult guardianship, supported decision-making, and elder abuse prevention—particularly in light of the limitations of Japan's existing adult guardianship system. Drawing on legal theory and comparative analysis, the study sought to clarify the concept of legal advocacy for vulnerable adults, positioned at the intersection of civil law and social security law, and employed a dual analytical framework combining the vulnerability—autonomy approach and a comparative legal examination of Japan and Australia. The central research question posed was: 'what is the structure and significance of adult support and protection legislation that respects the will and preferences of vulnerable adults with diminished mental capacity, and how can such a framework be effectively realized within a community-based support system?' To address this, five sub-questions were examined across individual chapters, and a legislative and policy framework—along with an operational model of community-based support—was elaborated through comparative analysis.

Three primary conclusions were drawn from the study.

First, the research confirmed the importance of establishing a legal framework that respects individuals' will and preferences. Chapter 2, building on the vulnerability–autonomy approach, emphasized that a capacity-based model of rights limitation, as codified in Japan's Civil Code, is no longer sufficient. Vulnerable adults at risk of harm require legal and policy-based support grounded in their dignity and autonomy. Internationally, the Convention on the Rights of Persons with Disabilities (CRPD) has influenced a paradigm shift away from guardianship systems and toward supported decision-making. Chapter 3 demonstrated that various countries are moving to curtail the use of guardianship while institutionalizing support measures aligned with their cultural and legal traditions. These reforms are underpinned by common normative principles such as 'necessity' and the 'least restrictive alternative.' Adult support and protection legislation, understood as a rights-based framework for legal advocacy, supports individuals through diverse legal options that prioritize their expressed will and preferences, while tailoring restrictions according to necessity and proportionality.

Second, the study emphasized the importance of constructing social norms to facilitate the implementation of supported decision-making, while reserving guardianship as a measure of last resort. Chapters 4 and 5 examined this development through a detailed analysis of the Guardianship and Administration Act 2019 (Vic). In the state of Victoria, supported decision-making has been incorporated into the guardianship framework and linked to national elder abuse prevention strategies. Institutional support mechanisms—including specialized tribunals, offices of public advocate, and state trustees—have played an essential role in facilitating this reform. By contrast, Japan's legal model has yet to internalize the CRPD's vision, highlighting the need for systemic transformation. This study presented a legislative proposal for a Japanese supported decision-making law and developed a conceptual model for adult support and protection legislation composed of five functions: reactive, proactive, assistive, advocacy, and normative/legal. These were situated within a framework balancing autonomy and protection, and personal and social dimensions. To advance from soft law (guidelines and pilot projects) to hard law (binding legislation), it is essential to refine supported decision-making mechanisms and promote standardized, legally enforceable practices based on empirical evidence and stakeholder input.

Third, the study clarified the operational foundation necessary for implementing adult support and protection legislation within a community-based support system. Chapters 1 and 5 stressed that legal systems should provide individuals with access to a range of supports beyond guardianship, coordinated through a single point of contact that integrates both social security and civil legal functions. Such systems require core agencies that perform multiple functions, including consultation, monitoring, informal assistance, and formal protective interventions, while maintaining confidentiality and coordinating with courts and municipalities. Depending on municipal delegation, these agencies may also take on oversight responsibilities. Thus, the study delineated the contours of a community-based support model in which core agencies, embedded in local networks, mediate between everyday life and legal protection, ensuring appropriate interventions while respecting autonomy and dignity. It is imperative that community-based support models address contemporary issues, including but not limited to single-living older people's loneliness, asset planning, end-of-life care, and funeral planning.

This research makes three key contributions to the field. First, it introduces a novel legal perspective on adult support and protection legislation—a domain that has remained underdeveloped and insufficiently conceptualized in Japanese legal discourse. By clarifying its definitions, scope, and position at the juncture of civil law and social security law, the study provides a new framework for understanding how to connect and overcome the fragmented systems of adult guardianship, supported decision-making, and elder abuse prevention. Second, the study offers a detailed analysis of the legislative process and content of Victoria's 2019 guardianship reform, drawing on Victorian experience to propose a stepwise legislative pathway for Japan. This includes the formation of social norms through guidelines, followed by the institutionalization of supported decision-making practices and their formal incorporation into law. The Victorian model, with its empirical foundations and integrated approach, serves as a valuable reference point for Japanese reform, which currently lacks a comparable evidence base. Third, the study highlights the critical role of core agencies in the community as the operational cornerstone of adult support and protection legislation. These agencies, positioned at the interface of formal legal systems and informal support networks, are essential for developing integrated, community-based safeguards for vulnerable adults. This dimension of institutional design remains insufficiently explored in Japan and requires further attention.

The uniqueness of this study lies in its presentation of a legislative roadmap for introducing supported decision-making into the Japanese legal system. By combining theoretical insight and comparative legal methodology, the study offers a legislative design that respects individuals' will and preferences, institutionalizes supported decision-making, and confines guardianship to a subsidiary role. The dual approach—grounded in the vulnerability–autonomy theory and comparative analysis with Australia—has not yet been adopted in Japanese legal scholarship or by the Expert Commission on adult guardianship reform. In this respect, the study represents a pioneering attempt to chart a path for legislative development.

Nonetheless, several issues remain to be addressed. First, safeguards for supported decision-making grounded in empirical practice are underdeveloped in Japan. To ensure the safe and effective implementation of such mechanisms, it is necessary to monitor Victoria's legislative developments and institutional practices closely. Second, the study did not explore comparative systems of financial and administrative assistance outside the guardianship framework, such as ombudsman models or representative payee systems. These are particularly relevant to contemporary legal needs and hold potential as supplementary or alternative mechanisms to guardianship. These areas require future comparative legal research to complete the vision of a comprehensive adult support and protection framework.

BIBLIOGRAPHY

A. Articles/Books/Reports Cited in the Text

A

2010 Adult Guardianship World Congress Organizing Committee [ed], *Autonomy and Protection in Adult Guardianship* (Nippon Hyoron Sha Co., Ltd., 2012).

Adult Protective Services (APS; Research and Development Division), *Early Impact of SB 2199 on the Adult Protective Services Program* (Online, 2000) <https://www.cdss.ca.gov/research/res/pdf/dapreports/APS-SB2199.pdf>.

Akanuma, Yasuhiro, 'Adult Guardian's Duties and Limitations' (2015) 1406 *Hanrei Times* 5, 15 (in Japanese).

Akimoto, Miyo, 'Support and Autonomy in Advocacy' (2004) 4 *Social Policy Research* 26, 50 (in Japanese).

Akimoto, Miyo and Atsushi Hirata, *Social Welfare and Advocacy: Theory and Practice for Human Rights* (Yuhikaku Publishing Co., Ltd., 2015) (in Japanese).

Alston, Bruce, 'Towards Supported Decision-Making: Article 12 of the Convention on the Rights of Persons with Disabilities and Guardianship Law Reform' (2017) 35 *Law in Context* 21, 43. https://doi.org/10.26826/law-in-context.v35i2.10.

Alwang, Jeffrey, Paul B. Siegel and Steen L. Jorgensen, 'Vulnerability: A View from Different Disciplines' (Social Protection Discussion Papers and Notes 23304, The World Bank, 2001).

Alzheimer Europe, *Legal Capacity and Decision Making: The Ethical Implications of Lack of Legal Capacity on the Lives of People with Dementia* (Alzheimer Europe, 2021) <https://www.alzheimer-europe.org/Ethics/Ethical-issues-in-practice/2020-Ethical-issues-linked-to-legal-capacity-and-decision-making-full-report>.

Anetzberger, Georgia J. and Morgan R. Thurston, 'Addressing Guardianship Abuse: The Roles of Adult Protective Services, Law Enforcement, and the Courts' (Conference Paper at the Fourth National Guardianship Summit in New York on May 10–14, 2021) <https://lawreview.syr.edu/wp-content/uploads/2022/09/369-421-Thurston-2.pdf>.

Aoki, Hitomi, 'Function of the Subsidiarity Principle in the Adult Guardianship System' (2016) 8 *Bulletin of Waseda University Institute of Advanced Study* 5, 25 (in Japanese).

———, 'From Representation to Support: A Consideration of Austrian Law Reform (1)' (2019) 26(1) *Toin Law Review* 53, 81 (in Japanese).

———, 'From Representation to Support: A Consideration of Austrian Law Reform (2)' (2020) 26(2) *Toin Law Review* 59, 75 (in Japanese).

Arai, Makoto, 'Construction of the Adult Guardianship Law System: What We Learn from the Comparison of the German Adult Guardianship Law and Japan's Adult Guardianship System' (2010) 33 *Practices of the Adult Guardianship* 5, 6.

———, 'The Convention on the Rights of Persons with Disabilities and the Adult Guardianship Law—The Tiger of the Front Gate, the Wolf of the Rear Gate' (2013) 28(1 and 2) *Chiba University Law Collection* 29, 61 (in Japanese).

———, 'Continuing Power of Attorney and Trusts' (2015) 8 *Journal of International Aging Law & Policy* 149, 176 <https://www.stetson.edu/law/agingjournal/media/JIALP-VOL8-FULL.pdf>.

———, 'Enactment of Act of Promotion of Adult Guardian System and Prospects for the Adult Guardian System' (2017) 1 *Disability Law* 51, 76 (in Japanese).

———, 'The Meaning of Personal Protection in Adult Guardianship and Its Memorandum: Considering International Trends' (2019) 79 *Adult Guardianship Practices* 4, 14 (in Japanese).

———, 'Japan Adult Guardianship Laws: Development and Reform Initiatives' in Lusina Ho and Rebecca Lee (eds), *Special Needs Financial Planning: A Comparative Perspective* (Cambridge University Press, English Edition, 2019) 61, 86.

———, 'The Adult Guardianship System Talks ⑮, III Enactment of the Adult Guardianship System Utilization Promotion Act, 3 Basic Plan Interim Verification Report' (2021) 2124 *Periodicals* 60, 64 (in Japanese)

———, *Formation and Development of the Adult Guardianship System* (Yuhikaku Publishing Co., Ltd., 2021) (in Japanese).

Arai, Makoto and Akira Homma, 'Guardianship for Adults in Japan: Legal Reforms and Advances in Practice' (2005) 24 *Australasian Journal on Ageing* 19, 24. <https://doi.org/10.1111/j.1741-6612.2005.00094.x>.

Arstein-Kerslake, Anna et al, 'Future Direction Is Supported Decision-Making' (2017) 37(1) *Disability Studies Quarterly* (Online) <https://dsq-sds.org/article/id/360/><https://doi.org/10.18061/dsq.v37i1.5070>.

Asagumo, Anri, 'Relational Autonomy, the Right to Reject Treatment, and Advance Directives in Japan' (2022) 14 *Asian Bioethics Review* 57–69 <https://doi.org/10.1007/s41649-021-00191-1>.

Asai, Atsushi, Taketoshi Okita and Seiji Bito, 'Discussions on Present Japanese Psychocultural-Social Tendencies as Obstacles to Clinical Shared Decision-Making in Japan' (2022) 14(2) *Asian Bioethics Review* 133–50 <https://doi.org/10.1007/s41649-021-00201-2>.

Ashida, Jun, 'Australian Intergovernmental Council: Method of Federal and State Government Coordination' (September 2018) 277 *Foreign Legislation* 77, 91 (in Japanese) <https://www.ndl.go.jp/jp/diet/publication/legis/2018/index.html>.

Australian Government, Attorney-General's Department, *National Register of Enduring Powers of Attorney: Public Consultation Paper* (Attorney-General's Department, April 2021) <https://www.ag.gov.au/rights-and-protections/consultations/national-register-enduring-powers-attorney>.

Australian Guardianship and Administration Council (AGAC), *Australian Adult Guardianship Orders 2023/24* (Report on Adult Guardianship and Ad-ministration/Financial Management Applications and New Orders, Web Page, February 2025) <https://www.agac.org.au/assets/images/AGAC-Guardian-ship_orders_Report-2023-2024_2025-03-03-021515.pdf>.

Australian Law Reform Commission (ALRC), *Equality, Capacity and Dis-ability in Commonwealth Laws Final Report* (ALRC Report No. 124, 2014) <https://www.agac.org.au/assets/images/AGAC-Guardianship_orders_Re-port-2023-2024_2025-03-03-021515.pdf> <https://www.alrc.gov.au/publication/equality-capacity-and-disability-in-commonwealth-laws-alrc-report-124/>

——, *Elder Abuse—A National Legal Response Final Report* (ALRC Report No. 131, 2017) <https://www.alrc.gov.au/publication/elder-abuse-a-national-legal-response-alrc-report-131/>.

Austrian Federal Ministry of Constitutional Affairs, Reforms, Deregulation and Justice, The Adult Protection Law. (Brochure in English, 2018) .

B

Bach, Michael and Lana Kerzner, *A New Paradigm for Protecting Autonomy, and the Right to Legal Capacity: Advancing Substantive Equality for Persons with Disabilities through Law, Policy and Practice* (The Report Commissioned by The Law Commission of Ontario, 2010) <https://supporteddecisionmaking. org/research_library/a-new-paradigm-for-protecting-autonomy-and-the-right-to-legal-capacity/>.

――――, *Supported Decision Making: A Roadmap for Reform in Newfoundland & Labrador Final Report* (Institute for Research and Development on Inclusion and Society (IRIS), 2020) <https://irisinstitute.ca/resource/supported-decision-making-a-roadmap-for-reform-in-newfoundland-labrador-final-report/>.

Bannistera, Emma Wynne and Sridhar Venkatapuram, 'Grounding the Right to Live in the Community (CRPD Article 19) in the Capabilities Approach to Social Justice' (Online, 2020) 69 *International Journal of Law and Psychiatry* 101551 <https://doi.org/10.1016/j.ijlp.2020.101551>.

Barry, Lise and Patrick Hughes, 'The New Serious Incident Response Scheme and the Responsive Regulation of Abuse in Aged Care' (2022) 29(1) *Journal of Law and Medicine* 465, 480 <https://pubmed.ncbi.nlm.nih.gov/35819386/>.

Barry, Lise and Susannah Sage-Jacobson, 'Human Rights, Older People and Decision Making in Australia' (2015) 9 *Elder Law Review* 1, 21 <https://ssrn. com/abstract=2717855>.

Barth, Peter, 'Reform of the Austrian Sachwalter Law' (Conference Material at the 4th WCAG2016 in Berlin in September 2016) <https://www.wcag2016. de/plenum-panels-arbeitsgruppen.html?L=1>.

Bartlett, Peter, 'At the Interface between Paradigms: English Mental Capacity Law and the CRPD' (2020) 11 *Frontiers in Psychiatry* 570735 <https://doi. org/10.3389/fpsyt.2020.570735>.

Beauchamp, Tom and James Childress, 'Principles of Biomedical Ethics: Marking Its Fortieth Anniversary' (2019) 19(11) *The American Journal of Bioethics* 9–12 <https://doi.org/10.1080/15265161.2019.1665402>.

Beaupert, Fleur, Linda Steele and Piers Gooding, 'Introduction to Disability, Rights and Law Reform in Australia: Pushing beyond Legal Future' in Fleur Beaupert, Linda Steele, and Piers Gooding (eds), *Disability, Rights and Law Reform in Australia* (The Federation Press, 2017) 1–14<https://doi.org/10.26826/law-in-context.v35i2.5>.

Bechyne, Gabrielle, 'Supported Decision-Making Agreements in Texas' (2020) 13(31) *Estate Planning and Community Property Law Journal* 311, 351 <https://ttu-ir.tdl.org/server/api/core/bitstreams/48260a9b-8d7c-4a61-a983-618830297444/content><https://hdl.handle.net/2346/89664>.

Bedford, Daniel, 'Vulnerability Refigured' in Daniel Bedford and Jonathan Herring (eds), *Embracing Vulnerability: The Challenges and Implications for Law* (Routledge, 2020) <https://doi.org/10.4324/9781351105705>.

Bedson, Lois, John Chesterman and Michael Woods, 'The Prevalence of Elder Abuse among Adult Guardianship Clients' (2018) 18 *Macquarie Law Journal* 15, 34 <http://classic.austlii.edu.au/au/journals/MqLawJl/2018/3.html>.

Benjamin, P. Davis and Eric Aldieri, 'Precarity and Resistance: A Critique of Martha Fineman's Vulnerability Theory' (2021) *Hypatia* 1, 17 <https://doi.org/10.1017/hyp.2021.25>.

Bigby, Christine and Jacinta Douglas, 'Supported Decision Making' in R. J. Stancliffe et al (eds), *Choice, Preference, and Disability: Promoting Self-Determination across the Lifespan* (Springer, 2020) 45, 66 <https://doi.org/10.1007/978-3-030-35683-5_3>.

Bigby, Christine et al, 'Delivering Decision Making Support to People with Cognitive Disability—What Has Been Learned from Pilot Programs in Australia from 2010 to 2015' (2017) 52 *Australian Journal of Social Issues* 222, 240 <https://doi.org/10.1002/ajs4.19>.

———, *Diversity, Dignity, Equity and Best Practice: A Framework for Supported Decision-Making* (Royal Commission into Violence, Abuse, Neglect and Exploitation of People with Disability, January 24, 2023) <https://disability.royalcommission.gov.au/publications/diversity-dignity-equity-and-best-practice-framework-supported-decision-making>.

Blake, Meredith et al, 'Supported Decision—Making for People Living with Dementia: An Examination of Four Australian Guardianship Laws' (2021) 28(2) *Journal of Law and Medicine* 389, 420 <https://pubmed.ncbi.nlm.nih.gov/33768748/>.

Boni-Saenz, Alexander A., 'Legal Age' (2022) 63(2/3) *Boston College Law Review* 521, 569 <https://ssrn.com/abstract=3949829>.

Bottomley, Steve, 'Mental Health Law Reform and Psychiatric Deinstitution-alization: The Issues in New South Wales' (1987) 10 *International Journal of Law and Psychiatry* 369, 362. <https://doi.org/10.1016/0160-2527(87)90019-7>

Boyle, Sam, 'Determining Capacity: How Beneficence Can Operate in an Autonomy-Focused Legal Regime' (2018) 26(1) *The Elder Law Journal* 35, 63 <https://theelderlawjournal.com/wp-content/uploads/2018/06/Boyle.pdf>.

Braun, Joan, 'Legal Interventions to Protect Vulnerable Adults: Can Relational Autonomy Provide a New Way Forward?' (2020) 12(2) *Elder Law Review* (Online) <https://ssrn.com/abstract=3698472>.

Brayley, John, 'Supported Decision-Making in Australia' (Conference Paper, Victorian Office of the Public Advocate, December 14, 2009)

———, 'Developing a Model of Practice for Supported Decision Making' (Office of the Public Advocate, South Australia: In Collaboration with the Julia Farr MS McLeod Benevolent Fund, 2011).

Brophy, Lisa et al, 'Community Treatment Orders and Supported Decision-Making' 10 *Frontiers in Psychiatry* Article 414 <PMCID: PMC6580382>.

Brosey, Dagmar, 'Court-Appointed Legal Representatives (Betreuer) in Germany: Quality Requirements and Their Implementation' (Conference Paper at 5th WCAG in Seoul in October 2018)

———, 'Aspects of the Reform of the German Legislation of Betreuung: Support and Representation of Adults Regarding to Legal Capacity in the German Law Reform' (American Bar Association, *Voice of Experience*, October 2021)<https://www.americanbar.org/groups/senior_lawyers/resources/voice-of-experience/2010-2022/aspects-reform-german-legislation-betreuung/>.

Brown, Hilary, 'The Role of Emotion in Decision-Making' (2011) 13(4) *The Journal of Adult Protection* 194, 202 <https://doi.org/10.1108/14668201111177932>.

Browning, Michelle, Christine Bigby and Jacinta Douglas, 'Supported Decision Making: Understanding How Its Conceptual Link to Legal Capacity Is Influencing the Development of Practice' (2014) 1(1) *Research and Practice in Intellectual and Developmental Disabilities* 34, 45 <https://doi.org/10.1080/23297018.2014.902726>.

————, 'A Process of Decision-Making Support: Exploring Supported Decision-Making Practice in Canada' (2020) *Journal of Intellectual & Developmental Disability* 138–49 <https://doi.org/10.3109/13668250.2020.1789269>.

Bryan, A. Liang and Fusako Seki, 'Protecting the Elderly: Policy Lessons from an Analysis of Japan and USA Approaches' (2009) 18(2) *Yokohama Law Review* 1, 37 <http://hdl.handle.net/10131/7026>.

Bryant, J. et al, 'Advance Care Planning Participation by People with Dementia: A Cross-Sectional Survey and Medical' (2021) *BMJ Supportive & Palliative Care* 1, 5 <https://doi.org/10.1136/bmjspcare-2020-002550>.

Burnett, Jason et al, 'Addressing Senior Financial Abuse: Adult Protective Services and Other Community Resources' in Ronan M. Factora (ed), *Aging and Money: Reducing Risk of Financial Exploitation and Protecting Financial Resources* (2nd ed, Springer, 2021) <https://doi.org/10.1007/978-3-030-67565-3>.

Burns, Fiona R., 'Elders and Testamentary Undue Influence in Australia' (2005) 28(1) *UNSW Law Journal* 145, 185 <http://www.austlii.edu.au/au/journals/UNSWLJ/2005/8.html>.

C

Carney, Terry, 'The Limits and the Social Legacy of Guardianship in Australia' (1898) 18(4) *Federal Law Review* 231, 266 <https://doi.org/10.1177/0067205X8901800403>.

————, 'Challenges to the Australian Guardianship and Administration Model' (2003) 2 *Elder Law Review* <http://classic.austlii.edu.au/au/journals/ElderLawRw/2003/8.html>.

————, 'Aged Capacity and Substitute Decision-Making in Australia and Japan' (2003) 2003/2004 *LAWASIA Journal* 1, 21 <https://search.informit.org/doi/10.3316/agispt.20050629>.

————, 'Guardianship, "Social" Citizenship and Theorising Substitute Decision-Making Law' in Israel Doron and Ann M. Soden (eds), *Beyond Elder Law: New Directions in Law and Aging* (Springer Science & Business Media, 2012) 1–17 <https://link.springer.com/chapter/10.1007/978-3-642-25972-2_1>.

————, 'Searching for Workable Alternatives to Guardianship for Vulnerable Populations?' (2015) 1(1) *Ethics, Medicine and Public Health* 113, 119 <http://doi.org/10.1016/j.jemep.2015.03.004>.

————, 'Prioritising Supported Decision-Making: Running on Empty or a Basis for Glacial-to-Steady Progress?' (2017) 6(4) *Laws* 6, 18 <https://doi.org/10.3390/laws6040018>.

————, 'Australian Guardianship Tribunals: An Adequate Response to CRPD Disability Rights Recognition and Protection of the Vulnerable over the Life Course?' (2017) 10(3) *Journal of Ethics in Mental Health* 1, 18 <https://ssrn.com/abstract=3011089>.

————, 'Supported Decision-Making in Australia: Meeting the Challenge of Moving from Capacity to Capacity-Building?' (2017) 35(2) *Disability, Rights and Law Reform in Australia* 44, 63 <https://www.latrobe.edu.au/lids/documents/SDM-LiDs-LTU-Roundtable-2016-Terry-Carney-Capacity-to-capacity-building.pdf>.

————, 'Vulnerability: False Hope for Vulnerable Social Security Clients?' (2018) 41(3) *The University of New South Wales Law Journal* 783, 817 (And Sydney Law School Research Paper No. 18/66) <https://ssrn.com/abstract=3266951>.

————, 'People with Dementia and Other Cognitive Disabilities: Relationally Vulnerable or a Source of Agency and Care?' (Online, 2020) 12(1) *Elder Law Review* <https://ssrn.com/abstract=3561294>.

————, 'Combating Elder Abuse: Any Role for Supported-Decision-Making, Adult Guardianship or Other Laws?' in Mala Kapur Shankardass (ed), *Combating Elder Abuse in Australia and India* (Nova Science Publishers, 2020) <https://ssrn.com/abstract=3805372>.

Carney, Terry and Peter Singer, 'Ethical and Legal Issues in Guardianship Options for Intellectually Disadvantaged People' (Australian Government Publishing Service, Human Rights Commission 3 Monograph Series No. 2, 1986) <https://humanrights.gov.au/__data/assets/file/0020/51482/Guardianship_for_intellectually_disadvantaged_people.pdf>.

Carney, Terry and David Tait, *The Adult Guardianship: Experiment Tribunals and Popular Justice* (The Federation Press, 1997).

Carney, Terry and Shih-Ning Then, 'Combating Elder Abuse: Any Role for Supported-Decision-Making, Adult Guardianship or Other Laws?' in Michelle Putnam and Christine Bigby (eds), *Handbook Ageing and Disability* (Routledge, 2021) <https://doi.org/10.4324/9780429465352>.

Carney, Terry et al, 'Realising "Will, Preferences and Rights": Reconciling Differences on Best Practice Support for Decision-Making?' (Online 2019) *Griffith Law Review* <https://doi.org/10.1080/10383441.2019.1690741>.

———, 'Paternalism to Empowerment: All in the Eye of the Beholder?' (2021) 38(3) *Disability & Society* 1, 21 <https://doi.org/10.1080/09687599.2021.1941781>.

Carolyn, Johnston and Jane Liddle, 'The Mental Capacity Act 2005: A New Framework for Healthcare Decision Making' (2007) 33(2) *Journal of Medical Ethics* 94–7 <https://doi.org/10.1136/jme.2006.016972>.

Carroll, Robyn and Anita Smith, 'Mediation in Guardianship Proceedings for the Elderly: An Australian Perspective' (2010) 28(1) *The Windsor Yearbook of Access to Justice* 53, 80 <https://ssrn.com/abstract=1817822>.

Castles, Margaret, 'A Critical Commentary on the 2017 ALRC Elder Abuse Report: Looking for an Ethical Baseline for Lawyers' (2018) 18 *Macquarie Law Journal* 115, 130 <https://www.mq.edu.au/__data/assets/pdf_file/0004/866308/Macquarie-Law-Journal_-Volume-18,-2018.pdf>.

Chamberlain, Stephanie et al, 'Going It Alone: A Scoping Review of Unbefriended Older Adults' (2018) 37(1) *Canadian Journal on Aging = La revue canadienne du vieillissement* 1, 11 <https://doi.org/10.1017/S0714980817000563>.

Chau, P.-L. and Jonathan Herring (eds), 'Sickness' in *Emergent Medicine and the Law* (Palgrave Macmillan, 2021) 195–210 <https://doi.org/10.1007/978-3-030-60208-6_6>.

Chen, Ben, 'Elder Financial Abuse: Capacity Law and Economics' (2020) 106 *Cornell Law Review* 1457, 1538 <https://ssrn.com/abstract=3710237>.

Chesterman, John, *Responding to Violence, Abuse, Exploitation and Neglect: Improving Our Protection of At-Risk Adults* (Report for Winston Churchill Memorial Trust of Australia, 2013) <https://www.churchilltrust.com.au/media/fellows/Chesterman_John_2012_Report.pdf>.

———, 'The Future of Adult Guardianship in Federal Australia' (2013) 66(1) *Australian Social Work* 26, 38 <https://doi.org/10.1080/0312407X.2012.715657>.

———, 'Modernising Adult Protection in an Age of Choice' (2014) 73(4) *Australian Journal of Public Administration* 517, 524 <https://doi.org/10.1111/1467-8500.12103>.

———, 'Supported Decision-Making' in Sue Field, Karen Williams and Carolyn Sappideen (eds), *Elder Law: A Guide to Working with Older Australians* (The Federation Press, 2018) 96–108.

———, 'Adult Guardianship and Its Alternatives in Australia' in Claire Spivakovsky, Kate Seear and Adrian Carter (eds), *Critical Perspectives on Coercive Interventions* (Routledge, 2018) 225–35 <https://doi.org/10.4324/9781315158693-19>.

———, 'The Future of Adult Safeguarding in Australia' (2019) 54(4) *Australian Journal of Social Issues* 360, 370 <https://doi.org/10.1002/ajs4.86>.

———, '"The Abuse of Older Australians (Elder Abuse)": Reform Activity and Imperatives' (2019) 73(3) *Australian Social Work* 381, 389 <https://doi.org/10.1080/0312407X.2019.1680715>.

———, 'Adult Safeguarding in Australia after the Disability Royal Commission' (2024) 11(1) *Research and Practice in Intellectual and Developmental Disabilities* 53–62 <https://doi.org/10.1080/23297018.2024.2316291>.

Chesterman, John and Lois Bedson, *Decision Time: Activating the Rights of Adults with Cognitive Disability* (Victorian OPA Report, March 1, 2021) <https://www.churchilltrust.com.au/fellow/john-chesterman-vic-2012/>.

Clough, Beverley, 'Disability and Vulnerability: Challenging the Capacity/Incapacity Binary' (2017) 16(3) *Social Policy and Society* 469, 481 <https://doi.org/10.1017/S1474746417000069>.

Cocks, Errol and Gordon Duffy, *The Nature and Purposes of Advocacy for People with Disabilities* (Edith Cowan University Publications, 1993/2011) <https://ro.ecu.edu.au/ecuworks/7172>.

Coleman, Thomas F., *Supported Decision-Making: My Transformation from a Curious Skeptic to an Enthusiastic Advocate* (Online, 2017) <https://tomcoleman.us/publications/sdm-essay-2017.pdf>.

Collingburn, Leanne and Deni Jokovic-Wroe, *Update on Elder Abuse and Coercive Control in Australia* (Web Page, June 13, 2024) <https://www.hopgoodganim.com.au/news-insights/update-on-elder-abuse-and-coercive-control-in-australia/>.

Commonwealth Attorney-General's Department, *The National Principles to Address Coercive Control in Family and Domestic Violence* (Web Page, March 5, 2024) <https://www.ag.gov.au/families-and-marriage/publications/national-principles-address-coercive-control-family-and-domestic-violence>.

Constantino, Renato, 'The Flag of Imagination: Peru's New Reform on Legal Capacity for Persons with Intellectual and Psychosocial Disabilities and the Need for New Understandings in Private Law' (2020) 14 *The Age of Human Rights Journal* 155, 180 <https://doi.org/10.17561/tahrj.v14.5482>.

Croucher, Rosalind F., 'Modelling Supported Decision Making in Commonwealth Laws—The ALRC's 2014 Report and Making It Work' (Conference Paper of AGAC in Sydney in October 18, 2016) <https://www.alrc.gov.au/news/modelling-supported-decision-making-in-commonwealth-laws-the-alrcs-2014-report-and-making-it-work/>.

———, 'Confronting Words: Driving a New Legal Lexicon of Disability' (2017) 35 *Law Context: A Socio-Legal Journal* 15, 20 <https://search.informit.org/toc/lic/35/2>.

———, 'Law Reform Agencies and Government: Independence, Survival and Effective Law Reform' (2018) 43(1) *University of Western Australia Law Review* 78, 91 <https://classic.austlii.edu.au/au/journals/UWALawRw/2018/5.html>.

Croucher, Rosalind F. and Julie MacKenzie, 'Framing Law Reform to Address Elder Abuse' (2018) 18 *Macquarie Law Journal* 5, 14 <https://www.mq.edu.au/__data/assets/pdf_file/0004/866308/Macquarie-Law-Journal_-Volume-18,-2018.pdf>.

Cukalevski, Emily, 'Supporting Choice and Control—An Analysis of the Approach Taken to Legal Capacity in Australia's National Disability Insurance Scheme' (2019) 8(2) *Disability Human Rights Law* 1, 19 <https://doi.org/10.3390/laws8020008>.

D

Dabove, Maria Isolina, 'Autonomy, Self-Determination, and Human Rights: Legal Safeguards in Argentina to Prevent Elder Abuse and Neglect' (2018) 32 *International Journal of Law, Policy and the Family* 80, 92 <https://doi.org/10.1093/lawfam/ebx017>.

Davidson, G. et al, 'An International Comparison of Legal Frameworks for Supported and Substituted Decision-Making in Mental Health Services' (2016) 44 *International Journal of Law and Psychiatry* 30, 40 <https://doi.org/10.1016/j.ijlp.2015.08.029>.

Davis, Benjamin P. and Eric Aldieri, 'Precarity and Resistance: A Critique of Martha Fineman's Vulnerability Theory' (2021) *Hypatia* 1, 17 <https://doi.org/10.1017/hyp.2021.25>.

Deane, Stephen, 'Elder Financial Exploitation: Why It Is a Concern, What Regulators Are Doing about It, and Looking Ahead' (U.S. Securities and Exchange

Commission/Office of the Investor Advocate, 2018) <https://www.sec.gov/files/elder-financial-exploitation.pdf>.

Degener, Thresia, 'A Huma Rights Model of Disability' in Peter Blanck and Eilionóir Flynn (eds), *Handbook of Disability Law and Human Rights* (Routledge, 2016) 31–49 <https://www.researchgate.net/publication/283713863_A_human_rights_model_of_disability>.

Delgado, Janet, 'Re-Thinking Relational Autonomy: Challenging the Triumph of Autonomy through Vulnerability' (2019) 5 *BIoethics Update* 50, 65 <https://doi.org/10.1016/j.bioet.2018.12.001>.

Diller, Rebekah and Leslie Salzman, 'Stripped of Funds, Stripped of Rights: A Critique of Guardianship as a Remedy for Elder Financial Harm' (2021) 24(2) *University of Pennsylvania Journal of Law and Social Change* 149, 194 <https://scholarship.law.upenn.edu/jlasc/vol24/iss2/2/>.

Dixon, Jeremy et al, 'Safeguarding People Living with Dementia: How Social Workers Can Use Supported Decision-Making Strategies to Support the Human Rights of Individuals During Adult Safeguarding Enquiries' (2021) 52(3) *The British Journal of Social Work* 1, 18 <https://doi.org/10.1093/bjsw/bcab119>.

Donnelly, Mary, *Healthcare Decision-Making and the Law—Autonomy, Capacity and the Limits of Liberalism* (Cambridge University Press, 2010) <https://doi.org/10.1017/CBO9780511760679>.

———, 'Dementia: A Legal Overview' in Charles Foster, Jonathan Herring and Israel Doron (eds), *The Law and Ethics of Dementia* (Hart Publishing, 2014) 271, 283 <https://www.bloomsbury.com/uk/law-and-ethics-of-dementia-9781782254300/>.

———, 'Best Interests in the Mental Capacity Act: Time to Say Goodbye?' (2016) 24(3) *Medical Law Review* 318, 332 <https://doi.org/10.1093/medlaw/fww030>.

———, 'Changing Values and Growing Expectations' (2017) 70(1) *Current Legal Problems* 305, 336 <https://doi.org/10.1093/clp/cux007>.

———, 'Deciding in Dementia: The Possibilities and Limits of Supported Decision-Making' (2019) 66 *International Journal of Law and Psychiatry* 101466 <https://doi.org/10.1016/j.ijlp.2019.101466>.

Donnelly, Mary and Caoimhe Gleeson, 'The Assisted Decision-Making (Capacity) Act 2015 in the Courts: Hearing the Voice of the Relevant Person' (2024) 8(2) *Irish Judicial Studies Journal* 47–66 <https://hdl.handle.net/10468/16849>.

Donnelly, Mary, Rosie Harding and Ezgi Tascioglu (eds), *Supporting Legal Capacity in Socio-Legal Context* (Hart Publishing, 2022) <https://www.bloomsbury.com/uk/supporting-legal-capacity-in-sociolegal-context-9781509940356/>.

Donnelly, Sarah and Marita O'Brien, 'Adult Safeguarding Legislation—The Key to Addressing Dualism of Agency and Structure? An Exploration of How Irish Social Workers Protect Adults at Risk in the Absence of Adult Safeguarding Legislation' (2022) 52(6) *The British Journal of Social Work* 3677–96. <https://doi.org/10.1093/bjsw/bcac003>.

Donnelly, Sarah et al, *Adult Safeguarding Legislation and Policy Rapid Realist Literature Review* (Health Service Executive, National Safeguarding Office and Trigraph Ltd., 2017) <http://hdl.handle.net/10197/9183>.

Doron, Israel, 'Elder Guardianship Kaleidoscope–A Comparative Perspective' (2002) 16(3) *International Journal of Law, Policy, and the Family* 368, 398 <https://ssrn.com/abstract=343901>.

———, 'From Elder Guardianship to Long-Term Legal Care: Law and Caring for the Elderly' (2002) Doctoral Dissertation, York University <https://doi.org/10.2139/SSRN.331580>.

———, 'A Multi-Dimensional Model of Elder Law: An Israeli Example' (2003) 28(3) *Ageing International* 242, 259 <https://ssrn.com/abstract=500522>.

———, 'A Multi-Dimensional Model of Elder Law' in I. Doron (ed), *Theories on Law and Ageing* (Springer, 2009) 59–74 <https://doi.org/10.1007/978-3-540-78954-3_5>.

Doron, Israel and Itai Apter, 'The Debate around the Need for an International Convention on the Rights of Older Persons' (2010) 50(5) *Gerontologist* 586–93 <https://doi.org/10.1093/geront/gnq016>.

Douglas, Jacinta and Christine Bigby, 'Development of an Evidence-Based Practice Framework to Guide Decision Making Support for People with Cognitive Impairment' (2020) 42(3) *Disability and Rehabilitation* 434, 441 <https://doi.org/10.1080/09638288.2018.1498546>.

Dow, Briony et al, 'Elder Abuse in Australia' in Mala Kapur Shankardass (ed), *International Handbook of Elder Abuse and Mistreatment* (Springer, 2020) 559–74 <https://doi.org/10.1007/978-981-13-8610-7_30>.

Duckett, Stephen and Anika Stobart, 'From Rationing to Rights: Creating a Universal Entitlement to Aged Care' (2021) 54(2) *The Australian Economic Review* 257, 265 <https://doi.org/10.1111/1467-8462.12424>.

Dunn, Michael C., Isabel C. H. Clare and Anthony J. Holland, 'To Empower or to Protect? Constructing the "Vulnerable Adult" in English Law and Public Policy' (2008) 28(2) *Legal Studies* 234, 253 <https://doi.org/10.1111/j.1748-121X.2008.00085.x>.

———, 'Living "a Life Like Ours"': Support Workers' Accounts of Substitute Decision-Making in Residential Care Homes for Adults with Intellectual Disabilities' (2010) 54(2) *Journal of Intellectual Disability Research* 144, 160 <https://doi.org/10.1111/j.1365-2788.2009.01228.x>.

Dworkin, Gerald, 'The Nature of Autonomy' (2015) 2015(2) *Nordic Journal of Studies in Educational Policy* Article 28479 <https://doi.org/10.3402/nstep.v1.28479>.

———, 'Paternalism' in Edward N. Zalta (ed), *The Stanford Encyclopedia of Philosophy* (Online 2020) <https://plato.stanford.edu/archives/fall2020/entries/paternalism/>.

E

Elwyn, Glyn et al, 'Shared Decision Making: A Model for Clinical Practice' (2012) 27(10) *Journal of General Internal Medicine* 1361–7 <https://doi.org/10.1007/s11606-012-2077-6>.

Enomoto, Hiroaki, 'Psychology of the Elderly' (2006) 70 *Japanese Journal of Research on Household Economics* 28, 37 (in Japanese) <http://kakeiken.org/journal/jjrhe/70/070_04.pdf>.

European Law Institute (ELI), 'European Commission's Public Consultation on the Initiative on the Cross-Border Protection of Vulnerable Adults: C. Inclusion of a Conflicts Rule on Ex Lege Powers of Representation' (2022) 17–18 <https://www.europeanlawinstitute.eu/fileadmin/user_upload/p_eli/Publications/ELI_Response_Protection_of_Adults.pdf>.

European Parliamentary Research Service (EPRS), *Protection of Vulnerable Adults—European Added Value Assessment* (Online, November 11, 2016) <https://doi.org/10.2861/664256>.

F

Fan, Ruiping, 'Self-Determination vs. Family-Determination: Two Incommensurable Principles of Autonomy' (1997) 11(3/4) *Bioethics* 309, 322 <https://doi.org/10.1111/1467-8519.00070>.

Field, Sue, Karen Williams and Carolyn Sappideen (eds), *Elder Law: A Guide to Working with Older Australians* (The Federation Press, 2018).

Fineman, Martha Albertson, *The Autonomy Myth: A Theory of Dependency* (The New Press, 2004).

——, 'The Vulnerable Subject: Anchoring Equality in the Human Condition' (2008) 20(1) *Yale Journal of Law & Feminism* 1, 23 <https://ssrn.com/abstract=1131407><https://openyls.law.yale.edu/entities/publication/9b33ed26-20b0-44b9-b256-b6e71242c661>.

——, '"Elderly" as Vulnerable: Rethinking the Nature of Individual and Societal Responsibility' (2012) 20 *Elder Law Journal* 71, 112 <https://papers.ssrn.com/sol3/papers.cfm?abstract_id=2088159>.

——, 'Introducing Vulnerability' in Martha Albertson Fineman and Jonathan W. Fineman (eds), *Vulnerability and the Legal Organization of Work* (Routledge, 2017) 1, 10 <https://doi.org/10.4324/9781315518572>.

——, 'Vulnerability and Inevitable Inequality' (2017) 4 *Oslo Law Review* 133, 149 <https://papers.ssrn.com/sol3/papers.cfm?abstract_id=3087441>.

——, 'Beyond Equality and Discrimination' (2020) 73 *SMU Law Review Forum* 51, 62 <https://doi.org/10.25172/slrf.73.1.7>.

——, 'Populations, Pandemics, and Politics' (2021) 21(3) *International Journal of Discrimination and the Law* 184, 190 <https://doi.org/10.1177/13582291211042212>.

Flavin, Theresa, 'Supported Decision Making for People Living with Dementia' (2020) 19(1) *Dementia* 95, 97 <https://doi.org/10.1177/1471301219876712>.

Fleming, Daniel J., and David J. Carter, *Voluntary Assisted Dying: Law? Health? Justice?* (ANU Press, 2022) <https://www.jstor.org/stable/j.ctv2bks5f6>.

FINRA, 'Addressing and Reporting Financial Exploitation of Senior and Vulnerable Investors.' (Web Page, June 2023). <https://www.finra.org/sites/default/files/2023-05/NASAA-SEC-FINRA-Training-Senior-Investor-Protection-June2023.pdf>.

FL-EUR, 'Country Reports and Questionnaire: Legal Protection and Empowerment of Vulnerable Adults' (n.d.) <https://fl-eur.eu/working_field_1__empowerment_and_protection/country-reports>.

Flynn, Eilionoir, *From Rhetoric to Action* (Cambridge University Press, 2013).

Frolik, Lawrence A., 'The Developing Field of Elder Law Redux: Ten Years after' (2002) 10 *The Elder Law Journal* 1, 14 <https://ssrn.com/abstract=1348080>.

———, 'How to Avoid Guardianship for Your Clients and Yourself!' (Social Science Research Network Electronic Paper Collection) (Online, 2013) <https://papers.ssrn.com/sol3/papers.cfm?abstract_id=2314589>.

Frolik, Lawrence and Alison Barnes, *Elder Law: Cases and Materials* (6th ed, LexisNexsis, 2015).

Fukuda, Tomoko, 'Incapacity Planning Used by Revocable Living Trust: Proposal on Estate Planning for Incapacitated People' (2018) 47 *Bulletin of Graduate Studies of Law, Chuo University* 23, 39 (in Japanese) <https://chuo-u.repo.nii.ac.jp/records/9214>.

———, 'Implications of Austrian New Adult Guardianship System' in Akihisa Shibuya et al (eds), *Practice and Promotion of Adult Guardianship and Civil Trust* (Nihon Kajo Publishing Co., Ltd., 2021) 465–77 (in Japanese)

G

Gamble, Keith Jacks et al, *The Causes and Consequences of Financial Fraud among Older Americans* (Boston College Center for Retirement Research, 2014) <http://crr.bc.edu/wp-content/uploads/2014/11/wp_2014-13.pdf>.

Ganner, Michael Ludwig, 'Austrian Guardianship Law—Status 2016 and Upcoming Reform' (Conference Paper at WCAG2016 in Berlin in September 2016) .

———, *Umfrage zum Erwachsenenschutzgesetzin* (Adult Protection Law Survey) (Web Page, University of Innsbruck, 2018) (in German) <https://www.uibk.ac.at/rtf/>.

———, 'The New Austrian Adult Protection Law of 2018.' (2020) 41 JULGAR 175–98 <https://julgar.pt/wp-content/uploads/2020/05/JULGAR41-08-MG.pdf>

————, 'Annotation of the German New Care Act' (2021) 15 *Quarterly Journal of Comparative Guardianship Law* 3, 12 (in Japanese, translated into Japanese by editor).

Gasparini1, Marina et al, 'The Evaluation of Capacity in Dementia: Ethical Constraints and Best Practice: A Systematic Review' (2021) 57(3) *Annali dell'Istituto Superiore di Sanità* 212, 225 <https://doi.org/10.4415 /ANN_21_03_04>.

Gilman, Laura, *Adults with Incapacity* (The Scottish Parliament, SPICe Briefing, January 2022) <https://www.parliament.scot/chamber-and-committees/ research-prepared-for-parliament/research-briefings/2022/1/11/sb-2202#dp30840>.

Glen, Kristin Booth, 'Supported Decision Making from Theory to Practice: Further Reflections on an Intentional Pilot Project' (2020) 13(1) *Albany Government Law Review* 24018 <https://www.albanygovernmentlawreview.org/ article/24018-supported-decision-making-from-theory-to-practice-further-re-flections-on-an-intentional-pilot-project>.

Godfrey, David, 'Challenges in Guardianship and Guardianship Abuse' (2021) 42(4) *Bifocal* 84, 86.

————, 'Using Alternatives to Guardianship to Defend against or Terminate Guardianship' (2021) <https://svlas.org/wp-content/uploads/2022/06/Alterna-tives-to-Guardianship-Ch-Summary-1.pdf>.

Gómez-Vírseda, Carlos, Yves de Maeseneer, and Chris Gastmans, 'Relational Autonomy: What Does It Mean and How Is It Used in End-of-Life Care? A Systematic Review of Argument-Based Ethics Literature' (2019) *BMC Medical Ethics* 76, 91 <https://doi.org/10.1186/s12910-019-0417-3>.

Gooding, Piers Michael, 'Supported Decision-Making: A Rights-Based Disability Concept and Its Implications for Mental Health Law' (2012) 20(3) *Psychiatry, Psychology and Law* 431, 451 <https://doi.org/10.1080/13218719.2012.71168 3><https://ssrn.com/abstract=2274478>

————, 'South Australian Supported Decision-Making Training: Adelaide' (National Resource Center for Supported Decision-Making, March 5, 2016) <https://supporteddecisionmaking.org/resource_library/ south-australian-supported-decision-making-training-adelaide-2/>.

Gooding, Piers Michael and Terry Carney A. O., 'Australia: Lessons from a Reformist Path to Supported Decision-Making' in Michael Bach and Nicolás Espejo Yaksic (eds), *Legal Capacity, Disability and Human Rights: Towards a*

Comprehensive Approach (Supreme Court of Mexico, Human Rights Division, 2021) <https://ssrn.com/abstract=3928342>.

Gordon, Robert M., 'The Emergence of Assisted (Supported) Decision-Making in the Canadian Law of Adult Guardianship and Substitute Decision-Making' (2000) 23(1) *International Journal of Law and Psychiatry* 61, 77 <https://doi.org/10.1016/S0160-2527(99)00034-5>.

———, 'Adult Protection Legislation in Canada: Models, Issues, and Problems' (2001) 24(2–3) *International Journal of Law and Psychiatry* 117, 134 <https://doi.org/10.1016/s0160-2527(00)00078-9>.

Gratton, Lynda and Andrew Scot (translated by Chiaki Ikemura), *The 100-Year Life: Living and Working in an Age of Longevity* (Toyokeizai-Shinposha, 2017) (in Japanese).

Gutterman, Alan, 'Convention on Human Rights of Older Persons' (June 29, 2021) <https://ssrn.com/abstract=3876618>.

H

Hall, Margaret Isabel, 'Mental Capacity in the (Civil) Law: Capacity, Autonomy and Vulnerability' (2012) 58(1) *McGill Law Journal* 1, 35 <https://ssrn.com/abstract=2083249>.

———, 'Relational Autonomy, Vulnerability Theory, Older Adults and the Law: Making It Real' (Online, 2020) 12 *Elder Law Review* <https://ssrn.com/abstract=5276084>.

———, 'Law and Dementia: Family Context and the Experience of Dementia in Old Age' in Beverley Clough and Jonathan Herring (eds), *Disability, Care and Family Law* (Routledge, 2021) 203–29 <https://doi.org/10.4324/9780429328015>.

Hamano, Ryo, 'Access to Justice in a Super Aging Society: Structure and Reform' (2020) 103 *Rikkyo Law Review* 129, 184 <https://doi.org/10.14992/00020214> (in Japanese).

Hansen, Kevin et al, 'Criminal and Adult Protection Financial Exploitation Laws in the United States: How Do the Statutes Measure Up to Existing Research?'

(2016) 42(3) *Mitchell Hamline Law Review* Article 3 <https://open.mitchell-hamline.edu/mhlr/vol42/iss3/3>.

Harada, Atsuko, 'American Law on the Prevention of Elderly Abuse: Elderly Abuse Prevention and Prosecution Law 2017' (2018) 276 *Foreign Legislation* 1, 20 <https://dl.ndl.go.jp/info:ndljp/pid/11100067> (in Japanese).

Harada, Keiichiro, 'Legal Evaluation of Community-Based Integrated Care System' (Special Feature: Reexamination of Laws and Policies Supporting Social Security: 1st Social Security Law Forum) (2019) 10 *Social Security Law Research* 91, 118 (in Japanese).

Harada, Masaki, 'Comprehensive Support System and Community-Based Welfare Plan: Conversion to Community-Based Welfare Administration' (Conference Paper at Japan Community Welfare Society 2017 Public Research Forum).

Harding, Rosie and Ezgi Taşcıoğlu, 'Supported Decision-Making from Theory to Practice: Implementing the Right to Enjoy Legal Capacity' (2018) 8(2) *Societies* 25, 42 <https://doi.org/10.3390/soc8020025>.

Haruna, Mitsu, 'Present Situations on the Responses of Care Managers to the Case of Elder Abuse: Issues Extracted from a Questionnaire Survey at Care Managers and Community General Support Centers' (2020) 28 *Hanazono University Faculty of Sociology Research Bulletin* 11, 19 (in Japanese) <https://cir.nii.ac.jp/crid/1050285299747707648?lang=en>.

———, 'Practice of Abuse Discovery and Report of Care Manager' (2021) 29 *Hanazono University Faculty of Sociology Research Bulletin* 1, 8 (in Japanese)

Hasuo, Hiroyuki, 'The Structure of <Autonomy> in Kant's Moral Philosophy: New Possibilities through Practice of "Duty of Love"' (2010) 6 *Civilization Structure Theory* 15, 34 <http://hdl.handle.net/2433/126713> (in Japanese).

Hayakawa, Seisuke, 'Caring and Vulnerable Agency' (2014) 3 *Studies on Action Theory* 1, 10 <https://actiontheories.wordpress.com/wp-content/uploads/2014/05/studies_on_action_theory_3_hayakawa.pdf>.

Hayashi, Maho and Naoyasu Obara, 'The Current Situation and Issues of Making Decisions for People Who Lack Capacity: Based on the Survey of Mental Capacity Act 2005' (2019) 60 *Memoirs of Beppu University* 89, 101 <https://ci.nii.ac.jp/naid/120006649818/>.

Herring, Jonathan, 'Relational Autonomy and Rape' in S. Day Sclater et al (eds), *Regulating Autonomy* (Oxford Legal Studies Research Paper No. 12, Hart Publishing, 2010) <https://ssrn.com/abstract=1551858>.

————, 'Elder Abuse: A Human Rights Agenda for the Future' in Israel Doron and Ann M. Soden (eds), *Beyond Elder Law: New Directions in Law and Aging* (Springer Science & Business Media, 2012) 175–97.

————, 'The Disability Critique of Care' (2014) 8 *Elder Law Review* Article 2 <http://classic.austlii.edu.au/au/journals/ElderLawRw/2014/2.html>.

————, *Vulnerable Adults and the Law* (Oxford University Press, 2016) <https://global.oup.com/academic/product/vulnerable-adults-and-the-law-9780198737278?cc=jp&lang=en&>.

————, *Legal Ethics* (2nd ed, Oxford University Press, 2016)

————, 'Compassion, Ethics of Care and Legal Rights' (2017) 13(2) *International Journal of Law in Context* 158, 171 <https://doi.org/10.1017/S174455231700009X>.

————, 'Ethics of Care and Disability Rights: Complementary or Contradictory?' in Loraine Gelsthorpe, Perveez Mody and Brian Sloan (eds), *Spaces of Care* (Hart Publishing, 2020) 165–82 <https://doi.org/10.5040/9781509929665.ch-009>.

Herring, Jonathan and Jesse Wall, 'Autonomy, Capacity and Vulnerable Adults: Filling the Gaps in the Mental Capacity Act' (2015) 35(4) *Legal Studies* 698, 719 <https://doi.org/10.1111/lest.12094>.

Higuchi, Norio, *Thinking about Medicine and Law* (in Japanese) (Yuhikaku Publishing Co. Ltd., 2007).

————, 'Legal Issues on Medical Interventions in Terminally Ill Patients' (2015) 25(1) *Medical Care and Society* 21, 34 (in Japanese) <https://doi.org/10.4091/iken.25.21>.

————, 'Elder Abuse and Responsibilities of Professionals' (2018) 8 *Journal of Law and Political Science* 134, 102

————, 'Current Status and Challenges of End-of-Life Care Legal Issues' (2020) 2(5) *Geriatrics* 579–84, 581 (in Japanese).

Higuchi, Norio and Fusako Seki (eds), *Elder Law: Legal Basics for a Super-Aged Society* (Tokyo University Press, 2019) (in Japanese).

Hirata, Atsushi, 'What Is Advocacy? Focusing on the Adult Guardianship System' (Lecture Paper at the Seminar on Social Welfare Sponsored by Public Interest Incorporated Foundation in Tokyo 23-City in November 12, 2010) (in Japanese) <https://www.tokyo-23city.or.jp/jigyo/kikaku/koza/h_22/221029.html>.

————, 'Issues and Challenges in the Elderly Abuse Prevention Act' (2010) 1411 *Monthly Jurist* 116, 121 (in Japanese).

————, *Advocacy and Welfare Practice Activities: Re-Questioning Concepts and Systems* (Akashi Shoten, 2012) (in Japanese).

————, 'The Ability to Make Decisions or to Judge Something' (2021) 24 *Meiji Law School Review* 1, 24 <https://meiji.repo.nii.ac.jp/records/11530> <http://hdl.handle.net/10291/21761> (in Japanese).

————, 'Current Status and Issues of Support Program for Self-Reliance in Daily Life Projects from the Perspective of Advocacy' (2021) *2021 Advocacy and Abuse Prevention* 28, 31 (in Japanese).

————, 'How to Protect the Rights of the Elderly' (2021) October 2021 *Monthly Welfare* 33, 38 (in Japanese).

Holmes, Alice L. et al, 'Integrity in Guardianship Decision Making: Applying the Will and Preferences Paradigm' (2022) 23(7) *Journal of the American Medical Directors Association* 1, 8 <https://doi.org/10.1016/j.jamda.2022.01.050>.

Honkasalo, Marja-Liisa, 'Vulnerability and Inquiring into Relationality' (2018) 43(3) *Suomen Antropologi (Journal of the Finnish Anthropological Society)* 1, 21 <https://journal.fi/suomenantropologi/issue/view/5645>.

Hopgood, Stephen, Jack Snyder and Leslie Vinjamuri, *Human Rights Futures* (Cambridge University Press, Reprint, 2018).

Hoshino, Eiichi, 'Adult Guardianship System and Legislative Process–Ask Professor Eiichi Hoshino' (2000) 1172 *Jurist* 2, 16 (in Japanese).

Ibrahim, Joseph E. and Marie-Claire Davis, 'Impediments to Applying the "Dignity of Risk" Principle in Residential Aged Care Services' (2013) 32(3) *Australasian Journal on Ageing* 188, 193 <https://doi.org/10.1111/ajag.12014>.

Ikeya, Hisao, 'Bioethics and Vulnerability' (2016) 10 *The Bulletin of Ryotokuji University* 105, 128 (in Japanese) <https://cir.nii.ac.jp/crid/1390009224760396928>.

Ikka, Tsusnakuni, 'Reconsideration of Hospital Ethics Committee' (2013) 23(1) *Bioethics* 23–30 (in Japanese).

Imura, Fumie, 'Reviewing the Adult Guardianship System from the Standpoint of Its Users' (2016) 4 *Bulletin of Rikkyo University Community Welfare Research Institute* 149, 169.

Inaba, Kazuto, 'Healthcare Decision-Making: Patients, Families, and Representatives in the Terminal Stage' (2003) 2(2) *Medicine, Life, Ethics, and Society.* Accessed March 27, 2025 (in Japanese) <https://www.med.osaka-u.ac.jp/pub/eth/OJ_files/OJ2-2/inaba.htm> (in Japanese).

Ishibashi, Toshiro, 'Advocacy Services and the Social Security Law' in Akira Moriyama and Nobuyuki Koike (eds), *Realization of Citizen's Guardianship* (Nihon Kajo Publishing Co., Ltd., 2014) 231, 299 (in Japanese).

———, 'The Community Comprehensive Care System, Mutual-Aid Society and the Academic Sphere of Social Security Law' (2019) 68 *Bulletin of the Faculty of Education Kumamoto University* 163, 171 (in Japanese).

Ishibashi, Toshiro et al, 'Development of a System to Support the Elderly, People with Disability, and People Living in Poverty in the Community' (2019) 26(1) *Administration* 1, 48 (in Japanese).

Ishiwata, Kazumi, 'Tsukui Yamayurien Incident and Supported-Decision Making: Community Life of People with Severe Disabilities' (2021) 17 *Journal of the Graduate of Toyo Eiwa University* 1, 12 (in Japanese).

Iwama, Nobuyuki, 'Adult Guardianship System and Social Welfare: Exploring New Possibilities from the Point of Contact' (2011) 627 *The Journal of Ohara Institute for Social Research* 19, 29 (in Japanese).

Iwashi, Kazuichiro, 'Autonomy and Protection of the Elderly in Germany' (2013) 85(7) [1061] *The Horitsu Jiho* 26, 32 (in Japanese).

Iwata, Futoshi, 'The Role of the Law in the Medical Care and Care of the Elderly in Australia: Focusing on the Recent Amendments to Victoria State Law' (2019) 80(1) *Comparative Law Research* 42, 55 (in Japanese).

Iyengar, Sheena and Mark R. Lepper, 'When Choice Is Demotivating: Can One Desire Too Much of a Good Thing?' (2000) 79(6) *Journal of Personality and Social Psychology* 995, 1006 <https://doi.org/10.1037//0022-3514.79.6.995>.

J

James, Krista, *Legal Definitions of Elder Abuse and Neglect* (Department of Justice Canada, 2019) <https://www.justice.gc.ca/eng/rp-pr/cj-jp/fv-vf/elder-aines/def/p4.html>. Modified on December 8, 2021.

James, Krista and Laura Watts, 'Understanding the Lived Experiences of Supported Decision-Making in Canada: Legal Capacity, Decision-Making and Guardianship' (Study Paper, Canadian Center for Elder Law (CCEL) Commissioned by the Law Commission of Ontario, March 2014) <https://www.bcli.org/project/understanding-lived-experience-supported-decision-making>.

Japan Federation of Bar Associations, *German Notary System Survey Report* (Japan Federation of Bar Associations, Consumer Affairs Committee, 2004) <http://yuigon.us/german.html> (in Japanese).

———, *From Adult Guardianship System to Supported Decision-Making— Aiming to Realize the Right to Self-Determination of People with Dementia and Disabilities* (No. 2 Subcommittee Keynote Report at the 58th Human Rights Protection Convention Symposium, Japan Federation of Bar Associations, 2015) (in Japanese).

Johnston, J. M. and Robert A. Sherman, 'Applying the Least Restrictive Alternative Principle to Treatment Decisions: A Legal and Behavioral Analysis' (1993) 16(1) *The Behavior Analyst* 103, 115 <https://doi.org/10.1007/bf03392615>.

Joosten, Melanie et al, *Seven Years of Elder Abuse Data in Victoria (2012–2019)* (National Ageing Research Institute in Partnership with Seniors Rights Victoria, 2020) <https://www.nari.net.au/elder-abuse-in-victoria>.

K

Kaljian, Diane, *Public Guardian and Collaboration in Three Countries: Models of Adult Protective Services* (Online, 2016) <https://mackcenter.berkeley.edu/sites/default/files/aas-2016-05-06/AAS/TOC-AAS-3.pdf>.

Kamiyama, Yasushi, 'Introduction of Public Adult Guardianship System in Japan: Refer to German Operation Scheme' (2010) 641 *The Journal of Ohara Institute for Social Research* 44, 58 (in Japanese).

———, 'Evaluation of Adult Guardianship System in International Monitoring of the Convention on the Rights of Persons with Disabilities' (2015) 2851 *Weekly Social Security* 48, 53 (in Japanese).

———, *Professional Guardian and Protection of Personal Affairs* (3rd ed, Civil Law Study Group, 2015) (in Japanese).

———, 'The Issues Based on the Basic Plan for Promoting the Adult Guardianship System' (2018) 20 *Clinical Legal Research* 107, 127 (in Japanese)

———, 'Trends in Uniform Review of Disqualification Clauses for Adult Guardians etc.' (2018) 72 [2975] *Weekly Social Security* 42, 47 (in Japanese).

———, 'Recent Policy Trends Regarding Supported Decision-Making in Japan' (2020) 72(4) [414] *The Doshisha Law Review* 445, 467 <https://doi.org/10.14988/00028092> (in Japanese).

———, 'Memorandum on the Medium to Long-Term Issues of Adult Guardianship: Toward Revision of Adult Guardianship Law' in Nobuhiro Oka et al (eds), *Development in the Civil Code and Trust Law in an Aged Society* (Nippon Hyoron Sha Co., Ltd., 2022) 468–89 (in Japanese).

Kanai, Naomi, 'Human Rights Violation in Private Area and Legal Regulation: Domestic Abuse and Enactment of Abuse Prevention Act' (2009) 30 *Journal of Political Science* 17, 41.

Kaneko, Osamu, 'Scope of Adult Guardianship and Obligation to Custody' (2010) 63(8) *Law Plaza* 9, 17 (in Japanese).

Kanter, Arlene S., 'Let's Try Again: Why the United States Should Ratify the United Nations Convention on the Rights of People with Disabilities' (2019) 35 *Touro Law Review* 301, 343 <https://ssrn.com/abstract=3373259>.

Kapp, Marshall B., 'Future Directions in Public Policy Relating to Elder Abuse' in XinQi Dong (ed), *Elder Abuse* (Springer, 2017) <https://doi.org/10.1007/978-3-319-47504-2>.

Kaspiew, Rae, Rachel Carson and Helen Rhoades, Elder Abuse: Understanding Issues, Frameworks and Responses (Research Report No. 35, Australian Institute of Family Studies, 2016/Correction, November 2, 2018) <https://aifs.gov.au/sites/default/files/rr35-elder-abuse.pdf>.

Kawakami, Mayu, 'Characteristics of Elderly Offenders in Japan—In Comparison with Study on Criminality of Elderly Offenders in the United States—' (2018) 47 *Graduate School Annual Report* 131, 149 (in Japanese) <https://chuo-u.repo.nii.ac.jp/records/9220>.

Kawakubo, Hiroshi, 'Social Security Law in the Light of Adult Guardianship and Advocacy' (2020) 12 *Review of Social Security Law* 3, 22 (in Japanese).

Kawano, Masateru, 'Basic Issues of "Welfare Advocacy in Community"' (1999) 66(2) *Journal of Law and Politics* 55, 84 (in Japanese).

———, 'Disability Law as a "New Social Law"' (2017) (1) *Disability Law* 9, 32 (in Japanese).

Kawashima, Takeyoshi, *Legal Consciousness in Law in Japan* (Iwanami Shoten, Publishers, 1967) (in Japanese).

———, 'The Legal Consciousness of Contract in Japan' (translated by Charles R. Stevens) (1974) 7 *Law in Japan* 1, 21 <https://heinonline.org/HOL/LandingPage?handle=hein.journals/lij7&div=5&id=&page=>.

Kayama, Yoshinori, 'About the Usefulness of the Assessment Sheet Devised by Akashi City: To Distinguish between the Adult Guardianship System and the Support Program for Self-Reliance in Daily Life' (2022) 805 *Hougaku Seminar* 61, 67 (in Japanese).

Kelly, Annemarie M. et al, 'Implementing Guardianship Policies in Special Needs Planning: Five Potential Positives' (2020) 74(6) *Journal of Financial Service Professionals* 49, 63 <https://www.emich.edu/cob/documents/faculty-profiles/guardianship-five-potential-positives.pdf>.

———, 'A 50-State Review of Guardianship Laws: Specific Concerns for Special Needs Planning' (2021) 75(1) *Journal of Financial Service Professionals* 59, 79 <https://www.emich.edu/cob/documents/kelly_2021_234.pdf>.

Khan, Abrahim H., 'Postulating an Affinity: Amartya Sen on Capability and Tagore' (2012) 19(1) *Annals of Neurosciences* 3, 7 <DOI: 10.5214/ans.0972.7531.180402>.

Kiguchi, Emiko, 'Trends in Domestic Discussions on Supported Decision-Making' (2017) 9 *Welfare and Social Development Study* 5, 12 <https://cir.nii.ac.jp/crid/1520572358670147456> (in Japanese).

Kiguchi, Emiko, Masaru Nagawa and Yukio Sakurai, 'Australian Guardianship and National Disability Insurance Scheme: Focusing on Supported Decision-Making Practices in the States of Victoria and New South Wales' (2020) 33 *Journal of Australian Studies* 1, 14 (in Japanese) <https://asaj.main.jp/publish/doc/kenkyu33/Kiguchi-Nagawa-Sakurai.pdf>.

Kikuchi, Yoshimi, *Social Security Law* (2nd ed, Yuhikaku Publishing Co., Ltd., 2014).

————, *Supporting Social Security: Rethinking <Community>* (Iwanami Publishers, 2019).

Killeen, Jan, *Supported Decision-Making: Learning from Australia* (Rights for Persons with Cognitive Disabilities: Learning from Australia, 2016) <https://elder-mediation.com.au/wp_files/wp-content/uploads/2014/03/Supported_Decision-making.pdf>.

Kirkemann, Boesen Jakob and Tomas Martin, *Applying a Rights-Based Approach: An Inspirational Guide for Civil Society* (The Danish Institute for Human Rights, 2007) <https://www.humanrights.dk/publications/applying-rights-based-approach>.

Kobayashi, Hiroshi, 'Creating a Place for Supported Decision-Making through the Transformation of Human Image' 64 *Adult Guardianship Practices* 21, 28 (in Japanese).

Koch, Martina, Esteban Piñeiro and Nathalie Pasche, '"Wir sind ein Dienst, keine Behörde." Multiple institutionelle Logiken in einem Schweizer Jugendamt—Ein ethnografisches Fallbeispiel aus der street-level bureaucracy' ('We Are a Service, Not an Authority': Multiple Institutional Logics in a Swiss Youth Welfare Office: An Ethnographic Case Study from Street-Level Bureaucracy) (2019) 20(2) *Forum: Qualitative Sozialforschung* Article 21 <https://doi.org/10.17169/fqs-20.2.3045>.

Kohn, Nina A., 'Elder Rights: The Next Civil Rights Movement' (2012) 21(2) *Temple Political and Civil Rights Law Review* 321, 328 <https://ssrn.com/abstract=2234106>.

————, 'A Civil Rights Approach to Elder Law' in Israel Doron and Ann Soden (eds), *Beyond Elder Law* (Springer, 2012) 19–34 <https://link.springer.com/chapter/10.1007/978-3-642-25972-2_2>.

————, 'Vulnerability Theory and the Role of Government' (2014) 26 *Yale Journal of Law and Feminism* 1, 27 <https://ssrn.com/abstract=2562737>.

————, 'Legislating Supported Decision-Making' (2021) 58 *Harvard Journal on Legislation* 313, 356 <https://ssrn.com/abstract=3768684>.

Kohn, Nina A. and Jeremy A. Blumenthal, 'A Critical Assessment of Supported Decision-Making for Persons Aging with Intellectual Disabilities' (2014) 7(1, Supplement) *Disability and Health Journal* S40, S43 <https://doi.org/10.1016/j.dhjo.2013.03.005>.

Kohn, Nina A., Jeremy A. Blumenthal and Amy T. Campbell, 'Supported Decision-Making: A Viable Alternative to Guardianship?' (2013) 117(4) *Pennsylvania State Law Review* 1111, 1157 <https://ssrn.com/abstract=2161115>.

Kohn, Nina A. and David English, 'Protective Orders and Limited Guardianships: Legal Tools for Sidelining Plenary Guardianship' (Conference Paper at the Fourth National Guardianship Summit in New York in May 10–14, 2021) <https://ssrn.com/abstract=3921123>.

Kolva, Elissa, Barry Rosenfeld and Rebecca Saracino, 'Assessing the Decision-Making Capacity of Terminally Ill Patients with Cancer' (2018) 26(5) *The American Journal of Geriatric Psychiatry* 523–31 <https://doi.org/10.1016/j.jagp.2017.11.012>.

Komine, Takao, 'Thinking about the 2025 Problem—Part 1: Population Change and the 2025 Problem' (2015) (Speech Delivered at the International Institute for Population Sciences in Tokyo, 2015) <https://www.npi.or.jp/en/research/2016/11/07130823.html>.

Kouy, BunRong, 'On Taiwan Patient Right to Autonomy Act: How Family Stimulates Autonomy' (2019) 67 *Applied Ethics Review* 187–212.

Kurrle, Susan and Gerard Naughtin, 'An Overview of Elder Abuse and Neglect in Australia' (2008) 20(2) *Journal of Elder Abuse & Neglect* 108, 125 <https://doi.org/10.1080/08946560801974521>.

Kusano, Masato, 'Current Status and Future of the Adult Guardianship System from the Perspective of the Family Court' (Special Feature: Practical Problems of the Adult Guardianship System) (2009) 47 *Japan Women's Bar Association Bulletin* 32, 36.

Kyle, Louise, 'Out of the Shadows: A Discussion on Law Reform for the Prevention of Financial Abuse of Older People' (2013) 7 *Elder Law Review* 1, 32 <http://classic.austlii.edu.au/au/journals/ElderLawRw/2013/4.html>.

L

Lacey, Wendy, 'Neglectful to the Point of Cruelty? Elder Abuse and the Rights of Older Persons in Australia' (2014) 36 *Sydney Law Review* 99, 130 <http://classic.austlii.edu.au/au/journals/SydLawRw/2014/4.html>.

Lacey, Wendy, Nicholas Procter and Kay Price, *Closing the Gaps: Enhancing South Australia's Response to the Abuse of Vulnerable Older People* (Office of the Public Advocate in Collaboration with the University of South Australia, 2011) <https://researchprofiles.canberra.edu.au/en/publications/closing-the-gaps-enhancing-south-australias-response-to-the-abuse>.

Lacey, Wendy et al, *Prevalence of Elder Abuse in South Australia: Final Report: Current Data Collection Practices of Key Agencies* (University of South Australia, Department of Health and Ageing (SA), 2017) <https://researchprofiles.canberra.edu.au/en/publications/prevalence-of-elder-abuse-in-south-australia-final-report-current/>.

Largent, Emily A. and Andrew Peterson, 'Supported Decision-Making in the United States and Abroad' (2021) 23(2) *Journal of Health Care Law & Policy* 271, 296 <https://digitalcommons.law.umaryland.edu/jhclp/vol23/iss2/7>.

Le Galès, Catherine and Martine Bungener, 'The Family Accompaniment of Persons with Dementia Seen through the Lens of the Capability Approach' (2019) 18(1) *Dementia* 55, 79 <https://doi.org/10.1177/1471301216657476>.

Leroi, Iracema et al, 'Dementia in "Super-Aged" Japan: Challenges and Solutions' (2018) 8(4) *Neurodegenerative Disease Management* 257–66 <https://doi.org/10.2217/nmt-2018-0007>.

Lewis, Melanie, 'Financial Elder Abuse in a Victorian Context: Now and into the Future' (Conference Paper at the Fourth National Conference on Elder Abuse Held in February 24–25, 2016).

Lewis, Virginia J. et al, 'Addressing Elder Abuse through Integrating Law into Health: What Do Allied Health Professionals at a Community Health Service in Melbourne, Australia, Think?' (2019) 39(2) *Australasian Journal on Ageing* e220, e225 <https://doi.org/10.1111/ajag.12720>.

Lichtenberg, Peter A., 'Financial Exploitation, Financial Capacity, and Alzheimer's Disease' (2016) 71(4) *American Psychologist* 312, 320 <https://www.apa.org/pubs/journals/releases/amp-a0040192.pdf>.

Lindsey, Jaime Tabitha, 'Protecting and Empowering Vulnerable Adults: Mental Capacity Law in Practice' (2018) Doctoral Dissertation, University of Birmingham <http://etheses.bham.ac.uk/id/eprint/8527>.

Lipp, Volker and Julian O. Winn, 'Guardianship and Autonomy: Foes or Friends' (2011) 5 *Journal of International Aging and Policy* 41, 56 <https://www.stetson.edu/law/agingjournal/media/JIALP-VOL5-FULL.pdf>.

Lombard, John and Hope Davidson, 'The Older Person's Experience of Autonomy in Healthcare Decision-Making in Ireland: The Relationship between Law, Policy, and Practice' (2022) 22(4) *Medical Law International* 1, 25 <https://doi.org/10.1177/09685332221109239>.

M

Mackay, Kathryn Jane, 'Adult Support and Protection (Scotland) Act 2007: Reflections on Developing Practice and Present Day Challenges' (2017) 19(4) *Journal of Adult Protection* 187, 198 <https://doi.org/10.1108/JAP-04-2017-0017>.

Mackenzie, Catriona, 'Relational Autonomy, Normative Authority and Perfectionism' (2008) 39 *Journal of Social Philosophy* 512, 533 <https://doi.org/10.1111/j.1467-9833.2008.00440.x>.

———, 'The Importance of Relational Autonomy and Capabilities for an Ethics of Vulnerability' in Catriona Mackenzie, Wendy Rogers and Susan Dodds (eds), *Vulnerability: New Essays in Ethics and Feminist Philosophy (Studies in Feminist Philosophy)* (Oxford University Press, 2014) 33–59 <https://doi.org/10.1093/acprof:oso/9780199316649.003.0002>.

————, 'Three Dimensions of Autonomy: A Relational Analysis' in Andrea Veltman and Mark Piper (eds), *Autonomy, Oppression, and Gender* (Oxford University Press, 2014) 15–41 <https://doi.org/10.1093/acprof:oso/9780199969104.003.0002>.

————, 'Feminist Innovation in Philosophy: Relational Autonomy and Social Justice' (2019) 72 *Women's Studies International Forum* 144–51 <https://doi.org/10.1016/j.wsif.2018.05.003>.

————, 'Vulnerability, Exploitation and Autonomy' in J. F. Childress and M. Quante (eds) *Thick (Concepts of) Autonomy* (Springer, 2022) 175–87 <https://doi.org/10.1007/978-3-030-80991-1_11>.

Maker, Yvette and Bernadette McSherry, 'Regulating Restraint Use in Mental Health and Aged Care Settings: Lessons from the Oakden Scandal' (2019) 44(1) *Alternative Law Journal* 29, 36 <https://doi.org/10.1177/1037969X18817592>.

Mandelstam, Michael, *Safeguarding Vulnerable Adults, and the Law* (Jessica Kingsley Publishers, 2008) <https://uk.jkp.com/products/safeguarding-vulnerable-adults-and-the-law>.

Martin, Wayne Michael et al, 'Towards Compliance with CRPD Art: 12 in Capacity/Incapacity Legislation across the UK' (The Essex Autonomy Project—Three Jurisdictions Report, 2016) <https://doi.org/10.13140/RG.2.2.10734.72002>.

Martinez-Pujalte, Antonio, 'Legal Capacity and Supported Decision-Making: Lessons from Some Recent Legal Reforms' (2019) 8(1) *Laws* 4 <https://doi.org/10.3390/laws8010004>.

Martinis, Jonathan et al, 'State Guardianship Laws and Supported Decision-Making in the United States after *Ross and Ross v. Hatch*: Analysis and Implications for Research, Policy, Education, and Advocacy' (2021) 34(1) *Journal of Disability Policy Studies* 8–16 <https://doi.org/10.1177/10442073211028586>.

Matsushita, Keiko, 'Advocacy by Adult Guardianship System: Establishment of the Significance and Role of Citizen Guardians' (2020) Doctoral Dissertation in Kansai University 1, 96 <https://doi.org/10.32286/00021343> (in Japanese).

Mattsson, Titti and Lottie Giertz, 'Vulnerability, Law, and Dementia: An Interdisciplinary Discussion of Legislation and Practice' (2020) 21(1) *Theoretical Inquiries in Law* 139, 159 <https://doi.org/10.1515/til-2020-0007>.

Mattsson, Titti and Mirjam Katzin, 'Vulnerability and Ageing' in Ann Numhauser-Henning (ed), *Elder Law: Evolving European Perspectives* (Monograph Book, 2017) <https://doi.org/10.4337/9781785369094.00014>.

McCallum, Ronald, *Research Report: The United Nations Convention on the Rights of Persons with Disabilities: An Assessment of Australia's Level of Compliance* (Royal Commission into Violence, Abuse, Neglect and Exploitation of People with Disability, 2020) <https://apo.org.au/node/308792>.

Meier, Philippe, 'The Swiss 2013 Guardianship Law Reform—A Presentation and a First Assessment in the Light of the Convention on the Rights of Persons with Disabilities' (Online 2013) 10 *Elder Law Review* <https://vvv.austlii.edu.au/au/journals/ElderLawRw/2016/3.pdf>.

Menon, Sumytra, 'Some Unresolved Ethical Challenges in Healthcare Decision-Making: Navigating Family Involvement' (2020) 12(1) *Asian Bioethics Review* 27, 36 <https://doi.org/10.1007/s41649-020-00111-9>.

Mikton, Christopher et al, 'Factors Shaping the Global Political Priority of Addressing Elder Abuse: A Qualitative Policy Analysis' (2022) 3(8) *The Lancet Healthy Longevity* e531, e539 <https://doi.org/10.1016/S2666-7568(22)00143-X>.

Minami, Takako, 'Characterization of the Voluntary Assisted Dying Legislation in the Australian State of Victoria' (2018) 28(1) *Bioethics* 40, 48 <https://doi.org/10.20593/jabedit.28.1_40> (in Japanese).

——, 'Issues Surrounding Voluntary Assisted Dying Laws in Australia' (2021) 34 *Journal of Australian Studies* 14, 29 <https://doi.org/10.20764/asaj.34.0_14> (in Japanese)

<https://www.jstage.jst.go.jp/article/asaj/34/0/34_14/_article/-char/en>.>.

Ministry of Justice of Japan, Civil Affairs Bureau Counselor's Office, *Commentary on Proposal Overview for Revision of Adult Guardianship System* (Kinzai Institute for Financial Affairs, Inc., 1998) (in Japanese).

Miwa, Madoka, 'The Concept of "Partnership" from Legal Perspective' (2015) 8 *Bulletin of Nanzan University 'Academia' Social Sciences* 99, 114 <https://doi.org/10.15119/00000497> (in Japanese).

——, 'Supervision of Guardianship' (2017) 12 *Bulletin of Nanzan University 'Academia' Social Sciences* 91, 111 <https://doi.org/10.15119/00001022> (in Japanese).

Miyazaki, Kazunori, 'Structural Analysis of "Basic Laws"' (2017) 5 *Public Policy Shibayashi* 43, 57.

Mizuho Information & Research Institute, Inc., *Survey Results on Management Support of Deposits and Savings, Property for People with Dementia* (Web Page, May 19, 2017) (in Japanese) <https://www.shojihomu.or.jp/list/seinenkoken>.

Mizuno, Noriko, 'Obligation of the Adult Guardian to Personal Protection' (Online, 2001) <http://www.law.tohoku.ac.jp/~parenoir/shinjou-kango.html> (in Japanese).

Mizushima, Toshihiko, 'Issues and Responses to Practice the Guidelines for Adult Guardians Based on Supported Decision-Making' (2021) (92) *Adult Guardianship Practices* 23, 31 (in Japanese).

———, 'Mission of the Guidelines for Adult Guardians Based on Supported Decision-Making' (2021) (142) *Social Welfare Research* 45, 54 (in Japanese).

———, 'Points of Supported Decision-Making Measures in the Second Term Basic Plan on for Promoting the Adult Guardianship System' (2022) 2022(2) *Law Plaza* 45, 49 (in Japanese).

Moir, Emily et al, 'Best Practice for Estimating Elder Abuse Prevalence in Australia: Moving towards the Dynamic Concept of "Adults at Risk" and away from Arbitrary Age Cut-Offs' (2017) 29(2) *Current Issues in Criminal Justice* 181, 190 <https://doi.org/10.1080/10345329.2017.12036095>.

Montgomery, Lorna et al, 'Implications of Divergences in Adult Protection Legislation' (2016) 18(3) *Journal of Adult Protection* 1, 16 <https://doi.org/10.1108/JAP-10-2015-0032>.

Morita, Tatsuya et al, 'Relational Autonomy in Advanced Care Planning' (2020) 30(5) *Palliative Care* 399, 402 (in Japanese).

Muramatsu, Naoko and Hiroko Akiyama, 'Japan: Super-Aging Society Preparing for the Future' (2011) 51(4) *The Gerontologist* 425, 432 <https://doi.org/10.1093/geront/gnr067>.

Murata, Akira, 'Thinking about "Mental Capacity": Attention to Be Paid to Defining "Mental Capacity"' (2016) 66(3) *Meijo Law Review* 183, 227 <http://law.meijo-u.ac.jp/staff/contents/66-3/660308_murata.pdf> (in Japanese).

Mutoh, Katsuhiro, 'Efficiency of the Diet Deliberation and the Representative System: How Should the Diet Deliberation Be Changed?: Report of the Hokkaido University Legislative Process Study Group' (2016) 66(5) *Hokkaido University Law Review* 186, 161 (in Japanese).

N

Nagano, Nobuko and Atsushi Ozawa, 'The Situation and Problems of the Guardianship Activities of Citizen Guardians: A Qualitative Analysis of Open-Ended Statements in the Questionnaire' (2021) 62(1) *Japanese Journal of Social Welfare* 52, 68 <https://doi.org/10.24469/jssw.62.1_52>.

Nagase, Osamu, 'The First Review of the Japan Report and Parallel Reports' (2021) 461 *New Normalization* (in Japanese) <https://www.dinf.ne.jp/d/2/424.html>.

Nagata, Yu, 'Progress and Issues of "Participation of Citizens" in Social Welfare' (2015) 123 *Social Welfare Studies* 19, 27 (in Japanese) <https://ci.nii.ac.jp/naid/40020549546>.

Nagawa, Masaru, 'Supported Decision-Making, Adult Guardianship System, and Guidelines (Draft) (Special Feature: Concepts of Decision-Making Support for Persons with Disabilities and Its Application to Adult Guardianship)' (2016) 64 *Adult Guardian Practices* 36, 44 (in Japanese).

Nakamura, Kyoko, 'A Study about on the Definition of "Elder Abuse" and the Help of Our Country: Suggestion from a British Legal System' (2014) Doctoral Dissertation, Kumamoto Gakuen University (in Japanese) <https://ci.nii.ac.jp/naid/500000919699>.

Nakamura, Masafumi, Asuka Okada and Chizuko Fujita, 'Review on "Cooperation" and "Collaboration" in the Field of Clinical Psychology: Focusing on the Differences of Their Definitions and Concepts' (2013) 7 *Journal of Graduate School of Human Science, Kagoshima Jyunshin University* 1, 13 <https://kjunshin.repo.nii.ac.jp/records/101> (in Japanese).

Nakayama, Shigeki, 'Consent and Intimate Relationships in Medical Care: From the Constitutional Perspective of "Respect for the Individual" (1)' (2024) 58(3) *Sendai Law Review* 269–96 <http://hdl.handle.net/10965/0002000266> (in Japanese).

National Adult Protective Services Association (NAPSA), *Adult Protective Services Recommended Minimum Program Standards* (NAPSA, 2013) <https://www.napsa-now.org/wp-content/uploads/2014/04/Recommended-Program-Standards.pdf>.

National Seniors Australia, *Scams and Financial Abuse Update: Snapshots from National Seniors Australia* (National Seniors Australia, 2022) <https://a.storyblok. com/f/119877/x/3849faa500/national-seniors-australia-2022-scams-and-financial-abuse-update-report.pdf>.

New South Wales Law Reform Commission (NSW LRC), *Review of the Guardianship Act 1987* (NSW LRC Report 145, 2018) <https://lawreform.nsw.gov.au/completed-projects/recent/guardianship/report-145.html>.

New South Wales Ombudsman, *Abuse and Neglect of Vulnerable Adults in NSW—The Need for Action* (NSW Ombudsman Report, 2018) <https://www.ombo.nsw.gov.au/reports/report-to-parliament/abuse-and-neglect-of-vulnerable-adults-in-nsw-the-need-for-action-2-november-2018>.

Ní Shé, Éidín et al, '"What Bothers Me Most Is the Disparity between the Choices That People Have or Don't Have": A Qualitative Study on the Health Systems Responsiveness to Implementing the Assisted Decision-Making (Capacity) Act in Ireland' (2020) 17(9) *International Journal of Environmental Research and Public Health* 3294, 3307 <https://doi.org/10.3390/ijerph17093294>.

Nishida, Kazuhiro, 'Procedures for Advocating and Relieving Social Security Rights' in Japan Society for Social Security Law (ed), *Social Security Law in the 21st Century* (Lecture, Social Security Law, Volume 1) (Horitsu Bunka Sha, 2001) 167, 193 (in Japanese).

——, 'Trends in Welfare Legislation on Guardianship and Responsibility and Role of Public: Based on Australian Law' (2015) 2636 *Weekly Social Security* 46, 51 (in Japanese).

Nishimori, Toshiki, 'Purpose of the Corporate Guardianship System from the Perspective of the Legislative Process-Focusing on the Deliberation of the Adult Guardianship Subcommittee-' (2013) 22(2) *Yokohama Law Review* 231, 255 (in Japanese).

Nishimura, Jun, 'Legal System of the Personal Social Services in Terms of Participation Support' (2018) 15(1) *Journal of Kanagawa University of Human Services* 1, 13 (in Japanese).

————, 'The Concept of Social Security and Philosophy of Reform' (2019) 3023 *Weekly Social Security* 48, 53 (in Japanese).

————, 'Legal Analysis of the Process of Social Service Provision: Tentative Study for Social Work Law' (2020) 14 *Annals of Public Policy* 119, 135 (in Japanese).

————, 'Ethics of Care and Social Security Law: For the Conversion from the Benefit-Centered Law to the Support-Centered Law' (2021) 18(1) *Journal of Kanagawa University of Human Services* 9, 18 (in Japanese).

Noda, Aiko et al, *Q & A for the Realization of a Diverse Society* (Gyosei Corporation, 2008) (in Japanese).

Noda, Hiroya, 'Logics and Issues Related to the Design of Community Welfare Advocacy Projects During the Project Formation Period' (2022) 70 *Bulletin of the Faculty of Education and Welfare, Aichi Prefectural University* 35, 48 (in Japanese).

————, 'Development and Characteristics of Support Program for Using Welfare Services in Services for Independence in Daily Living Program' (2022) 13 *Bulletin of the Graduate School of Human Development* 47, 59 (in Japanese).

Numhauser-Henning, Ann, *Elder Law: Evolving European Perspectives* (Edward Elgar Publishing, 2017) <https://doi.org/10.1017/S0144686X19000710>.

Nussbaum, Martha C., *Frontiers of Justice: Disability, Nationality, Species Membership* (Harvard University Press, 2006) <https://www.hup.harvard.edu/catalog.php?isbn=9780674024106>.

————, *Creating Capabilities: The Human Development Approach* (The Belknap Press of Harvard University Press, 2013) <https://www.hup.harvard.edu/catalog.php?isbn=9780674072350>.

O

Oba, Hikaru et al, 'The Economic Burden of Dementia: Evidence from a Survey of Households of People with Dementia and Their Caregivers' (2021) 18 *International Journal of Environmental Research and Public Health* 2717, 2727 <https://doi.org/10.3390/ijerph18052717>.

Obayashi, Keigo, 'What Is Public Welfare: Public Welfare as the Standard' (2022) 807 *Hougaku Seminar* 39, 44 (in Japanese).

Ochiai, Emiko, 'Why Does the "Japanese-Style Welfare Regime" Remain Familial? 4. Comments on the Report' (2015) 27(1) *Japanese Journal of Family Sociology* 61, 68 <https://doi.org/10.4234/jjoffamilysociology.27.61> (in Japanese).

Odaka, Tomoo, *The Ultimate in Law* (2nd ed, Yuhikaku Publishing Co., Ltd., 1965) (in Japanese).

Ogano, Shoichi, 'Development of Adult Guardianship Systems in Japan' (2013) 50(5) *Nihon Ronen Igakkai Zasshi (Journal of the Japan Geriatrics Society)* 638, 640 <https://doi.org/10.3143/geriatrics.50.638> (in Japanese).

———, 'The Role of Adult Guardianship System and Community Comprehensive Care: Community Symbiosis Society' (2020) 12 *Review of Social Security Law* 23, 48 (in Japanese).

Ogawa, Asao, 'End-of-Life Care for Dementia' (2019) 121 *Journal of Psychiatry* 289–97 (in Japanese).

Oguchi, Yoshiguchi et al, *Handbook of the Adult Guardianship Two Acts: Commentary on the Act on the Promotion of the Adult Guardianship System, the Civil Code and the Act on Revision of the Domestic Case Procedure* (Soseisha 2016) (in Japanese).

Ohe, Hiroshi, 'Rights and Relationships' (1999) 53 *St. Paul's Review of Law and Politics* 149, 178 (in Japanese).

Olney, Sue, and Helen Dickinson, 'Australia's New National Disability Insurance Scheme: Implications for Policy and Practice' (2019) 2(3) *Policy Design and Practice* 275, 290 <https://doi.org/10.1080/25741292.2019.1586083>.

Omori, Wataru, 'Significance and Promotion Measures of Participatory Administration' (2019) 11 *Journal of Urban Social Studies* 1, 13 (in Japanese).

Omura, Atsushi, 'Study Group on the Adult Guardianship System and Eiichi Hoshino: Eiichi Hoshino Research Material (Part 2)' (2017) 134(11) *Journal of the Law Association* 2254, 2280 (in Japanese).

O'Neill, Nick and Carmelle Peisah, 'Chapter 1—What Is Capacity?'; 'Chapter 5—The Development of Modern Guardianship'; and 'Chapter 8—Administration/ Financial Management' in Nick O'Neill and Carmelle Peisah (eds), *Capacity and the Law 2021 Edition* (Online, 2021) <http://austlii.community/foswiki/ Books/CapacityAndTheLaw/WebHome>.

Onyx, Jenny, Sue Kenny and Kevin Brown, 'Active Citizenship: An Empirical Investigation' (2012) 11(1) *Social Policy and Society* 55, 66 <https://doi. org/10.1017/S1474746411000406>.

Osawa, Michihiro, 'Cooperation of the Judiciary, Welfare Administration, and the Private in Adult Guardianship System Utilization Promotion' (2020) 15 *The Study of Social Well-Being and Development, Nihon Fukushi University Graduate Schools* 21, 32 <https://cir.nii.ac.jp/crid/1050565162622086784?lang=en (in Japanese).

O'shea, Tom, 'Critics of Autonomy' (Essex Autonomy Project: Green Paper Report, 2012) 1, 26 <https://autonomy.essex.ac.uk/resources/critics-of-autonomy/>.

Ota, Akiko, 'Revision of Medical Certificate Format and Practical Status after Introduction of Personal Information Sheet' (2020) 90 *Adult Guardianship Practices* 3, 14. (in Japanese)

P

Parker, Malcolm, 'Getting the Balance Right: Conceptual Considerations Concerning Legal Capacity and Supported Decision-Making' (2016) 13(3) *Journal of Bioethical Inquiry* 381, 393 <https://doi.org/10.1007/s11673-016-9727-z>.

Patterson, Kay, *Elder Abuse Is Everybody's Business* (Australian Human Rights Commission, June 15, 2018) <https://classic.austlii.edu.au/au/journals/ PrecedentAULA/2018/53.html>.

Paul, Shitangsu Kumar, 'Vulnerability Concepts and Its Application in Various Fields: A Review on Geographical Perspective' (2013) 8 *Journal of Life Earth Science* 63, 81 <https://doi.org/10.3329/jles.v8i0.20150>.

Penhale, Bridget et al, 'The Care Act 2014: A New Legal Framework for Safeguarding Adults in Civil Society' (2017) 19(4) *The Journal of Adult Protection* 169, 174 <https://doi.org/10.1108/JAP-06-2017-0024>.

Peterson, Andrew, Jason Karlawish and Emily Largent, 'Supported Decision Making with People at the Margins of Autonomy' (2020) 21(11) *The American Journal of Bioethics* 1, 15 <https://doi.org/10.1080/15265161.2020.1863507>.

Phillips, Rachel Mattingly, 'Model Language for Supported Decision-Making Statutes' (2020) 98 *Washington University Law Review* 615, 644 <https://open-scholarship.wustl.edu/law_lawreview/vol98/iss2/10>.

Pilliar, Andrew, 'Filling the Normative Hole at the Centre of Access to Justice: Toward a Person-Centred Conception' (2022) 55(1) *UBC Law Review* 149, 203 <https://ssrn.com/abstract=4100809>.

Plotkin, Daniel A. et al, 'Assessing Undue Influence' (2016) 44(3) *The Journal of the American Academy of Psychiatry and the Law* 344, 352 <PMID: 27644868>.

Poppe, Emily S. Taylor, 'Surprised by the Inevitable: A National Survey of Estate Planning Utilization' (2020) 53 *University of California Davis Law Review* 2511, 2560 <https://ssrn.com/abstract=3640621><https://lawreview.law.ucdavis.edu/sites/g/files/dgvnsk15026/files/media/documents/53-5_Poppe.pdf>.

Pryor, Kathy, 'Averting Financial Exploitation and Undue Influence through Legislation' (2016) 31(2) *Age in Action* 1, 6 <https://scholarscompass.vcu.edu/vcoa_case/75/>.

Putnam, Michelle et al, 'Understanding Ageing with Disability' in Michelle Putnam and Christine Bigby (eds), *Handbook on Ageing with Disabilities* (Routledge, 2021) <https://anrows.intersearch.com.au/anrowsjspui/handle/1/22027><https://www.taylorfrancis.com/chapters/edit/10.4324/9780429465352-1/understanding-ageing-disability-michelle-putnam-caitlin-coyle-lydia-ogden-christine-bigby>.

Q

Quah, Stella, *Families in Asia* (2nd ed, Routledge, 2008) <https://doi.org/10.4324/9780203888506>.

Quinn, Gerard, 'Personhood & Legal Capacity Perspectives on the Paradigm Shift of Article 12 CRPD' (Online, 2010) (Conference Paper at Conference on Disability and Legal Capacity under the CRPD in Harvard Law School, February 20, 2010) <https://www.fedvol.ie/_fileupload/Research/NDE%20Reading%20Lists/Harvard%20legal%20Capacity%20gq%20draft%202%20Gerard%20Quinn%20Feb%202010.pdf>.

———, 'Reflecting Will and Preference in Decision Making' (Conference Paper at Australian Guardianship and Administration Council (AGAC) Conference in Sydney in October 17–18, 2016)

Quinn, Gerard and Theresia Degener, *Human Rights and Disability* (Office of the High Commissioner for Human Rights UN, 2002) <https://www.ohchr.org/sites/default/files/Documents/Publications/HRDisabilityen.pdf>.

Quinn, Mary Joy, 'Undue Influence and Elder Abuse: Recognition and Intervention Strategies (CE)' (2002) 23(1) *Geriatric Nursing* 11, 17 <https://doi.org/10.1067/mgn.2002.122560>.

R

Ramsey-Klawsnik, Holly and Holly Ramsey-Klawsnik, *Understanding and Working with Adult Protective Services* (Online, May 2018) <https://www.dhs.wisconsin.gov/areaadmin/aps-staff-trng-comm-napsa-under-work-pt1-2018-05.pdf>.

Rawls, John, *A Theory Justice* (translated by Takashi Kawamoto et al) (2nd ed, Kinokuniya Bookstore, 2010) (in Japanese).

Reid, David et al, 'Form and Function: Views from Members of Adult Protection Committees in England and Wales' (2009) 11(4) *The Journal of Adult Protection* 20, 29 <https://doi.org/10.1108/14668203200900025>.

Ries, Nola M., 'When Powers of Attorney Go Wrong: Preventing Financial Abuse of Older People by Enduring Attorneys' (2018) 148 *Precedent* 9, 13 <http://classic.austlii.edu.au/au/journals/PrecedentAULA/2018/54.html>.

Ries, Nola M. and Elise Mansfield, 'Supported Decision-Making: A Good Idea in Principle but We Need to Consider Supporting Decisions about Voluntary Assisted Dying' in Daniel J. Fleming and David J. Carter (eds), *Voluntary Assisted Dying: Law? Health? Justice?* (ANU Press, 2022) 49–73.

Rogers, Wendy, Catriona Mackenzie and Susan Dodds, 'Why Bioethics Needs a Concept of Vulnerability' (2012) 5(2) *International Journal of Feminist Approaches to Bioethics* 11, 38 <https://www.jstor.org/stable/10.2979/intjfemappbio.5.2.11>.

Roth, Lenny, 'Adult Safeguarding Laws: Reviewing the Proposal for a NSW Ageing and Disability Commissioner' *NSW Parliamentary Research Service E-Brief Issue 3/2019* (Web Page, March 2019) <https://www.parliament.nsw.gov.au/researchpapers/Documents/Adult%20safeguarding%20laws.pdf>.

Royal Commission, *Royal Commission into Aged Care Quality and Safety* (Web Page, n.d.) <https://www.royalcommission.gov.au/aged-care>.

Royal Commission, *Roundtable—Supported Decision-Making and Guardianship—Summary Report (Auslan)* (October 21, 2022) <https://disability.royalcommission.gov.au/publications/roundtable-supported-decision-making-and-guardianship-summary-report-auslan>.

Royal Commission, *Publications—Final Report* (Web Page, September 28, 2023) <https://disability.royalcommission.gov.au/publications/final-report>.

Royal Commission into Violence, Abuse, Neglect and Exploitation of People with Disability, *Supported Decision-Making and Guardianship—Proposals for Reform Roundtable* (Web Page, June 3, 2022) <https://disability.royalcommission.gov.au/publications/supported-decision-making-and-guardianship-proposals-reform-roundtable>.

Ryan, Trevor, 'Is Japan Ready for Enduring Powers? A Comparative Analysis of Enduring Powers Reform' (2014) 9(1) *Asian Journal of Comparative Law* 241, 266 <https://doi.org/10.1017/S2194607800000995>.

———, 'Developments in Enduring Powers of Attorney Law in Australia' in Lusina Ho and Rebecca Lee (eds), *Special Needs Financial Planning: A Comparative Perspective* (Cambridge University Press, 2019) 179–211. <https://doi.org/10.1017/9781108646925.007>.

S

Saisho, Shinya, 'Socialization of Care in View of the Socialization of Adult Guardianship: Impact of Occupational Professionalization on the Family' (2016) 28(2) *Family Sociology Research* 148, 160 (in Japanese).

Saito, Osamu, 'Conceptual Framework and Analysis Method for Risk Trade-off Analysis Part 1: Conceptual Framework for Risk Trade-off Analysis' (2010) 20(2) *Journal of Japan Risk Research Journal* 97, 106 , <https://www.jstage.jst.go.jp/article/sraj/20/2/20_2_97/_pdf> (in Japanese).

Sakai, Yasushi, 'The Actual Situation and Problems of the Voluntary Guardianship System from the Viewpoint of Notary Practice' (2010) 12 *Journal of Asian Cultures* 279, 295.

Sakurai, Yukio, 'Social Design Concepts on "Dementia and Japan's Adult Guardianship System"' (2017) 8 *Social Design Review* 142, 147 <https://ci.nii.ac.jp/naid/40021158069>.

———, 'A Risk Analysis on Japan's Adult Guardianship System Practice against Principals and Adult Guardians' (2017) 9 *Journal of Urban Social Studies* 175, 184 (in Japanese) </https://www.city.setagaya.lg.jp/documents/6145/015.pdf>.

———, 'UN Convention on the Rights of Persons with Disabilities and Supported Decision-Making' (2017) 47 *The Graduate School Law Review, Nihon University* 276, 243 <https://ci.nii.ac.jp/naid/40021423820> (in Japanese).

———, 'Australia: Focusing on the State of Victoria' *Survey and Research Report on Adult Guardianship Law in Each Country* (Ministry of Justice Commissioned Research: Japan Institute of Business Law, 2017) 185, 195 (in Japanese).

———, 'Legal Challenge and Measures for Property Management of the Elderly: Focusing on Financial Exploitation and de facto Adult Guardianship' (2018) 48 *The Graduate School Law Review, Nihon University* 224, 176 <https://ci.nii.ac.jp/naid/40021765899> (in Japanese).

———, 'Adult Guardianship System in Australia and Its Recent Discussion Points' (2018) 7 *Quarterly Journal of Comparative Guardianship Law* 30, 41 <http://www.hikaku-kouken.or.jp/Hikakukokenhosei/Kikan_Hikakukokenhosei_7.pdf> (in Japanese).

———, 'An Essay on the Adult Protection System in Japan: Referring to Delaware State Law and the Revision of European Law' (2018) 8 *Quarterly Journal of Comparative Guardianship Law* 3, 21 (in Japanese).

———, 'The Role of Soft Law in the Ageing Society of the Twenty-First Century' (2018) 13(1) *The International Journal of Interdisciplinary Global Studies* 1, 10 <https://doi.org/10.18848/2324-755X/CGP/v13i01/1-10>.

———, 'The Ageing and Adult Protection Legislative System: A Comparative Law Study' (2019) 9(1) *The Journal of Aging and Social Change* 53, 69 <https://doi.org/10.18848/2576-5310/CGP/v09i01/53-69>.

———, 'Possible Roles of Elder Law in Super-Aged Society of Japan: Referring to Elder Law in the US' (2019) 10 *Quarterly Journal of Comparative Guardianship Law* 22, 44 <https://ci.nii.ac.jp/naid/40022050659> (in Japanese).

———, 'Safeguarding Law for Vulnerable Adults at Risk of Harm: Focusing on Elder Abuse' (2020) 13 *Quarterly Journal of Comparative Guardianship Law* 3, 32 (in Japanese).

————, 'Australian Adult Support and Protection for Vulnerable Adults: Through Law Reforms of Guardianship and Elder Abuse Legislation (Part I)' (2020) 25(2) *Yokohama Journal of Social Sciences* 119, 139 <https://doi.org/10.18880/00013445>.

————, 'Australian Adult Support and Protection for Vulnerable Adults: Through Law Reforms of Guardianship and Elder Abuse Legislation (Part II)' (2021) 25(4) *Yokohama Journal of Social Sciences* 97, 119 <https://doi.org/10.18880/00013705>.

————, 'Vulnerability Approach and Adult Support and Protection: Safeguarding Laws for Adults at Risk' (2021) 11(1) *The Journal of Aging and Social Change* 19, 34 <https://doi.org/10.18848/2576-5310/CGP/v11i01/19-34>.

————, 'Current Status and Issues of Japan's Adult Guardianship System in the Promotion Act: Focused on the Deliberation Process of the Basic Plan' (2021) 30(1) *Yokohama Law Review* 397, 432 (in Japanese) <https://doi.org/10.18880/00014059>.

————, 'The Idea of Adult Support and Protection Legislation in Japan: Multiple Options for Vulnerable Adults to Make Their Own Choices' (2021) 12(1) *The Journal of Aging and Social Change* 31, 47 <https://doi.org/10.18848/2576-5310/CGP/v12i01/31-47>.

————, 'Challenges of Property Management for Older Adults in Japan: Focusing on Financial Exploitation and Informal Arrangement' (2022) 12(2) *The Journal of Aging and Social Change* 1, 18 <https://doi.org/10.18848/2576-5310/CGP/v12i02/1-18>.

————,'Supported Decision-Making in the Japanese Context: Developments and Challenges' (2023) 3(1) *The Journal of Aging and Social Change* 151–69 <https://doi.org/10.18848/2576-5310/CGP/v13i01/151-169>.

————, 'The Role of Law and Bioethics in Human Life and Death: Japanese Medical Law in End-of-Life Care' (2024) 25(1) *Australian Journal of Asian Law* 89–105 <https://ssrn.com/abstract=4964356>.

————, 'The Political Process Involved in Formulating Healthcare Policy in Japan: With a Particular Focus on Advisory Councils, Interest Groups and Medical Officers' (2025) 15(1) *The Rest: Journal of Politics and Development* 82–96 <http://hdl.handle.net/10131/0002001605>.

Salzman, Leslie, 'Rethinking Guardianship (again): Substituted Decision Making as a Violation of the Integration Mandate of Title II of the Americans with Disabilities Act' (2009) 282 *Cardozo Working Paper* 156, 220 <https:// papers.ssrn.com/sol3/papers.cfm?abstract_id=1567132>.

———, 'Guardianship for Persons with Mental Illness—A Legal and Appropriate Alternative?' (2011) 4(2) *St. Louis University Journal of Health Law & Policy* 279, 330 <https://ssrn.com/abstract=1933809>.

Sanchez-Gonzalez, D. and C. Egea-Jimenez, 'Social Vulnerability Approach to Investigate the Social and Environmental Disadvantages: Its Application in the Study of Elderly People' (Online, 2011) 17(69) *Papeles de Población* <https://www.scielo. org.mx/scielo.php?pid=S1405-74252011000300006&script=sci_abstract&tlng=en>.

Santo, Nina, 'Breaking the Silence: Strategies for Combating Elder Abuse in California' (Online, 2000) 31 *McGeorge Law Review* 801, 838 <https://scholarlycommons.pacific.edu/mlr/vol31/iss3/11>.

Santos, Maria Angélica Bezerra dos et al, 'Factors Associated with Elder Abuse: A Systematic Review of the Literature' (2020) 25 *Ciência & Saúde Coletiva* 2153, 2175 <https://doi.org/10.1590/1413-81232020256.25112018>.

Sato, Koji, 'The Meaning of "Self-Determination" in the Constitutional Studies' (1990) 1989 *Legal Philosophy Annual Report* 76, 99 (in Japanese).

Sato, Noriko, 'Adoption du Pacs et Transformation de la Relation Intime Comme Lutte Symbolique' (Adoption of the PaCS and Transformation of the Intimate Relationship as a Symbolic Struggle) (2004) 112 *Philosophy* 1, 12 (in Japanese) <http://koara.lib.keio.ac.jp/xoonips/modules/xoonips/detail.php?koara_id=AN00150430-00000112-0003> (in Japanese).

Sato, Shoichi, 'Is Decision-Making Support Available?' (2016) 2016 *Annual Report of the Philosophy of Law* 57, 71.

———, 'Social Exclusion for Persons with Disabilities' (2019) 85 *Sociology of Law* 58, 73 (in Japanese).

Scholten, Matthé, 'Mental Capacity and Supported Decision-Making' in H. Helmchen, N. Sartorius and J. Gather (eds) *Ethics in Psychiatry: European Contributions* (Springer, 2025) 27–51<https://doi.org/10.1007/978-94-024-2274-0_3>.

Scholten, Matthe and Jakov Gather, 'Adverse Consequences of Article 12 of the UN Convention on the Rights of Persons with Disabilities for Persons with Mental Disabilities and an Alternative Way Forward' (2018) 44 *Journal of Medical Ethics* 226, 233 <https://doi.org/10.1136/medethics-2017-104414>.

Scholten, Matthe, Jakov Gather and Jochen Vollmann, 'Equality in the Informed Consent Process: Competence to Consent, Substitute Decision-Making, and Discrimination of Persons with Mental Disorders' (2021) 46(1) *Journal of Medicine and Philosophy* 108, 136 <https://doi.org/10.1093/jmp/jhaa030>.

Schwenzer, Ingeborg and Tomie Keller, 'A New Law for the Protection of Adults' in Bill Atkin (ed), *The International Survey of Family Law* (Jordan Publishing Ltd., 2013) 375, 386 <http://edoc.unibas.ch/dok/A6146169>.

Scottish Government, *Adults with Incapacity (Scotland) Act 2000: Proposals for Reform* (Proposal for Reform, January 2018) <https://www.gov.scot/publications/adults-incapacity-scotland-act-2000-proposals-reform/pages/4/>.

———, *Adult Support and Protection: Improvement Plan 2019–2022* (The Scottish Government, October 2019) <https://www.gov.scot/publications/adult-support-protection-improvement-plan-2019-2022/pages/7/>.

———, *Scottish Mental Health Law Review: Our Response* (Web Page, June 28, 2023) <https://www.gov.scot/publications/scottish-mental-health-law-review-response/>.

———, *Adults with Incapacity Amendment Act: Consultation Analysis Summary* (Web Page, January 27, 2025) <https://www.gov.scot/publications/adults-incapacity-amendment-act-summary-analysis-response-consultation/>.

Scottish Mental Health Law Review, *Final Report* (Web Page, September 30, 2022) <https://webarchive.nrscotland.gov.uk/20230327160310/https:/www.mentalhealthlawreview.scot/>.

Scottish Parliament, *Mental Health and Adults with Incapacity Law in Scotland—What Next?* (Web Page, June 13, 2021) <https://spice-spotlight.scot/2021/06/23/mental-health-and-adults-with-incapacity-law-in-scotland-what-next/>.

Seki, Fusako, 'Overview of the Elder Law' (2019) 35 *Social Security Law* 5, 19 (in Japanese).

———, 'Human Characteristics of the Elderly' in Norio Higuchi (ed), *Report: The Independence of the Elderly and Japanese Economy* (The 21st Century of Public Policy Institute, 2020) 19, 33 (in Japanese).

————, (ed/author) *Theory and Practice of Elder Law* (Chuokeizai-Sha Holdings, Inc., 2025) (in Japanese).

Sen, Amartya K., 'Capability and Well-Being' in Martha C. Nussbaum and Amartya Sen (eds), *Quality of Life* (Oxford University Press, 1992) 30–53 <https://doi.org/10.1093/0198287976.003.0003>.

————, (translated by Yukio Ikemoto, Hiroki Nogami and Jin Sato), *Inequality Examined* (Iwanami Publishers, 1999; Harvard University Press, 1992) (in Japanese).

————, 'Well-Being, Capability and Public Policy' (1994) 53(7/9) *Journal of Economists and Annuals of Economics* 333, 347 <https://www.jstor.org/stable/23247762>.

————, 'Human Rights and Capabilities' (2005) 6(2) *Journal of Human Development* 151, 166 <https://gsdrc.org/document-library/human-rights-and-capabilities/>.

————, *The Idea of Justice* (Penguin Books Ltd., 2009).

Series, Lucy, 'Relationships, Autonomy and Legal Capacity: Mental Capacity and Support Paradigms' (2015) 40 *International Journal of Law and Psychiatry* 80, 91 <https://doi.org/10.1016/j.ijlp.2015.04.010>.

————, 'Comment: Mental Capacity (Amendment) Act 2019 (UK)' (Online, 2020) 12(1) *The Elder Law Review* <PMID: 32066991; PMCID: PMC7025892>.

Séverine, Deneulin and Lila Shahani, *An Introduction to the Human Development and Capability Approach: Freedom and Agency* (Earthscan, 2009) <https://www.idrc.ca/en/book/introduction-human-development-and-capability-approach-freedom-and-agency>.

Shakespeare, Tom, 'The Social Model of Disability' in Lennard J. Davis (ed), *The Disability Studies Reader* (Routledge, 2010) 266–73 <http://thedigitalcommons.org/docs/shakespeare_social-model-of-disability.pdf>.

Shao, Jingjin et al, 'Why Are Older Adults Victims of Fraud? Current Knowledge and Prospects Regarding Older Adults' Vulnerability to Fraud' (2019) 31(3) *Journal of Elder Abuse & Neglect* 225, 243 <https://doi.org/10.1080/08946566.2019.1625842>.

Shelford, Leonard, *A Practical Treatise of the Law Concerning Lunatics, Idiots and Persons of Unsound Mind: With an Appendix of the Statutes of England, Ireland, and Scotland, Relating to such Persons; and Forms of Proceedings in Lunacy* (2nd ed, S. Sweet, 1847) <https://wellcomecollection.org/works/jy82g8sg>.

Sherman, Charles P., 'The Debt of the Modern Law of Guardianship to Roman Law' (1913) 12(2) *Michigan Law Review* 124, 131 <https://repository.law.umich.edu/mlr/vol12/iss2/3/>.

Sherman, Roger B., 'Guardianship: Time for a Reassessment' (1980) 49(3) *Fordham Law Review* 350, 378 <https://ir.lawnet.fordham.edu/flr/vol49/iss3/9>.

Sherwood-Johnson, Fiona, 'Constructions of "Vulnerability" in Comparative Perspective: Scottish Protection Policies and the Trouble with "Adults at Risk"' (2013) 28(7) *Disability & Society* 908, 921 <https://doi.org/10.1080/0968759 9.2012.732541>.

Shimada, Keiji, 'Participation and Coproduction' (2016) 42(457) *Monthly Review of Local Government* 1, 36 <https://doi.org/10.34559/jichisoken.42.457_1> (in Japanese).

Shimizu, Keisuke, 'Reading and Understanding the Supreme Court Decision of the Central Japan Railway Case-Including the Perspective of Adult Guardianship' (2016) 6 *Adult Guardianship Practices* 84, 93 (in Japanese).

———, 'The Convention on the Rights of Persons with Disabilities and Civil Law Theory' (2017) 14 *Adult Guardianship Law Review* 40, 50 (in Japanese).

———, 'Can the New Peruvian Law Protect the Rights of Persons with Disabilities? Based on the Trend of New Support System' (2021) 91 *Adult Guardianship Practices* 74, 80. (in Japanese)

Shimura, Takeshi, 'A Consideration on the Survival of Voluntary Agency Rights When the Person Is Incapacitated (Part 1)' (1996) 71(3) *Waseda Law Review* 1, 38 (in Japanese).

———, 'Underlying the Self-Decision Support Principle as an Alternative to the Adult Guardianship System in the United States (1 and 2): Seeking Suggestions from American Case Law, Enactment, and Theory to Japanese Law' (2021) 93 and 94 *Adult Guardianship Practices* 88–96 and 80–8 (in Japanese).

Sinclair, Craig, Sue Field and Meredith Blake, *Supported Decision-Making in Aged Care: A Policy Development Guideline for Aged Care Providers in Australia* (2nd ed, Cognitive Decline Partnership Centre, 2018) <https://cdpc.sydney.edu.au/wp-content/uploads/2019/06/SDM-Policy-Guidelines.pdf>.

Sinclair, Craig et al, *Supporting Decision-Making: A Guide for People Living with Dementia, Family Members and Carers* (Cognitive Decline Partnership

Centre, 2018) <https://cdpc.sydney.edu.au/wp-content/uploads/2019/06/SDM_Handbook_Online_Consumers-ReducedSize.pdf>.

———, 'Professionals' Views and Experiences in Supporting Decision-Making Involvement for People Living with Dementia' (2021) 20(1) *Dementia* 84, 105 <https://doi.org/10.1177/1471301219864849>.

Skowron, Paul, 'The Relationship between Autonomy and Adult Mental Capacity in the Law of England and Wales' (2019) 27(1) *Medical Law Review* 32, 58 <https://doi.org/10.1093/medlaw/fwy016>.

———, 'Giving Substance to "the Best Interpretation of Will and Preferences"' (2019) 62 *International Journal of Law and Psychiatry* 125, 134 <https://doi.org/10.1016/j.ijlp.2018.12.001>.

Smith, Anita, 'Developments in Australian Incapacity Legislation' (2018) 145 *Precedent* 4, 8 <http://classic.austlii.edu.au/au/journals/PrecedentAULA/2018/16.html>.

———, 'Tribunal Update: Compensation Where Loss Caused by Actions of an Attorney Using a Power of Attorney' (2019) 12 *Elder Law Review* 1–3. < https://classic.austlii.edu.au/au/journals/ElderLawRw/2019/17.pdf>

Sobode, Oluwaseun Rebecca et al, 'Shared Decision-Making in Adolescent Healthcare: A Literature Review of Ethical Considerations' (2024) 183 *European Journal of Pediatrics* 4195–203 <https://doi.org/10.1007/s00431-024-05687-0>.

Somes, Teresa, 'Identifying Vulnerability: The Argument for Law Reform for Failed Family Accommodation Arrangements' (Online, 2020) 12(1) *Elder Law Review* 1–39 <https://www.austlii.edu.au/au/journals/ElderLawRw/2019/8.pdf>.

Song, Peipei and Wei Tang, 'The Community-Based Integrated Care System in Japan: Health Care and Nursing Care Challenges Posed by Super-Aged Society' (2019) 13(3) *Bioscience Trends* 279, 281 <https://doi.org/10.5582/bst.2019.01173>.

South Australia, Office of the Public Advocate, *Closing the Gaps: Enhancing South Australia's Response to the Abuse of Vulnerable Older People* (Office of the Public Advocate in Collaboration with University of South Australia, 2011) <https://researchprofiles.canberra.edu.au/en/publications/closing-the-gaps-enhancing-south-australias-response-to-the-abuse/>.

Spreng, R. Nathan et al, 'Aging and Financial Exploitation Risk' in Ronan M. Factora (ed), *Aging and Money* (Springer, 2021) 55, 73 <https://doi.org/10.1007/978-3-030-67565-3_5>.

Stavert, Jill, 'Supported Decision-Making and Paradigm Shifts: Word Play or Real Change?' (2021) 11 *Frontier in Psychiatry* 1, 9 <https://doi.org/10.3389/fpsyt.2020.571005>.

Steinman, Kenneth J. and Georgia J. Anetzberger, 'Measuring the Diverse Characteristics of County Adult Protective Services Programs' (2022) 34(3) *Journal of Elder Abuse & Neglect* 153, 173 <https://doi.org/10.1080/0894656 6.2022.2092243>.

Stelma-Roorda, Rieneke, 'The Misuse or Abuse of Continuing Powers of Attorney: What Are Appropriate Safeguards?' (2021) 35(1) *International Journal of Law, Policy and the Family* 1, 25 <https://doi.org/10.1093/lawfam/ebab022>.

Stewart, Ailsa E., 'The Implementation of Adult Support and Protection (Scotland) Act (2007)' (2016) Doctoral Dissertation, University of Glasgow <http://theses.gla.ac.uk/7083/>.

Straehle, Christine, 'Introduction' in Christine Straehle (ed), *Vulnerability, Autonomy, and Applied Ethics* (Routledge, 2017) <https://doi.org/10.4324/9781315647418>.

Strickland, Karen et al, 'Supported Decision-Making to Assist Older Persons Experiencing Elder Abuse: An Integrative Review' (2021) 28(4) *Collegian* 447, 455 <https://doi.org/10.1016/j.colegn.2020.12.003>.

Suga, Fumie, 'Australia's Adult Guardianship System—From a Comparative Law Perspective' (2007) 20 *Adult Guardianship Practices* 106, 117 (in Japanese).

————, *The Doctrine of Autonomous Support in the English Adult Guardianship System: Towards a Society Pursuing the Best Interests* (Minerva Shobo, 2010) (in Japanese).

————, 'Comparative Legal Consideration on Adult Guardianship System in the International Trends: Suggestions for Reconsidering the Agency Decision System from the Idea of "Self-Determination Support"' (2014) 76 *Private Law* 198, 204 (in Japanese).

————, 'Reorganization of *Negotiorum Gestio* Theory for People with Inadequate Mental Capacity: An Attempt to Integrate Interpretation with the Adult

Guardianship System Based on a Person-Centered Approach' in Takanobu Igarashi et al (eds), *The History and Future of Civil Law* (Seibundo, 2014) 481–512 (in Japanese).

———, *New Consumer Law Research: Legal System and Enforcement System for Inclusion of Vulnerable Consumers* (Seibundo, 2018) (in Japanese).

Suga, Fumie and Ohara Institute for Social Affairs (Hosei University), *New Grand Design of Adult Guardianship System* (Hosei University Press, 2013) (in Japanese).

Sugita, Hiroko, 'A Study on the Supported Decision-Making System for the Elderly with Dementia (2): Focusing on the South Australian Legal System' (2021) 179 *The Graduate School Law Review* 71, 98 (in Japanese).

Sukimoto, Toyohiro, 'Contemporary Challenges of Larceny Committed against Relatives' (2009) 78 *Seijo Jurisprudence* 95, 120 (in Japanese).

Sunaga, June, 'Interpretation and Operation of the Adult Guardianship System and Legislative Issues' (2005) (Special Lecture at the 1st Annual Meeting of the Japan Adult Guardianship Law Association on May 29, 2004) 2 *Adult Guardianship Law Research* 3, 26.

T

Tahara, Shotaro, 'What Should Autonomous Agents Be Like? From the Individualistic to the Substantive Conception' (2017) 5 *Waseda Rilas Journal* 193, 203 <https://cir.nii.ac.jp/crid/1050282677447435136> (in Japanese).

———, 'Substantive Conceptions of Autonomy: An Approach Based on Shared Characteristics' (2022) 1 *Bulletin of the Faculty of Humanities, Ibaraki University. Studies in Social Sciences* 55, 76 (in Japanese).

Takikawa, Hirohide, 'Between Self-Decision and Self-Responsibility: A Philosophy of Law Consideration' (2001) September 2001 *Law Seminar* 32, 35 (in Japanese).

Tamam, Lut, Mehtap Bican and Necla Keskin, 'Impulse Control Disorders in Elderly Patients' (2014) 55(4) *Comprehensive Psychiatry* 1022, 1028 <https://doi.org/10.1016/j.comppsych.2013.12.003>.

Tamaruya, Masayuki, 'Japanese Wealth Management and the Transformation of the Law of Trusts and Succession' (2019) 33 *Trust Law International* 147, 168 <https://ssrn.com/abstract=3515207>.

Tanaka, Michihiro, 'Commentary on the French Civil Code: Family Law (5)' (2012) 62(4) *Journal of Law and Politics* 173, 195 <http://hdl.handle.net/10236/6778> (in Japanese).

Tanaka, Shigeaki, *Contemporary Jurisprudence* (Yuhikaku Publishing Co., Ltd., 2011) 442 (in Japanese).

Tang, Hang Wu, 'Singapore's Adult Guardianship Law and the Role of the Family in Medical Decision-Making' (2022) 36(1) *International Journal of Law, Policy and the Family* 1, 21 <https://doi.org/10.1093/lawfam/ebac002>.

Tang, Stephanie L., 'When Providers and Families Cannot Agree: A New Look at Due Process for End-of-Life Care Disputes' (2023) 61(1) *Houston Law Review* <https://ssrn.com/abstract=4454895>.

Taniguchi, Satoshi, 'A Study on an "Advance Healthcare Directive" in Ireland's Assisted Decision-Making (Capacity) Act 2015' (2020) 63(1) *The Economic Journal of Takasaki City University of Economics* 41, 71. (in Japanese)

Tayama, Teruaki, 'Legal Position of the Adult Guardianship System: Its Private Law and Public Law Aspects' in Kazutoshi Kobayashi, Hidefumi Kobayashi and Akira Murata (eds), *Legal Issues in an Ageing Society: A Collection of 80-Year-Old Commemorative Papers for Dr. Jun Sunaga* (Sakai Shoten, 2010) 1–29 (in Japanese).

———, (ed), *Adult Guardianship System and the Convention on the Rights of Persons with Disabilities* (Sanseido, 2012) (in Japanese).

———, *Commentary on Adult Guardianship System* (2nd ed, Sanseido, 2016) (in Japanese).

———, (ed), *Survey and Research Report on Adult Guardianship Law in Each Country* (Japan Ministry of Justice Commissioned Research: Japan Institute of Business Law, 2017) (in Japanese)

———, 'Ratification of the Convention on the Rights of Persons with Disabilities and the Adult Guardianship System' (2019) 30(1) *Geriatric Psychiatry Magazine* 27, 33 (in Japanese).

———, 'History, Current Status, and Future of the Adult Guardianship System in Japan' (2020) (Keynote Speech at the 17th Academic Conference, Japan Adult Guardianship Law Corporate Association (JAGA) in Tokyo in November 14, 2020) 18 *Adult Guardianship Study* 18, 27 (in Japanese).

Teaster, Pamela Booth and Stephanie Chamberlain, 'Public Guardianship: Policy and Practice' (2020) 1(1) *Journal of Elder Policy* 155, 174 <https://doi.org/10.18278/jep.1.1.8>.

Terada, Kimiyo, 'A Discussion of How Advocacy Is Conceptualized in Social Welfare Research in Japan' (2016) 15(2) *Niigata Journal of Health and Welfare* 27, 34 (in Japanese).

Teshima, Yutaka, *Introduction to Medical Law* (6th ed, Yuhikaku Publishing Co. Ltd., 2022). (in Japanese)

The American Bar Association Commission on Law and Aging, *Supporting Decision Making across the Age Spectrum* (Online, 2020) <https://www.americanbar.org/content/dam/aba/administrative/law_aging/2020-supporting-decision-making-final-report.pdf>.

The Arc of Northern Virginia and the Burton Blatt Institute at Syracuse University (BBI), *"I Learned That I Have a Voice in My Future" Summary, Findings, and Recommendations of the Virginia Supported Decision-Making Pilot Project* (The Arc and BBI, 2021)

The University of Tokyo, Policy Vision Research Center, *Study on Practical and Theoretical Systematization of Adult Guardians* (Research Report, March 2013) (in Japanese) <http://www.shimin-kouken.jp/materials/pdf/mhlw3_24.pdf>.

Thelin, Angelika, 'Care Ethics for Supported Decision-Making: A Narrative Policy Analysis Regarding Social Work in Cases of Dementia and Self-Neglect' (2021) 15(2) *Ethics and Social Welfare* 167, 184 <https://doi.org/10.1080/17496535.2020.1863998>.

Then, Shih-Ning, 'Evolution and Innovation in Guardianship Laws: Assisted Decision-Making' (2013) 35 *Sydney Law Review* 133, 166 <http://classic.austlii.edu.au/au/journals/SydLawRw/2013/6.html>.

Then, Shih-Ning and Christine Bigby, 'Supported Decision-Making and the Disability Royal Commission' (2024) 11(1) *Research and Practice in Intellectual and Developmental Disabilities* 86–106 <https://doi.org/10.1080/23297018.2 024.2330961>.

Then, Shih-Ning et al, 'Supporting Decision-Making of Adults with Cognitive Disabilities: The Role of Law Reform Agencies: Recommendations, Rationales and Influence' (2018) 61 *International Journal of Law and Psychiatry* 64, 75 <https://doi.org/10.1016/j.ijlp.2018.09.001>.

———, 'Moving from Support for Decision-Making to Substitute Decision-Making: Legal Frameworks and Perspectives of Supporters of Adults with Intellectual Disabilities' (2022) 37(3) *Law in Context* <https://doi.org/10.26826/law-in-context.v37i3.174>.

Trevelyan, E. J. et al, 'The Public Trustee in India, New Zealand, Australia, and England' (1916) 16(2) *Journal of the Society of Comparative Legislation* 110, 139 <https://www.jstor.org/stable/752415>.

Tsuchiya, Kohei, 'Citizen Guardian and Welfare Administration' (2016) 29(2) *Chuo Gakuin University Law Review* 211, 235 (in Japanese) <https://cgu.repo. nii.ac.jp/records/1186>.

U

Uchida, Takashi, *Civil Law I: General Rules and General Remarks on Property Rights* (4th ed, University of Tokyo Press, 2008).

UK Government, Department of Health, *No Secrets: Guidance on Developing and Implementing Multi-Agency Policies and Procedures to Protect Vulnerable Adults from Abuse* (2nd ed, Department of Health of UK, 2015) <https://www.gov. uk/government/publications/no-secrets-guidance-on-protecting-vulnerable-adults-in-care>.

UNESCO, 'Universal Declaration on Bioethics and Human Rights of 2005' (2005) <https://www.unesco.org/en/legal-affairs/universal-declaration-bioethics-and-human-rights>.

Unuma, Noriharu and Kaoru Sekine, 'A Study of Difficult Cases in Adult Guardianship: Analyses the Contents and Support Methods through Corporate Guardianship by the Council of Social Welfare' (2022) 12 *Kogakkan University of Japanese Studies* 1, 28 (in Japanese).

Uster, Ruth and Tadhg Stapleton, 'Overview of the Assisted Decision-Making (Capacity) Act (2015): Implications and Opportunities for Occupational Therapy'

(2018) 46(2) *Irish Journal of Occupational Therapy* 130, 140 <https://doi.org/10.1108/IJOT-08-2018-0013>.

V

Van Puymbrouck, L., *Supported Decision-Making in the U. S.: A White Paper* (The Council on Quality and Leadership Report, 2017) <https://c-q-l.org/resource-library/publications/cql-publications-for-free/data-analysis-briefs/supported-decision-making-in-the-united-states>.

Vásquez Encalada, Alberto, Kimber Bialik and Kaitlin Stober, 'Supported Decision Making in South America: Analysis of Three Countries' Experiences' (2021) 18(10) *International Journal of Environmental Research and Public Health* 5204 <https://doi.org/10.3390/ijerph18105204>.

Victoria, Law Institute Victoria, *ONE-VCAT: President's Review of the Victorian Civil and Administrative Tribunal* (VCAT Report, 2009) <https://catalogue.nla.gov.au/catalog/5448392>.

———, *The LIV Capacity Guidelines and Toolkit* (Concise Edition: November 2020, Full Version: 2018) (Online, Concise edition: November 2020) <https://www.liv.asn.au/download.aspx?DocumentVersionKey=3e89e8a7-cead-4efb-ba1e-d3682848213a&srsltid=AfmBOooDA0enVC5wigC07oiG5W03ef8EV5m4suhr-JPTL5x7qgxaVShTU>, Full Version <https://www.liv.asn.au/LawBooks/Law-book-subjects/LIV-Capacity-Guidelines-and-Toolkit>.

Victoria, Law Reform Commission (VLRC), *Guardianship: Final Report No. 24* (VLRC Report 24, 2012) <https://www.lawreform.vic.gov.au/wp-content/uploads/2021/07/Guardianship_FinalReport_Full-text.pdf>.

Victoria, Monash University, *Financial Abuse of Elders: A Review of the Evidence* (Web Page, June 2009) <https://www.eapu.com.au/uploads/research_resources/VIC-Financial_Elder_Abuse_Evidence_Review_JUN_209-Monash.pdf>.

Victoria, Parliament of Victoria, *Parliamentary Debates (HANSARD)* (Web Page) Legislative Assembly, Fifty-Eighth Parliament, First Session Wednesday, March 7, 2018 and Thursday, March 29, 2018; Legislative Assembly, Fifty-Ninth Parliament, First Session Wednesday, December 19, 2018 and Tuesday, May 28, 2019 <https://www.parliament.vic.gov.au/hansard/daily-hansard>.

Victoria State Trustees Ltd., Annual Reports (2014 - 2025)<https://www.statetrustees.com.au/forms-and-documents/?resources_type=annual-report,annual-report>

Victoria, Voluntary Assisted Dying Review Board, *Voluntary Assisted Dying Report of Operations (January to June 2021)* (Victoria State Government, September/December 2021) <https://www.health.vic.gov.au/voluntary-assisted-dying/voluntary-assisted-dying-review-board>.

Victorian Civil and Administrative Tribunal (VCAT), *Annual Reports (1999 - 2025) and Strategic Directions (Web Page, 2025)* <https://www.vcat.vic.gov.au/about-vcat/annual-reports-and-strategic-directions>

Victorian Office of the Public Advocacy (Victorian OPA), *Supported Decision-Making in Victoria* (OPA Report, October 2020) <https://www.publicadvocate.vic.gov.au/your-rights/your-healthcare/your-supported-medical-decisions>.

———, *Guardianship and Administration* (Victorian OPA Report, 2020) <https://www.publicadvocate.vic.gov.au/guardianship-and-administration/guardianship-and-administration-an-introduction>.

———, *Annual Report 2020–21* (Victorian OPA Report, 2021) <https://www.publicadvocate.vic.gov.au/opa-s-work/our-organisation/annual-reports/opa-annual-reports/359-opa-annual-report-2020-2021>.

———, *Community Visitors* (Web Page) <https://www.publicadvocate.vic.gov.au/opa-volunteers/community-visitors>.

———, *Annual Report 2023–24* (Victorian OPA Report, 2024) <https://www.publicadvocate.vic.gov.au/opa-s-work/our-organisation/annual-reports/opa-annual-reports/755-opa-annual-report-2023-2024>.

———, *Manipulation and Personal Autonomy* (Web Page, October 24, 2024) <https://www.publicadvocate.vic.gov.au/opa-s-work/research/745-manipulation-and-personal-autonomy>.

Victorian Ombudsman, *Investigation into State Trustees* (Online, June 2019) <https://www.ombudsman.vic.gov.au/our-impact/investigation-reports/investigation-into-state-trustees/>.

Vincent, Lanny, 'Differentiating Competence, Capability and Capacity' (2008) 16(3) *Innovating Perspectives* 1–2 <https://www.observatoriorh.org/sites/default/files/webfiles/fulltext/2016/competence_capability_and_capacity.pdf>.

Virokannas, Elina, Suvi Liuski and Marjo Kuronen, 'The Contested Concept of Vulnerability: A Literature Review' (2018) 23(2) *European Journal of Social Work* 327, 339 <https://doi.org/10.1080/13691457.2018.1508001>.

Vizard, Polly, Sakiko Fukuda-Parr and Diane Elson, 'Introduction: The Capability Approach and Human Rights' (2011) 12(1) *Journal of Human Development and Capabilities* 1, 12 <https://doi.org/10.1080/19452829.2010.541728>.

W

Wada, Tadashi et al, 'Detection of Elder Abuse in Japan Not Covered by the Elder Abuse Prevention Law in Comparison with WHO Definitions of Elder Abuse' (2022) 18(1) *Journal of the Japan Academy for the Prevention of Elder Abuse* 72, 86 (in Japanese).

Ward, Adrian D., 'Abolition of All Guardianship and Mental Health Laws?' (Online, April 14, 2014) *Law Society of Scotland* <http://www.journalonline.co.uk/Magazine/59-4/1013832.aspx>.

———, 'Legal Protection of Adults—An International Comparison' (Opening Address to the Fourth World Congress on Adult Guardianship Held in Erkner in September 14–17, 2016) <https://www.lawscot.org.uk/members/journal/issues/vol-61-issue-10/legal-protection-of-adults-an-international-comparison/>.

———, *Enabling Citizens to Plan for Incapacity* (Council of Europe, Online, 2017) <https://rm.coe.int/cdcj-2017-2e-final-rapport-vs-21-06-2018/16808b64ae>.

———, 'Scottish Government Review Extended and Delayed' and 'Mental Health Act Review in Scotland: Some Initial Observations' (2019) 93 *Mental Capacity Report: Scotland* (Online, April 2019) <https://www.39essex.com/sites/default/files/Mental-Capacity-Report-April-2019-Scotland.pdf>.

———, 'Adult Incapacity Law: Visions for the Future Drawn from the Unfinished Story of a New Subject with a Long History' (2020) 26 *International Journal of Mental Health and Capacity Law* 13, 34 <https://www.northumbriajournals.co.uk/index.php/ijmhcl/article/view/1092>.

Ward, Adrian D. et al, *Safeguarding Vulnerable Adults in Scotland* (British Association for Counselling and Psychotherapy (BACP), 2018) <https://www.bacp.co.uk/media/4291/bacp-safeguarding-vulnerable-adults-scotland-gpacp002-sep18.pdf>.

Watanabe, Akiko, *Adult Guardianship of Personal Custody* (Shinzansha Publisher, 2015). (in Japanese)

Watanabe, Ichiro, 'Aspects of the Adult Guardianship System from the Viewpoint of Local Governments-Citizen's Guardianship, Abuse Response, Support for the Elderly without Relatives, etc.' (2015) 3 *Quarterly Journal of Comparative Guardianship Law* 102, 131 (in Japanese).

———, 'Limitations of the Adult Guardianship System from the Safety Net Perspective: From Rescue to Preventive Advocacy' (2021) 15 *Quarterly Journal of Comparative Guardianship Law* 36, 63 (in Japanese).

Watson, Joanne et al, 'The Impact of the United Nations Convention on the Rights of Persons with Disabilities (CRPD) on Victorian Guardianship Practice' (2020) 44(12) *Disability and Rehabilitation* 2806–14 <https://doi.org/10.1080/09638288.2020.1836680>.

Weisbord, Reid K. and David Horton, 'The Future of Testamentary Capacity' (Online, 2021) *Washington and Lee Law Review*, Rutgers Law School Research Paper <https://ssrn.com/abstract=3964342>.

Werner, Shirli and Rachel Chabany, 'Guardianship Law Versus Supported Decision-Making Policies: Perceptions of Persons with Intellectual or Psychiatric Disabilities and Parents' (2015) 86(5) *American Journal of Orthopsychiatry* 486, 499 <https://doi.org/10.1037/ort0000125>.

White, Ben et al, 'The Legal Role of Medical Professionals in Decisions to Withhold or Withdraw Life-Sustaining Treatment: Part 1 (New South Wales)' (2011) 18(3) *Journal of Law and Medicine* 498, 522 <PMID: 21528737>.

———, 'Does the Voluntary Assisted Dying Act 2017 (Vic) Reflect Its Stated Policy Goals?' (2020) 43(2) *UNSW Law Journal* 417, 451 <https://doi.org/10.53637/QEQJ5610>.

Wiesel, Ilan et al, 'The Temporalities of Supported Decision-Making by People with Cognitive Disability' (2020) 23(7) *Social & Cultural Geography* 934–52 <https://doi.org/10.1080/14649365.2020.1829689>.

Williams, George, 'The Victorian Charter of Human Rights and Responsibilities: Origins and Scope' (2006) 30(3) *Melbourne University Law Review* 880, 905 <http://classic.austlii.edu.au/au/journals/MelbULawRw/2006/27.html>.

Williams, Karen and Sue Field, 'Advocacy and the Rights of the Vulnerable Older Person' (2021) 12 *Journal of Aging Law & Policy* 1, 37 <https://www.stetson.edu/law/agingjournal/media/JALP%20Vol.%2012.pdf>.

Willmott, Lindy et al, 'Guardianship and Health Decisions in China and Australia: A Comparative Analysis' (2017) 12(2) *Asian Journal of Comparative Law* 371, 400 <https://doi.org/10.1017/asjcl.2017.16>.

Wolfensberger, Wolf, 'A Contribution to the History of Normalization, with Primary Emphasis on the Establishment of Normalization in North America between 1967–1975' in Robert John Flynn and Raymond A. Lemay (eds) *A Quarter-Century of Normalization and Social Role Valorization: Evolution and Impact* (University of Ottawa Press, 1999) 3–69 <https://books.openedition.org/uop/2463>.

Wood, Erica, 'Recharging Adult Guardianship Reform: Six Current Paths Forward' (2016) 1(1) *Journal of Aging, Longevity, Law, and Policy* 8, 53 <https://digitalcommons.tourolaw.edu/jallp/vol1/iss1/5>.

Wood, Stacey and Peter A. Lichtenberg, 'Financial Capacity and Financial Exploitation of Older Adults: Research Findings, Policy Recommendations and Clinical Implications' (2017) 40(1) *Clinical Gerontologist* 3, 13 <https://doi.org/10.1080/07317115.2016.1203382>.

Woodlock, Delanie et al, *Voices against Violence Paper One: Summary Report and Recommendations* (Women with Disabilities Victoria, Office of the Public Advocate and Domestic Violence Resource Centre Victoria, 2014) <https://www.wdv.org.au/wp-content/uploads/2018/12/Voices-Against-Violence-Paper-One-Executive-Summary.pdf>.

Woolford, Marta H. et al, 'Applying Dignity of Risk Principles to Improve Quality of Life for Vulnerable Persons' (2020) 35(1) *International Journal of Geriatric Psychiatry* 122, 130 <https://doi.org/10.1002/gps.5228>.

Wright, Megan S., 'Dementia, Autonomy, and Supported Healthcare Decision Making' (2020) Penn State Law Research Paper No. 05-2019, 79 *Maryland Law Review* 257, 324 <http://doi.org/10.2139/ssrn.3354545>.

Wuth, Natalia, 'Enduring Powers of Attorney with Limited Remedies—It's Time to Face the Facts!' (2013) 7 *Elder Law Review* 1, 30 <http://classic.austlii.edu.au/au/journals/ElderLawRw/2013/3.html>.

X

Xue, Qian-Lie, 'The Frailty Syndrome: Definition and Natural History' (2011) 27(1) *Clinics in Geriatric Medicine* 1, 15 <https://doi.org/10.1016/j.cger.2010.08.009>.

Y

Yamaguchi, Aya, 'Case Study on the Actual Condition and Function of the Community Support Network for Legal Support for the Elderly' (2022) 105 *Rikkyo Law Review* 208, 240 (in Japanese).

Yamamoto, Katsuji, 'Study on the Definition of Elder Person Abuse' (2014) 50(2) *The Japanese Journal of Law and Political Science* 61, 78 <https://doi.org/10.20816/jalps.50.2_61> (in Japanese).

Yamanome, Akio, 'Interim Verification of the Basic Plan and the Future Prospects' (2020) 88 *Adult Guardianship Practices* 82, 89 (in Japanese).

Yamashiro, Kazuma, 'Mental Capacity of Contracting Parties and Consumer Law: Issues on Capacity-Type Contract Regulations' (Special Feature: Civil Code and Consumer Law) (2021) 9 *Review of Consumer Law* 83, 110 (in Japanese).

———, 'The Mental Capacity of Contracting Parties and Consumer Law: Following the Logic of CRPD in Private Law' (Japan Association of Private Law Symposium Material: Civil Code and Consumer Law in Transition) (2021) 1199 *NBL* 24, 31 (in Japanese).

Yamashita, Naoko and Akemi Nakazawa, 'Analysis of Research Trends and Prevention of Elderly Abuse Prevention' (2019) 60 *Bulletin of Wayo Women's University* 153, 161 (in Japanese).

Yamatani, Kiyohide, 'A Reconsideration of the Ombudsman System in Administrative Control Theory' (2021) 173 *Public Administration Review Quarterly* 37, 49 (in Japanese).

Yang, Yuexi et al, 'Confucian Familism and Shared Decision Making in End-of-Life Care for Patients with Advanced Cancers' (2022) 19 *International Journal of Environmental Research and Public Health* 10071 <https://doi.org/10.3390/ijerph191610071>.

Yon, Yongjie et al, 'Elder Abuse Prevalence in Community Settings: A Systematic Review and Meta-Analysis' (2017) 5(2) *Lancet Global Health* 147, 156 <https://doi.org/10.1016/S2214-109X(17)30006-2>

Yonemura, Shigeto, *Lectures on Medical Law* (Nippon Hyoron Sha Co., Ltd., 2016). (in Japanese)

———, 'Central Japan Railway Case: From Civil Law Perspective' (2017) 7 *Social Security Studies* 191, 211.

Yoshida, Ryuhei, 'Review of Capability Approach: For Limitation and the Future' (2020) 57 *Hokusei Review, the School of Social Welfare* 13, 23 (in Japanese) <https://ci.nii.ac.jp/naid/120006822619>.

Yoshinaka, Nobuhito, 'Origins of the Thought of Parens Patriae' (2006) 30(1) *Hiroshima Law Review* 29, 51 (in Japanese).

Young, Robert, *Personal Autonomy: Beyond Negative and Positive Liberty* (Routledge, 1986, reprint 2017) <https://philpapers.org/rec/YOUPAB>.

Z

Zammiello, Lisa, 'Don't You Know That Your Law Is Toxic? Britney Spears and Abusive Guardianship: A Revisionary Approach to the Uniform Probate Code, California Probate Code, and Texas Estates Code to Ensure Equitable Outcomes' (2021) 13(2) *Estate Planning & Community Property Law Journal* 587, 631 <https://hdl.handle.net/2346/89672>.

Zeilstra, Rebecca, 'Nudging and the Safeguards of the Rule of Law' (2024) 25(5) *German Law Journal* 750–71 <https://doi.org/10.1017/glj.2024.30>.

Zietlow, Kahli et al, 'Guardianship: A Medicolegal Review for Clinicians' (2022) 70(11) *Journal of the American Geriatrics Society* 3070–9 <https://doi.org/10.1111/jgs.17797>.

B. Cases

Australia

GIBBONS v. WRIGHT [1954] Hight Court of Australia 91 CLR 423, April 23, 1954 <http://www8.austlii.edu.au/cgi-bin/viewdoc/au/cases/cth/HCA/1954/17.html>

Blomley v. Ryan [1956] HCA 81; (1956) 99 CLR 362 (March 28, 1956) <http://www8.austlii.edu.au/cgi-bin/viewdoc/au/cases/cth/HCA/1956/81.html>

SA (Guardianship) [2008] VCAT 2345 (November 17, 2008) <http://www8.austlii.edu.au/cgi-bin/viewdoc/au/cases/vic/VCAT/2008/2345.html>

AC (Guardianship) [2009] VCAT 753 (May 8, 2009) <http://www8.austlii.edu.au/cgi-bin/viewdoc/au/cases/vic/VCAT/2009/753.html>

KLC (No 2) (Guardianship) [2009] VCAT 831 (May 7, 2009) <http://www8.austlii.edu.au/cgi-bin/viewdoc/au/cases/vic/VCAT/2009/831.html?query=%22guardianship%20list%22>

QBU [2008] NSWGT 18 (July 4, 2008) <http://www8.austlii.edu.au/cgi-bin/viewdoc/au/cases/nsw/NSWGT/2008/18.html>

Germany

The first court of the Federal Constitutional Court decided that the federal parliament violated Article 3.3, Paragraph 2 of the Basic Law (Constitution) on December 16, 2021 [1BvR 1541/20].

Japan

A Supreme Court of Japan ruling on business management, Supreme Court of Japan, Civil Code Vol. 15, No. 10, page 2629 in Japanese on November 30, 1961 <http://www.courts.go.jp/app/hanrei_jp/detail2?id=53758>

A Supreme Court of Japan ruling on business embezzlement defendant case, Supreme Court of Japan, Penal Code Vol. 66, No. 10, page 981 in Japanese on October 9, 2012 <http://www.courts.go.jp/app/hanrei_jp/detail2?id=82627>

A Supreme Court of Japan ruling on claims for damages, Supreme Court of Japan, Civil Code Vol. 69, No. 3, page 455 in Japanese on April 9, 2015 <http://www.courts.go.jp/app/hanrei_jp/detail2?id=85032>

A Supreme Court of Japan ruling on claims for damages, Supreme Court of Japan, Civil Code Vol. 70 No. 3 Pages 681 in Japanese on March 1, 2016 (*Hanrei Jiho* No. 1647, p. 1) <http://www.courts.go.jp/app/hanrei_jp/detail2?id=85714>

High Court of Nagoya, Civil Code (dismissal of adult guardian) No. 52, 2017 (Ra) on March 28, 2017 < https://cir.nii.ac.jp/crid/1520857690037705216?lang=en>.

The US

U.S. Supreme Court, *Shelton v. Tucker*, 364 U.S. 479(1960) <https://supreme.justia.com/cases/federal/us/364/479/>

Canterbury v. Spence, No. 22099 (D.C. Cir. 1972) <https://law.justia.com/cases/federal/appellate-courts/cadc/22099/22099.html>

Ross et al v. Hatch, Circuit Court for the City of Newport News, August 2, 2013 <https://static1.squarespace.com/static/5807a480d482e9eb1f5d9c54/t/589d-fae1ebbd1a291a24f734/1486748405298/03c-final-orders.pdf>

C. Legislation

Australia-Commonwealth

Aged Care Act 1997 <https://www.legislation.gov.au/C2004A05206/latest/text>

Aged Care Amendment (Security and Protection) Act 2007 <https://www.legislation.gov.au/C2007A00051/asmade/text>

Australian Human Rights Commission Act 1986 <https://www.austlii.edu.au/cgi-bin/viewdb/au/legis/cth/consol_act/ahrca1986373/>

Australian Mental Health Act 2014 <https://www.legislation.vic.gov.au/as-made/acts/mental-health-act-2014>

Human Rights (Parliamentary Scrutiny) Act 2011 <https://classic.austlii.edu.au/au/legis/cth/consol_act/hrsa2011409/>

Law Enforcement (Powers and Responsibilities) Act 2002 <https://classic.austlii.edu.au/au/legis/nsw/consol_act/leara2002451/>

National Disability Insurance Scheme Act 2013 (includes amendments up to: Act No. 131, 2017) <https://www.legislation.gov.au/Details/C2018C00276>

Australia-New South Wales (NSW)

Protected Estates Act 1983 (NSW) <https://legislation.nsw.gov.au/view/whole/html/inforce/2004-02-16/act-1983-179>

Mental Health Act 1983 (NSW) <https://classic.austlii.edu.au/au/legis/nsw/num_act/mha1983n178155.pdf>

Guardianship Act 1987 (No. 257 NSW) <https://legislation.nsw.gov.au/view/whole/html/inforce/current/act-1987-257>

Powers of Attorney Act 2003 (NSW) <https://legislation.nsw.gov.au/view/html/inforce/current/act-2003-053>

NSW Trustee and Guardian Act 2003 (NSW) <https://legislation.nsw.gov.au/view/whole/html/inforce/current/act-2009-049>

Civil and Administrative Tribunal Act 2013 (NSW) <https://legislation.nsw.gov.au/view/html/inforce/current/act-2013-002>

Ageing and Disability Act 2019 (No. 7 NSW) <https://legislation.nsw.gov.au/view/whole/html/inforce/current/act-2019-007>

Australia-South Australia

Office of the Ageing (Adult Safeguarding) Amendment Act 2018 (No. 34 SA) <http://classic.austlii.edu.au/au/legis/sa/num_act/oftasaa201834o2018441/>

Australia-Victoria

Charter of Human Rights and Responsibilities Act 2006 (Victoria) <http://www5.austlii.edu.au/au/legis/vic/consol_act/cohrara2006433/>

Court Services Victoria Act 2014 (No. 1 Victoria) <https://www.legislation.vic.gov.au/in-force/acts/court-services-victoria-act-2014/006>

Disability Act 2006 <https://www.legislation.vic.gov.au/in-force/acts/disability-act-2006/051>

Family Violence Protection Act 2008 (Victoria) <https://www.legislation.vic.gov.au/in-force/acts/family-violence-protection-act-2008/065>

Guardianship and Administration Act 1986 (Victoria) <https://www.legislation.vic.gov.au/in-force/acts/court-services-victoria-act-1986/089>

Personal Safety Intervention Order Act 2010 (Victoria) <https://www.legislation.vic.gov.au/in-force/acts/personal-safety-intervention-orders-act-2010/032>

Powers of Attorney Act 2014 (Victoria) <https://www.legislation.vic.gov.au/in-force/acts/powers-attorney-act-2014/007>

State Trustees (State Owned Company) Act 1994 (Victoria) <https://www.legislation.vic.gov.au/in-force/acts/state-trustees-state-owned-company-act-1994/031>

Victorian Civil and Administrative Tribunal Act 1998 (Victoria) <https://www.legislation.vic.gov.au/in-force/acts/victorian-civil-and-administrative-tribunal-act-1998/142>

Medical Treatment Planning and Decisions Act 2016 (No. 69 Victoria) <https://www.legislation.vic.gov.au/in-force/acts/medical-treatment-planning-and-decisions-act-2016/008>

Voluntary Assisted Dying Act 2017 (No. 61 Victoria) <https://www.legislation.vic.gov.au/in-force/acts/voluntary-assisted-dying-act-2017/005>

Guardianship and Administration Act 2019 (No. 13 Victoria) <https://www.legislation.vic.gov.au/in-force/acts/guardianship-and-administration-act-2019/005>

Austria

Civil Code: Adult Protection Law (*Erwachsenenschutzrecht*) <https://www.bmj.gv.at/themen/Zivilrecht/Erwachsenenschutz/Gesetzestexte.html> (in German)

Canada-British Columbia

Adult Guardianship Act [RSBC 1996] CHARTER 6 <https://www.bclaws.gov.bc.ca/civix/document/id/complete/statreg/96006_01>

Representation Agreement Act 1996/2000 <https://www.bclaws.gov.bc.ca/civix/document/id/complete/statreg/96405_01>

France

Civil Code <https://www.fd.ulisboa.pt/wp-content/uploads/2014/12/Codigo-Civil-Frances-French-Civil-Code-english-version.pdf>

Pacte Civil de Solidarité <https://www.gov.uk/government/publications/self-declaration-form-for-marriage-or-civil-partnership-pacs-in-france>

Germany

Civil Code (Guardianship and Care Law) <https://www.gesetze-im-internet.de/englisch_bgb/englisch_bgb.html>

Ireland

Powers of Attorney Act 1996 <https://www.irishstatutebook.ie/eli/1996/act/12/enacted/en/html>

Assisted Decision-Making (Capacity) Act (2015) <https://www.irishstatutebook.ie/eli/2015/act/64/enacted/en/html>

Japan

Act for the Mental Health and Welfare of the Persons with Mental Disorders (Act No. 123 of 1950) <https://www.japaneselawtranslation.go.jp/ja/laws/view/4235> (in Japanese/English)

Act for the Welfare of Persons with Intellectual Disabilities (Act No. 37 of 1960) <https://laws.e-gov.go.jp/law/335AC0000000037/20230401_504AC0000000104> (in Japanese)

Act for Partial Revision of the Civil Code (Act No. 149 of 1999) <https://www.shugiin.go.jp/internet/itdb_housei.nsf/html/housei/h146149.htm> (in Japanese)

Act of Guardianship Registration (Act No. 152 of 1999) <https://www.japaneselawtranslation.go.jp/ja/laws/view/3954/je> (in Japanese/English)

Act on Assurance of Medical Care for Elderly People (Act No. 80 of 1982) <https://www.japaneselawtranslation.go.jp/ja/laws/view/4903> (in Japanese/English)>

Act on Coordination (Act No. 151 of 1999) <https://hourei.ndl.go.jp/simple/detail?lawId=0000086186&current=-1> (in Japanese)

Act on Maintenance of Related Laws Optimization of Measures related to Restrictions on Rights of Adult Guardianship, etc. (Act No. 39 of 2019) (in Japanese) <https://www.shugiin.go.jp/internet/itdb_housei.nsf/html/housei/19820190614037.htm> (in Japanese)

Act on Promotion of Adult Guardian System 2016 (Act No. 29 of 2016) <https://laws.e-gov.go.jp/law/428AC1000000029> (in Japanese)

Act on Securement of Stable Supply of Elderly Persons' Housing (Act No. 26 of 2001) <https://laws.e-gov.go.jp/law/413AC0000000026> (in Japanese)

Act on Social Welfare for the Elderly (Act No. 133 of July 11, 1963) (in Japanese) <https://www.mhlw.go.jp/file/06-Seisakujouhou-12000000-Shakaiengokyoku- Shakai/sokusinhou.pdf>

Act on Specified Commercial Transactions (Act No. 57 of June 4, 1976) <https://laws.e-gov.go.jp/law/338AC0000000133> <https://www.japaneselawtranslation.go.jp/ja/laws/view/66> (in Japanese/English)

Act on the Comprehensive Support for the Daily and Social Life of Persons with Disabilities (Act No. 123 of November 7, 2005) <https://laws.e-gov.go.jp/law/417AC0000000123> (in Japanese)

Act on the Prevention, etc. of Child Abuse (Act No. 82 of 2000) <https://laws.e-gov.go.jp/law/412AC1000000082> (in Japanese)

Act on the Prevention of Spousal Violence and the Protection of Victims (Act No. 31 of 2001) <https://laws.e-gov.go.jp/law/413AC0100000031>(in Japanese)

Act on the Prevention of Elder Abuse, Support for Caregivers of Elderly Persons and Other Related Matters (Act No. 124 of 2005) <https://www.japaneselawtranslation.go.jp/en/laws/view/3929> (in English)

Act on the Prevention of Abuse of Persons with Disabilities and Support for Caregivers (Act No. 79 of June 24, 2011) <https://www.japaneselawtranslation.go.jp/en/laws/view/2773> (in English)

Act on Promotion of Use of Alternative Dispute Resolution (Act No. 151 of 2004) <https://www.japaneselawtranslation.go.jp/ja/laws/view/4589> (in Japanese/English)

Act on the Protection of Personal Information (Act No. 57 of May 30, 2003) <https://www.japaneselawtranslation.go.jp/ja/laws/view/130> (in Japanese/English)

Act on Voluntary Guardianship Contract (Act No. 150 of 1999) (in Japanese) <https://www.japaneselawtranslation.go.jp/ja/laws/view/4397> (in Japanese/English)

Act Partially Amending the Companies Act (Act No. 70 of 2019) <https://www.shugiin.go.jp/internet/itdb_housei.nsf/html/housei/20020191211070.htm> (in Japanese)

Attorney Act (Act No. 205 of June 10, 1949) <https://www.japaneselawtranslation.go.jp/ja/laws/view/4610> (in Japanese/English)

Banking Act (Act No. 59 of June 1, 1981) <https://www.japaneselawtranslation.go.jp/ja/laws/view/4498> (in Japanese/English)

Basic Act for Persons with Disabilities (Act No. 84 of May 21, 1970) (in Japanese/English) <https://www.japaneselawtranslation.go.jp/ja/laws/view/2436/je> (in Japanese/English)

Basic Consumer Act (Act No. 78 of May 30, 1968) <https://www.japanese-lawtranslation.go.jp/ja/laws/view/4934> (in Japanese/English)

Child Welfare Act (Act No. 164 of December 12, 1947) <https://www.japane-selawtranslation.go.jp/ja/laws/view/4035> (in Japanese/Englih)

Civil Code (Act No. 89 of April 27, 1896) <https://www.japaneselawtrans-lation.go.jp/ja/laws/view/4314> (in Japanese/English)

Commissioned Welfare Volunteers Act (Act No. 198 of 1948) <https://www.mhlw.go.jp/bunya/seikatsuhogo/minseiiin01/02a.html> (in Japanese)

Constitution of Japan (Promulgated in 1946 / Came into effect on May 3, 1947) <https://www.japaneselawtranslation.go.jp/ja/laws/view/174> (in Japanese/Englih)

Consumer Contract Act (Act No. 61 of May 12, 2000) <https://www.japane-selawtranslation.go.jp/ja/laws/view/4431> (in Japanese/English)

Consumer Safety Act (Act No. 50 of June 5, 2009) <https://www.japanese-lawtranslation.go.jp/ja/laws/view/2023> (in Japanese/English)

Domestic Relations Case Procedure Act (Act No. 52 of May 25, 2011) <https://www.japaneselawtranslation.go.jp/ja/laws/view/2323> (in Japanese/English)

Judicial Scrivener Act (Act No. 197, 1950) <https://laws.e-gov.go.jp/law/325AC1000000197> (in Japanese)

Long-Term Care Insurance Act (Act No. 123 of December 17, 1997) <https://www.japaneselawtranslation.go.jp/ja/laws/view/3807> (in Japanese/English)

Medical Care Act (Act No. 205 of July 30, 1948) <https://www.japaneselaw-translation.go.jp/ja/laws/view/4006> (in Japanese/English)

Notary Act (Act No. 53 of April 14, 1908) <https://www.japaneselawtranslation.go.jp/ja/laws/view/2619> (in Japanese/English)

Ordinance for Enforcement of the Act on Stabilization of Employment of Elderly Persons (Ordinance of the Ministry of Labour of Japan No. 24 of 1971) <https://www.japaneselawtranslation.go.jp/ja/laws/view/2622> (in Japanese/English)

Ordinance of Watching Over Elderly in Community (Kodaira 2017), (Nagareyama, 2015) <https://www.city.kodaira.tokyo.jp/reiki/reiki_honbun/g135RG00001214.

html])> (in Japanese); <https://www.city.nagareyama.chiba.jp/_res/projects/
default_project/_page_/001/009/610/tuite.pdf> (in Japanese)

Ordinance for Hope to Live with Dementia in Setagaya District (October 1,
2020) <https://www.city.setagaya.lg.jp/02087/2952.html>; <https://www.city.
setagaya.lg.jp/documents/2952/jourei.pdf> (in Japanese)

Penal Code (Act No. 45 of April 24, 1907) <https://www.japaneselawtransla-
tion.go.jp/en/laws/view/3581> (in Japanese/English)

Regulation for Enforcement of the Notary Act (Attorney-General's Office
Order No. 9 of June 1, 1949) <https://www.japaneselawtranslation.go.jp/ja/
laws/view/3559> (in Japanese/English)

Road Traffic Act (Act No. 105 of 1960) <http://www.japaneselawtranslation.
go.jp/laws/view/2962/en> (in Japanese/English)

Services and Supports for Persons with Disabilities Act (Act No. 123 of
November 7, 2005) <https://www.japaneselawtranslation.go.jp/ja/laws/view/143/
tb> (in Japanese/English)

Social Welfare Act (Act No. 45 of March 29, 1951) <https://www.japanese-
lawtranslation.go.jp/ja/laws/view/3813> (in Japanese/English)

State Redress Act (Act No. 125 of October 27, 1947) <https://www.japanese-
lawtranslation.go.jp/ja/laws/view/3785/tb> (in Japanese/English)

Trust Act (Act No. 108 of 2006) <https://www.japaneselawtranslation.go.jp/
ja/laws/view/4453> (in Japanese/English)

Peru

Civil Code <https://webfiles-sc1.blackbaud.com/files/support/helpfiles/npo-
connect/content/resources/attachments/peru-law-295-civil-code.pdf>

Singapore

Maintenance of Parents Act (Act 35 of 1995) <https://sso.agc.gov.sg/Act/
MPA1995>

Mental Capacity Act (Act 22 of 2008) <https://sso.agc.gov.sg/Act/MCA2008>

Mental Capacity (Amendment) Act 2016 (No. 10 of 2016) <https://sso.agc.gov.sg/Acts-Supp/10-2016/Published/20160530170000?DocDate=20160530170000>

Vulnerable Adults Act 2018 (No. 27 of 2018) <https://sso.agc.gov.sg/Act/VAA2018>

Switzerland

Civil Code <https://www.fedlex.admin.ch/eli/cc/24/233_245_233/en>

The US

Older American Act 1965 <https://www.congress.gov/crs-product/R43414>

Age Discrimination Act of 1975 <https://www.dol.gov/agencies/oasam/regulatory/statutes/age-discrimination-act>

Elder Justice Act 2009 <https://www.congress.gov/bill/111th-congress/senate-bill/795/text>

Elder Abuse Prevention and Prosecution Act 2017 <https://www.congress.gov/bill/115th-congress/senate-bill/178/text/rfh>

Senior Safe Act (Section 303, the Economic Growth, Regulatory Relief, and Consumer Protection Act) <https://www.congress.gov/bill/115th-congress/senate-bill/2155>

Supported Decision-Making Agreement Act of Texas (Texas State Act 1357 of 2015) <https://statutes.capitol.texas.gov/Docs/ES/htm/ES.1357.htm>

2005 Texas Human Resources Code CHAPTER 48 <https://statutes.capitol.texas.gov/Docs/HR/htm/HR.48.htm>

Title 16, Health and Safety, Individuals with Disabilities, Chapter 94A. Supported Decision-Making (Delaware State Act, Chapter 94a of 2016) <https://delcode.delaware.gov/title16/c094a/index.shtml>

Financial Industry Regulatory Authority (FINRA) Rule No. 2165 and No. 4512 in February 2018 <https://www.finra.org/rules-guidance/rulebooks/finra-rules/2165>

California Welfare and Institutions Code <https://leginfo.legislature.ca.gov/faces/codesTOCSelected.xhtml?tocCode=WIC&tocTitle=+Welfare+and+Institutions+Code+-+WIC>

Financial Exploitation Prevention Act in the State of Michigan <https://www.michigan.gov/difs/news-and-outreach/press-releases/2021/09/27/new-protections-in-place-for-vulnerable-adults-as-financial-exploitation-prevention-act-goes-into-e>

UK-England

Care Act 2014 <http://www.legislation.gov.uk/ukpga/2014/23/contents/enacted>

Mental Capacity Act 2005 <http://www.legislation.gov.uk/ukpga/2005/9/contents>

Code of Practice <https://www.gov.uk/guidance/code-of-practice>

Modern Slavery Act 2015 <http://www.legislation.gov.uk/ukpga/2015/30/contents/enacted>

UK-Scotland

Adults with Incapacity (Scotland) Act 2000 <https://www.legislation.gov.uk/asp/2000/4/contents>

Mental Health (Care and Treatment) (Scotland) Act 2003 <https://www.legislation.gov.uk/asp/2003/13/contents>

Adult Support and Protection (Scotland) Act 2007 <https://www.legislation.gov.uk/asp/2007/10/contents>

UK-Wales

Social Services and Well-being (Wales) Act 2014 <https://www.legislation.gov.uk/anaw/2014/4/contents>

D. Treaties

Council of Europe

Convention for the Protection of Human Rights and Fundamental Freedoms
<https://rm.coe.int/1680063765>

EU

Charter of Fundamental Rights of the European Union (2000/C 364/01)
<https://www.europarl.europa.eu/charter/pdf/text_en.pdf>

Convention for the Protection of Human Rights and Fundamental Freedoms
<chttps://www.eods.eu/library/CoE_European%20Convention%20for%20
the%20Protection%20of%20Human%20Rights%20and%20Fundamental%20
Freedoms_1950_EN.pdf>

Recommendation CM/Rec (2009) 11 of the Committee of Ministers to member
states on principles concerning continuing power of attorney and advance directives for
incapacity <https://rm.coe.int/questionnaire-cm-rec-2009-11-short-version/16807821a1>

Recommendation Rec (1999) 4 on Principles concerning the Legal Protection
of Incapable Adults <https://www.coe.int/t/dg3/healthbioethic/texts_and_docu-
ments/rec(99)4e.pdf>

Organization of American States (OAS)

American Convention on the Protection of Human Rights for the Elderly
<https://www.oas.org/en/sla/dil/inter_american_treaties_a-70_human_rights_
older_persons.asp>

The Hague Conference on Private International Law (HCCH)

The Hague Convention of January 13, 2000 on the International Protection of
Adults <https://www.hcch.net/en/instruments/conventions/full-text/?cid=71>

UN

Convention of December 13, 2006 on the Rights of Persons with Disabilities
<https://www.un.org/development/desa/disabilities/convention-on-the-rights-of-persons-with-disabilities.html>

Optional Protocol to the Convention on the Rights of Persons with Disabilities
<https://treaties.un.org/doc/Publication/CTC/Ch-15-a.pdf>

REFERENCE SURVEY

The way law reform reports are processed in Australia: This text was written by Terry Carney AO, Emeritus Professor of the University of Sydney in email correspondence with the author and is included here with his approval on July 20, 2021.

1. The 'reference' to the Law Reform Commission (LRC) comes from the Attorney-General and until issued, no inquiry can be held (very occasionally LRCs have their 'own motion' ability).

2. The LRC nearly always has a consultative process that involves (i) issues papers; (ii) a discussion paper; (iii) a final report.

3. The final report is tabled in Parliament and then published but is not self-executing in any way. It is coming from an independent body 'external to' the government.

4. As a matter of Parliamentary procedure, it is common for there to be a time limit set for the Government to issue its 'response' to the recommendations (often bland/uninformative).

5. At that point, many LRC reports effectively 'die.' No action is taken to introduce a Bill to change the law in any of the ways recommended by the LRC.

6. It is not uncommon, however, for an LRC Report to be suddenly rediscovered and acted on many years later; if political pressure builds up some action and the only blueprint for action (or the 'best' one) is whatever the LRC proposed.

7. When the government introduces a Bill based on (or partially on) an LRC report, it is treated in the same way as any other proposed reform:

    (1) There is an entirely formal 'first reading' of the Bill (takes a few minutes, is just its tabling).

    (2) Sometime later, there will be a 'second reading debate' on the Bill. It is 'at large' and starts with the Minister's 'Second Reading Speech' summarizing what the Bill is intended to achieve. There is usually

also an 'Explanatory Memorandum' to the Bill which will detail what each clause is designed to dov

(3)   At the end of the second reading debate (which is often adjourned and resumed), the House (or in upper chamber the 'Legislative Council') will go into 'committee stage.' This is where the Opposition and/or Government move and debate specific variations to the language of the original Bill.

(4)   Once done, the second reading vote adopts, and

(5)   There is a formal 'third reading' which clears passage in that chamber (ditto in upper chamber).

(6)   The Bill is then law subject to it going to the Governor in Council (the head of state plus a couple of Ministers for what is a rubber stamp process—i.e., it cannot do other than accept/endorse the will of the Parliament), and

(7)   Any proclamation of its date of effect (in many Acts [as the bill has now become] this is stipulated in a clause of the legislation; but all or some of those commencement dates may be devolved to the Executive and then published).

LIST OF PUBLICATIONS

Sakurai, Yukio. "Value of Legislation Providing Support and Protection to Vulnerable Adults: Vulnerability Approach and Autonomy." Doctoral dissertation, Yokohama National University, Japan, 2022. http://doi.org/10.18880/00014834.

Yukio Sakurai. "Value of Legislation Providing Support and Protection to Vulnerable Adults: Vulnerability Approach and Autonomy." Yokohama Law Review 33, no. 1 (2024): 215–252. [In Japanese]. https://doi.org/10.18880/0002001253.

Yukio Sakurai. "Current Status and Issues of Japan's Adult Guardianship System in the Promotion Act: Focused on the Deliberation Process of the Basic Plan." Yokohama Law Review 30, no. 1 (2021): 397–432. [In Japanese]. https://doi.org/10.18880/00014059.

Yukio Sakurai. "Vulnerability Approach and Adult Support and Protection: Based on Safeguarding Law for Adults at Risk." The Journal of Aging and Social Change 11, no. 1 (2021): 19–34. https://doi:10.18848/2576-5310/CGP/v11i01/19-34.

Yukio Sakurai. "The Ageing and Adult Protection Legislative System: A Comparative Law Study." The Journal of Aging and Social Change 9, no. 1 (2019): 53–69. https://doi.org/10.18848/2576-5310/CGP/v09i01/53-69.

Yukio Sakurai. "Australian Adult Support and Protection for Vulnerable Adults: Through Law Reforms of Guardianship and Elder Abuse Legislation (Part I)." Yokohama Journal of Social Sciences 25, no. 2 (2020): 119–139. https://doi.org/10.18880/00013445

Yukio Sakurai. "Australian Adult Support and Protection for Vulnerable Adults: Through Law Reforms of Guardianship and Elder Abuse Legislation (Part II)." Yokohama Journal of Social Sciences 25, no. 4 (2021): 97–119. https://doi.org/10.18880/00013705

Yukio Sakurai. "The Idea of Adult Support and Protection Legislation in Japan: Multiple Options for Vulnerable Adults to Make Their Own Choices." The Journal of Aging and Social Change 12, no. 1 (2021): 31–47. https://doi:10.18848/2576-5310/CGP/v12i01/31-47.

Yukio Sakurai. "Value of Legislation Providing Support and Protection to Vulnerable Adults: Consideration for a Core Agency and Supported Decision-Making." Journal of Aging Law and Policy 14 (2023): 43–96. http://hdl.handle.net/10131/0002000039. chrome-extension://efaidnbmnnnibpcajpcgl-clefindmkaj/https://www.stetson.edu/law/agingjournal/media/JALP%20Vol.%2014%20Final.pdf